Terrorism Studies

This new Reader aims to guide students through some of the key readings on the subject of terrorism and political violence.

In an age when there is more written about terrorism than anyone can possibly read in a lifetime, it has become increasingly difficult for students and scholars to navigate the literature. At the same time, courses and modules on terrorism studies are developing at a rapid rate. To meet this challenge, this wide-ranging Reader seeks to equip the aspiring student, based anywhere in the world, with a comprehensive introduction to the study of terrorism. Containing many of the most influential and groundbreaking studies from the world's leading experts, drawn from several academic disciplines, this volume is the essential companion for any student of terrorism and political violence.

The Reader, which starts with a detailed Introduction by the editors, is divided into seven sections, each of which contains a short introduction as well as a guide to further reading and student discussion questions:

- Terrorism in historical context
- Definitions
- Understanding and explaining terrorism
- Terrorist movements
- Terrorist behaviour
- Counterterrorism
- Current and future trends in terrorism.

This Reader will be essential reading for students of terrorism and political violence, and highly recommended for students of security studies, war and conflict studies and political science in general, as well as for practitioners in the field of counterterrorism and homeland security.

Contributors: David C. Rapoport, Isabelle Duyvesteyn, Jack P. Gibbs, Leonard Weinberg, Ami Pedahzur, Sivan Hirsch-Hoefler, Alex P. Schmid, Martha Crenshaw, Max Taylor, John Horgan, Magnus Ranstorp, C.J.M. Drake, Ehud Sprinzak, Jennifer S. Holmes, Sheila Amin Gutiérrez de Piñeres, Kevin M. Curtin, Xavier Raufer, Donatella della Porta, Robert A. Pape, Mia M. Bloom, Chris Dishman, Andrew Silke, Muhammad Haniff Bin Hassan, Gary Ackerman, Bruce Hoffman, John Mueller, Mohammed M. Hafez, Karla J. Cunningham, Jonathan Tonge, Lorenzo Vidino and Michael Barkun.

John Horgan is Director of the International Center for the Study of Terrorism at the Pennsylvania State University, where he is also Associate Professor of Psychology. Author of more than sixty publications, he is a leading expert on the psychology of terrorism. His books include *The Psychology of Terrorism* (2005), *The Future of Terrorism* (1999, with Max Taylor) and *Walking Away from Terrorism: Accounts of Disengagement from Radical and Extremist Movements* (2009).

Kurt Braddock is a Doctoral candidate in Communication Arts and Sciences at the Pennsylvania State University, where he is also a Graduate Research Assistant at the International Center for the Study of Terrorism.

Terrorism Studies

A Reader

**Edited by John Horgan
and Kurt Braddock**

Routledge
Taylor & Francis Group

LONDON AND NEW YORK

First published 2012
by Routledge
2 Park Square, Milton Park, Abingdon, Oxon, OX14 4RN

Simultaneously published in the USA and Canada
by Routledge
711 Third Avenue, New York, NY 10017

Routledge is an imprint of the Taylor & Francis Group, an informa business

British Library Cataloguing in Publication Data
A catalogue record for this book is available from the British Library

Library of Congress Cataloging-in-Publication Data
A catalog record has been requested for this book

ISBN: 978-0-415-45504-6 (hbk)
ISBN: 978-0-415-45505-3 (pbk)

Typeset in Baskerville
by RefineCatch Limited, Bungay, Suffolk

Printed and bound in Great Britain by
TJ International Ltd, Padstow, Cornwall

Contents

Introduction from the Editors

Prior to 2001, it was never too challenging to characterize the study of terrorism. The community of scholars was relatively small and the community of long-term experts even smaller. Even as late as 1988, Schmid and Jongman[1] determined that only 32 leading terrorism experts were steady contributors to "a collective body of knowledge of terrorism as a complex and interdisciplinary social and behavioural phenomenon."[2] In a more recent survey of the field, Magnus Ranstorp[3] explained how among these researchers, some boasted field experience in conflict zones, some had direct contact with the underground movements, and others still possessed pragmatic, "on-the-ground" counterterrorism or counterinsurgency experience from which to draw. Despite deep and extensive expertise within the small community of terrorism scholars, the scale of academic research projects was limited, with little funding available for all but those with the most urgently sought proposal ideas for research promised on the leanest of budgets.

However, terrorism research was very evidently multi-disciplinary even from those early days. Participating in a terrorism conference always guaranteed exciting and varied presentations from political scientists, psychologists, economists, public policy scholars, historians, religious experts, survivors of terrorist attacks, and on rare occasions, even former terrorists. The fact that "terrorism studies" (often incorrectly characterized as a discipline) has never been dominated by any particular academic perspective is one of its most exciting features. It can also, however, represent a daunting challenge. A graduate student in any particular field quickly realizes he or she will need to read about perspectives from other disciplines to grasp the complexity of terrorism.

Perhaps most characteristic of terrorism studies prior to 2001, however, was the relative ease with which new students could locate and access the field. While the latest terrorist attack always seemed to be the catalyst for a flood of rushed books, there had always been a straightforward route into the serious study of terrorism for scholars – primarily through one or both of the two academic journals that specialized in terrorism research.

The seminal terrorist event of the last forty years, the al-Qaeda operations of 11 September, 2001, sharply illustrated the extent to which the terrorism studies field has been sensitive to terrorist events. Immediately following the attacks, the study of terrorism was flooded by a variety of self-styled "experts" claiming to bring unique and valuable perspectives to the collective effort to understand and prevent political violence. However, the vast majority of those who flocked to terrorism studies in the wake of 9/11 were inexperienced. In a very short span of time, former academics from the Cold War era and war correspondents competed to provide their particular brands of expertise on al-Qaeda[4] and other groups designated as threats to the security of the United States. Their contributions to the research community were limited to second-hand accounts and assertions based on no empirical research protocol or valid data to speak of. As soon as the media frenzy following the attacks subsided, many of these commentators quickly moved on to other research agendas. Established academics left the world of terrorism research to take advantage of newly-formed government positions from which they would serve advisory roles. Those that stayed in academia were forced to adjust their theoretical models on international relations to account for the impact of terrorist groups.[5] In short, the universe of terrorism research in the years following 9/11 was a tumultuous one, characterized by high turnover among researchers and a relative underrepresentation of sound methodological practice. As a result, a major proportion of the literature produced on terrorism and political violence following 9/11 yielded an abundance of atheoretical speculation under the guise of expertise and insight.

Although the marked increase in literature produced in the wake of 9/11 can be largely attributed to the influx of inexperienced and transient researchers, there has always been a core of long-term dedicated scholars at the heart of terrorism studies. Researchers including Bruce Hoffman, Brian Jenkins, Martha Crenshaw, Andrew Silke, David Rapoport, Paul Wilkinson and others have provided a steadfast presence within terrorism studies that is dedicated to the empirical and nonpartisan pursuit of data-driven findings. Although the study of political violence has featured an ever-evolving core of researchers since its inception, the 9/11 attacks changed how established researchers within the field have approached the formal study of terrorism.

In a survey of terrorism research in the early 2000s, Silke[6] found that the ways in which the academic community approached the formal study of terrorism had begun to change relative to the years leading up to the 9/11 attacks. As an illustration of the limited number of resources available to researchers prior to 9/11, less than ten per cent of published articles related to terrorism and political violence were collaborative efforts in the 1990s. In contrast, studies that involve more than one author now comprise twenty per cent of the research published in major terrorism journals (e.g. *Terrorism and Political Violence, Studies in Conflict and Terrorism*). Although collaborative efforts still represent only one in five publications within terrorism studies, the increase in collaborative research "offers the potential for more ambitious, difficult, and rigorous research projects to be taken on by the field".[7] This becomes increasingly important as terrorism scholars attempt to perform complex analyses on multifaceted dynamic processes related to political violence.

The formal study of terrorism also appears to be gradually trending in a more quantitatively-driven direction. Silke found an increase of terrorism-related research that utilized descriptive and inferential statistics as a means to validate claims made by researchers.[8] Whereas nineteen per cent of terrorism-related articles used statistics prior to 9/11, that figure had jumped to almost twenty-six per cent after the attacks. Even with this modest increase, terrorism studies still lags significantly behind other related fields in its use of statistics. More than eighty per cent of the studies in forensic psychology and fifty per cent of the studies in criminology leverage some type of statistical analysis to provide evidence for the claims contained therein, whereas only about a quarter of the articles within terrorism studies have utilized statistics in the years following 9/11.

In addition to the shifting landscape of how research in terrorism studies has been performed, there have also been drastic changes in the focus of researchers. In the last ten years, there has been a substantial increase in the amount of attention paid to radical Islamic groups. Silke illustrated that only fourteen per cent of published articles focused on extreme Islamic groups prior to 9/11. After the attacks, however, that figure had jumped to fifty-seven per cent[9], more assuredly fuelled by the development of al-Qaeda. Still, several researchers have recognized the importance of identifying trends across terrorist groups, as research related to Irish republicanism, environmental and animal liberation, and Basque separatism has also increased in the last ten years.

As complex as past years of terrorism research have been, the future of terrorism studies looks to be equally, if not more complicated. In a discussion regarding future directions for terrorism research, Jongman[10] identified twenty-five general areas in which more extensive empirical research must be conducted if we are to gain a more thorough understanding of terrorism. Within these twenty-five areas, Jongman proposed *nearly five hundred* specific research questions that warrant future investigation. Many of Jongman's research questions have been taken up by other scholars within the terrorism research community. Others will surely be tackled in the years to come. If nothing else, it has become clear that as a field, terrorism studies has grown exponentially in recent years, and that growth shows little signs of abating.

Research has increased exponentially. Funding has become available for multi-million dollar projects involving teams of researchers distributed across national and international boundaries. The sheer volume of output has been staggering. There is absolutely no doubt about it: there is more information on terrorism in print than even the most dedicated and eager scholar could read in an entire lifetime. And still more information promises to be published daily. In light of the labyrinthine nature of terrorism studies, it can be no surprise that today's student seeking to "find out more" about terrorism in light of its changing nature faces unenviable questions – which journals should I read? How can I distinguish analysis from opinion? How will I know if I have found what I am looking for (especially if it lies outside my discipline)?

To equip students with the tremendous task of figuring out "where to start," we decided to develop this *Reader*. Our guiding task and the one that inspired us to develop this project, was to help the interested student take initial steps into the world of terrorism research. We wanted to do this by providing them with access, in one place, to some of the most influential, insightful, carefully developed and rigorous analyses of terrorist behaviour – from its causes, triggering factors, sustaining influences, to its trajectories, arcs, eventual consequences, and responses to all of those. In *Terrorism Studies: A Reader*, we have assembled a collection of influential and groundbreaking studies conducted by some of the world's leading experts in terrorism. Selected from a wide range of academic disciplines, the sections provided in this collection provide those students new to the study of terrorism the ability to ask critical questions and provide answers to such issues as:

- What is terrorism, and will we ever be able to resolve the problem of defining it?
- Why should we try to understand the tenets of terrorism and how does doing so help manage the problem better?
- What lessons can we learn from terrorist campaigns that ended hundreds, or even thousands of years ago?
- Why does terrorism, as a strategy, appear to be so effective?
- Why do some individuals participate in terrorism while others do not?
- How and why do terrorist organizations form, develop, and eventually disintegrate?
- What do terrorists say about themselves and others?
- How and why has suicide terrorism spread around the world?
- Is the use of nuclear terrorism by terrorists likely?
- What can we expect from terrorism in the future?

The articles and chapters we have selected for this collection were chosen because they represent empirically-rigorous attempts to answer these and other integral questions. These issues have been and will continue to be central to the study of terrorism for years to come, and while the research community has made greater progress on some questions than others, many of these contributions have spawned rich exchanges. The selection presented here contains ideas and arguments that present and build upon established theoretical assertions in the field, spur debate and discussion among academics, and contribute to the future development of empirical work within terrorism studies.

Our objective, however, is not only to provide a guide to students. We also wanted to provide assistance to those on the front lines of counterterrorism to learn more about what academics are doing to help bridge the once wide gap between theory, research and practice. It is now common for those involved in devising and implementing counterterrorism tactics, strategies and policies to reach out to the academic community not just for ideas and creative solutions to complex problems, but increasingly for research methods and analytical tools to help assess and evaluate the effectiveness of counterterrorism initiatives, in whatever form they take and at whatever level they are focused. We very deliberately had this audience in mind also as we developed the book.

When we started this project, the most daunting challenge was obvious: from the extraordinary body of quality research produced before and since 2001, which contributions would we select? We knew there would be exemplary work from talented researchers that we would be unable to include in this collection. In fact, when we began discussions with our colleagues at Routledge, our intention was to include nearly twice as many articles than were chosen for the final list. Even with almost sixty articles in our original catalog, we could easily have included far more. The decisions to cut particular readings involved several meetings, constant re-drafting of our initial proposal, and exchanges between the editors over the course of several weeks. Some articles would be inserted, removed a few days later, and later re-inserted again. We consistently found the length of our book expanding rather than shrinking. In the end, when we settled on the thirty items to be published in the book and presented to our readers, we decided that a useful compromise would be to recommend further reading at the beginning of each section. Taken together, we feel that the items selected for inclusion and suggestions for further reading provide a thorough and focused introduction into the world of terrorism research.

We owe thanks to Rebecca Brennan and Andrew Humphrys at Routledge for their encouragement in bringing this project to fruition. In addition, this book could not have been possible without the permissions of all the contributing authors, so to them, and those who granted us the necessary official permission to reprint their work, we say thank you. We also thank our colleagues at the International Center for the Study of Terrorism at the Pennsylvania State University.

The structure

Terrorism Studies: A Reader is divided into seven sections. Each section includes a brief introduction to that section, a series of learning objectives, the contributions themselves, and suggestions for further reading. The learning objectives are essentially a series of discussion questions and prompts associated with the material in each section. We developed these not only for students to help them reflect upon their understanding of the material but also for teachers as potential assignment topics or questions to prompt classroom discussion.

The sections are organized such that that the fundamental tenets of terrorism are presented first, with more specialized subject areas listed in the later sections. Before introducing attempts to define terrorism, we first explore the historical context and changing meaning of terrorism over time.

Section 1 provides context – perhaps the most important starting point from which we can bring the reader up to date with current thinking on the nature and identification of terrorism. Few are familiar with the immense historical context to terrorism. This section redresses that by providing some of the most influential literature underpinning just how important it is that we understand the historical continuity to terrorism before we can possibly make sense of today's (and perhaps tomorrow's) developments.

Section 2 introduces one of the crucial challenges in terrorism studies – how to define terrorism. A unique feature of this section will be a focus on the identification of practical solutions to this perennial challenge.

In Section 3, we move from identification and definition to explanation – what are some popular theories of terrorism and how successful have they been in understanding and explaining the phenomenon that we are attempting to study?

Section 4 provides detailed accounts of what terrorist movements are actually like, and what it is that they actually do. These readings represent some of the most detailed and painstakingly constructed case studies of some of the most prominent terrorist groups. Their depth will allow the reader to become familiar with the complexity of terrorist movements, as well as develop an appreciation of the value of the case study as a method of investigation.

Where Section 4 introduces terrorism at a group and organizational level, Section 5 examines the terrorists themselves. Contributions to this section investigate issues such as how and why individuals decide to become involved in terrorism within particular movements, how decisions are actually made while engaging in terrorist activity, and how terrorists view themselves and others. This section essentially introduces how the terrorist mind-set develops and is sustained.

In Section 6, we transition from conceptual, theoretical and methodological issues in terrorism studies to more practical matters. Here, we explore questions such as: What is the most effective way to respond to terrorism, and why? Research on counterterrorism frequently lacks this sense of critical self-awareness, particularly about the assumptions that underpin and drive arguments about "what works." The contributions assembled for this section were selected to allow for engagement with a mindfulness for the need to answer questions based upon evidence and recognition of the need for evaluation.

Finally, Section 7 describes some of the fundamental ways in which terrorism is currently developing. Although the earlier sections will contain readings that distinguish the "new" terrorism from the "old," this section explores these "new" characteristics in much greater detail. This section also considers the implications of these characteristics for potential new directions in counterterrorism.

If you are new to the study of terrorism, we understand that navigating the wealth of material within terrorism studies can be a daunting task. So, we welcome you and hope that *Terrorism Studies: A Reader* offers you an exciting and accessible first step into understanding this complex and challenging phenomenon.

John Horgan and Kurt Braddock
University Park, PA

Notes

1 Schmid, A., & Jongman, B. (1988). *Political terrorism: A new guide to actors, authors, concepts, databases, theories, and literature.* Amsterdam: Transaction Books.
2 Ranstorp, M. (2007). Mapping terrorism research: Challenges and priorities. In M. Ranstorp (Ed.) *Mapping terrorism research: State of the art, gaps, and future direction* (pp. 1–28). New York: Routledge.
3 Ibid.
4 Ranstorp, p. 3.
5 Ibid.
6 Silke, A. (2007). The impact of 9/11 on research on terrorism. In M. Ranstorp (Ed.) *Mapping terrorism research: State of the art, gaps, and future direction* (pp. 76–93). New York: Routledge.
7 Ibid p. 79.
8 Ibid pp. 80–81.
9 Ibid p. 85.
10 Jongman, B. (2007). Research desiderata in the field of terrorism. In M. Ranstorp (Ed.) *Mapping terrorism research: State of the art, gaps, and future direction* (pp. 255–291). New York: Routledge.

About the Editors

John Horgan is Director of the International Center for the Study of Terrorism at the Pennsylvania State University, where he is also Associate Professor of Psychology. Author of more than sixty publications, he is a leading expert on the psychology of terrorism. His books include *The Psychology of Terrorism* (2005), *The Future of Terrorism* (1999, with Max Taylor) and *Walking Away from Terrorism: Accounts of Disengagement from Radical and Extremist Movements* (2009).

Kurt Braddock is a Doctoral candidate in Communication Arts and Sciences at the Pennsylvania State University, where he is also a Graduate Research Assistant at the International Center for the Study of Terrorism.

Publisher's Acknowledgements

The publisher would like to thank the following for permission to reprint their material:

Rapoport, D. C. (1984). Fear and trembling: Terrorism in three religious traditions. *American Political Science Review, 78,* 658–677. © American Political Science Association, published by Cambridge University Press, reproduced with permission.

Duyvesteyn, I. (2004). How new is the new terrorism? *Studies in Conflict and Terrorism, 27,* 439–454. Taylor and Francis Ltd, (http://www.informaworld.com), reprinted by permission of the publisher.

Rapoport, D. C. (2004). Modern terror: The four waves. In A. Cronin & J. Ludes (Eds.), *Attacking terrorism: Elements of a grand strategy* (pp. 46–73). Washington, DC: Georgetown University Press. Reprinted with permission (www.press.georgetown.edu).

Gibbs, J. (1989). Conceptualization of terrorism. *American Sociological Review, 54,* 329–340. Reprinted with permission from the American Sociological Association; http://www.asanet.org.

Weinberg, L., Pedahzur, A., & Hirsch-Hoefler, S. (2004). The challenges of conceptualizing terrorism. *Terrorism and Political Violence, 16,* 777–794. Taylor and Francis Ltd (http://www.informaworld.com), reprinted by permission of the publisher.

Schmid, A. (1993). The response problem as a definition problem. In A. Schmid & R. Crelinsten (Eds.), *Western responses to terrorism* (pp. 7–13). London: Frank Cass. Reproduced by permission of Taylor and Francis Books UK.

Crenshaw, M. (1981). The causes of terrorism. *Comparative Politics, 13,* 379–399. Reprinted with permission.

Weinberg, L. (1991). Turning to terror: The conditions under which political parties turn to terrorist activities. *Comparative Politics, 23,* 423–438. Reprinted with permission.

Taylor, M., & Horgan, J. (2006). A conceptual framework for addressing psychological process in the development of the terrorist. *Terrorism and Political Violence, 18,* 1–17. Taylor and Francis Ltd, (http://www.informaworld.com), reprinted by permission of the publisher.

Ranstorp, M. (1994). Hizbollah's command leadership: Its structure, decision-making, and relationship with Iranian clergy and institutions. *Terrorism and Political Violence, 6,* 303–339. Taylor and Francis Ltd, (http://www.informaworld.com), reprinted by permission of the publisher.

Drake, C. (1991). The Provisional IRA: A case study. *Terrorism and Political Violence, 3,* 43–60. Taylor and Francis Ltd, (http://www.informaworld.com), reprinted by permission of the publisher.

Sprinzak, E. (1995). Right-wing terrorism in comparative perspective: The case of split delegitimization. In T. Bjorgo (Ed.), *Terrorism from the extreme right* (pp. 17–43). London: Frank Cass. Reproduced by permission of Taylor and Francis Books UK.

Holmes, J. S., Gutiérrez de Piñeres, S. A., & Curtin, K. M. (2007). A subnational study of insurgency: FARC violence in the 1990s. *Studies in Conflict and Terrorism, 30,* 249–265. Taylor and Francis Ltd, (http://www.informaworld.com), reprinted by permission of the publisher.

Raufer, X. (2003). Al Qaeda: A different diagnosis. *Studies in Conflict and Terrorism, 26,* 391–398. Taylor and Francis Ltd, (http://www.informaworld.com), reprinted by permission of the publisher.

della Porta, D. (1992). On individual motivations in underground political organizations. In Social movements and violence: Participation in underground organizations *(International Social Movement Research), 4,* 3–28. Reproduced with permission from Emerald Group Publishing Limited.

Crenshaw, M. (1992). Decisions to use terrorism: Psychological constraints on instrumental reasoning. In Social movements and violence: Participation in underground organizations *(International Social Movement Research), 4,* 29–42. Emerald Group Publishing Limited.

Pape, R. (2003). The strategic logic of suicide terrorism. *American Political Science Review, 97,* 21–42. © American Political Science Association, published by Cambridge University Press, reproduced with permission.

Bloom, M. (2004). Palestinian suicide bombing: Public support, market share, and outbidding. Reprinted by permission from *Political Science Quarterly, 119,* (Spring 2004): 61–88.

Pedahzur, A., & Ranstorp, M. (2001). A tertiary model for countering terrorism in liberal democracies: The case of Israel. *Terrorism and Political Violence, 13,* 1–26. Taylor and Francis Ltd, (http://www.informaworld.com), reprinted by permission of the publisher.

Dishman, C. (2005). The leaderless nexus: When crime and terror converge. *Studies in Conflict and Terrorism, 28,* 237–252. Taylor and Francis Ltd, (http://www.informaworld.com), reprinted by permission of the publisher.

Silke, A. (2005). Fire of Iolaus: The role of state countermeasures in causing terrorism and what needs to be done. In T. Bjorgo (Ed.), *Root causes of terrorism: Myths, reality, and ways forward* (pp. 241–255). Oxford, UK: Routledge. Reproduced by permission of Taylor and Francis Books UK.

Bin Hassan, M. H. (2006). Key considerations in counterideological work against terrorist ideology. *Studies in Conflict and Terrorism, 29,* 531–558. Taylor and Francis Ltd, (http://www.informaworld.com), reprinted by permission of the publisher.

Ackerman, G. (2005). WMD terrorism research: Whereto from here? *International Studies Review, 7,* 140–143. Reprinted with permission from John Wiley and Sons.

Hoffman, B. (2004). The changing face of Al Qaeda and the global war on terrorism. *Studies in Conflict and Terrorism, 27,* 549–560. Taylor and Francis Ltd, (http://www.informaworld.com), reprinted by permission of the publisher.

Mueller, J. (2005). Six rather unusual propositions about terrorism. *Terrorism and Political Violence, 17,* 487–505. Taylor and Francis Ltd, (http://www.informaworld.com), reprinted by permission of the publisher.

Hafez, M. (2007). Martyrdom mythology in Iraq: How jihadists frame suicide terrorism in videos and biographies. *Terrorism and Political Violence, 19,* 95–115. Taylor and Francis Ltd, (http://www.informaworld.com), reprinted by permission of the publisher.

Cunningham, K. J. (2007). Countering female terrorism. *Studies in Conflict and Terrorism, 30,* 113–129. Taylor and Francis Ltd, (http://www.informaworld.com), reprinted by permission of the publisher.

Tonge, J. (2004). "They haven't gone away, you know": Irish republican "dissidents" and "armed struggle". *Terrorism and Political Violence, 16,* 671–693. Taylor and Francis Ltd, (http://www.informaworld.com), reprinted by permission of the publisher.

Vidino, L. (2009). Homegrown jihadist terrorism in the United States: A new and occasional phenomenon? *Studies in Conflict and Terrorism, 32*, 1–17. Taylor and Francis Ltd, (http://www. informaworld.com), reprinted by permission of the publisher.

Barkun, M. (2007). Appropriated martyrs: The Branch Davidians and the radical right. *Terrorism and Political Violence, 19*, 117–124. Taylor and Francis Ltd, (http://www.informaworld.com), reprinted by permission of the publisher.

Every effort has been made to contact copyright holders for their permission to reprint material in this book. The publishers would be grateful to hear from any copyright holder who is not here acknowledged and will undertake to rectify any errors or omissions in future editions of this book.

Notes on Contributors

David Rapoport (Professor Emeritus, Department of Political Science, University of California, Los Angeles)
David Rapoport is Professor Emeritus in the Department of Political Science at the University of California, Los Angeles. He has authored and edited several books over his career, including *Inside Terrorist Organizations* (2001) and *Terrorism: Critical Concepts in Political Science* (2006). He is also the author of numerous peer-reviewed journal articles and book chapters. In addition, Dr Rapoport is the founder and co-editor of *Terrorism and Political Violence*, which according to ISI citations is the leading terrorism journal. Routledge has just published (2011) a festschrift on Dr Rapoport's works edited by Jean E. Rosenfeld entitled *Terrorism, Identity, and Legitimacy: The Four Waves Theory and Political Violence*.

Isabelle Duyvesteyn (Associate Professor, Department of History of International Relations, Utrecht University, Netherlands)
Isabelle Duyvesteyn is a senior lecturer-researcher (associate professor) in the Department of History of International Relations at Utrecht University in the Netherlands. Previously she has worked as a lecturer-researcher at the Royal Military Academy in the Netherlands and as researcher at the Netherlands Institute for International Relations. Currently she is engaged in a large-scale study of the history and effectiveness of modern counter-terrorism and counter-insurgency funded by the Netherlands Organisation for Scientific Research. Her research focuses on the nature of war and peace in the developing world and contemporary warfare and strategy. She has been involved with the production of several books, including *Modern War and the Utility of Force: Challenges, Methods, and Strategy* (Editor, with Jan Angstrom, 2010) and the forthcoming *Routledge Compendium to Insurgency and Counter-Insurgency* (Editor, with Paul B. Rich). Her work has been published in several journals, among others, *Civil Wars*, *Security Studies* and *Studies in Conflict and Terrorism*.

Jack P. Gibbs (Retiring Centennial Professor Emeritus and Acting Chair of the Department of Sociology, Vanderbilt University)
Jack P. Gibbs gained his PhD from the University of Oregon in 1957. His main research interests extend to the sociology of deviance, social control, human ecology, the sociology of law, and the methodology of theory construction. He has published several books on social control including *Colossal Control Failures: From Julius Caesar to 9/11* (2008).

Leonard Weinberg (Professor, Department of Political Science, University of Nevada, Reno)
Leonard Weinberg is a Professor in the Department of Political Science at the University of Nevada, Reno. He has published several books, including *Political Parties and Terrorist Groups* (2003,

2008), *Religious Fundamentalism and Political Extremism* (edited with Ami Pedahzur, 2004), and *What is Terrorism?* (with William Lee Eubank, 2006). In addition, Dr Weinberg has another book entitled *The End of Terrorism?* due to be published by Routledge and released in 2011.

Ami Pedahzur (Professor, Department of Government; Head of TIGER Lab, University of Texas at Austin)

Ami Pedahzur is Professor of Government and the head of the Terrorism, Insurgencies, & Guerillas in Education & Research Lab (T.I.G.E.R.) at the University of Texas at Austin. He has published widely on terrorism and counterterrorism, particularly with respect to Israel: *The Israeli Response to Jewish Extremism and Violence: Defending Democracy* (2002), *The Israeli Secret Services and the Struggle against Terrorism* (2009), *Suicide Terrorism* (2005), *Jewish Terrorism in Israel* (with Arie Perliger, 2011). Dr Pedahzur also serves as associate editor of *Studies in Conflict and Terrorism*, as well as member of the editorial boards of *Armed Forces & Society*, *Terrorism and Political Violence*, and *Civil Wars*.

Sivan Hirsch-Hoefler (Faculty of Political and Social Sciences, University of Antwerp, Belgium)

Sivan Hirsch-Hoefler is a member of the faculty in the Department of Political and Social Sciences at the University of Antwerp in Belgium. Formerly a post-doctoral fellow in the Government Department at Cornell University, Dr Hirsch-Hoefler has published in *Political Psychology*, *International Journal of Intercultural Relations*, *Israel Affairs*, and *Terrorism and Political Violence*.

Alex P. Schmid (Chair of Department of International Relations at University of St. Andrews)

Alex P. Schmid is Director of the Terrorism Research Initiative (TRI) and Editor of its electronic journal '*Perspective on Terrorism*'. He is currently a Fellow-in-Residence at the Netherlands Institute for Advanced Study in the Humanities and Social Sciences (NIAS). Previous positions included Director of the Centre for the Study of Terrorism and Political Violence (CSTPV) at the University of St. Andrews and Officer-in-Charge of the UN Terrorism Prevention Branch. His latest publication is *The Routledge Handbook of Terrorism Research* (2011).

Martha Crenshaw (Professor of Political Science by courtesy and Senior Fellow at Center for International Security and Cooperation and Freeman Spogli Institute for International Studies at Stanford University, Stanford, CA)

Martha Crenshaw is a senior fellow at the Center for International Security and Cooperation (CISAC) and the Freeman Spogli Institute for International Studies and a professor of political science by courtesy at Stanford University. She has written extensively on political terrorism for many years. Her more recent work includes *Explaining Terrorism: Causes, Processes, and Consequences* (2011), *The Consequences of Terrorism* (Editor, 2010), and The Obama Administration and Counterterrorism in *Obama in Office: The First Two Years* (Edited by James A. Thurber, forthcoming in 2011).

Max Taylor (Director of the Centre for the Study of Terrorism and Political Violence and Director of the E-Learning Programs, University of St. Andrews)

Dr Max Taylor is Professor of International Relations and the Director of the Centre for the Study of Terrorism and Political Violence (CSTPV) at the University of St. Andrews in Scotland. He is Editor of the journal *Terrorism and Political Violence*. Dr Taylor is widely published within terrorism studies, producing *The Future of Terrorism* (edited with John Horgan, 2000), *Terrorist Lives* (with Ethel Quayle, 1995), and *The Terrorist* (1988). He has also published articles related to the dynamics of terrorism in a number of peer-reviewed journals.

Magnus Ranstorp (Research Director, Centre for Asymmetric Threat Studies, Swedish National Defence College, Stockholm, Sweden)
Magnus Ranstorp is the Research Director for Asymmetric Threat Studies at the Swedish National Defence College in Stockholm, Sweden. He has published *Understanding Violent Radicalisation: Terrorist and Jihadist Movements in Europe* (2010), *Mapping Terrorism Research: State of the Art, Gaps, and Future Directions* (2007), and *Hizb'allah in Lebanon: The Politics of the Western Hostage Crisis* (1997).

Charles J.M. Drake
Charles Drake has a B.A. in Politics from the University of Lancaster and a PhD in International Relations from the University of St Andrews. He is the author of *Terrorists' Target Selection* (1998).

Ehud Sprinzak (Founding Dean, Lauder School of Government, Interdisciplinary Center in Herzliya, Israel; Professor Emeritus of Political Science, Hebrew University, Jerusalem, Israel)
Ehud Sprinzak (now deceased) was the founding Dean of the Lauder School of Government at the Interdisciplinary Center in Herzliya, Israel. He was also Professor Emeritus of Political Science at Hebrew University in Jerusalem, Israel. An expert on Israeli politics and terrorism, he published *Brother Against Brother: Violence and Extremism in Israeli Politics from Altalena to the Rabin Assassination* (1999), and *The Ascendance of Israel's Radical Right* (1991).

Jennifer S. Holmes (School of Economic, Political, and Policy Sciences, University of Texas at Dallas, TX)
Jennifer S. Holmes is an Associate Professor of Political Economy and Political Science and Associate Program Head of International Political Economy in the School of Economic, Political, and Policy Sciences at the University of Texas, Dallas. Dr Holmes' books include *Terrorism and Democratic Stability* (2001), *Terrorism and Democratic Stability Revisited* (2008), and *Guns, Drugs, and Development in Colombia* (with Sheila Amin Gutiérrez de Piñeres and Kevin Curtin, 2008).

Sheila Amin Gutiérrez de Piñeres (Professor of Economics and Political Economy, School of Economics, Political, and Policy Sciences, University of Texas at Dallas, TX)
Sheila Amin Gutiérrez de Piñeres is Professor of Economics and Political Economy in the School of Economics, Political, and Policy Sciences and Dean of Undergraduate Education, at the University of Texas, Dallas. She has authored or co-authored numerous scholarly journal articles in the areas of development economics, international economics, and Latin America in such journals as *Journal of Development Economics, Bulletin of Latin American Research, Latin American Politics and Society, Studies in Conflict and Terrorism, Applied Economics, Applied Economics Letters, International Journal of Public Administration, Review of Development Economics, Latin American Business Review, Terrorism & Political Violence, Agricultural Economics*, and *Journal of International Consumer Marketing*. Her book *Guns, Drugs, and Development in Colombia* with Jennifer Holmes and Kevin Curtin is now in print

Kevin M. Curtin (Associate Professor, Department of Geography and GeoInformation Science, George Mason University, Fairfax, VA)
Kevin M. Curtin is an Associate Professor in the Department of Geography and GeoInformation Science at George Mason University in Fairfax, Virginia. He writes extensively in the

peer-reviewed literature on the topics of network GIS, transportation geography, optimal facilities location, and GIS in the developing world.

Xavier Raufer (Director of Studies and Research, Department for the Study of the Contemporary Criminal Menace, University Panthéon-Assas, Paris, France; Associate Professor, Chinese People's Public Security University and Beijing Political Sciences and Law University, Beijing & Shenyang, People's Republic of China)
Xavier Raufer is the Director of Studies and Research in the Department for the Study of the Contemporary Criminal Menace at the University Panthéon-Assas in Paris. In addition, he is an Associate Professor at the Chinese People's Public Security University and Beijing Political Sciences and Law University in Beijing and Shenyang, China. Dr Raufer is the author and co-author of several works on criminology and terrorism. These include *Les Nouveaux Dangers Planétaires* (2009), *Le Noveau Chaos Mondial: Penser la Sécurité dans un Mondechaotique Principes et Perspectives* (with Alain Bauer, 2007), and *L'énigme al-Qaida* (2005).

Donatella della Porta (Professor of Sociology, Department of Political and Social Sciences, European University Institute, Florence, Italy)
Donatella della Porta is professor of sociology in the Department of Political and Social Sciences at the European University Institute in Florence, Italy. She is on leave of absence from the University of Florence, where she was full professor of Political Science, president of the corso di laurea in Administrative Sciences, and Director of the Department of Political Science and Sociology. Dr della Porta has authored or co-authored over eighty scholarly articles and contributed to over one hundred books related to social movements and political violence.

Robert A. Pape (Professor, Department of Political Science, Director, Chicago Project on Security and Terrorism, Director, Program for International Security Politics, University of Chicago, Chicago, IL)
Robert Pape is a professor within the Department of Political Science, Director of the Chicago Project on Security and Terrorism, and Director of the Program for International Security Politics at the University of Chicago in Chicago, Illinois. Specializing in international security affairs, Dr Pape's publications include the books *Dying to Win: The Strategic Logic of Suicide Terrorism* (2005) and *Bombing to Win: Air Power and Coercion in War* (1996); *Cutting the Fuse: The Explosion of Global Suicide Terrorism and How to Stop it* (University of Chicago Press, September, 2010) and articles "Why Economic Sanctions Do Not Work" (*International Security*, 1997), "The Determinants of International Moral Action" (*International Organization*, 1999), and "The True Worth of Air Power" (*Foreign Affairs*, March/April 2004).

Mia M. Bloom (Associate Professor of International and Women's Studies, Research Fellow, International Center for the Study of Terrorism, Penn State, University Park, PA)
Mia Bloom is Associate Professor of International Studies and Women's Studies at the Pennsylvania State University. She is a leading expert on suicide terrorism and author of *Dying to Kill: The Allure of Suicide Terror* (2005) and *Bombshell: The Many Faces of Women Terrorists* (2011). In addition to her work on terrorism, Dr Bloom researches ethnic conflict, the strategic use of rape in war, and child soldiers and has written *Living Together After Ethnic Killing* (2007) with Roy Licklider.

Chris Dishman (Southwest Region Director for the Department of Homeland Security's State and Local Program Office)
Chris Dishman holds a B.A. from the University of San Diego and an M.A. from the University of Pittsburgh. He is the Southwest Region Director for the Department of Homeland Security's

State and Local Program Office, which is located within the Office of Intelligence and Analysis. Chris oversees Texas, New Mexico, and Arizona and is responsible for facilitating information sharing between DHS and State and local officials.

Chris has written extensively about the relationship between terrorism and organized crime and other terrorist-related issues. He also pursues his interest in military history, including the Mexican War, and has written *The Battle of Monterrey* which was selected to be part of the University of Oklahoma's award winning military series, Campaigns & Commanders.

Andrew Silke (Professor and Chair of Criminology, Criminology Field Leader, Program Director for Terrorism Studies, School of Law, University of East London, London, UK)

Professor Andrew Silke (BSc Hons, AFBPsS, CSci, CPsych, PhD) holds a Chair in Criminology at the University of East London where he is the Field Leader for Criminology and the Program Director for Terrorism Studies. Professor Silke has published extensively on issues to do with terrorism, conflict, crime and policing in journals, books and the popular press. Some of his publications include *The Psychology of Counter-Terrorism* (2010), *Research on Terrorism: Trends, Achievements, and Failures* (editor, 2004), *Terrorists, Victims, and Society: Psychological Perspectives on Terrorism and its Consequences* (editor, 2003), as well as dozens of book chapters and peer-reviewed articles.

Muhammad Haniff Bin Hassan (Associate Research Fellow and Ph.D. candidate at the S. Rajaratnam School of International Studies (RSIS))

Muhammad Haniff Bin Hassan holds a M.Sc. in Strategic Studies at the Institute of Defence and Strategic Studies, Nanyang Technological University. He received his early education in Aljunied Islamic School. He then continued his tertiary education at the Faculty of Islamic Studies, National University of Malaysia, with honors in Syar'iah and Civil law.

Mr Haniff is also active in social activities as a member of the Islamic Religious Council Appeal Board, HSBC Insurance Islamic Advisory Board, Association of Islamic Religious Teachers and Scholars of Singapore (PERGAS), Management Committee of Al-Irsyad Islamic School, Resource Panel for Government Parliamentary Committee (Defence and Foreign Affairs) and Political Film Consultative Committee of Media Development Authority. He writes extensively in Berita Harian (a local Malay newspaper) and has also published articles in The Straits Times. He has published six books in his name and helped publish two books for PERGAS and the Islamic Religious Council of Singapore. He has a blog to counter misinterpretation of jihad by groups like Al-Qaeda at http://counterideology.multiply.com.

Gary Ackerman (Assistant Director for Research and Communication, National Consortium for the Study of Terrorism and Responses to Terrorism, University of Maryland, College Park, MD)

Gary Ackerman is Assistant Director for Research and Communication at the National Consortium for the Study of Terrorism and Responses to Terrorism (START) at the University of Maryland in College Park, MD. Prior to taking up his current position, he was Director of the Weapons of Mass Destruction Terrorism Research Program at the Center for Nonproliferation Studies in Monterey, California. His research encompasses various areas relating to terrorism and counterterrorism, including terrorist threat assessment, terrorist technologies and motivations for using chemical, biological, radiological, and nuclear (CBRN) weapons and the modeling and simulation of terrorist behavior. He is the co-editor of *Jihadists and Weapons of Mass Destruction* (CRC Press, 2009), author of several articles on CBRN terrorism and has testified on terrorist motivations for using nuclear weapons before the Senate Committee on Homeland Security.

Bruce Hoffman (Professor, Edmund A. Walsh School of Foreign Service; Director, Center for Peace and Security Studies; Director of the Security Studies Program, Georgetown University, Washington, DC)
Professor Bruce Hoffman is currently the Director of the Center for Peace and Security Studies, Director of the Security Studies Program, and a tenured professor at Georgetown University's Edmund A. Walsh School of Foreign Service at Georgetown University in Washington, DC. A revised and updated edition of his acclaimed 1998 book, *Inside Terrorism*, was published in May 2006 by Columbia University Press in the U.S. and S. Fischer Verlag in Germany. Foreign language editions of the first edition have been published in ten countries.

John Mueller (Woody Hayes Chair of National Security Studies, Mershon Center; Professor of Political Science, The Ohio State University, Columbus, OH)
Professor John Mueller is a Woody Hayes Chair of National Security Studies, Mershon Center and Professor of Political Science at the Ohio State University in Columbus, OH. His publications include *Atomic Obsession: Nuclear Alarmism from Hiroshima to Al-Qaeda* (2010), *Overblown: How Politicians and the Terrorism Industry Inflate National Security Threats, and Why We Believe Them* (2006), and *The Remnants of War* (2004). He also has a book forthcoming entitled *Terror, Security, and Money: Balancing the Risks, Benefits, and Costs of Homeland Security* (with Mark Stewart, 2011).

Mohammed M. Hafez (Associate Professor of National Security Affairs, Naval Postgraduate School)
Mohammed M. Hafez is an Associate Professor of National Security Affairs at the Naval Postgraduate School in Monterey, California. A specialist in Islamic movements and political violence, his books include *Why Muslims Rebel: Repression and Resistance in the Islamic World* (2003); *Manufacturing Human Bombs: The Making of Palestinian Suicide Bombers* (2006); and *Suicide Bombers in Iraq: The Strategy and Ideology of Martyrdom* (2007). Dr Hafez has also authored a number of book chapters and journal articles on Islamic movements, political radicalization, and jihadist ideologies.

Karla J. Cunningham (Full Political Scientist, RAND Corporation)
Karla J. Cunningham, Ph.D., is a Full Political Scientist at RAND, with expertise in political violence and political change. Drawing on applied backgrounds in intelligence and law enforcement, she studies factors that contribute to instability including terrorism, insurgency, organized crime, and unrest. She is the author of six published and two forthcoming publications on female terrorism including "Gender, Islam, and Conservatism" (in Kathleen Blee and Sandra McGee Deutsch, eds., *Women of the Right*).

Jonathan Tonge (Professor, Politics Department, University of Liverpool)
Jonathan Tonge is a Professor of Politics at the University of Liverpool in the United Kingdom. Professor Tonge has written on various aspects of British and Irish politics, publishing 14 books, including *Abandoning the Past? Republican and Loyalist Former Prisoners and Conflict Transformation in Northern Ireland* (with Peter Shirlow, James McAuley, and Catherine McGlynn, 2009), *Sinn Fein and the SDLP: From Alienation to Participation* (with Gerard Murray, 2005), *The New Northern Irish Politics* (2005), and *Northern Ireland: Conflict and Change* (2002, 1998). He has also authored or co-authored dozens of journal articles and book chapters.

Lorenzo Vidino (Fellow at the Center for Security Studies, ETH Zurich)
Lorenzo Vidino is a fellow at the Center for Security Studies, ETH Zurich and a visiting lecturer at the University of Zurich. Dr Vidino previously held fellowships at the RAND Corporation, the

Belfer Center for Science and International Affairs, Kennedy School of Government, Harvard University, the U.S. Institute of Peace, and the Fletcher School of Law and Diplomacy. He is the author of two books, including his latest, *The New Muslim Brotherhood in the West* (Columbia, 2010).

Michael Barkun (Syracuse University, Professor Emeritus, Political Science Department)
Michael Barkun is a Professor Emeritus in the Political Science Department at Syracuse University in Syracuse, New York. He has authored many works on religion, violence, and the relationship between them. His books include: *Chasing Phantoms: Reality, Imagination, and Homeland Security Since 9/11* (2011), *Culture of Conspiracy: Apocalyptic Visions of Contemporary America* (2003), *Religion and the Racist Right* (1997), *Crucible of the Millennium* (1986), and *Disaster and the Millennium* (1974).

Section 1

Terrorism in historical context

Readings

Rapoport, D. C. (1984). Fear and trembling: Terrorism in three religious traditions. *American Political Science Review, 78*, 658–677.

Duyvesteyn, I. (2004). How new is the new terrorism? *Studies in Conflict and Terrorism, 27*, 439–454.

Rapoport, D. C. (2004). The four waves of modern terrorism:. In A. Cronin & J. Ludes (Eds.), *Attacking terrorism: Elements of a grand strategy* (pp. 46–73). Washington, DC: Georgetown University Press.

Introduction

A contributor to this section, David Rapoport is a Professor of Political Science at the University of California, Los Angeles. One of the founding figures of terrorism studies, Rapoport once remarked that for most terrorism scholars, terrorism really has little if any history to speak of. For many researchers, there is a sense in which terrorism "began" on 11 September 2001. In this section you will receive a solid grounding in the history and development of terrorism through the ages. We will first examine Rapoport's "Fear and Trembling" article in which important historical case studies are presented, before moving to an issue that became quite controversial in the immediate years after 9/11 – that is, whether movements like al-Qaeda represented a truly "new" kind of terrorism. Isabelle Duyvesteyn tackles this critical issue and poses some interesting conclusions for how we might answer this question. We conclude with a second contribution from Rapoport, whose efforts to develop a theory of terrorism that argues for the phenomenon developing (and disappearing again) in "waves," have generated significant debate in the terrorism studies community and leads to some fascinating questions about what future "waves" might bring.

Discussion questions

At the end of this section you should be able to answer the following questions:

- What lessons can we learn from studying the history of terrorism?
- Can we really distinguish "new" from "old" terrorism?
- What are the strengths and weaknesses of Rapoport's Wave Theory of terrorism?

Further reading

Burleigh, M. (2009). *Blood and rage: A cultural history of terrorism.* New York: Harper.

Chaliand, G., & Blin, A. (2007). *The history of terrorism: From antiquity to al-Qaeda.* Berkeley, CA: University of California Press.

Clutterbuck, L. (2004). The progenitors of terrorism: Russian revolutionaries or extreme Irish republicans? *Terrorism and Political Violence, 16,* 154–181.

Crenshaw, M. (1995). *Terrorism in context.* University Park, PA: Pennsylvania State University Press.

Cronin, I. (2002). *Confronting fear: A history of terrorism.* New York: Thunders' Mouth Press.

Davis, M. (2007). *Buda's wagon: A brief history of the car bomb.* London: Verso.

Laqueur, W. (2001). *A history of terrorism.* New Brunswick, NJ: Transaction.

Shughart, W. F. (2006). An analytical history of terrorism, 1945–2000. *Public Choice, 128,* 7–39.

1 Fear and trembling

Terrorism in three religious traditions

David C. Rapoport

In 1933 *The Encyclopaedia of the Social Sciences* published fascinating, useful articles on assassination (Lerner) and terrorism (Hardman), which ended on a strange note, namely that the phenomena, which had reached an exceptionally high point at the turn of the century, were declining so much that the subjects would remain interesting only to antiquarians. Future events would be determined by classes and masses, because modern technology had made our world so complex that we had become increasingly *invulnerable* to determined actions by individuals or small groups. Terrorist activity became extensive again after World War II, not in Europe and America, as was the case earlier, but in western colonial territories, particularly in the Palestine Mandate, Cyprus, Malaya, Kenya, Vietnam, and Algeria. But the second edition of the *Encyclopedia*, which was published in 1968, ignored both subjects; perhaps the editors believed the prophecies in the earlier edition!

Academics returned to the subject when terrorist activity revived again in the center of the western world. The flow of articles and books began in the 1970s, and that flow continues to increase every year. A journal entitled *Terrorism* has been established, and many universities offer courses on the subject. As they did 50 years ago, political scientists dominate the field, and in some respects the conventional wisdom governing terrorist studies has not changed: the technological, not the political, environment is normally seen as the decisive determining condition for terrorist activity. Many contemporary studies begin, for example, by stating that although terrorism has always been a feature of social existence, it became "significant" for the first time in the 1960s when it "increased in frequency" and took on "novel dimensions" as an international or transnational activity, creating in the process a new "mode of conflict."[1] The most common explanation for this "new mode of conflict" is that now we are experiencing the cumulative impacts of specific developments in modern technology. Individuals and tiny groups have capacities that they previously lacked. Weapons are cheaper, more destructive, easier to obtain and to conceal. "The technological quantum jumps from the arrow to the revolver and from the gun to the Molotov Cocktail" (Hacker, 1976, p. ix). Modern communications and transport allow hitherto insignificant persons to coordinate activity quickly over vast spaces. Finally, by giving unusual events extensive coverage, the mass media complete the picture. "You can't be a revolutionary without a color TV: it's as necessary as a gun" (Rubin, 1970, p. 108).

It is in the nature of conventional wisdom that we never feel obliged either to examine or to demonstrate its propositions. The historical illustrations we provide are decorative, and we analyze contemporary experiences as though the statement declaring them *suis generis* is itself clear and at the same time provides the only evidence needed to establish the case! Although one can never be sure of what is meant by the term "modern terrorism," the characterizations normally focus on increases in the number of incidents or amounts of damage and on the fact that assaults transcend state borders. Because early experiences are insignificant in these respects, they are deemed irrelevant. One purpose of this article is to show that this view is simply wrong and that the past can provide materials for useful comparisons.

I shall do this by a detailed analysis of three groups: the Thugs, the Assassins, and the Zealots-Sicarii.[2] I have chosen them for several reasons. They are the examples most often cited to illustrate the ancient lineage of terrorism, but they are not discussed in our literature. We cite them because they are so well known elsewhere; no other early terror group has received as much attention. Ironically, although the words thug, assassin, and zealot have even become part of our vocabulary (often to describe terrorists), and most educated persons can identify the groups, they have never been compared.[3]

The cases are inherently interesting and peculiarly instructive. Each group was much more durable and much more destructive than any modern one has been; operating on an international stage, they had great social effects too. Yet the noose, the dagger, and the sword were the principal weapons they employed, travel was by horse or foot, and the most effective means of communication was by word of mouth. Although a relatively simple and common technology prevailed, each example displayed strikingly different characteristics. The critical variable, therefore, cannot be technology: rather, the purpose and organization of particular groups and the vulnerabilities of particular societies to them are decisive factors. Although the point may be more easily seen in these cases, it must be relevant, I shall argue, in our world too.

Furthermore, the three cases illustrate a kind of terror nowhere adequately analyzed in our theoretical literature, terror designated here as holy or sacred (cf. Laqueur, 1977; Price, 1977; Rapoport, 1971, 1977, 1982a; Thornton, 1964; Walter, 1969). Before the nineteenth century, religion provided the only acceptable justifications for terror, and the differences between sacred and modern expressions (differences of nature, not scale) raise questions about the appropriateness of contemporary definitions. The holy terrorist believes that only a transcendent purpose which fulfills the meaning of the universe can justify terror, and that the deity reveals at some early moment in time both the end and means and may even participate in the process as well. We see terrorists as free to seek different political ends in this world by whatever means of terror they consider most appropriate. This trait characterizes modern terrorism since its inception in the activities of Russian anarchists more than a century ago, and it is found also in many modern terrorist organizations in our century which have had important religious dimensions, i.e., the IRA, EOKA (Cyprus), the FLN (Algeria), and the Irgun (Israel). Sacred terror, on the other hand, never disappeared altogether, and there are signs that it is reviving in new and unusual forms.

As instances of sacred terror, the Thugs, the Assassins, and the Zealots-Sicarii seem remarkably different from each other, and hence they provide some orientation to the range of possibilities associated with the concept. On the other hand, each closely resembles other deviant groups within the same parent religion, Hinduism, Islam, and Judaism, and the three kinds of deviant groups reflect or distort themes distinctive to their particular major religion.[4] In the last respect, what seems to be distinctive about modern terrorists, their belief that terror can be organized rationally, represents or distorts a major theme peculiar to our own culture: a disposition to believe that any activity can be made rational.

I shall begin with a detailed analysis of the cases and in an extended conclusion draw out some implications and comparisons. My concern is largely with methods and doctrines, not the social basis of group activity. The order of the presentation (Thugs, Assassins, and Zealots-Sicarii) is designed to carry the reader from situations where only religious ends are served to one where the political purpose seems, but in fact is not, altogether dominant. The order also illustrates an irony, namely that there can be an inverse relationship between proximity in time and distance from us in spirit. Although extinguished in the nineteenth century, the Thugs seem wholly bizarre because they lacked a political purpose, and we invariably treat terror as though it could only serve one. The Assassins, who gave up terror in the thirteenth century, are comprehensible because their ends and methods remind us of nineteenth-century anarchists who originated modern rebel terror and were themselves conscious of affinities. But it is the Zealots-Sicarii, destroyed in the first century, who appear almost as our true contemporaries because they seem to have purposes and methods that we can fully understand. By means of provocation they were successful in generating a mass insurrection, an aim of most modern terrorists, but one that has probably never been achieved. The purpose of the Zealots-Sicarii, it seems, was to secure national liberation inter alia. The striking resemblances between their activities and those of terrorists with whom we are familiar will put us in a better position to conclude by elaborating the differences already suggested between holy and modern terror.

Thugs

"Terror," Kropotkin wrote, is "propaganda by the deed." We are inclined to think of it as a crime for the sake of publicity. When a bomb explodes, people take notice; the event attracts more attention than a thousand speeches or pictures. If the terror is sustained, more and more people will become interested, wondering why the atrocities occurred and whether the cause seems plausible. Hence virtually all modern conceptions of terrorism assume that the perpetrators only mean to harm their victims incidentally. The principal object is the public, whose consciousness will be aroused by the outrage.

For the holy terrorist, the primary audience is the deity, and depending upon his particular religious conception, it is even conceivable that he does not need or want to have the public witness his deed. The Thugs are our most interesting and instructive case in this respect. They intend their victims to experience terror and to express it visibly for the pleasure of Kali, the Hindu goddess of terror and destruction. Thugs strove to avoid publicity, and although fear of Thugs was wide-spread, that was the unintended result of their acts. Having no cause that they wanted others to appreciate, they did things that seem incongruous with our conception of how "good" terrorists should behave.

Indeed, one may ask, were the Thugs really terrorists? They are normally identified as such in the academic literature (DeQuincey, 1877; Freedman, 1982; Gupta, 1959; Laqueur, 1977; Lewis, 1967). As persons consciously committing atrocities, acts that go beyond the accepted norms and immunities that regulate violence, they were, according to one established definition, clearly terrorists.[5] Their deceit, unusual weapon (a noose), and practice of dismembering corpses (thereby preventing cremation or proper burial) made Thug violence outrageous by Hindu standards, or, for that matter, by those of any other culture. Cults of this sort may not exist anymore, but as the case of the Zebra Killers or the Fruit of Islam in San Francisco in 1975 demonstrates, the religious purposes of a group may prescribe murders that the public is not meant to notice.[6] A city was terrorized for months, but no one claimed responsibility. It is doubtful whether any American terrorist group produced as much panic as this one did, although terror may not have been its purpose.[7]

No one knows exactly when the Thugs (often called Phansigars or stranglers) first appeared. Few now believe that the ancient Sagartians, whom Herodotus (VII, 85) describes as stranglers serving in the Persian army, are the people whom the British encountered in India some 2500 years later.[8] But there is evidence that Thugs existed in the seventh century, and almost all scholars agree that they were vigorous in the thirteenth, which means that the group persisted for at least six hundred years.[9] By our standards, the durability of the Thugs is enormous; the IRA, now in its sixth decade, is by far the oldest modern terrorist group.

There are few estimates of the number of people killed by the Thugs. Sleeman (1933) offers a conservative figure of one million for the last three centuries of their history.[10] This figure seems too large, but half that number may be warranted, and that, indeed, is an astonishing figure, especially when one remembers that during the life of modern terrorist organizations, the deaths they cause rarely exceed several hundred, and it would be difficult to find one group that is directly responsible for more than ten thousand deaths.[11] The Thugs murdered more than any known terrorist group, partly because they lasted so much longer. Their impact on Indian economic life must have been enormous, although there is no way to calculate it. If the significance of a terrorist group is to be understood by these measures, the Thugs should be reckoned the most important ever known. The paradox is that, unlike most terrorist groups, they did not or could not threaten society for the simple reason that their doctrine made them attack individuals rather than institutions.

The reinterpretation of a cardinal Hindu myth and theme provided the Thugs with their peculiar purpose and method. Orthodox Hindus believed that in early times a gigantic monster devoured humans as soon as they were created. Kali (also known as Bhavani, Devi, and Durga) killed the monster with her sword, but from each drop of its blood another demon sprang up, and as she killed each one, the spilled blood continued to generate new demons. The orthodox maintained that Kali solved the problem of the multiplying demons by licking the blood from their wounds. But the Thugs believed that Kali sought assistance by making two men from her sweat who were given handkerchiefs from her garment in order to strangle the demons, that is, kill them without shedding a drop of blood. Upon completing their mission, they were commanded to keep the handkerchiefs for their descendants.

In Hindu mythology Kali has many dimensions. She represents the energy of the universe, which means, as the legend suggests, that she both sustains and destroys life. She is also the goddess of time, who presides over endless cycles in which both essential aspects of the life process are carried out. The Thug understood that he was obliged to supply the blood that Kali, his creator, required to keep the world in equilibrium. His responsibility was to keep himself alive as long as possible so that he could keep killing, and it has been estimated that each Thug participated in three murders annually: one claimed to have helped strangle 931 persons.[12] No one retired until he was physically unable to participate in expeditions. The logic of the cycle or balance required the brotherhood to keep its numbers relatively constant. New recruits came largely from the children of Thugs, and the deficiencies were made up by outsiders. The children were initiated into the tradition early by a carefully calculated gradual process—a circumstance that contributed to their resoluteness. Adult Thugs never seemed to experience revulsion, but sometimes the young did; invariably the cases involved those who witnessed events before they were supposed to. Drugs were used rarely, and then only among the young.

For obscure religious reasons Thugs attacked only travellers, and although they confiscated the property of their victims, material gain was not their principal concern, as indicated by their custom of "distinguish(ing) their most important exploits" not by the property gained but "by the number who were killed, the Sixty Soul Affair ... the Sacrifice of Forty" (Russell & Hira, 1916, vol. 4, p. 567). The legend of their origin also shows murder to be the Thugs' main business, murder in which the death agony was deliberately prolonged to give Kali ample time to enjoy the terror expressed by the victims. It was forbidden to take property without killing and burying its owner first. The Thugs judged the ordinary thief as morally unfit.[13] When religious omens were favorable, many without property were murdered. Similarly, unfavorable omens protected rich travellers.

Although murder was the Thugs' main object, they needed loot—enormous quantities of it— to pay princes who provided their expeditions with international sanctuaries. Without those sanctuaries the brotherhood would not have persisted for such a long time. As we have learned again and again in the contemporary world, when international sanctuaries are provided, relations between states are exacerbated constantly. After numerous frustrating experiences, British authorities decided that appropriate cooperation from neighboring native states was not forthcoming. Nor did recourse to doctrines of hot pursuit prove adequate (Sleeman, 1836, p. 48).[14] Ultimately, the international law governing piracy was utilized, enabling British officials to seize and punish Thugs wherever they were found. The cost was a more massive violation of the rights of independent states, culminating in a direct expansion of imperial jurisdictions, the result that critics of the policy feared most.

A striking feature of Thug operations was that virtually all activity was hemmed in by self-imposed restraints. From the moment he joined an annual sacred expedition until it was disbanded, a Thug was governed by innumerable rules, laid down by Kali, that specified victims, methods of attack, divisions of labor, disposal of corpses, distribution of booty, and training of new members. In a sense, there were no choices to be made because in dubious circumstances Kali manifested her views through omens.

British observers were impressed with the extraordinary "rationality" of the rules established. "Whatever the true source may be, (the system) is beyond all doubt the work of a man of genius, no ordinary man could have fenced and regulated it with so elaborate a code of rules—rules which the Thugs seem to believe are of divine origin, but in each of which we can trace a shrewd practical purpose" (Sleeman, 1839, p. 31).[15] "Ridiculous as their superstitions must appear … they serve the most important purposes of cementing the union of the gang, of kindling courage, and confidence; and by an appeal to religious texts deemed infallible of imparting to their atrocities the semblance of divine sanction" (A religion of murder, 1901, p. 512). "The precautions they take, the artifices they practice, the mode of destroying their victims, calculated at once to preclude any possibility of rescue or escape—of witnesses of the deed—of noises or cries for help—of effusion of blood and, in general of trades of murder. These circumstances conspire to throw a veil of darkness over their atrocities" (Sherwood, 1820, p. 263).

The list of persons immune from attack—women, vagabonds, lepers, the blind, the mutilated, and members of certain artisan crafts (all considered descendants of Kali, like the Thugs themselves)—suggests, perhaps, that the cult may once have had a political purpose. Nonetheless, there can be no politics without publicity.

Whatever purpose these rules were designed to serve, they could not be altered even when the life of the brotherhood was at stake, because they were perceived to be divine ordinances. Europeans, for example, were immune from attack—a prohibition that virtually enabled Thugs to escape attention. When the Thugs were discovered, the same rule kept them from retaliating directly against the small, relatively unprotected group of British administrators who ultimately exterminated them.[16] Their commitment to rules produced another unanticipated consequence: in the nineteenth century when some of its members became increasingly concerned with loot, the brotherhood became lax. This gave the British a unique opportunity to persuade older, more tradition-bound members that the ancient Thug belief that Kali would destroy the order when its members no longer served her required them now to help their goddess by becoming informers.

To us, a Thug is a brute, ruffian, or cut-throat, but the word originally signified deceiver, and the abilities of Thugs to deceive distinguish them radically from other related Hindu criminal associations, which also worshipped Kali but "exercised their (criminal) profession *without* disguise."[17] Thugs literally lived two very different sorts of lives, which continually amazed the British. For the greater portion of the year (sometimes 11 out of 12 months), Thugs were models of propriety, known for their industry, temperance, generosity, kindliness, and trustworthiness. British officers who unwittingly had employed them as guardians for their children lavishly praised the reliability of Thugs who had strangled hundreds of victims. An extraordinary capacity for deception was a cardinal feature of Thug tactics too. Long journeys in India always involved great hazards, requiring parties large enough to repel attacks by marauders. Groups of Thugs disguised as travellers, sometimes numbering as many as 60 persons, were often successful in persuading legitimate travellers to join forces, thereby increasing the security of all. In some cases, the intimate congenial associations would last months before the opportunity to strike occurred. (Strangling is a difficult art and requires exceptional conditions.) Usually, close contacts of this sort create bonds between people which make cold-blooded murder difficult. In fact, the striking way in which intimacy can transform relationships between potential murderers and their victims in our own day has stimulated academics to invent a new concept—the Stockholm syndrome (Lang, 1974). But the Thugs seemed indifferent to the emotions that make such transformations possible, testifying that pity or remorse never prevented them from acting. Nonetheless, their victims were never abused. The early judicial records and interviews do not provide a single case of wanton cruelty: the victims were sacrifices, the property of Kali, and, as in all religions, the best sacrifices are those offered without blemish.[18] "A Thug considers the persons murdered precisely in the light of victims offered up to the Goddess, and he remembers them, as a Priest of Jupiter remembered the oxen and as a Priest of Saturn the children sacrificed upon the altars" (Sleeman, 1836, p. 8).

Thugs believed that death actually benefitted the victim, who would surely enter paradise, whereas Thugs who failed to comply with Kali's commands would become impotent, and their families would become either extinct or experience many misfortunes. British observers admired the cheerfulness of convicted Thugs about to be hanged, sublimely confident that they would be admitted to paradise.[19] Thugs spoke also of the personal pleasure that their particular methods generated. "Do you ever feel remorse for murdering in cold blood, and after the pretense of friendship, those whom you have beguiled into a false sense of security?" a British interrogator asked. "Certainly not. Are you yourself not a hunter of big game, and do you not enjoy the thrill of the stalk, the pitting of your cunning against that of an animal, and are you not pleased at seeing it dead at your feet? So it is with the Thug, who indeed regards the stalking of men as a higher form of sport. For you *sahib* have but the instincts of wild beasts to overcome, whereas the Thug has to subdue the suspicions and fear of intelligent men … often heavily guarded, and familiar with the knowledge that the roads are dangerous. Game for our hunting is defended from all points save those of flattering and cunning. Cannot you imagine the pleasure of overcoming such protection during days of travel in their company, the joy in seeing suspicion change to friendship until that wonderful moment arrives. … Remorse, *sahib?* Never! Joy and elation often" (Sleeman, 1839, pp. 3–4).

Assassins

The Assassins (known also as Ismailis-Nizari) survived two centuries (1090–1275). Unlike the Thugs they had political objectives; their purpose was to fulfill or purify Islam, a community whose political and religious institutions were inseparable.[20] Although by Thug standards they inflicted few casualties and wrought negligible economic damage, the Assassins seriously threatened the governments of several states, especially those of the Turkish Seljuk Empire in Persia and Syria.

As Weber (1955, p. 2) pointed out, Islam has always been preeminently dedicated to delivering a moral message aimed at transforming social existence in *this* world. Terror in Islam, therefore, has an extra dimension not present in Hinduism. The Thugs were concerned with three parties (the assailant, his victim, and a deity), but the Assassins reached out to a fourth one as well, a public or a moral community whose sympathies could be aroused by deeds that evoked attention. They did not need mass media to reach interested audiences, because their prominent victims were murdered in venerated sites and royal courts, usually on holy days when many witnesses would be present.

To be noticed is one thing, to be understood is another, and when the object of a situation is to arouse a public, those threatened will try to place their own interpretations on the terrorist's message. Their opportunities to do so will be maximized if the assailant breaks down, or even if he tries to evade arrest. The doctrine of the Assassins seems constructed to prevent both possibilities. One who intends his act to be a public spectacle is unlikely to escape in any case. The Assassins prepared the assailant for this circumstance by preventing him from even entertaining the idea that he might survive. His weapon, which "was always a dagger, never poison, never a missile," seems designed to make certain that he would be captured or killed. He "usually made no attempt to escape; there is even a suggestion that to survive a mission was shameful." The words of a twelfth-century western author are revealing: "When, therefore, any of them have chosen to *die* in this way ... he himself [i.e., the Chief] hands them knives which are, so to speak, 'consecrated'" (Lewis, 1967, p. 127).

Martyrdom, the voluntary acceptance of death in order to "demonstrate the ... truth" to man, is a central, perhaps critical, method of message-giving religions, used both to dispel the doubts of believers and to aid proselytizing efforts. One cannot understand the Assassins without emphasizing the deeply embedded Muslim admiration for martyrs, particularly for those who die attempting to kill Islam's enemies. Assassin education clearly prepared assailants to seek martyrdom. The word used to designate the assailants—*fidayeen* (consecrated or dedicated ones)—indicates that they (like the victims of the Thugs) were considered religious sacrifices who freed themselves from the guilt of all sins and thereby gained "entry into paradise" (Kohlberg, 1976, p. 72).[21]

The Hindu image of history as an endless series of cycles makes Thuggee conceivable. Message-oriented religions are inclined to assume a unilinear view of history that may be fulfilled when all humans hear and accept the message. Because this aspiration is frustrated, these religions periodically produce millenarian movements predicated on the belief that an existing hypocritical religious establishment has so corrupted their original message that only extraordinary action can renew the community's faith.

Islamic millenarian movements are largely associated with the Shia (the minority), who believe that eventually a *Mahdi* (Messiah or Rightly Guided One) would emerge to lead a holy war (*jihad*) against the orthodox establishment to cleanse Islam. In the various Jewish and Christian messianic images violence may or may not appear, but "an *essential* part of the Mahdist theory regards the *jihad* in the sense of an armed revolutionary struggle, as the method whereby a perfected social order *must* be brought into being" (Hodgkin, 1977, p. 307; see also Kohlberg, 1976; MacEoin, 1982; Tyan, 1960). The believer's obligation is to keep his faith intact until the *Mahdi* summons him. To protect a believer among hostile Muslims until the moment arrives, the Shia permit pious dissimulation, *taqiyya*. The pure are allowed to conceal their beliefs for much the same reason that we condone deception during war. Should an opportunity materialize, the Shia must "use their tongues," or preach their faith openly; but not until the *Mahdi* arrives are they allowed to "draw the sword" (MacEoin, 1982, p. 121).

The Assassins apparently interpreted the injunction prohibiting swords against other Muslims to mean that the true believer could use other weapons, or perhaps even that he should do so in order to expedite the arrival of the *Mahdi*. In this respect, they resemble earlier Islamic millenarian groups, which always attached a ritual significance to particular weapons. Some eighth-century cults strangled their victims, and one clubbed them to death with wooden cudgels (Friedlaender,

1907, 1909; Watt, 1973, p. 48). In each case the weapon chosen precluded escape and invited martyrdom.

The Assassins originated from the more active Shia elements who "used their tongues," organizing missionaries or summoners to persuade fellow Muslims with respect to the true meaning of their faith. Although their roots were in Persia, many were educated in Egyptian missionary schools. When the capabilities of the Shia (Ismaili) state in Egypt to promote millenarian doctrines waned, the founder of the Assassins declared his independence, seized several impregnable mountain fortresses, and made them hospitable to all sorts of refugees. Here the Assassins developed a distinctive systematic Gnostic theology which promised a messianic fulfillment of history in a harmonious anarchic condition in which law would be abolished and human nature perfected.

Like the Thugs, the Assassins moved across state lines constantly. But the differences are important. The Thugs found it easy to make arrangements with princes who would protect them for profit and upon condition that they operate abroad. But the Assassins, aiming to reconstitute Islam into a single community again, were compelled by their doctrine to organize an international conspiracy that could not be planted in an existing Islamic state. Therefore, they had to establish their own state: a league of scattered mountain fortresses or city-states (Hodgson, 1955, p. 99).

For the first time in history, perhaps, a state found its principal raison d'être in organizing international terror. The state provided means for the creation of an efficient enduring organization that could and did recover from numerous setbacks. The earlier millenarian sodalities were too scattered, their bases were too accessible, and their consequent insignificance often made them unable to achieve even the acknowledgment of historians, which alone could make them known to us. Isolation gave the Assassins both the space and the time required to create a quasi-monastic form of life and to train leaders, missionaries, and *fidayeen*. When their popular support in urban centers evaporated after 50 years, the Assassins survived for still another century and a half and would have persisted much longer had not Mongol and Arab armies destroyed their state (Hodgson, 1955, p. 115).

To facilitate their work they organized an extensive network of supporting cells in sympathetic urban centers. Often key persons in the establishment provided internal access, support the Assassins gained through conversion, bribery, and intimidation. Since orthodox Muslims understood the importance of internal support, the Assassins manipulated apprehensions by implicating enemies as accomplices—a maneuver that multiplied suspicions and confusion.

A successful assassination policy depended upon establishing the purpose of a murder as a measure necessary to protect missionaries. Thus, one professional soldier likens the *fidayeen* to armed naval escorts, which never engage the enemy unless the convoy itself is attacked (Tugwell, 1979, p. 62). Victims were orthodox religious or political leaders who refused to heed warnings, and therefore provoked an attack by being scornful of the New Preaching, by attempting to prevent it from being heard, and by acting in ways that demonstrated complicity in Islam's corruption.

Assassin legends, like those of any millenarian group, are revealing. A most remarkable one concerned the victim-*fidayeen* relationship. Normally the movement placed a youthful member in the service of a high official. Through devotion and skill over the years he would gain his master's trust, and then, at the appropriate time, the faithful servant would plunge a dagger into his master's back. So preternatural did this immunity from personal or ordinary feelings seem to orthodox Muslims that they described the group as "hashish eaters" (*hashashin*), the source of our term assassin. (Although there is no evidence that drugs were used, the ability to use the doctrine of *taqiyya* and the fact that training began in childhood may help explain *fidayeen* behavior.) The legend is significant, too, for what it demonstrates about public responses. Everywhere Assassins inspired awe. Those favorably disposed to their cause would find such dedication admirable, whereas opponents would see it as hateful, repulsive, and inhuman fanaticism. Less obvious but much more interesting, perhaps, as a clue to responses of neutrals, is the transformation that the meaning of the term assassin underwent in medieval Europe, where initially it signified devotion and later meant one who killed by treachery (Lewis, 1967, p. 3).

The potential utility of an assassination policy is obvious. Dramatically staged assassinations draw immense attention to a cause. In the Muslim context too, the basis of power was manifestly personal. "When a Sultan died his troops were automatically dispersed. When an Amir died his lands were in disorder" (Hodgson, 1955, p. 84). When conceived as an alternative to war, assassinations can seem moral too. The assassin may be discriminating; he can strike the great and guilty, leaving the masses who are largely innocent untouched.

The problems created by an assassination policy become clear only in time. A series of assassinations must provoke immense social antagonism in the normal course of events; popular identification with some leaders will exist and assassinations themselves entail treachery. "There can be good faith even in war but not in unannounced murder. Though Muslims … commonly … used an assassination as an expedient, the adoption of … a regular and admitted (assassination) policy horrified them and has horrified men ever since" (Hodgson, 1955, p. 84). A similar logic moved Immanuel Kant (1948, p. 6) to describe belligerents who employ assassins as criminals; such a breach of faith intensifies hatred and diminishes the possibility of achieving a peace settlement before one party exterminates the other.[22]

As one might expect, the orthodox often responded by indiscriminately slaughtering those deemed sympathetic to the *fidayeen* (Hodgson, 1955, pp. 76–77, 111–113). The Assassins, however, reacted with remarkable restraint, eschewing numerous opportunities to reply in kind. Acts of urban terrorism occurred, the quarters of the orthodox were firebombed, but so infrequent were these incidents that one can only conclude that the rebels believed that another assassination was the only legitimate response to atrocities provoked by assassination.[23] The political consequence of this restraint was clear; after forty years, support for the Assassins among urban elements disappeared, and the massacres ceased (Hodgson, 1955, p. 115).

The commitment to a single, stylized form of attack is puzzling. Most of the Assassins' early millenarian predecessors found assassination attractive too, but other forms of terror were known.[24] More than any other millenarian group, the Assassins had resources to use other tactics and much to lose by failing to do so. Still, Assassin armies only protected their bases and raided caravans for booty, for it seems that Assassin doctrine made assassination and war mutually exclusive alternatives. The pattern is quite conspicuous during one of those strange periods in the movement's history when, for tactical reasons, it decided to become an orthodox community. "Instead of dispatching murderers to kill officers and divines, Hasan III sent armies to conquer provinces and cities; and by building mosques and bathhouses in the villages completed the transformation of his domain from a lair of assassins to a respectable kingdom, linked by ties of matrimonial alliance to his neighbors" (Hodgson, 1955, pp. 217–239; Lewis, 1967, p. 80). Assassin encounters with Christians also reflected the view that the dagger was reserved for those who betrayed the faith and the sword for persons who had never accepted it. When the Assassins first met invading Crusaders in Syria during the early twelfth century, they used their armies, not their *fidayeen* (Lewis, 1967, p. 108).

The peculiar reluctance to modify their tactics or to use their resources more efficiently probably had its origins, as the doctrines of all millenarian groups do, in reinterpretations of major precedents in the parent religion. To the millenarian, those precedents explain the religion's original success, and the abandonment of those precedents explains why there has been a failure to realize its promise. The life of Mohammed probably prescribed the model for Assassin strategy.

The group began, for example, by withdrawing to primitive places of refuge (*dar al-hijra*), a decision that "was a deliberate imitation of that archetype from Mohammed's own career," who fled to remote but more receptive Medina when he failed to convert his own people in Mecca. "Medina was the first *dar al-hijra* of Islam, the first place of refuge—whence to return in triumph to the unbelieving lands from which one had to flee persecuted" (Hodgson, 1955, pp. 79–80). Islam's calendar dates from this event, and the pattern of withdrawing in order to begin again became one that millenarian elements in Islam normally followed and in fact do still, as recent studies of Muslim terrorist groups in Egypt show (Hodgkin, 1977; Ibrahim, 1980).

Mohammed's unusual employment of military forces and assassins while in Medina seems particularly instructive.[25] Initially, the army had only two tasks, to defend the community against attacks and to raid caravans for booty. Simultaneously, he permitted (authorized?) assassinations of prominent persons within or on the fringes of Islam, "hypocrites" (*munafikun*) who had "provoked" attacks by displaying contempt for some aspect of Mohammed's teachings. Their deaths released hitherto latent sympathies for Islam among their followers.[26] The process of purifying, or consolidating the original nucleus of the faith, seemed to be the precondition of expansion. When Mohammed decided the community was ready to become universal, the army was given its first offensive role and assassinations ceased!

Other aspects of the assassination pattern may have seemed suggestive too. The assassins' deeds were means to compensate or atone for deficiencies in ardor. The ability to overcome normal inhibitions or personal attachments to the victim was a significant measure of commitment. In every case, for example, assassin and victim were kinsmen, and no stronger bond was known then.[27] The victims were not likely to defend themselves (e.g., they might be asleep or be women or old men), and they were often engaged in activities likely to evoke the assailant's compassion (e.g., they were playing with children or making love). As known associates of Mohammed, the assassins could only gain access to their victims by denying their faith or denouncing the Messenger of Allah.

A major difference between the earlier assassins and the later *fidayeen* is that one group returned to Mohammed for judgment, whereas the other actively sought martyrdom. In explaining this difference, remember that the origin of the *fidayeen* is in the Shia and Ismaili sects. Those groups link themselves to Ali and Husain, whom they consider Mohammed's true heirs. Ali and Husain were themselves both martyred after authorizing assassinations, and their martyrdoms became as central to their followers as Christ's passion is to Christians.

We do not have the primary sources to determine how the Assassins actually justified their tactics, but we know they saw themselves as engaged in a struggle to purify Islam and made extraordinary efforts to demonstrate that they acted defensively. The *fidayeen* put themselves in situations in which intimate bonds or personal feelings would be violated in order to demonstrate conviction. Assassin armies had one purpose in the *hijra*; later, they were likely to have another. The precedents were well known to anyone familiar with Mohammed's life and with the lives of figures most central to the Shia. Can there be justifications more compelling for believers than those that derive directly from the founders of their faith?

Zealots-Sicarii[28]

There are resemblances between the Assassins and the Zealots-Sicarii. Both were inspired by messianic hopes to seek maximum publicity. Both interpreted important events in the founding period of their religion as precedents for their tactics and to mean also that those who died in this struggle secured their places in paradise. Like the Assassins, the Sicarii (daggermen) were identified with a particular weapon, and both rebellions had an international character. Nonetheless, the differences between the two, which derive from variations in the content of their respective messianic and founding myths, are even more striking.

The Zealots-Sicarii survived for approximately 25 years, a brief existence by the standards of the Assassins, but their immediate and long-run influence was enormous. Holy terrorists are normally concerned with members of their own religious culture, but the Jews were also interested in generating a mass uprising against the large Greek population that lived in Judea and against the Romans who governed them both. The revolt proved disastrous and led to the destruction of the Temple, the desolation of the land, and the mass suicide at Masada. Moreover, Zealot-Sicarii activities inspired two more popular uprisings against Rome in successive generations, which resulted in the extermination of the large Jewish centers in Egypt and Cyprus, the virtual depopulation of Judea, and the final tragedy—the Exile itself, which exercised a traumatic impact on Jewish consciousness and became the central feature of Jewish experience for the next two thousand years, altering virtually every institution in Jewish life. It would be difficult to find terrorist activity in any historical period which influenced the life of a community more decisively.

The impact of the Jewish terrorists obviously stems from their ability to generate popular insurrections, an unusual capacity among religious terrorists which makes them particularly interesting to us because ever since the Russian Anarchists first created the doctrine of modern terror, the development of a *levee-en-masse* by means of provocation tactics has been the principal aim of most groups. Very few have succeeded, and none has had as much success as the Zealots-Sicarii did. Why were they so peculiar?

The nature of their messianic doctrines simultaneously suggested the object of terror and permitted methods necessary to achieve it. Jewish apocalyptic prophecies visualize the signs of the imminence of the messiah as a series of massive catastrophes involving whose populations, "the upsetting of all moral order to the point of dissolving the laws of nature" (Scholem, 1971, p. 12). This vision saturated Judaism for a generation preceding the genesis of Zealot-Sicarii activity, creating a state of feverish expectancy. "Almost every event was seized upon … to discover how and in what way it represented a Sign of the Times and threw light on the approach of the End of the Days. The whole condition of the Jewish people was psychologically abnormal. The strongest tales and imaginings could find ready credence" (Schonfield, 1965, p. 19). New messianic pretenders flourished everywhere, because so many people believed that the signs indicating a messianic intervention were quite conspicuous: Judea was occupied by an alien military power, and prominent Jews were acquiescing in "the desecration of God's name" or accepting the culture of the conqueror.

In all apocalyptic visions God determines the date of the redemption. Still, these visions often contain some conception that humans can speed the process. Prayer, repentance, and martyrdom are the most common methods. When these do not produce results and a period of unimaginable woe is perceived as the precondition of paradise, it will only be a matter of time before believers will act to force history, or bring about that precondition. Jewish terrorist activity appeared to have two purposes: to make oppression so intolerable that insurrection was inevitable, and, subsequently, to frustrate every attempt to reconcile the respective parties.

The names Zealot and Sicarii both derive from a much earlier model in Jewish history, Phineas, a high priest in the days of Moses. His zeal or righteous indignation averted a plague that afflicted Israel when the community tolerated acts of apostasy and "whoring with Moabite women." Taking the law into his own hands, he killed a tribal chief and his concubine who flaunted their contempt for God in a sacred site. Phineas is the only Biblical hero to receive a reward directly from God (*Numbers* 25:11). In purifying the community, his action prepared the way for the Holy War (*herem*) which God commanded Israel to wage against the Canaanites for the possession of the Promised Land. The Bible repeatedly refers to the terror that the *herem* was supposed to produce and to Israel's obligation to destroy all persons with their property who remain in the land, lest they become snares or corrupting influences. The word *herem*, it should be noted, designates a sacred sphere where ordinary standards do not apply, and in a military context, a *herem* is war without limits.[29]

The name Sicarii comes from the daggers (*sica*) used when the group first made its appearance. Rabbinic commentary indicates that Phineas used the head of his spear as a dagger, and the Sicarii normally assassinated prominent Jews, especially priests, who in their opinion had succumbed to Hellenistic culture. As in Phineas's case, these acts were also efforts to create a state of war readiness, and, more specifically, to intimidate priests who were anxious to avoid war with Rome and whose opposition could prevent it from materializing.

> The Sicarii committed murders in broad daylight in the heart of Jerusalem. The holy days were their special seasons when they would mingle with the crowd carrying short daggers concealed under their clothing with which they stabbed their enemies. Thus, when they fell, the murderers joined in cries of indignation, and through this plausible behavior, were never discovered. The first assassinated was Jonathan, the high-priest. After his death there were numerous daily murders. The panic created was more alarming than the calamity itself; everyone, as on the battlefield, hourly expected death. Men kept watch at a distance on their enemies and would not trust even their friends when they approached.
>
> (Josephus, 1926a, vol. 2, pp. 254–257)

Although their name reminds us of Phineas's weapon, his spirit and purpose were more decisive influences. Unlike the *fidayeen,* the Sicarii did not limit themselves to assassinations. They engaged military forces openly, often slaughtering their prisoners. They took hostages to pressure the priests and terrorized wealthy Jewish landowners in the hopes of compelling a land redistribution according to Biblical traditions. The Zealots illustrate the point even more clearly. Their Hebrew name signified the righteous indignation that Phineas personified, but they rarely plotted assassinations, and their principal antagonists were non-Jews who dwelled in the land. Phineas was also known for his audacity, which Zealot-Sicarii assaults often reflect. (It is not without interest that rage and audacity are qualities most admired and cultivated by modern terrorists.) Their atrocities occurred on the most holy days to exploit the potential for publicity therein, and, more important, to demonstrate that not even the most sacred occasions could provide immunity. Note, for example, Josephus's description of how the Sicarii massacred a Roman garrison, after it had secured a covenant (the most inviolable pledge Jews could make) that guaranteed the troops safe passage.

> When they had laid down their arms, the rebels massacred them; the Romans neither resisting, nor suing for mercy, but merely appealing with loud cries to the covenant! … The whole city was a scene of dejection, and among the moderates there was not one who was not racked with the thought that he should personally have to suffer for the rebels' crime. For to add to its heinousness the massacre took place on the sabbath, a day on which from religious scruples Jews abstain from even the most innocent acts.
>
> (Josephus, 1926a, vol. 2, p. 451)

The massacre electrified the Greeks, who constituted a significant portion of the population in Judea and were the local source of Roman recruitment. Jews in numerous cities were massacred, and everywhere the Greeks were repaid in kind. The action and the response illustrate vividly some salient differences between Muslim and Jewish terrorists. *Fidayeen* terror was an auxiliary weapon designed to protect their missions where the main work of the movement was done, converting the population to a particular messianic doctrine. Patient and deliberate, the Assassins acted as though they expected to absorb the Muslim world piecemeal. The Zealots and the Sicarii saw themselves not as the propagators of a doctrine but as revolutionary catalysts who moved men by force of their audacious action, exploiting mass expectations that a cataclysmic messianic deliverance was imminent.

To generate a mass uprising quickly and to sustain constantly increasing polarizing pressures, the Zealots-Sicarii developed an array of tactics unusual by Thug and Assassin standards. Participants (despite their contrary intentions) were pulled into an ever-escalating struggle by shock tactics which manipulated their fear, outrage, sympathy, and guilt. Sometimes these emotional affects were provoked by terrorist atrocities which went beyond the consensual norms governing violence; at other times they were produced by provoking the enemy into committing atrocities against his will.

Thugs and Assassin tactics always remained the same, but in the different phases of the Jewish uprising, striking changes occurred which seemed designed for specific contexts. The rebellion began with passive resistance in the cities. This tactic, of which the Jewish example may be the earliest recorded by historians, merits comment, for in our world (e.g., Cyprus and Northern Ireland), passive resistance has often appeared as an initial step in conflicts which later matured into full-scale terrorist campaigns.[30] Our experience has been that many who would have shrunk from violence, let alone terror, often embrace passive resistance as a legitimate method to rectify grievances, without understanding how the ensuing drama may intensify and broaden commitments by simultaneously exciting hopes and fanning smouldering hostilities.

In the Jewish case, before antagonisms had been sufficiently developed and when Roman military strength still seemed irresistible, passive resistance might have been the only illegal form of action that many Jews would willingly undertake. Initially, the confrontations involved Jewish claims, sometimes never before made, for respect due to their sacred symbols, and governments learned that, willy-nilly, they had backed, or been backed, into situations in which they either had to tolerate flagrant contempt for the law or commit actions that seemed to threaten the Jewish religion, the only concern that could unite all Jews. More often than one might expect, the Romans retreated in the face of this novel form of resistance. They admired the Jews' displays of courage, restraint, and intensity, and they learned how difficult and dangerous it was to break up demonstrations that included women and children (Josephus, 1926a, vol. 2, pp. 169, 195; 1926b, vol. 18, pp. 55, 269). They feared a rebellion that could engulf the eastern portion of the Empire, which was at least one-fifth Jewish and contained a significant class of Jewish sympathizers (*sebomenoi*, God-fearers) whose influence seemed to reach members of Rome's ruling circles.

The possibility that the conflict could become an international one troubled Rome. Judea was on the frontier next to Parthia, the last remaining major power in the ancient world. Parthia had intervened in earlier conflicts. Even if Parthia wanted to avoid involvement, she might find it difficult to do so because her Jewish population was large, and one Parthian client state had a Jewish dynasty that bore a special hatred for Rome. Parthian Jews were important figures in the early stage of the rebellion. The great annual pilgrimages of Parthian Jews to Jerusalem and the massive flow of wealth they contributed to maintain the Temple gave evidence of the strength of their tie to Judea, a bond that a modern historian compares to that which knitted American Jews to those in Palestine during the uprising against Britain.

For some time before the rebellion, Rome kept expanding the unusual exemptions given Jews, and the uprising was fueled partly by rising expectations. But Rome's anxiety to avoid a serious conflict simply made her more vulnerable to tactics calculated to produce outrage. Her restraint encouraged reckless behavior and weakened the case of Jewish moderates who argued that although Rome might be conciliatory, she was wholly determined to remain in Judea.

Large passive demonstrations against authority tend to produce violence unless both sides have discipline and foresight. When some on either side prefer violence, or when passive resistance is viewed not as an end in itself, but as a tactic that can be discarded when other tactics seem more productive, explosions will occur. Whatever the particular reason in this case, demonstrators soon became abusive, and bands of rock-throwing youths broke off from the crowds. When Roman troops (trying to be inconspicuous by discarding military dress and exchanging swords for wooden staves) were attacked, Roman discipline dissolved. The crowds panicked, and hundreds of innocent bystanders were trampled to death in Jerusalem's narrow streets. This pattern kept repeating itself, and the atrocities seemed especially horrifying because they normally occurred on holy days when Jerusalem was crowded with pilgrims, many of whom were killed while attending religious services. The massive outrage generated by Roman atrocities and the assassination campaign against the moderates finally intimidated reluctant priests into refusing to allow Roman sacrifices at the Temple. Rome viewed that act as a rejection of her sovereignty or as a declaration of war, and this gave the militants a plausible case that the war was indeed a *herem*.

When the war finally occurred, many on both sides hoped to conclude it quickly with a political settlement. These hopes were given a severe jolt early after the first military engagement. When the tiny Roman garrison in Jerusalem, which had laid down its arms for a covenant of safe passage, was massacred, a pattern of reprisal and counter-reprisal spread throughout the eastern portion of the Empire. Roman troops ran amuck. Yet when military discipline was finally restored, the Roman campaign quite unexpectedly was restrained. Military advantages were not pressed, as hope persisted that the olive branch offered would be seized. Understanding that most Jews wanted peace, Rome believed that the atrocities of Jew against Jew would eventually destroy the popular tolerance requisite for all terrorist movements. A significant Jewish desertion rate, including many important personalities, kept Roman hopes alive for negotiating a peace without strenuous military efforts. But various Jewish atrocities, which culminated in the cold-blooded murder of Roman peace envoys, led to the conclusion that only total war was feasible (Josephus, 1926a, vol. 2, p. 526).

Zealot-Sicarii strategy seemed admirably designed to provoke a massive uprising. Consecutive atrocities continually narrowed prospects for a political, or mutually agreeable, solution, serving to destroy the credibility of moderates on both sides while steadily expanding the conflict, which enlisted new participants. But no master hand can be detected in this process, and one can see it as an irrational process. Jewish terrorists reflect a bewildering assortment of forces. Several Zealot and at least two Sicarii organizations existed, and many other groups participated, but only a few can be identified. Then, as now, the effect of multiplicity was to encourage each element toward even more heinous atrocities, in order to prove the superiority of its commitments, and in time the groups decimated each other. As these extraordinary actions unfolded, the participating groups, like so many of their modern counterparts, found it necessary to make even more fantastic claims about their enemies and even more radical promises about the social reconstruction that would result from their victory. Ferrero's comment on the dynamics of the French Reign of Terror seems quite pertinent. "The Jacobins did not spill all that blood because they believed in popular sovereignty as a religious truth; rather they tried to believe in popular sovereignty as a religious truth because their fear made them spill all that blood" (1972, p. 100; cf. Josephus, 1926b, vol. 18, p. 269).

To focus on popular insurrection as the principal object, however, is to misconstrue the Zealot-Sicarii view. Insurrection was only a sign of messianic intervention, and because they were concerned with a divine audience, they did things that no one preoccupied with a human audience alone would dream of doing. The decision of Zealot leaders to burn the food supply of their *own* forces during Jerusalem's long siege becomes intelligible only if one believes that He might see it as proof that the faithful had placed all their trust in Him. God, therefore, would have no choice; was He not bound by His promise to rescue the righteous remnant? Because many thought God would be moved by their sufferings, the most profound disaster often created new hopes. When the Temple was burning (and the war irretrievably lost), a messianic impostor persuaded six thousand new recruits that the fire signified that the time for deliverance had finally arrived. Compared to the Thugs and Assassins, the Zealots-Sicarii seem free to choose their tactics, but how can one be free to follow an impossible goal?

Conclusion

These cases provide materials to broaden the study of comparative terrorism. Each contains parallels worth pondering, and the three together illustrate the uniqueness of sacred terror and thus provide a perspective for viewing modern terror and a glimpse of the latter's special properties.[31]

Our obliviousness to holy terror rests on a misconception that the distinction between it and the modern form is one of scale, not of nature or kind. A most conspicuous expression of this misconception is the conventional wisdom that terrorist operations require modern technology to be significant. There are relationships between changes in technology and changes in terrorist activity, but they have not been seriously studied. More important, every society has weapon, transport and communication facilities, and the clear meaning of our cases is that the decisive variables for understanding differences among the forms terror may take are a group's purpose, organization, methods, and above all the public's response to that group's activities.

This conclusion should shape our treatment of the dynamics of modern terrorism. There is no authoritative history of modern terrorism that traces its development from its inception more than a century ago. When that history is written, the cyclical character of modern terror will be conspicuous, and those cycles will be related not so much to technological changes as to significant political watersheds which excited the hopes of potential terrorists and increased the vulnerability of society to their claims. The upsurge in the 1960s, for example, would be related to Vietnam just as the activities immediately after World War II would appear as an aspect of the decline in the legitimacy of Western colonial empires. Since doctrine, rather than technology, is the ultimate source of terror, the analysis of modern forms must begin with the French, rather than the Industrial Revolution.

When the assumption concerning technology is abandoned, early cases seem more valuable as a source for appropriate parallels. We have already suggested a number of potentially instructive instances. For example, the Zealot-Sicarii case may be the only instance of a successful strategy that actually produced a mass insurrection—the announced objective of modern revolutionary terror. It illuminates predicaments inherent in this strategy while exposing aspects of societies especially vulnerable to it. It is worth noting that the problems illustrated by this particular experience concerned Menachem Begin greatly, because his strategy as the leader of the Irgun in the uprising against Britain was in part conceived to avoid "mistakes" made by the Zealots-Sicarii (Rapoport, 1982b, pp. 31–33).

The international context provides another parallel. It played a crucial role in sustaining the terror. The Thugs and Assassins had valuable foreign sanctuaries. Favorable, albeit different, international climates of opinion helped all three groups. In each case there was cooperation among terrorists from different countries; in one instance a state was actually directing an international terrorist organization, and in another there existed the threat of potential military intervention by an outside power. The problems posed and the constraints involved provide useful points of comparison with modern experiences. The difficulties in dealing with terrorists who have foreign sanctuaries and the ways in which those difficulties may exacerbate international relations are familiar. Rome's vulnerability to terror tactics reminds one of Western colonial empires after World War II, but the ultimate reason for the different outcomes was that Rome never doubted her right to rule. Britain's ability to exterminate the Thugs quickly in the nineteenth century was to a large extent the consequence of a favorable British and an indifferent international opinion. Perhaps the doubt expressed in the 1930s by a student of the Thugs that Britain could not have acted as decisively to deal with the same problem a century later was unwarranted, but the concern reflected a very different political environment, one that is even more deeply rooted today.[32]

How should we characterize sacred terror? Obviously there are enormous variations in its expressions which extend to purposes, methods, responses, and differences that derive from the ingenuity of the individual terror cult which in turn is limited by boundaries established by the original religion. In an odd, interesting way, the terrorist as a deviant highlights unique features of the parent religion that distinguish it from other religions, e.g., concepts of the relation of the divine to history and to social structure.

Because Hinduism provides no grounds for believing that the world can be transformed, the Thugs could neither perceive themselves nor could they be perceived as rebels. In imagining themselves obligated to keep the world in balance, they were part of the established order, though obviously not in it. In Islam and Judaism, the potentialities for radical attacks on institutions are inherent in the ambiguity of unfulfilled divine promises, which no existing establishment can reconcile fully with its own dominance. Because the promises are known to every member of the religious community, the Islamic or Jewish terrorist has a human audience not present in Hinduism. To reach this audience Islamic and Jewish terrorists must become visible and must either conquer all or be extinguished. There can be no such imperative with respect to the Thugs, as the extraordinarily long life of the order suggests. Initially the British were very reluctant to suppress the Thugs because they believed that it would be dangerous to disturb the local and foreign interests embedded in Thug activity. The decisive impetus was a rekindling of evangelical feeling in Victorian England which struck out at the world slave trade and was outraged by accounts of three ancient Hindu practices: infanticide, immolation of widows, and Thuggee. Under Hindu administration, Thuggee would have survived much longer.

If a particular religion creates boundaries for its terrorists, it follows that similarities within traditions will be as striking as differences among traditions. In the Hindu world, an ancient species of criminal tribes, all of which worshipped Kali, persisted. Each performed a particular criminal vocation, was committed to a special way of achieving it, and believed that its actions were legitimate by Hindu standards. The Thugs were unique among those tribes in not professing their practices openly; perhaps they could not have been able to survive the outrage and horror provoked by them. The Assassins' situation is more straightforward; they were the latest and most successful Muslim millenarian assassination cult and the only one that established a state, the mechanism required for thorough organization. The Assassins consummated a millenarian tradition of terror, but the Zealots-Sicarii appeared to have initiated one, which ended after three disastrous massive revolts in as many generations. Holy terrorists normally victimize members of the parent religion, but the Jews attacked non-Jews too, those who resided in the land. The concern with the land as the site of the messianic experience may be a distinguishing feature of Jewish terror. The conception of a war without limits in which large military forces are engaged probably had its roots in the extraordinary Holy War (*herem*), which, according to the Bible, God Himself authorized in the original conquest of Canaan. The belief that assimilation impeded messianic deliverance and that all members of the community were culpable gave Jewish terror a character that seemed indiscriminate, certainly by the standards of the Assassins, who held leaders responsible.

Sacred terrorists find their rationale in the past, either in divine instructions transmitted long ago or in interpretations of precedents from founding periods of the parent religions. Their struggles are sanctified with respect to purpose and with respect to means; this is why their violence must have unique characteristics. The very idea of the holy entails contrast with the profane, the normal, or the natural. The noose of the Thug and the dagger of the Assassin illustrate the point. It is difficult, in fact, to avoid feeling that the act of terror is holy just because one is acting against his natural impulses. The immunities of Assassins and Thugs to natural feelings (i.e., the Stockholm syndrome) astonished observers. But, unlike terrorists we are familiar with, they began training for their tasks as children. Our sources provide no information on the personal stress that the methods of the Jewish terrorists might have created for them, but perhaps it is relevant that the Bible relates instance after instance of individuals, including King Saul himself, who violate commands for indiscriminate destruction in the original *herem* to conquer Canaan.

Religion normally embodies ritual, and it does seem natural that rules prescribe every detail of Hindu and Islamic terror. As observers of the Thugs pointed out, those rules may have been rationally designed to resolve perennial practical problems, thus helping the groups to endure and become more effective. Still, divinely authorized rules cannot be altered even when they become destructive. So conspicuous were the Assassins' political concerns that an eminent historian has described them as the first to use "political terror" in a "planned systematic fashion" (Lewis, 1967, p. 269); but their religious mandate kept them committed to the same tactics even when they proved politically counterproductive. Jewish terror appears unique, being thoroughly anti-nomian and embracing a large variety of activities. The success in provoking insurrection and the freedom regarding means suggest that political considerations were paramount. But since their ultimate concern was to create *the* catastrophe that would compel God to redeem the righteous remnant, in the end they, like the Thugs and Assassins, continued to act in manifestly self-destructive ways.

The transcendent source of holy terror is its most critical distinguishing characteristic; the deity is perceived as being directly involved in the determination of ends and means. Holy terror never disappeared, and it seems to be reviving in new forms especially in, but not exclusive to, the Middle East. Still, modern terror, which began initially in the activities of *Narodnaya Volya*, a nineteenth-century Russian organization, now is much more common. The modern terrorist serves political ends to be achieved by human efforts alone, and he, not God, chooses the most appropriate ends and means. It is also true that modern terrorist organizations (especially the most durable and effective ones) are often associated with religious groups, for religion can be a major factor of ethnic identity. Although the IRA attracts Catholics and repels Protestants, its object is political, and no member believes that God participates in the struggle. The FLN in Algeria stressed its Muslim character, and EOKA in Cyprus was affiliated with the Greek Orthodox church, but the tactics in both cases were designed to appeal to various domestic and international audiences.

When the members of *Narodnaya Volya*, the first modern rebel terrorists, began their activities, they seemed to be engaged in a kind of sacred ritual. More specifically, they remind one of the Assassins. Highly ranked officials who symbolized the system and bore some responsibilities for its injustices were the victims, and the assailant hoped to attract moral sympathy through his own suffering, specifically by his willingness to accept death in a public trial where he could indict the system. Even his weapon—a hand-thrown bomb—suggests the *fidayeen*'s dagger because it forced face-to-face encounters virtually precluding escape, which persuaded many observers that his will to die was more compelling than his desire to kill (Ivianski, 1982). But, unlike the Assassins, the possibility of other terror tactics was visualized early by their contemporaries, and their initial patterns were soon discarded.

Modern terrorism has two unique, dominant features. Organizations and tactics are constantly modified, presumably to enhance effectiveness and terror is used for very different ends, ranging from those of anarchists with millenarian visions to anti-colonialists, to individuals who simply want to call attention to a particular situation that they find offensive. The early forms of sacred terror cannot be characterized this way. The ends are predetermined, and no real evidence exists that the participants learn to alter their behavior from others within their own tradition, let alone from those outside it.[33] Modern terrorists take their lessons from anyone, and in an important sense they constitute a single tradition which reflects and caricatures a much-observed tendency in our world to subject all activities to efficiency tests. Over the decades the tendency has been to choose methods that minimize the terrorist's risks; the targets, accordingly, are, increasingly, defenseless victims who have less and less value as symbols or less and less responsibility for any condition that the terrorists say they want to alter. The question is whether one can place a premium on reducing the assailant's risk without undermining his potential impact. The problem did not exist for the sacred terrorist, which may be one reason why he was so effective.

The desire to make terror "rational" dominated the first modern terrorist text, Nechaev's *Revolutionary Catechism*, produced before the birth of *Narodnaya Volya*. "The revolutionary (terrorist) … knows only one science: the science of destruction. For this reason, and only for this reason, he will study mechanics, chemistry, and perhaps medicine. But all day and night he studies the living science of peoples, their characteristics and circumstances, and all the phenomena of the present social order. The object is the same. The prompt destruction of this filthy order" (1971, p. 71). Nechaev's work is simply an exercise in technique, suggesting devices for provoking governments to savage their peoples until the latter can bear it no longer. It has had numerous successors, the latest and most notorious being Marighella's *Minimanual of the Urban Guerrilla*.

Although the disposition to apply standards of expediency distinguishes modern from holy terror, the presence of this disposition itself cannot mean that modern terrorists are rational. Some ends in principle may be impossible to achieve, like those of the anarchist; others may be so ill-considered that no means can be made rational—the situation, it seems, of the Baader Meinhoff group and the Italian Red Brigades. Sometimes, under the guise of expediency, the safety of the terrorist might become the prime concern. More fundamentally, the very idea of a rational or expedient terror may be contradictory, since by definition terror entails extranormal violence, and as such, is almost guaranteed to evoke wild and uncontrollable emotions. Indeed, the people attracted to it may be so intrigued by the experience of perpetrating terror that everything else is incidental.

Notes

1   "Terrorism is an activity that has probably characterized modern civilization from its inception. In the past decade, however, terrorist activity has increased in frequency and has taken on novel dimensions. For example, incidents are being employed more as a means of political expression and are becoming characterized by a transnational element" (Sandler, Tshirhart, & Cauley, 1983, p. 36). The phrase "new mode of conflict" was coined by Jenkins (1975). See also Mickolus (1980, Introduction) and Hacker (1976, Preface). As is often the case with conventional wisdom, the view is expressed without elaboration in the first paragraph or preface. To Gurr (1979, p. 23), the "conventional wisdom (concerning terrorism) is a fantasy accepted as an ominous political reality by (virtually) everyone." *Cf.* Rapoport (1982a, Introduction).

2   I do not distinguish Zealots from Sicarii, although they are distinctly different groups, as Smith (1971) demonstrates. The Sicarii terrorized mostly Jews, whereas the Zealots were more concerned with Romans and Greeks. But for our purposes this is not a critical distinction. A more extensive discussion

of the Jewish uprising appears in Rapoport (1982b). Horsley (1979a) is the only other essay I know which discusses the Jewish activity as terrorist activity.

3 The cases are so well known and interesting that Thomas DeQuincey (1877), a nineteenth-century Romantic writer and the first student of comparative terrorism, pointed out the importance of comparing them. DeQuincey himself concentrates on the *Sicarii* in various essays. Lewis (1967, chap. 6) compares the three briefly.

4 It would be useful to extend the analysis by treating Christian terror, but the materials are not as conveniently available. No single Christian terror group has caught the public imagination in a way that is comparable to those I have chosen. Unlike those groups discussed here, the numerous millenarian sects using terror in the late medieval period did not rely on hit-and-disappear tactics. Their terror was a sort of state terror; the sects organized their communities openly, taking full control of a territory, instituting gruesome purges to obliterate all traces of the old order, and organizing large armies, which waged holy wars periodically sweeping over the countryside and devastating, burning, and massacring everything and everyone in their paths. The military pattern reminds one of the Crusades, an unlimited or total war launched by the Papacy (Cohn, 1961; cf. Rapoport & Alexander, 1982), in which seven essays discuss relationships between sacred and modern justifications, focusing largely on Christian traditions.

5 Although the Thugs may do what they do because they know that ordinary Hindus regard such actions as terrifying and horrible, they want victims only to experience terror. The earliest contemporary discussions of terrorism emphasized the extranormal character of its violence as the distinguishing feature, but the importance of that distinction has been largely lost. Compare Thornton (1964), Walter (1969), Rapoport (1977), and Price (1977). Since terror is extranormal violence, it is likely to flow initially from a doctrine, and it tends to be a historical rather than a universal phenomenon. In recent years our definitions generally treat terror and violence as synonyms. (See, for example, Russell, 1979, p. 4.) Since violence is a universal phenomenon, it is not surprising that there is a tendency for those who do not distinguish between violence and terror to treat differences in the latter as largely differences in scale. Hostile sources compiled the materials for all three groups, which poses important questions of reliability. Specific footnotes for each case treat these problems, although obviously only historians of each period can assess the documents adequately. The pictures drawn for each group differ so dramatically that at the very least they represent archetypes of specific religious traditions.

6 When early twentieth-century Hindu terrorist groups used Kali to justify their activities, secrecy was shunned because they had a political purpose, the independence of India (Pal, 1932).

   Because terror can give the perpetrator joy, it can be undertaken for its own sake. An example might be the Tylenol killer in the fall of 1982, who laced capsules with arsenic, terrorizing the American public and drug industry in the process. Publicity would be important in this case of terror for terror's sake only if the terrorist desired an audience too.

7 The experience is described in a reasonably accurate, overly gruesome bestseller (Clark, 1979). The group apparently believed that a race war would develop from its efforts, and perhaps at this point it would become visible.

8 Primary sources on the Thugs are extensive. Numerous archival and published government materials exist for virtually every year from 1826 to 1904, the latter being the termination date of the special Indian institution created to deal with Thuggee and related problems, The Thag and Dakaiti Department. By 1850 Thug activity itself ceased almost entirely. Pfirrmann (1970) is the only person who has examined all the primary source materials. His conclusions are substantially those offered by W. H. Sleeman, the remarkable officer who made the Thugs an issue in British politics, contrived the special methods used to destroy them, and proved to be a perceptive sociologist of religion. Sleeman's six published books (1836, 1839, 1840, 1893, 1858, and 1849) are listed in order of their pertinence. Two useful nineteenth-century secondary accounts based on Sleeman are Hutton (1857) and Thornton (1837). The best twentieth-century books published before Pfirrmann are Sleeman (1933) and Bruce (1968).

   The Thugs have captured literary imaginations. Meadows Taylor, a British officer with Sleeman, wrote a bestselling novel (1839) which was reprinted several times. Wilkie Collins's novel, *The Moonstone*, has gone through eleven editions at least, and John Masters (1952) has provided the latest fictional account.

9 The thirteenth-century writings of Jalalu-d din Firoz Khilji, Sultan of Delhi, refer to the banishment of a thousand persons generally identified as Thugs. But before their demise, not much was known about them. Afterward, the thoroughness of British officials, trial records, and police informants provided much material. Although the information was compiled by British police administrators and the Thugs

were denied public trials, legal counsel, and the right to question witnesses, the picture developed from this information was accepted completely for more than a century. Recently, it was challenged by Gupta (1959) and Gordon (1969), who believe that the group developed only when the British arrived. Gupta provides no evidence for this view, and Pfirrmann is justified in simply brushing it aside as a polemic. Gordon's thesis seems more substantial and depends on allegations of inconsistencies in the primary sources. His essay was published too late for Pfirrmann to evaluate, but I found that the inconsistencies cited come largely from Gordon's tendency to take quotations out of context, which may explain why he did not develop the thesis in subsequent writings and why it has been ignored by others.

10   The estimate is incorporated in J. L. Sleeman's title (1933). Every estimate flounders because we don't know the age of the organization or its size in various periods. It is generally assumed that the number remained constant because the group was largely hereditary. In my view, the administrative chaos that prevailed in the wake of the Moghul Empire's collapse when the British arrived gave the brotherhood unusual opportunities for new victims and swelled its ranks, which suggests that Sleeman's "conservative estimate" represents a maximum, not a minimum, one.

11   When terrorist activities are part of a larger military struggle (i.e., Vietnam and Algeria), we have no reliable statistics on the terror alone. In situations when terror alone prevails (e.g., Cyprus, Aden, Northern Ireland) the casualties terrorists inflict rarely exceed three figures.

12   "Bhowanee is happy and most so in proportion to the blood that is shed. ... Blood is her food. ... She thirsts for blood!" (Sleeman, 1836, p. 36). The estimates made by various British officials are compiled in a review article which also provides a list of 20 leading Thugs who murdered 5120 persons, an average of 256 each (A religion of murder, 1901)!

13   "There are many thieves in my village but I would not go with them. My father Assa used to counsel me against the thieves saying—do not join them, they take money without thugging. Go with Thugs. If I had a (farthing) by Thuggee, I would take it, but never by theft" (Pfirrmann, 1970, p. 70). Another on-the-spot observer, Sir John Malcolm (1823, vol. 2, p. 187), suggested that robbery was the prime concern, "their victims ... are always selected for having property. ..." But the evidence seems to be clearly against him.

14   To allay Hindu anxieties concerning Thug reprisals, the British waived many rights of the defendants. Individuals could be convicted simply for being members of the group and then would be interned for the rest of their lives on grounds that they perceived Thuggee as a religious obligation and would always continue to do so. Thomas Macauley probably drew up the legislation. The rationale is explained by Hervey (1892, vol. 2, pp. 443–451 and Appendixes E and F). In World War II Gillie (1944) contended that the principles should be revived to dispose of Nazi leaders, and to some extent they were embodied at Nuremberg.

15   No serious argument has been made that the Thugs ever had a political purpose. Russell and Hira (1916) conclude that the immunities were probably linked with Hindu concepts of luck and impurities, although the immunities may have represented tribes from which Thugs originated or disguises Thugs often assumed.

16   Thirty to forty Europeans normally participated in these operations against some 10,000 Thugs. A few assassination attempts against officials occurred, but the assailants lost their nerve, so pervasive must have been the taboo. As far as we know, the Thugs murdered only one or two European travellers.

17   "So far from shrinking at the appellation, when one of them is asked who he is, he will coolly answer that he is a robber" (Hutton, 1961, p. 127).

18   The prolongation of the death agony (the only exception?) was required by Thug doctrine.

19   Apparently the major anxiety of Thugs was that they might be hung by a person of a lower caste (Spry, 1837, vol. 2, chap. 5).

20   For the convenience of readers unfamiliar with Islamic references, I shall refer to the Nizari by their more familiar name, Assassins. When I refer to sympathetic elements, I have in mind the Shia and especially the Ismaili, the groups from which the Assassins originated. Orthodox Muslims are Sunni.

Few Assassin documents have survived, and our picture of the sect is reconstructed mostly from bitterly hostile orthodox chroniclers who obviously could not pierce the veil of secrecy, even if they had wanted to do so. Poonawala (1977) provides the most recent bibliography of sources and secondary works. Many item are annotated. The difficulties of the contemporary historian are aptly described in Hodgson (1955, pp. 22–32). Universally recognized as the best source, Hodgson's work was later sharpened (1968). My analysis is based largely on these accounts and on Lewis (1940, 1967).

21   The reference is to Shia doctrine, but it applies equally to the Assassins.

22   "A state ought not during war to countenance such hostilities as would make mutual confidence in a subsequent peace impossible such as employing assassins, poisoners, breaches of capitulation, secret

instigations to treachery and rebellion in the hostile state … (for there must be) some kind of confidence in the disposition of the enemy even in the midst of war, or otherwise … the hostilities will pass into a war of extermination. … Such a war and … all means which lead to it, must be absolutely forbidden." (*Cf.* Vattel, I, 19, 233.)

23 The sect, of course, was the subject of many allegations, but it was never charged with instigating counter-atrocities against groups or classes. Its targets were almost invariably individuals. The sober Sunni view was that the Nizari wanted "to destroy Islam but not necessarily any … Muslims" (Hodgson, 1955, p. 123).

24 The Azraqites apparently practiced indiscriminate slaughter, arguing that every member of a family of unbelievers was an unbeliever (Watt, 1973, p. 22).

25 The initial assassination, that of Asma bent Marwan, was occasioned by Mohammed's question, "Will no one rid me of (her)?" Henry II encouraged his knights in the same way when he grumbled about Becket. But how different were the results! Becket was martyred, the knights were punished, and the English king did penance. For a discussion of Greco-Roman and Christian attitudes toward assassination, see Rapoport (1971, chap. 1).

   Six assassinations are discussed by Rodinson (1971, chap. 5). They are also described by Watt (1956), but because Watt's references are scattered throughout the text and fewer details are provided, it is more difficult to perceive patterns.

26 In the Koran, the term hypocrite (*munafikun*) refers to those whose fidelity and zeal Mohammed could not rely upon, persons "in whose hearts there is sickness, weakness, and doubt … who had joined Islam perhaps reluctantly … usually members of the aristocracy" (Buhl, 1913). Most of those assassinated were Jews, but Mohammed's "Constitution of Medina" clearly indicates that his original community included Jews, and initially he intended to bring Islam as close as possible to Judaism. When that policy failed, the assassinations were an essential aspect of the struggle to separate the two religious bodies and to gain converts out of the Jewish tribes. The process is illustrated in the aftermath of the first assassination, that of a Jewish poetess by 'Umayr, her kinsmen: "'Umayr returned to his own clan, which was in a great uproar. Decide what is to be done with me, but do not keep me waiting! No one moved. … That was the day when Islam first showed its power over the Banu Katma. 'Umayr had been the first among them to become a Muslim. On the day the daughter of Marwan was killed, the men of the Banu Khatma were converted because of what they saw of the power of Islam" (Ibn Hisham quoted by Rodinson, 1971, p. 171).

27 Margoliouth (1923, p. 116) notes that Muslim initially meant "traitor, one who handed over his kinsmen or friends to their enemies," and that "Mohammed … displayed great ingenuity" in transforming its meaning into "one who handed over his own person to God." The new religion, he believes, could not survive without challenging the kin bond; and "Islam, as appears from the most authorized traditions, had the effect of making men anxious … to signalize their faith by parricide or fratricide" (p. 265). The traditional or orthodox interpretations of these incidents is that the assailants, shamed by their kinsmen's behavior, acted on their own initiative.

28 No terrorist campaign before the nineteenth century is better known, and virtually all our information comes from Josephus Flavius, a Jewish commander who later became a Roman supporter and portrays the Zealots and *Sicarii* as provoking the popular uprising when no irreconcilable issues divided Roman and Jew. How reliable is Josephus? Historians have always disagreed. He has been seen as a "mere Roman apologist," and the accounts he challenges have vanished. His description, like those of all ancient historians, wildly exaggerates statistics and contains inconsistencies which serve explicit didactic purposes. Still, moderns increasingly find him credible, except on particular matters where good reason to mistrust him exists. When his sources can be checked, he "remains fairly close to the original. Even when he modifies the source to suit a certain aim, he still reproduces the essence of the story. More important, he does not engage in the free invention of episodes … like other (ancient) authors …" (Cohen, 1979, p. 233). All other extant sources, Roman and Jewish materials alike, are more hostile to the rebels than Josephus himself was. Although some say "that Josephus' good faith as a historian cannot be seriously questioned" (Shutt, 1961, p. 123), most agree that despite other concerns he truly had "an interest as a historian in the course of events themselves" (Bilde, 1979, p. 201).

   The second issue is which of Josephus' different and contradictory assessments of motives is most credible? I have followed the modern tendency in playing down the criminal and personal motives Josephus gives to the rebels in order to emphasize their religious and political concerns. And I have taken seriously his frequently repeated contention, which some scholars question, that the terrorists forced their will on reluctant parties. The process of polarizing a society by exploiting latent hostilities through shock tactics was not understood well by the nineteenth- and early twentieth-century commentators on

Josephus who knew of no terror campaigns with which to compare the revolt. More recent scholars display less skepticism on this point. My earlier study (1982b) is a step-by-step analysis of the dynamic presupposed by Josephus' account, and the description above is based upon that essay.

The literature on the revolt is quite extensive. The following articles (in addition to those cited above) were particularly helpful: Applebaum (1971), Betz et al. (1974), Borg (1971), Farmer (1956), Grant (1973), Hengel (1961), Horsley (1979b), Kingdom (1970, 1971), Kohler (1905), Roth (1959), Smallwood (1976), Stern (1973), Thackeray (1967), and Zeitlin (1967).

29 For a convenient discussion of the *herem* and its revival by the Zealots-Sicarii as reflected in the Dead Sea Scrolls, see de Vaux (1972, pp. 258–267). The later conception had new elements: the war would be a war to end all wars, it would involve all men, and the enemy was under Satan's influence.

30 Rapoport (1982b, pp. 36–37) discusses relationships between the process described here and modern campaign experiences. For a general discussion of passive resistance and terrorism, see Thornton (1964, p. 75).

31 A third reason for studying sacred terror is that there are direct links between some of its concepts and those that animate modern forms (Dugard, 1982).

32 In 1933, J. L. Sleeman wrote, "it is of interest to speculate as to what the procedure would be today were such an organization of murder to be discovered in India, and imagination runs riot at the long vista of Royal Commissions, Blue, Red, and White Books, Geneva Conferences and the political capital which would be made of it, the procrastination and the delay, tying the hands of those on the spot, and the world propaganda which would ensure. ... Thuggee could shelter behind disunited party government" (p. 103).

33 The Crusades are the major exception, for they were inspired by the *herem* and undertaken to regain the Holy Land in order to initiate a messianic era.

References

A religion of murder. *Quarterly Review,* 1901, *194,* 506–513.

Applebaum, S. The Zealots: the case for revaluation. *Journal of Roman Studies,* 1971, *61,* 155–170.

Betz, O., Haacker, K., & Hengal, M. *Josephus-Studien.* Gottingen: Vanderhoeck and Ruprecht, 1974.

Bilde, P. The causes of the Jewish War according to Josephus. *Journal for the Study of Judaism,* 1979, *10,* 179–202.

Borg, M. The currency of the term "Zealot." *Journal of Theological Studies,* 1971, 22, 504–513.

Buhl, Fr Munafikun. *Encyclopedia of Islam.* London: Luzac, 1913.

Bruce, C. *The Stranglers.* London: Longmans, 1968.

Clark, H. *Zebra.* New York: Merek, 1979.

Cohen, S. J. D. *Josephus in Galilee and Rome.* Leiden: Brill, 1979.

Cohn, N. *The pursuit of the millenium: revolutionary messianism in medieval and reformation Europe and its bearing on modern totalitarian movements.* New York: Harper Torchbooks, 1961.

Collins, W. *The moonstone.* London: Tinsley, 1868.

DeQuincey, T. Supplementary paper on murder considered as one of the fine arts. In *Works.* Boston: Houghton Mifflin, 1877.

Dugard, J. International terrorism and the Just War. In D. C. Rapoport & Y. Alexander (Eds.). *The morality of terrorism: religions and secular justifications.* New York: Pergamon, 1982.

Farmer, W. R. *Maccabees, Zealots, and Josephus.* New York: Columbia University Press, 1956.

Ferrero, G. *The principles of power.* New York: Arno, 1972.

Freedman, L. Z. Why does terrorism terrorize? In D. C. Rapoport & Y. Alexander (Eds.). *The rationalization of terrorism.* Frederick, Md.: University Publications of America, 1982.

Friedlaender, I. The heterodoxies of the Shi-ites in the presentation of Ibh Hazm. *Journal of the American Oriental Society,* 1907, *28,* 1–80; 1909, *29,* 1–183.

Gillie, D. R. Justice and Thugs. *The Spectator.* 1944, *172,* 567–568.

Gordon, S. N. Scarf and sword: Thugs, marauders and state formation in 18th century Malwa. *Indian Journal of Economic and Social History,* 1969, *6,* 403–429.

Grant, J. *The Jews in the Roman world.* London: Wiedenfeld, 1973.

Gupta, H. A critical study of the Thugs and their activities. *Journal of Indian History,* 1959, *38,* 167–176.

Gurr, T. Some characteristics of terrorism. In M. Stohl (Ed.), *The politics of terrorism*. New York: Dekker, 1979.

Hacker, F. *Crusaders, criminals, and crazies*. New York: Norton, 1976.

Hardman, J. Terrorism. *Encyclopaedia of the Social Sciences*. New York: Macmillan, 1933.

Hengel, M. *Die Zeloten*. Leiden: Brill, 1961.

Herodotus. *Persian Wars*.

Hervey, J. *Some records of crime*. London: Sampson Low, 1892.

Hodgkin, T. Mahdism, Messianism and Marxism in the African setting. In P. Gutkind & P. Waterman (Eds.). *African social studies: A radical reader*. New York: 1977.

Hodgson, M. G. S. The Ismaili state. In W. B. Fisher (Ed.), *The Cambridge history of Iran*. Cambridge: Cambridge University Press, 1968.

Hodgson, M. G. S. *The order of Assassins*. The Hague: Mouton, 1955.

Horsley, R. A. Josephus and the bandits. *Journal for the Study of Judaism*, 1979, *10*, 38–63. (b)

Horsley, R. A. The *Sicarii*; ancient Jewish "terrorists." *Journal of Religion*, 1979, *59*, 435–458. (a)

Hutton, J. *A popular account of the Thugs and Dakoits*. London: W. H. Allen, 1857.

Hutton, J. H. *Caste in India*. Oxford: Clarendon Press, 1961.

Ibrahim, S. Anatomy of Egypt's militant Islamic groups. *International Journal of Middle Eastern Studies*, 1980, *12*, 423–453.

Ivianski, Z. The moral issue: some aspects of individual terror. In D. C. Rapoport & Y. Alexander (Eds.), *The morality of terrorism: religious and secular justifications*. New York: Pergamon, 1982.

Jenkins, B. *International terrorism: a new mode of conflict*. Los Angeles: Crescent, 1975.

Josephus. The Jewish War. In *Works*. Loeb Classical Library. London: Heinemann, 1926 (a).

Josephus. Antiquities of the Jews. In *Works*. Loeb Classical Library. London: Heinemann, 1926. (b)

Kant, I. *Perpetual peace*. M. Smith (Trans.). New York: Liberal Arts, 1948.

Kingdom, H. Origin of the Zealots. *New Testament Studies*, 1971, *79*, 74–61.

Kingdom, H. Who were the Zealots? *New Testament Studies*, 1970, *17*, 68–72.

Kohlberg, E. The development of the Imami Shii doctrine of *Jihad*. *Deutschen Morgenlandischen Gesellschaft Zeitschrift*, 1976, *126*, 64–82.

Kohler, K. Zealots. *The Jewish Encyclopedia*. New York: Funk & Wagnalls, 1905.

Lang, D. A reporter at large: the bank drama (Swedish hostages). *The New Yorker*, 1974, 50(40), 56–126.

Laqueur, W. *Terrorism*. Boston: Little Brown, 1977.

Lerner, M. Assassination. *Encyclopaedia of the Social Sciences*. New York: Macmillan, 1933.

Lewis, B. *The Assassins: a radical sect in Islam*. London: Nicholson and Weidenfeld, 1967.

Lewis, B. *Origins of Ismailism*. Cambridge: Cambridge University Press, 1940.

MacEoin, D. The Babi concept of the Holy War. *Religion*, 1982, *12*, 93–129.

Malcolm, J., Sir. *A memoir of Central India*. London: Kingsbury, Parbury and Allen, 1823.

Marighella, C. *For the liberation of Brazil*. Harmondsworth: Penguin, 1972.

Margoliouth, D. S. *Mohammed and the rise of Islam*. London: G. P. Putnam, 1923.

Masters, J. *The deceivers*. New York: Viking, 1952.

Mickolus, E. F. *Transnational terrorism: a chronology of events*. Westport, Conn.: Greenwood, 1980.

Nechaev, S. The revolutionary catechism. In D. C. Rapoport, *Assassination and terrorism*. Toronto: Canadian Broadcasting Corp., 1972.

Pal, B. *Memories of my life and times*. Calcutta: Modern Book Agency, 1932.

Pfirrmann, G. *Religioser charakter und organisatin der Thag-Bruederschaften*. Tuebingen: Ph.D. dissertation, 1970.

Poonawala, K. *Biobibliography of Ismaili literature*. Malibu, Calif.: Undena, 1977.

Price, H., Jr. The strategy and tactics of revolutionary terrorism. *Comparative Studies in Society and History*, 1977, *19*, 52–65.

Rapoport, D. C. Introduction. Religious terror. In D. Canadian Broadcasting Corp., 1971.

Rapoport, D. C. The politics of atrocity. In Y. Alexander & S. Finger (Eds.), *Terrorism: Interdisciplinary perspectives*. New York: John Jay, 1977.

Rapoport, D. C. Introduction. Religious terror. In D. C. Rapoport & Y. Alexander, *The morality of terrorism: religious and secular justifications*. New York: Pergamon, 1982. (a)

Rapoport, D. C. Terror and the messiah; an ancient experience and modern parallels. In D. C. Rapoport & Y. Alexander (Eds.), *The morality of terrorism: Religious and secular justifications*. New York: Pergamon, 1982. (b)

Rapoport, D. C. & Alexander, Y. (Eds.). *The morality of terrorism: Religious and secular justifications*. New York: Pergamon Press, 1982.

Rodinson, M. *Mohammed*. London: Penguin, 1971.

Roth, C. The Zealots and the war of 66–70. *Journal of Semitic Studies*, 1959, *4*, 332–334.

Rubin, J. *Do it*. New York: Simon and Schuster, 1970.

Russell, C. A., Banker, L. J., & Miller, B. H. Out-inventing the terrorist. In Y. Alexander, D. Carlton, and P. Wilkinson (Eds.), *Terrorism: theory and practice*. Boulder, Colo.: Westview, 1979.

Russell, R. V., & Hira, L. *The tribes and castes of the Central Provinces of India*. London: Macmillan, 1916.

Sandler, T., Tshirhart, J. T., & Cauley, J. A theoretical analysis of transnational terrorism. *American Political Science Review*, 1983, 77, 36–54.

Scholem, G. *The messianic idea in Judaism*. New York: Schocken, 1971.

Schonfield, J. *The Passover plot*. New York: Geis, 1965.

Sherwood, R. On the murderers called P'hansigars. *Asiatic Researchers*, 1820, *13*, 250–281.

Shutt, R. J. H. *Studies in Josephus*. London: S.P.C.K. 1961.

Sleeman, J. L. *Thugs; or a million murders*. London S. Low and Marston, 1933.

Sleeman, W. H. *Ramaseeana*. Calcutta: Huttman, 1836.

Sleeman, W. H. *The Thugs or Phansigars of India*. Philadelphia: Carey and Hart, 1839.

Sleeman, W. H. *Report on the depredations committed by the Thug gangs of Upper and Central India*. Calcutta: Huttman, 1840.

Sleeman, W. H. *A journey through the kingdom of Oudh in 1849–1850*. London: Bentley, 1858.

Sleeman, W. H. *Rambles and recollections of an Indian official*, V. A. Smith (Ed.). Westminster: Constable, 1893.

Smallwood, E. J. *The Jews under Roman rule*. Leiden: Brill, 1976.

Smith, M. Zealots and *Sicarii*: their origins and relations. *Harvard Theological Review*, 1971, *64*, 1–19.

Spry, H. *Modern India*. London: Whitaker, 1837.

Stern, J. Zealots. *Encyclopedia Judaica Yearbook*. New York: Macmillan, 1973.

Taylor, M. *Confessions of a Thug*. London: R. Bentley, 1839.

Taylor, M. *The story of my life*. London: Oxford University Press, 1920.

Thackeray, H. St. J. *Josephus, the man and the historian*. New York: repr. Ktva, 1967.

Thornton, E. *Illustrations and practices of the Thugs*. London: W. H. Allen, 1837.

Thornton, T. P. Terror as a weapon of political agitation. In H. Eckstein (Ed.), *Internal War*. New York: Free Press, 1964.

Tugwell, M. *Revolutionary propaganda and possible counter-measures*. Kings College, University of London: Ph.D. dissertation, 1979.

Tyan, E. Djihad. *Encyclopedia of Islam*. Leiden: Brill, 1960.

Vattel, E. *The law of nations*. London: Newbery, 1760.

de Vaux, R. *Ancient Israel*. New York: McGraw-Hill, 1972.

Walter, E. V. *Terror and resistance: a study of political violence*. New York: Oxford University Press, 1969.

Watt, M. W. *The formative period of Islamic thought*. Edinburgh: University Press, 1973.

Watt, M. W. *Mohammed at Medina*. Oxford: Clarendon Press, 1956.

Weber, M. *The sociology of religion*. E. Fischoff (Ed.). London: Methuen, 1955.

Zeitlin, S. The Sicarii and the Zealots. *Jewish Quarterly Review*, 1967, *57*, 251–270.

2 How new is the new terrorism?

Isabelle Duyvesteyn

New terrorism is a concept that has recently been used by many and questioned by few; "Many contemporary studies begin ... by stating that although terrorism has always been a feature of social existence, it became 'significant' ... when it 'increased in frequency' and took on 'novel dimensions' as an international or transnational activity, creating in the process a new 'mode of conflict.'"[1] This quote makes sense in light of the terrorist attacks of 11 September 2001, were it not that it was written in the early 1980s describing a situation starting in the 1960s.[2] The present generation is thus not the only one perceiving terrorism to be fundamentally new.

What does it mean when something is labeled new? David Rapoport has argued that the label new even in the 1960s was not contentious: "we analyze contemporary experiences as though the statement declaring them *sui generis* is itself clear and at the same time provides the only evidence needed to establish the case!"[3] "New" can signify that a phenomenon has not been witnessed before, such as the discovery of a new star in a far-away galaxy. Alternatively, the label "new" can rightly be applied when it concerns seen-before phenomena but an unknown perspective or interpretation is developed, such as the theory of relativity or the idea that the earth is round. In the case of the arguments that are presented about the new terrorism the first understanding of new is prominent, that is, among others the fanaticism and ruthlessness of the Al Qaeda terrorists, who are held responsible for the devastating terrorist attacks, has not been seen before. This article will argue that from a historical perspective there are several reasons to be hesitant about the application of the label new.

While the label new has not been hotly debated in regard to terrorism, the concept of terrorism itself has.[4] The concept of terrorism has, in the past, been pronounced dead, analytically useless, and only valid in the eye of the beholder. Despite all the problems, the term and concept continue to be used. This continued use, perhaps because of the lack of a viable alternative, suggests that the term does seem to be able and useful to describe or denote a social phenomenon.

A study by Alex Schmid compared a large number of existing definitions of terrorism he had come across in his investigations.[5] The factor that in a quantitative perspective carried most agreement in these definitions was violence (over 80%). The second most common element of "political" that was contained in definitions of terrorism already showed a lot less agreement (65%). Fear or terror as the third element could only be found in 51% of the definitions. The limited extent of the agreement is an indication of how contentious the term is analytically.[6]

Apart from being difficult to define, the term should also be judged from the perspective of the beholder. This refers to the too often quoted cliché that one man's terrorist is another man's freedom fighter. Put in the words of Noam Chomsky, "we have to qualify the definition of 'terrorism' given in official sources: the term applies only to terrorism against *us*, not the terrorism we carry out against *them*."[7] Terrorism is thus often a pejorative term.

When terrorism is such a semantic, terminological, and conceptual minefield, why is it still used in academic study? The aim of this article is to demonstrate that a substantial input by historians in the debate about the nature of terrorism has been lacking. The dominating influence of social and political science has had as a result that the label new has largely gone unquestioned but more importantly that a systematic, large-scale, and cross-case comparison of historical cases has to date not been written. This has not only hampered the understanding of the phenomenon of terrorism, but has prevented the development of insights into patterns, trends, and transformations of terrorism in the modern period. First, the article will briefly survey the state of terrorism research in order to outline what is known about the phenomenon. Two main fields of study that have devoted substantial attention to the subject of terrorism, social science—in particular psychology—and political science will be discussed. Each of these fields will be reviewed in order to appreciate the debates that have ensued here. After this brief survey of the field, the main part of the article will challenge the current dominant view on the newness of terrorism.

The study of terrorism

Although it has been another often quoted cliché about terrorism that it is as old as history, the academic interest in the subject only seriously took off in the early 1970s.[8] In particular, political science has dominated the field since that period.[9] However, other fields such as social science, psychology, criminology, law, and military and communication studies have made contributions as well. Despite these scholarly endeavors, judgments on the overall state of terrorism research have not been favorable. As Alex Schmid has stated, "[m]uch of the writing in the crucial areas of terrorism research … is impressionistic, superficial and at the same time often also pretentious, far-reaching generalizations on the basis of episodal evidence."[10] Furthermore, "[p]erhaps as much as 80 percent of the literature is not research-based in any rigorous sense; instead it is too often narrative, condemnatory and prescriptive."[11] Despite this criticism, some important insights have been gained.

Social science

The main psychological explanations for terrorism have focused on the link between frustration and aggression, group dynamics, and individual psychological dispositions. In the 1970s Robert Ted Gurr developed the Relative Deprivation Theory. This theory contends that when there is frustration about the relative position of individuals in terms of what they have and their perceptions of what they ought to have, that is, deprivation, the chances of seeing violence increase.[12] When this situation is compounded by an ideology inciting uprising and violence and the chances and opportunities arise for doing so, persons willing to engage in terrorism will. This theory has been extensively criticized; nevertheless it shows in which direction the terrorism experts have been looking for evidence of the origins of violent and terrorist acts.

As for the field of psychology, while terrorists have been found to mostly operate in small groups,[13] there is no evidence of a terrorist personality, nor has there been a consistent finding of abnormality or derangement in persons involved in the undertaking.[14] Terrorism is mainly a small-group activity and has a tendency to involve groupthink and group dynamics, which are much more likely to occur than individual psychological abnormalities.[15] Several attempts have been made to develop a terrorist profile. Based on data gathered from press reports on 350 individual terrorists in the period 1968–1976, the following profile has been compiled: "They are in the main, single, male, 22 to 25 years old … university trained, reared in an urban environment, middle to upper class in social origin, and anarchist or Marxist in ideology."[16] The exceptions were Germany, where there were more female terrorists active; Japan, where the average age was older; and Northern Ireland, where the origin was of the lower social strata. Furthermore, "the vast majority of terrorists with university backgrounds have studied in the humanities and non-technical fields," with exceptions for Iran and Turkey.[17] Despite heavy criticism over the years, especially concerning its testability, this profile does not seem far off the mark when surveying the material that has come out in the media on, for example, the Al Qaeda terrorists.

Not only the individual terrorist and the interaction in groups have received attention in the field of psychology, the effects of terrorism have also been studied. There are indications of a copycat or contamination effect of terrorism.[18] Most of the studies in this area, however, focus on individual coping mechanisms.[19] One example is the Stockholm syndrome, where the victim starts to identify with the terrorist. Also the after-effects in victims have been studied, which can be long-lasting, both mentally and physically.

Political science

Whereas the social sciences have devoted considerable attention to actor-focused perspectives of terrorism, political science has presented many purpose-focused studies. The purposes or aims of terrorist movements have often been cloaked in left-wing/right-wing dichotomies. In particular, left-wing terrorism, that is, inspired by Marx, Lenin, Mao, anarchism, or nihilism has received attention.[20] This is not to suggest that the political scientist has not had an eye for the actors perpetrating terrorist acts. Especially the distinction between state and non-state actors is important in this respect, for example, the terrorism of the Nazi and Stalinist states.[21]

Apart from divisions into left-wing and right-wing terrorism, nationalist, separatist, irredentist, ethnic, and religious motivations have been offered as explanations for terrorism. Although during the 1960s and 1970s the debate was heavily focused on left-wing terrorism, since the 1990s the bulk of the literature concerns religious terrorism. In particular, the 1993 World Trade Center bombing in New York, the sarin gas attack in the Tokyo subway by the Japanese Aum Shinrikyo sect, and the Oklahoma City bombing by the Christian-inspired Timothy McVeigh were instrumental in putting this perspective on the research agenda.[22] Overall the political science approach is characterized by eclecticism. It has borrowed theories from other fields such as Robert Ted Gurr's Relative Deprivation Theory[23] and, furthermore, it has adopted characteristically the case study approach. Among the most investigated case studies are the Northern Irish and Algerian examples.[24]

Historical research

Walter Laqueur is generally credited with linking history and terrorism.[25] Laqueur himself has expressed doubt, however, about the usefulness of the study of terrorism's history. Although "[t]he history of terrorism remains an essential key to understanding the phenomenon"[26] at the same time he has argued that "all this history has to be recalled for the simple reason that an analysis of the roots of terrorism at the beginning of the twentieth century cannot be based exclusively on the experience of earlier phases."[27] Ironically, one of the founding fathers of the historical approach to terrorism has serious reservations about the usefulness of studying the phenomenon in a historical perspective. This does seem to be a wider shared opinion: "For most commentators terrorism has no history, or at least they would have us believe that the 'terrorist problem' had no significance until the 1960s, when the full impact of modern technology was felt, endowing most individuals as individuals or as members of small groups, with capacities they never had before."[28] These doubts and reservations have led to a state of affairs in which a thorough study of the history of modern terrorism is completely lacking.[29]

Several attempts in the direction of historical analysis of terrorism have been made. There are authoritative encyclopaedias that cover the whole of the modern period, notably the excellent work done by Martha Crenshaw and John Pimlott.[30] However, these are works of reference and lack systematic analysis and cross-time comparisons. Furthermore, historical anthologies about terrorism exist.[31] Although presenting important documents and texts, they do not meet the specifics of historical studies either. Also, a very limited number of studies exist that try to map the development of terrorism. Notable is Andrew Sinclair's study, *An Anatomy of Terror*.[32] His book, however, aims to be comprehensive by starting in antiquity, but lacks analysis and critical examination of competing sources. Furthermore, Martin Miller has made an attempt to study the intellectual origins of modern terrorism in the nineteenth century.[33] He points out that the institutionalization, organization, and intellectual and theoretical foundations shifted in this period from tyrannicide to more limitless terrorism. Unfortunately he has limited himself to only the nineteenth century. Finally, many terrorism studies do start with an obligatory historical introduction but these are in the majority of the cases not based on independent historical research and only function as a stepping stone toward discussing other aspects of the phenomenon.[34]

In general there are several problems with the literature on terrorism. First, there is very little building on previous work that has been done in the field.[35] Terrorism seems to be an area of expertise built around big names and individual projects. Second, there exists a strong temptation to predict the future. The fact that those predictions were not always on the mark can be illustrated by the following example. In the 1968 International Encyclopaedia of the Social Sciences, the concept of terrorism was completely missing. David Rapoport speculated that the editors seemed to have believed the prediction of the experts in the previous 1933 edition that read that 'assassinations and acts of terror were declining so much that in the future the subjects would be interesting to historians or antiquarians only."[36] Prediction, however, if at all undertaken by social scientists should be based on thorough investigation of the subject including a basis of historical trends, patterns, and development and this is, as noted, what the field needs. The current research agenda will now be discussed, and it will be demonstrated where and how historical studies could contribute to and shed a different light on the discussion of the nature of terrorism.

The research agenda

The terrorist attacks of 11 September 2001 have given rise to what can almost be called a tidal wave of literature trying to understand, if not explain, the surprise attacks on the American mainland. Characteristic of this literature is the qualification of the attacks as part of a new chapter in the history of terrorism. This is not to stress that the label new is inextricably linked to the events of 11 September. As already noted the term new had been used extensively before and in particular in the mid-1990s the term resurfaced in the debate.[37] The now widespread stress on the new character of terrorism might be due to the enormity of the shock and the damage that was suffered that September day, both physically and emotionally. Another explanation might be that the high production rate has been caused by ambitious and eager scientists who aim to contribute to the debate. Or, less idealistically, they see an opportunity to establish their reputation.[38] All seem to regard the use of the label new as a way to originality.

The new terrorism is supposedly new because of the following prominent features.[39] First, the perpetrators of terrorism act transnationally and operate in loosely organized networks. Second, they are inspired by religion and are seen as religious fanatics. Third, they seek weapons to attack as many people as possible, notably weapons of mass destruction. Fourth, their victims are not carefully selected but their targeting is indiscriminate. On the basis of arguments pertaining to the actors, their motivation, the instruments they use, and the effects they aim to achieve, several questions will now be raised concerning the extent of the "newness" of the new terrorism.[40]

The actors

The actors carrying out the new terrorism are said to operate transnationally. They are not bound by national ties or sentiments but are loosely organized in the form of networks and with their own channels of finance. This is in contrast to traditional terrorism, which was supposed to be characterized by a purely national and territorial focus and a hierarchical organization. Examples are said to be the Irish Republican Army (IRA) and the Basque ETA movement.

Three points can be raised here. First, the actors responsible for the terrorist attacks of 11 September 2001 were also focused on national and territorial aspects similar to the traditional terrorists. Second, the traditional terrorists also operated transnationally to a significant extent. Third, the traditional terrorists' organizational structure was in several cases also based on networks.

To start with the last point, a network structure is not exclusive to the new terrorism. An important historical example forms the anarchist movement in the nineteenth century, which was active most notably in imperial Russia and France. This anarchist organization was responsible for several high-profile attacks among others against heads of state. The organization was network- instead of hierarchically based.[41] Furthermore, even in the twentieth century terrorist organizations used the network structure. David Tucker argues that the PLO and Hezbollah operate fundamentally as networks with very little formal central control being exercised.[42]

Furthermore, there is evidence that terrorists received support from outside sponsors, such as princes and other wealthy individuals even in antiquity.[43] In the historic literature this transnational aspect is a given and is not adequately realized by the authors from the new terrorism school.[44] More recently, the transnational nature of many traditional terrorist organizations can be read from, for example, the Irish Republican Army (IRA) in the United Kingdom and the Rote Armee Fraktion (RAF) in Germany. These groups trained with the Palestinian Liberation Organization fighters in the Middle East, among others in Libya. These contacts led to Palestinian groups hijacking an airplane, which landed in Somalia in 1977 in order to put pressure on the German government to release RAF comrades from jail.[45] The Somali liberation attempt by the German GSG9 Special Forces cost the lives of several involved.[46] Another example is the Japanese Red Army, which was fighting in the 1970s to bring about a more just world according to a Marxist agenda. They carried out attacks in three continents. Even though they never had a true base in Japan itself, they managed to carry out attacks at Lod Airport in Israel, a Shell refinery in Singapore, and the French embassy in The Hague. They even enjoyed support from, among others, the North Korean regime.[47]

Finally, the national and territorial aspects of the new terrorists have also not received the attention they deserve. For example, the territorial aspects of the members of the Al Qaeda organization and Osama bin Laden's wider group of supporters can be read from their main preoccupations. First, the main aim of bin Laden and his fighters is the establishment of a Caliphate that stretches at least from North Africa to Southeast Asia. This is decidedly a territorial aim that overlaps with the present settlement of the community of believers, the Umma.

Second, they are concerned with the occupation by the United States of the holiest places of Islam. American troops have since the end of the Second Gulf War been stationed in Saudi Arabia, the land of Mecca and Medina.[48] The fighters have an axe to grind with the regimes that have allowed such a state of affairs to develop, among others the Saudi Arabian rulers and the Egyptian regime. These concerns can be seen as highly national and territorial. It is true that the church and state or rather, the mosque and the state are not separate in most Arab states. The distinction between the national, territorial, and the religious can therefore be problematic. The acceptance by political Islam of the nation-state makes the distinction impossible.[49] However, it does not discredit the existence of territorial claims of these groups.

Third, it has been argued, in particular by Lawrence Freedman, that the sanctuary that the Taliban regime provided in Afghanistan is decidedly territorial in orientation: "The description of Al-Qaeda as being a non-state was not accurate in that it had gained its base and sanctuary in Afghanistan by effectively sponsoring and then taking over the Taliban regime, and through the gradual integration of its fighters with those of the Taliban."[50] The terrorist organization needed and used the state as a staging base for its operations.[51]

Fourth, the Al Qaeda fighters are also concerned with U.S. support for the state of Israel and its policies toward the Palestinians, among others the occupation of Palestinian land. The fact that American support enables the Israeli state to continue to suppress the Palestinian population is abhorrent to bin Laden and his supporters. Some argue, however, that the Palestinian cause has been pragmatically adopted by bin Laden *cum suis* to increase the appeal and popularity of the movement.[52]

Not only the Al Qaeda terrorists but also the convicted terrorist for the Oklahoma bombing in 1995 claimed to fight against undue interference from the national American government in the lives of ordinary Americans. This can also be seen as national and territorial in focus. Government agents had besieged the compound of the religious sect of David Koresh, the Branch Davidians, in Waco, Texas. According to Timothy McVeigh, the main perpetrator, this action was against the freedoms that are granted to the American people in the United States constitution. The involvement of American national governmental agencies was abhorrent to him. The focus was for this "new terrorist" also decidedly national.

It can thus be questioned in the light of the presence of earlier network structures, the transnational nature, and territorial and national concerns of both the old and the new terrorists whether there is not more continuity than change. Essential continuity in territorial focus, transnational links, and network structures are indicated to exist. The religious can be territorially and even nationally oriented for the new terrorists, transnational operations and ties do not preclude a national and territorial focus for the old terrorists, and network structures have been in operation before. What then is so new about the new terrorism?

The aims

Religion and fanaticism are said to be the main motivators for the new terrorists. The growth of religiously inspired terrorist organizations is said to overlap with the end of the Cold War.[53] Earlier forms of terrorism were supposed to be characterized by political motivations, such as nationalism and extreme left-wing ideologies. The choice of targets of the old terrorists reflected their ideas and was highly symbolic. Two sets of question marks are in order here. First, the presumably old or traditional terrorists were not a-religious. The IRA, for example, had an almost exclusive Catholic membership. Furthermore, Irgun was a Jewish terrorist organization, EOKA in Cyprus was inspired by the Greek Orthodox Church, and the FLN fighters in Algeria were exclusively Muslim. Second, the new terrorists are not purely motivated by religion. As has already been noted, national and territorial characteristics also play a role.

Religious terrorism as a concept has several problematic aspects. First, when religion and more specifically the beliefs of the *individual* are central to the terrorism under investigation, it can be questioned why acts of violence happen at all. If all that was of concern to the individual was his or her personal relationship with God, "the primary audience is the deity ... it is even conceivable that he does not want to have the public witness his deed."[54] In several historical cases, the perpetrators of terrorist acts guided solely by religious motivations based on this personal relationship showed that their desire to die in order to please God was far greater than their willingness to kill others.[55] This is clearly not the case in the 11 September attacks, the example of Timothy McVeigh, and the Japanese Aum Shinrikyo sect. The Japanese terrorists, notably, who left sarin gas on the Tokyo underground, had gotten off the train just before the gas was released. Their willingness to take the lives of innocent bystanders was larger than their willingness to sacrifice their own lives in order to please their spiritual leader. The fact that self-sacrifice is not always present points to a possible second interpretation of religious terrorism.

Killing the infidels or non-believers or reordering the world according to a spiritual ideal, many observers have pointed out, form the main aims in religious terrorist acts. If this desire is inherent in a particular religion, the question needs to be answered why this feature is so prominent here and now that it is perceived as new. Religion is usually a factor that plays a large role in times of insecurity. Some have argued that the process of globalization causes such insecurity. The use of terrorism might even be an attempt to use an idealized past that never existed as an expression of the threat that is felt to be emanating from globalization. It can form a defensive mechanism.[56] However, religiously inspired terrorism aimed at killing others has existed for millennia. According to Rapoport, in the pre-modern age, religion was the only acceptable justification for terrorism.[57] Even during those days, making a distinction between religious terrorism and secular expressions was wholly artificial.[58] Is religious terrorism, when it has existed for millennia and has justified killing non-believers, then really new?

Not only can the conception of the religious factor itself be challenged, the aims of the new terrorist organizations themselves can also in many respects be seen as political.[59] Many have doubted whether the new terrorists have any clear goals, let alone political goals, at all:

> The nihilism of their [Al Qaeda's] means—the indifference to human costs—takes their actions out of the realm of politics, but even out of the realm of war itself. The apocalyptical nature of their goals makes it absurd to believe they are making demands at all. They are seeking the violent transformation of an irremediably sinful and unjust world.[60]

The argument that religious terrorists have no motivation because the achievement of their goal is impossible seems untenable.

A distinction should be made between short-term and long-term goals. Short-term goals seem highly attainable, that is, provocation, publicity, and hurting the enemy. Long-term goals and whether they are achievable should only be judged by the standards of those who carry out the terrorist acts. The long-term objectives for Al Qaeda and other religious groups are similar to the traditional terrorist organizations, such as the Rote Armee Fraktion or the anarchist movement. How likely was it for them to achieve their goal of revolutionary change or establishing a society based on anarchist principles? Experts have not denied the RAF or the anarchist movement a goal in their descriptions of their activities. Why should Aum Shinrikyo be denied a goal? Why are their preparations for the coming of the Apocalypse any less real than the actions to precipitate the advent of world revolution?

The fact that the aims of the 11 September attacks go directly against American interests does not negate their political nature. On close inspection of bin Laden's intellectual origins not Islam the religion but Islam the political interpretation based on the specific teachings of Sayyid Qutb are dominant.[61] It cannot be denied that religion has played a role in the formulation of the terrorist targets. However, these are translated to clear political positions related to clear political targets, the spread of political Islam, and the establishment of the Caliphate.

Religion is a problematic label because it implies a monocausal explanation that does not do justice to rich practice of terrorist activity. Several motivations usually play a role in terrorist organizations. As noted, the IRA was nationalist, predominantly Catholic, but at one point in its existence also Marxist in orientation. This also points to the fact that the traditional terrorist organizations were also marked by religion. Several examples of old terrorist organizations that had distinct religious characteristics and audiences have been named earlier. As Walter Laqueur has argued,

> A mystical element has been noted in nineteenth-century Russian terrorism, an element also present in Irish, Rumanian, Japanese, and Arab terrorists. These terrorists' belief in their cause has a religious quality; the idea of martyrs gaining eternal life appears in Irish terrorism from the very beginning, and it has been pronounced among the Shiite and other Muslims.[62]

The distinction between motivations thus becomes artificial, perhaps even subject to Western bias and leads to simplifications. It should not be forgotten that Marxism, anarchism, and their different variants that were adhered to by several of the old terrorist groups all had universal claims and were applicable to all societies, transcending national boundaries. Links between these organizations existed and state sponsorship did occur.

The new terrorism can both be seen as political and religious at the same time. These factors overlap to a large extent. Furthermore, as the historic examples have hinted, this is not a new phenomenon. The old terrorism also contained religious elements and qualities and some groups fighting to realize ideological aims, such as Marxism, had universal application. Also in respect to the aims terrorists strive to realize, more continuity is indicated to exist than hitherto might have been realized.

The instruments and effects

The means that the terrorists use are said to have changed. No longer is it the case that terrorists kidnap individuals, hijack airplanes or carry out bomb attacks, with only a relatively small number of victims. The instruments that the new terrorists use, among others weapons of mass destruction, are aimed at inflicting as much damage as possible and killing many innocent civilians.

Three important questions need clarification for these claims to be substantiated. First, to what extent are the new terrorists actually using weapons of mass destruction? Second, did traditional terrorists always limit themselves in terms of weaponry and third, in terms of the number of victims? When traditional terrorists used conventional instruments, such as small weaponry and explosives, large numbers of victims were often the result. One of the most notable examples is the attack in 1983 on the U.S. barracks in Lebanon, which cost the lives of over 200 American Marines and was carried out with a truckload of conventional explosives.[63] The scale of attacks of the old terrorists has increased as well. The Omagh bombing in Northern Ireland in 1998, for example, which killed 28, was the largest number in one incident of Northern Irish terrorism.[64] As for the number of victims terrorist attacks claim, it should be noted that at least since the beginning of the 1980s, the number of victims has been on the rise. This clearly does not overlap with the claimed development of the new terrorism since the 1990s.[65] Even before the advent of religious terrorists the effects of terrorist activities had been described as horrific and without bounds.[66]

Regarding the first question, the instruments the new terrorists use still continue to rely, to a large extent, on conventional arms.[67] Conventional explosives are the most important means with which attacks are carried out, for example, a bomb made of fertilizer in Oklahoma. One of the effects of the collapse of the Soviet Union has been that the central control has been lost over all kinds of weaponry, not only nuclear material but also chemical and biological components.[68] In addition to weapons material the know-how has also proliferated. It is therefore not surprising that experts continue to speculate if and how individuals with bad intentions have been able to lay their hands on these goods. However, the use of weapons of mass destruction certainly does not constitute a trend, as some experts have tried to make everyone believe. With the exception of the sarin gas attack in Tokyo and the anthrax letters sent in the aftermath of 11 September 2001 in the United States, both of which were strongly indicated to have mainly national sources, there are no other examples of the use of these weapons. This does not mean that they should not be expected in the future. However, two cases do not form a trend.

Even without weapons of mass destruction the new terrorists have been characterized as becoming more and more lethal. It cannot be denied that there is a statistical link between Islamic groups and a high number of fatalities in their terrorist attacks.[69] At the same time, however, the continued use of conventional weaponry, the use of bombs and airplanes, does not automatically lead to more deaths and destruction. The explanation that has been offered by the new terrorism school has been that the choice of targets has changed. It is no longer the individual representative or a symbolic target but the increasingly indiscriminate nature of the targeting that makes the new terrorism stand out in destructiveness.

However, the evidence so far does not completely support this contention. The targets are still largely symbolic. Buildings and structures continue to be selected for their symbolic value, that is, the World Trade Center as a symbol of Western capitalism or the Oklahoma Federal Building symbolizing Federal power. Furthermore, individuals remain important targets for the new terrorists, allegedly the American president in the White House during the 11 September 2001 attack and Paul Wolfowitz, American Deputy Secretary of Defense and Sergio Vieira de Mello, the United Nations special representative in Bagdad.

It should be asked whether the terrorists have changed or whether the world has changed in which they operate. Does the increase in the numbers of deaths resulting from terrorism form a conscious choice of the terrorists, a choice for new targets with high casualties, as stressed by the new terrorism school, or is it a result of the technological progress and the increased effectiveness of the instruments and a necessity to strike harder to achieve the same result? Did the invention of dynamite in the nineteenth century also signal a new era in the history of terrorism because dynamite and hand grenades continued to be used to kill heads of state and other public figures in the nineteenth century?[70] Is it not inherent in the logic of terrorism that the attacks need to be larger and more extreme in order to achieve the same or a larger effect? When the means become available, the terrorist expressions will inevitably become more extreme. What Brian Jenkins argued several years ago, "terrorists want a lot of people watching, not a lot of people dead," no longer seems to apply.[71] However, it is also a truism that the more people are dead, the more will be watching.

In order for a lot of people to be watching, the terrorists need the media. The role of the media should not be discounted here.[72] The effects of terrorist attacks are greatly enlarged when round the clock news services on television, Internet, and radio report on the terrorist activities. Terrorists thrive by media attention. This has been the case throughout the nineteenth and twentieth centuries. The global news media, the product of modernization, however, has given it a quantitative impetus. If the terrorists simply use the means that have become available in a world that has changed around them and need to strike harder to make their point, how new is the new terrorism?

Although globalization on the one hand has been perceived as having a negative influence of spreading unwanted Western dominance around the world, the terrorists, on the other hand, also benefited from the fruits it offered—international travel, communications, and ideas about weaponry. In order for terrorism not to be considered new it is implied that they should not have moved with the times.[73] It could very well be the case that because of a change in the external factors a change in the phenomenon of terrorism is perceived to have taken place and not because of the terrorists' own making or conscious choice.

The effect the new terrorists are supposedly after is the extermination of the enemy, whereas traditional terrorists had been concerned with bringing across a message and striving for change; often revolutionary change. A surprise effect and publicity was what the traditional terrorists sought. However, annihilating the enemy was important for many traditional terrorists as well and bringing the state or government to its knees or even working toward its collapse does not seem to be so different from the interpretation of the new terrorists. The immediate effect that is aimed for in the old and new terrorist attacks is still geared toward achieving surprise and publicity. The idea of propaganda by deed and the strategy of provocation have antecedents in the nineteenth century but are more applicable than ever in the early twenty-first century.[74] The fact that not every attack is claimed is not new but adds to the surprise effect and uncertainty that the attackers aim to achieve. Al Qaeda does not seem to consistently claim the attacks for which it is responsible, to make it harder for the victims, among others the United States, to retaliate.[75]

With respect to the means that are used, more continuity than change can be argued to exist. The number of terrorist victims has been on the rise for at least two decades, which does not overlap with the rise of the new terrorists. The use of weapons of mass destruction is not an inherent feature of the new terrorism and certainly does not constitute a trend. The new terrorists use predominantly the same weaponry as the traditional terrorists and continue to select symbolic targets such as powerful individuals and important structures. The increased lethality and destructiveness of terrorism can also be explained not only by a gradual increase in the effectiveness of the means in the modern period, but more importantly by the inherent necessity in terrorist actions to strike harder to reach the same effect. There is little evidence that the new terrorists and their predecessors differ in respect to surprise and publicity as effects they are after. Furthermore, the annihilation of the enemy continues to be of paramount importance, a characteristic shared by both the old and the new terrorists.

Preliminary conclusions and suggestions for an alternative research agenda

There are several important continuities between the old and new terrorism, which fundamentally question the distinction that is implied by the use of the two terms. Continuity exists in territorial focus, transnational links, and network structures, which mark both the old forms of terrorism and the new. The overlap between important aims that the terrorist organisations set themselves also constitutes continuity. Political, ideological, and religious themes strongly overlap, making clear goal-oriented distinctions problematic, if not impossible. Continuity further exists in the increase in scale and number of victims, which has been taking place over a number of years and is not just a recent phenomenon. The use of weapons of mass destruction might be a threat in the future, and we should be well aware of this, but it does not form an inherent feature of the new terrorism. The new terrorists do not differ fundamentally from their ancestors in the type of weaponry they use. Surprise, provocation, and publicity are what the terrorists are after and essential continuity exists here as well.

Some have argued that it might not be the separate features of the new terrorism that have not been seen before but the combination of these characteristics that makes terrorism new[76] and, it is argued, more dangerous. Often the most dangerous element is perceived to be the choice for weapons of mass destruction,[77] which, as has been pointed out, is based on an extremely limited number of cases. If the presence of one fundamental characteristic can already be questioned, how strong are the claims of the remaining combination of characteristics? It seems that the argument for a combination of characteristics making terrorism new is mostly inspired by the activities of Al Qaeda and leaves out the other cases.

If indeed it is the combination of factors that assures terrorism's newness, then this should be confirmed on the basis of rigorous empirical tests, which to date have not been systematically carried out. To further substantiate the claims made in this contribution, a proper historical investigation should be made into the history of terrorism. What is called for is a structured investigation, using where possible primary source material, into the development of terrorism in the modern period, that is, the nineteenth and twentieth centuries. Such a longitudinal study should incorporate several variables that are crucial for the understanding of the phenomenon, among others, the actors, their organizational structure, the instruments they use, the effects they manage to achieve, and the measures that are taken against them. Only with such a multivariate analysis can claims regarding terrorism and the extent of trends and transformations, including its newness, be substantiated.

Several requirements of this historical investigation can be formulated on the basis of the arguments presented in this article. First, it should be presumed that the terrorism, which is the subject of analysis, can be rationally understood.[78] This means that even though beliefs are seen as important in the use of violence, it is presumed that these beliefs can be rationally comprehended.[79] This rational understanding, even when disagreeing with the fundamentals of the belief, should be used as an explanatory factor.

Second, a thematic or typological approach to terrorism is not the most productive way to investigate the phenomenon. Assigning motivations such as religion cannot be objective because terrorist activities are often not claimed and motivations are often multiple and overlapping. Separating out a motivation becomes thus almost impossible.[80] In the literature, actor- and purpose-based typologies dominate.[81] Even refined and multivariate typologies cannot do justice to the rich practice. As Schmid noted: "As long as terrorism is conceptualized as extremism of ends rather than means, the concept cannot be relieved of its ideological baggage."[82] By avoiding a thematic typology, at least an attempt can be made to attenuate this problem.

Third, reactions to and measures against terrorist activities should be taken into account because of the action and reaction cycle between the terrorists and the authorities charged with combating them. This forms an exchange process. The counter-measures define the space that is left for terrorists to operate in. Especially discussions about asymmetric responses should be incorporated here.[83]

The label "new" should only be applied when on the basis of historical research the phenomenon has not been seen before or when it is the subject of a new historical interpretation. This contribution has indicated that in both cases this might turn out to be ultimately problematic. Terrorism is part of daily reality. Using the label new might give expression to the pain and trauma that is suffered as a result of terrorist activity. However, using the label new does not always help in clarifying and comprehending what is actually occurring in the world today.

Notes

1 David C. Rapoport, "Fear and Trembling; Terrorism in Three Religious Traditions," *American Political Science Review*, 78(3) (1984), pp. 658–677, p. 658.

2 The label new has been used many times before; even at the beginning of the twentieth century with the advent of nationalist political violence this same label was used. Walter Laqueur, *The New Terrorism: Fanatics and the Arms of Mass Destruction* (London: Phoenix, 2001), p. 20.

3   Rapoport, "Fear and Trembling," p. 659.
4   Not only terrorism has been labelled new in the past ten years. There has, for example, also been talk of "new wars." See Mary Kaldor, *New and Old Wars: Organized Violence in a Global Era* (Cambridge: Polity, 1999). This proposition has also been questioned: Mats Berdal, "How 'New' are 'New Wars'? Global Economic Change and the Study of Civil War," *Global Governance* 9 (2003), pp. 477–502. Isabelle Duyvesteyn and Jan Angstrom (eds.), *The Nature of Modern War: Clausewitz and his Critics Revisited* (Stockholm: Swedish National Defence College, 2003). Isabelle Duyvesteyn, *Clausewitz and African War: Politics and Strategy in Liberia and Somalia* (London: Taylor and Francis, 2004).
5   Alex P. Schmid and Albert J. Jongman et al., *Political Terrorism; A New Guide to Actors, Authors, Concepts, Data Bases, Theories and Literature* (New Brunswick, NJ: Transaction, 1988), pp. 5–6.
6   This is not only a problem for academic studies but also and perhaps more so for government and law in order to put a stop to terrorist activities. See for example, John F. Murphy, *State Support of International Terrorism: Legal, Political and Economic Dimensions* (Boulder, CO: Westview, 1989).
7   Noam Chomsky, "Who are the Global Terrorists?," in Ken Booth and Tim Dunne (eds.), *Worlds in Collision: Terror and the Future of Global Order* (Basingstoke: Palgrave MacMillan, 2002), pp. 128–137, p. 131. Italics in original.
8   Walter Laqueur, *No End to War: Terrorism in the Twenty-First Century* (New York: Continuum, 2003), p. 138. Schmid, *Political Terrorism*, 177. Schmid claims that "more than 85% of all books on the topic have been written since 1968." See also the bibliography of Edward F. Mickolus, *The Literature of Terrorism: A Selective Annotated Bibliography* (Westport, CT: Greenwood, 1993), which only lists titles from the 1970s.
9   Rapoport, "Fear and Trembling," p. 658. Schmid, *Political Terrorism*, p. 207.
10 Schmid, *Political Terrorism*, p. 177.
11 Ibid., p. 177.
12 Robert Ted Gurr, *Why Men Rebel* (Princeton, NJ: Princeton University Press, 1970).
13 Martha Crenshaw, "The Psychology of Political Terrorism," in Margaret Hermann (ed.), *Political Psychology: Contemporary Problems and Issues* (San Francisco, CA: Jossey-Bass, 1986), pp. 379–413, p. 389.
14 Ibid., p. 385.
15 Jerrold Post, "Terrorist Psycho-logic: Terrorist Behavior as a Product of Psychological Forces," in Walter Reich (ed.), *Origins of Terrorism; Psychologies, Ideologies, Theologies, States of Mind* (Washington DC: Woodrow Wilson Center Press, 1998).
16 Charles A. Russell, Leon J. Barker Jr., and Bowman H. Miller, "Out-Inventing the Terrorist," in Yonah Alexander, David Carlton, and Paul Wilkinson (eds.), *Terrorism: Theory and Practice* (Boulder, CO: Westview, 1979), pp. 3–42, p. 8. See also Charles A. Russell and Bowman H. Miller, "Profile of a Terrorist," *Terrorism: An International Journal* 1(1) (1977).
17 Russell, Barker, and Miller, "Out-Inventing the Terrorist," p. 8.
18 Manus I. Midlarsky, Martha Crenshaw, and Fumihiko Yoshida, "Why Violence Spreads: The Contagion of International Terrorism," *International Studies Quarterly* 24(2) (1980), pp. 262–298.
19 Crenshaw, "The Psychology of Political Terrorism."
20 See for example Martha Crenshaw's book *Terrorism in Context*, which only includes left-wing terrorism, while the book purports to discuss the whole phenomenon of terrorism. Martha Crenshaw (ed.), *Terrorism in Context* (University Park 1995).
21 Daniel Goldhagen, *Hitler's Willing Executioners: Ordinary Germans and the Holocaust* (London: Little Brown, 1996).
22 Mark Juergensmeyer, *Terror in the Mind of God: The Global Rise of Religious Violence* (Berkeley, CA: University of California Press, 2001).
23 See also Kent Layne Oots and Thomas C. Wiegele, "Terrorist and Victim: Psychiatric and Physiological Approaches from a Social Science Perspective," *Terrorism; An International Journal* 8(1) (1985), pp. 1–32, p. 4.
24 Martha Crenshaw Hutchinson, *Revolutionary Terrorism: The FLN in Algeria 1954–1962* (Stanford, CA: Stanford University Press, 1978). John Bowyer Bell, *The Irish Troubles, A Generation of Violence 1967–1992* (Dublin: Gill and MacMillan, 1993).
25 Schmid, *Political Terrorism*, p. 181.
26 Laqueur, *No End to War*, p. 7.
27 Ibid., p. 29.
28 David C. Rapoport, "Introduction," in David C. Rapoport and Yonah Alexander (eds.), *The Morality of Terrorism: Religious and Secular Justifications* (New York: Columbia University Press, 1989), p. xii.
29 One will look in vain for the historical approach to terrorism in Schmid's handbook. See also: Rapoport, "Fear and Trembling," p. 672.

30 Martha Crenshaw and John Pimlott, *Encyclopedia of World Terrorism* (Armonk, NY: Sharpe, 1997). See also Harvey W. Kushner, *Encyclopedia of Terrorism* (Thousand Oaks, CA: Sage, 2003).

31 Walter Laqueur, *The Terrorism Reader, A Historical Anthology* (London: Wildwood House, 1979).

32 Andrew Sinclair, *An Anatomy of Terror: A History of Terrorism* (London: MacMillan, 2003).

33 Martin A. Miller, "The Intellectual Origins of Modern Terrorism in Europe," in Crenshaw, *Terrorism in Context*, pp. 27–62.

34 See Bruce Hoffman, *Inside Terrorism* (London: Gollancz, 1998) and Laqueur, *The New Terrorism*.

35 Crenshaw, "The Psychology of Political Terrorism," p. 381

36 Rapoport, "Introduction," p. xi.

37 See for example, Steven Simon and Daniel Benjamin, "America and the New Terrorism," *Survival* 42(1) (Spring 2000), pp. 59–75.

38 This does not seem to be uncommon in this field: Schmid, *Political Terrorism*, p. 180.

39 Laqueur, *No End To War*, pp. 8–9. Simon and Daniel, "American and the New Terrorism," p. 66. David Tucker, "What is New About the New Terrorism and How Dangerous is It?," *Terrorism and Political Violence* 13(3) (2001), pp. 1–14.

40 Strangely enough, what could be seen as truly new forms of terrorism, ecoterrorism and narcoterrorism, two phenomena clearly linked to societal developments in the last half of the twentieth century have hardly been studied in this light. Perhaps new also has a connotation of extremely dangerous and threatening. For another approach to questioning the newness of terrorism see Thomas Copeland, "Is the 'New Terrorism' Really New?: An Analysis of the New Paradigm for Terrorism," *Journal of Conflict Studies* 21(2) (2000) pp. 7–27. Copeland argues that "the new terrorism is primarily a US policy frame," p. 22.

41 See also Bruce Hoffman, "Change and Continuity in Terrorism," *Studies in Conflict and Terrorism* 24 (2001), pp. 417–428, p. 426, footnote 1.

42 Tucker, "What is New About the New Terrorism," pp. 3–4.

43 Rapoport, "Fear and Trembling," p. 658.

44 Crenshaw claims that the transnational nature of the phenomenon has made terrorism a difficult subject to study; Crenshaw, "The Psychology of Political Terrorism," p. 383. Rapoport, "Fear and Trembling," p. 673.

45 Tatjana Botzat, *Ein deutscher Herbst: Zustande, Dokumente, Berichte, Kommentare* (A German Autumn: Circumstances, Documents, Reports and Commentary) (Frankfurt: Neue Kritik, 1978).

46 J. Paul de B. Taillon, *Hijacking and Hostages: Government Responses to Terrorism* (New York: Praeger, 2002).

47 Laqueur, *The New Terrorism*, p. 182.

48 The United States now intends to withdraw its troops from Saudi Arabia.

49 Juergensmeyer, *Terror in the Mind of God*.

50 Lawrence Freedman, "A New Type of War," in Ken Booth and Tim Dunne (eds.), *Worlds in Collision: Terror and the Future of Global Order* (Basingstoke: Palgrave MacMillan, 2002), pp. 37–47, p. 38. Thomas Copeland stresses that state sponsorship of terrorist movements in general continues both actively and passively (safe havens and condoning criminal activities). Copeland, "Is the 'New Terrorism' Really New?," p. 13.

51 This also questions the globalisation argument that has stressed the irrelevance of state actors. See Kaldor, *New and Old Wars*.

52 Samuel R. Berger and Mona Sutphen, "Commandeering the Palestinian Cause; Bin Laden's Belated Concern," in James F. Hoge Jr. and Gideon Rose (eds.), *How Did This Happen: Terrorism and the New War* (New York: Public Affairs, 2001), pp. 123–128.

53 Simon and Benjamin, "America and the New Terrorism," p. 59.

54 Rapoport, "Fear and Trembling," p. 660.

55 For an example of such a terrorist organization, see the "Thugs" in what is now India. The Thugs worshipped the Hindu Goddess of destruction and terror, Kali. Rapoport, "Fear and Trembling," p. 660.

56 Giles Kepel, *The Revenge of God: The Resurgence of Islam, Christianity and Judaism in the Modern World* (Cambridge: Polity, 1994).

57 Rapoport, "Fear and Trembling," p. 658.

58 Miller, "The Intellectual Origins," p. 30.

59 John Gearson, "The Nature of Modern Terrorism," *Political Quarterly* 73(4), Supplement I (2002), pp. 7–24, p. 21.

60 Michael Ignatieff, "It's War—But It Does not have to be Dirty," *Guardian*, 1 October 2001.

61 Paul Berman, *Terror and Liberalism* (New York: Norton, 2003).

62 Laqueur, *The New Terrorism*.

63 Robert Fisk, *Pity the Nation: Lebanon at War* (London: Deutsch, 1990), pp. 39–40.

64 James Dingley, "The Bombing of Omagh, 15 August 1998; The Bombers, their Tactics, Strategy and Purpose Behind the Incident," *Studies in Conflict and Terrorism* 24(6) (2001), pp. 451–466.

65 Hoffman, *Inside Terrorism*, pp. 94, 201. David Tucker has noted that the conclusion of a rise in mass-casualty attacks seems to be based on a very small number of cases. Tucker, "What is New About the New Terrorism," p. 6. He also notes that conventional warfare has become more lethal in terms of civilian casualties in the course of the twentieth century; why should unconventional war in the shape of terrorism not?, p. 9.

66 Miller, "The Intellectual Origins," p. 31.

67 Hoffman, "Change and Continuity in Terrorism."

68 Jessica Stern, *The Ultimate Terrorists* (Cambridge, MA: Harvard University Press, 1999).

69 Hoffman, *Inside Terrorism*, pp. 94, 201.

70 Miller, "The Intellectual Origins."

71 Brian M. Jenkins, *International Terrorism: A New Kind of Warfare* (Santa Monica, CA: Rand, 1974), p. 4.

72 A lot of research is being conducted into the role of the media and conflict. See for example, W. P. Strobel, *Late Breaking Foreign Policy: The News Media's Influence on Peace Operations* (Washington D.C.: United States Institute of Peace Press, 1997). L. Minear, C. Scott, and Th. G. Weiss, *The News Media, Civil War and Humanitarian Action* (Boulder, CO: Lynne Rienner, 1994).

73 This revolves around the age-old debate in the social sciences between agency or structure as determinate factor.

74 Miller, "The Intellectual Origins."

75 According to some the feature of not claiming attacks is increasing. Gearson, "The Nature of Modern Terrorism," p. 11.

76 See for this suggestion E. R. Muller, R. F. J. Spaay, and A. G. W. Ruitenberg, *Trends in Terrorisme* (Trends in Terrorism) (Alphen aan den Rijn: Kluwer, 2003), p. 211. See for an example based on Al Qaeda, David Martin Jones, "Out of Bali; Cybercaliphate Rising," *The National Interest* 71 (2003), pp. 75–85.

77 Tucker, "What is New About the New Terrorism," p. 9.

78 See Martha Crenshaw, "The Logic of Terrorism, Terrorist Behavior as a Product of Strategic Choice," in Reich, *Origins of Terrorism*. This point of view is not always shared: Stern, *The Ultimate Terrorists*, in particular chapter five. Laqueur, *The New Terrorism*, p. 91.

79 See for rational choice theory, Herbert Simon, *Models of Man: Social and Rational: Mathematical Essay on Rational Human Behavior in a Social Setting* (New York: John Wiley, 1957). Michael Allingham, *Rational Choice* (Basingstoke: MacMillan, 1999).

80 Chris Quillen, "A Historical Analysis of Mass Casualty Bombers," *Studies in Conflict and Terrorism* 25 (2002), pp. 279–292.

81 Schmid, *Political Terrorism*, in particular the chapter "Terrorism and Related Concepts: Typologies."

82 Ibid., p. 56.

83 Andrew Mack, "Why Big Nations Lose Small Wars: The Politics of Asymmetric Conflict," *World Politics* 26(1) (1974), pp. 175–200.

3   The four waves of modern terrorism

David C. Rapoport

September 11, 2001, is the most destructive day in the long, bloody history of terrorism. The casualties, economic damage, and outrage were unprecedented. It could turn out to be the most important day too, because it led President Bush to declare a "war (that) would not end until every terrorist group of global reach has been found, stopped, and defeated."[1]

However unprecedented September 11 was, President Bush's declaration was not altogether unique. Exactly 100 years ago, when an anarchist assassinated President William McKinley in September 1901, his successor Theodore Roosevelt called for a crusade to exterminate terrorism everywhere.[2]

No one knows if the current campaign will be more successful than its predecessors, but we can more fully appreciate the difficulties ahead by examining features of the history of rebel (nonstate) terror. That history shows how deeply implanted terrorism is in our culture, provides parallels worth pondering, and offers a perspective for understanding the uniqueness of September 11 and its aftermath.[3] To this end, in this chapter I examine the course of modern terror from its initial appearance 125 years ago; I emphasize continuities and change, particularly with respect to international ingredients.[4]

The wave phenomena

Modern terror began in Russia in the 1880s and within a decade appeared in Western Europe, the Balkans, and Asia. A generation later the wave was completed. Anarchists initiated the wave, and their primary strategy—assassination campaigns against prominent officials—was adopted by virtually all the other groups of the time, even those with nationalist aims in the Balkans and India.

Significant examples of secular rebel terror existed earlier, but they were specific to a particular time and country. The Ku Klux Klan (KKK), for example, made a striking contribution to the decision of the federal government to end Reconstruction, but the KKK had no contemporary parallels or emulators.[5]

The "Anarchist wave" was the first global or truly international terrorist experience in history;[6] three similar, consecutive, and overlapping expressions followed. The "anticolonial wave" began in the 1920s and lasted about forty years. Then came the "New Left wave," which diminished greatly as the twentieth century closed, leaving only a few groups still active today in Nepal, Spain, the United Kingdom, Peru, and Colombia. In 1979 a "religious wave" emerged; if the pattern of its three predecessors is relevant it could disappear by 2025, at which time a new wave might emerge. The uniqueness and persistence of the wave experience indicates that terror is deeply rooted in modern culture.

The wave concept—an unfamiliar notion—is worth more attention. Academics focus on organizations, and there are good reasons for this orientation. Organizations launch terror campaigns, and governments are always primarily concerned to disable those organizations.[8] Students of terrorism also focus unduly on contemporary events, which makes us less sensitive to waves because the life cycle of a wave lasts at least a generation.[9]

What is a wave? It is a cycle of activity in a given time period—a cycle characterized by expansion and contraction phases. A crucial feature is its international character; similar activities occur in several countries, driven by a common predominant energy that shapes the participating groups' characteristics and mutual relationships. As their names— "Anarchist," "anticolonial," "New Left," and "Religious"—suggest, a different energy drives each.

Each wave's name reflects its dominant but not its only feature. Nationalist organizations in various numbers appear in all waves, for example, and each wave shaped its national elements differently. The Anarchists gave them tactics and often training. Third-wave nationalist groups displayed profoundly left-wing aspirations, and nationalism serves or reacts to religious purposes in the fourth wave. All groups in the second wave had nationalist aspirations, but the wave is termed anticolonial because the resisting states were powers that had become ambivalent about retaining their colonial status. That ambivalence explains why the wave produced the first terrorist successes. In other waves, that ambivalence is absent or very weak, and no nationalist struggle has succeeded.

A wave is composed of organizations, but waves and organizations have very different life rhythms. Normally, organizations disappear before the initial wave associated with them does. New Left organizations were particularly striking in this respect—typically lasting two years. Nonetheless, the wave retained sufficient energy to create a generation of successor or new groups. When a wave's energy cannot inspire new organizations, the wave disappears. Resistance, political concessions, and changes in the perceptions of generations are critical factors in explaining the disappearance.

Occasionally an organization survives its original wave. The Irish Republican Army (IRA), for example, is the oldest modern terrorist organization—emerging first in 1916, though not as a terror organization.[10] It then fought five campaigns in two successive waves (the fourth struggle, in the 1950s, used guerrilla tactics).[11] At least two offshoots—the Real IRA and Continuity IRA— are still active. The Palestine Liberation Organization (PLO), founded in 1964, became active in 1967. When the Viet Cong faded into history, the international connections and activity of the PLO made it the preeminent body of the New Left wave, although the PLO pursued largely nationalist ends. More recently, elements of the PLO (e.g., Fatah) have become active in the fourth wave, even though the organization initially was wholly secular. When an organization transcends a wave, it reflects the new wave's influence—a change that may pose special problems for the group and its constituencies, as we shall see.

The first three waves lasted about a generation each—a suggestive time frame closest in duration to that of a human life cycle, in which dreams inspiring parents lose their attractiveness for children.[12] Although the resistance of those attacked is crucial in explaining why terror organizations rarely succeed, the time span of the wave also suggests that the wave has its own momentum. Over time there are fewer organizations because the enterprise's problematic nature becomes more visible. The pattern is familiar to students of revolutionary states such as France, the Soviet Union, and Iran. The inheritors of the revolution do not value it in the same way its creators did. In the anticolonial wave, the process also seems relevant to the colonial powers. A new generation found it much easier to discard the colonial idea. The wave pattern calls one's attention to crucial political themes in the general culture—themes that distinguish the ethos of one generation from another.

There are many reasons the first wave occurred when it did, but two critical factors are conspicuous and facilitated successive waves. The first was the transformation in communication and transportation patterns. The telegraph, daily mass newspapers, and railroads flourished during the last quarter of the nineteenth century. Events in one country were known elsewhere in a day or so. Prominent Russian anarchists traveled extensively, helping to inspire sympathies and groups elsewhere; sometimes, as the journeys of Peter Prodhoun indicate, they had more influence abroad than at home. Mass transportation made large-scale emigrations possible and created diaspora communities, which then became significant in the politics of both their "new" and "old" countries. Subsequent innovations continued to shrink time and space.

A second factor contributing to the emergence of the first wave was doctrine or culture. Russian writers created a strategy for terror, which became an inheritance for successors to use, improve, and transmit. Sergei Nechaev was the leading figure in this effort; Nicholas Mozorov, Peter Kropotkin, Serge Stepniak, and others also made contributions.[13] Their efforts perpetuated the wave. The KKK had no emulators partly because it made no effort to explain its tactics. The Russian achievement becomes even more striking when we compare it to the practices of the ancient religious terrorists who always stayed within their own religious tradition—the source of their justifications and binding precedents. Each religious tradition produced its own kind of terrorist, and sometimes the tactics within a tradition were so uniform that they appear to be a form of religious ritual.[14]

A comparison of Nechaev's *Revolutionary Catechism* with Osama bin Laden's training manual, *Military Studies in the Jihad Against the Tyrants*, shows that they share one very significant feature: a paramount desire to become more *efficient* by learning from the experiences of friends and enemies alike.[15] The major difference in this respect is the role of women. Nechaev considers them "priceless assets," and indeed they were crucial leaders and participants in the first wave. Bin Laden dedicates his book to protecting the Muslim woman, but he ignores what experience can tell us about female terrorists.[16] Women do not participate in his forces and are virtually excluded in the fourth wave, except in Sri Lanka.

Each wave produces major technical works that reflect the special properties of that wave and contribute to a common modern effort to formulate a "science" of terror. Between Nechaev and bin Laden there were Georges Grivas, *Guerrilla War*, and Carlos Marighella, *Mini-Manual of the Urban Guerrilla*, in the second and third waves, respectively.

"Revolution" is the overriding aim in every wave, but revolution is understood in different ways.[17] Revolutionaries create a new source of political legitimacy, and more often than not that meant national self-determination. The anticolonial wave was dominated by this quest. The principle that a people should govern itself was bequeathed by the American and French revolutions. (The French Revolution also introduced the term *terror* to our vocabulary.)[18] Because the definition of "the people" has never been (and perhaps never can be) clear and fixed, however, it is a source of recurring conflict even when the sanctity of the principle is accepted everywhere. Revolution also can mean a radical reconstruction of authority to eliminate all forms of equality—a cardinal theme in the first wave and a significant one in the third wave. Fourth-wave groups use a variety of sacred texts or revelations for legitimacy.

This chapter treats the great events precipitating each wave and the aims and tactics of participating groups. The focus, however, is the international scene. I examine the interactions of the five principal actors: terrorist organizations; diaspora populations; states; sympathetic foreign publics; and, beginning with the second wave, supranational organizations.[19]

First wave: creation of a doctrine

The creators of modern terrorism inherited a world in which traditional revolutionaries, who depended on pamphlets and leaflets to generate an uprising, suddenly seemed obsolete. The masses, Nechaev said, regarded them as "idle word-spillers."[20] A new form of communication (Peter Kropotkin named it "Propaganda by the Deed") was needed—one that would be heard and would command respect because the rebel took action that involved serious personal risks that signified deep commitment.

[The anarchist analysis of modern society contained four major points. It noted that society had huge reservoirs of latent ambivalence and hostility and that the conventions society devised to muffle and diffuse antagonisms generated guilt and provided channels for settling grievances and securing personal amenities. By demonstrating that these conventions were simple historical creations, however, acts once declared immoral would be hailed by later generations as noble efforts to liberate humanity. In this view, terror was thought to be the quickest and most effective means to destroy conventions. By this reasoning, the perpetrators freed themselves from the paralyzing grip of guilt to become different kinds of people. They forced those who defended the government to respond in ways that undermined the rules the latter claimed to respect.[21] Dramatic action repeated again and again invariably would polarize the society, and the revolution inevitably would follow—or so the anarchists reasoned.]

An incident that inspired the turbulent decades to follow illustrates the process. On January 24, 1878, Vera Zasulich wounded a Russian police commander who abused political prisoners. Throwing her weapon to the floor, she proclaimed that she was a "terrorist, *not* a killer."[22] The ensuing trial quickly became that of the police chief. When the court freed her, crowds greeted the verdict with thunderous applause.[23]

A successful campaign entailed learning how to fight and how to die, and the most admirable death occurred as a result of a court trial in which one accepted responsibility and used the occasion to indict the regime. Stepniak, a major figure in the history of Russian terrorism, described the Russian terrorist as "noble, terrible, irresistibly fascinating, uniting the two sublimities of human grandeur, the martyr and the hero."[24] Dynamite—a recent invention—was the weapon of choice because the assailant usually was killed too, so it was not a weapon a criminal would use.[25]

Terror was violence beyond the moral conventions used to regulate violence: the rules of war and punishment. The former distinguishes combatants from noncombatants, and the latter separates the guilty from the innocent. Invariably, most onlookers would label acts of terror atrocities or outrages. The rebels described themselves as terrorists, not guerrillas, tracing their lineage to the French Revolution. They sought political targets or those that could affect public attitudes.[26] Terrorism was a strategy, not an end. The tactics used depended upon the group's political objective and on the specific context faced. Judging a context constantly in flux was both an art and a science.

The creators of this strategy took confidence from contemporary events. In the Russian case, as well as in all subsequent ones, major unexpected political events dramatized new government vulnerabilities. Hope was excited, and hope is always an indispensable lubricant of rebel activity.[27] The turn of events that suggested Russian vulnerability was the dazzling effort of the young Czar Alexander II to transform the system virtually overnight. In one stroke of the pen (1861) he freed the serfs (one-third of the population) and promised them funds to buy their land. Three years later he established limited local self-government, "westernized" the judicial system, abolished capital punishment, and relaxed censorship powers and control over education. Hopes were aroused but could not be fulfilled quickly enough, as indicated by the fact that the funds available for the serfs to buy land were insufficient. In the wake of inevitable disappointments, systematic assassination strikes against prominent officials began—culminating in the death of Alexander himself.

Russian rebels encouraged and trained other groups, even those with different political aims. Their efforts bore fruit quickly. Armenian and Polish nationalist groups committed to assassination emerged in Russia and used bank robbery to finance their activities. Then the Balkans exploded, as many groups found the boundaries of states recently torn out of the Ottoman Empire unsatisfactory.[28] In the West, where Russian anarchists fled and found refuge in Russian diaspora colonies and among other elements hostile to the czarist regime, a campaign of anarchist terror developed that influenced activities in India too.[29] The diaspora produced some surprising results for groups still struggling in Russia. The Terrorist Brigade in 1905 had its headquarters in Switzerland, launched strikes from Finland (an autonomous part of the Russian empire), got arms from an Armenian terrorist group Russians helped train, and were offered funds by the Japanese to be laundered through American millionaires.[30]

The high point of the first wave of international terrorist activity occurred in the 1890s, sometimes called the "Golden Age of Assassination"—when monarchs, prime ministers, and presidents were struck down, one after another, usually by assassins who moved easily across international borders.[31] The most immediately affected governments clamored for international police cooperation and for better border control, a situation President Theodore Roosevelt thought ideal for launching the first international effort to eliminate terrorism:

> Anarchy is a crime against the whole human race, and all mankind should band together against the Anarchist. His crimes should be made a crime against the law of nations … declared by treaties among all civilized powers.[32]

The consensus lasted only three years, however. The United States refused to send a delegation to a St. Petersburg conference to consider a German/Russian-sponsored protocol to meet these objectives. It feared that extensive involvement in European politics might be required, and it had no federal police force. Italy refused too, for a very different and revealing concern: If anarchists were returned to their original countries, Italy's domestic troubles might be worse than its international ones.

The first great effort to deal with international terrorism failed because the interests of states pulled them in different directions, and the divisions developed new expressions as the century developed. Bulgaria gave Macedonian nationalists sanctuaries and bases to aid operations in the Ottoman Empire. The suspicion that Serbia helped Archduke Franz Ferdinand's assassin precipitated World War I. An unintended consequence of the four terrible years that followed was a dampened enthusiasm for the strategy of assassination.

Second wave: mostly successful, and a new language

A wave by definition is an international event; oddly, however, the first one was sparked by a domestic political situation. A monumental international event, the Versailles Peace Treaty that concluded World War I, precipitated the second wave. The victors applied the principle of national self-determination to break up the empires of the defeated states (mostly in Europe). The non-European portions of those defeated empires, which were deemed not yet ready for independence, became League of Nations "mandates" administered directly by individual victorious powers until the territories were ready for independence.

Whether the victors fully understood the implications of their decisions or not, they undermined the legitimacy of their own empires. The IRA achieved limited success in the 1920s,[33] and terrorist groups developed in all empires except the Soviet Union (which did not recognize itself as a colonial power) after World War II. Terrorist activity was crucial in establishing the new states of Ireland, Israel, Cyprus, and Algeria, among others. As empires dissolved, the wave receded.

Most terrorist successes occurred twenty-five years after Versailles, and the time lag requires explanation. World War II reinforced and enlarged the implications of Versailles. Once more the victors compelled the defeated to abandon empires; this time the colonial territories were overseas (Manchuria, Korea, Ethiopia, Libya, and so forth) and were not made mandates. The victors began liquidating their own empires as well, and in doing so they generally were not responding to terrorist activity, as in India, Pakistan, Burma, Ceylon, Tunisia, Egypt, Morocco, the Philippines, Ghana, and Nigeria—which indicated how firmly committed the Western world had become to the principle of self-determination. The United States had become the major Western power, and it pressed hardest for eliminating empires. As the cold war developed, the process was accelerated because the Soviets were always poised to help would-be rebels.[34]

The terror campaigns of the second wave were fought in territories where special political problems made withdrawal a less attractive option. Jews and Arabs in Palestine, for example, had dramatically conflicting versions of what the termination of British rule was supposed to mean. The considerable European population in Algeria did not want Paris to abandon its authority, and in Northern Ireland the majority wanted to remain British. In Cyprus, the Turkish community did not want to be put under Greek rule—the aim of Ethniki Organosis Kyprion Agoniston (EOKA)—and Britain wanted to retain Cyprus as a base for Middle East operations.

The problem of conflicting aspirations was reflected in the way the struggles were or were not settled. The terrorists did get the imperial powers to withdraw, but that was not the only purpose of the struggle. Menachem Begin's *Irgun* fought to gain the entire Palestine mandate but settled for partition.[35] IRA elements have never accepted the fact that Britain will not leave Northern Ireland without the consent of the territory's population. EOKA fought to unify Cyprus with Greece (*enosis*) but accepted an independent state that EOKA tried to subvert for the sake of an ever-elusive *enosis*. Algeria seems to be the chief exception because the Europeans all fled. The initial manifesto of the Front de Libération Nationale, Algeria (FLN) proclaimed, however, that it wanted to retain that population and establish a democratic state; neither objective was achieved.[36]

Second-wave organizations understood that they needed a new language to describe themselves because the term *terrorist* had accumulated so many negative connotations that those who identified themselves as terrorists incurred enormous political liabilities. The Israeli group *Lehi* was the last self-identified terrorist group. Begin, leader of the *Irgun* (*Lehi*'s Zionist rival)—which concentrated on purpose rather than means—described his people as "freedom fighters" struggling against "government terror."[37] This self-description was so appealing that all subsequent terrorist groups followed suit; because the anticolonial struggle seemed more legitimate than the purposes served in the first wave, the "new" language became attractive to potential political supporters as well. Governments also appreciated the political value of "appropriate" language and began to describe all violent rebels as terrorists. The media, hoping to avoid being seen as blatantly partisan, corrupted language further. Major American newspapers, for example, often described the same individuals alternatively as terrorists, guerrillas, and soldiers in the same account.[38]

Terrorist tactics also changed in the second wave. Because diaspora sources contributed more money, bank robberies were less common. The first wave demonstrated that assassinating prominent political figures could be very counterproductive, and few assassinations occurred in the second wave. The Balkans was an exception—an odd place especially when one considers where World War I started.[39] Elsewhere only *Lehi* (the British renamed it the Stern Gang) remained committed to a strategy of assassination. *Lehi* was much less effective than its two competitors, however, which may have been an important lesson for subsequent anticolonial movements. Martyrdom, often linked to assassination, seemed less significant as well.

The new strategy was more complicated than the old because there were more kinds of targets chosen, and it was important to strike them in proper sequence. Second-wave strategy sought to eliminate the police—a government's eyes and ears—first, through systematic assassinations of officers and/or their families. The military units replacing them, second-wave proponents reasoned, would prove too clumsy to cope without producing counter-atrocities that would increase social support for the cause. If the process of atrocities and counter-atrocities were well planned, it could favor those perceived to be weak and without alternatives.[40]

Major energies went into guerrilla-like (hit-and-run) actions against troops—attacks that still went beyond the rules of war because weapons were concealed and the assailants had no identifying insignia.[41] Some groups, such as the Irgun, made efforts to give warnings in order to limit civilian casualties. In some cases, such as Algeria, terror was one aspect of a more comprehensive rebellion that included extensive guerrilla forces.

Compared to terrorists in the first wave, those in the second wave used the four international ingredients in different and much more productive ways. Leaders of different national groups still acknowledged the common bonds and heritage of an international revolutionary tradition, but the heroes invoked in the literature of specific groups were overwhelmingly national heroes.[42] The underlying assumption seemed to be that if one strengthened ties with foreign terrorists, other international assets would become less useful.

Diaspora groups regularly displayed abilities not seen earlier. Nineteenth-century Irish rebels received money, weapons, and volunteers from the Irish-American community, but in the 1920s the exertions of the latter went further and induced the U.S. government to exert significant political influence on Britain to accept an Irish state.[43] Jewish diaspora communities, especially in the United States, exerted similar leverage as the horror of the Holocaust was finally revealed.

Foreign states with kindred populations also were active. Arab states gave the Algerian FLN crucial political support, and those adjacent to Algeria offered sanctuaries from which the group could stage attacks. Greece sponsored the Cypriot uprising against the British and against Cyprus when it became a state. Frightened Turkish Cypriots, in turn, looked to Turkey for aid. Turkish troops then invaded the island (1974) and are still there.

Outside influences obviously change when the purpose of the terrorist activity and the local context are perceived differently. The different Irish experiences illustrate the point well. The early effort in the 1920s was seen simply as an anticolonial movement, and the Irish-American community had its greatest or most productive impact.[44] The diaspora was less interested in the IRA's brief campaigns to bring Northern Ireland into the Republic during World War II or, later, during the cold war. Conflicting concerns weakened overseas enthusiasms and influences.

As the second wave progressed, a new, fifth ingredient—supranational organization—came into play. When Alexander I of Serbia was assassinated in Marseilles (1934), the League of Nations tried to contain international terror by drafting two conventions, including one for an international court (1937). Neither came into effect. Two League members (Hungary and Italy) apparently encouraged the assassination and blocked the antiterror efforts.[45] After World War II, the United Nations inherited the League's ultimate authority over the colonial mandates— territories that were now scenes of extensive terrorist activity. When Britain decided to withdraw from Palestine, the UN was crucial in legitimizing the partition; subsequently all anticolonial terrorists sought to interest the UN in their struggles. The new states admitted to the UN were nearly always former colonial territories, and they gave the anticolonial sentiment in that body more structure, focus, and opportunities. More and more participants in UN debates regularly used Begin's language to describe anticolonial terrorists as "freedom fighters."[46]

Third wave: excessive internationalism?

The major political event stimulating the third, or "New Left," wave was the agonizing Vietnam War. The effectiveness of the Viet Cong's "primitive weapons" against the American goliath's modern technology rekindled radical hopes that the contemporary system was vulnerable. Groups developed in the Third World and in the Western heartland itself, where the war stimulated enormous ambivalence among the youth about the value of the existing system. Many Western groups—such as American Weather Underground, the West German Red Army Faction (RAF), the Italian Red Brigades, the Japanese Red Army, and the French Action Directe—saw themselves as vanguards for the Third World masses. The Soviet world encouraged the outbreaks and offered moral support, training, and weapons.

As in the first wave, radicalism and nationalism often were combined, as evidenced by the struggles of the Basques, Armenians, Corsicans, Kurds, and Irish.[47] Every first-wave nationalist movement had failed, but the linkage was renewed because ethnic concerns always have larger constituencies than radical aspirations have. Although self-determination ultimately obscured the radical programs and nationalist groups were much more durable than other groups in the third wave, none succeeded, and their survivors will fail too. The countries concerned—Spain, France, the United Kingdom, and Turkey—simply do not consider themselves to be colonial powers, and the ambivalence necessary for nationalist success is absent.

When the Vietnam War ended in 1975, the PLO replaced the Viet Cong as the heroic model. The PLO originated after the extraordinary collapse of three Arab armies in the six days of the 1967 Middle East war; its existence and persistence gave credibility to supporters who argued that only terror could remove Israel. Its centrality for other groups was strengthened because it got strong support from Arab states and the Soviet Union and made training facilities in Lebanon available to the other groups.

The first and third waves had some striking resemblances. Women in the second wave had been restricted to the role of messengers and scouts; now they became leaders and fighters once more.[48] "Theatrical targets," comparable to those of the first wave, replaced the second wave's military targets. International hijacking is one example. Terrorists understood that some foreign landing fields were accessible. Seven hundred hijackings occurred during the first three decades of the third wave.[49]

Planes were hijacked to secure hostages. There were other ways to generate hostage crises, however, and the hostage crisis became a third-wave characteristic. The most memorable episode was the 1979 kidnapping of former Italian Prime Minister Aldo Moro by the Red Brigades. When the government refused to negotiate, Moro was brutally murdered and his body dumped in the streets. The Sandinistas took Nicaragua's Congress hostage in 1978—an act so audacious that it sparked the popular insurrection that brought the Somoza regime down a year later. In Colombia the M-19 tried to duplicate the feat by seizing the Supreme Court on April 19,1985, but the government refused to yield and in the struggle nearly 100 people were killed; the terrorists killed eleven justices.

Kidnappings occurred in seventy-three countries—especially in Italy, Spain, and Latin America. From 1968 to 1982 there were 409 international kidnapping incidents yielding 951 hostages.[50] Initially hostages gave their captors political leverage, but soon another concern became more dominant. Companies insured their executives, and kidnapping became lucrative. When money was the principal issue, kidnappers found that hostage negotiations were easier to consummate on their terms. Informed observers estimate the practice "earned" $350 million.[51]

The abandoned practice of assassinating prominent figures was revived. The IRA and its various splinter organizations, for example, assassinated the British ambassador to Ireland (1976) and Lord Mountbatten (1979) and attempted to kill prime ministers Thatcher (1984) and Major (1991).[52] The Palestinian Black September assassinated the Jordanian prime minister (1971) and attempted to assassinate Jordan's King Hussein (1974). Black September killed the American ambassador when it took the Saudi embassy in Khartoum (1973). Euskadi ta Askatasuna (Basque Nation and Liberty; ETA) killed the Spanish prime minister in the same year.

First- and third-wave assassinations had a different logic, however. A first-wave victim was assassinated because he or she held a public office. New Left-wave assassinations more often were "punishments." Jordan's prime minister and king had forced the PLO out of their country in a savage battle. Similarly, the attempt against British Prime Minister Margaret Thatcher occurred because she was "responsible" for the death of the nine IRA hunger strikers who refused to be treated as ordinary criminals.[53] Aldo Moro was assassinated because the Italian government refused to enter hostage negotiations. The German Red Army Faction provided a second typical pattern: 15 percent of its strikes involved assassination. Although the RAF did not seek the most prominent public figures, it did kill the head of the Berlin Supreme Court and a well-known industrialist.[54]

For good reason, the abandoned term "international terrorism" was revived. Again the revolutionary ethos created significant bonds between separate national groups—bonds that intensified when first Cuban and then PLO training facilities were made available. The targets chosen reflected international dimensions as well. Some groups conducted more assaults abroad than on their home territories; the PLO, for example, was more active in Europe than on the West Bank, and sometimes more active in Europe than many European groups themselves were. Different national groups cooperated in attacks such as the Munich Olympics massacre (1972) and the kidnapping of OPEC ministers (1975), among others.

On their own soil, groups often chose targets with international significance. Strikes on foreign embassies began when the PLO attacked the Saudi embassy in Khartoum (1973). The Peruvian group *Tupac Amaru*—partly to gain political advantage over its rival *Sendero Luminoso* (The Shining Path)—held seventy-two hostages in the Japanese Embassy for more than four months (1996–1997) until a rescue operation killed every terrorist in the complex.

One people became a favorite target of most groups. One-third of the international attacks in the third wave involved American targets—a pattern reflecting the United States' new importance. American targets were visible in Latin America, Europe, and the Middle East, where the United States supported most governments under terrorist siege.[55]

Despite its preeminent status as a target, cold war concerns sometimes led the United States to ignore its stated distaste for terror. In Nicaragua, Angola, and elsewhere the United States supported terrorist activity—an indication of how difficult it was to forgo a purpose deemed worthwhile even when deplorable tactics had to be used.

Third-wave organizations discovered that they paid a large price for not being able to negotiate between the conflicting demands imposed by various international elements.[56] The commitment to a revolutionary ethos alienated domestic and foreign liberal elements, particularly during the cold war. The IRA forfeited significant Irish American diaspora support during the third wave. Its initial goal during the third wave was a united socialist Ireland, and its willingness to accept support from Libya and the PLO created problems. Most of all, however, the cold war had to end before the Irish diaspora and an American government showed sustained interest in the Irish issue again and assisted moves to resolve the conflict.

Involvement with foreign groups made some terrorist organizations neglect domestic constituencies. A leader of the 2nd of June, a German anarchist body, suggested that its obsession with the Palestinian cause induced it to attack a Jewish synagogue on the anniversary of *Kristall Nacht*—a date often considered the beginning of the Holocaust. Such "stupidity," he said, alienated potential German constituencies.[57] When the power of the cooperating terrorist entities was very unequal, the weaker found that its interest did not count. Thus, the German Revolutionary Cells, hijacking partners of the Popular Front for the Liberation of Palestine (PFLP), could not get help from their partners to release German prisoners. "(D)ependent on the will of Wadi Haddad and his group," whose agenda was very different from theirs after all, the Revolutionary Cells terminated the relationship and soon collapsed.[58]

The PLO, always a loose confederation, often found international ties expensive because they complicated serious existing divisions within the organization. In the 1970s Abu Iyad, PLO founding member and intelligence chief, wrote that the Palestinian cause was so important in Syrian and Iraqi domestic politics that those states felt it necessary to capture organizations within the PLO to serve their own ends. That made it even more difficult to settle for a limited goal, as the Irgun and EOKA had done earlier.

Entanglements with Arab states created problems for both parties. Raids from Egyptian-occupied Gaza helped precipitate a disastrous war with Israel (1956), and the *fidayeen* were prohibited from launching raids from that territory ever again. A Palestinian raid from Syria brought Syria into the Six-Day War, and ever afterward Syria kept a tight control on those operating from its territories. When a PLO faction hijacked British and American planes to Jordan (1970) in the first effort to target non-Israelis, the Jordanian army devastated the PLO, which then lost its home. Finally, an attempted assassination of an Israeli diplomat in Britain sparked the 1982 invasion of Lebanon and forced the PLO to leave a home that had given it so much significance among foreign terrorist groups. (Ironically, the assassination attempt was organized by Abu Nidal's renegade faction associated with Iraq—a group that had made two previous attempts to assassinate the PLO's leader Yasser Arafat.) Subsequently, Tunisia—the PLO's new host—prohibited the PLO from training foreign groups, and to a large extent the PLO's career as an effective terrorist organization seemed to be over. Paradoxically, the Oslo Accords demonstrated that the PLO could achieve more of its objectives when it was less dangerous.[59]

To maintain control over their own destiny, states again began to "sponsor" groups (a practice abandoned in the second wave), and once more the sponsors found the practice costly. In the 1980s Britain severed diplomatic relations with Libya and Syria for sponsoring terrorism on British soil, and France broke with Iran when it refused to let the French interrogate its embassy staff about assassinations of Iranian émigrés. Iraq's surprising restraint during the 1991 Gulf War highlighted the weakness of state-sponsored terror. Iraq did threaten to use terror—a threat that induced Western authorities to predict that terrorists would flood Europe.[60] If terror had materialized, however, it would have made bringing Saddam Hussein to trial for crimes a war aim, and the desire to avoid that result is the most plausible explanation for the Iraqi dictator's uncharacteristic restraint.

The third wave began to ebb in the 1980s. Revolutionary terrorists were defeated in one country after another. Israel's invasion of Lebanon (1982) eliminated PLO facilities to train terrorist groups, and international counterterrorist cooperation became increasingly effective.

As in the first wave, states cooperated openly and formally in counterterror efforts. The United States, with British aid, bombed Libya (1986) because of its role as a state sponsor, and the European Community imposed an arms embargo. The international cooperation of national police forces sought at St. Petersburg (1904) became more significant as Trevi—established in the mid-1970s—was joined in this mission by Europol in 1994. Differences between states remained, however; even close allies could not always cooperate. France refused to extradite PLO, Red Brigade, and ETA suspects to West Germany, Italy, and Spain, respectively. Italy spurned American requests to extradite a Palestinian suspect in the seizure of the *Achille Lauro* cruise ship (1984), and Italy refused to extradite a Kurd (1988) because Italian law forbids capital punishment whereas Turkish law does not. The United States has refused to extradite some IRA suspects. Events of this sort will not stop until that improbable day when the laws and interests of separate states are identical.

The UN's role changed dramatically in the third wave. Now "new states"—former colonial territories—found that terrorism threatened their interests, and they particularly shunned nationalist movements. Major UN conventions from 1970 through 1999 made hijacking, hostage taking, attacks on senior government officials, "terrorist bombing" of a foreign state's facilities, and financing of international activities crimes. A change of language is some indication of the changed attitude. "Freedom fighter" was no longer a popular term in UN debates, and the term *terrorism* actually was used for the title of a document: "International Convention for the Suppression of Terrorist Bombing" (1997).[61] Evidence that Libya's agents were involved in the Pan Am Lockerbie crash produced a unanimous Security Council decision obliging Libya to extradite the suspects (1988), and a decade later when collective sanctions had their full effects Libya complied; this episode will continue to shape UN responses to Libya's terrorist activities.

Yet very serious ambiguities and conflicts within the UN remained, reflecting the ever-present fact that terror serves different ends—and some of those ends are prized. Ironically, the most important ambiguity concerned the third wave's major organization: the PLO. It received official UN status and was recognized by more than 100 states as a state that is entitled to receive a share of the Palestine Mandate.

(Fatah)

Fourth wave: how unique and how long?

As its predecessor began to ebb, the "religious wave" gathered force. Religious elements have always been important in modern terror because religious and ethnic identities often overlap. The Armenian, Macedonian, Irish, Cypriot, French Canadian, Israeli, and Palestinian struggles illustrate the point.[62] In these cases, however, the aim was to create secular states.

Today religion has a vastly different significance, supplying justifications and organizing principles for a state. The religious wave has produced an occasional secular group—a reaction to excessive religious zeal. Buddhists in Sri Lanka tried to transform the country, and a terrorist response among the largely Hindu Tamils aims at creating a separate secular state.

Islam is at the heart of the wave. Islamic groups have conducted the most significant, deadly, and profoundly international attacks. Equally significant, the political events providing the hope for the fourth wave originated in Islam, and the successes achieved apparently influenced religious terror groups elsewhere.[63]

Although there is no direct evidence for the latter connection, the chronology is suggestive. After Islam erupted, Sikhs sought a religious state in the Punjab. Jewish terrorists attempted to blow up Islam's most sacred shrine in Jerusalem and waged an assassination campaign against Palestinian mayors. One Jew murdered twenty-nine Muslim worshippers in Abraham's tomb (Hebron, 1994), and another assassinated Israeli Prime Minister Rabin (1995). Aum Shinrikyo—a group that combined Buddhist, Hindu, and Christian themes—released nerve gas on the Tokyo subway (1995), killing 12 people and injuring 3,000 and creating worldwide anxiety that various groups would soon use weapons of mass destruction.

Christian terrorism, based on racist interpretations of the Bible, emerged in the amorphous American "Christian Identity" movement. In true medieval millenarian fashion, armed rural communes composed of families withdrew from the state to wait for the Second Coming and the great racial war. Although some observers have associated Christian Identity with the Oklahoma City bombing (1995), the Christian level of violence has been minimal—so far.

Three events in the Islamic world provided the hope or dramatic political turning point that was vital to launch the fourth wave. In 1979 the Iranian Revolution occurred, a new Islamic century began, and the Soviets made an unprovoked invasion of Afghanistan.

Iranian street demonstrations disintegrated the Shah's secular state. The event also was clear evidence to believers that religion now had more political appeal than did the prevailing third-wave ethos because Iranian Marxists could only muster meager support against the Shah. "There are no frontiers in Islam," Ayatollah Khomeini proclaimed, and "his" revolution altered relationships among all Muslims as well as between Islam and the rest of the world. Most immediately, the Iranians inspired and assisted Shiite terror movements outside of Iran, particularly in Iraq, Saudi Arabia, Kuwait, and Lebanon. In Lebanon, Shiites—influenced by the self-martyrdom tactic of the medieval Assassins—introduced suicide bombing, with surprising results, ousting American and other foreign troops that had entered the country on a peace mission after the 1982 Israeli invasion.

The monumental Iranian revolution was unexpected, but some Muslims had always believed that the year would be very significant because it marked the beginning of a new Islamic century. One venerable Islamic tradition holds that a redeemer will come with the start of a new century—an expectation that regularly sparked uprisings at the turn of earlier Muslim centuries.[64] Muslims stormed the Grand Mosque in Mecca in the first minutes of the new century in 1979, and 10,000 casualties resulted. Whatever the specific local causes, it is striking that so many examples of Sunni terrorism appeared at the same time in Egypt, Syria, Tunisia, Morocco, Algeria, the Philippines, and Indonesia.

The Soviet Union invaded Afghanistan in 1979. Resistance strengthened by volunteers from all over the Sunni world and subsidized by U.S aid forced the Soviets out by 1989—a crucial step in the stunning and unimaginable disintegration of the Soviet Union itself. Religion had eliminated a secular superpower, an astonishing event with important consequences for terrorist activity[65] in that the third wave received a decisive blow. Lands with large Muslim populations that formerly were part of the Soviet Union—such as Chechnya, Uzbekistan, Kyrgyzstan, Tajikistan, and Azerbaijan—became important new fields for Islamic rebels. Islamic forces ignited Bosnia. Kashmir again became a critical issue, and the death toll since 1990 has been more than 50,000.[66] Trained and confident Afghan veterans were major participants in the new and ongoing conflicts.

"Suicide bombing," reminiscent of anarchist bomb-throwing efforts, was the most deadly tactical innovation. Despite the conventional wisdom that only a vision of rewards in paradise could inspire such acts, the secular Tamil Tigers were so impressed by the achievement in Lebanon that they used the tactic in Sri Lanka to give their movement new life. From 1983 to 2000 they used suicide bombers more than all Islamic groups combined, and Tamil suicide bombers often were women—a very unusual event in the fourth wave.[67] Partly to enhance their political leverage at home, Palestinian religious groups began to use suicide bombers, compelling secular PLO elements to emulate them.

The fourth wave has displayed other distinctive international features. The number of terrorist groups declined dramatically. About 200 were active in the 1980s, but in the next decade the number fell to 40.[68] The trend appears to be related to the size of the primary audiences (nation versus religion). A major religious community such as Islam is much larger than any national group. Different cultural traditions also may be relevant. The huge number of secular terrorist groups came largely from Christian countries, and the Christian tradition has always generated many more religious divisions than the Islamic tradition has.[69] Islamic groups are more durable than their third-wave predecessors; the major groups in Lebanon, Egypt, and Algeria have persisted for two decades and are still functioning.[70] These groups are large organizations, and bin Laden's al-Qaeda was the largest, containing perhaps 5,000 members with cells operating in seventy-two countries.[71] Larger terrorist groups earlier usually had nationalist aims—with a few hundred active members and a few thousand available for recruitment. The PLO was a special case at least in Lebanon, where it had about 25,000 members and was trying to transform itself into a regular army. Likewise, most al-Qaeda recruits served with the Taliban in the Afghan civil war.

The American role too changed. Iran called the United States the "Great Satan." Al-Qaeda regarded America as its chief antagonist immediately after the Soviet Union was defeated—a fact not widely appreciated until September 11.[72] From the beginning, Islamic religious groups sought to *destroy* their American targets, usually military or civilian installations, an unknown pattern in the third wave. The aim was U.S. military withdrawal from the Middle East. U.S. troops were driven out of Lebanon and forced to abandon a humanitarian mission in Somalia. Attacks on military posts in Yemen and Saudi Arabia occurred. The destroyer USS *Cole* experienced the first terrorist strike against a military vessel ever (2000). All of the attacks on the U.S. military in the Arabian Peninsula and Africa drew military responses; moreover, Americans did not withdraw after those incidents. The strikes against American embassies in Kenya and Tanzania (1998) inflicted heavy casualties, and futile cruise missile attacks were made against al-Qaeda targets—the first time missiles were used against a group rather than a state. As Peter Bergen has noted, "The attacks, however, had a major unintended consequence: They turned bin Laden from a marginal figure in the Muslim world to a global celebrity."[73] Strikes on American soil began in 1993 with a partially successful effort on the World Trade Center. A mission to strike on the millennial celebration night seven years later was aborted.[74] Then there was September 11.

Al-Qaeda was responsible for attacks in the Arabian Peninsula, Africa, and the American homeland. Its initial object was to force U.S. evacuation of military bases in Saudi Arabia, the land containing Islam's two holiest sites. The Prophet Muhammed had said that only one religion should be in the land, and Saudi Arabia became a land where Christians and Jews could reside only for temporary periods.[75] Al-Qaeda's aim resonates in the Sunni world and is reflected in its unique recruiting pattern. Most volunteers come from Arab states—especially Egypt, Saudi Arabia, and Algeria—and the Afghan training camps received Sunnis from at least sixty Muslim and non-Muslim countries. Every previous terrorist organization, including Islamic groups, drew its recruits from a single national base. The contrast between PLO and al-Qaeda training facilities reflects this fact; the former trained units from other organizations and the latter received individuals only.

Beyond the evacuation of bases in Islam's Holy Land, al-Qaeda later developed another objective—a single Islamic state under the Sharia. Bin Laden gave vigorous support to Islamic groups that were active in various states of the Sunni world—states that many Muslims understand to be residues of collapsed colonial influence. Just as the United States refused to leave Saudi Arabia, it helped to frustrate this second effort by aiding the attacked states. The United States avoided direct intervention that could inflame the Islamic world, however. The support given to states attacked had some success, and perhaps September 11 should be understood as a desperate attempt to rejuvenate a failing cause by triggering indiscriminate reactions.[76]

The response to September 11 was as unprecedented as the attack itself. Under UN auspices, more than 100 states (including Iran) joined the attack on Afghanistan in various ways. Yet no one involved expected the intervention to be so quick and decisive. Afghanistan had always been difficult for invaders. Moreover, terrorist history demonstrates that even when antiterrorist forces were very familiar with territories containing terrorists (this time they were not), entrenched terrorists still had considerable staying power.

There are many reasons why al-Qaeda collapsed so quickly in Afghanistan. It violated a cardinal rule for terrorist organizations, which is to stay underground always. Al-Qaeda remained visible to operate its extensive training operations,[77] and as the Israelis demonstrated in ousting the PLO from Lebanon, visible groups are vulnerable. Moreover, al-Qaeda and the PLO were foreign elements in lands uncomfortable with their presence. Finally, al-Qaeda did not plan for an invasion possibility. The reason is not clear, but there is evidence that its contempt for previous American reactions convinced it that the United States would avoid difficult targets and not go to Afghanistan.[78]

The PLO regrouped in Tunisia, on condition that it would abandon its extensive training mission. Could al-Qaeda accept such limits, and if it did, would any state risk playing Tunisia's role? Pakistan's revolving-door policy suggests a much more likely reaction. Once al-Qaeda's principal supporter, Pakistan switched under U.S. pressure to give the coalition indispensable aid.

As of this writing, the world does not know what happened to al-Qaeda's leadership, but even if the portion left can be reassembled, how can the organization function without a protected sanctuary? Al Zawahiri, bin Laden's likely successor, warned his comrades before the Afghan training grounds were lost that "the victory … against the international alliance will not be accomplished without acquiring a … base in the heart of the Islamic world."[79] Peter Bergen's admirable study of al-Qaeda makes the same point.[80]

The disruption of al-Qaeda in Afghanistan has altered the organization's previous routine. Typically, al-Qaeda sleeper cells remained inactive until the moment to strike materialized, often designated by the organization's senior leadership. It was an unusual pattern in terrorist history. Normally cells are active and, therefore, need more autonomy so that police penetration in one cell does not go beyond that unit. Cells of this sort have more freedom to strike. They generally will do so more quickly and frequently, but the numbers and resources available to a cell constantly in motion limit them to softer or less protected targets. If direction from the top can no longer be a feature of al-Qaeda, the striking patterns will necessarily become more "normal."[81] Since the Afghan rout, strikes have been against "softer," largely unprotected civilian targets. As the destruction of tourist sites—such as the ancient synagogue in Tunisia and the nightclubs in Bali, Indonesia—suggests, however, the organization displays its trademark by maximizing casualties.

Concluding thoughts and questions

Unlike crime or poverty, international terrorism is a recent phenomenon. Its continuing presence for 125 years means, however, that it is rooted in important features of our world. Technology and doctrine have played vital roles. The latter reflects a modern inclination to rationalize activity or make it efficient, which Max Weber declared a distinctive feature of modern life. A third briefly noted factor is the spread of democratic ideas, which shapes terrorist activity in different ways—as suggested by the fact that nationalism or separatism is the most frequently espoused cause.[82]

The failure of a democratic reform program inspired the first wave, and the main theme of the second was national self-determination. A dominant, however confused, third-wave theme was that existing systems were not truly democratic. The spirit of the fourth wave appears explicitly antidemocratic because the democratic idea is inconceivable without a significant measure of secularism.

For many reasons, terrorist organizations often have short lives; sometimes their future is determined by devastating tactical mistakes. A decision to become visible is rare in the history of terror, and the quick success of the coalition's Afghan military campaign demonstrates why. If al-Qaeda successfully reconstructs itself, it may discover that it must become an "ordinary" terrorist group living underground among a friendly local population. That also suggests but, alas, does not demonstrate that its strikes will become more "ordinary" too.

No matter what happens to al-Qaeda, this wave will continue, but for how long is uncertain. The life cycle of its predecessors may mislead us. Each was inspired by a secular cause, and a striking characteristic of religious communities is how durable some are. Thus, the fourth wave may last longer than its predecessors, but the course of the Iranian revolution suggests something else. If history repeats itself, the fourth wave will be over in two decades. That history also demonstrates, however, that the world of politics always produces large issues to stimulate terrorists who regularly invent new ways to deal with them. What makes the pattern so interesting and frightening is that the issues emerge unexpectedly—or, at least, no one has been able to anticipate their tragic course.

The coalition assembled after September 11 was extraordinary for several reasons. September 11 was not only an American catastrophe: the World Trade Center housed numerous large foreign groups, and there were many foreign casualties. The UN involvement climaxed a transformation; it is hard to see it as the same organization that regularly referred to terrorists as freedom fighters forty years ago.

The only other coalition against terrorism was initiated a century ago. It aimed to make waves impossible by disrupting vital communication and migration conditions. Much less was expected from its participants, but it still fell apart in three years (1904). Will the current coalition last longer? September 11 will not be forgotten easily,[83] and the effort is focused now on an organization—a much easier focus to sustain.

When the present campaign against al-Qaeda and the small groups in Asia loosely associated with it concludes, what happens next? No organization has been identified as the next target, and until that happens one suspects that the perennial inclination for different states to distinguish groups according to the ends sought rather than the means used may reappear. Kashmir and Palestine are the two most important active scenes for terrorist activity. In Kashmir, Islamic insurgents are seriously dividing two important members of the coalition. India considers them terrorists, but Pakistan does not. War between those states, both possessing nuclear weapons, will push the coalition's war against terror aside. Successful outside mediation may produce a similar result because that would require some acceptance of the insurgents' legitimacy. The Israeli-Palestinian conflict has a similar meaning; so many important states understand the issue of terror there differently.

Islam fuels terrorist activity in Kashmir, but the issue—as in Palestine, where religious elements are less significant—is a local one. To what extent are other organizations in the fourth wave local too? How deeply can the coalition afford to get involved in situations where it will be serving the interests of local governments? Our experience supporting governments dealing with "local" terrorists has not always served our interests well, especially in the Islamic world.

The efforts of Aum Shinrikyo to use weapons of mass destruction has made American officials feel that the most important lesson of this wave is that those weapons will be used by terrorists against us.[84] September 11 intensified this anxiety even though suicide bombers armed with box cutters produced that catastrophe, and the history of terrorism demonstrates that cheap, easy to produce, portable, and simple to use weapons have always been the most attractive.

The fourth wave's cheap and distinctive weapon is suicide bombing. The victory in Lebanon was impressive, and suicide bombers have been enormously destructive in Sri Lanka and Israel. Driving foreign troops out of a country is one thing, however; compelling a people to give up a portion of its own country (Sri Lanka) or leave its own land (Israel) is another. In the latter case, the bombers' supporters seem to be suffering a lot more than their enemies are.

How does September 11 affect our understanding of foreign threats? This is a serious question that needs more discussion than it has received. Nechaev emphasized that the fear and rage rebel terror produced undermined a society's traditional moral conventions and ways of thinking. He was thinking of the domestic context, and indeed the history of modern terrors shows that domestic responses frequently are indiscriminate and self-destructive.[85] Can the same pattern be observed on the international scene?

The 2003 invasion of Iraq suggests that Nechaev's observation is apt for the international scene as well. The justifications for the war were that Iraq might give terrorists weapons of mass destruction or use them itself against the West—considerations that are applicable to a variety of states, as the "axis of evil" language suggests. After September 11 the United States scrapped the deterrence doctrine, which we developed to help us cope with states possessing weapons of mass destruction and served us well for more than fifty years. Preemption seemed to fit the new age better. Deterrence worked because states knew that they were visible and could be destroyed if they used the dreaded weapons. Underground terrorist groups do not have this vulnerability, which is why preemption has been an important part of police counterterrorist strategy since the first wave. Deterrence is linked to actions, whereas preemption is more suitable when intentions have to be assessed—a task always shrouded in grave ambiguities. Is there any reason to think the crucial distinction between states and terrorist groups has disappeared, however, and that we should put decisions of war and peace largely in the hands of very imperfect intelligence agencies?

The significance of the Iraqi war for the war against terrorism remains unclear. The coalition's cohesion has been weakened, and the flagging fortunes of Islamic groups could be revived. Both possibilities are more likely if preemption is employed against another state or if the victory in Iraq ultimately is understood as an occupation.

Notes

An earlier version of this essay was published in *Current History* (December 2001): 419–425. Another version was delivered at the annual John Barlow Lecture, University of Indiana, Indianapolis. I am indebted to Jim Ludes, Lindsay Clutterbuck, Laura Donohue, Clark McCauley, Barbara Rapoport, and Sara Grdan for useful comments, even those I did not take. The problems in the essay are my responsibility.

1 On September 20, 2001, the president told Congress that "any nation that continues to harbor or support terrorism will be regarded as a hostile regime. [T]he war would not end until every terrorist group of global reach has been found, stopped, and defeated."

2 See Richard B. Jensen, "The United States, International Policing, and the War against Anarchist Terrorism," *Terrorism and Political Violence* (hereafter *TPV*) 13, no. 1 (spring 2001): 5–46.

3 No good history of terrorism exists. Schmid and Jongman's monumental study of the terrorism literature does not even list a history of the subject. See *Political Terrorism: A New Guide to Actors, Authors, Concepts, Theories, DataBases, and Literature*, rev. ed. (New Brunswick, N.J.: Transaction Books, 1988).

4 I lack space to discuss the domestic sphere, which offers important parallels as well. The unusual character of terrorist activity made an enormous impact on national life in many countries beginning in the latter part of the nineteenth century. Every state affected in the first wave radically transformed its police organizations as tools to penetrate underground groups. The Russian *Okhrana*, the British Special Branch, and the FBI are conspicuous examples. The new organizational form remains a permanent, perhaps indispensable, feature of modern life. Terrorist tactics, *inter alia*, aim at producing rage and frustration, often driving governments to respond in unanticipated, extraordinary, illegal, socially destructive, and shameful ways. Because a significant Jewish element, for example, was present in the several Russian terrorist movements, the *Okhrana* organized pogroms to intimidate Russian Jews, compelling many to flee to the West and to the Holy Land. *Okhrana* fabricated *The Protocols of Zion*, a book that helped stimulate a virulent anti-Semitism that went well beyond Russia. The influence of that fabrication continued for decades and still influences Christian and Islamic terrorist movements today.

Democratic states "overreacted" too. President Theodore Roosevelt proposed sending all anarchists back to Europe. Congress did not act, but more than a decade later President Wilson's Attorney General Palmer implemented a similar proposal and rounded up all anarchists to ship them back "home," regardless of whether they had committed crimes. That event produced the 1920 Wall Street bombing, which in turn became the justification for an immigration quota law that for decades made it much more difficult for persons from southern and eastern European states (the original home of most anarchists) to immigrate—a law Adolph Hitler praised highly. It is still too early to know what the domestic consequences of September 11 will be. The very first reactions suggested that we had learned from past mistakes. The federal government made special efforts to show that we were not at war with Islam, and it curbed the first expressions of vigilante passions. The significance of subsequent measures seems more problematic, however. Our first experience with terror led us to create important new policing arrangements. Now Congress has established a Department of Homeland Security with 170,000 employees—clearly the largest change in security policy in our history. No one knows what that seismic change means. One casualty could be the Posse Comitatus law, which prohibits the military forces from administering civil affairs—a law that ironically was passed because we were unhappy with military responses to KKK terrorist activity after the Civil War! A policy of secret detentions, a common reaction to serious terrorist activities in many countries, has been implemented. Extensive revisions of immigration regulations are being instituted. Prisoners taken in Afghanistan are not being prosecuted under the criminal law, reversing a long-standing policy in virtually all states including our own. Previous experiences suggest that it will take time for the changes to have their effect because so much depends on the scope, frequency, and duration of future terrorist activity.

5 David M. Chalmers, *Hooded Americanism: The History of the Ku Klux Klan*, 3d ed. (Durham, N.C.: Duke University Press, 1987), 19.

6 The activities of the Thugs and Assassins had international dimensions but were confined to specific regions; more important, there were no comparable groups operating at the same time in this region or elsewhere. See David C. Rapoport, "Fear and Trembling: Terror in Three Religious Traditions," *American Political Science Review* 78, no. 3 (1984): 658–677.

7 The lineage of rebel terror is very ancient, going back at least to the first century. Hinduism, Judaism, and Islam produced the Thugs, Zealots, and Assassins, respectively; these names still are used to designate terrorists. Religion determined every purpose and each tactic of this ancient form. See Rapoport, "Fear and Trembling."

8 By far most published academic articles on terrorism deal with counterterrorism and with organizations. Judging by my experience as an editor of *TPV*, the proportions increase further in this direction if we also consider articles that are rejected.

9 See note 1.

10 The rebels fought in uniform and against soldiers. George Bernard Shaw said, "My own view is that the men who were shot in cold blood … after their capture were prisoners of war." Prime Minister Asquith said that by Britain's own standards, the rebels were honorable, that "they conducted themselves with great humanity … fought very bravely and did not resort to outrage." The *Manchester Guardian* declared that the executions were "atrocities." See my introduction to part III of David C. Rapoport and Yonah Alexander, eds., *The Morality of Terrorism: Religious Origins and Ethnic Implications*, 2d ed. (New York: Columbia University Press, 1989), 219–227.

11 Guerrillas carry weapons openly and wear an identifying emblem—circumstances that oblige a state to treat them as soldiers.

12 Anyone who has tried to explain the intensity of the 1960s experience to contemporary students knows how difficult it is to transmit a generation's experience.

13 Nechaev's "Revolutionary Catechism" is reprinted in David C. Rapoport, *Assassination and Terrorism* (Toronto: CBC, 1971). See Michael Bakunin and Peter Kropotkin, *Revolutionary Pamphlets* (New York: Benjamin Bloom, 1927); Nicholas Mozorov, *Terroristic Struggle* (London, 1880); Serge Stepniak, *Underground Russia: Revolutionary Profiles and Sketches from Life* (New York, 1892).

14 See Rapoport, "Fear and Trembling."

15 It took time for this attitude to develop in Islam. If one compares bin Laden's work with Faraj's *Neglected Duty*—a work primarily written at the beginning of the fourth wave to justify the assassination of Egyptian President Sadat (1981)—the two authors seem to be in different worlds. Faraj cites no experience outside the Islamic tradition, and his most recent historical reference is to Napoleon's invasion of Europe. See David C. Rapoport, "Sacred Terror: A Case from Contemporary Islam," in *Origins of Terrorism*, ed. Walter Reich (Cambridge: Cambridge University Press, 1990), 103–30. I am grateful to Jerry Post for sharing his copy of the bin Laden treatise. An edited version appears on the Department of Justice website www.usdoj.gov/ag/trainingmanual.htm.

16 Bin Laden's dedication reads as follows:
Pledge, O Sister

To the sister believer whose clothes the criminals have stripped off:
To the sister believer whose hair the oppressors have shaved.
To the sister believer whose body has been abused by the human dogs.
…
Covenant, O Sister … to make their women widows and their children orphans. …

17 I ignore right-wing groups because more often than not they are associated with government reactions. I also ignore "single issue" groups such as the contemporary antiabortion and Green movements.

18 The term *terror* originally referred to actions of the Revolutionary government that went beyond the rules regulating punishment in order to "educate" a people to govern itself.

19 Vera Figner, the architect of Narodnaya Volya's foreign policy, identifies the first four ingredients. The fifth was created later. For a more extensive discussion of Figner, see David C. Rapoport, "The International World as Some Terrorists Have Seen It: A Look at a Century of Memoirs," in *Inside Terrorist Organizations*, 2d ed. (London: Frank Cass, 2001), 125*ff.*

20 Nechaev, "Revolutionary Catechism."

21 An equivalent for this argument in religious millennial thought is that the world must become impossibly bad before it could become unimaginably good.

22 Adam B. Ulam, *In the Name of the People* (New York: Viking Press, 1977), 269 (emphasis added).

23 Newspaper reports in Germany the next day interpreted the demonstrations to mean that a revolution was coming. See *New York Times*, 4 April 1878.

24 Stepniak, *Underground Russia*, 39–40.

25 The bomb was most significant in Russia. Women were crucial in Russian groups but sometimes were precluded from throwing the bomb, presumably because bombers rarely escaped. Other terrorists used the bomb extensively but chose other weapons as well.

26 A guerrilla force has political objectives, as any army does, but it aims to weaken or destroy the enemy's military forces first. The terrorist, on the other hand, strikes directly at the political sentiments that sustain the enemy.

27 Thomas Hobbes may have been the first to emphasize hope as a necessary ingredient of revolutionary efforts. The first chapter of Menachem Begin's account of his experience in the Irgun contains the most moving description of the necessity of hope in terrorist literature. Menachem Begin, *The Revolt: Story of the Irgun* (Jerusalem: Steinmatzky's Agency, 1997).

28 There were many organizations: the Internal Macedonian Revolutionary Organization, Young Bosnia, and the Serbian Black Hand.

29 See Peter Heehs, *Nationalism, Terrorism, and Communalism: Essays in Modern Indian History* (Delhi: Oxford University Press, 1998), chap. 2.

30 The Japanese offer to finance Russian terrorists during the Russo-Japanese War (1905) encouraged Indian terrorists to believe that the Japanese would help them too. Heehs, *Nationalism, Terrorism, and Communalism*, 4. The Russians turned the Japanese offer down, fearing that knowledge of the transaction during a time of war would destroy their political credibility.

31 Italians were particularly active as international assassins, crossing borders to kill French President Carnot (1894), Spanish Premier Casnovas (1896), and Austrian Empress Elizabeth (1898). In 1900 an agent of an anarchist group in Patterson, New Jersey, returned to Italy to assassinate King Umberto.

32 Jensen, "The United States, International Policing, and the War against Anarchist Terrorism," 19.

33 The IRA's success in 1921 occurred when the British recognized the Irish state. Northern Ireland remained British, however, and the civil war between Irish factions over the peace settlement ended in defeat for those who wanted to continue until Northern Ireland joined the Irish state

34 For an interesting and useful account of the decolonialization process, see Robert Hager, Jr., and David A. Lake, "Balancing Empires: Competitive Decolonization in International Politics," *Security Studies* 9, no. 3 (spring 2000): 108–148. Hager and Lake emphasize that the literature on decolonization "has ignored how events and politics within the core (metropolitan area) shaped the process" (145).

35 Begin said that his decision was determined by the fact that if he pursued it, a civil war among Jews would occur, indicating that most Jews favored partition. Begin, *The Revolt*, chapters 9 and 10.

36 Alistair Home, *A Savage War of Peace* (London: Macmillan, 1977), 94–96.

37 Begin, *The Revolt*.

38 For a more detailed discussion of the definition problem, see David C. Rapoport, "Politics of Atrocity," in *Terrorism: Interdisciplinary Perspectives*, ed. Yonah Alexander and Seymour Finger (New York: John Jay Press, 1987), 46.

39 Alexander I of Yugoslavia (1934) was the most prominent victim, and historians believe that Hungary and Italy were involved in providing help for Balkan terrorists. Begin points out in *The Revolt* that it was too costly to assassinate prominent figures.

40 The strategy is superbly described in the film "Battle of Algiers," based on the memoirs of Yaacev Saadi, who organized the battle. Attacks occur against the police, whose responses are limited by rules governing criminal procedure. In desperation, the police set a bomb off in the Casbah, inadvertently exploding an ammunition dump and killing Algerian women and children. A mob emerges screaming for revenge, and at this point the FLN has the moral warrant to attack civilians. There is another underlying element that often gives rebel terrorism in a democratic world special weight. The atrocities of the strong always seem worse than those of the weak because people believe that the latter have no alternatives.

41 See note 11.

42 See Rapoport, "The International World as Some Terrorists Have Seen It."

43 Irish Americans have always given Irish rebels extensive support. In fact, the Fenian movement was born in the American Civil War. Members attempted to invade Canada from the United States and then went to Ireland to spark rebellion there.

44 World War I, of course, increased the influence of the United States, and Wilson justified the war with the self-determination principle.

45 Martin David Dubin, "Great Britain and the Anti-Terrorist Conventions of 1937," *TPV* 5, no. 1 (spring 1993): 1.

46 See John Dugard, "International Terrorism and the Just War," in Rapoport and Alexander, *Morality of Terrorism*, 77–78.

47 Basque Nation and Liberty (ETA), the Armenian Secret Army for the Liberation of Armenia (ASALA), the Corsican National Liberation Front (FNLC), and the IRA.

48 The periods of the first and third waves were times when the rights of women were asserted more strenuously in the general society.

49 Sean Anderson and Stephen Sloan, *Historical Dictionary of Terrorism* (Metuchen, N.J.: Transaction Press, 1995), 136.

50 Although bank robbing was not as significant as in the first wave, some striking examples materialized. In January 1976 the PLO, together with its bitter enemies the Christian Phalange, hired safe breakers to help loot the vaults of the major banks in Beirut. Estimates of the amount stolen range between $50 and $100 million. "Whatever the truth the robbery was large enough to earn a place in the *Guinness Book of Records* as the biggest bank robbery of all time"; James Adams, *The Financing of Terror* (New York: Simon and Schuster, 1986), 192.

51 Adams, *Financing of Terror*, 94.

52 The attack on Major actually was an attack on the cabinet, so it is not clear whether the prime minister was the principal target (Lindsay Clutterbuck, personal communication to author).

53 The status of political prisoner was revoked in March 1976. William Whitelaw, who granted it in the first place, ranked it as one of his "most regrettable decisions."

54 Anderson and Sloan, *Historical Dictionary of Terrorism*, 303.

55 Sometimes there was American support for terrorist activity (e.g., the Contras in Nicaragua).

56 When a disappointed office-seeker assassinated President Garfield, Figner's sympathy letter to the American people said that there was no place for terror in democratic states. The statement alienated elements of her radical constituency in other countries.

57 Michael Baumann, *Terror or Love* (New York: Grove Press, 1977), 61.

58 Interview with Hans J. Klein in Jean M. Bourguereau, *German Guerrilla: Terror, Rebel Reaction and Resistance* (Sanday, U.K.: Cienfuegos Press, 1981), 31.

59 Abu Nidal himself was on a PLO list of persons to be assassinated.

60 W. Andrew Terrill, "Saddam's Failed Counterstrike: Terrorism and the Gulf War," *Studies in Conflict and Terrorism* 16 (1993): 219–232.

61 In addition to four UN conventions there are eight other major multilateral terrorism conventions, starting with The Tokyo Convention of 1963, dealing with the aircraft safety. See http://usinfo.state.gov/topical/pol/terror/conven.htm and http://untreaty.un.org/English/Terrorism.asp.

62 Khachig Tololyan, "Cultural Narrative and the Motivation of the Terrorist," in Rapoport, *Inside Terrorist Organizations*, 217–233.

63 See David C. Rapoport, "Comparing Militant Fundamentalist Movements and Groups," in *Fundamentalisms and the State*, ed. Martin Marty and Scott Appleby (Chicago: University of Chicago Press, 1993), 429–461.

64 To those in the West the most familiar was the nineteenth-century uprising in the Sudan, which resulted in the murder of legendary British General "Chinese" Gordon.

65 This was not the first time secular forces would help launch the careers of those who would become religious terrorists. Israel helped Hamas to get started, thinking it would compete to weaken the PLO.

To check left-wing opposition, President Sadat released religious elements from prison that later assassinated him.

66 Peter Bergen, *Holy War Inc.: Inside the Secret World of Osama Bin Ladin* (New York: Free Press, 2001), 208.

67 In the period specified, Tamil suicide bombers struck 171 times; the combined total for all thirteen Islamic groups using the tactic was 117. Ehud Sprinzak cites the figures compiled by Yoram Schweitzer in "Rational Fanatics," *Foreign Policy* (October 2001): 69. The most spectacular Tamil act was the assassination of Indian Prime Minister Rajiv Gandhi. (Religion did not motivate the notorious Kamikaze attacks during World War II either.) The example of the Tamils has other unusual characteristics. Efforts to make Sri Lanka a Buddhist state stimulated the revolt. Although Tamils largely come from India, there are several religious traditions represented in the population, and religion does not define the terrorists' purpose.

68 See Ami Pedahzur, William Eubank, and Leonard Weinberg, "The War on Terrorism and the Decline of Terrorist Group Formation," *TPV* 14, no. 3 (fall 2002): 141–147.

69 The relationship between different religious terror groups is unusual. Groups from different mainstream traditions (Christianity, Islam, etc.) do not cooperate. Even traditional cleavages within a religion—as in Shiite and Sunni Islam, for example—sometimes are intensified. Shiite terror groups generally take their lead from Iran regarding aid to Sunnis. Iran has helped the Palestinians and is hostile to al-Qaeda and the Saudi religious state.

70 I have no statistical evidence on this point.

71 Rohan Gunaratna, *Inside Al Qaeda: Global Network of Terror* (New York: Columbia University Press, 2002), 97.

72 The stated object of al-Qaeda is to recreate a single Muslim state, and one could argue that if the United States had withdrawn military units from the Muslim world, the attacks would have ceased. What if the issue really was the impact of American secular culture on the world?

73 Bergen, *Holy War Inc.*, 225.

74 Those attacks, as well as the expected attacks that did not materialize, are discussed in a special volume of *TPV* 14, no. 1 (spring 2002) edited by Jeffrey Kaplan, titled *Millennial Violence*. The issue also was published as a book: *Millennial Violence: Past, Present, and Future* (London: Frank Cass, 2002).

75 Bernard Lewis, "License to Kill," *Foreign Affairs* (November/December 1998).

76 For a very interesting discussion of the circumstances that provoke American military responses to terrorist attacks, see Michelle Mavesti, "Explaining the United States' Decision to Strike Back at Terrorists," *TPV* 13, no. 2 (summer 2001): 85–106.

77 If the organization understood its vulnerability, it might have thought that an attack on the sovereignty of the state protecting it was unlikely. One reason the Taliban government refused a repeated UN demand to expel al-Qaeda was because without al-Qaeda support it could not survive local domestic opposition. Because most al-Qaeda recruits served in the Taliban forces in the ongoing civil war, the Taliban must have felt that it had no choice. Clearly, however, there must have been a failure to plan for an invasion possibility; the failure to resist is astonishing otherwise.

78 Gunaratna, *Inside Al Qaeda*.

79 Quoted by Nimrod Raphaeli, "Ayman Muhammad Rabi Al-Zawahiri: The Making of an Arch-Terrorist," *TPV* 14, no. 4 (winter 2002): 1–22.

80 Bergen, *Holy War Inc.*, 234.

81 The Spaniards conquered the Aztecs and Incas easily, but the United States had more difficulty with the less powerful but highly decentralized native Americans. Steven Simon and Daniel Benjamin make a different argument, contending that bin Laden's group is uniquely decentralized and therefore less likely to be disturbed by destroying the center. See "America and the New Terrorism," *Survival* 42, no. 2 (2000): 156–157.

82 We lack a systematic comparison of the aims sought by organizations in the history of modern terror.

83 September 11 has had an impact on at least one terrorist group: The Tamils found diaspora financial support suddenly disappearing for suicide bombing—an opportunity the Norwegians seized to bring them to the bargaining table again.

84 See David C. Rapoport, "Terrorism and Weapons of the Apocalypse," *National Security Studies Quarterly* 5, no. 3 (summer 1999): 49–69, reprinted in Henry Sokolski and James Ludes, *Twenty-First Century Weapons Proliferation* (London: Frank Cass, 2001), 14–33.

85 See note 3.

Section 2

Definitions

Readings

Gibbs, J. P. (1989). Conceptualization of terrorism. *American Sociological Review, 54*, 329–340.

Weinberg, L., Pedahzur, A., & Hirsch-Hoefler, S. (2004). The challenges of conceptualizing terrorism. *Terrorism and Political Violence, 16*, 777–794.

Schmid, A. P. (1993). The response problem as a definition problem. In A. Schmid & R. Crelinsten (Eds.), *Western responses to terrorism* (pp. 7–13). London: Frank Cass.

Introduction

Now that you have a historical context to the development of terrorism through the centuries, we move to one of the most difficult and contentious issues in the study of terrorism – how to define it. As part of this journey, we will discover what kinds of challenges make it difficult for us to arrive at a consensus definition. It should come as no surprise that this is an issue that has generated enormous debate in the terrorism studies literature. We have carefully selected the three publications presented in this section. If, by the end of these readings, you find the complexity of terrorism so challenging as to pose almost overwhelming difficulty in defining it, then you can rest assured that you have successfully engaged with these contributions. If it was easy to define terrorism, we would have arrived at an agreed-upon definition a long time ago. Our intention with this section is to expose you to the complex nature of the phenomenon (through the chapters by Gibbs and Weinberg, Pedahzur, and Hirsch-Hoefler) while also giving you exposure to some very practical steps by a scholar (Schmid) who has spent many years studying the debate about definitions.

Discussion questions

By the end of this section you should be able to answer the following questions:

- Why is it difficult to define terrorism?
- Is the old adage "one man's terrorist is another man's freedom fighter" accurate?
- Is it more useful to have a broader or narrower definition of terrorism? Why?

Further reading

Fletcher, G. P. (2006). The indefinable concept of terrorism. *Journal of International Criminal Justice, 4*, 894–911.

Hoffman, B. (2006). *Inside terrorism* (2nd ed.). New York: Columbia University Press.

Kennedy, R. (1999). Is one person's terrorist another person's freedom fighter? Western and Islamic approaches to 'just war' compared. *Terrorism and Political Violence, 11*, 1–21.

Perry, N. J. (2003). Numerous federal legal definitions of terrorism: The problem of too many grails. *Journal of Legislation, 30*, 249.

Primoratz, I. (1990). What is terrorism? *Journal of Applied Philosophy, 7*, 129–138.

Silke, A. (1996). Terrorism and the blind men's elephant. *Terrorism and Political Violence, 8*, 12–28.

Sinnott-Armstrong, W. (1991). On Primoratz's definition of terrorism. *Journal of Applied Philosophy, 8*, 115–120.

Sproat, P. A. (1991). Can the state be terrorist? *Studies in Conflict & Terrorism, 14*, 19–29.

4 Conceptualization of terrorism

Jack P. Gibbs

Definitions of terrorism are controversial for reasons other than conceptual issues and problems. Because labeling actions as "terrorism" promotes condemnation of the actors, a definition may reflect ideological or political bias (for lengthy elaboration, see Rubenstein 1987). Given such considerations, all of which discourage attempts to define terrorism, it is not surprising that Laqueur (1977, p. 5) argued that

> a comprehensive definition of terrorism … does not exist nor will it be found in the foreseeable future. To argue that terrorism cannot be studied without such a definition is manifestly absurd.

Even granting what Laqueur implies—that terrorism is somehow out there awaiting definition— it is no less "manifestly absurd" to pretend to study terrorism without at least some kind of definition of it. Leaving the definition implicit is the road to obscurantism.

Even if sociologists should overcome their ostensible reluctance to study terrorism (for a rare exception, see Lee 1983), they are unlikely to contribute to its conceptualization. The situation has been described succinctly by Tallman (1984, p. 1121): "Efforts to explicate key concepts in sociology have been met with stifling indifference by members of our discipline."

There are at least two reasons why sociologists commonly appear indifferent to conceptualizations. First, Weber and Parsons gave the work a bad name in the eyes of those sociologists who insist (rightly) on a distinction between substantive theory and conceptual analysis. Second, conclusive resolutions of conceptual issues are improbable because the *ultimate* justification of any definition is an impressive theory that incorporates the definition. Nonetheless, it is crippling to assume that productive research and impressive theories are possible without confronting conceptual issues and problems. The argument is not just that theorizing without definitions is sterile, nor merely recognition that theory construction and conceptualization should go hand in hand. Additionally, one can assess definitions without descending to purely personal opinion, even when not guided by a theory.

Systematic tests of a theory require definitions of at least *some* of the theory's constituent terms; but test findings, even those based on the same units of comparison, will diverge if each definition's empirical applicability is negligible, meaning if independent observers disagree when applying the definition to identify events or things. To illustrate, contemplate a question about any definition of terrorism: How much do independent observers agree in judging whether or not President Kennedy's assassination was terrorism in light of the definition? As subsequent illustrations show, simple definitions may promote agreement in answers to the Kennedy question and yet be objectionable for theoretical reasons; but the immediate point is that an empirically applicable definition does not require a theory. By contrast, given evidence that a definition promises negligible empirical applicability, no theory can justify that definition.

Still another "atheoretical" criterion is the definition's consistency with convention. That criterion cannot be decisive, because it would preclude novel definitions; but it is important when the field's professionals must rely on "outsiders" for data and, hence, presume appreciable congruence between their definitions and those of the outsiders. That consideration is particularly relevant here, because in analyzing terrorism social scientists often rely on reports of government officials, journalists, and historians.

Conceptual issues and problems haunt virtually all major terms in the social and behavioral sciences, and any definition is ambiguous if it does not answer questions bearing on those issues and problems. There are at least five such questions about terrorism. First, is terrorism *necessarily* illegal (a crime)? Second, is terrorism *necessarily* undertaken to realize some particular type of goal and, if so, what is it? Third, how does terrorism *necessarily* differ from conventional military operations in a war, a civil war, or so-called guerrilla warfare? Fourth, is it *necessarily* the case that only opponents of the government engage in terrorism? Fifth, is terrorism *necessarily* a distinctive strategy in the use of violence and, if so, what is that strategy?

The questions are answered in light of a subsequent definition of terrorism, but more than a definition is needed. The pursuit of a theory about terrorism will be furthered by describing and thinking about terrorism and all other sociological phenomena in terms of one particular notion, thereby promoting the recognition of logical and empirical associations. The most appropriate notion is identified subsequently as "control," but a defense of that identification requires a definition of terrorism (*not* of "terror").

A definition of terrorism

Terrorism is illegal violence or threatened violence directed against human or nonhuman objects, provided that it:

1   was undertaken or ordered with a view to altering or maintaining at least one putative norm in at least one particular territorial unit or population;
2   had secretive, furtive, and/or clandestine features that were expected by the participants to conceal their personal identity and/or their future location;
3   was not undertaken or ordered to further the permanent defense of some area;
4   was not conventional warfare and because of their concealed personal identity, concealment of their future location, their threats, and/or their spatial mobility, the participants perceived themselves as less vulnerable to conventional military action; *and*
5   was perceived by the participants as contributing to the normative goal previously described (*supra*) by inculcating fear of violence in persons (perhaps an indefinite category of them) other than the immediate target of the actual or threatened violence and/or by publicizing some cause.

Clarification, issues, and problems

In keeping with a social science tradition, most definitions of terrorism are set forth in a fairly brief sentence (see, e.g., surveys by Oots 1986, pp. 5–8, and Schmid and Jongman 1988, pp. 32–38). Such definitions do not tax the reader's intellect or patience, but it is inconsistent to grant that human behavior is complex and then demand simple definitions of behavioral types.

The illegality of terrorism. Rubenstein's definition (1987, p. 31) is noteworthy if only because it makes no reference to crime or illegality: "I use the term 'terrorism' … to denote *acts of small-group violence for which arguable claims of mass representation can be made.*" However, even granting that terrorism is an illegal action, there are two contending conceptions of crime, one emphasizing the *reactions* of officials as the criterion and the other emphasizing normative considerations (e.g., statutory law). Because of space limitations, it is not feasible to go much beyond recognizing the two contending conceptions. It must suffice to point out that an action may be illegal or criminal (in light of statutes and/or reactions by state officials) because of (1) where it was planned; (2) where it commenced; and/or (3) where it continued, especially in connection with crossing a political boundary. Such distinctions are relevant even when contemplating the incidence of terrorism.

One likely reaction: But why is terrorism *necessarily* a crime? The question suggests that *classes* of events or things exist independently of definitions. Thus, it may appear that "stones" and "humans" denote ontologically *given* classes, but in the context of gravitational theory stones and humans are *not* different. However, to insist that all definitions are *nominal* is not to imply that conventional usage should be ignored; and, again, the point takes on special significance when defining terrorism. The initial (unnumbered) part of the present definition is consistent with most other definitions and also with this claim: most journalists, officials, and historians who label an action as "terrorism" evidently regard the action as illegal or criminal. However, it is not denied that two populations may differ sharply as to whether or not a particular action was a crime. As a *necessary* condition for an action to be terrorism, only the statutes and/or reactions of officials in the political unit where the action was planned or took place (in whole or in part) need identify the action as criminal or illegal.

Violence and terrorism. Something like the phrase "violence or threatened violence" appears in most definitions of terrorism (see Schmid and Jongman 1988, p. 5). As in those definitions, the phrase's key terms are here left as primitives; and whether they must be defined to realize sufficient empirical applicability can be determined only by actual attempts to apply the definition.

Despite consensus about violence as a *necessary* feature of terrorism, there is a related issue. Writers often suggest that only humans can be targets of violence, but many journalists, officials, and historians have identified instances of destruction or damage of nonhuman objects (e.g., buildings, domesticated animals, crops) as terrorism. Moreover, terrorists pursue their ultimate goal through inculcation of fear and humans do fear damage or destruction of particular nonhuman objects.

The ultimate goal of terrorists. The present definition indicates that terrorists *necessarily* have a goal. Even though it is difficult to think of a human action that is not goal oriented, the consideration is controversial for two reasons. One reason is the allegation that terrorists are irrational or mentally ill (see, e.g., Livingston 1978, pp. 224–239; and Livingstone's commentary, 1982, p. 31 on Parry), which raises doubts as to whether terrorists have identifiable goals. The second reasons why part 1 of the definition is controversial: many sociologists, especially Durkheimians, do not emphasize the purposive quality of human behavior, perhaps because they view the emphasis as reductionism. In any case, a defensible definition of virtually any term in sociology's vocabulary requires recognition of the relevance of internal behavior (e.g., perception, beliefs, purpose). Thus, without part 1 of the present definition, the distinction between terrorism and the *typical* robbery becomes obscure. The typical robber does not threaten violence to maintain or alter a putative norm; he or she is concerned only with behavioral control in a particular situation.

A defensible definition of a norm is not presumed (see Gibbs 1981, pp. 9–18, for a litany of difficulties). Rather, it is necessary only that at least one of the participants (those who undertake the violent action or order it) view the action as contributing to the maintenance or alteration of some law, policy, arrangement, practice, institution, or shared belief.

Part 1 of the definition is unconventional only in that goals of terrorists are *not* necessarily political. Many definitions create the impression that all terrorism is political (for a contrary view, see Wilkinson 1986, p. 51), but the very term "political terrorism" suggests at least two types.[1] The concern of social scientists with terrorism typologies is premature (see e.g., the commentary by Oots [1986, pp. 11, 30] on Mickolus's notions of international, transnational, domestic, and interstate terrorism). No terrorism typology amounts to a *generic* definition (see the survey in Schmid and Jongman 1988, pp. 39–59), and without the latter the former is bound to be unsatisfactory.

Military operations and terrorism. To repeat a previous question: How does terrorism *necessarily* differ, if at all, from conventional military operations in a war, civil war, or so-called guerrilla warfare? The question cannot be answered readily because there are no clearly accepted definitions of conventional military operation, war, civil war, and guerrilla warfare.[2] "Guerrilla" is especially troublesome because journalists are prone to use the word without defining it but such as to suggest that it is synonymous with terrorism (a usage emphatically rejected by Laqueur 1987 and Wilkinson 1986).

Conventional military operations differ from terrorism along the lines indicated by parts 2, 3, and 4 of the definition.[3] However, the definition does not preclude the possibility of a transition from terrorism to civil war. One tragic instance was the Easter Rising in Ireland (1916), when rather than perpetuate the terrorism tradition, a small group of Irish seized and attempted a permanent defense of government buildings in Dublin, vainly hoping that the populace would join them in open warfare. Today, it is terrorism rather than civil war that haunts Northern Ireland, and the term "guerrilla warfare" has no descriptive utility in that context.

Terrorism as a special strategy. One feature of terrorism makes it a distinctive (though not unique) strategy in violence. That feature is described in part 5 of the definition.

Part 5 is controversial primarily because it would exclude action such as this threat: "Senator, if you vote for that bill, it will be your death warrant." Why would such a threat not be terrorism? A more theoretically significant answer is given subsequently. Here it must suffice to point out that scores of writers have emphasized "third-party" or "general" intimidation as an essential feature of terrorism;[4] and journalists, officials, or historians only rarely identify "dyadic intimidation" (X acts violently toward Y but *not* to control Z's behavior) as terrorism.

"State terrorism" as a special issue. Zinam's definition (1978, pp. 244–245) illustrates one of many reasons why definitions of terrorism are so disputable: "[Terrorism is] the use or threat of violence by individuals or organized groups to evoke fear and submission to obtain some economic, political, sociopsychological, ideological, or other objective." Because the definition would extend to the imposition of legal punishments by government officials to prevent crimes through *general* deterrence, in virtually all jurisdictions (see Morris 1966, p. 631) some aspects of criminal justice would qualify as terrorism; and Zinam's definition provides no basis for denying that it would be "state terrorism."[5] Even granting that a state agent or employee acts for the state only when acting at the direction or with the consent of a superordinate, there is still no ostensible difference between the use or threat of violence in law enforcement and Zinam's terrorism.

Had Zinam defined terrorism as being *necessarily* illegal or criminal, then many instances of violence by a state agent or employee at the direction or with the consent of a superordinate would not be terrorism. However, think of the numerous killings in Nazi Germany (Ernst Roehm, the Storm Troop head being a well-known victim) during the Night of the Long Knives (June 30, 1934). Hitler ordered the slaughter, and *at the time* the killings were illegal in light of German statues; but Hitler publicly acknowledged responsibility, and the only concealment was that perceived as necessary to surprise the victims.[6] Surely there is a significant difference between such open, blatant use of coercion by a state official (dictator or not) and the situation where regime opponents are assassinated but officials disavow responsibility and the murders are so secretive that official complicity is difficult to prove. The "rule of terror" of Shaka, the famous Zulu chief, is also relevant. Shaka frequently ordered the execution of tribal members on a seemingly whimsical basis, but the orders were glaringly public (see Walter 1969). Shaka's regime illustrates another point: in some social units there may be no obvious "law" other than the will of a despot, in which case there is no basis to describe the despot's violence as illegal. The general point: because various aspects of government may be *public* violence, to label all of those aspects "terrorism" is to deny that terrorism has any secretive, furtive, or clandestine features.

Given the conceptual issues and problems that haunt the notion of state terrorism, it is hardly surprising that some writers attribute great significance to the notion, while others (e.g., Laqueur 1987, pp. 145–146) seem to reject it. The notion is not rejected here, and the following definition does not make it an extremely rare phenomenon. State terrorism occurs when and only when a government official (or agent or employee) engages in terrorism, as previously defined, at the direction or with the consent of a superordinate, but one who does *not* publicly acknowledge such direction or consent.

The foregoing notwithstanding, for theoretical reasons it may prove desirable to limit the proposed definition of terrorism (*supra*) to *nonstate* terrorism and to seek a quite different definition of *state* terrorism. Even so, it will not do to presume that all violence by state agents is terrorism. The immediate reason is that the presumption blurs the distinction between terrorism and various kinds or aspects of law enforcement. Moreover, it is grossly unrealistic to assume that all instances of genocide or persecution along racial, ethnic, religious, or class lines by state agents (including the military) are terrorism regardless of the means, goals, or circumstances. Nor is it defensible to speak of particular regimes (e.g., Stalin's, Hitler's, Pol Pot's) as though all of the related violence must have been state terrorism. For that matter, granted that the regimes were monstrous bloodbaths, it does not follow that the state agents in question made no effort whatever to conceal any of their activities and/or their identity.[7] Readers who reject the argument should confer with American journalists who attempted to cover Stalin's Soviet Union, Hitler's Germany, or Pol Pot's Cambodia. Similarly, it is pointless to deny that secretive, clandestine, or furtive actions have been characteristic of "death squads" (many allegedly "state") in numerous Latin American countries over recent decades. It is commonly very difficult to prove that such groups murder with the knowledge and/or consent of state officials; but the difficulty is one justification for identifying the murders as terrorism, even though the state-nonstate distinction may be debatable in particular instances.

Difficulties in empirical application

One likely objection to the present definition of terrorism is its complexity; but, again, demands for simplicity are inconsistent with human behavior's complexity. Nonetheless, application of the definition does call for kinds of information that may not be readily available. Reconsider a previous question: Was President Kennedy's assassination terrorism? The present definition does not permit an unequivocal answer, largely because there are doubts about the goals of the assassination and whether or not it was intimidation. If terrorism were defined as simply "the illegal use or threat of violence," an affirmative answer to the Kennedy question could be given; but the definition would also admit (*inter alia*) all robberies and many child abuses. Similarly, the phrase "for political purposes" would justify an affirmative answer to the Kennedy question; but the implication would be a tacit denial of *apolitical* terrorism, and divergent interpretations of "political" are legion. Finally, although a definition that specifically includes "murder of a state official" would maximize confidence in an affirmative answer to the Kennedy question, there must be doubts about the feasibility of such an "enumerative" definition of terrorism. And what would one make of the murder of a sheriff by his or her spouse?

The general point is that a *simple* definition of terrorism tends to delimit a class of events so broad as to defy valid generalizations about it (reconsider mixing presidential assassinations, robberies, and child abuses) or so vague that its empirical applicability is negligible. In the latter connection, the Kennedy illustration indicates the need to grant this methodological principle: the congruence dimension (but not the feasibility dimension) of a definition's empirical applicability is enhanced when independent observers agree that the definition cannot be applied in a particular instance because requisite information is not available. If that principle is not granted, sociologists will try to make do with simple definitions and whatever data are readily available.

Presumptive and possible terrorism. Comparative research on terrorism commonly is based on the use of the term "terrorism" by journalists or officials. Hence, insofar as the use of data on *presumptive* terrorism can be justified, a definition's utility is enhanced by its correspondence with the use of the term "terrorism" by journalists and officials. Although only potentially demonstrable, my claim is that the present definition corresponds more with such use of the term than does any simpler definition, such as: terrorism is illegal violence.

Even when terrorism research is based on *descriptions* of violent events, as in newspaper stories, there may be cases that can be designated as *possible* terrorism even though the information is not complete; and a definition's empirical applicability can be assessed in terms of agreement among independent observers in such designations. In that connection, the present definition points to the kind of information needed for truly defensible research on terrorism, which is not the case when investigators try to make do with a much simpler definition, or no definition at all.

Toward a theory of terrorism

The present definition of terrorism does not answer any of a multitude of questions, such as: Why does the incidence of terrorism vary among political units and over time? Although it is an illusion to suppose that any definition answers empirical questions,[8] a definition may be much more conducive than are alternatives to thinking about phenomena; if so, the definition furthers the pursuit of a theory.

Recognizing relations

Unlike an isolated proposition, a theory requires preliminary observations and considerable thought. The observations depend on the way the phenomenon in question has been con-ceptualized, and some conceptualizations facilitate recognition of logical connections and/or possible empirical associations.

When a definition comprises several distinct parts, it is commonly all the more difficult to recognize relations between the phenomenon defined and other phenomena. The solution is to think about all parts of the definition in terms of a particular notion, one that can be used to think also about diverse phenomena in the field's subject matter. Explication of the strategy is furthered by this diagram: $X <—Y—> Z$, where X is the phenomenon defined, Z is any other phenomenon in the field's subject matter, and Y is the notion used to think about both X and Z. Thinking about X and Z serves no purpose unless it suggests a relation between them. If the relation is a logical connection, it furthers the field's conceptual unification; but substantive theory is advanced primarily by recognition of a possible empirical association, especially one having explanatory implications. Whether there are explanatory implications depends not just on the way that the two phenomena have been defined and on the choice of the notion but also on the explanatory mechanism.

Strategic explanatory mechanisms for sociology

In formulating theories sociologists rarely identify the *type* of explanatory mechanism, and the relative merits of contenders are rarely debated. Unfortunately, space limitations permit only a few observations on three major possibilities.

Strict causation. Possibly excluding the period when functionalism was dominant, strict causation has been sociology's most common explanatory mechanism. It is also the most difficult to describe, due in part to debates (particularly from Hume onward) over the nature of causation. So a simple *residual* definition must suffice: strict causation is the mechanism if the explanation neither makes reference to selective survival nor emphasizes the purposive quality of human behavior. As such, strict causation includes direct, indirect or sequential (i.e., intervening variables), multiple, and reciprocal causation.

Doubts about strict causation as sociology's sole explanatory mechanism grow when one contemplates variation in the incidence of terrorism. Consider two illustrative assertions: (1) an increase in urbanization causes an increase in terrorism; and (2) an increase in stratification causes an increase in terrorism. Both assertions tax credulity; and credulity would not be furthered by substituting other structural variables, nor by invoking multiple, sequential, or reciprocal causation rather than direct causation (see surveys by Laqueur 1987, pp. 172–173; Schmid and Jongman 1988, pp. 61–135; and Wilkinson 1986, pp. 93, 102, 197, 213).

Selective survival. Contemplate Durkheim's assertion (1949, especially p. 257) that an increase in material (population) density results in an increase in the division of labor. How could the relation be strict causation? One answer: it is not strict causation; rather, insofar as a positive empirical association holds between the two variables, it is through selective survival. Specifically, the probability of a society's survival is greater if an increase in material density is accompanied or followed by an increase in the division of labor, even though the association was not anticipated (i.e., it was not purposive).

A "selective survival" explanation can be described this way: some patterns or uniformities exist because exceptions to them tend to be eliminated. Although the explanatory mechanism requires no reference to the internal behavior (perception, intention, etc.) of the participants, the term "eliminated" (or "survival") is not limited to the purely biological sphere. After all, no one is confused when it is said that a particular marriage did not survive or that various 19th-century U.S. occupations have been eliminated during this century.

Functionalist theories in sociology are studies in *implicit* resort to selective survival as the explanatory mechanism; but there is no mystery as to why the mechanism is commonly left implicit, nor why Davis (1959) saw fit to defend functionalism by emphasizing "functional analysis" rather than "functional explanation." The notion of a functional explanation cannot be clarified and made distinctive without invoking selective survival; but most functionalist theories appear incredible when translated something like this: the institution or practice in question (i.e., the *explicandum*) is necessary for the survival of the larger system. Credulity would be sorely taxed by a functional theory of terrorism. Imagine someone even suggesting that terrorism is necessary for a country's survival.

The purposive quality of human behavior. Any theory that emphasizes the purposive quality of human behavior is likely to be criticized as being "teleological." That label should be avoided if only because it gives rise to extreme arguments, as when Catton (1966, pp. 5, 11) dismisses teleological theories or explanations on the grounds that they have some *future* state (a goal) causing *present* behavior. However, the term "purposiveness" is not used here as a synonym for "teleological"; instead, it is used to denote all major types of internal behavior, such as perception and belief, the argument being that such behaviors enter into the pursuit of goals.

Identification of "purposiveness" as an explanatory mechanism is consistent with symbolic interactionism, one of sociology's perennial major perspectives. Yet the subjectivism of some versions of symbolic interactionism is so extreme as to suggest that *only one* explanatory mechanism is relevant for sociology. To the contrary, the purposiveness mechanism can be combined with the other two, and defensible sociological theories may require such combinations. Consider, for example, an explanation of "armed and organized groups," which are identified as police or military in English-speaking social units. The international ubiquity of such groups suggests that a country's survival is jeopardized by civil war or conquest without armed and organized opposition to militant secessionists or invaders. Even so, such groups are studies in purposiveness. As for combining strict causation and purposiveness, environmental features make certain human practices difficult; but the consequences may depend on whether and how the relation is perceived. Marvin Harris (1979, p. 105) unwittingly supplied an illustration: "Rainfall agriculture leads to dispersed, multicentered forms of production. Hence it is doubtful that any pristine state even developed on a rainfall base." Harris could not bring himself to recognize that would-be rulers may perceive the difficulty of controlling a dispersed population. Yet an extreme position need not be taken. A population's actual spatial distribution is a causal factor in perception, and *imperceptive* would-be rulers may be eliminated.

Conceptualization of control

In light of the foregoing arguments, there is a need for a notion that (1) facilitates describing and thinking about not only terrorism but also any sociological subject and (2) is compatible with all three explanatory mechanisms. Control is the most promising candidate, but its conceptualization is crucial.

The immediate issue is the choice of the term "control" rather than "social control." The latter is only a subclass of the class "control over human behavior"; and unless control is defined so as to include not only that class but also biotic control (e.g., domestication of plants) and inanimate control (e.g., making or using tools), it is doubtful whether the notion facilitates describing and thinking about sociology's subject matter.

The prevailing conception of social control, the "counteraction of deviance" conception, is conducive to thinking of terrorists as *objects* but not also as *agents* of social control. Moreover, well-known advocates (e.g., Parsons 1951, pp. 297, 321) of the conception deny the relevance of internal behavior. Thus, if the practice of wearing a wedding ring is conducive to marital fidelity and infidelity is deviant, then the practice is social control even if the connection is recognized only by a sociologist observer. So the counteraction-of-deviance conception of social control is alien to terrorism's purposive quality and to *attempts* to suppress terrorism.

A generic definition of attempted control. If only because sociologists should study both successes and failures in control, *attempted control* is the key term. That point takes on special significance in the case of terrorism. Describing and thinking about terrorism require recognition more of what terrorists attempt to control than what they actually control.

Defined generically, attempted control is *overt* behavior by a human in the belief that (1) the behavior increases or decreases the probability of some subsequent condition and (2) the increase or decrease is desirable. To clarify, the commission or omission of an act is overt behavior; and "a subsequent condition" may be an organism's behavior (external or internal) *or* the existence, location, composition, color, size, weight, shape, odor, temperature, or texture of some object or substance, be it animate or inanimate, observable or unobservable.

Durkheim's disciples will be prone to nurse this reservation: the definition makes intention relevant. The objection ignores the point that sociologists use an army of terms that imply intention, such as *reaching, turning,* and *saluting.* For that matter, while some reference to internal behavior is essential to maintain the distinction between success and failure in control (according to the counteraction-of-deviance conception, there are no failures in social control), the present definition does not limit attempted control to intentional behavior in the sense of conscious and deliberate. To illustrate, while drivers ordinarily are unaware of holding the steering wheel, who would deny that they hold *in the belief that* it reduces the probability of an undesirable subsequent condition? Recognition of an "affective" quality (i.e., desirable vs. undesirable) will antagonize both extreme behaviorists and Durkheimians, but consider the consequences of ignoring it. When someone robs a bank, he or she presumably acts in the belief that his or her behavior increases the probability of being injured, which is a cognitive belief. So when a man backs out of a bank with gun in hand and is shot by a police officer, did the gunman "control" the police officer? To answer affirmatively is to embrace an absurdity, the inevitable outcome of avoiding reference to internal behavior (in this case, an *affective* belief) when defining types of behavior.

Types of human control. For reasons given later, social control is a very important type of control when describing or thinking about terrorism. However, that is the case only if the counteraction-of-deviance conception of social control is rejected, and it is imperative to distinguish social control from other types of control over human behavior.

In attempting *self-control* an individual acts in the belief that the action increases the probability that his or her subsequent behavior will be as desired (e.g., perhaps greater diligence at work) or decreases the probability of undesirable behavior (e.g., perhaps smoking). Although that definition is consistent with the "challenge" conception of self-control (overcoming fears or vices), various mundane acts, such as lifting the phone receiver before dialing or setting an alarm clock, are also attempted self-control.

Attempted *proximate control* most commonly takes the form of a command or a request, but coercion and certain kinds of threats are also proximate control; and they are especially relevant in analyzing terrorism. However, even though the target of proximate control may be an aggregate, as when a terrorist leader shouts an order to a bomb squad, there is no third party (i.e., no human intermediary, no reference to someone).

Attempted *sequential control* is a command or request by one human to another in the belief that (1) it increases the probability of a subsequent command or request by another human to still other humans and (2) the increase is desirable. A chain of commands is the most common form of sequential control, and sequential control warrants recognition if only because that form is virtually a defining characteristic of an organization. For that reason alone, sequential control is relevant in analyzing terrorist groups and governmental agencies that attempt to suppress terrorism.

Attempted *social control* is overt behavior by a human, the first party, in the belief that (1) the behavior increases or decreases the probability of a change in the behavior of another human or humans, the second party in either case; (2) the overt behavior involves a third party but not in the way of a sequential control; and (3) the increase or decrease is desirable. The definition is clarified by subsequent observations on terrorism; but some clarification can be realized at this point by considering one of the five inclusive types of social control (Gibbs 1981, pp. 77–109), because those types are distinguished primarily in terms of how a third party is involved. In all instances of attempted *vicarious* social control, the first party attempts to punish the third party, reward the third party, or somehow rectify the third party's behavior, always presuming that such action will influence the second party's behavior. Vicarious social control is the basis of general deterrence, which enters into criminal justice policy in virtually all jurisdictions (see Morris 1966, p. 631). Less obvious, terrorists also often resort to deterrent vicarious social control as an integral component of their intimidation strategy.

Some logical connections and possible empirical associations

The initial (unnumbered) part of the definition (*supra*) suggests this question: Why is terrorism illegal? Terrorism is a violent act, but state officials seek a monopoly on violence, especially violence with a negligible probability or retaliation (see Weber 1978, p. 314, though note that Weber ignored the probability of retaliation). So the question's answer: Terrorism is illegal because it jeopardizes the control exercised by superordinate state officials (legislators, monarchs, despots, or others) *or* is an attempt by those officials to realize a goal that they perceive as realizable through legal means, if at all, by incurring the loss of something they value more than the goal.

Why do terrorists—state or nonstate—resort to secretive, furtive, and/or clandestine violence? Because they seek goals that they perceive as realizable only through such violence or only through legal means that entail unacceptable losses. What are such goals? Why do terrorists pursue them? Why do terrorists perceive secretive, furtive, and/or clandestine violence as an essential means of countercontrol? A theory is needed to answer such questions; but a theory will not be realized unless social scientists take the questions seriously, and no theory will be defensible if inconsistent with Walter's statement (1969, p. 13) about violence: "the proximate aim is to instill terror; the ultimate end is control."

More on goals. In seeking to maintain or alter some putative norm, dissidents may have so little popular support in the country as a whole (e.g., the United Kingdom in the case of England, Wales, Scotland, and Northern Ireland) and/or such determined opposition from state officials that the dissidents come to perceive violence as the only means of realizing that goal. However, the amount of popular support and official opposition depend not just on the *evalutive* standards of the public and/or officials but on the extent to which they view the dissidents' goal as realistic. They will not view the goal as realistic if they are baffled by related statements. Contemplate the characterization of terrorists in West Germany (see Becker 1988, p. 24) *of themselves* as fighters for "the uprooted masses" of the Third World. Even if officials should agree that West Germany is responsible for the plight of Third World countries, they are unlikely to know what would satisfy the terrorists.

Even if the "acceptability" and "realizability" of dissident goals partially determine whether the dissidents become terrorists, those considerations are not to be judged by social scientists. It is entirely a matter of the way that the public and/or officials perceive those goals. Yet sociologists can further the pursuit of a theory about terrorism by undertaking research on this question: What conditions promote or impede perceptions by the public and officials of the goals of dissidents as acceptable and realizable?

Another major question about violence. Parts 2, 3, and 4 of the definition indicate how terrorism differs from lethal conflicts commonly identified as wars or civil wars. But why is "covertness" so characteristic of terrorism? What writers commonly label as terrorist groups or organizations (nonstate) rarely comprise more than a few hundred members, which precludes more than electoral success. Because nonstate terrorists resort to violence, they are certain to be targets of attempted control by the police and/or the military; and their small number alone precludes successful countercontrol measures akin to open warfare. Various tactics of concealment—all types of counter-control—offer the only hope of survival, and various features of "international terrorism" are manifestations of those tactics.

Officials engaged in state terrorism are not endangered by conventional military or police action, but they are concerned with concealing their personal identity. Although a theory is needed to specify the conditions in which state officials resort to terrorism, their reliance on concealment is not puzzling. Even a homicidal despot is likely to recognize that the *appearance* of legitimacy may be essential for the regime's survival.

Concealment is purposive behavior, and no notion rivals control when it comes to forcing recognition of purposiveness. Yet the notion does not lead to an extreme position as far as explanatory mechanisms are concerned. Should the concealment tactics of terrorists fail or should their bravado lead them to extremely reckless behavior, they are virtually certain to be killed or incapacitated; but terrorists do not just happen to be killed or incapacitated, which is to say that the notion of control remains relevant. The related question for sociology is thus: What conditions (e.g., degree of urbanization) influence the efficacy of the concealment tactics of terrorists?

The strategy of terrorism reconsidered. When terrorists inflict injuries or destroy property, they aim to promote fear throughout some population (e.g., legislators, factory owners), and thereby control that population's behavior. To what end? The answer depends on the putative norm that the terrorists are attempting to alter or maintain; but whatever it may be, the terrorists employ deterrent vicarious social control.

Why do terrorists engage in that type of control? Their small number and vulnerability to retaliation make attempts at proximate control ineffective; indeed, social control is distinctive in that it offers a means for the few to control the many. Sequential control is not an alternative because the "normative position" of terrorists severely limits the range of their authority. Normative considerations are also relevant in contemplating this question: Why *deterrent* vicarious social control rather than some other subtype or type? Because violence (including related coercion, physical punishment, etc.) is the principal alternative when there is no normative basis (e.g., authority, appeals to evalutive standards) for control. Should it be objected that assassination may be a means to a political goal without the element of intimidation, the objection ignores a multitude of definitions that make intimidation a necessary feature of terrorism. Moreover, such a definition need not even suggest that terrorism is the only means to a political goal, not even the only violent means. Finally, by what logic are *all* assassinations instances of terrorism?

What do terrorists hope to gain through deterrent control? One common answer is "concessions" (see, e.g., Oots 1986, p. 81), but that answer ignores a strategy that several writers have attributed to terrorists (see, e.g., Laqueur 1987; Wilkinson 1986). Briefly, terrorists aim to provoke officials to such extreme repressive measures (e.g., censorship, preventive detention) that the government loses popular support and falls. The "provocational" strategy is based on modulative social control, wherein the first party (terrorists in this case) uses the influence of the third party (the public at large in this case) on the second party (government officials in this case). The immediate significance of the provocative strategy is the possibility of its failure. In employing the strategy, terrorists evidently assume that the government will fall because it increasingly departs from the rule of law, but some powerful faction may consider the rule of law secondary to suppression of terrorism and stage a *coup d'état* because of the government's "underreaction" to terrorism. Such was the case when the military toppled Uruguay's liberal democratic government, crushed the terrorists (the *Tupamaros*), and remained in power.

The provocational strategy has implications for a theory concerning variation in the incidence of terrorism. A failure in the strategy may be more important than success. Specifically, if the outcome is an authoritarian regime, the incidence of terrorism may decline because repressive measures become more effective. That possibility poses a sociological question, but some sociologists will not be inclined to do research on the question because they evidently think of officials as thumb-twiddling spectators when the *status quo* is challenged violently (see, e.g., Skocpol 1979). To the contrary, in numerous countries officials have responded effectively to terrorism (see, e.g., Laqueur 1987). Hence, a theory's validity is jeopardized if it does not recognize that variation in terrorism may to some extent reflect variation in the effectiveness of attempts to control it. Indeed, where there is scarcely any rule of law, why would terrorists employ the provocational strategy? That question is relevant in contemplating the ostensible rarity of terrorism in Marxist countries (see Laqueur 1987, p. 302).

Summary and conclusion

An impressive theory of terrorism requires more than a conceptualization that confronts issues and problems. A definition of terrorism must promise empirical applicability and facilitate recognition of logical connections and possible empirical associations. Such recognition requires a notion that facilitates describing and thinking about terrorism; and the notion must be compatible with each of three possible explanatory mechanisms: strict causation, selective survival, and purposiveness.

The notion of control is the most promising candidate. Although that notion has no equal when it comes to underscoring human behavior's purposive quality, it is not alien to any particular explanatory mechanism. All of sociology's subject matter can be described and thought of in terms of control (at least as it has been conceptualized here), and the notion is particularly relevant in the study of terrorism. That phenomenon and attempts to prevent it are nothing less than one vast attempt at control.

Notes

1   As pointed out by Laqueur (1987, pp. 19, 118), much of the terrorism in the American labor movement (e.g., the bombing of the *Los Angeles Times* building in 1910) was attacked even by the left as "commercial, not idealistic"; and "there was no intention of overthrowing the government, killing the political leadership or changing the political system." To insist that an effort (violent or otherwise) to alter working conditions or wages in a particular context (e.g., a publishing corporation) is "political" only illustrates indiscriminate use of that term. To be sure, it may be that an impressive theory about terrorism must be limited to "political terrorism," but the necessity for such limitation cannot be known *a priori*.
2   The question is *not* how terrorists differ from military personnel, insurgents, rebels, revolutionaries, or guerrillas. The distinction is irrelevant for present purposes because the concern is not with defining "a terrorist." The terms "terrorist" and "terrorists" are used occasionally in this paper in the loose sense of "an individual or individuals who have engaged in terrorism," but it is recognized that a more elaborate definition is needed.
3   The secretive, furtive, and/or clandestine features of terrorism (part 2 of the present definition) are not limited to the violent action itself. They also pertain to previous and subsequent actions (nonviolent), even the lifestyle of the participants. Consider Clark's observation (1986, p. 300) on members of a terrorist organization dedicated to Basque separatism: "The great majority of the members of ETA continue to live at home, either with their parents or (if they were married) with their spouses and children, and to work at their regular employment. …"
4   For example, Oots (1986, p. 81) makes intimidation central in his definition of terrorism, but numerous writers suggest that "seeking publicity" is also an essential strategy in terrorism. Hence, reference is made in the present definition (the last part of it) to "publicizing some cause." Actually, the two strategies—intimidation and publicization—are virtually inseparable.
5   Should it be argued (see, e.g., Wilkinson 1986, p. 23, and Zinam 1978, p. 241) that violence is *by definition* illegal, what of a killing in an Anglo-American case of undisputed justifiable homicide? To deny that the killing was violence would be arbitrary in the extreme and contrary to conventional use of the term "violence." Indeed, why submit to an unconventional usage that makes "illegitimate violence" redundant and "legitimate violence" contradictory? Perhaps more importantly, what term is the appropriate descriptive label for undisputed justifiable homicide or the *legitimate* use of force by a police officer? If the answer is "coercion," there is no corresponding convention; and when kidnappers bind their victims, surely that action is coercion.
6   The suggestion is not that Nazi state terrorism ended with the Night of the Long Knives (June 30, 1934). Note, however, that writers on "Nazi terror" (e.g., Noakes 1986) are prone to avoid an explicit definition

of terrorism. Such phrases as "use of terror" (Noakes 1986, p. 67) and "siege of terror" (Walter 1969, p. 7) should not be equated with "terrorism," and they are conducive to misunderstandings.

7   When perpetrators of violence attempt to conceal their personal identity, the attempt alone is indicative of illegality; and the secretive, furtive, and/or clandestine features of terrorism (part 2 of the definition) are more decisive than conjectures about legality. When there are doubts on the part of observers as to the legality of some violent act, the concealment of the personal identity of the actor or actors should be treated as evidence of illegality.

8   It is also an illusion to suppose that social scientists have anything even approaching an adequate theory of terrorism (see commentaries by Laqueur 1987, p. 165; Schmid and Jongman 1988, p. 61; and Wilkinson 1986, p. 96).

References

Becker, Jillian. 1988. *Terrorism in West Germany.* London: Institute for the Study of Terrorism.

Catton, William R. 1966. *From Animistic to Naturalistic Sociology.* New York: McGraw-Hill.

Clark, Robert P. 1986. "Patterns in the Lives of ETA Members." pp. 283–309 in *Political Violence and Terror,* edited by Peter H. Merkl. Berkeley: University of California Press.

Davis, Kingsley. 1959. "The Myth of Functional Analysis as a Special Method in Sociology and Anthropology." *American Sociological Review* 24:757–772.

Durkheim, Emile. 1949. *The Division of Labor in Society.* New York: Free Press.

Gibbs, Jack P. 1981. *Norms, Deviance, and Social Control.* New York: Elsevier.

Harris, Marvin. 1979. *Cultural Materialism.* New York: Random House.

Laqueur, Walter. 1977. *Terrorism.* London: Weidenfeld and Nicolson.

———. 1987. *The Age of Terrorism.* London: Weidenfeld and Nicolson.

Lee, Alfred M. 1983. *Terrorism in Northern Ireland.* Bayside, NY: General Hall.

Livingston, Marius H., ed. 1978. *International Terrorism in the Contemporary World*. Westport, CT: Greenwood.

Livingstone, Neil C. 1982. *The War Against Terrorism.* Lexington, MA: Heath.

Morris, Norval. 1966. "Impediments of Penal Reform." *University of Chicago Law Review* 33:627–656.

Noakes, Jeremy. 1986. "The Origins, Structure and Function of Nazi Terror." pp. 67–87 in *Terrorism, Ideology, and Revolution,* edited by Noel O'Sullivan. Brighton, England: Harvester.

Oots, Kent L. 1986. *A Political Organization Approach to Transnational Terrorism.* Westport, CT: Greenwood.

Parsons, Talcott. 1951. *The Social System.* New York: Free Press.

Rubenstein, Richard E. 1987. *Alchemists of Revolution.* London: I.B. Tauris.

Schmid, Alex P. and Albert J. Jongman. 1988. *Political Terrorism.* Rev. ed. Amsterdam: North-Holland.

Skocpol, Theda. 1979. *States and Social Revolution.* London: Cambridge University Press.

Tallman, Irving. 1984. Book Review. *Social Forces* 62:1121–1122.

Walter, Eugene V. 1969. *Terror and Resistance.* New York: Oxford University Press.

Weber, Max. 1978. *Economy and Society.* 2 vols., continuous pagination. Berkeley: University of California Press.

Wilkinson, Paul. 1986. *Terrorism and the Liberal State.* 2nd ed. New York: New York University Press.

Zinam, Oleg. 1978. "Terrorism and Violence in Light of a Theory of Discontent and Frustration." pp. 240–268 in *International Terrorism in the Contemporary World,* edited by Marius H. Livingston. Westport, CT: Greenwood.

5 The challenges of conceptualizing terrorism

Leonard Weinberg, Ami Pedahzur and Sivan Hirsch-Hoefler

Few terms or concepts in contemporary political discourse have proved as hard to define as terrorism. When the subject itself appeared, or reappeared, in the late 1960s and early 1970s, various professional commentators noted the difficulties involved in articulating a definition which could gain wide agreement among those concerned with the subject. One writer, Walter Laqueur, simply threw up his hands, arguing that terrorism had appeared in so many different forms and under so many different circumstances that a comprehensive definition was impossible. An observer would simply know it when s/he saw it.[1] Almost 30 years later, and after the publication of thousands of books and articles on the subject, another leading figure in the field noted that "... the problem of defining terrorism has hindered analysis since the inception of studies in the early 1970s" and has shown few signs of abating as we enter the twenty-first century.[2] Why has the term been so hard to define? Why has the concept evaded definitional efforts of so many for so long?

Some answers seem obvious. For one thing, 'terrorism' has been widely used for purposes of political effect. Somewhat paradoxically, Menachem Begin, as the leader of the Irgun (Lehi's Zionist rival) in postwar Palestine, was the first to see the propaganda advantage in referring to his followers as "freedom fighters" rather than terrorists. Afterwards, terrorist groups adopted this appealing description and called themselves freedom fighters, understanding the propaganda advantage.[3] The term terrorism became confused during what David C. Rapoport has labeled terrorism of the "second-wave,"[4] since organizations understood that they needed a new language to describe themselves.

The term had accumulated so many negative connotations that those who identified themselves as such incurred enormous political liabilities.[5] The application of the term to the activities of a group, organization or state institution conveys opprobrium. Naturally, those to whom it is applied regard it as an accusation and often seek to turn the tables on their accusers by labeling them as the "real" terrorists. The resulting war of words simply adds to the ambiguity and compounds the confusion. Often the polemic involves confusion, unintended or deliberate, between ends and means. A particular group or organization cannot be waging a terrorist campaign because it hopes to achieve some (self-defined) noble purpose.[6]

More important, though, for purposes of serious analysis, the term terrorism has been subject to virtually all the sins to which complex concepts are heir. Here are just a few. First, following the work of W. B. Gallie and William Connolly, terrorism has become an "essentially contested concept," one whose meaning lends itself to endless dispute but no resolution.

To quote Connolly:

> When the disagreement does not simply reflect different readings of evidence within a fully shared system of concepts, we can say that a conceptual dispute has arisen. When the concept

involved is appraisive … when the practice described is internally complex in that its characterization involves reference to several dimensions, and when the agreed and contested rules of application are relatively open, enabling parties to interpret even those shared rules differently as new and unforeseen situations arise, then the concept in question is 'an essentially contested concept'. Such concepts 'essentially involve endless disputes about their proper uses on the part of their users'.[7]

The assumption on the part of the disputants over meaning is that if they only argue their cases long and hard enough, a real or essential definition will emerge. But 30 years of contesting the meaning of terrorism has produced no such result. For Connolly and Gallie, this outcome may simply be the consequence of the nature of such concepts.

Second, terrorism as a concept also seems to suffer from 'border' and 'membership' problems. Where does terrorism stop and other forms of political violence begin, guerrilla warfare or urban guerrilla warfare, for example? The same acts, such as air piracy or assassinations, may be considered terrorist acts on some occasions but not on others, usually based upon the assumed motivations of the perpetrators or the social standing of their victims.[8]

Further, terrorism suffers from "stretching" and "traveling" problems, some literal, others of an analytic character. In regard to the former, some writers seem to identify terrorism based on the physical or social distance between the act in question and the observer. If, for instance, an act of political violence occurs at a significant distance (geographically or psychologically) from the observer, the tendency is to give it a more neutral or benign name. The same act carried out closer to home becomes terrorism.

Considering the stretching and traveling capacity of the term for analytic purposes, writers now deal with terms such as "narco-terrorism" and "cyber-terrorism": the latter rarely involves any reference to violence or the threat of violence. The problem is, as Collier and Mahon put it:

> When scholars take a category developed from one set of cases and extend it to additional cases, the new cases may be sufficiently different that the category is no longer appropriate in its original form. If this problem arises, they may adapt the category by climbing the ladder of generality, thereby obeying the law of inverse variation. As they increase the extension, they reduce the intension to the degree necessary to fit the new contexts.[9]

The choices are often between stretching the concept to the point of vagueness or inventing a new term to cover a wider range of activities, for example, low intensity conflict.

Confronted by doubt and uncertainty of this magnitude, we have concluded that the best way to make the definitional problem manageable is to follow Alex Schmid's advice and divide the discussion of non-state terrorism into separate "arenas of discourse." Schmid identifies four such arenas. First, there is the academic arena where scholars struggle to stipulate a definition useful for conducting research on the topic. Second, there are the state's statements about 'terrorism' including those expressed in the form of laws, judicial rulings and regulations. Next, for Schmid, is the public debate on the subject. By this he means the various ways the mass media choose to label and interpret the concept. Fourth, we may be exposed to "(t)he discussion of those who oppose many of our societies' values and support or perform acts of violence and terrorism against what they consider repressive states."[10]

Unfortunately, Schmid's categories are not mutually exclusive. There appears to be significant overlap between the first and fourth arenas, in particular. Such leading advocates and practitioners of what many would call terrorism, as Abimael Guzman (the founder of Peru's Shining Path) and

Antonio Negri (the leader of the Italian Armed Autonomy) began their careers as academics. On the other side of the ledger, there are a number of individuals who retired from careers in terrorism to become part of the academic world. (Law, sociology and political science seem to be favorite destinations.)

There are still others, including the Italian Front Line and the Red Brigade leadership, who have participated in both arenas simultaneously. In fact, this may have contributed to the downfall of the groups involved. Observers have noted that the rhetoric, the public communiqués of these groups became progressively more obscure and unintelligible, the longer they continued to function. The groups lost whatever ability they had possessed to win the support of workers and peasants because they could not make themselves understood. The incomprehensible rhetoric is frequently attributed to the fact that the groups' members lost touch with external reality, the longer they were required to operate on a clandestine basis.[11] However, it is possible that the communiqués and other messages intended for public consumption were simply written by professors who confused the first and fourth arenas as a result of long-term exposure to both.

Despite this methodological problem we think it would still be helpful if we attempted to limit our discussion of 'terrorism' to the academic arena. A good place to start is with the definition Alex Schmid proposed in the volume he edited with Albert Jongman, *Political Terrorism: A New Guide to Actors, Authors, Concepts, Data bases, Theories and Literature:*

> Terrorism is an anxiety-inspiring method of repeated violent action, employed by (semi-) clandestine individual, group, or state actors, for idiosyncratic, criminal, or political reasons, whereby—in contrast to assassination—the direct targets of violence are not the main targets. The immediate human victims of violence are generally chosen randomly (targets of opportunity) or selectively (representative or symbolic targets) from a target population, and serve as message generators. Threat—and violence—based communication processes between terrorist (organization), (imperiled) victims, and main target (audiences(s)), turning it into a target of terror, a target of demands, or a target of attention, depending on whether intimidation, coercion, or propaganda is primarily sought.[12]

Schmid's definition was refined from reactions he received from scholars who responded to a questionnaire he had mailed them. The respondents had originally produced 109 separate definitions. The latter consisted of twenty-two "definitional elements" which Schmid then ranked in order of the frequency with which they appeared in the questionnaires. The comprehensive definition he proposed (see above) reflected sixteen of these twenty-two "definitional elements."[12]

Our own approach to investigating the academic domain of terrorism discourse is somewhat different than Schmid's. Like him, we have relied on what the experts tell us terrorism means but we do not rely on questionnaire responses in identifying the concept's definitional elements. Instead, we have based our inquiry on what contributors to leading professional journals in the field of terrorism tell us the word means to them.

To be more specific, we sought definitions from three journals whose contents we scrutinized. We examined all the articles in *Terrorism* (New York: Crane Russak & Company), from 1977 through 1991 and then (Minneapolis, MN: John Scherer), 1982–1983, 1986–1989; *Terrorism and Political Violence* (London: Frank Cass) from 1990 through 2001; and *Studies in Conflict and Terrorism* (London: Taylor and Francis) from 1992 through 2001.[13]

Our review of these journals yielded a total of seventy-three definitions (drawn from fifty-five articles) (See Appendix A). How do these compare to the 109 definitions with their twenty-two constituent elements Schmid's questionnaire produced?

Frequencies of definitional elements of terrorism

A brief examination of Table 5.1 reveals wide differences in the relative strength of the 22 definitional elements Schmid reports when compared to the journal contributors' suggested definitions. In two instances, elements 9 ("extra-normality, in breach of accepted rules, without humanitarian constraints") and 12 ("arbitrariness, impersonal, random character, indiscriminate"), which emerged as important constituents of Schmid's definition, received no mention at all in the relevant journal articles. Another element, 10 ("coercion, extortion, induction of compliance"), which appeared in 28 percent of the definitions in Schmid's survey, was mentioned in less than 6 percent of the journal definitions.

If we match this difference to discrepancies in references to two other elements, we may discern something of a pattern. The journal-based definitions were also much less likely to mention the arousal of fear and terror (element 3) and "psychological effects and anticipated reactions" (element 5) as important components. In general, then, the journal contributors placed much less emphasis on the psychological aspects of terrorism, a theme which, of course, has loomed large in general discussions of the topic over the years. One obvious explanation for the paucity of references to these psychological elements among the journal articles might be the paucity of psychologists. But this does not seem to be the case. About the same proportion of contributors to the journals as respondents to the Schmid survey identified themselves as psychologists.[14]

Table 5.1 Frequencies of definitional elements of "Terrorism"

Element	Schmid & Jongman Survey (1988) frequency (%)	Our survey (2002) frequency (%)
1. Violence, Force	83.5	71
2. Political	65	60
3. Fear, Terror emphasized	51	22
4. Threat	47	41
5. Psychological effects and (anticipated) reactions	41.5	5.5
6. Victim-Target differentiation	37.5	25
7. Purposive, Planned, Systematic, Organized action	32	11
8. Method of combat, strategy, tactic	30.5	31.5
9. Extranormality, in breach of accepted rules, without humanitarian constrains	30	0
10. Coercion, extortion, induction of compliance	28	5.5
11. Publicity aspect	21.5	18
12. Arbitrariness, impersonal, random character, indiscrimination	21	0
13. Civilians, noncombatants, neutrals, outsiders as victims	17.5	22
14. Intimidation	17	11
15. Innocence of victims emphasized	15.5	10
16. Group, movement, organization as perpetrator	14	29
17. Symbolic aspect, demonstration to others	13.5	5.5
18. Incalculability, unpredictability, unexpectedness of occurrence of violence	9	1
19. Clandestine, covert nature	9	7
20. Repetitiveness, serial or campaign character of violence	7	0
21. Criminal	6	5.5
22. Demands made on third parties	4	1

Note: The Schmid & Jongman survey consists of 22 elements drawn from 109 definitions. Our survey consists of 73 definitions drawn from 55 articles collected from three journals.

Are there aspects of the meaning of terrorism on which Schmid's respondents and the journal writers actually agree? Yes; in fact high percentages of the experts in both categories (20 percent or more) identify terrorism as a method of combat or a tactic (element 8), involving a threat (element 4) of force and violence (element 1) used for a political (element 2) purpose. The pursuit of publicity (element 11) is mentioned somewhat less frequently but members of both groups seem to agree that it is part of the definition of terrorism. So it is possible to discern a consensus among academics who study the subject, to this extent. Terrorism is a politically motivated tactic involving the threat or use of force or violence in which the pursuit of publicity plays a significant role. This consensus definition stresses terrorism as an activity, a method of conduct, over the psychological. And, surprisingly, given our own understanding, neither the distinction between combatants and non-combatants nor between immediate target and wider audience is mentioned.

In addition to the comparison between Schmid's respondents and the contributors to professional terrorism journals, it is essential to examine whether there are significant differences among the journals themselves in the way terrorism has been defined.

Table 5.2 shows the frequency of definitional elements of the term terrorism according to the three journals analyzed in this article. However, to test whether differences among those three journals are significant, we also performed an analysis of variance (One way ANOVA). Significant differences were found with relation to: *threat* ($F (2, 70) = 4.49$, $p < .05$) and *method of combat/strategy /tactics* ($F (2, 70) = 8.75$, $p < .001$). In terms of *threat* (m = 2.00, sd = .00) *SCT* journal presents the highest mean (e.g., highest rate of non-usage of this category). In terms of method of *combat/ strategy/tactics* (m = 1.87, sd = .34), Terrorism present the highest mean.

The significance in the *threat* element resulted from the differences between *SCT* and *Terrorism* (*p* = .01) and between the *SCT* and *TPV* (*p* = .04). The significant differences in the *tactics* element resulted from the difference between *Terrorism* and *SCT* (*p* = .00) and between *Terrorism* and *TPV* (*p* = .02). To summarize the comparison of definitional elements among the professional terrorism journals, we may say that significant differences were found with relation to two categories: *threat* and *tactics*. More specifically, *SCT* did not at all use the *threat* category in the definition for the term terrorism, while in the case of *tactics*, *Terrorism* presented the highest rate of non-usage of this category.

Regarding the various definitions presented in these three journals, it seems that, despite the need for serious conceptual work, only few articles really grapple with the problem of definition. Most of them just place a definition in the text as a matter of formality and, in fact, never pay attention to it again. Nevertheless, we believe that even though most of the articles used in developing our data file did not grapple with the problem of definition, it is still very important to

Table 5.2 Frequencies of definitional elements of "Terrorism" according to the three journals

Elements	Terrorism N = 38	Studies in Conflict and Terrorism N = 10	Terrorism and Political Violence N = 25
1. Violence	68%	80%	72%
2. Political	63%	50%	60%
3. Fear	21%	20%	24%
4. Threat	50%	0%	44%
5. Victim	16%	50%	28%
6. Tactic	13%	70%	44%
7. Civilians	16%	30%	28%
8. Movement	24%	40%	32%

Note: Our survey consists of 73 definitions drawn from 55 articles collected from three journals.

examine these definitions as they appear, mainly from the academic point of view, as vital and relevant literature on the perception of terrorism.

As in most discussions of terrorism, even those taking place in the academic domain, we should pay some attention to the point of view of the observer. Who is defining the term and where does s/he come from?

In both cases, we are dealing with academics. A modest six of the seventy-three professional journal contributors were non-academics, and only one of Schmid's respondents identified

Frequencies of definitional elements of "Terrorism" according to writer's professional affiliation (Figure 5.1)

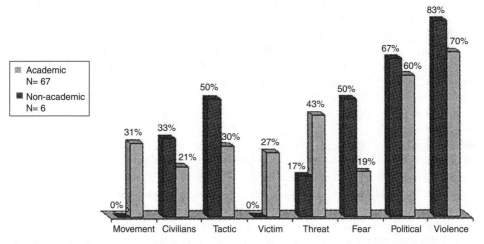

Figure 5.1 The Survey consists of 73 definitions drawn from 55 articles collected from three journals.

Frequencies of definitional elements of "Terrorism" according to writer's region (Figure 5.2)

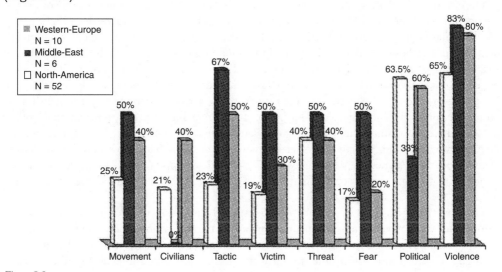

Figure 5.2

himself/herself as a journalist; the rest reported various academic specialties. Second, we are dealing overwhelmingly with North American and Western European academics. (What seems to us a modest number, only five of the contributors were Israeli.) There were a handful of respondents in both groups who fell outside the Western orbit, but the preponderance of both respondents and contributors was based in these regions, with the United States far and away furnishing the largest contingents. Consequently, we understand that the consensus over the definition of terrorism among academic specialists is not universal but one grounded in the view of Westerners, and Americans in particular.

The question which emerges is whether or not country of origin makes a difference in definition. In order to answer this crucial question, we examined the frequencies of definitional elements of terrorism according to writer's region. Looking at Figure 5.2, we may see that country of origin does play a role in the way scholars in the professional journals define the term terrorism. For example, scholars from the Middle East never mentioned (0%) the element "civilians", while scholars from Western Europe and North America mentioned this element more frequently (40% and 21%, respectively). In contrast, half of the scholars from the Middle East mentioned the element "fear" in their definitions for the term, while less than a quarter of scholars from Western Europe and North America used it. However, although there are differences in the definitional elements used by the writers, as shown from Figure 5.2, the most popular element among all ethnic groups was violence.[15]

Before offering an assessment of the merits or deficiencies of the consensus definition, we should reflect for a moment on why there were such wide differences between Schmid's respondents and the contributors to the professional terrorism journals. (This is particularly true since we would expect that there would be some overlap between the two groups.)

We readily admit to engaging in speculation, but an accounting based on the times at which the studies were conducted may be relevant to our understanding. Schmid's survey was carried out in 1985. Respondents would necessarily have based their reactions to terrorism on activities or operations which had occurred earlier, that is from the late 1960s onwards. For the most part, those responding to Schmid's questionnaire would have obtained their understanding from observing what David C. Rapoport has labeled terrorism of the "third wave."[16]

The events on which these observers would have based their definitions would have encompassed the operations of the left-wing revolutionary groups of Latin America and Western Europe (e.g., the Tupamaros, the Red Army Faction, the Red Brigades) along with such secular nationalist organizations as those linked to the Palestine Liberation Organization (PLO), the Irish Republican Army (IRA), Basque Homeland and Liberty (ETA), and a long list of others. These were organizations which wanted, to use Brian Jenkins' famous phrase, "a lot of people watching, not a lot of people dead." The type of operations they carried out frequently involved taking prominent individuals hostage (e.g., Aldo Moro, the former Italian prime minister, Sir Geoffrey Jackson, the British Ambassador to Uruguay, Patty Hearst, the newspaper heiress) and holding them for ransom; another method was seizing members of the public and demanding the release of imprisoned colleagues in exchange (e.g., 1972 Munich Olympics); and spectacular acts of air piracy in which the perpetrators demanded various political concessions in exchange for the release of the plane and its passengers.

Third wave terrorism also engendered widespread discussion of such phenomena as the "Stockholm syndrome," brain-washing, the process of hostage negotiations, and the role of the mass media in reporting the events which came to be labeled terrorism. In short, the late 1960s through the early 1980s was a time during which terrorism seemed to elicit the discussion of psychological issues. Consequently, we should probably not be surprised that such definitional elements as "fear and terror" along with "psychological effects and anticipated reactions" appear so frequently among the responses to Schmid's questionnaire.

Rapoport and other observers have called our attention to the emergence of a "New Terrorism."[17] Rapoport, in particular, refers to a "fourth wave" of terrorism which was ignited by the Iranian Revolution of 1979–1980 but which really took hold during the mid-1980s. This "new" or fourth wave of terrorism has been dominated by religious concerns, and especially Islamist ones. By contrast to its predecessor(s), the new terrorists have been willing to inflict mass casualties, kill large numbers of people, and use or attempt to use unconventional weapons to achieve this end. Furthermore, from an organizational perspective, the new terrorists have tended to rely less on hierarchical and more on horizontally articulated and network-based forms than those active in the 1960s and 1970s.

Frequencies of definitional elements of "Terrorism" according to years of publication (Table 5.3)

The articles in the three professional terrorism journals which we have used to compare with the respondents to Schmid's 1985 questionnaire clearly cover a wider time span than the latter. The questionnaire respondents would have been aware of the early phases of the new terrorism, but the experiences on which their definitions were based would far more likely have been derived from the events of the previous decades or Rapoport's Third Wave. The journal contributions, on the other hand, would include the observations of writers who were able to look back at the terrorist phenomenon from the 1990s and the early years of the new millennium, after the "new terrorism" was well underway and after some of the dramatic attacks associated with it had already been committed.

We interpret this distinction, with some overlap in time for both sets of observers to be sure, to mean that the definitions of terrorism proposed by the journal contributors would be less likely to pay attention to such acts as hostage-taking and kidnapping, in which the mental states of the victims and perpetrators would be central considerations. They might also be somewhat less likely to have available various autobiographies, memoirs, and written reflections that third wave terrorists furnished in abundance. Therefore, we suspect that the journal contributors' definitions were less psychology focused than the questionnaire respondents. But this is, of course, a post hoc explanation of our own.

Table 5.3 Frequencies of definitional elements of "Terrorism" according to years of publication

1997–2001 N = 16	1992–1996 N = 11	1987–1991 N = 23	1982–1986 N = 13	1977–1981 N = 10	Element
69%	91%	83%	54%	50%	1. Violence
44%	64%	74%	69%	40%	2. Political
19%	36%	17%	8%	40%	3. Fear
0%	54.5%	70%	46%	20%	4. Threat
37.5%	36%	26%	8%	10%	5. Victim
62.5%	54.5%	13%	8%	30%	6. Tactic
19%	45.5%	22%	23%	0%	7. Civilians
31%	54.5%	17%	38.5%	10%	8. Movement

Note: Our survey consists of 73 definitions drawn from 55 articles collected from three journals.

The consensus definition to emerge from our merger of the two academic sources is as follows: *Terrorism is a politically motivated tactic involving the threat or use of force or violence in which the pursuit of publicity plays a significant role.* Is this definition good or bad, helpful or not?

One criterion for evaluating definitions of terrorism has been suggested by Schmid. This standard is whether or not advocates and opponents, authorities and their challengers, agree over its merits.[18] Whatever else they disagree over, they would share a common understanding when they use the word terrorism. But even if we remain within the academic domain, it seems unlikely that the consensus definition will satisfy some professorial critics. They regard the word itself as a snare and a delusion, a semantic device by which the state and its agents divert attention from their own crimes. For those members of academia who wish to express their solidarity with the sufferings of the oppressed, "… it is clear that so-called terrorism is the logical and just resistance of the people against state terrorism, capitalism, racism, sexism and imperialism."[19] "Terrorism" in and of itself is simply a way of changing the subject by transforming victims into perpetrators.

Frequencies of definitional elements of "Terrorism" according to writer's academic field (Table 5.4)

In a sense, academic critics of the very idea of terrorism have a point. What we have identified as a consensus definition bears a relatively strong resemblance to the way states, and law enforcement agencies, in particular, regard the phenomenon. For instance, Hoffman reports that the US Federal Bureau of Investigation defines terrorism as "… the unlawful use of force or violence against persons or property to intimidate or coerce a Government, the civilian population, or any segment thereof, in furtherance of political and social objectives. …"[20] And British law (circa 1974) specifies that "… terrorism is the use of violence for political ends, and includes any use of violence for the purpose of putting the public or any section of the public in fear."[21] Whether or not the resemblance between the definitions provided by the academic domain and by the state is good or bad depends upon the point of view of the observer. However, it is relatively common, in international law, for example, for academic discussions of legal concepts to find their way into the statute books or into international conventions.

Is the consensus definition helpful to those who wish to study terrorism? By ignoring the psychological element, by, in effect, taking the terror out of terrorism, the definition facilitates observation of the phenomenon. It is easier to study politically driven actions than internal mental conditions. But, of course, the consensus definition suffers from serious flaws. Sartori's observations make good sense in this case: "The rules for climbing and descending along a ladder of abstraction

Table 5.4 Frequencies of definitional elements of "Terrorism" according to the writer's academic field

Element	Political science $N = 22$	Sociology $N = 7$	Communication $N = 1$	Psychology $N = 7$	History $N = 3$	International relations $N = 3$	Philosophy $N = 1$	Law $N = 5$	Other $N = 5$
1. Violence	73%	86%	100%	43%	67%	67%	0%	80%	100%
2. Political	59%	57%	100%	29%	67%	67%	100%	100%	60%
3. Fear	18%	29%	0%	29%	33%	33%	0%	40%	40%
4. Threat	41%	71%	100%	29%	33%	33%	100%	40%	20%
5. Victim-	41%	57%	0%	0%	0%	0%	0%	0%	0%
6. Tactic	41%	14%	100%	43%	33%	33%	100%	0%	40%
7. Civilians	23%	57%	0%	14%	33%	33%	0%	0%	20%
8. Movement	36%	43%	100%	0%	33%	33%	0%	20%	0%

Note: Our survey consists of 73 definitions drawn from 55 articles collected from three journals.

are thus very simple rules. … We make a concept more abstract and more general by lessening its properties or attributes …"[22]

The consensus definition is highly general. It seems too vague, in other words. It also suffers from border problems. The definition includes no distinction between combatants and non-combatants as targets of violence and, as a consequence, no way of discriminating between terrorism and, for example, guerrilla warfare of the type US forces are currently experiencing in Iraq. Nor, for that matter, does it permit us to separate the highly planned operations of small, clandestine groups from large-scale attacks carried out by large aggregations intended to attract publicity to a cause.

The cost of achieving consensus among academic analysts of terrorism is a definition which has climbed too high on the ladder of abstraction to discriminate among different types of politically driven violence aimed at achieving publicity. Thus, unless we are willing to label as terrorism a very wide range of violent activities, we may be better off finding another governing concept or looking elsewhere for a definition.

Appendix A List of the articles used in developing our data file

Name of author	Name of article	Year of publication	Name of journal
1. Conrad V. Hassel	Terror: The Crime of The Privileged—An Examination and Prognosis	1977	Terrorism
2. Brian Jenkins	Research Note: Rand's Research on Terrorism	1977	Terrorism
3. Thomas M. Franck	International Legal Action Concerning Terrorism	1978	Terrorism
4. Abraham Kaplan	The Psychodynamics of Terrorism	1978	Terrorism
5. Gerald Holton	Reflections on Modern Terrorism	1978	Terrorism
6. J.K. Zawodny	Internal Organizational Problems and the Sources of Tensions of Terrorist Movements as Catalysts of Violence	1978	Terrorism
7. Stephen Sloan, Richard Keaney & Charles Wise	Learning about Terrorism: Analysis, Simulations, and Future Directions	1978	Terrorism
8. Frederick J. Hacker	Terror and Terrorism: Modern Growth Industry and Mass Entertainment	1980	Terrorism
9. L. C. Green	Aspects of Terrorism	1981	Terrorism
10. Gerald W. Hopple	Transnational Terrorism: Prospects For a Casual Modeling Approach	1982	Terrorism
11. Lawrence Zelic Freedman	Why Does Terrorism Terrorize?	1983	Terrorism
12. Terrorist Research and Analytical Center	FBI Analysis of Terrorist Incidents in the United States—1982	1984	Terrorism
13. Brent L. Smith	Antiterrorism Legislation in the United States: Problems and Implication	1984	Terrorism
14. Allan S. Nanes	Congressional Developments	1984	Terrorism
15. L. John Martin	The Media's Role in International Terrorism	1985	Terrorism
16. Robert H. Kupperman	Terrorism and National Security	1985	Terrorism
17. Michael Gunter	Contemporary Armenian Terrorism	1985	Terrorism
18. Edward A. Lynch	International Terrorism: The Search for a Policy	1987	Terrorism
19. Julius Emeka Okolo	Nigerian Politics and the Dikko Kidnap Affair	1987	Terrorism
20. Ruth Linn	Terrorism, Morality and Soldiers' Motivation to Fight: An Example from the Israeli Experience in Lebanon	1988	Terrorism
21. Michele Wilson & John Lynxwiler	Abortion Clinic Violence as Terrorism	1988	Terrorism
22. Jae Taik Kim	North Korean Terrorism: Trends, Characteristics, and Deterrence	1988	Terrorism
23. Jeffrey Ian Ross	Attributes of Domestic Political Terrorism in Canada, 1960–1985	1988	Terrorism

Appendix A (Continued)

Name of author	Name of article	Year of publication	Name of journal
45. Wayne G. Reilly	The Management of Political Violence in Quebec and Northern Ireland: A Comparison	1994	Terrorism and Political Violence
46. Ehud Sprinzak	Right Wing Terrorism in a Comparative Perspective: The Case of Split Delegitimization	1995	Terrorism and Political Violence
47. Avishag Gordon	Terrorism and Computerized Databases: An Examination of Multidisciplinary Coverage	1995	Terrorism and Political Violence
48. Andrew Silke	Terrorism and the Blind Men's Elephant	1996	Terrorism and Political Violence
49. Bruce Hoffman	The Confluence of International and Domestic Trends in Terrorism	1997	Terrorism and Political Violence
50. Matthew G. Devost, Brian K. Hougthon & Neal Allen Pollard	Information Terrorism: Political Violence in the Information Age	1997	Terrorism and Political Violence
51. Thomas J. Badey	Defining International Terrorism: A Pragmatic Approach	1998	Terrorism and Political Violence
52. Ariel Merari	Terrorism as a Strategy of Struggle: Past and Future	1999	Terrorism and Political Violence
53. Max Taylor and John Horgan	Future Developments of Political Terrorism in Europe	1999	Terrorism and Political Violence
54. Jerrold M. Post, Keven G. Ruby & Eric D. Shaw	From Car Bombs to Logic Bombs: The Growing Threat From Information Terrorism	2000	Terrorism and Political Violence
55. Clive Walker	Briefing on the Terrorism Act 2000	2000	Terrorism and Political Violence

Note: Our survey consists of 55 articles collected from three journals.

Notes

1 Walter Laqueur, *Terrorism* (Boston: Little, Brown 1977) p. 5.
2 Martha Crenshaw, "The Psychology of Terrorism" *Political Psychology* 21/2 (2000) p. 406.
3 David C. Rapoport, "The Four Waves of Modern Terrorism" in Audrey Cronin and James Ludes (eds), *Attacking Terrorism: Elements of a Grand Strategy* (Washington, DC: Georgetown University Press 2004) p. 54; David C. Rapoport "Introduction to Part I" in David C. Rapoport and Yonah Alexander (eds), *The Morality of Terrorism: Religious and Secular Justifications* (New York: Pergamon Press 1982) pp. 3–11.
4 The second wave of terrorism, also known as the "Anti-Colonial Wave," began in the 1920s and crested in the 1960s. All groups in the second wave struggled against colonial powers that had become ambivalent about retraining their colonial status. The second wave receded largely as the colonial powers disappeared (Rapoport, "The Four Waves of Modern Terrorism").
5 Rapoport, "The Four Waves of Modern Terrorism," p. 54. Moreover, as Rapoport explained, "Because the anti-colonial struggle seemed more legitimate than the purposes served in the first wave, the 'new' language became attractive to potential political supporters as well. Governments also appreciated the political value of 'appropriate' language and began to describe all violent rebels as terrorists. The media, hoping to avoid being seen as blatantly partisan, corrupted language further. Major American newspapers, for example, often described the same individuals alternatively as terrorists, guerrillas, and soldiers in the same account" (p. 54).
6 See, for example, Boaz Ganor, "Defining Terrorism: Is One Man's Terrorist Another Man's Freedom Fighter?" *Annual Editions: Violence and Terrorism 03/04* (Guilford, CT: Dushkin 2003) pp. 11–19.
7 William Connolly, *The Terms of Political Discourse* 3rd ed. (Princeton: Princeton University Press 1993) p. 10. The idea comes from W.B. Gallie, "Essentially Contested Concepts" in Max Black (ed), *The Importance of Language* (Ithaca: Cornell University Press 1969) pp. 121–146.
8 See, for example, Giovanni Sartori, *Social Science Concepts* (Beverly Hills: Sage Publications 1984) pp. 28–35.
9 David Collier and James Mahon, "Conceptual 'Stretching' Revisited: Adapting Categories in Comparative Analysis," *The American Political Science Review* 87:4 (1993) p. 846.
10 Alex Schmid, "The Response Problem as a Definition Problem," *Terrorism and Political Violence* 4:4 (1992) pp. 7–25.
11 See, for example, Donatella della Porta, "Left-Wing Terrorism in Italy," in Martha Crenshaw (ed), *Terrorism in Context* (University Park, PA: Pennsylvania State University Press 1995) pp. 105–159.
12 Alex Schmid, Albert Jongman et al., *Political Terrorism* (New Brunswick, NJ: Transaction Books, 1988) p.28. Schmid is in the process of updating this work, see, "The Problem of Defining Terrorism" (a paper presented at a conference on Terrorism and Security Studies, George Marshall Defense Center, Garmisch Germany, June 28 2004) pp. 1–30.
13 Our research attempted to define terrorism throughout the last two decades. In order to do so, we extensively collected all articles from three central journals (*Terrorism; Terrorism and Political Violence; Studies in Conflict and Terrorism*) that pertain to the matter at hand. Initially, the data we collected were divided into different categories that did not only include the context of the article but included information about its author, as well. Within the context of the article we examined the subject of the article, its focus, its research method (i.e., qualitative/quantitative case study, qualitative/quantitative comparative research, qualitative/quantitative theoretical research), its nature (i.e., conceptual, analytic, theoretical or case-study), and whether it constructs a typology, a theory, or a definition. In addition to the article's context we noted the author's professional affiliation, field of education, and place of residence. These categories allowed for a wide observation of the phenomenon of terrorism. The second step of our research was to extract from the 110 articles found relevant, the various definitions for terrorism. Within 55 articles, the 73 definitions that originated were examined according to twenty-two elements revealed in the work done by Schmid & Jongman (1988). It was this type of incongruity which led to the main question of our research: Are the entire twenty-two elements needed in order to reach a substantial definition of terrorism or are there definitional elements that may have been crucial in the past, but are no longer relevant in the present?
14 Schmid reported that, of his 58 respondents, 10% said they were psychologists (Scmid and Jongman, p. 207), while 7 of the 55 authors of the journal articles were identified with that profession.
15 In order to determine whether differences according to country of origin are significant, we considered performing an analysis of variance (ANOVA, for example). However, due to the small number of scholars in each origin (e.g., two scholars from Africa, three scholars from Australia and six scholars from the Middle East) we were unable to perform this kind of statistical test.

16 David Rapoport, "The Fourth Wave: September 11 in the History of Terrorism" *Current History* (December 2001) pp. 419–424.
17 See, for example, Bruce Hoffman, *Inside Terrorism* (New York: Columbia University Press 1999) pp. 86–129.
18 Schmid, "The Response Problem as a Definition Problem," p. 11.
19 Ibid.
20 Hoffman, p. 38.
21 Schmid, "The Response Problem as a Definition Problem," p. 9.
22 Giovanni Sartori, "Concept Misinformation in Comparative Politics," *The American Political Science Review* LXIV/4 (December 1970) p. 1041.

6 The response problem as a definition problem

Alex P. Schmid

The definition of what constitutes "terrorism" varies from society to society, from government to government and, to a lesser degree, even from academic author to academic author. Such diversity of definition is problematic when one strives to develop a common policy against "terrorism". If one country has a broad definition and the other a narrow one, a clear and consistent consensual policy will be an elusive goal. How can we escape from this definitional quagmire?

Four arenas of discourse on "Terrorism"

We can begin by distinguishing four different arenas of discourse on non-state terrorism:

1   The academic discourse. The universities offer an intellectual forum where scholars can discuss terrorism without being suspected of sympathizing with terrorists.
2   The state's statements. The official discourse on terrorism by those who speak in the name of the state.
3   The public debate on terrorism. The way our open societies are structured, this arena is largely co-extensive with the views and suggestions met in the media.
4   The discussion of those who oppose many of our societies' values and support or perform acts of violence and terrorism against what they consider repressive states.[1]

Taking each arena in turn:

1.   When academic scholars look at terrorism, their perspective – as researchers, not necessarily in their role as citizens – differs from that of those charged with law enforcement against insurgent terrorists. To use a distinction of T. R. Gurr: the latter are "firefighters", while the former should be mere "students of combustion". Their distance should allow them more perspective.

   Over the past few years, this author has attempted to discover what the academic perspective on terrorism is by communicating with other members of the research community. The instruments used were lengthy questionnaires mailed to many authors in the field. On this basis, an academic consensus definition of "terrorism" is attempted. I was glad to find considerable academic acceptance of its basic elements. No less than 81 per cent of the respondents from the academic community found my first attempt at definition partially or fully acceptable.[2] The comments and criticism of over 50 scholars helped me to refine and reconceptualize this first definition. The result is the following definition:

   Terrorism is an anxiety-inspiring method of repeated violent action, employed by (semi-) clandestine individual, group or state actors, for idiosyncratic, criminal or political reasons, whereby – in contrast to assassination – the direct targets of violence are not the main targets. The immediate human victims of violence are generally chosen randomly (targets of opportunity) or selectively (representative or symbolic targets) from a target population, and serve as message generators. Threat- and violence-based communication processes between terrorist (organisation), (imperiled) victims, and main targets are used to manipulate the main target (audience(s)), turning it into a target of terror, a target of demands, or a target of attention, depending on whether intimidation, coercion, or propaganda is primarily sought.[3]

2. Such a precise but lengthy definition is not likely to be used by governments. Compare this 'academic' definition with two government definitions, the German and the British:

German Federal Republic, Office for the Protection of the Constitution (1985): "Terrorism is the enduringly conducted struggle for political goals, which are intended to be achieved by means of assaults on the life and property of other persons, especially by means of severe crimes as detailed in art. 129a, section 1 of the penal code (above all: murder, homicide, extortionist kidnapping, arson, setting off a blast by explosives) or by means of other acts of violence, which serve as preparation of such criminal acts";[4]

United Kingdom (1974): "For the purposes of the legislation, terrorism is the use of violence for political ends, and includes any use of violence for the purpose of putting the public or any section of the public in fear".[5]

The British definition, in particular, is very broad and could be interpreted to include conventional war as well as nuclear deterrence. Unfortunately, the "European" TREVI (Terrorism, Radicalism, Extremism and political Violence) group definition has been modelled on the British one, except that it excludes the contingency of war: "Terrorism is defined as the use, or the threatened use, by a cohesive group of persons of violence (short of warfare) to effect political aims".[6] The European Convention to Combat Terrorism (1977) did not use any definition in order not to get stuck in a political debate. It simply listed crimes and "depoliticized" these in order to circumvent restrictions on extradition. However, this avoidance of the problem was no solution as various controversies around extradition in the following years made clear.

3. What is the image of terrorism in the media? In another questionnaire, editors of news agencies, television, radio and the press were asked what kind of (political) violence their medium labelled 'terrorism'. Table 6.1 summarises which particular acts of violence these editors defined as acts of terrorism and reveals a declining consensus about labelling certain acts of violence as 'terrorism'.

While the European Convention for the Suppression of Terrorism assumes all hijackings to be acts of terrorism for the purposes of extradition,[7] editors do make a distinction between a hijacking for escape and one for coercive bargaining. In this particular case, I think that the majority of editors are closer to the mark than the drafters of the European convention. If you are sitting in an aircraft and the hijacker only asks the pilot to fly to Rome instead of Tirana, you will feel much less terrorised than when he or she demands the liberation of 700 prisoners from the Iranian government. In the first case, the pilot can, through a change of behaviour, escape from the threat of being killed. In the second case, his and the passengers' attitude or behaviour does not matter, since the addressee is not identical with the threatened group of people.

Table 6.1 Answers to the question: "What kind of (political) violence does your medium commonly label 'Terrorism'?"

Type of violence using	Percentage of editors label 'terrorism'
Hostage taking	80%
Assassination	75%
Indiscriminate bombing	75%
Kidnapping	70%
Hijacking for coercive bargaining	70%
Urban guerrilla warfare	65%
Sabotage	60%
Torture	45%
Hijacking for escape	35%

Other categories mentioned by individual respondents were: murder by an organisation; land mines; attacks on security forces in rural areas and robbery.

In the same way, a kidnapping can be terroristic or not. When only money is asked from an abducted millionaire, the situation is less frightening than when political concessions are asked from a government in return for the victim, as when the German industrialist Hanns-Martin Schleyer was abducted by the German Red Army Faction in 1977. Apparently some hijackings and kidnappings are more terroristic than others. The same goes for 'assassination'. Some political assassinations are performed to kill a political opponent whose policies are contrary to those of the murderer. The murder of John F. Kennedy was not terroristic in this sense. A terroristic assassination, on the other hand, involves more parties than the killer and his victim. There are three parties instead of two (see Figure 6.1).

As Figure 6.1 makes clear, there is a difference between the target of violence and the target of terror, between the victim and the opponent. The specific victim does not matter as much as with a traditional assassination. In a terroristic murder, one victim can easily be substituted for another since the effect on the ultimate target is what really counts. Hence one has to distinguish between a common assassination and one in the context of terrorism by

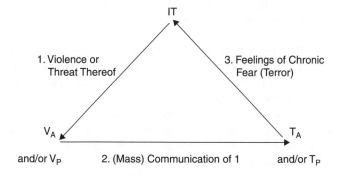

(IT = Insurgent Terrorism; V_A = Victim Belonging to the Camp of the State Authorities; V_P = Victim Being Part of the Public; T_A = The Authorities as Target; T_P = The Public as Target)

Figure 6.1 The Triangle of Insurgent Terrorism

Source: Alec P. Schmid and Janny de Graaf, *Violence as Communication: Insurgent Terrorism and the Western News Media* (Beverly Hills: Sage, 1982), p. 176.

labelling the first "individuated political murder" and the second "de-individuated political murder".[8] In the first case, the victim usually knew his opponents and the threat posed to him before he was killed. In the second case, the victim is often not aware that he is a party to a conflict and the attack on his life comes unexpectedly.

Here we also arrive at the reason why terrorism terrorises. It does so because we are caught by surprise and are victimised arbitrarily and without provocation from our side. Suddenly, we are "struck with terror". Terror, then, is a state of mind. Terrorism is the calculated causing of extreme anxiety of becoming a victim of arbitrary violence and the exploitation of this emotional reaction for manipulative purposes.

4.   I am aware that this is not the way the terrorists themselves and their sympathizers would describe their activities. During the AEGEE/COMT conference in Leiden some graffiti-painters calling themselves the "Revolutionary Commando Marinus van der Lubbe" sent a letter to the local newspaper wherein they expressed their solidarity with the oppressed people in, among other places, Palestine, Ireland, Central America and Kurdistan. Literally, they said: 'It is clear that so-called terrorism is the logical and just resistance of the people against state terrorism, capitalism, racism, sexism and imperialism'.[9] Some contemporary terrorists call themselves "freedom fighters", members of the anti-imperialist resistance, or "Defense League".

There is nothing new in this: in the Second World War the German occupation force called members of the Dutch resistance "terrorists" while the latter's self-image was that they were patriots and resistance fighters. The point I wish to make here is that these terms are not exclusive. They are "definitions" with different focal points: one in terms of means, the other in terms of goals.

Terrorism as the "peacetime equivalent of war crimes"

Which definition is the right one? A good definition is one to which many can agree. A broad definition – like "terrorism is violence for political purposes" – is likely to be objected to by more people than a narrow one since it turns more practitioners of violence into terrorists. An academic definition which is too detailed, may be impractical. What is needed is a legal definition to which many can agree. I submit that such a legal definition already exists in the category of "war crimes".[10]

Fotion and Elfstrom (1986) have concluded that "In contrast to the lack of clarity about what constitutes war, there is broad international agreement about what actions count as war crimes."[11] It would be wise to profit from this consensus. Included among the acts prohibited by the laws of war are attacks on persons taking no active part in hostilities. This also includes members of the armed forces who have laid down their arms. The protection of the non-combatant and the innocent stand at the core of international humanitarian law as codified in the Hague Regulations and Geneva Conventions. The rules of war prohibit not only violence against captives but also hostage-taking as well as most other atrocities committed by terrorists.[12]

Terrorists have elevated practices which are excesses of war to the level of routine tactics. They do not engage in combat, as soldiers do. They strike preferably the unarmed.[13] The attack on the undefended is not an unsought side-effect but a deliberate strategy. Categorising acts of terrorism as war crimes is also appropriate in the sense that terrorists consider themselves as being at war with Western democracies.[14] What makes them different from soldiers, however, is that they do not carry their arms openly and that they do not discriminate between armed adversaries and noncombatants. Since they are not fighting by the rules of war they turn themselves into war criminals. Terrorism distinguishes itself from conventional and to some extent also from guerrilla warfare through the disregard for principles of chivalry and humanity contained in the Hague Regulations and Geneva Conventions.

I believe that Western policy-makers would do well to choose a restricted legal definition of terrorism as "peacetime equivalents of war crimes". Such a definition might exclude some forms of violence and coercion (such as attacks on the military, hijackings for escape and destruction of property) currently labelled "terrorism" by some governments. However, a narrow and precise definition of terrorism is likely to find broader support than one that includes various forms of violent dissent and protest short of terrorist atrocities.

Other, lesser forms of political violence (e.g., against property) will still be illegal by national laws. However, terrorist offences could be considered federal crimes against humanity, requiring special treatment. If we have clarity on this front, nobody will be able to confuse terrorists and freedom fighters. "Freedom fighters" who adhere to the rules of war should be given privileged treatment. "Freedom-fighters" targeting civilians, on the other hand, should be dealt with as war criminals. Extradition problems, which now arise out of different interpretations about who is a terrorist, could then disappear. The good motive (like the fight for self-determination, freedom and democracy) can then no longer exculpate the bad deed of violence against the unarmed, the disarmed and the neutral bystanders.

The European Convention for the Suppression of Terrorism has been plagued by the lack of distinction between a "criminal offence" and a "political offence".[15] By placing narrowly defined acts of terrorism in the context of "war crimes", the dilemma of attributing a given act of violence to the criminal or political sphere disappears. Acts of terrorism, like war crimes, could be dealt with by a special European tribunal with special jurisdiction on terroristic offences.

Notes

1 This classification has been inspired by Philip Schlesinger, Graham Murdock and Philip Elliott, *Televising 'Terrorism': Political Violence in Popular Culture* (London: Comedia, 1983). Schlesinger *et al.* differentiate between the official perspective, the alternative perspective, the populist perspective and the opposition perspective.

2 Alex P. Schmid, Albert J. Jongman *et al.*, *Political Terrorism: A New Guide to Actors, Authors, Concepts, Data Bases, Theories, and Literature* (Amsterdam: North-Holland Publishing, 1988), p. 2.

3 Schmid *et al.*, *Political Terrorism*, p.28.

4 Ministry of the Interior. *Verfassungsschutzbericht 1984* (Bonn: Bundesministerium des Innern, 1985), p. 17n.

5 Prevention of Terrorism (Temporary Provisions) Act of 1974; cited in E.F. Mickolus, *The Literature of Terrorism* (Westport, CT: Greenwood Press, 1980), p. 295.

6 *Handelingen* (Dutch Parliamentary Proceedings) II, 1986/87, Bijlagen 19700, Hoofdstuk VI nr.30, p. 5, as cited in Peter Klerks, *Terreur Bestrijding in Nederland 1970–1988* (Amsterdam: Ravijn, 1989), p. 22.

7 Article 1, *Europees Verdrag tot bestrijding van terrorisme*, 1977.

8 Schmid *et al.*, *Political Terrorism* (note 2).

9 *Leidsch Dagblad*, 17 March 1989.

10 To my knowledge, Alfred P. Rubin was the first to relate terrorism to the laws of war. See: A. P. Rubin, 'Terrorism and the Law of War', *Denver Journal of International Law and Politics* 17/2–3 (1983), p. 219.

11 N. Fotion and G. Elfstrom, *Military Ethics: Guidelines for Peace and War* (Boston: RKP, 1986), p. 260.

12 L.P. Bremer III, 'Terrorism and the Rule of War', US Dept. of State, Bureau of Public Affairs, Current Policy No.947 (Text of address 23 April 1987), p. 3.

13 Of the 782 international terrorist incidents listed by the US State Dept. for 1985, the smallest group of victims (7 per cent) consisted of military men; the largest group (27.5 per cent) consisted of 'other', that is, other than military and other than diplomats (9.5 per cent), politically affiliated and non-official public targets (7.25 per cent), private party (15.4 per cent) and business (23.75 per cent); US Dept. of State, 1986, p. 3 (see also Jongman, this volume).

14 I have discussed this theme in more detail in A.P. Schmid, 'Force or Conciliation? An Overview of Some Problems Associated With Current Anti-Terrorist Response Strategies', *Violence, Aggression and Terrorism* 2/2 (1988), pp. 152–155.

15 See M. Zagari (Rapporteur), *Verslag namens de Commissie juridische zaken en rechten van de burger over de bestrijding van het terrorisme*, Europees Parlement. Zittings-documenten, Document A2-155/89, 2 May 1989, p. 14. (See also Zagari in A. Schmid & R. Crelinsten (Eds) *Western responses to terrorism* London: Frant Cass p. 291, for an English version of this text.)

Section 3

Understanding and explaining terrorism

Readings

Crenshaw, M. (1981). The causes of terrorism. *Comparative Politics, 13,* 379–399.
Weinberg, L. (1991). Turning to terror: The conditions under which political parties turn to terrorist activities. *Comparative Politics, 23,* 423–438.
Taylor, M., & Horgan, J. (2006). A conceptual framework for addressing psychological process in the development of the terrorist. *Terrorism and Political Violence, 18,* 1–17.

Introduction

In her article "The Causes of Terrorism," Martha Crenshaw considers the social setting, driving conditions, logic, reasoning and motivations for individuals and groups to become involved with terrorism. One of several key lessons from Crenshaw's article is the need to appreciate how, in order to explain terrorism, we must consider it at a number of different levels. There is the terrorist group, of course, but that group is comprised of people whose motivation, background factors and individual psychology we must also bear in mind when trying to explain it. Ten years later, in the same journal, *Comparative Politics,* Leonard Weinberg also addressed key issues relevant for understanding and explaining terrorism. In his article "Turning to Terror," Weinberg examines the relationship between political parties and terrorist groups, and examines the factors that give rise to a peaceful group turning towards a violent strategy. In his analysis, he asserts, "terrorist groups do not emerge from thin air." As with Crenshaw's article, Weinberg carefully considers the environmental setting in which terrorist groups emerge, and also examines the relationship *between* terrorist groups and the political parties that represent them. Our final contribution to this section is by two psychologists – Max Taylor and John Horgan. They recognize the need to understand the psychology of the terrorist, but rather than attempt to explain terrorism at the level of the individual, place far greater emphasis on the interaction between the terrorists, the organizational context to which they belong, as well as the environmental setting that heavily influences what they do (and do not do). They conclude by presenting an overarching framework for understanding how terrorism develops, and just like many other scholars, highlight the challenges in explaining terrorism from one perspective alone.

Discussion questions

By the end of this section you should be able to answer the following questions:

* What causes terrorism?
* How are terrorist groups and political parties linked to each other?
* Why do we need to understand terrorism at multiple levels?

Further reading

Bjorgo, T. (Ed). (2005). *Root causes of terrorism: Myths, reality, and ways forward.* London: Routledge.

Crenshaw, M. (Ed.). (2010). *Explaining terrorism: Causes, processes and consequences.* London: Routledge.

Gupta, D. (2005). Toward an integrated behavioral framework for analyzing terrorism: Individual motivations to group dynamics. *Democracy and Security, 1,* 5–31.

Krueger, A. B., & Malecova, J. (2003). Education, poverty, and terrorism: Is there a causal connection? *Journal of Economic Perspectives, 17,* 119–144.

Silke, A. (2003). *Terrorist, victims, and society: Psychological perspectives on terrorism and its consequences.* Hoboken, NJ: Wiley.

Victoroff, J. (Ed.). (2006). *Tangled roots: Social and psychological factors in the genesis of terrorism.* Washington, DC: IOS Press.

7 The causes of terrorism

Martha Crenshaw

Terrorism occurs both in the context of violent resistance to the state as well as in the service of state interests. If we focus on terrorism directed against governments for purposes of political change, we are considering the premeditated use or threat of symbolic, low-level violence by conspiratorial organizations. Terrorist violence communicates a political message; its ends go beyond damaging an enemy's material resources.[1] The victims or objects of terrorist attack have little intrinsic value to the terrorist group but represent a larger human audience whose reaction the terrorists seek. Violence characterized by spontaneity, mass participation, or a primary intent of physical destruction can therefore be excluded from our investigation.

The study of terrorism can be organized around three questions: why terrorism occurs, how the process of terrorism works, and what its social and political effects are. Here the objective is to outline an approach to the analysis of the causes of terrorism, based on comparison of different cases of terrorism, in order to distinguish a common pattern of causation from the historically unique.

The subject of terrorism has inspired a voluminous literature in recent years. However, nowhere among the highly varied treatments does one find a general theoretical analysis of the causes of terrorism. This may be because terrorism has often been approached from historical perspectives, which, if we take Laqueur's work as an example, dismiss explanations that try to take into account more than a single case as "exceedingly vague or altogether wrong."[2] Certainly existing general accounts are often based on assumptions that are neither explicit nor factually demonstrable. We find judgments centering on social factors such as the permissiveness and affluence in which Western youth are raised or the imitation of dramatic models encouraged by television. Alternatively, we encounter political explanations that blame revolutionary ideologies, Marxism-Leninism or nationalism, governmental weakness in giving in to terrorist demands, or conversely government oppression and the weakness of the regime's opponents. Individual psychopathology is often cited as a culprit.

Even the most persuasive of statements about terrorism are not cast in the form of testable propositions, nor are they broadly comparative in origin or intent. Many are partial analyses, limited in scope to revolutionary terrorism from the Left, not terrorism that is a form of protest or a reaction to political or social change. A narrow historical or geographical focus is also common; the majority of explanations concern modern phenomena. Some focus usefully on terrorism against the Western democracies.[3] In general, propositions about terrorism lack logical comparability, specification of the relationship of variables to each other, and a rank-ordering of variables in terms of explanatory power.

We would not wish to claim that a general explanation of the sources of terrorism is a simple task, but it is possible to make a useful beginning by establishing a theoretical order for different types and levels of causes. We approach terrorism as a form of political behavior resulting from the deliberate choice of a basically rational actor, the terrorist organization. A comprehensive explanation, however, must also take into account the environment in which terrorism occurs and address the question of whether broad political, social, and economic conditions make terrorism more likely in some contexts than in others. What sort of circumstances lead to the formation of a terrorist group? On the other hand, only a few of the people who experience a given situation practice terrorism. Not even all individuals who share the goals of a terrorist organization agree that terrorism is the best means. It is essential to consider the psychological variables that may encourage or inhibit individual participation in terrorist actions. The analysis of these three levels of causation will center first on situational variables, then on the strategy of the terrorist organization, and last on the problem of individual participation.

This paper represents only a preliminary set of ideas about the problem of causation; historical cases of terrorism are used as illustrations, not as demonstrations of hypotheses. The historical examples referred to here are significant terrorist campaigns since the French Revolution of 1789; terrorism is considered as a facet of secular modern politics, principally associated with the rise of nationalism, anarchism, and revolutionary socialism.[4] The term *terrorism* was coined to describe the systematic inducement of fear and anxiety to control and direct a civilian population, and the phenomenon of terrorism as a challenge to the authority of the state grew from the difficulties revolutionaries experienced in trying to recreate the mass uprisings of the French Revolution. Most references provided here are drawn from the best-known and most-documented examples: Narodnaya Volya and the Combat Organization of the Socialist-Revolutionary party in Russia, from 1878 to 1913; anarchist terrorism of the 1890s in Europe, primarily France; the Irish Republican Army (IRA) and its predecessors and successors from 1919 to the present; the Irgun Zwai Leumi in Mandate Palestine from 1937 to 1947; the Front de Libération Nationale (FLN) in Algeria from 1954 to 1962; the Popular Front for the Liberation of Palestine from 1968 to the present; the Rote Armee Fraktion (RAF) and the 2nd June Movement in West Germany since 1968; and the Tupamaros of Uruguay, 1968–1974.

The setting for terrorism

An initial obstacle to identification of propitious circumstances for terrorism is the absence of significant empirical studies of relevant cross-national factors. There are a number of quantitative analyses of collective violence, assassination, civil strife, and crime,[5] but none of these phenomena is identical to a campaign of terrorism. Little internal agreement exists among such studies, and the consensus one finds is not particularly useful for the study of terrorism.[6] For example, Ted Robert Gurr found that "modern" states are less violent than developing countries and that legitimacy of the regime inhibits violence. Yet, Western Europe experiences high levels of terrorism. Surprisingly, in the 1961–1970 period, out of 87 countries, the United States was ranked as having the highest number of terrorist campaigns.[7] Although it is impractical to borrow entire theoretical structures from the literature on political and criminal violence, some propositions can be adapted to the analysis of terrorism.

To develop a framework for the analysis of likely settings for terrorism, we must establish conceptual distinctions among different types of factors. First, a significant difference exists between *preconditions*, factors that set the stage for terrorism over the long run, and *precipitants*, specific events that immediately precede the occurrence of terrorism. Second, a further classification divides preconditions into enabling or permissive factors, which provide opportunities for terrorism to happen, and situations that directly inspire and motivate terrorist campaigns. Precipitants are similar to the direct causes of terrorism.[8] Furthermore, no factor is neatly compartmentalized in a single nation-state; each has a transnational dimension that complicates the analysis.

First, modernization produces an interrelated set of factors that is a significant permissive cause of terrorism, as increased complexity on all levels of society and economy creates opportunities and vulnerabilities. Sophisticated networks of transportation and communication offer mobility and the means of publicity for terrorists. The terrorists of Narodnaya Volya would have been unable to operate without Russia's newly established rail system, and the Popular Front for the Liberaton of Palestine could not indulge in hijacking without the jet aircraft. In Algeria, the FLN only adopted a strategy of urban bombings when they were able to acquire plastic explosives. In 1907, the Combat Organization of the Socialist-Revolutionary party paid 20,000 rubles to an inventor who was working on an aircraft in the futile hope of bombing the Russian imperial palaces from the air.[9] Today we fear that terrorists will exploit the potential of nuclear power, but it was in 1867 that Nobel's invention of dynamite made bombings a convenient terrorist tactic.

Urbanization is part of the modern trend toward aggregation and complexity, which increases the number and accessibility of targets and methods. The popular concept of terrorism as "urban guerrilla warfare" grew out of the Latin American experience of the late 1960s.[10] Yet, as Hobsbawn has pointed out, cities became the arena for terrorism after the urban renewal projects of the late nineteenth century, such as the boulevards constructed by Baron Haussman in Paris, made them unsuitable for a strategy based on riots and the defense of barricades.[11] In preventing popular insurrections, governments have exposed themselves to terrorism. P.N. Grabosky has recently argued that cities are a significant cause of terrorism in that they provide an opportunity (a multitude of targets, mobility, communications, anonymity, and audiences) and a recruiting ground among the politicized and volatile inhabitants.[12]

Social "facilitation," which Gurr found to be extremely powerful in bringing about civil strife in general, is also an important permissive factor. This concept refers to social habits and historical traditions that sanction the use of violence against the government, making it morally and politically justifiable, and even dictating an appropriate form, such as demonstrations, coups, or terrorism. Social myths, traditions, and habits permit the development of terrorism as an established political custom. An excellent example of such a tradition is the case of Ireland, where the tradition of physical force dates from the eighteenth century, and the legend of Michael Collins in 1919–1921 still inspires and partially excuses the much less discriminate and less effective terrorism of the contemporary Provisional IRA in Northern Ireland.

Moreover, broad attitudes and beliefs that condone terrorism are communicated transnationally. Revolutionary ideologies have always crossed borders with ease. In the nineteenth and early twentieth centuries, such ideas were primarily a European preserve, stemming from the French and Bolshevik Revolutions. Since the Second World War, Third World revolutions—China, Cuba, Algeria—and intellectuals such as Frantz Fanon and Carlos Marighela[13] have significantly influenced terrorist movements in the developed West by promoting the development of terrorism as routine behavior.

The most salient political factor in the category of permissive causes is a government's inability or unwillingness to prevent terrorism. The absence of adequate prevention by police and intelligence services permits the spread of conspiracy. However, since terrorist organizations are small and clandestine, the majority of states can be placed in the permissive category. Inefficiency or leniency can be found in a broad range of all but the most brutally efficient dictatorships, including incompetent authoritarian states such as tsarist Russia on the eve of the emergence of Narodnaya Volya as well as modern liberal democratic states whose desire to protect civil liberties constrains security measures. The absence of effective security measures is a necessary cause, since our limited information on the subject indicates that terrorism does not occur in the communist dictatorships; and certainly repressive military regimes in Uruguay, Brazil, and Argentina have crushed terrorist organizations. For many governments, however, the cost of disallowing terrorism is too high.

Turning now to a consideration of the direct causes of terrorism, we focus on background conditions that positively encourage resistance to the state. These instigating circumstances go beyond merely creating an environment in which terrorism is possible; they provide motivation and direction for the terrorist movement. We are dealing here with reasons rather than opportunities.

The first condition that can be considered a direct cause of terrorism is the existence of concrete grievances among an identifiable subgroup of a larger population, such as an ethnic minority discriminated against by the majority. A social movement develops in order to redress these grievances and to gain either equal rights or a separate state; terrorism is then the resort of an extremist faction of this broader movement. In practice, terrorism has frequently arisen in such situations: in modern states, separatist nationalism among Basques, Bretons, and Québeçois has motivated terrorism. In the colonial era, nationalist movements commonly turned to terrorism.

This is not to say, however, that the existence of a dissatisfied minority or majority is a necessary or a sufficient cause of terrorism. Not all those who are discriminated against turn to terrorism, nor does terrorism always reflect objective social or economic deprivation. In West Germany, Japan, and Italy, for example, terrorism has been the chosen method of the privileged, not the downtrodden. Some theoretical studies have suggested that the essential ingredient that must be added to real deprivation is the perception on the part of the deprived that this condition is not what they deserve or expect, in short, that discrimination is unjust. An attitude study, for example, found that "the idea of justice or fairness may be more centrally related to attitudes toward violence than are feelings of deprivation. It is the perceived injustice underlying the deprivation that gives rise to anger or frustration."[14] The intervening variables, as we have argued, lie in the terrorists' perceptions. Moreover, it seems likely that for terrorism to occur the government must be singled out to blame for popular suffering.

The second condition that creates motivations for terrorism is the lack of opportunity for political participation. Regimes that deny access to power and persecute dissenters create dissatisfaction. In this case, grievances are primarily political, without social or economic overtones. Discrimination is not directed against any ethnic, religious, or racial subgroup of the population. The terrorist organization is not necessarily part of a broader social movement; indeed, the population may be largely apathetic. In situations where paths to the legal expression of opposition are blocked, but where the regime's repression is inefficient, revolutionary terrorism is doubly likely, as permissive and direct causes coincide. An example of this situation is tsarist Russia in the 1870s.

Context is especially significant as a direct cause of terrorism when it affects an elite, not the mass population. Terrorism is essentially the result of elite disaffection; it represents the strategy of a minority, who may act on behalf of a wider popular constituency who have not been consulted about, and do not necessarily approve of, the terrorists' aims or methods. There is remarkable relevance in E.J. Hobsbawn's comments on the political conspirators of post-Napoleonic Europe: "All revolutionaries regarded themselves, with some justification, as small elites of the emancipated and progressive operating among, and for the eventual benefit of, a vast and inert mass of the ignorant and misled common people, which would no doubt welcome liberation when it came, but could not be expected to take much part in preparing it."[15] Many terrorists today are young, well-educated, and middle class in background. Such students or young professionals, with prior political experience, are disillusioned with the prospects of changing society and see little chance of access to the system despite their privileged status. Much terrorism has grown out of student unrest; this was the case in nineteenth-century Russia as well as post-World War II West Germany, Italy, the United States, Japan, and Uruguay.

Perhaps terrorism is most likely to occur precisely where mass passivity and elite dissatisfaction coincide. Discontent is not generalized or severe enough to provoke the majority of the populace to action against the regime, yet a small minority, without access to the bases of power that would permit overthrow of the government through coup d'état or subversion, seeks radical change. Terrorism may thus be a sign of a stable society rather than a symptom of fragility and impending collapse. Terrorism is the resort of an elite when conditions are not revolutionary. Luigi Bonanate has blamed terrorism on a "blocked society" that is strong enough to preserve itself (presumably through popular inertia) yet resistant to innovation. Such self-perpetuating "immobilisme" invites terrorism.[16]

The last category of situational factors involves the concept of a precipitating event that immediately precedes outbreaks of terrorism. Although it is generally thought that precipitants are the most unpredictable of causes, there does seem to be a common pattern of government actions that act as catalysts for terrorism. Government use of unexpected and unusual force in response to protest or reform attempts often compels terrorist retaliation. The development of such an action-reaction syndrome then establishes the structure of the conflict between the regime and its challengers. There are numerous historical examples of a campaign of terrorism precipitated by a government's reliance on excessive force to quell protest or squash dissent. The tsarist regime's severity in dealing with the populist movement was a factor in the development of Narodaya Volya as a terrorist organization in 1879. The French government's persecution of anarchists was a factor in subsequent anarchist terrorism in the 1890s. The British government's execution of the heros of the Easter Rising set the stage for Michael Collins and the IRA. The Protestant violence that met the Catholic civil rights movement in Northern Ireland in 1969 pushed the Provisional IRA to retaliate. In West Germany, the death of Benno Ohnesorg at the hands of the police in a demonstration against the Shah of Iran in 1968 contributed to the emergence of the RAF.

This analysis of the background conditions for terrorism indicates that we must look at the terrorist organization's perception and interpretation of the situation. Terrorists view the context as permissive, making terrorism a viable option. In a material sense, the means are placed at their disposal by the environment. Circumstances also provide the terrorists with compelling reasons for seeking political change. Finally, an event occurs that snaps the terrorists' patience with the regime. Government action is now seen as intolerably unjust, and terrorism becomes not only a possible decision but a morally acceptable one. The regime has forfeited its status as the standard of legitimacy. For the terrorist, the end may now excuse the means.

The reasons for terrorism

Significant campaigns of terrorism depend on rational political choice. As purposeful activity, terrorism is the result of an organization's decision that it is a politically useful means to oppose a government. The argument that terrorist behavior should be analyzed as "rational" is based on the assumption that terrorist organizations possess internally consistent sets of values, beliefs, and images of the environment. Terrorism is seen collectively as a logical means to advance desired ends. The terrorist organization engages in decision-making calculations that an analyst can approximate. In short, the terrorist group's reasons for resorting to terrorism constitute an important factor in the process of causation.[17]

Terrorism serves a variety of goals, both revolutionary and subrevolutionary. Terrorists may be revolutionaries (such as the Combat Organization of the Socialist-Revolutionary Party in the nineteenth century or the Tupamaros of the twentieth); nationalists fighting against foreign occupiers (the Algerian FLN, the IRA of 1919–1921, or the Irgun); minority separatists combatting indigenous regimes (such as the Corsican, Breton, and Basque movements, and the Provisional IRA); reformists (the bombing of nuclear construction sites, for example, is meant to halt nuclear power, not to overthrow governments); anarchists or millenarians (such as the original anarchist movement of the nineteenth century and modern millenarian groups such as the Red Army faction in West Germany, the Italian Red Brigades, and the Japanese Red Army); or reactionaries acting to prevent change from the top (such as the Secret Army Organization during the Algerian war or the contemporary Ulster Defence Association in Northern Ireland).[18]

Saying that extremist groups resort to terrorism in order to acquire political influence does not mean that all groups have equally precise objectives or that the relationship between means and ends is perfectly clear to an outside observer. Some groups are less realistic about the logic of means and ends than others. The leaders of Narodnaya Volya, for example, lacked a detailed conception of how the assassination of the tsar would force his successor to permit the liberalization they sought. Other terrorist groups are more pragmatic: the IRA of 1919–21 and the Irgun, for instance, shrewdly foresaw the utility of a war of attrition against the British. Menachem Begin, in particular, planned his campaign to take advantage of the "glass house" that Britain operated in.[19] The degree of skill in relating means to ends seems to have little to do with the overall sophistication of the terrorist ideology. The French anarchists of the 1890s, for example, acted in light of a well-developed philosophical doctrine but were much less certain of how violence against the bourgeoisie would bring about freedom. It is possible that anarchist or millenarian terrorists are so preoccupied with the splendor of the future that they lose sight of the present. Less theoretical nationalists who concentrate on the short run have simpler aims but sharper plans.

However diverse the long-run goals of terrorist groups, there is a common pattern of proximate or short-run objectives of a terrorist strategy. Proximate objectives are defined in terms of the reactions that terrorists want to achieve in their different audiences.[20] The most basic reason for terrorism is to gain recognition or attention—what Thornton called advertisement of the cause. Violence and bloodshed always excite human curiosity, and the theatricality, suspense, and threat of danger inherent in terrorism enhance its attention getting qualities. In fact, publicity may be the highest goal of some groups. For example, terrorists who are fundamentally protesters might be satisfied with airing their grievances before the world. Today, in an interdependent world, the need for international recognition encourages transnational terrorist activities, with escalation to ever more destructive and spectacular violence. As the audience grows larger, more diverse, and more accustomed to terrorism, terrorists must go to extreme lengths to shock.

Terrorism is also often designed to disrupt and discredit the processes of government, by weakening it administratively and impairing normal operations. Terrorism as a direct attack on the regime aims at the insecurity and demoralization of government officials, independent of any impact on public opinion. An excellent example of this strategy is Michael Collins's campaign against the British intelligence system in Ireland in 1919–21. This form of terrorism often accompanies rural guerrilla warfare, as the insurgents try to weaken the government's control over its territory.

Terrorism also affects public attitudes in both a positive and a negative sense, aiming at creating either sympathy in a potential constituency or fear and hostility in an audience identified as the "enemy." These two functions are interrelated, since intimidating the "enemy" impresses both sympathizers and the uncommitted. At the same time, terrorism may be used to enforce obedience in an audience from whom the terrorists demand allegiance. The FLN in Algeria, for example, claimed more Algerian than French victims. Fear and respect were not incompatible with solidarity against the French.[21] When terrorism is part of a struggle between incumbents and challengers, polarization of public opinion undermines the government's legitimacy.

Terrorism may also be intended to provoke a counterreaction from the government, to increase publicity for the terrorists' cause and to demonstrate to the people that their charges against the regime are well founded. The terrorists mean to force the state to show its true repressive face, thereby driving the people into the arms of the challengers. For example, Carlos Marighela argued that the way to win popular support was to provoke the regime to measures of greater repression and persecution.[22] Provocative terrorism is designed to bring about revolutionary conditions rather than to exploit them. The FLN against the French, the Palestinians against Israel, and the RAF against the Federal Republic all appear to have used terrorism as provocation.

In addition, terrorism may serve internal organizational functions of control, discipline, and morale building within the terrorist group and even become an instrument of rivalry among factions in a resistance movement. For example, factional terrorism has frequently characterized the Palestinian resistance movement. Rival groups have competed in a vicious game where the victims are Israeli civilians or anonymous airline passengers, but where the immediate goal is influence within the resistance movement rather than the intimidation of the Israeli public or international recognition of the Palestinian cause.

Terrorism is a logical choice when oppositions have such goals and when the power ratio of government to challenger is high. The observation that terrorism is a weapon of the weak is hackneyed but apt. At least when initially adopted, terrorism is the strategy of a minority that by its own judgment lacks other means. When the group perceives its options as limited, terrorism is attractive because it is a relatively inexpensive and simple alternative, and because its potential reward is high.

Weakness and consequent restriction of choice can stem from different sources. On the one hand, weakness may result from the regime's suppression of opposition. Resistance organizations who lack the means of mounting more extensive violence may then turn to terrorism because legitimate expression of dissent is denied. Lack of popular support at the outset of a conflict does not mean that the terrorists' aims lack general appeal. Even though they cannot immediately mobilize widespread and active support, over the course of the conflict they may acquire the allegiance of the population. For example, the Algerian FLN used terrorism as a significant means of mobilizing mass support.[23]

On the other hand, it is wrong to assume that where there is terrorism there is oppression. Weakness may mean that an extremist organization deliberately rejects nonviolent methods of opposition open to them in a liberal state. Challengers then adopt terrorism because they are impatient with time-consuming legal methods of eliciting support or advertising their cause, because they distrust the regime, or because they are not capable of, or interested in, mobilizing majority support. Most terrorist groups operating in Western Europe and Japan in the past decade illustrate this phenomenon. The new millenarians lack a readily identifiable constituency and espouse causes devoid of mass appeal. Similarly, separatist movements represent at best only a minority of the total population of the state.

Thus, some groups are weak because weakness is imposed on them by the political system they operate in, others because of unpopularity. We are therefore making value judgments about the potential legitimacy of terrorist organizations. In some cases resistance groups are genuinely desperate, in others they have alternatives to violence. Nor do we want to forget that nonviolent resistance has been chosen in other circumstances, for example, by Gandhi and by Martin Luther King. Terrorists may argue that they had no choice, but their perceptions may be flawed.[24]

In addition to weakness, an important rationale in the decision to adopt a strategy of terrorism is impatience. Action becomes imperative. For a variety of reasons, the challenge to the state cannot be left to the future. Given a perception of limited means, the group often sees the choice as between action as survival and inaction as the death of resistance.

One reason for haste is external: the historical moment seems to present a unique chance. For example, the resistance group facing a colonial power recently weakened by a foreign war exploits a temporary vulnerability: the IRA against Britain after World War I, the Irgun against Britain after World War II, and the FLN against France after the Indochina war. We might even suggest that the stalemate between the United States and North Vietnam stimulated the post-1968 wave of anti-imperialist terrorism, especially in Latin America. There may be other pressures or catalysts provided by the regime, such as the violent precipitants discussed earlier or the British decision to introduce conscription in Ireland during World War I.

A sense of urgency may also develop when similar resistance groups have apparently succeeded with terrorism and created a momentum. The contagion effect of terrorism is partially based on an image of success that recommends terrorism to groups who identify with the innovator. The Algerian FLN, for example, was pressured to keep up with nationalists in Tunisia and Morocco, whose violent agitation brought about independence in 1956. Terrorism spread rapidly through Latin America in the post-1968 period as revolutionary groups worked in terms of a continental solidarity.

Dramatic failure of alternative means of obtaining one's ends may also fuel a drive toward terrorism. The Arab defeat in the 1967 war with Israel led Palestinians to realize that they could no longer depend on the Arab states to further their goals. In retrospect, their extreme weakness and the historical tradition of violence in the Middle East made it likely that militant nationalists should turn to terrorism. Since international recognition of the Palestinian cause was a primary aim (given the influence of outside powers in the region) and since attacks on Israeli territory were difficult, terrorism developed into a transnational phenomenon.

These external pressures to act are often intensified by internal politics. Leaders of resistance groups act under constraints imposed by their followers. They are forced to justify the organization's existence, to quell restlessness among the cadres, to satisfy demands for revenge, to prevent splintering of the movement, and to maintain control. Pressures may also come from the terrorists' constituency.

In conclusion, we see that terrorism is an attractive strategy to groups of different ideological persuasions who challenge the state's authority. Groups who want to dramatize a cause, to demoralize the government, to gain popular support, to provoke regime violence, to inspire followers, or to dominate a wider resistance movement, who are weak vis-à-vis the regime, and who are impatient to act, often find terrorism a reasonable choice. This is especially so when conditions are favorable, providing opportunities and making terrorism a simple and rapid option, with immediate and visible payoff.

Individual motivation and participation

Terrorism is neither an automatic reaction to conditions nor a purely calculated strategy. What psychological factors motivate the terrorist and influence his or her perceptions and interpretations of reality? Terrorists are only a small minority of people with similar personal backgrounds, experiencing the same conditions, who might thus be expected to reach identical conclusions based on logical reasoning about the utility of terrorism as a technique of political influence.

The relationship between personality and politics is complex and imperfectly understood.[25] Why individuals engage in political violence is a complicated problem, and the question why they engage in terrorism is still more difficult.[26] As most simply and frequently posed, the question of a psychological explanation of terrorism is whether or not there is a "terrorist personality," similar to the authoritarian personality, whose emotional traits we can specify with some exactitude.[27] An identifiable pattern of attitudes and behavior in the terrorism-prone individual would result from a combination of ego-defensive needs, cognitive processes, and socialization, in interaction with a specific situation. In pursuing this line of inquiry, it is important to avoid stereotyping the terrorist or oversimplifying the sources of terrorist actions. No single motivation or personality can be valid for all circumstances.

What limited data we have on individual terrorists (and knowledge must be gleaned from disparate sources that usually neither focus on psychology nor use a comparative approach) suggest that the outstanding common characteristic of terrorists is their normality. Terrorism often seems to be the connecting link among widely varying personalities. Franco Venturi, concentrating on the terrorists of a single small group, observed that "the policy of terrorism united many very different characters and mentalities" and that agreement on using terrorism was the cement that bound the members of Narodnaya Volya together.[28] The West German psychiatrist who conducted a pretrial examination of four members of the RAF concluded that they were "intelligent," even "humorous," and showed no symptoms of psychosis or neurosis and "no particular personality type."[29] Psychoanalysis might penetrate beneath superficial normality to expose some unifying or pathological trait, but this is scarcely a workable research method, even if the likelihood of the existence of such a characteristic could be demonstrated.

Peter Merkl, in his study of the pre-1933 Nazi movement—a study based on much more data than we have on terrorists—abandoned any attempt to classify personality types and instead focused on factors like the level of political understanding.[30] An unbiased examination of conscious attitudes might be more revealing than a study of subconscious predispositions or personalities. For example, if terrorists perceive the state as unjust, morally corrupt, and violent, then terrorism may seem legitimate and justified. For example, Blumenthal and her coauthors found that "the stronger the perception of an act as violence, the more violence is thought to be an appropriate response."[31] The evidence also indicates that many terrorists are activists with prior political experience in nonviolent opposition to the state. How do these experiences in participation influence later attitudes? Furthermore, how do terrorists view their victims? Do we find extreme devaluation, depersonalization, or stereotyping? Is there "us versus them" polarization or ethnic or religious prejudice that might sanction or prompt violence toward an out-group? How do terrorists justify and rationalize violence? Is remorse a theme?

The questions of attitudes toward victims and justifications for terrorism are especially important because different forms of terrorism involve various degrees of selectivity in the choice of victims. Some acts of terrorism are extremely discriminate, while others are broadly indiscriminate. Also, some terrorist acts require more intimate contact between terrorist and victim than others. Thus, the form of terrorism practiced—how selective it is and how much personal domination of the victim it involves—would determine the relevance of different questions.

Analyzing these issues involves serious methodological problems. As the Blumenthal study emphasizes, there are two ways of analyzing the relationship between attitudes and political behavior.[32] If our interest is in identifying potential terrorists by predicting behavior from the existence of certain consciously held attitudes and beliefs, then the best method would be to survey a young age group in a society determined to be susceptible. If terrorism subsequently occurred, we could then see which types of individuals became terrorists. (A problem is that the preconditions would change over time and that precipitants are unpredictable.) The more common and easier way of investigating the attitudes-behavior connection is to select people who have engaged in a particular behavior and ask them questions about their opinions. Yet attitudes may be adopted subsequent, rather than prior, to behavior, and they may serve as rationalizations for behavior engaged in for different reasons, not as genuine motivations. These problems would seem to be particularly acute when the individuals concerned have engaged in illegal forms of political behavior.

Another problem facing the researcher interested in predispositions or attitudes is that terrorists are recruited in different ways. Assuming that people who are in some way personally attracted to terrorism actually engage in such behavior supposes that potential terrorists are presented with an appropriate opportunity, which is a factor over which they have little control.[33] Moreover, terrorist groups often discourage or reject potential recruits who are openly seeking excitement or danger for personal motives. For instance, William Mackey Lomasney, a member of the Clan na Gael or American Fenians in the nineteenth century (who was killed in 1884 in an attempt to blow up London Bridge) condemned the "disgraceful" activities of the hotheaded and impulsive Jeremiah O'Donovan Rossa:

> Were it not that O'Donovan Rossa has openly and unblushingly boasted that he is responsible for those ridiculous and futile efforts … we might hesitate to even suspect that any sane man, least of all one professedly friendly to the cause, would for any consideration or desire for notoriety take upon himself such a fearful responsibility, and, that having done so, he could engage men so utterly incapable of carrying out his insane designs.[34]

Lomasney complained that the would-be terrorists were:

> such stupid blundering fools that they make our cause appear imbecile and farcical. When the fact becomes known that those half-idiotic attempts have been made by men professing to be patriotic Irishmen what will the world think but that Irish revolutionists are a lot of fools and ignoramuses, men who do not understand the first principles of the art of war, the elements of chemistry or even the amount of explosive material necessary to remove or destroy an ordinary brick or stone wall. Think of the utter madness of men who have no idea of accumulative and destructive forces undertaking with common blasting powder to scare and shatter the Empire.[35]

Not only do serious terrorists scorn the ineptitude of the more excitable, but they find them a serious security risk. Rossa, for example, could not be trusted not to give away the Clan na Gael's plans for terrorism in his New York newspaper articles. In a similar vein, Boris Savinkov, head of the Combat Organization of the Socialist-Revolutionary party in Russia, tried to discourage an aspirant whom he suspected of being drawn to the adventure of terrorism:

> I explained to him that terrorist activity did not consist only of throwing bombs; that it was much more minute, difficult and tedious than might be imagined; that a terrorist is called upon to live a rather dull existence for months at a time, eschewing meeting his own comrades and doing most difficult and unpleasant work—the work of systematic observation.[36]

Similar problems in analyzing the connection between attitudes and behavior are due to the fact that there are role differentiations between leaders and followers. The degree of formal organization varies from the paramilitary hierarchies of the Irgun or the IRA to the semiautonomous coexistence of small groups in contemporary West Germany or Italy or even to the rejection of central direction in the nineteenth century anarchist movement in France. Yet even Narodnaya Volya, a self-consciously democratic group, observed distinctions based on authority. There are thus likely to be psychological or background differences between leaders and cadres. For example, a survey of contemporary terrorist movements found that leaders are usually older than their followers, which is not historically unusual.[37] In general, data are scant on individual terrorist leaders, their exercise of authority, the basis for it, and their interactions with their followers.[38]

Furthermore, if there is a predisposition to terrorism, the terrorism-prone individual who obtains psychic gratification from the experience is likely to be a follower, not a leader who commands but does not perform the act.

An alternative approach to analyzing the psychology of terrorism is to use a deductive method based on what we know about terrorism as an activity, rather than an inductive method yielding general propositions from statements of the particular. What sort of characteristics would make an individual suited for terrorism? What are the role requirements of the terrorist?

One of the most salient attributes of terrorist activity is that it involves significant personal danger.[39] Furthermore, since terrorism involves premeditated, not impulsive, violence, the terrorist's awareness of the risks is maximized. Thus, although terrorists may simply be people who enjoy or disregard risk,[40] it is more likely that they are people who tolerate high risk because of intense commitment to a cause. Their commitment is strong enough to make the risk of personal harm acceptable and perhaps to outweigh the cost of society's rejection, although defiance of the majority may be a reward in itself. In either case, the violent activity is not gratifying per se.

It is perhaps even more significant that terrorism is a group activity, involving intimate relationships among a small number of people. Interactions among members of the group may be more important in determining behavior than the psychological predispositions of individual members. Terrorists live and make decisions under conditions of extreme stress. As a clandestine minority, the members of a terrorist group are isolated from society, even if they live in what Menachem Begin called the "open underground."[41]

Terrorists can confide in and trust only each other. The nature of their commitment cuts them off from society; they inhabit a closed community that is forsaken only at great cost. Isolation and the perception of a hostile environment intensify shared belief and commitment and make faith in the cause imperative. A pattern of mutual reassurance, solidarity, and comradeship develops, in which the members of the group reinforce each other's self-righteousness, image of a hostile world, and sense of mission. Because of the real danger terrorists confront, the strain they live under, and the moral conflicts they undergo, they value solidarity highly.[42] Terrorists are not necessarily people who seek "belonging" or personal integration through ideological commitment, but once embarked on the path of terrorism, they desperately need the group and the cause. Isolation and internal consensus explain how the beliefs and values of a terrorist group can be so drastically at odds with those of society at large. An example of such a divorce from social and political reality is the idea of the RAF that terrorism would lead to a resurgence of Nazism in West Germany that would in turn spark a workers' revolt.[43]

In their intense commitment, separation from the outside world, and intolerance of internal dissent, terrorist groups resemble religious sects or cults. Michael Barkun has explained the continued commitment of members of millenarian movements, a conviction frequently expressed in proselytizing in order to validate beliefs, in terms of the reinforcement and reassurance of rightness that the individual receives from other members of the organization. He also notes the frequent practice of initiation rites that involve violations of taboos, or "bridge-burning acts," that create guilt and prevent the convert's return to society. Thus the millenarian, like the terrorist group, constitutes "a community of common guilt."[44] J. Bowyer Bell has commented on the religious qualities of dedication and moral fervor characterizing the IRA: "In the Republican Movement, the two seemingly opposing traditions, one of the revolution and physical force, and the other of pious and puritanical service, combine into a secular vocation."[45]

If there is a single common emotion that drives the individual to become a terrorist, it is vengeance on behalf of comrades or even the constituency the terrorist aspires to represent. (At the same time, the demand for retribution serves as public justification or excuse.) A regime thus encourages terrorism when it creates martyrs to be avenged. Anger at what is perceived as unjust persecution inspires demands for revenge, and as the regime responds to terrorism with greater force, violence escalates out of control.

There are numerous historical demonstrations of the central role vengeance plays as motivation for terrorism. It is seen as one of the principal causes of anarchist terrorism in France in the 1890s. The infamous Ravachol acted to avenge the "martyrs of Clichy," two possibly innocent anarchists who were beaten by the police and sentenced to prison. Subsequent bombings and assassinations, for instance that of President Carnot, were intended to avenge Ravachol's execution.[46] The cruelty of the sentences imposed for minor offenses at the "Trial of the 193," the hanging of eleven southern revolutionaries after Soloviev's unsuccessful attack on the tsar in 1879, and the "Trial of the 16" in 1880 deeply affected the members of Narodnaya Volya. Kravchinski (Stepniak) explained that personal resentment felt after the Trial of the 193 led to killing police spies; it then seemed unreasonable to spare their employers, who were actually responsible for the repression. Thus, intellectually the logic first inspired by resentment compelled them to escalate terrorism by degrees.[47] During the Algerian war, the French execution of FLN prisoners; in Northern Ireland, British troops firing on civil rights demonstrators; in West Germany, the death of a demonstrator at the hands of the police—all served to precipitate terrorism as militants sought to avenge their comrades.

The terrorists' willingness to accept high risks may also be related to the belief that one's death will be avenged. The prospect of retribution gives the act of terrorism and the death of the terrorist meaning and continuity, even fame and immortality. Vengeance may be not only a function of anger but of a desire for transcendence.

Shared guilt is surely a strong force in binding members of the terrorist group together. Almost all terrorists seem compelled to justify their behavior, and this anxiety cannot be explained solely by reference to their desire to create a public image of virtuous sincerity. Terrorists usually show acute concern for morality, especially for sexual purity, and believe that they act in terms of a higher good. Justifications usually focus on past suffering, on the glorious future to be created, and on the regime's illegitimacy and violence, to which terrorism is the only available response. Shared guilt and anxiety increase the group's interdependence and mutual commitment and may also make followers more dependent on leaders and on the common ideology as sources of moral authority.

Guilt may also lead terrorists to seek punishment and danger rather than avoid it. The motive of self-sacrifice notably influenced many Russian terrorists of the nineteenth century. Kaliayev, for example, felt that only his death could atone for the murder he committed. Even to Camus, the risk of death for the terrorist is a form of personal absolution.[48] In other cases of terrorism, individuals much more pragmatic than Kaliayev, admittedly a religious mystic, seemed to welcome capture because it brought release from the strains of underground existence and a sense of content and fulfillment. For example, Meridor, a member of the Irgun High Command, felt "high spirits" and "satisfaction" when arrested by the British because he now shared the suffering that all fighters had to experience. He almost welcomed the opportunity to prove that he was prepared to sacrifice himself for the cause. In fact, until his arrest he had felt "morally uncomfortable," whereas afterwards he felt "exalted."[49] Menachem Begin expressed similar feelings. Once, waiting as the British searched the hotel where he was staying, he admitted anxiety and fear, but when he knew there was "no way out," his "anxious thoughts evaporated." He "felt a peculiar serenity mixed with incomprehensible happiness" and waited "composedly," but the police passed him by.[50]

Vera Figner, a leader of the Narodnaya Volya, insisted on physically assisting in acts of terrorism, even though her comrades accused her of seeking personal satisfaction instead of allowing the organization to make the best use of her talents. She found it intolerable to bear a moral responsibility for acts that endangered her comrades. She could not encourage others to commit acts she would not herself commit; anything less than full acceptance of the consequences of her decisions would be cowardice.[51]

It is possible that the willingness to face risk is related to what Robert J. Lifton has termed "survivor-guilt" as well as to feelings of group solidarity or of guilt at harming victims.[52] Sometimes individuals who survive disaster or escape punishment when others have suffered feel guilty and may seek relief by courting a similar fate. This guilt may also explain why terrorists often take enormous risks to rescue imprisoned comrades, as well as why they accept danger or arrest with equanimity or even satisfaction.

It is clear that once a terrorist group embarks on a strategy of terrorism, whatever its purpose and whatever its successes or failures, psychological factors make it very difficult to halt. Terrorism as a process gathers its own momentum, independent of external events.

Conclusions

Terrorism per se is not usually a reflection of mass discontent or deep cleavages in society. More often it represents the disaffection of a fragment of the elite, who may take it upon themselves to act on the behalf of a majority unaware of its plight, unwilling to take action to remedy grievances, or unable to express dissent. This discontent, however subjective in origin or minor in scope, is blamed on the government and its supporters. Since the sources of terrorism are manifold, any society or polity that permits opportunities for terrorism is vulnerable. Government reactions that are inconsistent, wavering between tolerance and repression, seem most likely to encourage terrorism.

Given some source of disaffection—and in the centralized modern state with its faceless bureaucracies, lack of responsiveness to demands is ubiquitous—terrorism is an attractive strategy for small organizations of diverse ideological persuasions who want to attract attention for their cause, provoke the government, intimidate opponents, appeal for sympathy, impress an audience, or promote the adherence of the faithful. Terrorists perceive an absence of choice. Whether unable or unwilling to perceive a choice between terrorist and nonterrorist action, whether unpopular or prohibited by the government, the terrorist group reasons that there is no alternative. The ease, simplicity, and rapidity with which terrorism can be implemented and the prominence of models of terrorism strengthen its appeal, especially since terrorist groups are impatient to act. Long-standing social traditions that sanction terrorism against the state, as in Ireland, further enhance its attractiveness.

There are two fundamental questions about the psychological basis of terrorism. The first is why the individual takes the first step and chooses to engage in terrorism: why join? Does the terrorist possess specific psychological predispositions, identifiable in advance, that suit him or her for terrorism? That terrorists are people capable of intense commitment tells us little, and the motivations for terrorism vary immensely. Many individuals are potential terrorists, but few actually make that commitment. To explain why terrorism happens, another question is more appropriate: Why does involvement continue? What are the psychological mechanisms of group interaction? We are not dealing with a situation in which certain types of personalities suddenly turn to terrorism in answer to some inner call. Terrorism is the result of a gradual growth of commitment and opposition, a group development that furthermore depends on government action. The psychological relationships within the terrorist group—the interplay of commitment, risk, solidarity, loyalty, guilt, revenge, and isolation—discourage terrorists from changing the direction they have taken. This may explain why—even if objective circumstances change when, for example, grievances are satisfied, or if the logic of the situation changes when, for example, the terrorists are offered other alternatives for the expression of opposition—terrorism may endure until the terrorist group is physically destroyed.

Notes

1　For discussions of the meaning of the concept of terrorism, see Thomas P. Thornton, "Terror as a Weapon of Political Agitation," in Harry Eckstein, ed. *Internal War* (New York, 1964), pp. 71–99; Martha Crenshaw Hutchinson, "The Concept of Revolutionary Terrorism," *Revolutionary Terrorism: The FLN in Algeria, 1954–1962* (Stanford: The Hoover Institution Press, 1978) chap. 2; and E. Victor Walter, *Terror and Resistance* (New York, 1969).

2　Walter Laqueur, "Interpretations of Terrorism—Fact, Fiction and Political Science," *Journal of Contemporary History*, 12 (January 1977), 1–42. See also his major work *Terrorism* (London: Weidenfeld and Nicolson, 1977).

3　See, for example, Paul Wilkinson, *Terrorism and the Liberal State* (London: Macmillan, 1977), or J. Bowyer Bell, *A Time of Terror: How Democratic Societies Respond to Revolutionary Violence* (New York, 1978).

4　This is not to deny that some modem terrorist groups, such as those in West Germany, resemble premodern millenarian movements. See specifically Conor Cruise O'Brien, "Liberty and Terrorism," *International Security*, 2 (1977), 56–67. In general, see Norman Cohn, *The Pursuit of the Millenium* (London: Secker and Warburg, 1957), and E.J. Hobsbawm, *Primitive Rebels: Studies in Archaic Forms of Social Movement in the 19th and 20th Centuries* (Manchester: Manchester University Press, 1971).

5　A sampling would include Douglas Hibbs, Jr., *Mass Political Violence: A Cross-National Causal Analysis* (New York, 1973); William J. Crotty, ed. *Assassinations and the Political Order* (New York, 1971); Ted Robert Gurr, *Why Men Rebel* (Princeton, 1971), and Gurr, Peter N. Grabosky, and Richard C. Hula, *The Politics of Crime and Conflict* (Beverly Hills, 1977).

6　For a summary of these findings, see Gurr, "The Calculus of Civil Conflict," *Journal of Social Issues*, 28 (1972), 27–47.

7　Gurr, "Some Characteristics of Political Terrorism in the 1960s," in Michael Stohl, ed. *The Politics of Terrorism* (New York, 1979), pp. 23–50 and 46–47.

8　A distinction between preconditions and precipitants is found in Eckstein, "On the Etiology of Internal Wars," *History and Theory*, 4 (1965), 133–162. Kenneth Waltz also differentiates between the framework for action as a permissive or underlying cause and special reasons as immediate or efficient causes. In some cases we can say of terrorism, as he says of war, that it occurs because there is nothing to prevent it. See *Man, the State and War* (New York, 1959), p. 232.

9　Boris Savinkov, *Memoirs of a Terrorist*, trans. Joseph Shaplen (New York: A. & C. Boni, 1931), pp. 286–287.

10　The major theoreticians of the transition from the rural to the urban guerrilla are Carlos Marighela, *For the Liberation of Brazil* (Harmondsworth: Penguin Books, 1971), and Abraham Guillen, *Philosophy of the Urban Guerrilla: The Revolutionary Writings of Abraham Guillen*, trans. and edited by Donald C. Hodges (New York, 1973).

11　Hobsbawm, *Revolutionaries: Contemporary Essays* (New York, 1973), pp. 226–227.

12　Grabosky, "The Urban Context of Political Terrorism," in Michael Stohl, ed., pp. 51–76.

13　See Amy Sands Redlick, "The Transnational Flow of Information as a Cause of Terrorism," in Yonah Alexander, David Carlton, and Wilkinson, eds. *Terrorism: Theory and Practice* (Boulder, 1979), pp. 73–95. See also Manus I. Midlarsky, Martha Crenshaw, and Fumihiko Yoshida, "Why Violence Spreads: The Contagion of International Terrorism," *International Studies Quarterly*, 24 (June 1980), 262–298.

14　Monica D. Blumenthal, et al., *More About Justifying Violence: Methodological Studies of Attitudes and Behavior* (Ann Arbor: Survey Research Center, Institute for Social Research, University of Michigan, 1975), p. 108. Similarly, Peter Lupsha, "Explanation of Political Violence: Some Psychological Theories Versus Indignation," *Politics and Society*, 2 (1971), 89–104, contrasts the concept of "indignation" with Gurr's theory of relative deprivation, which holds that expectations exceed rewards (see *Why Men Rebel*, esp. pp. 24–30).

15　Hobsbawm, *Revolutionaries*, p. 143.

16　Luigi Bonanate, "Some Unanticipated Consequences of Terrorism," *Journal of Peace Research*, 16 (1979), 197–211. If this theory is valid, we then need to identify such blocked societies.

17　See Barbara Salert's critique of the rational choice model of revolutionary participation in *Revolutions and Revolutionaries* (New York, 1976). In addition, Abraham Kaplan discusses the distinction between reasons and causes in "The Psychodynamics of Terrorism," *Terrorism—An International Journal*, 1, 3 and 4 (1978), 237–254.

18 For a typology of terrorist organizations, see Wilkinson, *Political Terrorism* (New York, 1975). These classes are not mutually exclusive, and they depend on an outside assessment of goals. For example, the Basque ETA would consider itself revolutionary as well as separatist. The RAF considered itself a classic national liberation movement, and the Provisional IRA insists that it is combatting a foreign oppressor, not an indigenous regime.

19 Bell presents a succinct analysis of Irgun strategy in "The Palestinian Archetype: Irgun and the Strategy of Leverage," in *On Revolt: Strategies of National Liberation* (Cambridge [Ma.], 1976), chap. 3.

20 See Thornton's analysis of proximate goals in "Terror as a Weapon of Political Agitation," in Eckstein, ed. pp. 82–88.

21 Walter's discussion of the concept of "forced choice" explains how direct audiences, from whom the victims are drawn, may accept terrorism as legitimate; see *Terror and Resistance*, pp. 285–289.

22 See Marighela, *For the Liberation of Brazil*, pp. 94–95. The West German RAF apparently adopted the idea of provocation as part of a general national liberation strategy borrowed from the Third World.

23 See Hutchinson, *Revolutionary Terrorism*, chap. 3, pp. 40–60.

24 See Michael Walzer's analysis of the morality of terrorism in *Just and Unjust Wars* (New York, 1977), pp. 197–206. See also Bernard Avishai, "In Cold Blood," *The New York Review of Books*, March 8, 1979, pp. 41–44, for a critical appraisal of the failure of recent works on terrorism to discuss moral issues. The question of the availability of alternatives to terrorism is related to the problem of discrimination in the selection of victims. Where victims are clearly responsible for a regime's denial of opportunity, terrorism is more justifiable than where they are not.

25 See Fred I. Greenstein, *Pesonality and Politics: Problems of Evidence, Inference, and Conceptualization* (Chicago, 1969).

26 See Jeffrey Goldstein, *Aggression and Crimes of Violence* (New York, 1975).

27 A study of the West German New Left, for example, concludes that social psychological models of authoritarianism do help explain the dynamics of radicalism and even the transformation from protest to terrorism. See S. Robert Lichter, "A Psychopolitical Study of West German Male Radical Students," *Comparative Politics*, 12 (October 1979), pp. 27–48.

28 Franco Venturi, *Roots of Revolution: A History of the Populist and Socialist Movements in Nineteenth Century Russia* (London: Weidenfeld and Nicolson, 1960), p. 647.

29 Quoted in *Science*, 203, 5 January 1979, p. 34, as part of an account of the proceedings of the International Scientific Conference on Terrorism held in Berlin, December, 1978. Advocates of the "terrorist personality" theory, however, argued that terrorists suffer from faulty vestibular functions in the middle ear or from inconsistent mothering resulting in dysphoria. For another description see John Wykert, "Psychiatry and Terrorism," *Psychiatric News*, 14 (February 2, 1979), 1 and 12–14. A psychologist's study of a single group, the Front de Libération du Québec, is Gustav Morf, *Terror in Quebec: Case Studies of the FLQ* (Toronto: Clarke, Irvin, and Co., 1970).

30 Peter Merkl, *Political Violence Under the Swastika: 581 Early Nazis* (Princeton, 1974), 33–34.

31 Blumenthal, et al., p. 182.

32 Ibid., p. 12. Lichter also recognizes this problem

33 Ibid., pp. 12–13.

34 William O'Brien and Desmond Ryan, eds. *Devoy's Post Bag*, vol. II (Dublin: C.J. Fallon, Ltd., 1953), p. 51.

35 Ibid., p. 52.

36 Savinkov, *Memoirs*, p. 147.

37 Charles A. Russell and Bowman H. Miller, "Profile of a Terrorist," *Terrorism—An International Journal*, 1 (1977), reprinted in John D. Elliott and Leslie K. Gibson, eds. *Contemporary Terrorism: Selected Readings* (Gaithersburg, Md.: International Association of Chiefs of Police, 1978), pp. 81–95.

38 See Philip Pomper's analysis of the influence of Nechaev over his band of followers: "The People's Revenge," *Sergei Nechaev* (New Brunswick [N.J.], 1979), chap. 4.

39 A Rand Corporation study of kidnappings and barricade-and-hostage incidents concluded that such tactics are not necessarily perilous, while admitting that drawing statistical inferences from a small number of cases in a limited time period (August, 1968 to June, 1975) is hazardous. See Brian Jenkins, Janera Johnson, and David Ronfeldt, *Numbered Lives: Some Statistical Observations from 77 International Hostage Episodes,* Rand Paper P-5905 (Santa Monica: The Rand Corporation, 1977).

40 Psychiatrist Frederick Hacker, for example, argues that terrorists are by nature indifferent to risk; see *Crusaders, Criminals and Crazies* (New York, 1976), p. 13.

41 Menachem Begin, *The Revolt* (London: W.H. Allen, 1951).

42 J. Glenn Gray, "The Enduring Appeals of Battle," *The Warriors: Reflections on Men in Battle* (New York, 1970), chap. 2, describes similar experiences among soldiers in combat.

43 Statements of the beliefs of the leaders of the RAF can be found in *Textes des prisonniers de la Fraction armée rouge et dernières lettres d'Ulrike Meinhof* (Paris: Maspéro, 1977).

44 Michael Barkun, *Disaster and the Millennium* (New Haven, 1974), pp. 14–16. See also Leon Festinger, et al., *When Prophecy Fails* (New York, 1964).

45 Bell, *The Secret Army* (London: Anthony Blond, 1970), p. 379.

46 Jean Maitron, *Histoire du mouvement anarchiste en France (1880–1914)* (Paris: Societe universitairé d'éditions et de librairie, 1955), pp. 242–243.

47 S. Stepniak (pseudonym for Kravchinski), *Underground Russia: Revolutionary Profiles and Sketches from Life* (London: Smith, Elder, and Co., 1882), pp. 36–37; see also Venturi, pp. 639 and 707–708.

48 See "Les meurtriers délicats" in *L'Homme Révolté* (Paris: Gallimard, 1965), pp. 571–579.

49 Ya'acov Meridor, *Long is the Road to Freedom* (Tujunga [Ca.]: Barak Publications, 1961), pp. 6 and 9.

50 Begin, p. 111.

51 Vera Figner, *Mémoires d'une révolutionnaire*, trans. Victor Serge (Paris: Gallimard, 1930), pp. 131 and 257–262.

52 Such an argument is applied to Japanese Red Army terrorist Kozo Okamoto by Patricia Steinhof in "Portrait of a Terrorist," *Asian Survey*, 16 (1976), 830–885.

8 Turning to terror

The conditions under which political parties turn to terrorist activities

Leonard Weinberg

At first view political parties and terrorist groups would seem to have little in common with one another.[1] For a long time parties have been celebrated, if not always by voters then certainly among political scientists, as indispensable components of a democratic political order, as institutions that afford the means by which economic and social differences in society may be resolved peacefully. Terrorist groups, by contrast, are regarded as organizations whose use of violence is intended to circumvent or destroy the democratic political process. At times leaders of terrorist groups even exhibit some sensitivity for the higher regard in which political parties are held. Thus, spokesmen for the *Sendero Luminoso* (Shining Path) movement in Peru deny that Shining Path is the correct name of their organization. The bourgeois press may call it Shining Path, but its spokesmen prefer their organization to be known as the Communist Party of Peru.[2]

In addition to their choice of strategies, one peaceful, the other violent, and the reputations they enjoy among those committed to the principles of democratic government, there are other obvious ways in which parties and terrorist groups seem to differ. Structurally, the latter are thought to be small clandestine bands whose adherents do everything they can to evade public notice until such time as they are prepared to carry out an operation. On the other hand, political parties are conceived as large and often bureaucratized organizations which perform their various tasks in full public view with an eye to mobilizing voters and winning elections.

Ostensibly parties and terrorist groups would seem to share at least one thing in common: a commitment to the achievement of some political goal or public purpose. Yet, though few observers would deny that parties are political organizations *par excellence*, a good deal of the analysis to which terrorist groups have been subjected has challenged the authenticity of their public purposes. In some instances, observers have sought to depoliticize terrorist groups by emphasizing the private psychological needs of their members. Beginning with such figures as Dostoevski and Lombroso in the nineteenth century and continuing into the 1980s, there has been a tendency to see terrorist groups less as political organizations than as mental asylums whose public slogans disguise their inmates psychopathologies.[3] Other analysts have achieved the same result by reporting instances when terrorist groups have deteriorated into or have developed links with criminal gangs whose armed struggles have more to do with pecuniary considerations than politics.[4]

Even the circumstances surrounding the emergence of modern terrorism over the last third of the nineteenth century provide reasons for rejecting any commonality between parties and terrorist groups. The appeals of anarchism, whose followers were responsible for many of the assassinations, bombings, and other acts of terrorist violence that marked this era, were based on an explicit rejection of the political party as an institution capable of achieving the revolutionary liberation of the European working classes from their oppressors. From the anarchist perspective, the structural needs of political parties, for example, discipline and hierarchy, were signs of authoritarian domination to whose elimination from the wider society they were committed.[5]

In sum, these preliminary remarks suggest their author has chosen a singularly unpromising subject about which to write. But as in love, so too in politics, first impressions may be somewhat misleading. A closer inspection will provide greater grounds for optimism.

To begin, political parties and terrorist groups appear to thrive in roughly similar environments. Neither competing parties nor terrorist organizations are able to endure in closed societies ruled by strong authoritarian regimes. Despite the difference they display in relation to democratic political processes, it is in relatively open societies with self-restrained if not always democratic governments that both seem to do well. Indeed, as recent experiences in Turkey, Argentina, and Uruguay suggest, serious terrorist problems can be resolved quite rapidly when democracy is ended by the military's seizure of power.

Second, it is not true that terrorist groups are necessarily small clandestine bands while modern political parties consistently have large memberships and conduct their business in public. The Montoneros in Argentina, Hizbollah (the party of God) in Lebanon, and the Tamil Tigers in Sri Lanka are all groups which have attracted thousands of followers despite their having been responsible for many well-publicized terrorist operations.[6] The particular operations may be carried out by a handful of individuals, but the size of the band need not be the same as that of the organization of which it is a part. Furthermore, terrorist groups need not operate in total clandestinity. Some countries sympathetic to the terrorists' causes have provided them sanctuaries from which they may conduct their political activities in a perfectly open manner. Even where this is not the case, groups such as the Italian Red Brigades and Front Line were able to make use of privately owned radio stations (for example, Radio Sherwood) to convey their views to the public.

If terrorist groups are not always small or clandestine, political parties need not be large and open. In many democracies there are minor parties with few members and meager support in the electorate.[7] In various dictatorships where open political competition is prohibited, parties are compelled either to operate on an underground basis or conduct their work from locations in exile. The cases of Fascist Italy and Spain under Franco's rule are illustrative.

Nor is it true political parties invariably pursue their goals by peaceful means. As Duverger reminded us many years ago, some devotee parties develop militias or private armies in order to protect their public meetings and intimidate their opponents.[8] And as recent events in Lebanon suggest, this practice has not been confined to the emergence of fascism during the interwar period in Europe. Certainly Leninist parties with revolutionary aspirations have been willing to employ violence when their leaders believe the appropriate conditions are at hand.

On the other side of the ledger, terrorist groups by definition are organizations that commit acts of terrorist violence. But they need not do this indefinitely. At least some of them have abandoned the armed struggle and sought to pursue their goals by peaceful means. Recent rhetoric suggests such a "strategic shift" may be occurring within the PLO.[9]

The tendency to question the authenticity of terrorist groups' commitments to political goals has been matched by a body of literature that casts similar doubts on party organizations. The observations of Dostoevski and Lombroso et al. have their echoes in the writings of Michels and Lasswell with their assertions concerning the private material and psychological needs of party politicians.[10] Furthermore, linkages between political parties and criminal organizations are not totally unheard of phenomena in some western democracies at the present time.[11]

Even the historical division between parties and terrorist groups may not be as clear as it appears initially. During the 1870s in Czarist Russia members of the People's Will *(Narodny Volya)*, widely regarded as the first modern terrorist group, thought of themselves as belonging to a political party.[12] And at the beginning of the twentieth century the Russian Social Revolutionaries, which aspired to become a mass socialist party, formed the Combat Organization for the purpose of waging a campaign of terror against representatives of the autocracy until such time as a constituent assembly was selected by democratic means.[13]

At this stage of the inquiry the reader may be persuaded that political parties and terrorist groups have more in common with one another than was suspected initially. But to say that on occasion they may display certain similarities is not the same as asserting the existence of links or ties between the two types of organizations. Detecting the latter is the purpose of this investigation.

Before pursuing this inquiry, though, it may be helpful to review some of the prevailing understandings concerning the organizational careers of parties and terrorist groups from their origins to their ends. By engaging in this exercise, we may gain a better grasp of the problem with which we are confronted.

Organizational careers of parties and terrorist groups

Political scientists have developed clear understandings of the conditions which promote the formation of political parties. In reviewing the literature some observers classify the prevailing explanations under three general headings: institutional, historical crises, and modernization theories.[14] According to the first line of reasoning, the formation of parties, at least in the western world, was associated with the achievement of a more powerful role for parliament and the extension of the franchise to progressively wider segments of the population, with particular emphasis on the latter. Factions within and political associations of various kinds outside parliament took advantage of these changing conditions to develop the organizational means of getting their sympathizers elected to office and calling their views to public attention. Thus, political parties were born.[15]

The particular crises which some observers believe have inspired political party formation are ones involving legitimacy, integration, and participation.[16] In the first case, challenges to the authority of those in power (traditional monarchies in eighteenth and nineteenth century Europe and colonial administrations in twentieth century Africa and Asia) by small oppositional elites led the latter to mobilize popular support in an effort to establish representative institutions or bring an end to foreign domination. In the course of these struggles political parties were organized. Parties have also emerged in the context of integration crises. Commonly, groups and associations seeking to represent various regionally based ethnic or religious communities have formed parties as part of their efforts to achieve local self-rule or independence from the larger nation. Also, parties have been formed to pursue the opposite goal, that of achieving some measure of national unity in countries composed of diverse tribal, ethnic, and religious groups. Finally, the growing sense that some segment of a national population, for example, the working class, has been denied the right to participate in the political process has led its champions to create parties as a means of winning the franchise and having its interests taken into consideration.

Other analysts discuss the emergence of political parties in the context of the modernization of society. Lipset and Rokkan, for instance, refer to the impact of two revolutions, national and industrial.[17] According to this understanding, efforts by modernizing elites in eighteenth and nineteenth century Europe to establish a unified nation-state were met by opposition from traditional religious institutions and tradition-bound agrarian notables. In addition, the industrialization of the economy, bringing with it a host of concomitant changes, had the effect of causing the formation of new classes in society. In short, the national and industrial revolutions stimulated the development or caused the proliferation of a variety of social cleavages between center and periphery, state and church, agriculture and industry, worker and owner. Political parties emerged as organizations designed to express the interests in the political arena of those segments of the population affected by these modernizing trends.

All three sets of explanations intended to account for political party formation share a common broad perspective. Parties are seen as the product of important changes in the structure of state and society. But party formation need not be the outcome of such developments. The historical record abounds with instances of new parties emerging from unresolvable factional disagreements within existing ones. Alternatively, new parties have been formed as the result of mergers between existing ones. A number of factors may be at work here, but some analysts pay particular attention to incentives provided by modifications in electoral laws, especially those determining how the votes are counted.[18]

In general, the situation with respect to the appearance of terrorist groups in politics is different. Some influential observers believe this phenomenon defies explanation, while others look to idiosyncratic events for the origins of terrorist groups. The matter seems less settled than is true for the genesis of political parties.

A few analysts have argued that, in view of their small size and the fact they have emerged in so many different historical and societal contexts, it is impossible to generalize about what causes terrorist groups to come into being.[19] It has been asked rhetorically whether it is possible to deduce the Symbionese Liberation Army from changes in the demographic characteristics of the state of California. According to this line of reasoning, the social science tools used to explain outbreaks of mass violence, riots, popular protests, revolutions, and civil wars are inappropriate when the dependent variable is a group consisting of no more than one or two dozen individuals. The reader is referred to the protagonists' autobiographies or the fictions of Conrad and O'Casey.

At the other extreme are analysts who believe they have identified the single most important or even exclusive cause of terrorist group activity: conspiracy. From this perspective, most contemporary terrorist groups are the product of a scheme devised by the Soviets and their allies to destabilize the western democracies by providing support for tiny bands of alienated and violent individuals located within the NATO countries or in Third World nations sympathetic to the West.[20] Whatever its merits and deficiencies, at one time this account won the endorsement of an American secretary of state and a few other influential figures elsewhere.

Yet these two efforts, one emphasizing randomness and the other conspiracy, to account for the appearance of terrorist groups are hardly the only ones available to the reader. Other analysts have provided commentaries which fit more comfortably into the explanatory apparatus of the social sciences and which exhibit some similarities to the accounts of the origins of political parties.

For some, the modernization of society has been identified as a permissive factor in the stimulation of terrorist group activity.[21] The modern urban environment offers terrorists a multiplicity of attractive targets. The modern mass media provide opportunities for terrorist groups to communicate their ideas to different audiences. In addition to offering attractive targets, modern forms of mass transportation make it easy for terrorists to move from one site to another in the course of carrying out their various operations.

Also according to this interpretation, terrorist groups, like political parties, often though not always emerge in response to broad social cleavages and discontents. The unattended grievances of various ethnic and religious minorities furnish the most obvious examples. In these instances, however, the discontents are usually not deep enough by themselves to provoke the organization of a popularly based mass movement or political party.

In the political realm the explanations diverge. As we have noted, the rise of political parties is often associated with the extension of the franchise and enhanced opportunities for mass participation. But according to this analysis, the formation of terrorist groups is linked to the performances of regimes that frustrate demands for broadened participation, if not to all, then to some segments of the population.

In fact, the body of writing these remarks seek to summarize stresses the relationship between failure and the recourse to terrorism. Terrorism and terrorist groups emerge in situations where alienated and highly motivated elites confront the indifference of the population they hope to lead in challenging those in positions of power. As one observer puts it: "Perhaps terrorism is most likely to occur precisely where mass passivity and elite dissatisfaction coincide."[22] Other commentaries in this vein link the rise of terrorist groups to the collapse of mass movements, particularly student based ones, whose leaders were unable to achieve their goals or sustain the emotions associated with their causes.[23]

As against the accounts concerning the formation of political parties, those seeking to explain the initiation of terrorist groups commonly refer to some dramatic event(s) that provides a sufficient shock to cause a group of individuals to embark on the terrorist path. Massacres, acts of indiscriminate repression by the police or military, a disastrous political setback often provide the immediate stimulus for the decision. Political parties seem more likely to be the products of longer periods of gestation.

After parties and terrorist groups make their appearances in the political arena, their observers have devoted enormous attention to their relationships with other forces in their environments. In the case of terrorist groups these discussions have been focused on their ties to various sympathetic governments in the Middle East and elsewhere with incentives to support their activities covertly.[24] Similarly, the literature provides discussion of the antagonistic relationship between the groups and those governments they seek to threaten. The symbiotic relationship between terrorists and the mass media, particularly television, has been the subject of extended commentary. Important things have been written about the physical and psychological impact of terrorist events on victims who have been taken captive. There are also accounts, usually speculative, of the effects of terrorist operations in mobilizing the support of social classes, ethnic communities, and issue publics, whose diverse causes the terrorist groups attempt to champion.[25]

The linkages between political parties and other elements in their environments come close to being the stock in trade of those interested in the study of party politics.[26] Certainly no brief commentary could conceivably do the topic justice.

Much has been written about the relationships parties have developed with interest groups of one type or another. Certainly a major focus of concern has been the capacity of parties to win control of governmental institutions at national and subnational levels. The competitive relationships parties often have with one another have hardly gone unnoticed. And obviously the same may be said in connection with the sources of support parties achieve in the relevant national populations.

Except for fleeting references, little attention has been paid to links between parties and terrorist organizations. Terrorism is, after all, not an ideology but a technique, one of a repertoire of techniques that political groups may employ to advance their interests, be they the installation of a dictatorship of the proletariat or the closing down of abortion clinics. Thus, it seems at least conceivable that the two types of political organizations may have more to do with one another than is reflected in the contemporary literature.

One thing parties and terrorist groups clearly have in common is the experience of failure. Not only do they often fail to achieve their ostensible political aims, but they frequently cease to exist as well.

The most widely discussed end of terrorist groups is defeat or preemption.[27] The authorities with whom the terrorists are in conflict succeed in destroying their organizations and arresting or killing their members. A long list of modern terrorist groups have met their end in this manner.

But defeat is hardly the only way in which these groups cease to exist. The literature also refers to their collapse for predominantly internal reasons as well. Instances of "burnout" or disintegration are not uncommon. The commitments of the members to the group may wane as the result of a host of factors. Boredom, an excess of ideological debate, factional divisions, the arrest, death, or defection of comrades, an inability to recruit new members, and public expressions of hostility by segments of the population whose support the terrorists thought they had or hoped to win, all of these demoralizing occurrences have contributed to a decision to abandon the struggle and end the group's violent activities.

Finally, there have been instances in which a terrorist group has made a "strategic shift." These are situations where the organization itself may persist but its leaders make a decision to pursue their objectives by means other than terrorism. This decision may be reached because the violence has proven to be ineffective or because it has outlived its usefulness. New circumstances may require different techniques, other approaches. A desire to achieve respectability in domestic or international politics may trigger the reaction.

Among the several ways in which political parties end, the one that appears closest to the experiences of terrorist groups is repression. On occasion democratic regimes have been replaced by authoritarian ones whose leaders, often military, then compel the dissolution of all existing political parties. In other cases, one political party will win control of the state and then use this power to eliminate its erstwhile rivals in the system. And even in the democracies, individual parties whose outlooks are regarded as extremist, subversive, or anticonstitutional have been banned.

But as with terrorist groups, so too with political parties, there are circumstances when the end comes even in the absence of external coercion. One study devoted to the careers of all political parties in the western democracies dating back to 1828 reports that 42 percent (142 of 369) of parties that contested at least one election proved to be ephemeral; they disappeared without leaving any traces.[28] Even among those 195 parties that succeeded in becoming "institutionalized" (that is, contested more than three elections), there was a considerable number of disappearances. Twenty-three percent of these institutionalized parties (45 of 195) eventually ceased their endeavors. The reasons adduced to explain these disappearances reflect a combination of internal and external factors including poor electoral performances, an inability to achieve participation in government, such changes in the rules of the game as the introduction of proportional representation, and the collapse of political regimes brought on by defeat in war and foreign occupation.

For those parties in the western democracies that have managed to persist, the record suggests that many have undergone structural modifications. Specifically, their histories have been marked by mergers with other parties and splits in which factions separate themselves to form new parties.

Recent concern about the decline of parties in the western democracies has stimulated a discussion about possible replacements, organizations that may come to perform certain tasks previously played by the parties.[29] Among these potential replacements, reference is made to environmental protection organizations, citizen action groups, and various ethnic and religious associations. Some of these groups have evolved into new alternative political parties, while others have not. There is no reference in this discussion to the possibility that terrorist groups may seek on occasion to replace parties that display diminished capacities to fulfill their tasks.

Linkages between political parties and terrorist groups

The point of this limited effort to review what seem to be widely accepted understandings concerning the origins and ends of parties and terrorist groups, as well as their relationships with other forces in their environments, is to emphasize how sporadically the views of each type of organization take the other into consideration. It is hard to say why this is the case, because the record suggests there has been a variety of instances, both historical and contemporary, where ties have clearly existed. Let us examine a few of the available cases.

First, there is the example of the Russian Social Revolutionaries, that is, of a political party deliberately causing the formation of a subsidiary group, the Combat Organization, in order to pursue the party's goals by terrorist means.[30] In this case the terrorist group retained its affiliation with the parent organization.

Second, there are circumstances in which the relationship is reversed: where a terrorist group promotes the formation of a political party. In Ireland the IRA sponsored the formation of a political wing, Sinn Fein, during the course of that nation's struggle for independence.[31] As with the Social Revolutionaries, so too in this case the tie persisted over time.

Third, as the result of growing dissatisfaction with the direction in which the leadership is taking it, there have been cases where a faction within a political party has severed its link and formed an independent terrorist group. One example: in Italy during the 1950s the New Order emerged as a consequence of a split within the neo-fascist Italian Social Movement.[32] The New Order's militants decided in favor of autonomy because they believed the Social Movement's national leadership was pursuing a strategy for a right-wing revival that was both tepid and hopeless.

Next, it is possible for a terrorist group to undergo a strategic shift, conclude its violent operations, and reconstitute itself as a political party which then participates in the democratic electoral process. For example, the Irgun in mandatory Palestine staged a revolt against British rule involving various acts of terrorism. After the achievement of Israeli independence, it was reorganized as the Herut party, whose leader, Menachem Begin, eventually became prime minister.[33]

There are still other career possibilities to contemplate. Some political organizations may go through a complete life cycle experience, beginning as political parties which then spin off or form terrorist groups with the latter, sometime later, then giving up violence in favor of rejoining or promoting the formation of a competitive political party. Developments in the Basque region of Spain suggest that such a process is at work.[34] Last, the possibilities to this point have treated parties and terrorist groups as causes and effects of one another, with each alternating as dependent and independent variables. But there may be situations in which both parties and terrorist groups are the products of a third force: a political movement. Here the movement's followers may divide themselves into those who favor legal party-political means to achieve its goals and others who believe this approach will prove fruitless and, as a consequence, choose the terrorist alternative. In these circumstances, a political party and a terrorist group may be in competition with one another for the support of the movement's followers and potential sympathizers in the population. This pattern was observable in the case of the new left *Lotta Continua* (Struggle Continues) movement in Italy during the 1970s, with some adherents promoting a political party, the Democratic Proletarians, to contest elections, while others followed the terrorist path into *Prima Linea* (Front Line).[35]

Of course, references to a few cases used for illustrative purposes in no way furnishes evidence about how prevalent the general phenomenon itself may be. How common are the sorts of ties between political parties and terrorist groups suggested by the possibilities described above?

To answer this question, at least initially, information about the characteristics of violent political organizations was obtained from Peter Janke's *World Directory* of guerrilla and terrorist organizations. Supplementary information was drawn also from John Thackrah's *Encyclopedia of Terrorism and Political Violence* and George Rosie's *The Directory of International Terrorism*.[36] Janke's handbook and the other compendia provide valuable sketches of all such violent organizations known to their authors. The accounts, though, have their limitations. For one, they are likely biased in favor of groups able to endure for some time. Ephemeral bands whose members commit a few violent acts before passing from the scene seem less likely to be included. The second deficiency, from our perspective, is that the principal source, Janke's *Directory*, includes guerrilla and other violent political groups as well as the terrorist ones. Little can be done to compensate for the absence of the ephemeral bands. On the other hand, an effort will be made shortly to narrow this analysis exclusively to groups that pursue terrorist strategies.

According to the Janke *Directory*, there were a total of 563 violent organizations that sought to challenge incumbent political regimes between 1945 and the early 1980s. Of this total, slightly more than 19 percent (110) exhibited links to political parties of the sorts mentioned earlier. Thus, based on these data the general phenomenon appears to be relatively common. But this claim is not restricted to the relationship between parties and groups pursuing terrorist means to advance their aims. The 110 organizations include ones that employed other forms of violence. Such Sub-Saharan African organizations as the Zimbabwe African National Union, which waged a protracted guerrilla campaign in order to end white domination in Southern Rhodesia and then became the country's ruling political party, are included. The same is true for such groups as the Christian Phalangist party in Lebanon, whose leadership formed a militia in order to participate in that nation's civil war and fight against militias organized by various Muslim parties seeking to change the status quo. The *Directory* also includes a number of cases from Southeast Asia and elsewhere where Communist parties launched insurgencies in their anticolonial struggles against British or French rule. In short, there were an abundance of cases involving ties between parties and violent political groups whose operations did not usually encompass what is commonly regarded as terrorism.

It is possible, however, to confine this analysis exclusively to terrorist groups. Martha Crenshaw recently compiled a subset of seventy-five organizations drawn from the Janke *Directory* whose violent strategies she judged to be terrorist in character.[37] If we limit the analysis to these seventy-five terrorist groups, it becomes possible to make a number of useful observations.

To begin, a total of twenty-seven of the seventy-five terrorist groups identified by Crenshaw exhibited links to political parties of the kind discussed earlier (see Table 8.1). In terms of frequency, then, ties between terrorist groups and political parties are substantially more common (36 percent to 19.1 percent) than those between parties and violent political organizations in general. Table 8.2 presents a distribution of these twenty-seven groups based on the particular type of relationship they have or had with political parties. As may be seen, the most frequent occurrence is for a faction of a party, often its youth branch, to break away from its parent body for the purpose of waging a terrorist campaign. There are some situations, though, in which the affiliation between the terrorist group and the political party is retained.

In addition to their relationships with one another, it is possible to make other observations about the parties and terrorist groups involved. So far as the ideological outlooks of the parties are concerned, the dominant perspective is a leftist one. Though there are some exceptions, for example, the Turkish Grey Wolves that operated under the auspices of the right-wing National Action party and the Liberation Tigers of Tamil Eelam in Sri Lanka that emerged from a separatist party (the Tamil United Liberation Front), most of the party-related groups (nineteen of the twenty-seven) defined themselves as belonging in the Marxist-Leninist tradition (often Castroite, Maoist, or Trotskyite), for example, the People's Liberation Army in Argentina, the Naxalites in India, and GRAPO in Spain.

No systematic effort was undertaken to assemble data on the electoral performances of the parties related to the terrorist groups. In some cases the parties were prohibited by law from

Table 8.1 Terrorist Groups with Links to Political Parties

Revolutionary Popular Vanguard (VPR) – Brazil
National Liberating Action (ALN) – Brazil
People's Revolutionary Army (ERP) – Argentina
Black Panthers – United States
Prima Linea – Italy
First of October Anti-Fascist Resistance Group (GRAPO) – Spain
Shining Path – Peru
Armed Revolutionary Action (ARA) – Portugal
Grey Wolves – Turkey
Armed Forces of National Liberation (FALN) – Venezuela
Movement of the Revolutionary Left (MIR) – Venezuela
Communist Party of India-Marxist-Leninist (Naxalites) – India
Fadayeen-e-Khalq – Iran
Armed Revolutionary Nuclei – Italy
Liberation Tigers of Tamil Eelam – Sri Lanka
Red Brigades (BR) – Italy
Irish National Liberation Army (INLA) – Northern Ireland
Armed Revolutionary Forces of Colombia (FARC) – Colombia
April 19 Movement (M-19) – Colombia
National Liberation Army (ELN) – Colombia
Popular Liberation Army (EPL) – Colombia
Movement of the Revolutionary Left (MIR) – Chile
Farabundo Marti National Liberation Front – El Salvador
New People's Army – Philippines
Provisional Irish Republican Army – Northern Ireland
Basque Homeland and Freedom (ETA) – Spain
Rebel Armed Forces (FAR) Guatemala

participating in the electoral process. This was true for the Guatemalan Labor party that aided in the formation of the Rebel Armed Forces (FAR) and the ERP-related Workers' Revolutionary party in Argentina, among others. There were a few cases, however, where the parties displayed considerable prowess in attracting voter support. In Venezuela, the Movement of the Revolutionary Left (MIR) began as a dissident faction within the Democratic Action party, a pro-Castro organization represented by 73 deputies in the country's legislature at the time (1960) the split

Table 8.2 Relationship between Terrorist Groups and Political Parties

Type of Relationship	Numbers
faction of political party breaks away to create separate terrorist group	14 (VPR, ALN, FLAN, MIR, Naxalites, Fedayeen-e-Khalq, Armed Revolutionary Nuclei, Liberation Tigers, BR, INLA, FARC, M-19, ELN, EPL)
collective party decisions to launch terrorist campaign through use of subsidiary unit and abandon non-violent politics	8 (ERP, GRAPO, FARC, ARA, Shining Path, FAR, New People's Army, Farabundo Marti Liberation Front)
party leadership decides to engage in terrorism and conventional politics simultaneously	3 (Provisional IRA, Grey Wolves, Black Panthers)
alternation over time, party to terrorist group to party	1 (ETA)
political movement spawns both party and terrorist group	1 (Prima Linea)
	27

occurred. Likewise, the identically named MIR in Chile defected from that nation's Socialist party at the time the latter was a significant electoral force. And at the point (1978) the Tamil Tigers was organized in Sri Lanka, the Tamil United Liberation Front was the single largest opposition party represented in parliament. Nonetheless, this writer has the impression but can not prove that the more common experience has been for the terrorism-related parties to fare poorly at the polls. For example, Sinn Fein, the political wing of the IRA in Northern Ireland, and Herri Batasuna, which plays an analogous role vis-à-vis ETA in the Basque provinces of Spain, have averaged approximately 10 percent of the vote in recent elections held in their respective regions. In Italy, the *Prima Linea* related Democratic Proletarians won less than 2 percent of the vote in the crucial 1976 national elections; the neo-fascist Italian Social Movement, from which the Armed Revolutionary Nuclei emerged, received the support of slightly over 6 percent of the electorate in the same contest. Likewise, in Colombia presidential candidates supported by the same Communist party from which the Armed Revolutionary Forces and Popular Liberation Army had come received less than 3 percent of the vote in the 1974 and 1978 national elections.

This observation serves to call our attention to another attribute of parties with linkages to terrorist groups. Some of the parties themselves began as dissident splinters of larger and more electorally successful parties. Maoist or Trotskyite dissidents within large left parties separated themselves from the maternal party out of a belief it had abandoned the revolutionary cause and ignored the alleged revolutionary aspirations of the masses. Of course this is largely speculation, but the decision to pursue a terrorist strategy may take place in a context where efforts to demonstrate the masses' untapped revolutionary yearnings are frustrated by the fact that the parties' appeals for support are rejected by the voters. Unexpectedly poor showings at the polls may lead to the conclusion that the entire electoral enterprise is a fraud or that the large maternal left party's opportunism and commitment to reform within the existing order have blinded the masses to their real interests. At this point, some or all members of the party may reach the conclusion that a new correlation of forces may be achieved through the pursuit of a terrorist strategy.

Some evidence accumulated by Crenshaw permits us to make an observation about the characteristics, not of the parties, but of the terrorist groups exhibiting links to them. The concern here is with their duration. The seventy-five terrorist groups reported in her study displayed considerable variation in their survival rates. The generalization that presents itself from the data reported in Table 8.3 is that those terrorist groups with party political links seem to have been more successful, if we measure success by persistence, in waging their armed struggles than those groups lacking these relationships. It is not immediately apparent why this should be the case. Perhaps the experience of having belonged (or of belonging) to a party equipped the terrorists with an array of organizational skills useful in sustaining the violent groups. Or the fact that the longer lasting terrorist organizations were more likely to exhibit relationships with political parties

Table 8.3 Duration of Party and Nonparty Linked Terrorist Groups

Duration	Party Linked		Non-Party	
	Number	*(Per Cent)*	*Number*	*(Per Cent)*
1 to 5 years	2	(7)	8	(17)
5 to 10 years	6	(22)	18	(38)
over 10 years	19	(70)	22	(46)
	27	(100)	48	(100) N = 75

H = 267.85   df = 1   p ≤ .001

may be symptomatic of their enjoying greater popular support. If the latter is true, the groups involved may have had an easier time in recruiting new members and in obtaining logistical aid from well-wishers. There may have been a larger pool of such individuals upon which to draw than was true for terrorist groups lacking party political ties. If we accept endurance as a measure of success for a terrorist group and high voter support one for a political party, it may be that institutionally the violent groups were more successful than the parties to which they had ties. We are, of course, in a highly speculative realm, but if these inferences hold, the decision to embark on the terrorist path discloses considerable rationality by those who made it.

To the extent these comments have some bearing on the causes of the relationship(s) between political parties and terrorist groups, they focus on factors largely internal to the organizations themselves. It seems wise at this stage of the inquiry to ask ourselves where the phenomenon of party-terrorist linkage is most prevalent: in what sorts of polities and in which regions of the world does the relationship(s) seem most common?

The central tendencies of the two regional distributions (see Table 8.4) of terrorist organizations appear to be different. The highest percentages of terrorist groups lacking ties to political parties are to be found in Europe and the Middle East. By contrast, it is clearly Latin America where the party-terrorism relationship is found most frequently. Why? It might be reasoned that terrorist groups lacking party ties would be found in areas of the world where parties, as forms of political expression, are relatively rare phenomena. Conversely, we might expect the relationship to exist most commonly in party-rich environments, that is, in nations and regions where parties of all types grow in abundance. If this were true, it follows that the phenomenon would occur most frequently in Europe. But the evidence suggests this is only partially true. Western Europe displays a relatively high proportion of party-linked terrorist groups but is the modal location of nonparty ones as well. In Latin America, another party-rich environment, the relationship is reversed. That is, there are some terrorist groups lacking party ties, but it is the region of the world where an absolute majority of party-related terrorist groups are to be found. Why should this be the case? A review of the particular countries where these relationships exist may provide an answer.

There are eighteen nations (see Table 8.5) in which terrorist groups displaying this characteristic are found. Aside from the fact that half of them are Latin American, they seem to share another attribute. The striking thing about these countries is not so much their geographic location as the political conditions prevailing within them. To be sure there are some exceptions, for example, India and Italy, but for the most part (thirteen of the eighteen countries) they are nations whose political regimes underwent transformations either before, during, or after the party-linked terrorist groups emerged. In some cases—Portugal, Spain, Peru, El Salvador, Venezuela—the

Table 8.4 Regional Distribution of Party and Nonparty Linked Terrorist Groups

Region	Party Linked		Non-Party	
	Number	*(Per Cent)*	*Number*	*(Per Cent)*
Europe	7	(26)	18	(37)
Africa	0	(0)	0	(0)
Middle East	2	(7)	14	(29)
South Asia	2	(7)	1	(2)
Far East	1	(4)	2	(4)
North America	1	(4)	6	(13)
Latin America	14	(52)	7	(15)
	27	(100)	48	(100) N = 75

$$X^2 = 15.88, \quad 6df, p \leq .01$$

Table 8.5 Nations Where Party Linked Terrorist Groups Are Located

Nation	Number of Groups
Brazil	2
Argentina	1
United States	1
Italy	3
Spain	2
Peru	1
Portugal	1
Turkey	1
Venezuela	2
India	1
Iran	1
Sri Lanka	1
Northern Ireland	2
Colombia	4
Chile	1
El Salvador	1
Philippines	1
Guatemala	1
	27

transition was from dictatorship to democracy. In another, Iran, it was from monarchy to Islamic republic. In still another instance, Chile, the transition was from democracy to dictatorship. Argentina, Brazil, Colombia, Guatemala, Turkey, and the Philippines experienced multiple changes: from democracy to dictatorship to democracy. For the most part, then, we seem to be dealing with cases of regime instability, circumstances in which there is considerable uncertainty about the strength and persistence of the existing order.

Why do we find this evident relationship between the presence of party-linked terrorist groups and regime instability? One obvious response is that these terrorist groups caused or at least contributed to the instability. Why did the military intervene in Turkey in 1980 if not to put an end to the terrorist violence whose perpetrators included the Grey Wolves? An alternative though not necessarily competing explanation makes some sense.

In transitional political environments, ones in which the military has seized power and outlawed some or all political parties or where an authoritarian regime shows signs of breakdown, and when the affected nation faces an uncertain future, it seems reasonable to believe there will be considerable confusion among members of contending political forces concerning the appropriate strategies to be pursued. Some members of recently outlawed parties, ones which can no longer openly appeal to an electorate, may opt for the terrorist alternative (Brazil). Or in conditions where dictatorships seem likely to give way to democracy, underground political parties and terrorist groups may come to consider open partisan politics as a plausible path to follow (Spain, Portugal). Under certain circumstances both terrorism and electoral politics may be employed simultaneously until the outcome becomes clear. Thus, it may be the transitional context which promotes the relationship between political parties and terrorist groups.

Conclusions

The data on which these judgments have been based are admittedly fragmentary. Most studies concerning the relationship between political violence and the political order have used comparative rates of violent events as the basis upon which to reach conclusions.[38] Instead, in this investigation groups and organizations have served as the units of analysis. Despite the difference in approach and notwithstanding other limitations, it seems possible to make a number of summary observations.

First, terrorist groups and political parties have more to do with each other than might have been suspected on the basis of a review of the relevant literature. Links between these types of political organizations appear to have been relatively common in recent decades. Second, terrorist groups do not emerge from thin air, nor do they necessarily disappear into air at the conclusion of their adventures; rather, their appearances and disappearances often are associated with developments internal to individual political parties and to changes in the system within which they pursue their various objectives.

Political parties most likely to stimulate the formation of terrorist groups seem to share at least two things in common. First, irrespective of size, organizational vitality, or ideological bent, they all appear to be parties with grandiose goals to achieve. These may involve the formation of a new independent state for a people presently without one or the installation of a dictatorship of the proletariat. But whatever their ultimate aims, it seems clear the parties involved hold exceedingly high aspirations. The terrorist impulse, manifested by the party itself or a dissident faction within it, may be caused by frustrations growing out of the gap between the party's self-defined task and its immediate political prospects. Grandiose objectives coupled with meager support at the polls would seem to be a circumstance in which thoughts of terrorism might come to the minds of a party's most enthusiastic members. On the other hand, it also seems reasonable to believe that a party which experiences some success in winning voter support but compromises or even abandons its grandiose goals in the process is susceptible to the terrorist impulse as well. Those within the party most strongly committed to its original objectives may see themselves as the victims of betrayal and choose armed struggle instead of further debate with leaders who, they believe, have been corrupted by the system.

There is a second requirement needed for a party or faction thereof to turn to terror. In addition to having grandiose plans, the party's doctrine must emphasize the illegitimacy of the prevailing political order. In monarchy, military junta, or parliamentary democracy, the party which stresses the illegitimacy of the incumbent regime will furnish a justification for terrorist violence to some members most drawn to the party's high ambitions. When the incumbent regime is viewed not only as illegitimate, but weak as well, the likelihood of party-linked terrorism would seem to increase. Furthermore, a regime which attempts to repress such a party and fails increases the chances of its becoming the target of a party-linked terrorist campaign. The act of repression will likely confirm the party's sense of its own important mission (if it was not important why would the government make the effort to eliminate it?) and simultaneously emphasize the regime's own fears and vulnerabilities.

As a final thought it may be helpful in the analysis of this subject to stress the mutability of political strategies. Waging public electoral campaigns on behalf of candidates for office and conducting terrorist operations are techniques for winning power that may seem to have little to do with one another. But given the appropriate circumstances, one can replace the other or both may be used simultaneously. And the organizations that employ them may undergo chameleon-like transformations as well.

Notes

1   The amount of writing concerning the meanings of "terrorism" and "political party" is nearly oceanic in volume. If an attempt was made to review this literature it would prove impossible to undertake the

task at hand. Nevertheless, there is an obvious need to clarify our terms. Accordingly, terrorism will be understood as a type of politically motivated violence threatened or committed by private individuals for the purpose of influencing the behavior of an audience(s) wider than its immediate victims. Terrorist groups are organizations that rely, partially or exclusively, on this technique to achieve their political ends. Some definitions of political party restrict its meaning to organizations which accept the legitimacy of the prevailing political order or ones that operate in national contexts where an atmosphere supportive of pluralism exists. If this judgment was accepted, extremist parties active in the democracies and democratic parties operating illegally in authoritarian settings (for example, Pinochet's Chile) would fail the test. For our purposes, let us consider a political party to be a modern organization seeking to win or retain political power on the basis of some general understanding of the public interest through the mobilization of popular support on behalf of these endeavors. Often, though not always, the latter involves participation in elections.

2   *Revolution in Peru* (Berkeley: The Committee to Support the Revolution in Peru, 1985), p. 1.

3   See, for example, John Crayton, "Terrorism and the Psychology of the Self," in Lawrence Freedman and Jonah Alexander, eds., *Perspectives on Terrorism* (Wilmington: Scholarly Resources, 1983), pp. 33–41; or Jillian Becker, *Hitler's Children* (Philadelphia: J. P. Lippincott, 1977).

4   James Adams, *The Financing of Terror* (New York: Simon and Schuster, 1986).

5   James Joll, *The Anarchists* (Boston: Little, Brown, 1964), pp. 84–114.

6   See, for example, Richard Gillespie, *Soldiers of Peron* (Oxford: Clarendon Press, 1982), pp. 257–258.

7   Stephen Fisher, "The 'Decline of Parties' Thesis and the Role of Minor Parties," in Peter Merkl, ed., *Western European Party Systems* (New York: The Free Press, 1980), pp. 609–613.

8   Maurice Duverger, *Political Parties* (New York: John Wiley, 1954), pp. 36–39.

9   Martha Crenshaw, "How Terrorism Ends," paper presented at the annual meeting of the American Political Science Association, Chicago, September 1987, pp. 10–11.

10 Robert Michels, *Political Parties* (New York: Viking Press, 1959); and Harold Lasswell, *Power and Personality* (New York: Viking Press, 1962).

11 See, for example, James Walston, *The Mafia and Clientelism: Roads to Rome in Post-War Calabria* (London: Routledge, 1988).

12 Astrid von Borcke, "Violence and Terror in Russian Revolutionary Populism: The Narodnaya Volya, 1870–1883," in Wolfgang Mommsen and Gerhard Hirschfeld, eds., *Social Protest: Violence in Nineteenth and Twentieth Century Europe* (New York: St. Martin's Press, 1982), pp. 48–62.

13 Maureen Perrie, "Political and Economic Terror in the Tactics of the Russian Socialist-Revolutionary Party before 1914," in Mommsen and Hirschfeld, eds., pp. 63–79.

14 Klaus von Beyme, *Political Parties in Western Democracies* (New York: St. Martin's Press, 1985), pp. 14–26; see also Joseph LaPalombara and Myron Weiner, "The Origins and Development of Political Parties," in Joseph LaPalombara and Myron Weiner, eds., *Political Parties and Political Development* (Princeton: Princeton University Press, 1966), pp. 3–42.

15 See especially M. I. Ostrogorski, *Democracy and the Organization of Political Parties* (New York: Anchor Books, 1964).

16 La Palombara and Weiner, pp. 14–19.

17 Seymour Lipset and Stein Rokkan, "Cleavage Structures, Party Systems and Voter Alignments," in Seymour Lipset and Stein Rokkan, eds., *Party Systems and Voter Alignments* (New York: The Free Press, 1967), pp. 13–23.

18 F. A. Hermens, "The Dynamics of Proportional Representation," in Harry Eckstein and David Apter, eds., *Comparative Politics* (New York: The Free Press, 1963), pp. 254–280.

19 Walter Laqueur, *The Age of Terrorism*, rev. ed. (Boston: Little, Brown, 1987), p. 142–173.

20 See, for example, Claire Sterling, *The Terror Network* (New York: Holt, Rinehart & Winston, 1981).

21 Martha Crenshaw, "The Causes of Terrorism," *Comparative Politics*, 13 (July 1981), 379–399.

22 Ibid., p. 384. See also Richard Rubenstein, *Alchemists of Revolution* (New York: Basic Books, 1987), pp. 65–85.

23 Manfred Hildermeier, "The Terrorist Strategies of the Socialist-Revolutionary Party in Russia, 1900–1914," in Mommsen and Hirschfeld, eds., p. 86.

24 See, for example, Benjamin Netanyahu, ed., *Terrorism: How the West Can Win* (New York: Farrar, Strauss, Giroux, 1986).

25 Martha Crenshaw, ed., *Terrorism, Legitimacy and Power* (Middletown: Wesleyan University Press, 1983), pp. 1–29.

26 For an overview, see Kay Lawson, ed., *Political Parties and Linkage* (New Haven: Yale University Press, 1980).

27 Crenshaw, "How Terrorism Ends," pp. 8–9.
28 Richard Rose and Thomas Mackie, "Do Parties Persist or Fail? The Big Trade-Off Facing Organizations," in Kay Lawson and Peter Merkl, eds., *When Parties Fail* (Princeton: Princeton University Press, 1988), pp. 533–558.
29 Lawson and Merkl, eds., pp. 3–12.
30 Hildermeier, pp. 80–87.
31 J. Bowyer Bell, *The Secret Army: The IRA 1916–1979* (Cambridge, Mass.: MIT Press, 1980), pp. 16–17.
32 Rosario Minna, "II Terrorismo di Destra," in Donatella della Porta, ed., *Terrorismi in Italia* (Bologna: II Mulino, 1984), pp. 32–39.
33 J. Bowyer Bell, *Terror out of Zion* (New York: Avon Books, 1977), pp. 432–433.
34 Joseba Zulaika, *Basque Violence* (Reno: University of Nevada Press, 1988), pp. 98–101.
35 Mino Monicelli, *L'Ultrasinistra in Italia: 1968–1978* (Bari: Laterza, 1978).
36 Peter Janke, *Guerrilla and Terrorist Organizations: A World Directory and Bibliography* (New York: Macmillan, 1983); John Thackrah, *Encyclopedia of Terrorism and Political Violence* (London: Routledge and Keegan Paul 1987); and George Rosie, *The Directory of International Terrorism* (New York: Paragon House, 1986).
37 Crenshaw, "How Terrorism Ends," pp. 39–42.
38 See, for example, G. Bingham Powell, Jr., *Contemporary Democracies* (Cambridge, Mass.: Harvard University Press, 1982), pp. 154–174.

9 A conceptual framework for addressing psychological process in the development of the terrorist

Max Taylor and John Horgan

It is increasingly accepted that if we think of terrorism as something conducted by evil people whose intention is to destroy "our" way of life, we are vulnerable to making serious errors of analysis that may consequently deflect policy down flawed paths.[1] Efforts to understand terrorism in terms of abnormal, individual, or other special motivations similarly seem inappropriate, and to the extent that psychology can contribute to this debate, there seems to be little or no evidence of particular or distinctive individual qualities being associated with the terrorist.[2] On the other hand, we see across the heterogeneity of groups that use terrorism today what seems to be an unending flow of recruits, who seem capable of engaging in levels of increasingly extreme violence, including suicide. How can this, and the issues that emerge from it, be understood, if not in terms of psychopathology or evil individual action and motivation?

Perhaps some of the difficulties we face arise from the assumption that terrorism is something to be understood out of its social and political context, and which furthermore can be characterised as a psychological state of some kind disconnected from context and history; this necessarily leads to a focused attempt to identify unique and/or personal qualities. However, an under-explored alternative to an account in terms of individual qualities is to see involvement in terrorism, at least in psychological terms, as a process rather than a state; this implies a focus not on the individual and their presumed psychological or moral qualities, but on process variables such as the changing context that the individual operates in, and also the relationships between events and the individual as they affect behaviour. Such an approach would be consistent with the way we tend to see other forms of problematic behaviour.[3] A further major benefit that follows from this is that our attention switches to attempts to identify the essentially practical matters (i.e., about things that can be changed) rather than seeking to address qualities of people (i.e., personality or "evil traits") that draw on essentially intangible mentalistic concepts, and that are by definition resistant to change. Moving our level of explanation away from properties to processes seems to offer tangible rewards beyond just conceptual adequacy and may offer a different approach, for example, to the development of more practical and efficient counterterrorism initiatives.

Terrorism as process

What does "seeing terrorism as a process" imply? In general terms, a process refers to a sequence of events, involving steps or operations that are usually ordered and/or interdependent. To use a term like "process" to describe activities like terrorism implies what we describe as terrorism to be actions of some kind associated with other actions and reactions, often expressed in some sort of reciprocal relationship (in an immediate sense between the various actors involved, such as governments, terrorists, media, politicians, the public, and also perhaps in a more long-term sense in terms of sociological, psychological, and political forces). The nature of that reciprocity may of course be expressed in a variety of ways, but it is important to note, however, that specifying or identifying the elements of the process does not necessarily imply a simple deterministic account, despite the ease with which such accounts may follow from post hoc analyses of events.

In addition, describing activities in terms of a process also implies a potential for some form of modelling of the events and their relationships. Modelling can take a variety of forms, and perhaps a continuum can be expressed between identifying and expressing mathematical or statistical probabilities about the relationships between events, and conceptual models of events and their relationships in terms of conceptual structures expressed as hypothetical constructs and intervening variables. And finally, and this relates to the point made in the opening section about the dangers of "special" explanations of both terrorism and those who engage in it, viewing terrorism as a process also reflects an acknowledgement that the extreme violence associated with terrorism may have its origins in relatively mundane and apparently unrelated activities.[4]

While some analyses of processes describing events may perhaps integrate perspectives from a variety of contexts, others may focus on particular discipline or problem perspectives. On the other hand, it may be that understanding some processes will necessarily draw on perspectives from particular disciplines or professions. The nature of the activity, the perspective taken, the degree of conceptual complexity and understanding are presumably variables that will affect this. Given this, there is a sense in which what we identify as a process is an expression of a set of (formal or informal) rules describing the expression of whatever the activity we are concerned about is in actual life. However, to paraphrase Wittgenstein, we might also assume that like the rules of a game, the rules describing a process are neither right nor wrong, neither true nor false: they are merely useful for the particular applications in which we apply them. If this is the case, so clearly our level of analysis and the assumptions we make about starting points for analysis and end products will influence our process analysis.

If we follow this through, it will imply at least from a psychological perspective a clearer understanding of the terrorist in his or her environment, and significantly, in order to do this, a much more explicit bringing together of political and psychological analyses. Indeed, perhaps such an analysis will also bring the study of terrorism within a broader ecological framework, embracing psychological factors within their political context. For example, recent insights in criminology related to the concept of *affordance*[5] may merit further exploration, in terms of understanding the environmental and contextual structuring of terrorist behaviour. By doing this, we will be drawn into developing a clearer but inevitably complex sense of the relationship between political context (and especially its ideological qualities), organisational framework, and the individual by breaking down the process into parts, and examining the relationship between them, from the "lens" of social, political, civil society, and temporal frames of reference. This is not a new agenda: H. H. A. Cooper[6] described the need to consider terrorism as a "creature of its own time and place," yet this is increasingly less obvious in contemporary thinking about the development of terrorism. It is important to stress that in adopting one "lens" through which to view the problem, however, we cannot ignore other equally legitimate "lenses."[7] But, if we are to engage with a sense of process, then temporal dimensions are clearly of critical significance.

Developing this perspective into what will be a complex, multilayered analysis is a major endeavour beyond the scope of this paper and, more importantly, well beyond the scope of currently available empirical evidence. However we can, by way of illustration, at least explore some of the implications of this approach in simpler forms. As a starting point, we will explore from primarily a theoretical perspective an aspect of terrorism as a process that seems to follow from the above—a conceptual framework to understand involvement and engagement with terrorism. What follows assumes the existence of a movement that the potential terrorist might engage with; there may or may not be some measure of commonality of process in other circumstances such as exiting from terrorism, or in the emergence of new terrorist movements. However, it must be emphasised that as already noted, a serious limiting factor is the lack of empirical knowledge about the area, and about the individuals concerned. Considerable effort has gone into the development of chronologies, and in the construction of very general case studies; but neither yields the kind of information that might illustrate the issues of concern here. However, by embarking on a theoretical and conceptual discussion in potentially empirically verifiable terms, we can at least contribute to the creation of a systematic research agenda.

Frameworks of engagement with terrorism

Given the lack of sound empirical knowledge, we need to be explicit about the validity of the assumptions made. Perhaps a useful starting point for what follows is the assumption that terrorists are ordinary people (to the extent that they are not distinguishable from other "ordinary" people) who make choices in the contexts in which they find themselves (discussed at length by Taylor[8]). A further assumption is that choices made by individuals are meaningful for the person making those choices. One of the great challenges when thinking about the terrorist and terrorism is that despite identifying potential broad putative predisposing factors in terms of educational attainment, income levels, and other potential causal agents,[9] these essentially correlated qualities in themselves do not account for why, given apparent commonalities of experience, one individual engages with the process of terrorism and another does not (discussed at length by Horgan).[10] This problem is not unique to analyses of terrorism, and is probably the same for most (if not all) life choices made by individuals.[11] However, a failure to recognise this represents an absolutely critical failure to address what must be the central rate-limiting factor in the core quality of terrorism and its expression—regardless of ideology, politics, or social processes, terrorism necessarily has to involve an individual *with the opportunity* (including the capacity to make a choice) to engage in terrorist behaviour however we define it. The answer to why one person and not another becomes involved in terrorism is not simply a matter to dismiss as a technical psychological issue, and therefore of less significance. The answer to why a person becomes involved in terrorism (as opposed to those who do not who share similar backgrounds and contexts) is central to addressing the problem of terrorism; the answer lies within the psychological and emotional context of the individual on which the bigger and essentially non-psychological forces of opportunity and context operate. But the critical point to make is that it is in a meaningful and transparent answer to this as a process that our understanding of terrorism as well as the terrorist needs to begin.

How then do we understand that facilitating context to terrorism? Regardless of the views that might be taken on a definition of terrorism, there is broad acceptance on the minimal position that one of the defining qualities of what terrorists do (i.e., "terrorist acts") is that it is a form of problematic and perhaps abnormal (*viz* a relatively uncommon) violent behaviour. This is not to say that the terrorist is abnormal in a clinical sense, but rather that he (or she) does things that are unlikely and unusual; terrorist violence is both relatively rare and also something generally not approved of. Not only terrorists engage in violent behaviour, of course, and sometimes it might be difficult to distinguish between terrorist violence and criminal violence, as Alex Schmid notes.[12] But this may suggest that the frame of reference for understanding at least the violent elements of terrorism may be shared with other kinds of violence and aggression, and therefore we might benefit from looking at terrorist violence in the way we look at other forms of problematic aggressive behaviour.[13]

A further important point to note is that engaging with terrorist behaviour may for the individual involve some risk, but equally that person presumably also gains some benefit. Benefit need not be seen in financial terms, but might include amongst other things peer or significant other approval, a sense of satisfaction, or a sense of personal agency.[14] Again, this of course is not unique to terrorists—we are quite familiar with other examples of problematic behaviours that involve risk, but where the risk in the individual decisional calculus is outweighed by personal benefit. Driving fast might be one such example; downloading child pornography from the Internet might be another. We also know that emotional arousal is known to impede or change decision making (by increasing risk taking for example) in ways that may be relevant to understanding the pressure towards violence in the immediate decisional calculus facing the terrorist prior to engagement.[15] Indeed, we should also note that not even the way terrorist violence is instrumental is unique in this sense, for our society is replete with examples of the use of instrumental violence for financial gain (armed robbery), sexual gain (rape), personal power (domestic violence), social control and compliance with the law (police activity), and entertainment (boxing); sometimes these activities are solitary, sometimes undertaken co-operatively as part of groups. Other examples could be developed to illustrate the point that in many, if not all respects, what terrorists actually engage with is not in itself unique, although in contemporary examples the scale and extent of the mayhem caused may be. Even one of the worrying features of contemporary terrorism, that is, instrumental mass deaths, occurs outside of what we tend to label "terrorism" (in the actions of a state through its army at war, as for example in Iraq, or in the use of genocide as an instrument of policy, as in the war in Bosnia). It seems to be the focused non-state political instrumentality that is critical, and which we normally identify as one of the defining qualities of terrorism. But following from that, a number of issues arise—does this political instrumentality come *before* engagement with terrorism, or is this political instrumentality (as distinct from a more general recognition of the instrumentality of violence) a *product* of, rather than a cause of, continued terrorist activity? Or, more likely, does the answer to questions like this change over time, dependant on degree of exposure and involvement with terrorist life styles and activities? Given the emphasis here on process, the latter seems a more likely explanation.

Pathways into, through and out of terrorism

Embedded in the above discussion of process is the notion of a pathway. The criminological literature has extensively used this concept to address issues related to understanding engagement with criminal behaviour from a developmental context,[16] and an essential quality of the concept is that it implies a sense of change or process towards (or away from) criminal engagement. Essential to understanding this is the concept of "trajectory," which is the pathway of development for the individual marked by a sequence of transitions. Every trajectory has an entry point, success point, and the element of timing; transitions refer to the life events themselves that are embedded in the trajectories. Transitions can consist of sudden critical points, but may also relate to more complex, long-term processes of change. There is considerable debate about whether or not "trajectories" can be identified in early life as predisposing influences in the development of pathways to criminal behaviour; resolution to this issue, however, does not necessarily influence the significance of the concept itself.

The sense of incremental and changing involvement implied by the concept of pathway to crime seems to correspond to such little knowledge we have about the formation of the terrorist. It also offers a broad platform for understanding in essentially social learning terms how more general deviant behaviour might emerge. Karsten Hundeide,[17] for example, describes the incremental process through which youngsters become committed insiders of counter-culture youth groups. Interestingly and significantly, Hundeide places the debate within the broader context of Community of Practice rather than anything special or distinctive to counter-culture groups. Communities of Practice are informal social learning environments for the individuals involved within which members exchange experience and views, developing each other's tacit knowledge into conversations and knowledge that allow its transmission: "Over time, this collective learning results in practices that reflect both the pursuit of our enterprises and the attendant social relations. These practices are thus the property of a kind of community created over time by the sustained pursuit of a shared enterprise."[18]

Notions like Community of Practice offer ways of understanding the role and informal transmission of practice and knowledge in a variety of situations, including terrorism. Specifically, it augments and extends our sense of the social processes involved in engagement with terrorism. What is also interesting in the concept of Community of Practice is that it offers a structure to understand the emergence of ideological and social control in contexts where there are no necessary face-to-face meetings.[19]

Community of Practice also offers a way of understanding the transmission of implicit and explicit knowledge such as ideology between members as the framework within which behaviour is developed, and further it helps us to understand the informal processes that facilitate ideology influencing behaviour and practice. Central to understanding the influence of ideology is the role of language, ritual, and practices, and we might draw on Althusserian notions about meaning and representation expressed through language and practice to place this within a broader conceptual context. As Stuart Hall[20] notes, "ideologies are the framework of thinking and calculations about the world—the 'ideas' that people use to figure out how the social world works, what their place is in it and what they ought to do"—another way of expressing this in behavioural and psychological concepts reflecting the significance of language might be in terms of rule governance (as briefly discussed later).

A broad outline of a process model describing involvement with terrorism is presented in Figure 9.1.

This diagram illustrates in a general sense the wide array of influences acting upon the individual, and the way in which those influences may affect behavioural choices. The central core of the diagram illustrates the effect on cognitions, and subsequent behaviour, of the various factors. It is consistent with efforts to model other forms of aggressive behaviour drawing on notions of process[21] based on cognitive-behaviour principles.

As a means of developing the process approach further, a further figure is presented below to illustrate potential relationships of more specific factors constituting the processes involved in the formation of terrorism and the terrorist at a point of engagement or choice, expressed as a conceptual pathway individuals might take to and with terrorism. Figure 9.2 illustrates the processes that might underpin forms of terrorist involvement, particularly initial and later stages of involvement. The influences affecting individual choices towards terrorism are necessarily complex, and do not readily fit into single dimensions. For the sake of simplicity, three critical process variables[22] have been identified that might relate to both the development of, and engagement with, terrorism:

1. Setting events
2. Personal factors
3. Social/political/organisational context

Setting events relate to essentially past contextual influence. These influences are effectively unchangeable, in that they have happened as part of the individual's socialisation into family, work, religion, society, and culture. They represent the context from which the individual comes, and may in part correspond to the sort of correlational factors identified in surveys and the like that look

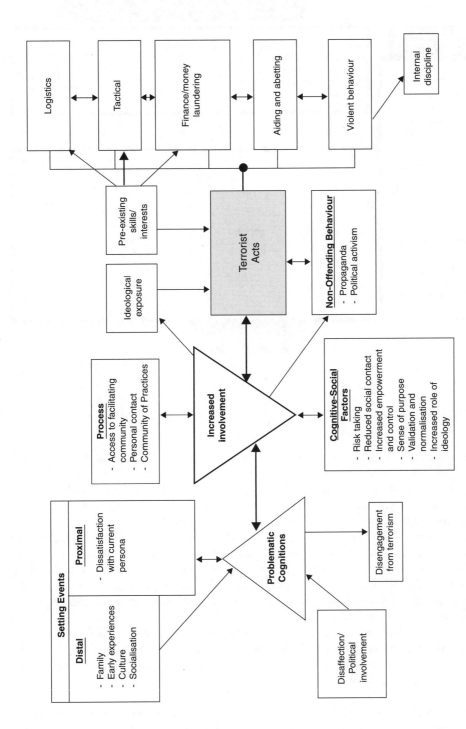

Figure 9.1 A diagrammatic model of terrorist involvement.

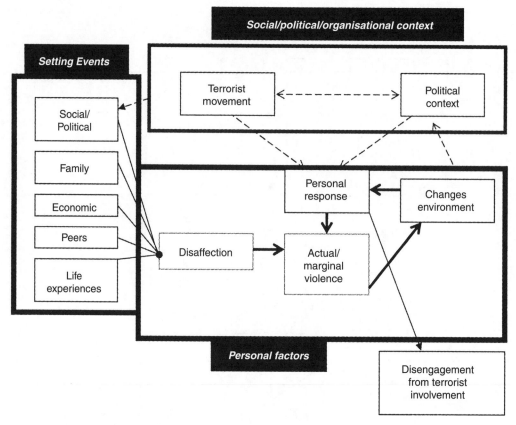

Figure 9.2 Involvement with terrorism.

for commonalities of experience between terrorists that might be expressed as the "trajectory" qualities to terrorism.[23] In a sense these factors are the precursors of immediate causal influences, but tend to be so general as to have little predictive value. They clearly contribute to the behavioural choices of an individual, and may provide important direction and motivation, but they cannot be said in any meaningful way to "cause" or result in choices of a particular set of actions.

Notions of *cause* and *choice* are clearly central to this discussion, and an important point relevant to this has been made by Ronald V. Clarke and Marcus Felson.[24] Drawing on analyses of crime, they make a critical distinction, which is relevant to understanding terrorist behaviour, between "criminal involvement" and "criminal events." Criminal involvement they refer to as "the processes through which individuals choose to become initially involved in particular forms of crime, to continue and to desist from that involvement." Different stages of involvement therefore imply different decisional factors, and need to be considered as separate. As for criminal event decisions, "the decision processes involved in the commission of a particular crime (i.e. the criminal event) are dependent upon their own special categories of information"[25] An important corollary of this distinction is that

> involvement decisions are characteristically multistage and extend over substantial periods of time. Event decisions, on the other hand, are frequently shorter processes, utilising more circumscribed information largely relating to immediate circumstances and situations.[26]

Although these distinctions were made with respect to criminal behaviour, it has been argued that they are clearly relevant to our consideration of terrorist behaviour.[27] The distal factors identified in Figure 9.1 as elements of the terrorist's decisional pathway are clearly related to Clarke and Felson's concept of criminal involvement factors.

Personal factors relate to the psychological and environmental context the individual experiences at the time of whatever quality of involvement he or she has. Critical elements might include an individual's emotional state (perhaps as an element in its own right, or, as below, as an element of what is described in the diagrams as "disaffection" or distance from social constraints relating to immediate political or ideological contexts), immediate experiences (such as perceived negative contact with security forces), or peer pressure. The precise factors will presumably vary from individual to individual, and furthermore will change as a result of the individual's experiences and continued involvement with terrorism and its consequences. Although there may be some overlap, personal factors can be distinguished from setting events in terms of immediacy and salience.

Social/political/organisational context refers to a feature of the individual's external social context that is specifically concerned with political expression and ideology, and/or the organisational expression of that ideology. Given that both political and organisational qualities impinge on the individual's experience of social context, some elements of this may be included in, or at least influenced by, the individual's distal context, and similarly they may also impinge on personal factors (in the sense, for example, of joining an organisation to acquire status). However, there is a clear sense in which political, ideological, and organisational issues come together in terrorism to form a distinctive and critical quality perhaps not so evident in other areas of social living. This seems to be the most significant factor that distinguishes terrorist from criminal violence, and it might be hypothesised that it is in accessing this quality that the process that changes the disaffected and troubled individual into a terrorist may lie.

The influence of ideology in a psychological sense has been little explored with respect to terrorism. As noted earlier, Hall[28] describes ideology as "the framework for thinking and calculations about the world—the 'ideas' that people use to figure out how the social world works, what their place is in it and what they *ought* to do." In a psychological sense, this implies influences on an individual's cognitive state, a point noted by Aaron T. Beck[29] in his paper on terrorism: "Ideology concentrates their thinking and controls their actions." For Beck, ideology implies not only cognitive influences, but that it operates as a process, changing or "controlling" behaviour; ideology therefore might be expressed in forms of cognitive structure, but it also has a sense of content that may exercise significance influence over behaviour. From a different context, as noted earlier, Louis Althusser also emphasises the significance of meaning and representation expressed through language and social action and practice. Taylor[30] and Taylor and Horgan[31] explored the role of rule governance as one way of understanding the behavioural process that might be involved in ideological control over behaviour, and it may be that further empirical exploration of this would yield valuable results.

The relative influence of these factors will vary between individuals, and as the individual becomes involved in his or her *particular* pathway to terrorism. What this therefore points to is a focus on the individual in context, and a concern with the experiences of the individual as the processes impinge on them. In practical terms, it may offer opportunities for structured intervention related to particular processes, or events; but what it also serves to do in conceptual terms is to offer a systematic means of identifying process variables, and aiding exploration of how these variables might interact given the individual's particular circumstances. Perhaps most significantly, it addresses at least one of the rate-limiting elements in the dynamic of terrorism.

Involvement

Figure 9.2 schematically describes how we might conceptualise the principle factors at work in an individual's initial involvement with terrorism using the factors outlined above.

In the initial stage of involvement, the features of setting events and personal factors seem likely to be most influential. Setting events may provide the context to choices made in terms of involvement with, knowledge and expectations of, and access to ideologies and organisations involved in terrorism, but the critical element that distinguishes those who engage actively with terrorism relates to the particular personal context the individual finds him- or herself in, and the interaction of that with setting events and the social/political/organisational context—the Community of Practice, to use Hundeide's term. However we might conceptualise the choices an individual might make (one of which of course may be to disengage from potential terrorist involvement), the reciprocal relationship amongst violence, environmental change, and the consequences of that environmental change in personal terms seems to be a critical factor to focus on, along with the nature and qualities of exposure to the social/political/organisational context. It is these circumstances that describe the involvement factors referred to by Clarke and Felson.[32]

The pathway taken might be structured (as in the case, for example, of a highly organised terrorist group like the Provisional IRA (PIRA)) where initiates and new recruits were exposed to a probationary period, where recruits were tested and assessed, and where involvement (for many) was shaped by formal training activities through attendance at training camps and programmes; alternatively, and for other kinds of groups (for example, the kind described by Marc Sageman[33]), it might be more informal, in some cases involving almost a form of apprenticeship training (from which again notions of Community of Practice are drawn). It is important to note, however, that case studies of terrorist involvement, such as there are, suggest that in all cases, an important developmental element is ideological and political exposure.[34] Whilst action and activity might be the route by which people initially engage with terrorism, the recruit has to learn about the particular ideology and "meaning" their behaviour has within the terrorist movement's context. And it seems to be that sense of meaning that strengthens the process of involvement, and gives it direction.

The ultimate expression of this may be found in the case of the suicide bomber. Evidence suggests that the short training programmes given to involve suicide bombers may serve this purpose. The use of intensive video presentations associated with discussion and peer pressure spread over two or three days serves to engage the initiate with the incremental process of further involvement. These may be associated with other kinds of social processes that confirm, strengthen, and sustain involvement, and close off (or at least narrow down) potential "escape" routes on what essentially becomes a continuum of successive "points of no return."[35] Comparison might be made with other similar processes that serve to initiate individuals into high risk and socially problematic behaviour—the "grooming" process used to initiate children into sexual behaviour by paedophiles, for example, might draw on similar processes, although spread out over longer time periods.

We might hypothesise that over time, the relative weight of influence between "personal" and "social/political/organisational" changes, and the origins in personal disaffection may change in terms of the balance of influence they each exert over the individual terrorist (at whatever stage of the process), or at least be diluted. Parallel with (and perhaps replacing) this, there is an increase in explicit political and ideological involvement and activism, which has the effect of "institutionalising" and internalising the social/political/organisational factors, bringing those more clearly and firmly within the individual's decisional calculus.

In the later development of terrorism, perhaps mediated by personal responses to individual involvement in terrorism, we might hypothesize that the significance of social/political/organisational context grows in importance in the individual decisional calculus, and the influence of setting events and personal factors diminish. Indeed, our knowledge of terrorist formation suggests that explicitly (through training) and implicitly (through attribution of meaning), political ideology and organisational factors become increasingly influential in determining the individual's behaviour and the choices made, and this might also be described as reflecting a growing sense of meaning to action as well as acceptance into the social group[36] (real or virtual). What we might also see is a growing together of political and personal factors, in the sense that individual qualities absorb and become part of the ideological and social context; in the diagram, personal factors and social/political/ideological context become merged.

The processes outlined above broadly describe in theoretical terms what we know about terrorist engagement and involvement and might be represented as a kind of "psychology of terrorism." Individual terrorists do not appear "fully fledged" as terrorists; they *become* terrorists through involvement in terrorism, they have to be trained both in terms of what they do (the mechanics of their trade as it were) and in terms of how they make sense of what they do (ideological formation). The aspirant terrorist comes from somewhere physically and psychologically, and he belongs in a social context that is outside of terrorist life (if only by virtue of not having "crossed the boundary" to illegality). The committed terrorist, in contrast, has already crossed that boundary, has acquired skills and knowledge that binds him or her closer to illegality and to the terrorist organisation, and these factors weigh heavily in the decisional calculus. Incidentally, the influence of the organisation and ideology can also be seen in the way in which political involvement in the later stages of development can represent a form of disengagement from terrorist violence,[37] where engagement in the political process can substitute for violent terrorist engagement (as in the recent case of some of the PIRA leadership for example). The above discussion, therefore, describes one sense of what the notion of process in terrorism might mean, exploring the essentially psychological dimension of engagement.

Thus far, this paper has assumed (or perhaps more accurately, taken for granted and not expressed) a sense of what a terrorist might do, although in Figure 9.1 there was some general indication of differentiation of function. However, quite clearly involvement with terrorism relates to a variety of activities and behaviours as the above discussion of incremental progression and process implies. Some kinds of involvement may have the dramatic quality of direct engagement with violence, others may be less directly involved but still central to creating the potential for violence (through construction of bombs or transport of munitions, for example), and yet others may be involved in activities which may not even be illegal, yet still vital for the conduct of terrorism (such as political activism and community involvement). A simple way of expressing this is in terms of a linear dimension expressing a sense of distance from the terrorist violent event, as can be seen in the following Figure 9.3. It draws on a sense of the structure of mature terrorist

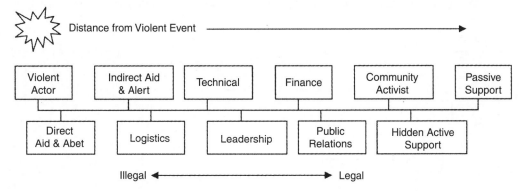

Figure 9.3 Linear depiction of terrorist roles.

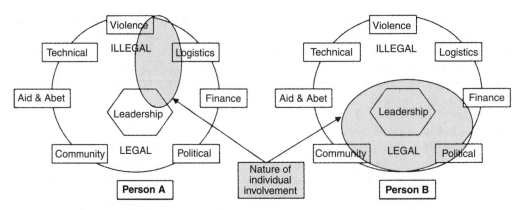

Figure 9.4 Relationship between the individual and different terrorist roles.

groups such as PIRA,[38] but in principle the sense of kinds of individual involvement applies to any terrorist movement.

The actual relationship between individuals and the functions they might occupy will be complex and multifaceted. For example, an individual may hold a variety of roles simultaneously, and almost certainly will occupy different roles over time as their terrorist "career" develops. This of course is implied by the concept of process as discussed above. An alternative way of expressing the relationships between the individual and roles may be seen in Figure 9.4. In this figure, seven of the activities identified in Figure 9.3 are focused on; there is no necessary reason for the order in which they are presented around the circle, although some activities might tend to cluster together more naturally than others (financing, political and community activism, for example).

The first (Person A) describes someone who is primarily involved in violent activity and associated logistical work. That person may also have an input into leadership activities. Person B in contrast has a much broader leadership, community, and political role. Person A's activities are almost wholly illegal, whereas Person B's are almost wholly legal—yet in the terms presented here, both fall within the broad concept of terrorist.

It is important to note that none of these diagrams take into account the dynamic temporal qualities of process, which implies a migration of function for the individual between the various activities over time. The following Figure 9.5 schematically illustrates a potential temporal quality to the function migratory process for Person A above.

The above categories of activities require more systematic work to identify their qualities and to validate their inclusion. Indeed, some kinds of terrorist involvement may have different factors

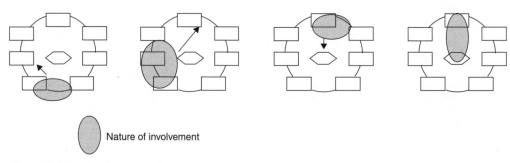

Figure 9.5 Migration between roles.

associated with them, particularly sleepers, or "walk in"[39] terrorists, and these are areas that merit much more investigation and analysis. The clustering of kinds of involvement for individuals requires more exploration, but such analysis and explorations may yield added value in terms of risk analysis and preventative initiatives. Furthermore, an added benefit from this approach is that it would also offer a means of developing a typology of terrorist engagement, which may have a further bearing on risk analysis and preventative activities.

Conclusions

This discussion would appear to suggest a clear research agenda related to gaining information about a) *decisional contexts* and b) *the choices of individuals* who have gone through, or are experiencing, these processes and c) the nature and implications for individuals of *different kinds of involvement* in terrorism. Furthermore, it suggests research methodologies that will enable a focus on the influences and factors that impinge on the individual in his or her life context, offering the opportunity to develop a systematic base for the development of both preventative and counterterrorism strategies. Given the relatively low frequency of terrorist events, and the difficulty of accessing information, aggregation of individual case studies seems to be the most likely strategy to follow; however, it follows from the above that the subjects of case studies need to illustrate broader kinds of involvement than either leadership or active violent roles. The analytical framework of Case Study and Theory Development described by Alexander George and Andrew Bennett[40] offers one promising methodology to employ.

In summary, the following points can be made:

1   There is never one route to terrorism, but rather there are individual routes, and furthermore those routes and activities as experienced by the individual *change* over time (hence the idea of a process). One further important route about which we know relatively little is disengagement from terrorism, particularly in the early formative stages of involvement, an issue of clear relevance in the development of counterterrorism strategies;
2   The conceptual framework presented here assumes that terrorism works at both an individual *and* political level, through *behaviour* acting on the environment sustained and focused by *ideology*, and the effect of that on subsequent behaviour;
3   The significant element in strengthening engagement with terrorism and giving it direction is the increased role of the social/political/organisational context (and especially as expressed through ideology) in exerting control over behaviour.

This account is closely allied to that which might follow from an analysis based on the Rational Choice Perspective applied to terrorism.[41] This approach emphasises the role of consequences to behavioural choices as the central determinant to behaviour change, and also draws on more traditional Cognitive Behavioural models of understanding behaviour. Taylor[42] explored the use of Rational Choice concepts in terrorism, and other authors have extended this drawing on primarily economic contexts, rather than psychological. A further central research issue emerging from the above relates to how we might understand the effects of ideology and organisational influences on the individual. Explorations of accounts grounded in empirical evidence, such as rule governance and relational frame theory,[43] may offer fruitful avenues for further conceptual development.

While the conceptual framework presented here offers a way of analysing and understanding terrorism and the actions of the terrorist within a political, ideological, and temporal framework, it also serves as an account of a "psychology of terrorism." Perhaps its overall contribution, however, is that it establishes a clear and unambiguous position for psychology within an interdisciplinary approach for developing an understanding of the emergence of terrorist behaviour and the sense of how group and other influences impinge upon the individual—this is, after all, what a "psychology of terrorism" ultimately implies: it recognises that individual experience is necessarily unique, but offers a framework for understanding that uniqueness *within* broader contextual political processes. What is even more important, however, is that by improving our understanding of the processes involved we may begin to develop empirically based strategies to interfere with and change the effects of those processes to result, for those individuals involved, in activities other than violence—a rather different kind of counterterrorism agenda than those currently practiced.

In terms of preventing and controlling terrorist behaviour, however, a further important corollary of this approach is that the opportunities to influence the process outcomes, at least in the short term, need to focus on changing the expression of the process in behaviour as they impinge on the individual at critical decisional points, rather than a focus on changing the processes themselves. As in the case of criminal behaviour, it is necessary to identify in terrorism the rate-limiting factors related to opportunity that can change the choices made for the potential terrorist from violence to other means of expression. In practical and immediate terms, limiting the opportunities for terrorist behaviour and focusing on the elements of the decisional calculus preceding potential terrorist action seems a more sensible strategy than seeking to change either presumed individual qualities or broad societal processes. However, to effect the agenda outlined here, we clearly need to move away from naive notions of "defeating" terrorism, to a more sophisticated analysis that will facilitate both the reduction of terrorism and the development of preventative strategies.

Notes

1   For example, D. Rothe and S. L. Muzzatti, "Enemies Everywhere: Terrorism, Moral Panic and US Civil Society," *Critical Criminology* 12 (2004): 327–350; also see J. Stern, "Fearing Evil," *Social Research* 71 (2004): 1111–1126.

2   See, for example, John Horgan, *The Psychology of Terrorism* (London: Routledge, 2005); Andrew Silke, ed., *Terrorists, Victims and Society: Psychological Perspectives on Terrorism and its Consequences* (Chichester, England: John Wiley, 2003); Max Taylor, *The Terrorist* (London: Brassey's, 1988).

3   See, for example, Ethel Quayle and Max Taylor, "A Cognitive Behavioural Model of Problematic Internet Use in People with a Sexual Interest in Children," *Cyber Psychology and Behaviour* 6 (2003): 93–106; Max Taylor and Ethel Quayle, "The Internet and Abuse Images of Children: Search, Precriminal Situations and Opportunity," in Richard Wortley and Stephen Smallbone, eds., *Situational prevention of Child Sexual Abuse: Crime Prevention Studies*, Vol. 19 (jointly published by Criminal Justice Press, Monsey, NY, and Willan Publishing, Cullompton, Devon, 2005). These papers address kinds of problematic behaviour that differs from terrorism, but illustrate commonalities in terms of *process* explanations.

4   See, for example, J. Horgan (see note 2 above), 86–94.

5   James Jerome Gibson, *The Ecological Approach to Visual Perception* (Boston: Houghton Mifflin, 1979); M. Taylor and E. Quayle (see note 3 above).

6   H. H. A. Cooper, "Voices from Troy: What Are We Hearing?" in *Outthinking the Terrorist—An International Challenge: Proceedings of the 10th Annual Symposium on the Role of Behavioural Science in Physical Security* (Washington, D.C.: Defence Nuclear Agency, 1985), 95.

7   Walter Reich, "Understanding Terrorist Behavior: The Limits and Opportunities of Psychological Enquiry," in Walter Reich, ed., *Origins of Terrorism: Psychologies, Ideologies, Theologies, States of Mind* (New York: Cambridge University Press, 1990), 261–279.

8   Max Taylor, "Rational Choice, Behaviour Analysis and Political Violence," in Ronald V. Clarke and Marcus Felson, eds., *Routine Activity and Rational Choice: Advances in Criminological Theory*, Vol. 5 (Piseataway, NJ: Transaction Press, 1992), 159–178.

9   For example, see A. Testas, "Determinants of Terrorism in the Muslim World: An Empirical Cross-Sectional Analysis," *Terrorism and Political Violence* 16 (2004): 252–273; A. B. Krueger and J. Maleckova,

"Education, Poverty, Political Violence and Terrorism: Is There a Causal Connection?," *NBER Working Paper No. 9074* (July 2002); T. R. Gurr and T. Björgo, "Economic Factors that Contribute to Terrorism in Social and Political Context: Final Report May 1, 2005," *International Summit on Democracy, Terrorism and Security*, Club de Madrid, March 8–11, 2005.

10 See J. Horgan (see note 2 above), especially Chapter 4, "Becoming a Terrorist."

11 Max Taylor and Ethel Quayle, *Terrorist Lives* (London: Brassey's, 1994).

12 Alex P. Schmid, "The Links between Transnational Organized Crime and Terrorist Crimes," *Transnational Organized Crime* 2 (1996): 40–82.

13 We tend to distinguish between terrorist violence and other forms of violence not only conceptually, but also in terms of how we treat convicted terrorists compared to other violent offenders; it would be interesting to know, for example, if the release of terrorist prisoners resulting from the implementation of the Good Friday Agreement in Northern Ireland was preceded by programmes of violence reduction and control, as might be expected when other violent offenders are released, and if not, why not?

14 W. Güth, "Bounded Rational Decision Emergence—A General Perspective and Some Selective Illustrations," *Journal of Economic Psychology*, 21 (2000): 433–458.

15 See, for example, J. A. Bouffard, "The Influence of Emotion on Rational Decision Making in Sexual Aggression," *Journal of Criminal Justice* 30 (2002): 121–124.

16 See, for example, D. P. Farrington and R. Loeber, "Risk Factors for Delinquency Over Time and Place," *Youth Update* 17 (1999): 4–5.

17 Karsten Hundeide, "Becoming a Committed Insider," *Culture and Psychology* 9 (2003): 107–127.

18 E. Wenger, "Communities of Practice: Learning as a Social System," *Systems Thinker* (1988). Retrieved 14 September 2005 from http://www.co-i-l.com/coil/knowledgegarden/cop/lss.shtml. A useful resource for the concepts of Community of Practice can be found at http://www.co-I-l.com/coil/index.shtml

19 See, for example, http://www.sfu.ca/cscd/cli/default.htm for how notions of community of practice can be applied to collaborative learning.

20 S. Hall, "Signification, Representation, Ideology: Althusser and the Post-Structuralist Debates," *Critical Studies in Mass Communication* 2 (1985): 91–114.

21 See, for example, A. R. Beech and Y. Ward, "The Integration of Etiology and Risk in Sexual Offenders: A Theoretical Framework," *Aggression and Violent Behavior* 10 (2004): 31–63 and N. Henry, T. Ward and M. Hirshberg, "A Multifactorial Model of Wartime Rape," *Aggression and Violent Behavior* 9 (2004): 535–562.

22 These variables are drawn from the Cognitive Behaviour Therapy (CBT) literature. See Aaron T. Beck, *Cognitive Therapy and the Emotional Disorders* (New York: International University Press: 1976) and L. Y. Abramson, G. I. Metalsky and L. B. Alloy, "Hopelessness Depression: A Theory-Based Subtype of Depression," *Psychological Review* 96 (1989): 358–372 for a broad introduction to this area and to the conceptual thinking underlying these variables.

23 J. Horgan (see note 2 above) discusses these factors as they might relate to some individuals having a greater "openness to socialisation into terrorism" than others, but as with the discussion presented here, argues that they are not only too broad to hold predictive validity, but are frequently a source of significant bias in recalled accounts of initial involvement in terrorism. The relevance of their identification, therefore, ought to be interpreted with caution.

24 Ronald V. Clarke and Marcus Felson, "Introduction: Criminology, Routine Activity, and Rational Choice," in Ronald V. Clarke and Marcus Felson, eds., *Routine Activity and Rational Choice: Advances in Criminological Theory, Volume 5* (New Piscataway, NJ: Transaction, 1993), 1–14.

25 Ibid., 6.

26 Ibid.

27 M. Taylor (see note 2 above); M. Taylor (see note 8 above); also see Chapter 5 ("Being a Terrorist") of J. Horgan (see note 2 above).

28 S. Hall (see note 20 above), 99.

29 Aaron T. Beck, "Prisoners of Hate," *Behaviour Research and Therapy* 40 (2002): 209–216, 210.

30 M. Taylor (see note 8 above).

31 M. Taylor and J. Horgan, "The Psychological and Behavioural Bases of Islamic Fundamentalism," *Terrorism and Political Violence* 13 (2001): 37–71.

32 Ronald V. Clarke and Marcus Felson (see note 24 above).

33 Marc Sageman, *Understanding Terror Networks* (Philadelphia: University of Pennsylvania Press, 2004).

34 Biographies and autobiographies of terrorists seem to suggest this to be the case in examples ranging from Baader-Meinhof members, such as that of Michael Baumann (in M. Baumann, *Terror or Love?*

Bommi Baumann's Own Story of His Life as a West German Urban Guerrilla (New York: Grove Press, 1977)) to more contemporary examples such as Abimael Guzmán (in Simon Strong, *Shining Path: Terror and Revolution in Peru* (New York: Times Books, 1992)) and Timothy McVeigh (by Lou Michel and Dan Herbeck, *American Terrorist: Timothy McVeigh and the Oklahoma City Bombing* (New York: Regan Books, 2001)).

35 Examples might be "psychological traps" (see J. Z. Rubin, "Psychological Traps," in Roy J. Lewicki, David M. Saunders, John W. Minton, eds., *Negotiation: Readings, Exercises, and Cases* (Boston: McGraw-Hill, 1999), 399–407) and "Groupthink" (Irving L. Janis, *Victims of Groupthink* (Boston: Houghton Mifflin, 1972); Irving L. Janis, *Groupthink: Psychological Studies of Policy Decisions and Fiascoes, 2nd Ed.* (Boston: Houghton Mifflin, 1982)). For a specific discussion of suicide bombings, see Ariel Merari, "Social, Organisational and Psychological Factors in Suicide Terrorism," in Tore Björgo, ed., *Root Causes of Terrorism: Myths, Realities, Ways Forward* (London: Routledge, 2005). Merari identifies three elements of suicide terrorism: indoctrination (ideology), group commitment, and personal commitment—elements that correspond broadly to the processes identified in this paper. Temporal factors also seem to be important—he notes that 93% of all attacks occur within one month of initial contact and consent, with 33% occurring within ten days. Group forces and the influence of ideology through what Merari describes as "indoctrination" rather than psychopathology seem to characterise the processes the suicide bomber is exposed to.

36 M. Sageman (see note 33 above) describes the significance of this in the context of initial involvement in Al Qaeda.

37 See J. Horgan, "Leaving Terrorism Behind: An Individual Perspective," in A. Silke, ed., *Terrorists, Victims and Society: Psychological Perspectives on Terrorism and Its Consequences* (Chichester, England: Wiley, 2003), 109–130.

38 J. Horgan and M. Taylor, "The Provisional Irish Republican Army: Command and Functional Structure," *Terrorism and Political Violence* 9 (1997): 1–32.

39 See the discussion in B. McAllister, "Al Qaeda and the Innovative Firm: Demythologising the Network," *Studies in Conflict and Terrorism* 27 (2004): 297–319.

40 Alexander L. George and Andrew Bennett, *Case Studies and Theory Development in the Social Sciences* (Cambridge, MA: MIT Press, 2005).

41 See, for example, M. Taylor (see note 8 above); J. Horgan (see note 2 above); M. Harrison, "The Logic of Suicide Terrorism" (August 2003), retrieved 21 September 2005 from http://www.securitymanagement. com/library/Suicide_Harrison0803.pdf; M. Harrison, "An Economist Looks at Suicide Terrorism," retrieved 21 September 2005 from http://www2.warwick.ac.uk/fac/soc/economics/staff/faculty/ harrison/papers/terrorism.pdf.

42 M. Taylor (see note 8 above).

43 The following discuss approaches to rule governance and terrorism: M. Taylor and J. Horgan (see note 27 above); M. R. Dixon, S. Dymond, R. A. Rehfeldt, B. Roche and K. R. Zlomke, "Terrorism and Relational Frame Theory," *Behavior and Social Issues* 12 (2003): 129–147; for a technical introduction see Stephen C. Hayes, ed., *Rule-Governed Behavior: Cognition, Contingencies and Instructional Control* (New York: Plenum, 1989), 153–190. See also Steven C. Hayes, Reville Niccolls, Akihiko Masuda, and Alyssa K. Rye, "Prejudice, Terrorism, and Behavior Therapy," *Cognitive and Behavioral Practice 9*, 296–301, 2002.

Section 4

Terrorist movements

Readings

Ranstorp, M. (1994). Hizbollah's command leadership: Its structure, decision-making, and relationship with Iranian clergy and institutions. *Terrorism and Political Violence, 6*, 303–339.

Drake, C. J. M. (1991). The Provisional IRA: A case study. *Terrorism and Political Violence, 3*, 43–60.

Sprinzak, E. (1995). Right-wing terrorism in a comparative perspective: The case of split delegitimization. In T. Bjorgo (Ed.), *Terrorism from the extreme right* (pp. 17–43). London: Frank Cass.

Holmes, J. S., Gutiérrez de Piñeres, S. A., & Curtin, K. M. (2007). A subnational study of insurgency: FARC violence in the 1990s. *Studies in Conflict and Terrorism, 30*, 249–265.

Raufer, X. (2003). Al Qaeda: A different diagnosis. *Studies in Conflict and Terrorism, 26*, 391–398.

Introduction

Now, having delved into the conceptual tenets of terrorism studies, this section provides detailed accounts of what terrorist movements are actually like, and what it is that they actually do. The articles selected here represent some of the best case studies of prominent terrorist groups the world has yet seen. The variety of the groups sampled, as well as the depth to which they are investigated will bring to light the complexity of terrorist movements and will allow you to develop an appreciation of the case study as a methodological tool for exploring terrorism.

In the first selection, Magnus Ranstorp investigates Hizbollah, a radical Islamic group based in Lebanon. Ranstorp's approach to studying Hizbollah illuminates the extent to which some terrorist groups develop ties between their members and foreign entities and how those ties affect the behaviour of the group. Next, we turn to C. J. M. Drake's case study of one of the most prominent terrorist organizations of the last fifty years, the Provisional Irish Republican Army. Written prior to the Good Friday Agreement of 1998 that served as a precursor to the disbanding of the Provisional IRA, this piece stands as a poignant look back at the "Long War" in its waning years. We then turn to Ehud Sprinzak's chapter on right-wing terrorism. Sprinzak's work identifies unique features of right-wing terrorism and explains how right-wing leaning individuals turn to terrorism through a process by which they perceive a conflict with multiple entities. Next, Jennifer Holmes, Sheila Amin Gutiérrez de Piñeres and Kevin M. Curtin examine the factors that have been theorized as causal of insurgency. More specifically, the authors provide a series of econometric analyses that seek to explain the insurgency fueled by the Fuerzas Armadas Revolucionares de Colombia (FARC). In the last article selected for this section, Xavier Raufer takes a look at the most notorious terrorist movement in the world today – al-Qaeda. Raufer asks some of the most basic questions about al-Qaeda: What is it? How have recent geopolitical changes paved the way for its emergence? How do its members perceive their actions, their enemies, and the world around them?

In taking a closer look at the movements themselves, this section will help you understand how different groups are motivated and sustained. Perhaps more importantly, this section illustrates that no two terrorist groups are the same, and that to defeat any one group requires a unique response tailored to the context in which they operate.

Discussion questions

By the end of this section, you should be able to answer:

* Why do some terrorist groups endure for long periods of time while others don't?
* How is al-Qaeda different to the Provisional IRA?
* What factors give rise to right-wing terrorism?

Further reading

Alonso. R. (2007). *The IRA and armed struggle.* London: Routledge.

Barton, G. (2004). *Indonesia's struggle: Jemaah Islamiyah and the soul of Islam.* Sydney, Australia: University of New South Wales Press.

Dingley, J. (2001). The bombing of Omagh, 15 August 1998: The bombers, their tactics, strategy, and purpose behind the incident. *Studies in Conflict and Terrorism, 24,* 451–465.

Joshi, M. (1996). On the razor's edge: The Liberation Tigers of Tamil Eelam. *Studies in Conflict and Terrorism, 19,* 19–42.

Leader, S. H., & Probst, P. (2003). The Earth Liberation Front and environmental terrorism. *Terrorism and Political Violence, 15,* 37–58.

Olson, K. B. (1999). Aum Shrinrikyo: Once and future threat? *Emerging Infectious Diseases, 5,* 513–516.

Ortiz, R. (2002). Insurgent strategies in the post-Cold War: The case of the Revolutionary Armed Forces of Colombia. *Studies in Conflict and Terrorism, 25,* 127–143.

Silke, A. (1997). Honour and expulsion: Terrorism in nineteenth-century Japan. *Terrorism and Political Violence, 9,* 58–81.

Taji-Farouki, S. (2000). Islamists and the threat of jihad: Hizb ut-Tahrir and al-Muhajiroun on Israel and the Jews. *Middle Eastern Studies, 36,* 21–46.

Weinberg, L., & Eubank, W. L. (1989). Leaders and followers in Italian terrorist groups. *Terrorism and Political Violence, 1,* 156–176.

Woodworth, P. (2001). Why do they kill? The Basque conflict in Spain. *World Policy Journal, 18,* 1–12.

10 Hizbollah's command leadership

Its structure, decision-making, and relationship with Iranian clergy and institutions

Magnus Ranstorp

For over 12 years the pro-Iranian Hizbollah organization in Lebanon has been the main terrorist nemesis of Western governments and Israel, inflicting blow after blow against its self-proclaimed enemies of Islam through suicide-attacks, hostage-takings, and other forms of terrorism.[1] While the unrelenting campaign of violence has led to the association and image of Hizbollah in the West as a crazy and fanatical religious group, bent on martyrdom through suicide operations and randomly abducting foreigners, under the assumed strict control and direction of Iran's clerical establishment, Hizbollah's use of terrorism has been anything but disorganized or solely Iranian-orchestrated. On the contrary, Hizbollah mastery of political violence served as the basic ingredient in its rapid and calibrated transformation from a small rag-tag revolutionary militia into a major military actor and, since 1992, a political player within post civil-war Lebanon. Simultaneously, Hizbollah's close ideological and material support from Iran has been instrumental in the movement's success in fighting and buying its way into the hearts and minds of the Shiite community in Lebanon.

Yet the nature of the Iranian-Hizbollah relationship has been far from monolithic but rather bound by both the dynamics of a series of formal and informal networks of personal contacts between Hizbollah (the party of God) and Iranian clergyman. These were initially forged by their shared theological experience in Najaf, Iraq, and grew into close personal friendships which fundamentally shaped the movement's ideological outlook as well as serve to regulate its past and current behaviour.[2] Consequently, the approach of viewing both Hizbollah and Iran as unitary rational actors is not only based on a misconception but also ignores the political reality of the internal dimensions of Lebanon's civil war. It also disregards the permanent projection of clerical factionalism in Iran onto the Lebanese arena through Hizbollah activity, especially in terms of hostage-taking of foreigners.[3] As a militant Islamic organisation, the Hizbollah is far from a uniform body as displayed by continuous *clerical factionalism* between its leading members over the direction of the movement and the constant readjustments of the movement's position within Lebanon's warring factions. In turn, this is influenced by the shifting dynamics of the relationship with Iranian clergy and institutions at work within the movement.[4] Any closer understanding of the Hizbollah as an organization requires an indepth analysis of the nature and dynamics of Hizbollah's command leadership balanced against the dynamics of its institutionalized relationship with Iran and, to a lesser extent, Syria.

Hizbollah's command leadership

The origins and development of the Hizbollah movement in Lebanon represent the most important and successful example of Islamic Iran's efforts to export its pan-Islamic brand of revolution beyond its own borders. Hizbollah's radicalization of the Lebanese Shia community and its declared allegiance to the Islamic Republic of Iran and Ayatollah Khomeini underlined the movement's close ideological and spiritual deference to Iran. However, the Hizbollah is not a monolithic body with total subservience to Iran but rather a coalition of Lebanese Shiite clerics, who each have their own views and networks of followers as well as ties to Iran's clerical establishment. Although leading Hizbollah clergy and Iranian officials deny that the movement had a clearly defined organizational structure, the Hizbollah was governed on the national and local level by the supreme political-religious leadership, composed of a small and select group of Lebanese *uluma*.[5] Apart from ensuring strict obedience by followers to decisions taken by the Hizbollah leadership, the authority of the Hizbollah *uluma* extends all the way to the religious and political authority of Iran's Ayatollah Khomeini to whom they appeal for guidance and directives in cases when Hizbollah's collective leadership fail to reach a consensus.[6]

On the first anniversary of the martyrdom of Sheikh Ragheb Harb, on 16 February 1985, Hizbollah publicly announced for the first time not only its ideological programme and strategy in a manifesto[7] but also appeared as a unified organization with the assembly of the entire Hizbollah command leadership.[8] Although the Hizbollah revealed only the position of Sheikh Ibrahim al-Amin as its official spokesman, the movement was secretly governed by a supreme religious body, which had been instituted by Iran's Fazlollah Mahallati in 1983, fashioned after the upper echelons of Iran's clerical leadership.[9] The composition of the highest authority within this supreme religious body in Lebanon reflected the core group of individual Shiite clergy who helped found Hizbollah in July 1982.[10] Apart from the position of Hussein al-Musawi, as the only non-clerical member of the religious leadership, the composition of Hizbollah's leadership council also reflected the religious authority of these clergymen in terms of their command of a substantial number of followers in each of the three main Shiite regions in Lebanon: Bekaa Valley; Beirut; and southern Lebanon.[11]

Bekaa Valley

In the Bekaa Valley area the Hizbollah is headed by Sheikh Subhi al-Tufayli,[12] who was considered the highest religious authority in Baalbek as evident by his nomination as "president of the Islamic Republic" in Baalbek in 1984,[13] and Sheikh Abbas al-Musawi.[14] Along with Hussein al-Musawi and his *Islamic Amal*,[15] these two religious figures occupied not only the most senior positions as spiritual leaders of the Hizbollah in the Bekaa but also acted as liaison with the Iranian Pasdaran Revolutionary Guards Corps and Iran while maintaining overall control over Hizbollah's irregular and semi-regular military units.[16] Sheikh al-Tufayli acted as the head of the Hizbollah headquarters in Baalbek and was the movement's main liaison with Tehran.[17] Sheikh al-Musawi was operational head of Hizbollah's Special Security Apparatus and the movement's military wing, the *Islamic Resistance*.[18] Another main leader of Hizbollah military activity in the Bekaa was Sheikh Husayn al-Khalil, who maintained a senior position within Hizbollah's command leadership.[19] Al-Khalil acted as operational co-ordinator of Hizbollah's military units in co-operation with *Islamic Amal*, which was subordinated organisationally within Hizbollah from 1984 onwards under the personal authority of Husayn al-Musawi.[20] A lesser Hizbollah figure in the Bekaa with an important function was Mustafa Mahmud Madhi, who is responsible for the arms shipments received from Iran at the Sheikh Abdallah barracks.[21]

Beirut

In Beirut and the surrounding suburbs the Hizbollah was headed by Sheikh Muhammad Hussein Fadlallah, the overall spiritual guide of the movement, who mustered a substantial following

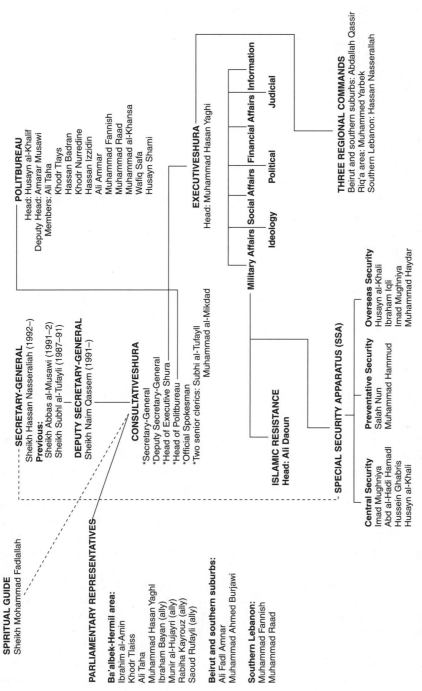

SPIRITUAL GUIDE
Sheikh Mohammad Fadlallah

PARLIAMENTARY REPRESENTATIVES

Ba'albek-Hermil area:
Ibrahim al-Amin
Khodr Tlaiss
Ali Taha
Muhammad Hasan Yaghi
Ibraham Bayan (ally)
Munir al-Hujayri (ally)
Rabiha Kayrouz (ally)
Saoud Rufayli (ally)

Beirut and southern suburbs:
Ali Fadl Amnar
Muhammad Ahmed Burjawi

Southern Lebanon:
Muhammad Fannish
Muhammad Raad

SECRETARY-GENERAL
Sheikh Hassan Nasseraliah (1992–)
Previous:
Sheikh Abbas al-Musawi (1991–2)
Sheikh Subhi al-Tufayli (1987–91)

DEPUTY SECRETARY-GENERAL
Sheikh Naim Qassem (1991–)

CONSULTATIVESHURA

*Secretary-General
*Deputy Secretary-General
*Head of Executive Shura
*Head of Politbureau
*Official Spokesman
*Two senior clerics: Subhi al-Tufayll
Muhammad al-Mikdad

POLITBUREAU
Head: Husayn al-Khalif
Deputy Head: Amarar Musawi
Members: Ali Taha
Khodr Tlays
Hassan Badran
Khodr Nurredine
Hassan Izzidin
Ali Ammar
Muhammad Fannish
Muhammad Raad
Muhammad al-Khansa
Wafiq Safa
Husayn Shami

EXECUTIVESHURA
Head: Muhammad Hasan Yaghi

Military Affairs | Social Affairs | Financial Affairs | Information
Ideology | Political | Judicial

ISLAMIC RESISTANCE
Head: Ali Daoun

SPECIAL SECURITY APPARATUS (SSA)

Central Security
Imad Mughniya
Abd al-Hadi Hamadl
Hussein Ghabris
Husayn al-Khali

Preventative Security
Salah Nun
Muhammad Hammud

Overseas Security
Husayn al-Khali
Ibraham Iqli
Imad Mughniya
Muhammad Haydar

THREE REGIONAL COMMANDS
Beirut and southern suburbs: Abdallah Qassir
Riq'a area: Muhammed Yarbek
Southern Lebanon: Hassan Nasserallah

Figure 10.1 The structure and leadership of Hizbollah

within existing Shiite religious institutions and other Shiite radical movements.[22] While Sheikh Fadlallah denies any official position within Hizbollah, the main leaders were seen to be Sheikh Ibrahim al-Amin, the official spokesman,[23] and Sheikh Hassan Nasserallah, who mustered support from the activists within the movement and were operationally responsible for certain aspects involving military and terrorist operations.[24] Both Sheikh al-Amin and Sheikh Nasserallah acted as liaison officers with Iran through its embassy in Beirut,[25] most notably with Muhammad Nurani, the *chargé d'affaires* between 1981 and 1985.[26] Another senior Hizbollah cleric was Sheikh Muhammad Ismail al-Khaliq, who is the personal representative of Iran's Ayatollah Montazeri in Lebanon.[27]

Southern Lebanon

In southern Lebanon the Hizbollah was headed by Sheikh Raghib Harb until his death in 1984.[28] While he was succeeded by Sheikh Abd al-Karim Obeid as Imam of Jibshit and in his position within the Hizbollah's command leadership,[29] the regional leadership of the movement is divided between local commanders and religious clergymen in the Hizbollah districts of Nabatiya and Sidon-Zahrani in southern Lebanon, most notably under the direction of Sheikh Afif al-Nabulsi and Sheikh Muhammad Fannish.[30] Hizbollah's military units in southern Lebanon are headed by local commanders, who recruit young Shiites from the villages with in-depth knowledge of the local terrain.[31] The military units of *Islamic Resistance* (*al-muqawama al-islamiyya*) are composed of a total of 300–400 core fighters and at least 1,500 armed sympathisers.[32] While Hizbollah's military actions against Israel were initiated by the local field commanders, all military activity was subject to approval by Hizbollah's military command, headed by 12 senior Hizbollah clergymen.[33]

Majlis al-Shura

These prominent regional Hizbollah clergymen and commanders were represented on the *Majlis al-Shura*, the supreme decision-making authority of the Hizbollah on the national level, that was first convened on 28 May 1986, on a regular basis.[34] Within the *Majlis al-Shura*, there are seven specialised committees dealing with ideological, financial, military, political, judicial, informational and social affairs.[35] In turn, the *Majlis al-Shura* and these seven committees are replicated in each of Hizbollah's three main regional and operational areas. They function as the principal governing body on local daily efforts.[36] All Hizbollah activity is regulated by decisions taken by the main *Majlis al-Shura*, which issued general directives to the regions, which in turn were left to implement the decisions on the operational level. While Sheikh Fadlallah presided over the national *Majlis al-Shura* as its overall leader in his capacity as spiritual leader of Hizbollah, the main clergymen who exercise control over the movement are the ones responsible for a specific committee or portfolio.[37]

In 1989 new organs were added, the *Executive Shura*, which ranks after the *Majlis al-Shura* as the second highest leadership authority, and a *Politbureau*, a supervisory organ which co-ordinates the work of the various committees under the *Jihad al-Bina'* (Holy Reconstruction Organ). These changes have meant a "Lebanonization" of the Hizbollah where the control of the overall organization has been made more open and expanded.[38] The control of specific portfolios has become more important and increasingly subject to factionalism.[39] Although Hizbollah's newly-established central decision-making body has led to a greater openness within the organization, in conjunction with an effort by Hizbollah to raise its profile and move into mainstream Lebanese politics, it continues to maintain strict operational secrecy in the field of military and security affairs.[40]

Special security apparatus

Within the military committee on Hizbollah's main *Majlis al-Shura* and in the three regional areas, there exists a separate body, the so-called Special Security Apparatus (SSA), responsible for intelligence and security matters.[41] In turn, the Hizbollah's security apparatus is divided into three subgroups: the central security apparatus, the preventative security apparatus and an overseas security apparatus.[42] While Sheikh al-Musawi was the overall head of Hizbollah's SSA until late 1985,[43] the central security apparatus is headed by Imad Mughniya and Abd al-Hadi Hamadi and was responsible for Hizbollah's hostage-taking activity of foreigners during the 1980s.[44] On the operational level, it was mainly family members from both the Mughniya and Hamadi clans that were involved in the hostage-takings which ensured loyalty to the senior commanders and secrecy surrounding the operations.[45] Apart from Mughniya and Hamadi, other senior members of the national central security apparatus were Sheikh Hussein Ghabris, who acted as Mughniya's deputy, and Sheikh Hussein Khalil, who was the main liaison between Hizbollah's security and intelligence.[46] This division of Hizbollah's SSA has also been effective in the infiltration of its own members within rival movements and in the elimination of military and political opponents in Lebanon.[47] Hizbollah's national preventative security apparatus was headed by Salah Nun and Muhammad Hammud and was in charge of the personal security of prominent Hizbollah clergymen.[48] The functions of Hizbollah's central security apparatus and the overseas security apparatus, in charge of special operations abroad, overlapped as Hussein Khalil, Ibrahim Aqil, Imad Mughniya, Muhammad Haydar, Kharib Nasser and Abd al-Hamadi, were the senior commanders of the Hizbollah operations in Europe.[49] Waid Ramadan acted as the chief coordinator of Hizbollah with Iran concerning these European operations.[50] During the frequent absence of Mughniya from Lebanon, the influence of his *de facto* deputy, Ali Karekeh, increased within the SSA.[51]

While Hizbollah's SSA managed to maintain operational secrecy due to its use of mainly family and clan members, this can also be attributed to the previous experience by some of its commanders in Fatah Force 17, the Palestinian Liberation Organization's intelligence and security organization.[52] In particular, Imad Mughniya had not only been the personal bodyguard of Sheikh Fadlallah before he was elevated within the Hizbollah after the successful hijacking of TWA 847 at Beirut in 1985, but also served with Force 17 as a lieutenant prior to Israel's invasion in 1982.[53] The decision by Hizbollah's SSA to abduct foreign citizens was usually initiated at the highest level in the main *Majlis al-Shura* within the Hizbollah through consultation with its senior clergy and two permanent representatives from Iran.[54] After reaching concensus of the future nationality of the hostage, Hizbollah's *Majlis al-Shura* delegated either specific details of a certain individual intended for abduction or broadly issued directives relating to the nationality and profession of victim to the commanders of Hizbollah national SSA.[55] A similar method was used with regard to military operations by the *Islamic Resistance*, formed in 1983, whereby the attacks were initiated by local commanders with confirmation from the supreme *Majlis al-Shura*.[56]

Liaison with Iran

In making the abductions authorized by Hizbollah's national SSA, the operational officers maintained close liaison with official representatives from Iran's embassies in Beirut and Damascus as well as with Pasdaran (Iranian Revolutionary Guards Corps) officials.[57] While Muhammad Haydar was Hizbollah's main liaison with the Pasdaran, three senior Hizbollah operatives liaised with Iranian intelligence, VEVAK, most notably Hussein al-Khalil.[58] Apart from the well-known and close role of Ali Akbar Mohtashemi, the former Iranian ambassador to Syria and Interior Minister, in both the formation of the Hizbollah and continued guidance over the movement,[59]

Iranian diplomatic staff provided intelligence on targets while the Iranian Pasdaran supplied weaponry and training.[60] Although Iran's embassy in Beirut was previously active with Hizbollah under the helm of Muhammad Nurani, the Iranian *chargé d'affaires*, most of the liaison for security reasons between Hizbollah and Iran occurred through the Iranian embassy in Syria.[61] However, Ali Akbar Rahimi and Muhammad Javad of the Iranian embassy in Beirut maintained close liaison with Hizbollah's national SSA.[62] The role of the Iranian embassy in Beirut assumed increased importance over the mission in Damascus due to the constraints imposed by the Amal-Hizbollah clashes.[63] While Iran's military attaché in Damascus coordinated activities between Iran's Pasdaran contingent in Baalbek and its headquarters in the Syrian border village of Zebdani,[64] the Pasdaran contingent and Iran's military attaché in Beirut were involved not only in supplying the cadres of Hizbollah SSA with training and military equipment[65] but also in its hostage-taking activity, as evident by their role in the initiation as well as interrogation and housing of some of the foreign hostages.[66]

The role of the Pasdaran with Hizbollah was formally institutionalized through, and controlled by, the presence of a high-ranking Iranian Revolutionary Guard Corps (IRGC) representative on the *Majlis al-Shura*.[67] Despite attempts by Iran's clerical establishment to impose a degree of clerical control over the Pasdaran,[68] the Lebanese contingent has shown a capacity for institutional autonomy and radicalism by its previous and present commanders, most notably Hosein Deqan,[69] in terms of conforming to the wishes of the political leadership in Iran, especially *vis-à-vis* the release of Western hostages.[70] In particular, this was evident by the efforts of Iran's President Rafsanjani to assign a more loyal and pliable IRGC unit to the Pasdaran contingent in 1989.[71]

Liaison with Syria

The Hizbollah command leadership and its security and intelligence service were also in close liaison with Syrian military intelligence[72] which actively participated in the planning of Hizbollah actions until the withdrawal of the Multinational Forces from Beirut in early 1984.[73] Syria pursued a calibrated policy of tacit co-operation with Hizbollah and support for its abductions of foreigners, as long as they were in accordance with Syrian strategic interests in Lebanon. Simultaneously it was forced to clamp down on Hizbollah in order to reassert Syrian hegemony and to limit Iran's influence and avoid a military confrontation with Israel.[74] While Syria has pursued a public policy of disassociation from Hizbollah's hostage-taking activity, its relationship with the movement's SSA was pursued by Syrian military intelligence, under the command of Brigadier Ghazi Kan'an.[75] As Syria has been in firm control over the Bekaa area from which Pasdaran and Hizbollah operate, Syrian military intelligence not only facilitated the transfer of hostages to Baalbek from Beirut, but also acted as a conduit for the release of the foreign hostages through the hands of Syrian military intelligence officers.[76] A main liaison between Hizbollah and Syrian military intelligence was Mustafa Dirani, the former head of Amal's security service who defected from Amal in late 1988 and joined Hizbollah in 1989.[77]

The relationship between Hizbollah's SSA and Syrian military intelligence has been characterized by periods of conflict and cooperation, largely dictated by the shifting internal situation in Lebanon.[78] While Syrian sanction for the presence of Pasdaran and tolerance towards Hizbollah activity has often depended on its relationship with Iran, coupled with Syrian complicity in drug-trafficking in Lebanon,[79] the friction between Syria and Hizbollah has been manifest by retaliatory abductions and the threat, or actual use, of military force.[80] Apart from direct Syrian military intervention throughout the use of its proxy Amal, in the search for foreign hostages, Syria increased the pressure on both the Hizbollah and the Pasdaran by confining them to the Bekaa area or searched for the hostages in Hizbollah safe-houses in Beirut and its southern suburbs.[81] However, friction between Syria and Hizbollah over the hostage-taking of foreigners was the exception rather than the norm, as displayed by their co-ordination of military operations against Israel[82] and co-operation in the release of hostages. At any rate, Syria controlled the surrounding territory of the Bekaa and authorized not only the presence of the Pasdaran and the Hizbollah, but also their movement beyond this area. In particular, Syria continues to supply weapon consignments to Hizbollah for its anti-Israel operations through a fixed route: from Tehran to Damascus and onwards under Syrian protection to Beirut's southern suburbs and then to Hizbollah strong-holds near the security zone.[83]

Clerical factionalism

Apart from the Hizbollah decision-making apparatus and the institutionalized relationship with Iran and Syria through military and civilian channels at work in Lebanon, Hizbollah's mechanism for hostage-taking of foreigners was also subject to influence from clerical factionalism within the organization itself and to a web of clerical relationships extending from members of the national *Majlis al-Shura* to various clergy within Iran's civilian and military establishment.[84] While the clerical factionalism within Hizbollah can be monitored by the ascendancy or demotion of clergyman over the leadership of the movement, as shown by the election of a new Hizbollah Secretary-General every two years, it is also a guide to not only the direction of the movement in Lebanon but also to the affiliation and loyalty of Hizbollah's leadership with clerical factions and institutions in Iran.[85] Although the Hizbollah command leadership is a cohesive organization, the main differences between leading Hizbollah clergymen are over methods rather than aims, as evidently displayed by the 1988 dispute between Sheikh al-Tufayli and Sheikh Fadlallah over the question of the feasibility of the establishment of an Islamic republic in Lebanon.[86] Similarly, Sheikh al-Tufayli has been at the heart of a dissident faction within the command leadership over the issue of a new leader of the movement in the wake of the February 1992 assassination of Sheikh al-Musawi. This faction also vehemently objected to Hizbollah members taking part in the Lebanese parliamentary elections held between 23 August and 6 September 1992, in which the movement won 12 out of 128 seats.[87] However, the position of the Secretary-General and his deputy are fundamental to monitor for an understanding of Hizbollah as they directly control all the affairs of the movement and are *ex-officio* in charge, and have direct access to, clerical commanders of the regional *Majlis al-Shuras*.[88]

While Hizbollah's national *Majlis al-Shura* was established in 1986, no particular leading cleric emerged as undisputed leader until the ascendancy of Sheikh Subhi al-Tufayli in late 1987, a noted radical with particularly close personal ties with Ali Akbar-Mohtashemi in Iran.[89] Sheikh al-Tufayli's position as leader of the Hizbollah remained uncontested until the death of Ayatollah Khomeini in June 1989, when the organization faced unprecedented challenges with Lebanon and, consequently, displayed intensified rivalry between Hizbollah clergymen over the position and direction of the movement.[90] As a result of meetings held in Tehran in October and December 1989, Hizbollah submitted to major structural changes, as seen in the establishment of an *Executive Shura*, also known as the Supreme Shura.[91] While the composition of the new *Executive Shura* corresponds with the so-called *Consultative Shura*, or the *Majlis al-Shura*, the former decision-making body assumed the second highest authority of the Hizbollah and set mainly strategic matters in the overall administration of the movement.[92] It also led to the establishment of a *"Politbureau"*, a supervisory committee composed of 15 clergy in charge of Hizbollah's co-ordination of recruitment, propaganda and support services on the regional and local level.[93]

Although Sheikh al-Tufayli retained his position as Secretary-General of the Hizbollah in December 1989, the meetings underlined strong clerical factionalism within the hierarchy.[94] In particular, the meetings revealed intense rivalry between the nominated leadership and elements from *Lebanese al-Da'wa*, the *Islamic Resistance*, and members of the Special Security Apparatus, as evident by their rejection of the main decisions at the meeting and the delay in the reappointment for another two years of Sheikh Subhi al-Tufayli until the December 1989 meeting.[95] The militant position of Sheikh Hassan Nasserallah was also revealed by his vocal opposition to compromises made with Amal in 1989 by his clerical colleagues.[96] The structural changes within the leadership also led to the dismissal of four leading Hizbollah officials while it bolstered the positions of Sheikhs al-Tufayli, Naim Qassem, and Nasserallah within the leadership of Hizbollah's national *Majlis al-Shura*.[97] Under the renewed command of Sheikh al-Tufayli, the Hizbollah leadership was considered closer to Iran's radical faction, led by Ali Akbar-Mohtashemi, than to Hashemi Rafsanjani.[98]

While the tenure of Sheikh al-Tufayli as leader of Hizbollah was marked by friction with Iran's newly-elected president, the election of Sheikh al-Musawi as the Secretary-General of Hizbollah, and Sheikh al-Amin as his deputy in May 1991[99] came after settlement of the uncertainty within Hizbollah ranks concerning disarmament of all Lebanese militias in accordance with implementation of the Ta'if agreement.[100] The appointment of Sheikh Abbas al-Musawi, the former head of the *Islamic Resistance*,[101] came as a response to a *quid pro quo* arrangement between the organization and Iran and Syria which permitted the movement to maintain their armed presence in the South and in the eastern Bekaa, as it claimed to be a resistance movement rather than a militia.[102] Unlike his predecessor, Sheikh al-Musawi appeared to be more pragmatic as evident by the fact that he presided over Hizbollah through the denouement of the Western hostage crisis[103] while he readjusted the organization's grand strategic aim from creating an Islamic Republic of Lebanon through armed struggle to a willingness to participate in mainstream Lebanese politics.[104] Although his pragmatism reflected Hizbollah's effort to confront the challenges posed by a post-militia phase of Lebanese politics[105] and that the position of Sheikh al-Musawi was closer to the line of Iran's Hashemi Rafsanjani than that of his clerical colleagues within the Hizbollah, it was also the result of increased Iranian influence and pressure.[106]

The assassination of Sheikh al-Musawi

The assassination of Sheikh al-Musawi by Israeli missile-firing helicopters on 16 February 1992, after he and some other high-ranking Hizbollah officials attended an annual memorial service in the village of Jibshit in order to mark the eighth anniversary of the death of Sheikh Harb,[107] strengthened Hizbollah's militancy and allegiance to Iran's more radical clergy.[108] In an attempt to assure its own cadres that al-Musawi's death had not seriously affected the organization, Hizbollah immediately announced the election of Sheikh Nasserallah as the new leader.[109] However, internal rivalry between Nasserallah factions and those supporting al-Tufayli became apparent through the influence and intervention of Iran in the appointment of the new Hizbollah leader.[110] Despite the fact that Nasserellah received a majority vote in *Majlis al-Shura* elections in May 1991 to the post of Secretary-General of the movement, which he yielded to Sheikh al-Musawi out of "humility", Shiekh Nasserallah bolstered his own position within the *Majlis al-Shura* under Sheikh al-Musawi's leadership as he held control over finances and military matters, thereby restricting the maneuvrability of Sheikh al-Musawi and turning himself into the real *de facto* leader.[111] Sheikh Nasserallah also maintained a far closer relationship with Iran's revolutionist faction, most notably with Ali-Akbar Mohtashemi, than his predecessor.[112] However, Iranian pressure to appoint Sheikh Nasserallah to the post of the incumbent Secretary-General of Hizbollah over the hardline contender and previous leader, Sheikh al-Tufayli, came after Nasserallah had assured Iranian officials that he was in full compliance with their wishes and orders. This led to an intense internal Hizbollah dispute with dissident factions loyal to al-Tufayli.[113]

In particular, the internal rivalry within the Hizbollah leadership came over the decision by certain leaders to participate in Lebanon's parliamentary elections, held between 23 August and 6 September 1992. The followers of the al-Tufayli faction vehemently objected that it abandoned the movement's pan-Islamic goal of resistance against Israel by redirecting the movement's focus towards Lebanese internal politics.[114] While threats of sabotage by Sheikh al-Tufayli to Hizbollah's participation in the parliamentary elections failed to materialise,[115] challenges to the leadership of Sheikh Nasserallah by al-Tufayli supporters in the Bekaa area assumed the form of independent resistance attacks against Israel immediately following the procurement by Hizbollah of 12 electoral seats out of 128 in the Lebanese parliamentary elections.[116] As a consequence, the divisions within the Hizbollah, in the wake of the death of Sheikh al-Musawi, have been between Nasserallah's efforts to reorientate the party of God more towards political rather than military activity through acceptance of the realities of Lebanon's systems, and the dissident faction led by Sheikh al-Tufayli, supported by the Iranian revolutionist faction, towards undermining the more moderate position of the new Secretary-General and to press on with a perpetual jihad against Israel at all costs.[117] While Nasserallah has stressed his commitment to the armed strategy of the *Islamic Resistance* against Israel, he also underlined that Hizbollah's parliamentary participation was geared towards "[t]rying to topple the government through peaceful means".[118] Hizbollah's participation as a party represented in the Lebanese parliament was also a joint Hizbollah-Iranian strategy to legitimize the movement in order to guarantee its survival and insulate itself from internal/external persecution in post-civil war Lebanon.[119]

The internal rivalry between Nasserallah and al-Tufayli clearly demónstrated the existence of clerical factionalism within the hierarchy of the movement. It also underlined the importance of understanding divisions among its leaders and their ability to muster a substantial number of followers as a guide to the activity of the movement as well as allegiances of dissident factions.[120] In this particular rivalry, the fact that Sheikh Nasserallah comes from southern Lebanon rather than, as his predecessors, from the Bekaa area meant that he was more susceptible to losing control over the loyalty of commanders and fighters of the *Islamic Resistance*. Most of them come from the Bekaa and pledge closer allegiance to Sheikh al-Tufayli.[121] This became apparent by Nasserallah's replacement of military commanders in southern Lebanon and separation of the *Islamic Resistance* from the political framework of the Hizbollah for operational expediency and security after the assassination of Sheikh al-Musawi.[122] However, the failure of Sheikh al-Tufayli to regain the leadership of the Hizbollah in its leadership elections in May 1991, February 1992, and April 1993 have led to an erosion in the influence of the extremist and radical camp of the movement which is parallel to the decline of its closest allies in Iran, the revolutionist faction under the leadership of Hojjatolislam Mohtashemi. As a result, Hizbollah appointments of a new Secretary-General demonstrated that election of a particular senior Party of God cleric not only depended on the relevance of his previous experience to a current situation confronting the movement within Lebanon and, on the level of support and followers the candidate manage to muster within the movement, but also on his closer links with particular factions and institutions within Iran's clerical establishment.[123]

Hizbollah's relationship with Iranian clerics and institutions

Apart from the influence of close personal relationships, the conduct of both formal and informal consultations between Hizbollah clergymen and Iranian officials occurs through a variety of channels and institutions.[124] While official Iran has attempted to exert influence over Hizbollah activity through various Iranian agencies at work in the movement, ranging from the Pasdaran contingent and Iran's personal representatives in Damascus and Beirut to Iran's Foreign Ministry and the Martyr's Foundation, Hizbollah clergymen are also influenced by individual Iranian clergy with personal and political aspirations, at times, contrary to the official position and policy of Iran's ruling clerical elite.[125] The degree of divergence between Hizbollah's subordination, in principle, to the supreme religious and political authority of Ayatollah Khomeini and the disobedience and disagreements displayed within the Party of God's ranks towards Iran's official leadership and its willingness to sacrifice ideology to achieve pragmatic foreign and domestic policy objectives, depends on Hizbollah's and individual clergymen's interaction with official Iranian institutions as well as on clerical factionalism in Iran. In turn, any discord or harmony in Hizbollah's relationship with Iran is influenced by the impact of Iranian clerical factionalism on the institutions at work in the Party of God.

As a revolutionary movement, the pan-Islamic ideological position of the Hizbollah and its command leadership is naturally attuned to the revolutionist faction within Iran's clerical establishment. This closeness in radical ideology stemmed from the position of Ayatollah Khomeini. It also mirrors the involvement by several Iranian members of the revolutionist factions with prominent Lebanese Shiite clerics both prior to and, more importantly, in the formation and development of Hizbollah in Lebanon.[126] The personal relationships between some Iranian clergymen and Hizbollah's command leadership, forged at the religious centers in Najaf and in Qum as well as in Lebanon during the early 1970s, translated not only into their close involvement in the actual formation of the Party of God in 1982, but also into the appointments of these Iranian clergy to the official Iranian institutions at work in Hizbollah.[127] This facilitated the rapid growth and expansion of Hizbollah and also forged ties to the inner sanctum of Iran's clerical establishment. The movement also became gradually susceptible to clerical factionalism in Iran, as evident by the dismissal and appointment of Iran's radical clergy within these Iranian institutions.[128]

The role of Ali-Akbar Mohtashemi

Among the most influential and strongest relationship between an individual Iranian clergyman and the Hizbollah command leadership was the role of Ali-Akbar Mohtashemi, the former Iranian ambassador to Syria and former Interior Minister.[129] Apart from his pivotal role in the creation of the Hizbollah in 1982[130] and his role as liaison between Iran and the movement in Lebanon during his tenure in Syria until 1986,[131] Mohtashemi's radical position in ideological terms has resonated within the movement in Lebanon, especially when Hizbollah has been at odds with the official Iranian leadership.[132] While Mohtashemi has cultivated a broad base of support within the movement, his closest relationship within Hizbollah's command leadership has been with the radical activists, most notably Sheikh al-Tufayli and Sheikh Nasserallah.[133] Hizbollah's spiritual leader, Sheikh Fadlallah, reportedly was not a supporter of Mohtashemi.[134] Although the promotion of Mohtashemi as Interior Minister within Iran's clerical establishment in 1986 meant the loss of his position as Iranian representative within Hizbollah's national *Majlis al-Shura*, he maintained an independent relationship with the movement's leadership, as evident from his frequent visits to Lebanon and Syria as well as his outspoken views on the Party of God's position with particular reference to the abduction and release of foreign hostages.[135] Although the dismissal of Mohtashemi in the post-Khomeini cabinet, under the leadership of Hashemi Rafsanjani, in 1989 weakened his influence within Iran's clerical establishment,[136] it also translated into an attempt by Mohtashemi to upstage Rafsanjani's pragmatic foreign policy, through Hizbollah, by blocking the release of Western hostages.[137] Notwithstanding the prominent role of Mohtashemi in the initiation of abduction of foreigners, his influence over radical clergy within

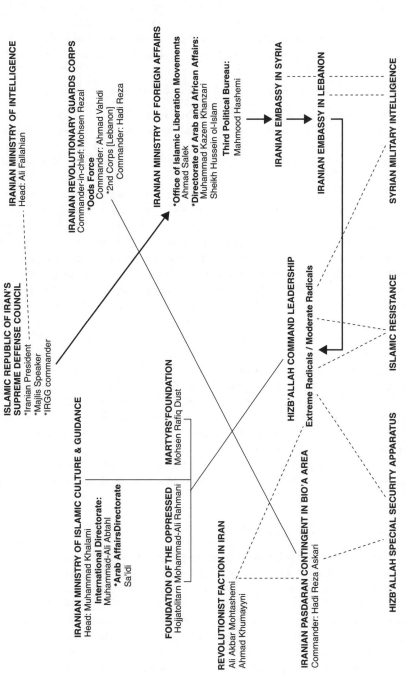

Figure 10.2 Iranian institutions at work within the Hizbollah

Hizbollah provided him with an instrument to both sabotage moderate and pragmatic overtures by the Iranian leadership in the foreign policy arena as well as to bolster his position within the clerical factionalism in Iran.[138] However, Mohtashemi's ability to manipulate Hizbollah activity was limited by changes in the Party of God's position within Lebanon, as evident by the denouement of the hostage-crisis in 1991 despite long opposition from Mohtashemi, and by the presence of a more pragmatic Hizbollah leader, Sheikh al-Musawi, in charge of the organization.[139]

Ayatollah Montazeri and the Office of Islamic Liberation Movements

Another prominent Iranian cleric for the Hizbollah is Khomeini's designated heir, Ayatollah Husayn Ali Montazeri.[140] Apart from his early active role in the promotion of Iranian involvement in Lebanon through Hizbollah, Montazeri's position as supervisor of the *Office of Islamic Liberation Movements*, operated by his relative Mehdi Hashemi and in charge of co-ordination of Iran's revolutionary support and activity abroad, provided him with an official channel to Hizbollah's command leadership.[141] As the *Office of Islamic Liberation Movements* had been originally a formal arm of the Revolutionary Guard until 1983,[142] it was transformed into a semi-independent institution of the IRGC headed by Montazeri's protégé, Mehdi Hashemi, which co-ordinated the operational co-operation between Iran and the Hizbollah.[143] Hashemi's efforts to foment revolutionary activity and terrorism abroad damaged Iran's war effort against Iraq and led to his arrest in 1986. The retaliatory abductions of American hostages and revelation of the US-Iranian arms-for-hostages deal by Ayatollah Montazeri's personal representative in Lebanon, Sheikh Ismail al-Khaliq,[144] coupled with the kidnapping of Iyad Mahmoud, the Syrian *chargé d'affaires* to Iran, clearly showed the connection between Iranian clerical factionalism and Hizbollah activity.[145] It also led to the final separation of the *Office of Islamic Liberation Movements* from the IRGC[146] and its transfer to the Ministry of Foreign Affairs in late 1986, in an effort by Rafsanjani to achieve greater Iranian control over Hizbollah activity.[147]

This was also evident by Rafsanjani's appointment of Hojjatolislam Khosrowshahi in 1987 to head the *Office of Islamic Liberation Movements*,[148] and the nomination of Rafsanjani's brother, Mahmud Hashemi, to head the Lebanon desk within Iran's Ministry of Foreign Affairs.[149] Mohtashemi established his own parallel institution with its own budget to aid the movement,[150] thus making Hizbollah's official links to the revolutionary Iranian clergy more difficult.[151] Even worse, the dismissal of Khomeini's designated heir Montazeri in March 1989 and the death of Ayatollah Khomeini three months later left the movement in disarray over its future position in Lebanon.[152]

Iranian Ministry of Foreign Affairs

While Montazeri maintained relations with Hizbollah through another Iranian institution, the Ministry of Islamic Guidance,[153] several radical Iranian clergy held senior positions within Iran's Ministry of Foreign Affairs and strongly supported the movement in Lebanon. Among the most helpful foreign ministry officials has been the Director for Arab Affairs, Hosein Sheikh-ol-Islam, who coordinated with the Pasdaran to place its members in Iranian embassies abroad and participate in Hizbollah operations.[154] Another radical ally of Hizbollah was Javad Mansuri, Undersecretary for Cultural and Consular Affairs in the Ministry of Foreign Affairs, who controlled the Iranian embassies abroad.[155] After the appointment of Rafsanjani in 1989, both Sheikh-ol-Islam's and Mansuri's positions were formally demoted in the Ministry of Foreign Affairs.[156] As a consequence, Hizbollah downgraded the role and influence of the Iranian ambassadors to Syria and Lebanon on both its *Executive* and *Consultative* Shuras.[157]

Martyrs' Foundation and Foundation of the Oppressed

Other influential Iranian institutions at work within the Hizbollah are the *Martyrs' Foundation*, under the command of Ayatollah Mehdi Karrubi, and the *Foundation of the Oppressed*, headed by Hojjatolislam Mohammad Ali-Rahmani.[158] These two Iranian institutions have helped the families of those killed in the revolution and redistributed goods and money to lower class families in need. They are funded from the government, religious trusts and by income from the confiscation of exiled Iranians' properties. They also serve as a channel for Iran's substantial injection of resources to the Hizbollah in Lebanon.[159] Iran's financial contributions, which averaged $60 million a year, were vital for the Hizbollah in running an array of social and financial services for the Shia community, including religious schools, hospital clinics, agricultural co-operatives and building projects.[160] The Hizbollah religious *hawzats* and mosques have served a vital role in the indoctrination process of countless young Shi'ites and are reinforced by Iranian support for Hizbollah's three radio stations, one television station and two publications.[161]

The Party of God's organ *Jihad al-Bina* (Holy Reconstruction Organ) serves as the main co-ordinating body, divided into eight committees, for the social and financial needs of the movement's members.[162] Through Iran's generous financial support, the *Islamic Health Committee* established two major hospitals in Baalbek and in the southern suburbs of Beirut in 1986 and an array of medical centres and pharmacies throughout the various regions in Lebanon.[163] The *Financial Aid Committee*, in close co-operation with the *Martyrs' Foundation*, distributed over $90 million between 1982 and 1986 to families whose dependents had died or were wounded, and the *Martyrs' Foundation* provides approximately $225,000 monthly to martyrs' families.[164] Apart from aid to those who had fallen or were wounded in the fight against the enemies of Islam, the *Financial Aid Committee* has extended generous loans intended for marriages, school expenses, and small business ventures.[165] The importance of the *Reconstruction Committees* has been made obvious by the repair during 1988–1991 of over 1,000 homes in southern Lebanon damaged by Israel attacks.[166] Apart from Hizbollah's dependence on Iranian financial support to sustain these services and projects, the Party of God's ability to capture the hearts and minds of the Shia community, through a skilful combination of financial inducements and ideological indoctrination, partially depended on Iran's willingness to extend available resources. Likewise, in the armed struggle the Pasdaran provided the Hizbollah with other military-related equipment and resources.[167] Iranian aid to Hizbollah steadily increased from $30 million in 1985 to over $64 million in 1988.[168]

However, these aid institutions were subject to Iranian clerical factionalism.[169] In particular, the involvement of Ayatollah Mehdi Karrubi in the 5 April 1988 hijacking of KU422 by Hizbollah pointed to an effort by the Iranian cleric to influence the forthcoming Iranian *Majlis* elections.[170] Control over Iranian funds to the Party of God, through the leader of the *Martyrs' Foundation*, was also used by Hashemi Rafsanjani in 1989 in an effort to control Hizbollah. This was evident in his move to downgrade support for the movement in Lebanon and by the dismissal of Ayatollah Karrubi, who was replaced by the only non-radical former IRGC Minister and Rafsanjani's nephew, Mohsen Rafiq Dust.[171] In the wake of the release of the remaining Western hostages in 1991, reports spoke of much reduced Iranian aid to Hizbollah, in some cases as high a reduction as 90 per cent.[172] Although Iran has faced financial constraints since the 1988 end of the First Gulf War, Hizbollah's expansion of its social services and financial assistance to the Lebanese Shiites would indicate otherwise.[173] In fact, evidence would suggest that Iran's current annual financial contribution to the Hizbollah amounts to over $100 million in order to sustain its vast non-military activities and to renew as well as expand its weapons arsenal.[174]

The Iranian Revolutionary Guards corps (Pasdaran)

Although Hizbollah's command leadership has been affected by the availability of Iranian financial and material resources, the institution of the *Revolutionary Guards* was least affected by Iranian clerical factionalism and remained the most reliable and loyal ally of Hizbollah.[175] As demonstrated by the Pasdaran contingent in Lebanon, it has remained the most radical and least pliable Iranian institution with close ties to Iran's clerical revolutionist faction.[176] The Pasdaran's semi-institutional autonomy from the civilian leadership in Iran has meant that Hizbollah has been able to resist attempts of co-option by Iran through support from the IRGC.[177] Attempts by Iranian political leaders to exert pressure on the IRGC contingent in Lebanon, as seen in proposals for its withdrawal and the release of the remaining hostages in Lebanon in 1991, were unsuccessful.[178] This became apparent through the assurance of Hadi Reza Askari, commander of the Iranian Pasdaran contingent, that it would remain in Lebanon until Israel withdrew its troops from southern Lebanon.[179] The lack of control by Iran's political leadership over IRGC support for Hizbollah was clearly revealed by the Pasdaran's close training and military support of the Party of God and its repeated armed clashes during 1987–1990 with Amal,[180] despite official efforts by Iran to broker an end to the conflict in order to preserve its relationship with Syria.[181] As the IRGC's Lebanon contingent was led and manned by the most ideologically-radical military officials and demonstrated a degree of institutional autonomy from civilian political control, it enabled Hizbollah to exercise a certain independence, at times in violation of specific orders, in terms of its activity in Lebanon, especially in the abduction and release of foreign hostages.[182] However, the political necessity of close affiliation with Iran's official leadership for its continued survival in Lebanon under the Ta'if agreement contributed to Hizbollah's decision, under the helm of Sheikh Nasserallah, to hand over the Sheikh Abdallah barracks in Baalbek to the Lebanese Army in the summer of 1992. Meanwhile the organization retained a base for training and weaponry storage in the eastern Bekaa in close co-operation with Pasdaran officials.[183]

Iran and the hostage-taking

Notwithstanding the various influences of factionalism within Hizbollah and the Iranian clerical establishment, coupled with the movement's relationship with Iranian and Syrian military institutions, Hizbollah and official Iran co-ordinated some of the movement's abductions of foreigners, from a convergence of mutual interests, through a formally defined chain of command from Iran to the Party of God.[184] At the highest level in Iran, the Islamic Republic's *Supreme Defense Council*, which is the central decision-making body of the military-security establishment,[185] is the main vehicle for policy formulation, decisions and guidance to Hizbollah relating to hostage-taking in Lebanon and operations abroad.[186] While this Council, composed of the Iranian President, *Majlis* Speaker and IRGC commander, is formally in charge of policy formulation *vis-à-vis* Hizbollah, implementation of specific operational directives was delegated to the *Office of Islamic Liberation Movements*.[187] In turn, this body delegated the specific tasks through Iran's diplomatic representatives in Damascus and, to a lesser extent, Beirut as well as to the Pasdaran contingent in Lebanon.[188] Although Iran's operational policy with Hizbollah remained particularly close until the removal of Mehdi Hashemi in the autumn of 1986 and the reassignment of Mohtashemi from his post as ambassador to Syria to Minister of Interior, it became increasingly subject to clerical factionalism in Iran. The reassignment of the *Office for Islamic Liberation Movements* to Iran's Ministry of Foreign Affairs, and the appointment of Hojjatolislam Khosrowshahi to head the control-mechanism of Iran's official contacts with Hizbollah, underlined not only the clerical factionalism in Iran but also that control over the organization's activity was exercised both through official Iranian institutions and independent channels loyal to the revolutionist faction within Iran's clerical establishment.[189]

In particular, it has been suggested that Iran, in an attempt to control Hizbollah abductions, recalled senior Hizbollah SSA commanders to Iran in April 1987 either because of increased disagreements between Hizbollah and Iran over the movement's claims for independence or as a safety precaution to prevent their capture by Syrian intelligence in Lebanon due to their involvement in attacks against the Syrian armed forces in west Beirut.[190] It would seem likely that Imad Mughniya and Abd al-Hadi Hamadi remained in Iran for training and security reasons rather than for detention, as both were subsequently elevated within Hizbollah's operational command leadership.[191] This can further be supported by the parallel Iranian efforts to upgrade the Hizbollah's military capability through increased funding and sophisticated weaponry.[192]

The future of Hizbollah terrorism

A fuller understanding of the behaviour of the Hizbollah as a militant Shiite organization depends not only on the depth and allegiance of closely forged relationships between individual Hizbollah leaders and Iranian clergy but also on the adaptability of a particular Hizbollah leader to suit the movement's activity to the political requirements of the region within which it operates. As a result, it was demonstrated that any analysis of Hizbollah requires both an understanding of the movement itself, in terms of its decision-making apparatus, and the mechanisms of its institutionalised relationship with Iran and, to a lesser extent, Syria through military and civilian channels at work within Lebanon.

The transformation of the Hizbollah from a revolutionary movement to a political party in post-civil war Lebanon raises the question whether the movement has abandoned the use of political violence to achieve its wider pan-Islamic goals. The Party of God has demonstrated a mastery of political violence in its quest to enhance its position and agenda within Lebanon and beyond, and also demonstrated it was very susceptible of, and adaptable to, changes within its own surroundings. Yet, the Hizbollah finds itself again at another crossroads in terms of its survival, particularly in the aftermath of the Gaza-Jericho First Agreement between Israel and PLO as well as in the wake of a wider resolution to the Arab-Israeli conflict. Every sign indicates that the movement has retained the same degree of its pan-Islamic zeal and militancy to prevent its demise within Lebanon. While Hizbollah's reorientation in activity, substituting hostage-taking for participation within the political process, occurred to suit the realities of a post-civil war Lebanon, the movement has also escalated its committment and struggle to confront Israel and achieve its pan-Islamic goal of liberating Jerusalem, both within Lebanon and beyond.[193] Although this may lead to increased factionalism within the Hizbollah and its future course,[194] the intensification of the movement's attacks against Israel in southern Lebanon can be attributed to efforts to sabotage any prospects for any Arab-Israeli peace, which would *de facto* jeopardize its very existence and its accomplishments hitherto within Lebanon.[195]

The most immediate critical issue for the organization's future role and existence as a revolutionary military and political party in Lebanon is whether the bilateral negotiations between Syria and Israel produce a peace agreement. Its first condition would be the suspension of Hizbollah's armed resistance. While Syria has used Hizbollah's activities and resistance as an important card in negotiations with Israel, there are already signs that Syria would not hesitate to crack-down on the Party of God in order to achieve its wider interests in the region despite the Iranian-Syrian relationship.[196] Although the evidence suggests that Syria has not allowed new military shipments for Hizbollah, the movement has an arsenal that would enable it to continue its military activities for five years without feeling a need for new weapons.[197] Hizbollah has also circumvented even its dependence on Iranian weapons consignments through the purchase of advanced weaponry from various arms dealers in Lebanon, particularly "Sagger" anti-tank missiles.[198]

Hizbollah has increased its Islamic extremism by continuing its guerrilla attacks against Israel in southern Lebanon and also launched a new form of terrorism, car-bomb attacks. These have been specifically aimed against Israeli high-profile targets outside the Middle East since March 1992, most notably in South America and Europe, both in revenge for Israeli actions against the Hizbollah as well as to sabotage any emerging signs of Arab-Israeli peace.[199] Although the Party of God discovered that it can subvert the system from within through its participation within Lebanese domestic politics, its vanguard position of Islamic extremism with its messianic aspirations for the establishment of an Islamic republic in Lebanon and the eradication of Israel, means that the movement for the moment will intensify its attacks against Israel through bombs to avert any emerging Arab-Israeli *rapprochement*. This will be the emphasis rather than on any more hostage-taking against the West. Ultimately, the degree to which the movement's position is threatened, coupled with the ability of Iran to sustain its revolutionary pan-Islamic zeal at home and abroad, will determine the means and levels of violence employed by the Hizbollah in the future.

Notes

1   The term Hizbollah, meaning "the party, or adherents, of God", originally appeared in the Holy Quran (V, 61/56; LVIII, 22) which promises triumph for believers (Party of God) over the unbelievers Hizb al-shaytan (Party of the Devil). The symbol of the Hizbollah involves the writing of "Hizballah" integrated into an arm holding an automatic assault rifle, the Holy Quran, and the olive branch, set against the background of a globe (symbolizing the pan-Islamic nature of the movement). Also see "An Open Letter: The Hizballah", *Jerusalem Quarterly*, No. 48 (Fall 1988), pp. 11–16.

2   This is mainly due to the fact that most of Hizbollah's clerical elite studied at the theological college of Najaf and were profoundly influenced by Ayatollah Khomeini during his exile in Najaf between 1964 and 1978. For a brief discussion, see Shimon Shapira, "The Origins of Hizb'allah", *The Jerusalem Quarterly*, Vol. 46 (Spring 1988), pp. 115–130; and Augustus Richard Norton, "Lebanon: The Internal Conflict and the Iranian Connection", in John L. Esposito (ed.), *The Iranian Revolution: Its Global Impact* (Miami, FL: Florida University Int. Press, 1990), p. 125.

3   See Ali al-Kurani, *Tariqat Hizballah fil-amal al-islami* (Beirut, 1986); *Valeurs Actuelles*, 6 April 1987; and *Le Monde*, 25 Oct. 1986. The importance of understanding clerical factionalism in Iran was aptly described by Graham Fuller: "[t]he Iranian political and social systems decree that one deal with personalities and not with institutions, the personal relationship to this day transcends any formal or institutionalized relationship", see Graham Fuller, *The "Center of the Universe": The Geopolitics of Iran* (Boulder, CO: Westview Press, 1991), p. 20.

4   As advanced by John Calabrese: "[f]rom the days of Musa Sadr, the Iranian-Lebanese Shia connection has been built on a network of personal contacts and relationships. Hezbollah as an 'organization', Iran as a 'state', and the 'association' between them have been, and still are, impenetrable and unfathomable: knowing what they are depends on knowing who the key personalities are within them, and how these key players relate to one another", see John Calabrese, "Iran II: The Damascus Connection", *World Today* (Oct. 1990), p. 189. Also see *al-Shira*, 27 Sept. 1993.

5   For Hizbollah and Iranian denials of an organisational structure, see *Monday Morning*, 14 Jan. 1985; and *al-Nahar al-Arabi wal-Duwali*, 10 June 1986.

6   See Marius Deeb, *Militant Islamic Movements in Lebanon: Origins, Social Basis and Ideology* (Occas. Paper Series, Center for Contemp. Arab Studies, Georgetown Univ., Washington, DC, Nov. 1986), p.16.

7   For a full text of the manifesto, see *Nass al-risla al-maftuha allati wajjaha allah ila al-mustad 'afiri fi lubnan wa al-alam* (Text of Open Letter Addressed by Hizb Allah to the Downtrodden in Lebanon and in the World), repr in Augustus Richard Norton, *Amal and the Shi'a: Struggle for the Soul of Lebanon* (Austin, TX: Univ. of Texas Press, 1987), pp. 167–187.

8   Hizbollah's command leadership attended a meeting at Shyah in the southern suburbs of Beirut, where Hizbollah's official spokesman read the "Open Letter Addressed by the Hizbollah to the Oppressed/

Downtrodden in Lebanon and in the World", see Gilles Delafon, *Beyrouth: Les Soldats de l'Islam* (Paris: Stock, 1989), p.90.

9 For details, see Amir Taheri, *Holy Terror: The Inside Story of Islamic Terrorism* (London: Sphere Books, 1987), p. 125. Also see Shimon Shapira, "Shi'ite Radicalism in Lebanon: Historical Origins and Organizational, Political and Ideological Patterns" MA thesis (Hebrew), (Tel Aviv Univ.: Dayan Center for Middle Eastern and African Studies, May 1987). Hojjatolislam Fazlollah Mahallati had trained in the PLO guerrilla training camps in Lebanon and was appointed Pasdaran Supervisor until his death in a 1986 plane crash, see Nikola Schahgaldian, *The Iranian Military Under the Islamic Republic* (Santa Monica, CA.: RAND Corp. 1987), pp.119–121.

10 See Shapira (note 2), pp.114–130; and *al-Dustur*, 6 Nov. 1989.

11 See Israeli Defense Forces Spokesman (IDFS), 18 Feb. 1986; and *Davar*, 6 Nov. 1989.

12 Sheikh Subhi al-Tufayli was born in 1948 in the village of Brital in the Bekaa area and spent nine years studying theology in Najaf (Iraq) and briefly in Qom (Iran), see *Davar*, 25 Nov. 1983; *al-Nashra*, 5 Dec. 1984: *Ha'aretz*, 10 Jan. 1984; *Ha'aretz*, 4 June 1984; *al-Dustur*, 31 March 1985; *Ha'aretz*, 1 April 1985; and *International Herald Tribune*, 27 March 1987.

13 See *Ha'aretz*, 4 June 1984; and *al-Nashra*, 5 Dec. 1983.

14 Abbas al-Musawi was born in 1952 in Nabishit near Baalbek and studied at the Inst. for Islamic Studies in Tyre 1969–1970. Thereafter he moved to Najaf where he studied under Muhammad Baqer al-Sadr until his return to Lebanon in 1978, see *Ma'aretz*, 14 June, 1984; and *al-Shira*, 17 March 1986. Abbas al-Musawi also heads the Islamic College at Baalbek.

15 See *Ma'aretz*, 24 Oct. 1983; *Ma'aretz*, 6 Nov. 1983; *al-Nahar al-Arabi*, 10 June 1985; *Washington Post*, 14 Feb. 1986; *Noveau Magazine*, 15 Nov. 1986; *al-Nahar*, 14 Nov. 1986; *Foreign Report*, 30 July 1987; *al-Safir*, 17 Aug. 1987; *al-Shira*, 8 Aug. 1988; and *Independent*, 30 Aug. 1989. Hussein al-Musawi is related to Abbas al-Musawi, see *Davar*, 25 Dec. 1983.

16 See *al-Dustur*, 31 March 1985; *al-Ittihad*, 4 Dec. 1986; *International Herald Tribune*, 27 March 1987; *Ma'aretz*, 14 June 1987; *Ha'aretz*, 29 Nov. 1987; *La Revue du Liban*, 30 Jan. 1988; *Ha'aretz*, 22 Feb. 1988; *Independent*, 30 Aug. 1989; and *Ha'aretz*, 17 Dec. 1989.

17 See *International Herald Tribune*, 27 March 1987; *Ha'aretz*, 29 Nov. 1987, *Ma'aretz*, 14 June 1987; and *Ha'aretz*, 22 Feb. 1988. Sheikh al-Tufayli is also responsible for Hizbollah's financial assets, see *Ha'aretz*, 21 Aug. 1991.

18 See *Foreign Report*, 30 July 1987; *Davar*, 2 Oct. 1987; *Ha'aretz*, 2 Oct. 1987; *Ma'aretz*, 14 June 1984; *al-Hayat*, 27 Nov. 1989; *Ha'aretz*, 17 Dec. 1989; and *Independent*, 7 March 1990. Al-Musawi was head of internal security within Hizbollah's SSA from 1983–1985. In late 1985 until April 1988, al-Musawi was the head of the *Islamic Resistance*. See *Middle East Reporter*, 7 Nov. 1987. For Hizbollah-Pasdaran military march in Baalbek, see *Radio Monte Carlo*, 14 Dec. 1987. In June 1987 Abbas al-Musawi was transferred from the Bekaa area to Tyre to set up hideouts to which Western hostages could be transferred from Beirut and to weaken Amal's position in the area, see *Foreign Report*, 30 July 1987.

19 See *Independent*, 30 Aug. 1989; *al-Hayat*, 27 Nov. 1989; *Ha'aretz*, 17 Dec. 1989; and *FBIS*, 30 Nov. 1989. Sheikh Husayn al-Khalil became also the head of the Hizbollah Politbureau in 1989–1990, see *Lebanon Report* 4/3 (March 1993).

20 See *Ha'aretz*, 20 March 1987; and *al-Anba*, 18 Feb. 1984. The military leader of *Islamic Amal* is Abu Yahia, see *Associated Press*, 18 Nov. 1983; and *Israeli Defense Forces Spokesman*, 3 Feb. 1984.

21 See *Ha'aretz*, 21 June 1987. According to Norton (note 7), the Hizbollah had in 1985 M-113 APCs, Sagger anti-tank weapons, GRAD rockets, and artillery pieces, see Norton, p. 205 n. 36. Also see Xavier Raufer, *Atlas Mondial de L'Islam Activiste* (Paris: La Table Ronde, 1991): p. 147. On 28 Nov. 1991 the Hizbollah used for the first time a shoulder-held SAM-7 anti-aircraft missile made in Eastern Europe at an Israeli C-47 aircraft, see *Foreign Report*, 5 Dec. 1991. For a detailed overview of those weapons and their use in terrorist operations, see "MANPADs: The Potential for Use as a Terrorist Tactic", in *Terrorist Tactics and Security Practices* (Washington, DC: Dept. of State, Bureau of Diplomatic Security, Feb. 1994): pp. 67–113. It also uses ex-Soviet "Sagger-3" anti-tank missiles and American M-72 light anti-tank weapons, see *Foreign Report*, 20 May 1993; and *Ha'aretz*, 14 April 1993. For Hizbollah possession of LAW (Light Anti-Tank Weapon) shoulder-fired missiles, see *Jerusalem Domestic Service*, 28 Aug. 1984. The main weapon used against Israeli targets by the Hizbollah is the Katyusha rocket (or BM-21), a Soviet-designed solid propellant rocket with a range of approx. 13 miles, see IDF Spokesman, 6 June 1994.

22 See *Davar*, 25 Nov. 1983; *Ma'aretz*, 30 Oct. 1983; *Ha'aretz*, 27 Nov. 1983; *Ha'aretz*, 2 Feb. 1984; and *Ha'aretz*, 3 June 1984. Sheikh Fadlallah was born in 1934 at Najaf (Iraq). A descendant of a family of clergymen, Sheikh Fadlallah hails from Aynata, a southern Lebanese town near the Shiite center of Bint Jbail. For a full biographical account, see Martin Kramer, "Muhammad Husayn Fadlallah", *Orient*:

German Journal for Politics and Economics of the Middle East 26/2 (June 1985): pp.147–149; and "Leadership Profile: Sheikh Muhammad Husayn Fadlallah" *Defense & Foreign Affairs Weekly* 23–29 June 1986): p. 7.

23 Sheikh Ibrahim al-Amin was born in 1952 in the village of Nabi Ayla near Zahle and educated at Najaf (Iraq) and Qum (Iran). Al-Amin was formerly the representative of the Amal movement in Iran until he attacked Nabi Berri for participating in the National Salvation Committee, see *Washington Post*, 13 Dec. 1983; *al-Watan al-Arabi*, 11 Dec. 1987; *Independent*, 30 Aug. 1989; and *al-Hayat*, 27 Nov. 1989. Also see *al-Shira*, 17 March 1986; *Ma'aretz*, 14 June 1986; and *Liberation*, 19 March 1985.

24 Sheikh Hassan Nasserallah was born in 1953 at Bazuriyah in southern Lebanon and is considered one of the founders of Hizbollah. He returned to Beirut in the early 1970s, after graduating from both the religious academy of Najaf in Iraq and Qum in Iran, and served as a group official in Lebanese *al-Da'wa* and later in the Amal movement. He became Hizbollah's mobilization officer in the Bekaa and later served as commander of Hizbollah's fighters against the Amal, see *AFP* 1520 GMT 18 Feb. 92 – BBC/SWB/ME/1309, 20 Feb. 1992; *Independent*, 15 June 1992; and *al-Shira*, 8 Nov. 1993. Also see: *al-Qabas*, 20 July 1989; *Ha'aretz*, 7 Aug. 1989, *Independent*, 30 Aug. 1989; *al-Anba*, 27 Nov. 1989; *al-Hayat*, 27 Nov. 1989; FBIS, 30 Nov. 1989; and *Ha'aretz*, 17 Dec. 1989. Nasserallah has considerable influence over Hizbollah activists in west and south Beirut, within the *al-Da'wa* trend and in the *Islamic Resistance*, see *Ha'aretz*, 17 Dec. 1989.

25 See *Independent*, 7 March 1990; and *al-Shira*, 17 March 1986.

26 See *Foreign Report*, 30 July 1987, and *al-Shira*, 19 Sept. 1988.

27 See al-Nahar, 6 Feb. 1989. For a useful discussion of al-Khaliq's influence within Hizbollah, see Shapira (note 9).

28 Sheikh Ragheb Harb was born in 1952 in the village of Jibshit. Apart from having studied under Sheikh Muhammad Hussein Fadlallah, Sheikh Harb played a prominent role in Iran as one of the drafters of Islamic Iran's Constitution, see Chibli Mallat, "Religious Militancy in Contemporary Iraq: Muhammad Baqer as-Sadr and the Sunni-Shia paradigm", *Third World Quarterly* 10/2 (April 1988), p.721. Also see *Politique International*, April 1984; and *Liberation*, 19 March 1985.

29 See *al-Shira*, 17 March, 1986; *Independent*, 30 Aug. 1989; and *Jerusalem Post*, 30 July 1989. Sheikh Obeid remained the Imam of Jibshit and regional military commander of *Islamic Resistance* until his abduction by elite Israeli military units on 28 July 1989, see Samuel M. Katz, *Soldier Spies: Israeli Military Intelligence* (Novato, CA: Presidio Press, 1992), pp.344. Sheikh Ahmed Ali Taleb is the temporary Imam of Jibshit in Sheikh Obeid's absence, see *The Times*, 10 May 1990.

30 See Ali al-Kurani, *Tariqat Hizballah fil-amal al-islami* (Beirut: 1986); *al-Shira*, 17 March 1986; Israeli Government Press Office, 5 July 1985; *al-Nahar*, 7 June 1985; *al-Nahar*, 9 June 1985; Israeli Defense Forces Spokesman, 19 Feb. 1986; *al-Nahar*, 16 June 1985; and *US News & World Report*, 9 Feb. 1987. Also see Deeb (note 6), pp.18–19.

31 See *Ha'aretz*, 13 May and 15 May 1987; *Ma'aretz*, 15 June 1987; *Ha'aretz*, 21 June 1987; *Jerusalem Post*, 13 Nov. 1987; and *Le Point*, 3 Aug. 1987. According to various estimates, Hizbollah's military strength numbered: 2,500 in the Bekaa, 1,000 in Beirut, and 500 in southern Lebanon, see *Jerusalem Post*, 8 Jan. 1988; and *Ha'aretz*, 22 Sept. 1986. For useful overview of training of new Hizbollah fighters, see *Yediot Aharanot*, 16 July 1993.

32 See *Foreign Report*, 5 Dec. 1991. Newly-trained Hizbollah and *Islamic Amal* received approx. £200 per month, see *The Times*, 14 Nov. 1987; *al-Shira*, 18 Jan. 1993; *Yediot Aharanot*, 16 July 1993; and *Independent*, 3 Aug. 1989. The Hizbollah has a standing militia of 3,500 men and a reserve of over 25,000 men, see *Defense & Diplomacy* (May 1989), p. 56. Also see *al-Majallah*, 15–21 Aug. 1993.

33 See *Ha'aretz*, 15 May and 21 June 1987. In 1988, the Hizbollah decided to form secret cells to execute specific military operations under cultural and religious cover, see *Voice of Lebanon*, 14 April 1988. Decision-making authority is divided between section commanders and military forces headquarters in Baalbek, see *Davar*, 11 Jan. 1987. Until his death in Aug. 1988, assassinated by Amal, Sheikh Ali Karim was the head of the Hizbollah operations center in south Lebanon, see *Foreign Report*, 13 Aug. 1988. Muhammad Fannish has also been the commander for southern Lebanon, see *US News & World Report*, 9 Feb. 1987. In 1993 the *Islamic Resistance* became a separate and ultra-secret organisation with a new command structure which conceals the identity of the three or four top leaders. The new structure came as a result of a secret review in the aftermath of security breaches, see *Foreign Report*, 13 May 1993. For a useful analysis of Hizbollah operations, see Martin Kramer, "Sacrifice and Fratricide in Shiite Lebanon", *Terrorism and Political Violence* 3/3 (Autumn 1991), pp. 30–47.

34 See *al-Shira*, 2 April, 1986; *Ha'aretz*, 2 April 1986; *al-Watan al-Arabi*, 11 Dec. 1987. The members of the *Majlis al-Shura* were: Ibrahim al-Amin; Ibrahim al-Laquim; Zuheir Kanj; Imad Mughenya; Hassan

Nasserallah; Ali Yasin; Hassan Malik; Yussef Sbeit; Khaidar Tlais; Ali Atwa; Haj Hussein Khalil; Muhammad al-Hamsa Suleiman Yahfufi; Ali Karim; Abbas al-Mussawi; Subhi al-Tufayli; Ali Yunes; Hassan Trad; Muhammad Mikdad; Waal Ramadan; Said Shaaban; and Hussein al-Musawi.

35 See As'ad AbuKhalil, "Hizbollah in Lebanon: Islamisation of Leninist Organisational Principles", *Middle Eastern Studies* 27/3 (July 1991), p.397. Also see *Davar*, 11 Jan. 1987.

36 See Marius Deeb, "Shia Movements in Lebanon: Their Formation, Ideology, Social Basis, and Links with Iran and Syria", *Third World Quarterly* 10/2 (April 1988): p.693. Also see "Hizbollah", in US Dept. of Defense (DOD), *Terrorist Group Profiles*, Nov. 1988, p. 15.

37 Private communication with Dr Yossi Olmert, Director, Government Press Office, Israel, 30 Dec. 1991. Also see *Davar*, 11 Jan. 1987. Sheikh Fadlallah himself contends that he controls 70 per cent of Hizbollah's power, policy, and decisions, see *al-Shira*, 27 Sept. 1993.

38 See A. Nizar Hamzeh, "Lebanon's Hizbullah: From Islamic Revolution to Parliamentary Accomodation", *Third World Quarterly* 14/2 (1993), pp. 321–337. For previous criticism of the secretive nature of Hizbollah's leadership by one of the movement's members, Ali al-Kurani, see *Tariqat Hizb'allah fi-l-'Amal-il-Islami*. To become a Hizbollah member, a prospective candidate passes through the stages of "mobilization" which means at least a year's education during which the individual is closely observed. After this, actual membership (al-Intizam) involves further responsibilities, see *al-Shira*, 17 March 1987; and *Ha'aretz*, 31 May 1985. New Hizbollah recruits must fulfill four conditions: member of a Shi'ite sect; under the age of 22; literate; and physical ability. For details, see *Yediot Aharanot*, 16 July 1993. Hizbollah's political cadres are numbered at over 3,000, see *al-Majallah*, 15–21 Aug. 1993.

39 Under the new structure, the *Consultative Shura* is composed of the following positions: Secretary-General; Deputy Secretary-General; Head of *Executive Shura*; Head of *Politbureau*; a spokesman; and two other members. The *Executive Shura* is composed of the following positions: Head of *Executive Shura*; Finance; Education; Health; Trades Union Affairs; Social Affairs; Security; Military Affairs; and Information, see *Lebanon Report* 4/3 (March 1993): p.6. Under the leadership of Sheikh Subhi al-Tufayli, the *Majlis al-Shura* expanded to over 20 members. For membership, see *al-Watan al-Arabi*, 11 Dec. 1987. This number was reduced to eight by Sheikh Abbas al-Musawi in 1991.

40 It is estimated that the *Islamic Resistance* is composed of approx. 5,000 fighters in 1994, see *Independent*, 8 May 1994.

41 For information concerning Hizbollah's SSA, see Rolf Tophoven, "Der Tod eines Terroristen – Hintergrunde und Konsequenzen", *Terrorismus*, Nr.3 (March 1992): pp.1–4; *al-Hayat*, 27 Nov. 1989; *Wall Street Journal*, 16 Aug. 1989; *New York Times*, 14 March 1986; *Washington Post*, 15 May 1990; *Le Figaro*, 4 Dec. 1989; *Independent*, 26 April 1988; *al-Majallah*, 15–21 Aug. 1993; and *Ha'aretz*, 29 Jan. 1988. In addition, information on the Hizbollah SSA was collected by the author during interviews with high-ranking Israeli officials in the Ministries of Defence and Foreign Affairs, Tel Aviv, 25 Aug.–10 Sept. 1991.

42 Private communication with Dr Yossi Olmert, Director, Government Press Office, Israel, 30 Dec. 1991. This was also confirmed in unattributable interviews with senior IDF officials in Israel (Aug./Sept. 1991) and a senior counter-terrorism official at the Dept. of State, Washington, DC, 4 Sept. 1993. The central security apparatus is further divided into two groups responsible for either East or West Beirut, see Roger Faligot and Remi Kauffer, *Les Maîtres Espions* (Paris: Robert Laffont, 1994), p.485.

43 See *Ma'aretz*, 14 June 1986; *Independent*, 7 March 1990; and *al-Watan al-Arabi*, 11 Dec. 1987.

44 See *Independent*, 9 Oct. 1991; *Le Figaro*, 4 Dec. 1989; *Yediot Aharanot*, 24 June 1988; *Independent*, 26 April 1988; *al-Nahar al-Arabi wal-Duwali*, 16 Jan. 1989; *Wall Street Journal*, 16 Aug. 1989; *Jerusalem Post*, 25 Jan. 1987; *al-Shira*, 27 June 1989; *FBIS*, 30 Nov. 1989; *Ma'aretz*, 2 Feb. and 27 Feb. 1986; *Independent*, 28 Jan. 1987; and *Los Angeles Times*, 26 Nov. 1988.

45 See *Wall Street Journal*, 16 Aug. 1989; and *Le Figaro*, 4 Dec. 1989. Another prominent leader is Muhammad Ali Mikdad, see *Ma'aretz*, 28 June 1987; and *Ma'aretz*, 8 July 1987.

46 For information on Nun and Khalil, see *Wall Street Journal*, 16 Aug. 1989; *Davar*, 8 Feb. 1989; *Independent*, 30 Aug. 1989; *al-Anba*, 27 Nov. 1989; *FBIS*, 30 Nov. 1989; *Radio Free Lebanon*, 27 Jan. 1989; *al-Hayat*, 27 Nov. 1989; and *Ha'aretz*, 17 Dec. 1989. Also see Faligot and Kauffer (note 42), p.485. For Khalil's close relationship with Qassem, see *Wall Street Journal*, 16 Aug. 1989.

47 E.g., the Amal movement dismissed some leading members after discovering their dual allegiance to Hizbollah, see *BBC*, 13 April 1988. A leading Amal official, Mustafa Dirani, the then head of Amal's security service, defected in 1988, see *Ha'aretz*, 4 Dec. 1988.

48 See *Radio Free Lebanon*, 22 March 1986; *Radio Free Lebanon*, 9 Sept. 1986; and *al-Watan al-Arabi wal-Duwali*, 11 Dec. 1987. For dismissal of Hizbollah security after infiltration of Hizbollah and a foiled assassination

attempt on Sheikh Muhammad Hussein Fadlallah in 1989, see *al-Anba*, 27 Nov. 1989; *Hadashot*, 25 Oct. 1989; and *FBIS*, 17 Dec. 1989.

49 See *Le Point*, 1 June 1987; *al-Sharq al-Awsat*, 21 Nov. 1991; *Le Quotidien de Paris*, 27–28 Jan. 1990; *Yediot Aharanot*, 1 July 1987; *Le Point*, 3 Aug. 1987; *Defense & Armament Heracles*, Nov. 1989; *Independent*, 7 March 1990; and *Frankfurter Allgemeine Zeitung*, 17 March 1986.

50 See *Le Point*, 15 June 1987; and *Le Point*, 3 Aug. 1987.

51 See *Foreign Report*, 22 Aug 1991. For Mughniya's absence from Lebanon (Oct.–Dec. 1987 in northern Iran; in Jan. 1988 at Qum; and his return to Lebanon in July 1990), see: *Voice of the Oppressed*, 6 Sep. 1991; *Ma'ariv*, 11 Oct. 1991; and *Reuters*, 4 Oct. 1991.

52 See *Wall Street Journal*, 16 Aug. 1989; *Ha'aretz*, 29 Jan. 1988; *Jerusalem Post*, 14 April 1988; and *Ma'aretz*, 14 April 1988. Another important Hizbollah clan with close ties to Force 17 is the Mikdad family, see *Ma'aretz*, 8 July 1987. This was also confirmed in an unattributable interview with a former senior Fatah adviser in Cairo, Egypt, who had personally known Imad Mughniya until his defection to Hizbollah (Cairo, Egypt, April 1994).

53 For Imad Mughniya's position, see: *Los Angeles Times*, 26 Nov. 1988; *Davar*, 6 May 1988; *Le Point*, 3 Aug. 1987; *Davar*, 6 May 1988; *Independent*, 26 April 1988; and *Ma'aretz*, 27 Feb. 1986. Also see Neil Livingstone and David Halevy, *Inside the PLO* (London: Hale 1990): pp.262–270. For Hizbollah's relationship with Force 17, see *Ma'ariv*, 17 Oct. 1986; *Le Matin*, 29 Jan. 1987; *Ma'aretz*, 31 March 1987; and *Keyhan*, 12 Feb. 1987. Also see *Voice of Israel* 1000 GMT 29 July 94–BBC/*SWB*/ME/2062, 1 Aug. 1994.

54 Unattributable interview with senior official in Israel's Ministry of Defence, 27 Aug. 1991, Tel Aviv, Israel.

55 Unattributable interview with senior official in US Dept. of State, Washington, DC, 4 Oct. 1993.

56 See Shapira (note 9). Also see *Ma'aretz*, 15 June 1987; and *Ha'aretz*, 21 June 1986. This information was confirmed in an unattributable interview with a former Israeli military intelligence officer, Tel Aviv, Aug. 1991.

57 See Ronald Perron, "The Iranian Islamic Revolutionary Guards Corps", *Middle East Insight* (June/July 1985), pp.35–39; *US News & World Report*, 6 March 1989; *Ha'aretz*, 30 Sept. 1984; *New York Times*, 29 Dec. 1989; *Ma'aretz*, 8 July 1987; and *Le Point*, 3 Aug. 1987. The Pasdaran's financial official in Lebanon is Abu-Khalil, see *al-Majallah*, 15 Aug. 1993.

58 See Faligot and Kauffer (note 42) p.485. Also see *al-Watan al-Arabi*, 12 Feb. 1993.

59 For Mohtashemi's role, see Robin Wright, *In the Name of God: The Khomeini Decade* (NY: Simon & Schuster, 1989), p.122. Also see *Washington Post*, 15 May 1990; and *al-Majallah*, 15 Aug. 1993.

60 See *Yediot Aharanot*, 24 June 1988; *Le Quotidien de Paris*, 27–28 Jan. 1990; *Ma'aretz*, 8 July 1987; *Ma'aretz*, 28 June 1986. For Pasdaran establishment of military centers in the Bekaa valley, see *Radio Free Lebanon*, 6 July 1984. For Pasdaran training of Hizbollah to improve the quality of attacks against Israel, see *FBIS*, 26 Jan. 1993.

61 See *Independent*, 7 March 1990; *Ha'aretz*, 30 Sep. 1984; and *Foreign Report*, 30 July 1987. Muhammad Nurani served as *charge d'affairés* in the Iranian embassy in Beirut 1980–1985. He returned to Beirut in May 1987, see *Foreign Report*, 30 July 1987.

62 See *Independent*, 7 March 1990.

63 See Maskit Burgin, Anat Kurz and Ariel Merari, *Foreign Hostages in Lebanon*, JCSS Memorandum no.25 – Aug. 1988 (Tel Aviv: Tel Aviv Univ., 1988): p. 14, n.4.

64 See *Jeune Afrique*, 25 Jan. 1984; *al-Amal*, 19 May 1984; *Le Point*. 11 May 1987; and *Ha'aretz*, 21 June 1987.

65 In July 1984 the Iranian Pasdaran established six military centres in the Bekaa for training Hizbollah and Islamic Amal fighters, see *Radio Free Lebanon*, 6 July 1984.

66 See *Jeune Afrique*, 25 Jan. 1984; *Washington Post*, 19 Jan. 1992; *US News & World Report*, 6 March 1989; *Washington Post*, 8 Jan. 1990; and *FBIS*, 28 Aug 1990.

67 See *al-Shira*, 17 March 1986; *Independent*, 7 March 1990; and *Davar*, 11 Jan. 1987. For IRGC recruitment of Hizbollah operatives in Iran's embassy in Beirut, see *IDF Radio*, 13 Oct. 1987.

68 See Kenneth Katzman, *The Warriors of Islam: Iran's Revolutionary Guards* (Oxford: Westview Press, 1993).

69 See *Middle East Reporter*, 1 Sep. 1984; and *Jeune Afrique*, 25 Jan. 1984.

70 See *al-Sharq al-Awsat*, 18 April 1989; *AFP*, 16 May 1988; *al-Majallah*, 19–25 April 1989; *New York Times*, 23 April 1990; *Washington Post*, 8 Jan. 1990; *New York Times*, 29 Dec. 1989; *New York Times*, 10 Oct. and 22 May 1989.

71 See *Washington Post*, 8 Jan. 1990; *The Echo of Iran*, No.26 (Feb. 1990), p. 12; and Farhang Jahanpour, "Iran I: Wars Among the Heirs", *The World Today* (Oct. 1990), p. 186.

72 In the early 1980s Syrian officials from Rifa'at Assad's "Special Forces Brigades" trained Hizbollah and *Islamic Amal* members in the Bekaa area, see *Middle East Defense News*, 16 May 1988. Also see: *Ma'ariv*, 22 Sep. 1986; and *al-Qabas*, 15 June 1988; *Independent* 22 June 1988; *al-Anba*, 7 April 1990; and *Jeune Afrique*, 7 May 1986. Also see Carl Anthony Wege, "Assad's Legions: The Syrian Intelligence Services", *International Journal of Intelligence and Counter Intelligence* 4/1 (Spring 1990), pp.91–100.

73 See *Ma'ariv*, 27 March 1983; and *Foreign Report*, 27 Oct. 1983. Also see R. Avi-Ran, *Syrian Involvement in Lebanon (1975–1985)*, (Tel-Aviv: Jaffee Center for Strategic Studies, Tel Aviv Univ. 1986).

74 See Yosef Olmert, "Iranian-Syrian Relations: Between Islam and Realpolitik", in David Menashri (ed.), *The Iranian Revolution and the Muslim World* (Boulder, Co: Westview Press, 1990), pp.171–188; William Harris, "Syria in Lebanon", in Altaf Gauhar (ed.) *Third World Affairs 1988* (London: Third World Fdn., 1988). Also see *al-Anwar*, 27 Feb. 1987. E.g., Syria warned Hizbollah in 1985 about its overt activity, urging the establishment of an Islamic Republic, by threatening to kill Sheikh Fadlallah unless this activity was ceased, see *Ma'aretz*, 10 March and 19 March 1985.

75 See *al-Dustur*, 5 March 1990; *Jeune Afrique*, 7 May 1986; *Le Nouvel Observateur*, 28 March–3 April 1986; *IRNA*, 25 Oct. 1991; and *Jeune Afrique*, 25 April 1984. For a useful overview of Syrian intelligence, see Middle East Watch, *Syria Unmasked* (London: Yale UP, 1991), pp.38–51.

76 In June 1988 a Hizbollah delegation (Ibrahim al-Amin; Subhi al-Tufayli; Hussein al-Musawi; and Khalil) held consultations with senior Syrian officials on future operations, see *al-Qabas*, 15 June 1988. For Syria's role as conduit in the release of hostages, see *Jerusalem Post*, May 17, 1985; *International Herald Tribune*, 1 Nov. 1986; *Yediot Aharanot*, 5 May 1988; *al-Aharam*, 26 March 1987; *Ha'aretz*, 4 May 1986; *Jerusalem Post*, 7 Aug. 1989; *Defense & Foreign Affairs Weekly*, 11 Sept. 1988; *Ha'aretz*, 1 April 1987; and *Ma'aretz*, 24 Feb. 1989.

77 Mustafa Dirani defected from Amal after the Feb. 1988 kidnapping of US Marine Corps officer Lt. Col. William Higgins. For information on Dirani's role, see *Ma'aretz*, 24 Feb. 1989; *Davar*, 28 Feb. 1988; *Defense and Foreign Affairs Weekly*, 15 July 1985; *Davar*, 10 Nov. 1987; and *Yediot Aharanot*, 25 Feb. 1988. Another leading Amal member, who defected to the Hizbollah, is Akel Hamiye. He was responsible for six hijackings between 1979 and 1982 and was appointed Amal military commander in 1984. Hamiye emerged as a leading figure during the negotiations over TWA 847 hijacking. In 1985 he established with Mustafa Dirani, the *Believers Resistance Movement*. Hamiye defected from Amal in 1987 and was appointed leader in Hizbollah, see *Ha'aretz*, 17 Feb. 1987; *Davar*, 10 and 13 Nov. 1987; *Washington Post*, 8 Oct. 1988; and *Yediot Aharanot*, 25 Feb. 1988. On 21 May 1994 Israel abducted Dirani from his home in Qaser al-Naba in the eastern Bekaa, see *Independent on Sunday*, 22 May 1994; and *Sunday Times*, 22 May 1994.

78 See Shireen T. Hunter, "Iran and Syria: From Hostility to Limited Alliance", in Hooshang Amirahmadi and Nader Entessar (eds.), *Iran and the Arab World* (London: Macmillan, 1993), pp.198–216.

79 In Lebanon's Syrian-controlled Bekaa valley, Hizbollah clans openly cultivate hashish and opium, which are refined and sent on to be distributed through the Dahiya suburban district of Beirut, see *Foreign Report*, 11 Oct. 1990; and *Wall Street Journal*, 24 March 1988. Another transit point is Syria and Syria's Defense Minister, Mustafa Talas, revealed that he provided transit documents with his signature to drugtraffickers in Baalbek in order to provide free passage for them between Lebanon and Syria, see *Hadashot*, 10 May 1991. Hizbollah clergymen encouraged the drug trade as it serves to weaken the three great enemies of Islam, see *Foreign Report*, 11 Oct. 1990. For Syria's involvement in drug-trafficking, see *Middle East Defense News*, 16 May 1988; and James Wyllie, "Assad's Tightrope", *Jane's Intelligence Review* 5/10 (Oct. 1993), p.465. Also see *Le Point*, 11 Sept. 1989; *al-Shira*, 5 Feb 1990; *Yediot Aharanot*, 5 Feb. 1992; and *Le Figaro*, 30–31 May 1992. Also see Rachel Ehrenfeld, *Narcoterrorism* (NY: Basic Books, 1990), pp. 52–73; and US Dept. of State, *International Narcotics Control Strategy Report* (Washington, DC.: Bureau of Int. Narcotics Matter, March 1988), pp.218–220.

80 For incidents of Hizbollah-Syrian frictions, see *Jerusalem Post*, 29 Nov. 1987; *Le Matin*, 28 Nov. 1987; *Ma'aretz*, 13 Feb. 1987; *Washington Post*, 30 June 1987; *International Herald Tribune*, 4 March 1988; *Observer*, 8 Dec. 1991; and *Ma'aretz*, 2 March 1987. A prominent example is the Syrian arrest warrant against Imad Mughniya, see *Ha'aretz*, 29 Jan. 1988.

81 See *BBC*, 3 Dec. 1988; *International Herald Tribune*, 20 June 1987; and *Jerusalem Post*, 20 Aug. 1987.

82 E.g., Sheikh Subhi al-Tufayli met Syrian leader. Hafez al-Assad who promised support and supply of weapons for the organization. The two also agreed that all Hizbollah military operations would be coordinated with the Syrian headquarters in Lebanon, see *al-Shira* and *Ma'aretz*, 14 June 1987; and *Ma'aretz*, 15 June 1987.

83 See *Yediot Aharanot*, 16 July 1993; and *Ha'aretz*, 14 April 1993.

84 See Calabrese (note 4), p.189; and *FBIS*, 5 Dec. 1989.

85 See *Liberation*, 19 March 1985; *Jeune Afrique*, 7 May 1986; and *The Lebanon Report* 4/3 (March 1993), pp. 6–7.

86 While Sheikh Subhi al-Tufayli, supported by Sheikh Ibrahim al-Amin, argued that an Islamic republic should be established as soon as possible and all means should be pursued for this purpose, Sheikh Fadlallah disagreed, see *La Revue du Liban*, 30 Jan. 1988; *Ha'aretz*, 22 Feb. 1988; and *Ha'aretz*, 29 Nov. 1987. For wider dispute between al-Tufayli and Fadlallah, see *al-Shira*, 27 Sept. 1993.

87 Sheikh Subhi al-Tufayli threatened that his supporters would burn voting centres in his home village of Brital, see *al-Shira*, 2 Aug. 1992. For rivalry over the post of Secretary-General of the movement, see *Foreign Report*, 30 April 1992. For efforts by Sheikh al-Tufayli of undermining the position of Sheikh Nasserallah, see *Foreign Report*, 5 Nov. 1992.

88 E.g., the Deputy Secretary-General is in charge of the financial military affairs of the movement, see *Foreign Report*, 13 June 1991. The regional commanders of the Hizbollah are Hajj Abdallah Qassir (Beirut and the southern suburbs); Sheikh Muhammad Yazbek (Bekaa); and Sheikh Hassan Nasserallah (southern Lebanon), see *The Lebanon Report* 4/3 (March 1993), p.6. Another key position within the Hizbollah is the head of the *Executive Shura*.

89 While Sheikh Fadlallah's position was temporarily diminished, the position of Sheikh Subhi al-Tufayli was bolstered as he served as a spokesman for the Iranian position in the organization, see *Ha'aretz*, 29 Nov. 1987. Also see *al-Watan al-Arabi wal-Duwali*, 11 Dec. 1987; and *MENA*, 3 Nov. 1987.

90 This led to the assembly of over 200 Hizbollah representatives from the Bekaa, south Beirut, the *Islamic Resistance*, the senior clergy within *Majlis al-Shura* and others in Iran, see *al-Anba*, 27 Nov. 1989. For Hizbollah factionalism in Sept./Oct. 1989, see *Hadashot*, 25 Oct. 1989; and *al-Majallah*, 15 Aug. 1993.

91 The *Executive Shura* consists of nine leading Hizbollah clergy, see *al-Hayat*, 27 Nov. 1989; and *Ha'aretz*, 17 Dec. 1989.

92 Private communication with Dr Yossi Olmert, Director, Government Press Office, Israel, 30 Dec. 1991. Also see *FBIS*, 30 Nov. 1989. The composition of the nine-man *Deciding Shura* is: Hajj Muhammad Hassan Yaghi (President); Fadl Zayn al-Din (Finance); Husayn al-Hajj Hasan (Education); Nabil Sulayman (Health); Ghanim Salim (Trades Union Affairs); Sultan As'ad (Social Affairs); Hajj Abd al-Hadi Hamadi (Security); Mustafa Badreddin (Military Affairs); and Hajj Ali Rashid (Information), see *The Lebanon Report* 4/3 (March 1993), p.6.

93 The first *chairman* of the *Politbureau* was Muhammad Fannish (later Hussein al-Khalil and the other members correspond to the composition of the real decision-making body, see *Foreign Report*, 13 June 1991. The other members of the *Politbureau* are: Sayyid Ammar Musawi (Vice-President); Sheikh Ali Taha; Sheikh Khodr Tlays; Sheikh Hassan Badran; Sheikh Khodr Nurredine; Sheikh Hassan Izzidin; Hajj Ali Ammar; Hajj Muhammad Fannish; Hajj Muhammad Ra'ad; Hajj Muhammad al-Khansa; Hajj Wafiq Safa; Hajj Husayn Shami, see *The Lebanon Report* 4/3 (March 1993): p.6.

94 The clerical factionalism developed into three main conflicting positions supported by members of the movement. The first position, led by Subhi al-Tufayli; Abbas al-Musawi; and Hussein al-Musawi, called for a public and open declaration of Hizbollah's position and for co-operation with pro-Syrian leftist organizations in Lebanon as well as with pro-Iranian Muslim bodies. They also called for a collective leadership. The second position, led by Hassan Nasserallah and Ibrahim al-Amin, called for a centralized party structure, tighter party discipline, while rejecting the formation of an open and public leadership apparatus. This position also opposed any extension of Hizbollah's involvement in the developments in the wider Lebanese arena and urged a jihad against those who opposed their efforts for an Islamic Lebanon. The third position, led by Naim Qassem; Hussein Korani; Muhammad Raad; and Hussein Khalil, rejected the suggestion of an overture of the leadership. For Hizbollah factionalism at the meetings, see *al-Anba*, 27 Nov. 1989; *al-Ahd*, and *al-Hayat*, 27 Oct. 1989; and *Ha'aretz*, 17 Dec. 1989. This was also confirmed in an unattributable interview with a senior IDF official, Tel Aviv, Sept. 1991.

95 See *FBIS*, Nov. 30, 1989; and Assaf Kfoury, *Arabies*, Dec. 1992. The most prominent representatives of the al-Da'wa trend within the main *Majlis al-Shura* are Hassan Nasserallah; Naim Qassem; and Muhammad Raad, see *al-Shira*, 27 Sept. 1993.

96 See *Middle East Contemporary Survey* (1988), pp.193–194; and *al-Shira*, 8 Nov. 1993.

97 The four dismissed leaders were Ibrahim al-Amin; Hussein al-Musawi; Hussein Khalil; and Abd al-Hadi Hamadi. In the case of Khalil and Hamadi, a major reason for their dismissal was security infiltrations into party ranks, discovered after a failed assassination attempt on Sheikh Fadlallah, see *al-Anba*, 27 Nov. 1989; and *Foreign Report*, 14 Dec. 1989.

98 See *al-Anba*, 27 Nov. 1989; *Ha'aretz*, 17 Dec. 1989; and *FBIS*, 30 Nov. 1989.

99 See *Voice of Lebanon*, Beirut 1015 GMT 21 May 91 – BBC/*SWB*/ME/1079 23 May 1991. For Hizbollah's "democratization process", see *Jerusalem Report*, 1 Aug. 1991. Under Sheikh al-Tufayli's tenure as Sec.

Gen., the number of members of the *Majlis al-Shura* grew to include over 20 Hizbollah members. However, with the appointment of Sheikh Abbas al-Musawi, the number was reduced to eight, see *The Lebanon Report* 4/3 (March 1993), p.7.

100 For insights on Hizbollah's concern over disarmament, see *Voice of the Oppressed* 0630 GMT 24 March 1991 – BBC/*SWB*/ME/1030, 26 March 1991. See also interview with Sheikh Subhi al-Tufayli, *Voice of the Oppressed* 0530 GMT 8 May 1991 – BBC/SWB/ME/1068, 10 May 1991.

101 For al-Musawi's position as leader of Hizbollah's military wing, see *Ha'aretz*, 2 Oct. 1987; and *Independent*, 7 March 1990.

102 For agreement, see *Financial Times*, 17 Feb. 1992; and *Voice of the Oppressed*, 0630 GMT 30 April 1991 – BBC/*SWB*/ME/1061, 2 May 1991. For Hizbollah's justification of retaining its armed presence in the South, see *Voice of Lebanon* 1715 GMT 21 April 91 – BBC/*SWB*/ME/1053, 23 April 1991; and *Voice of the Oppressed* 0530 GMT 4 May 1991 – BBC/*SWB*/ME/1064, 6 May 1991. Also see *al-Shira*, 18 March 1991.

103 For a useful insight to Hizbollah's view on the achievements of hostage-taking, see *Voice of the Oppressed* 0550 GMT 16 Aug. 1991 – BBC/*SWB*/ME/1153, 17 Aug. 1991.

104 See *Jerusalem Report*, 1 Aug. 1991; *Independent* 9 Oct. 1991; and *al-Hayat*, 25 May 1991.

105 A major strategy by the Hizbollah was to: "mould the organizational body in a manner that makes it compatible with the emerging regional and international developments and harmonious with the new Iranian leadership", see *al-Hayat*, 25 May 1991. Hizbollah's existence as a resistance movement also meant that it had to escalate its confrontation with Israel in southern Lebanon. This has been clearly evident by the dramatic rise in the number of attacks made by the *Islamic Resistance* against Israel. In 1991 Hizbollah carried out 52 attacks, compared to 19 the previous year. In 1992 the *Islamic Resistance* launched 63 attacks and in 1993, 158 attacks, see "Hizbullah", *IDF Spokesman*, 6 June 1994; and *Jerusalem Post*, 4 Jan. 1994.

106 Unattributable interviews with the high-ranking counter-terrorism officials at Israel's Ministry of Defense, Tel Aviv, Israel, Aug. 1991; and Office for Counterterrorism, US Dept. of State, Oct. 1993. Also see *Foreign Report*, 13 June 1991. For Iranian hints of a global deal to release Western hostages three months prior to the first release of John McCarthy, see *Sawt al-Kuwayt al-Duwali*, 9 May 1991.

107 For details concerning the assassination of Sheikh al-Musawi, see *Terrorismus*, No. 1, March 1992. For excerpts of Sheikh Abbas al-Musawi's speech in Jibshit, see *Radio Free Lebanon*, 1645 GMT 16 Feb. 1992 – BBC/*SWB*/ME/1307, 18 Feb. 1992.

108 See *Foreign Report*, 30 April 1992.

109 An announcement made by the Beirut-based pro-Hizbollah radio, *Voice of the Oppressed*, 1250 GMT 18 Feb. 1991 – BBC/*SWB*/ME/1398, 19 Feb. 1992. The election had been conducted by the members of the *Supreme Shura* at a meeting in Baalbek, see *AFP* in English 1520 GMT 18 Feb 1992 – BBC/*SWB*/ME/1309, 20 Feb. 1992. The Hizbollah was careful to underline that the decision by the *Supreme Shura* to elect Sheikh Nasserallah was unanimous, see *Voice of the People* 1239 GMT Feb 1992 – BBC/*SWB*/ME/1318, 2 March 1992.

110 See *Foreign Report*, 30 April 1992; and *Foreign Report*, 8 Oct. 1992.

111 For Sheikh Nasserallah's strengthened position under the tenure of Sheikh al-Musawi, see *al-Hayat*, 21 May 1991. At the end of 1989 Nasserallah had bolstered his position with Iran, who wanted him to fulfill a senior role in the next stage of Iranian policy in Lebanon, see *al-Qabas*, 20 July 1989.

112 Unattributable interview with official in Israel's Ministry of Foreign Affairs, 3 Sept. 1991. In an interview with Sheikh Hassan Nasserallah, he is asked to elaborate on his links with Ayatollah Mohtashemi, see *Voice of the People* 1239 GMT 28 Feb. 1992 – BBC/*SWB*/ME/1318, 2 March 1992.

113 See *Foreign Report*, 30 April 1992; *Foreign Report*, 8 Oct. 1992; and *Foreign Report*, 5 Nov. 1992. Sheikh Nasserallah spent a period in Qum, Iran, after the Amal-Hizbollah ceasefire to project his image as obedient to Iranian officials, see *al-Shira*, 8 Nov. 1993. Sheikh Nasserallah reshuffled some of the leaders of Hizbollah's military wing to ensure loyalty. In particular, Ali Daoun replaced Hajj Hassan Hubollah as commander in south Lebanon. Nasserallah also promoted Sheikh Nuhad Kushman to head military-security affairs. Also see *al-Watan al-Arabi*, 7 Jan. 1994. Nasserallah also transferred responsibility of Palestinian affairs from Khader Selim to Haj Abbas Ruhani.

114 See *Foreign Report*, 30 April 1992; *Foreign Report*, 8 Oct. 1992; *Foreign Report*, 5 Nov. 1992; *Foreign Report*, 15 May 1993; *al-Shira*, 13 July 1992; and *al-Shira*, 2 Aug. 1992. For Nasserallah's difficulty in justifying the decision to participate in the parliamentary elections, see *al-Shira*, 8 Nov. 1993. Also see interview with Sheikh Nasserallah, *al-Diyar*, 19 Dec. 1993.

115 Sheikh al-Tufayli threatened to burn the voting-centres in his home village of Brital, see *al-Shira*, 2 Aug. 1992.

116   For the Hizbollah operation, initiated by Sheikh al-Tufayli, near the village of Kaoukaba which killed 5 IDF soldiers and wounded 5 others on 25 Oct. 1992, see *Foreign Report*, 5 Nov. 1992. In the parliamentary elections, Hizbollah won four seats in the Baalbek-Hermil area (Hizb'allah politbureau members: Ibrahim al-Amin; Khodr Tiaiss; and Mohammad Yaghi); two scats in the southern suburbs of Beirut (politbureau members: Ali Amnar; and Mohammad Burjawi); and two seats in southern Lebanon (politbureau members: Mohammad Fannish; and Mohammad Raad). In addition, four seats were captured by non-Hizbollah members who were loyal to Hizbollah, For details, see *Foreign Report*, 17 Sept. 1992.

117   See *Foreign Report*, 7 Oct. 1993. Also see *al-Ahd*, 25 Feb. 1994; and *al-Watan al-Arabi*, 7 Jan. 1994. E.g., it was alleged that Hussayn al-Musawi, head of *Islamic Amal*, was considering joining forces with this opposition due to the poor financial position of the movement.

118   For Nasserallah's statement, see *AFP* 1230 GMT 24 Feb. 1994 – BBC/*SWB*/ME/1932, 26 Feb. 1994. For Nasserallah's blueprint of the movement's future political strategy towards Lebanon, see: *IRNA* 1745 GMT 13 Oct 92 – BBC/*SWB*/ME/1512, 15 Oct. 1992.

119   This was stressed by Rafsanjani in meetings with Hizbollah leaders, see *al-Majallah*, 15 Aug. 1993. As admitted by Sheikh Nasserallah: "[o]ur entry to the ranks of parliamentary representatives gives us the opportunity to defend our resistance on the political plane", see *Ettela'at*, 13 Feb. 1993.

120   E.g., the appointment of Hajj Husayn Khalil as the president of the *Politbureau* was in alignment with Hizbollah's new profile in Lebanon as he was known for his close ties to Syria and as he had coordinated the movement's long-term relations with Damascus, see *The Lebanon Report* 4/3 (March 1993), p.7.

121   See *Foreign Report*, 30 April 1992. This is also apparent by the relegation of Sheikh Subhi al-Tufayli to a position as a mere member of the main *Majlis al-Shura* without any specific portfolio. Also see *al-Watan al-Arabi*, 7 Jan. 1994.

122   See *Foreign Report*, 13 May 1993.

123   See *The Lebanon Report*, 4/3 (1993): p.6; *al-Shira*, 27 Sept. 1993; and *al-Majallah*, 15 Aug. 1993.

124   See *US News & World Report*, 6 March 1989.

125   See Martin Kramer, "Redeeming Jerusalem: The Pan-Islamic Premise of Hizbollah", in Menashri, *Iranian Revolution and the Muslim World* (note 74), pp.105–131.

126   See *Le Figaro*, 18 April 1990; *Lettre Persane*, No.46 (June 1986); *Le Nouvel Observateur*, 28 March–3 April 1986; *Valeurs Actuelles*, 1 April 1986; *al-Sharq al-Awsat*, Feb. 1989; and *al-Majallah*, 5–11 Nov. 1983.

127   See Raufer (note 21), pp.132–133; *al-Majallah*, 5–11 Nov. 1983; and *Jeune Afrique*, 7 May 1986.

128   See *Keyhan*, 18 Sept. 1986; *Valeurs Actuelles*, 6 April 1987; and *Le Monde*, 25 Oct. 1986.

129   See *New York Times*, 27 Aug. 1989; *al-Shira*, 17 March 1986; and *al-Shira*, 19 Sept. 1988. For Mohtashemi's stay in Najaf under Ayatollah Khomeini and his closely forged friendships with future Hizbollah leaders, see *Independent*, 23 Oct. 1991. Mohtashemi had been Ayatollah Khumayyni's personal secretary during the latter's exile in Paris, see *al-Majallah*, 15 Aug. 1993.

130   For Mohtashemi's role in the creation of Hizbollah, see *al-Watan al-Arabi*, 11 Dec. 1987; *Davar*, 11 Jan. 1987; *Foreign Report*, 30 July 1987; *al-Shira*, 19 Sept. 1988; *Ha'aretz*, 7 Aug. 1989; and *Washington Post*, 7 July 1988.

131   See *Foreign Report*, 20 June 1985; *New York Times*, 2 Nov. 1983; and *New York Times*, 5 Oct. 1984. Mohtshemi was replaced by Hojjatolislam Hassan Akhtari as Iran's ambassador to Damascus, see *New York Times*, 1 Sept. 1986; and *al-Majallah*, 15 Aug. 1993.

132   See *Washington Post*, 8 Jan. 1990; *al-Shira*, 19 Sept. 1988; and *Independent*, 23 Oct. 1991.

133   See *Voice of the People* 1239 GMT 28 Feb. 1992 – BBC/*SWB*/ME/1318, 2 March 1992; *FBIS*, 30 Nov. 1989; and *al-Anba*, 27 Nov. 1989.

134   See *al-Anba*, 29 Nov. 1989.

135   For a debate within the Iranian *Majlis* on Mohtashemi's independent efforts, see *FBIS*, 23 Sept. 1988. Also see *Ha'aretz*, 17 Dec. 1989.

136   See *New York Times*, 10 Oct. 1989; and *New York Times*, 14 March 1990.

137   See *al-Anba*, 27 Nov. 1989; *FBIS*, 30 Nov. 1989; and *Ha'aretz*, 17 Dec. 1989. For details of Mohtashemi's three-week visit to Lebanon with Hizbollah leaders, see *AP*, 26 Oct. 1989.

138   See *Independent*, 23 Oct. 1991; *Wall Street Journal*, 16 Aug. 1989; and *Washington Post*, 15 May 1990.

139   See *al-Hayat*, 25 May 1991; *Jerusalem Report*, 1 Aug. 1991; *al-Anba*, 27 Nov. 1989; and *FBIS*, 30 Nov. 1989.

140   For Hizbollah's ties with Montazeri, see *Ha'aretz*, 30 Sept. 1984; *al-Dustur*, 22 Dec. 1986; *al-Ahd*, 30 Nov. 1986; *Foreign Report*, 13 Dec. 1984; *Financial Times*, 8 Dec. 1984; and *International Herald Tribune*, 8–9 Dec. 1984.

141   Both Mohammad Montazeri and Mehdi Hashmi had obtained guerrilla training in Lebanon before 1979 and were deeply involved in promoting the Iranian Pasdaran's presence, see *Paris Lettre Persane*, No.46 (June 1986), pp.6–10. Also see Shireen T. Hunter, "Iran and the Spread of Revolutionary Islam", *Third World Quarterly* 10/2 (April 1988); pp.743–744; and Dilip Hiro, *Between Marx and Muhammad* (NY: HarperCollins, 1994), p.284.

142   See *FBIS*, 5 Nov. 1986. Also see Faligot and Kauffer (note 42), p.412. Under the auspices of the *Office of Islamic Liberation Movements*, Hizbollah held its first plenary meeting in 1983 in which the movement's charter and constitution for a future Islamic regime in Lebanon were drafted, see *al-Majallah*, 15 Aug. 1993.

143   See Hazhir Teimourian, "The Mullah Goes Back to the Mosque", *The Middle East* (May 1989): pp.20–21; *FBIS*, 28 Oct. 1986; and *New York Times*, 18 March 1987. Also see Alvin H. Bernstein, "Iran's Low-Intensity War Against the United States". *Orbis*, No. 1 (Spring 1986), pp.149–150.

144   See *al-Shira*, 3 Nov. 1986 and *al-Dustur*, 22 Dec. 1986

145   See *Washington Post*, 4 Feb. 1987; and George Joffe, "Iran, the Southern Mediterranean and Europe: Terrorism and Hostages", in Anoushiravan Ehteshami and Manshour Varasteh (eds.), *Iran and the International Community* (London: Routledge, 1991), p. 85.

146   See: *IRNA*, 18 March 1987; and Bruce Hoffman, *Recent Trends and Future Prospects of Iranian Sponsored International Terrorism*, R-3783-USDP (Santa Monica, CA: RAND Corporation, 1990): p.26.

147   See *Foreign Report*, 18 Dec. 1986; *Bulvar*, 16 Nov. 1986; and *Marmara*, 25 Nov. 1986.

148   Khosrowshahi was a noted protégé of Rafsanjani, see Pierre Pean, *La Menace* (Paris: Fayard, 1987), p.262. Also see *al-Dustur*, 11 June 1990.

149   See Nassif Hitti, "Lebanon in Iran's Foreign Policy: Opportunities and Constraints", in Hooshang Amirahmadi and Nader Entessar (eds.) *Iran and the Arab World* (London: Macmillan, 1993), pp. 188–189. Also see *al-Majallah*, 15 Aug. 1993.

150   After 1986 the Office of Islamic Liberation Movements operated with a budget of 150 million, see *al-Watan al-Arabi*, 12 Feb. 1993.

151   See *Foreign Report*, 18 Dec. 1986; and *Le Monde*, 25 Oct. 1986.

152   See *al-Anba*, 27 Nov. 1989; *al-Hayat*, 27 Nov. 1989; and *Ha'aretz*, 17 Dec. 1989.

153   See Shireen T. Hunter "Iran and the Spread of Revolutionary Islam", *Third World Quarterly* 10/2 (April 1988), pp.743–744.

154   See *US News & World Report*, 6 March 1989; *Independent*, 1 July 1987; *Keyhan*, 5 Dec. 1985; *Nouvel Observateur*, 30 Oct. 1983; and *Le Monde*, 6–7 Nov. 1983. For the close relationship between Sheikh-ol-Islam and Mohtashemi, see *IRNA*, 7 Nov. 1982; and *Radio Damascus*, 9 Nov. 1982. Also see *al-Watan al-Arabi*, 27 Nov. 1992.

155   See *al-Dustur*, 12 Feb. 1990; and *al-Dustur*, 16 Oct. 1990.

156   See Katzman (note 68), pp.125–126. Also see *al-Dustur*, 12 Feb. 1990.

157   Private communication with Dr Yossi Olmert, Director, Government Press Office, Israel, 20 Dec. 1991. Also see *FBIS*, 30 Nov. 1989.

158   See Raufer (note 21), pp.180–182. Also see *The Times*, 1 June 1985.

159   See Norton (note 7), pp.104–105. Also see *al-Dustur*, 14 Oct. 1985; *al-Shira*, 15 March 1986; and Raufer (note 21), p.150.

160   See *Middle East International*, No.315 (19 Dec. 1987); *Financial Times*, 25 July 1987; *al-Dustur*, 14 Oct. 1985; *al-Shira*, 19 Sept. 1988; *Jerusalem Post*, 22 July 1987; and *al-Musawwar*, 17 Sept. 1987. In 1994 it was estimated that Hizbollah received £40 million annually from Iran, see *Independent*, 8 May 1994.

161   See *al-Nahar al-Arabi wal-Duwali*, 19 Sept. 1989. Hizbollah's TV station is called *al-Manar* (the Beacon) while its three radio station are called: *Voice of the Oppressed*; *Voice of Faith*; and *Voice of Struggle*. Its main daily publication is *al-Ahd* and a monthly publication *al-Bilad*. The director of *al-Manar* is Sheikh Ali Daber. For an insight into *al-Manar*'s programmes, see *Sunday Times*, 19 July 1992.

162   For a useful overview, see A. Nizar Hamzeh, "Lebanon's Hizbullah: From Islamic Revolution to Parliamentary Accomodation", *Third World Quarterly* 14/2 (1993), pp.327–328.

163   For an overview, see *al-Ahd*, 1 Aug. 1989.

164   See *al-Ahd*, 23 Jan. 1987; and "Details about 'Hizballah' and Its Leaders", *Middle East Reporter*, 22 March 1986. For a lower figure to martyr's families, see *The Times*, 14 Nov. 1987. The founder of the *Martyr's Foundation* was Ali Amnar, who currently serves as one of Hizbollah's parliamentary delegates (note 116). For his profile, see *The Lebanon Report* 3/12 (Dec. 1992), p.7.

165   For details, see Norton (note 2), p.127. For a detailed list of payments for social services of over $2 million made by the office of Ayatollah Mohammad Hussein Fadlallah in 1992, see *al-Nahar*,

4 Jan. 1993. For a summary of a report by the Muslim Treasury, a financial institution operated by the Hizbollah, detailing extended loans, see *al-Ahd*, 15 Jan. 1993. Also see *al-Shira*, 18 Jan. 1993.

166   See *al-Ahd*, 7 Feb. 1988; and *al-Shira*, 31 Aug. 1992. Also see *Middle East*, (Feb. 1993), pp.12–13.

167   See *Ha'aretz*, 21 June 1987; *Jerusalem Post*, 13 Nov. 1987; *al-Musawwar*, 17 Sept. 1987; *Voice of Lebanon*, 29 Oct. 1987; and *Jerusalem Post*, 22 July 1987. According to *al-Dustur*, approximately one-third of Iran's financial support for liberation movements is allocated to the Hizbollah in Lebanon, see *al-Dustur*, 14 Oct. 1985. Iran's financial aid to the Hizbollah is channelled through the Iranian embassies in Damascus and Beirut, see *al-Shira*, 18 Jan. 1993.

168   See *Middle East Defense News*, 1 May 1988; and John L. Esposito, *The Islamic Threat: Myth or Reality?* (Oxford: OUP 1992), p.147. Also see *Liberation*, 19 March 1985; *al-Shira*, 19 Sept. 1988; *al-Musawwar*, 17 Sept. 1987; and *Financial Times*, 25 July 1987.

169   See *al-Sharq al-Awsat*, 18 April 1989; and *Washington Post*, 22 Sept. 1988.

170   See Sean K. Anderson, "Iranian State-Sponsored Terrorism", *Conflict Quarterly* (Fall 1991), pp. 19–34.

171   See *FBIS*, 7 Sept. 1989; *Teheran Domestic Service*, 6 Sept. 1989; *Washington Post*, 22 Sept. 1988; *al-Sharq al-Awsat*, 18 April 1989; and *al-Watan al-Arabi*, 6 April 1993.

172   See Robin Wright, "Islam's New Political Face", *Current History* 90/552 (Jan. 1991), p.28.

173   See *Middle East* (Feb. 1993), pp.12–13; and *Middle East* (Feb. 1992), p.13. E.g., the delay in Iranian financial assistance to Hizbollah in Oct. 1993 was caused by a financial crisis in the Bank of Iran rather than any Iranian attempts to reduce aid to the movement, see *Radio Monte Carlo* 1700 GMT 7 Apr 1994 – BBC/*SWB*/ME/1967, 9 April 1994.

174   In 1992 it was alleged that Iran's financial aid to Hizbollah amounted to $120 million, see *al-Majallah*, 15 Aug. 1993. Also see *al-Ahram*, 8 Dec. 1992.

175   See *al-Sharq al-Awsat*, 18 April 1989; *al-Majallah*, 19–25 April 1989; *New York Times*, 23 April 1990; *New York Times*, 29 Dec. 1989; *Washington Post*, 8 Jan. 1990; and *New York Times*, 22 May 1989. The importance of the Iranian clergy within the Pasdaran was discussed by the author and Dr Martin Kramer at the Jaffee Center for Strategic Studies, Tel Aviv Univ., 1 Sept. 1991. For the role of Iranian Pasdaran contingent in the formation of Hizbollah's armed cells, political organization, and security agency, see *al-Majallah*, 15 Aug. 1993.

176   The most notable supporters are Ahmad Khumayyni and Mohtashemi, see Katzman (note 68): and Nikola Schahgaldian, *The Iranian Military Under the Islamic Republic* (Santa Monica, CA.: RAND Corp. 1987); and *Washington Post*, 7 Jan. 1990. The *al-Quds*, the IRGC units operating abroad, is headed by Gen. Ahmad Vahidi, see *al-Ahram*, 8 Dec. 1988.

177   See *Jeune Afrique* (Jan. 1984); *Washington Post*, 7 Jan. 1990; and Robin Wright, "A Reporter at Large", *New Yorker*, 5 Sept. 1988.

178   Rafsanjani offered more weaponry and authority to the Pasdaran, which would enable it to pursue more hardline political and military objectives in the strengthening of the Islamic revolution and its spread to other countries, see *Wall Street Journal*, 27 April 1990; *New York Times*, 16 Oct. 1991; *Jane's Defence Weekly*, 16 Nov. 1991; *al-Majallah*, 19–25 April 1989; and *Washington Post*, Jan. 1992.

179   For statements, see *Reuters*, 10 April and 12 April 1991.

180   It was reportedly activist members with *al-Da'wa* allegiance which began attacks on Amal, see *al-Nahar*, 19 Jan. 1989.

181   The Iranian mediation team was led by the Foreign Minister, Velyati, and the only non-radical Pasdaran leader, Mohsen Rafiq Dust, see *al-Sharq al-Awsat*, 18 April 1989; and *AFP*, 16 May 1988.

182   See *Independent*, 1 July 1987; *Wall Street Journal*, 16 Aug. 1989; and *Washington Post*, 15 May 1990.

183   See *al-Nahar*, 31 July 1992; and *Independent*, 8 May 1994.

184   See *Independent*, 30 Aug. 1989; *al-Shira*, 17 March 1986; *Ha'aretz*, 2 April 1986; and *al-Watan al-Arabi*, 11 Dec. 1987.

185   See Sean K. Anderson, "Iranian State-Sponsored Terrorism", *Conflict Quarterly* 11/4 (Fall 1991), p.29.

186   See Norton (note 7), pp.101–102. Also see *al-Shira*, 15 March 1986; *al-Watan al-Arabi*, 11 Dec. 1987; *al-Madinah*, 11 June 1990; and *al-Majellah*, 20 April 1988. For a useful overview of Iran's subversive activities through the ministries of Foreign Affairs, Islamic Guidance, and Intelligence, see *al-Watan al-Arabi*, 27 Nov. 1992. Also see *L'Express*, 22 Aug. 1991.

187   See Pierre Pean, *La Menace* (Paris: Fayard, 1987).

188   See: *al-Shira*, 15 March 1986; *Ma'aretz*, 30 Sept. 1984; and *Middle East Reporter*, 22 March 1986.

189   See *Ha'aretz*, 20 March 1987; *Ma'aretz*, 10 Nov. 1987; and *Ha'aretz*, 29 Nov. 1987.

190   See *al-Ittihad*, 31 Jan. 1988; *Davar*, 1 Feb. 1988; *Ha'aretz*, 29 Jan. 1988; *al-Ittihad*, 15 Jan. 1988; and *Davar*, 13 Nov. 1987.

191   See *Le Figaro*, 4 Dec. 1989; *Independent*, 26 April 1988; *al-Ittihad*, 15 Jan. 1988; and *Radio Free Lebanon*, 5 July 1990.

192   See *al-Ray*, 27 Dec. 1987; *Jerusalem Post*, 13 Nov. 1987; and *Ha'aretz*, 14 April 1993.

193   For Hizbollah's continued pan-Islamic commitments, as outlined by Sheikh Muhammad Fannish, see *al-Hayah*, 17 April 1992. Also see *al-Safir*, 4 Aug. 1993; and *al-Wasat*, 2–8 May 1994.

194   For rumours of a split within Hizbollah, see *al-Diyar*, 19 Dec. 1993.

195   For Nasserallah's concerns of the movement's future, see *al-Ahd*, 25 Feb. 1994. Also see *al-Wasat*, 23–29 Aug. 1993; and *al-Nahar*, 30 July 1994.

196   E.g., Syria arrested 11 Hizbollah fighters during a violent demonstration in Baalbek to mark Jerusalem Day, the first time this occurred. See: *FBIS*, 13 April 1994. Also see *FBIS*, 16 Feb. 1994.

197   See *al-Majallah*, 15–21 Aug. 1993.

198   See *Ha'aretz*, 14 April 1992.

199   In retaliation for Israel's assassination of Sheikh al-Musawi, the Hizbollah detonated a car-bomb outside Israel's embassy in Buenos Aires on 17 March 1992, which caused 30 deaths and 252 injuries, see *Ha'aretz*, 20 March 1992. With the conclusion of an Israeli-Jordanian peace agreement in July 1994, Hizbollah, with the assistance of Iran, also carried out car bomb-attacks in Argentina, Panama, and in London, see *Sunday Telegraph*, 31 July 1994; *FBIS*, 10 Aug. 1994; *al-Sharq al-Awsat*, 30 July 1994; and *al-Watan al-Arabi*, 10 Aug. 1994.

11 The Provisional IRA

A case study

Charles J. M. Drake

The tradition of militant republican nationalism in Ireland dates back to the United Irishmen of the 1790s. The Provisional Irish Republican Army (PIRA) is the result of a split in the Irish Republican Army (IRA) which occurred in 1969. Under the treaty of 1921 which ended a three-year guerrilla war with the IRA, the British government withdrew their forces from 26 of the 32 counties of Ireland. In those 26 predominantly Catholic counties the Irish Free State was established, with the British monarch as titular head of state. In the other six north-eastern counties which overall, though not individually, had a Protestant majority, the British ruled but locally governed state of Northern Ireland was established. A civil war was waged across the 26 counties in 1922–1923, in which the Free State forces defeated the anti-treaty Republicans. Following this some of the Republicans reformed as the IRA and its political equivalent Sinn Fein. The IRA waged a sporadic terrorist campaign across Ireland to little avail. After 1948 when the Free State declared itself a republic, the IRA largely confined its military actions to Northern Ireland whilst maintaining its headquarters in Dublin.

The IRA denied the legitimacy of the parliaments in Dublin and Belfast, and denied the right of Britain to rule or govern Northern Ireland. They held that the legitimate government of Ireland rested with those members of Dáil Éireann (the Irish Parliament) who had voted against accepting the treaty in December 1921, the other deputies being deemed traitors. In December 1938 the surviving anti-treaty deputies transferred their responsibilities to the ruling body of the IRA, the IRA Army Council, thus making it the legitimate government of Ireland from a republican perspective.[1]

In the mid-1960s some of the IRA Army Council, led by the Chief of Staff, Cathal Goulding, tried to move the IRA away from what they saw as futile efforts to end partition by force alone. They believed that in order to unite Ireland it would be necessary to form a left-wing, non-sectarian workers' movement across Ireland as a whole. The Catholic and Protestant workers together would overthrow capitalism in Ireland and establish a united Irish socialist state.[2] This move split the IRA for two reasons. First, it offended the conservatism and Catholicism of many members of the IRA and Sinn Fein throughout Ireland.[3] Second, it ignored the special position of the IRA in Northern Ireland as the defender of the urban Catholic enclaves during sectarian riots such as those of 1920–1922 and 1935.[4]

The IRA reforms of the 1960s led to many men leaving the organisation. This, allied to the lack of weaponry caused by the marginalisation of the IRA's' military role, meant that when sectarian rioting broke out in August 1969 the IRA was unable to protect the northern Catholics.[5] The northern IRA had long felt that the IRA Army Council, dominated as it was by southerners, was remote from the problems which they faced.[6] In December 1969 the IRA Special Convention voted to end abstentionism and send elected Sinn Fein candidates to the parliaments in Dublin, Belfast, and London. To traditional IRA men this was tantamount to recognising the legitimacy of these bodies and thus of partition. Accordingly, several northerners and traditionalists, led by Sean MacStiofain, split off to form the PIRA, followed the next month by the formation of Provisional Sinn Fein (PSF).[7]

The basic ideology of PIRA is fairly similar to that of the pre-1960s IRA. The "treachery" of the IRA Army Council in 1969 in recognising the illegitimate parliaments in Dublin and Belfast meant that the mantle of the legitimate government of Ireland passed to the PIRA Army Council.[8] According to the PIRA official handbook, "The Green Book", one of the main objects of the PIRA is "[to] support the establishment of an Irish Socialist Republic based on the 1916 Proclamation."[9]

The PIRA considers itself to be the republican vanguard, responsible for protecting the integrity of the republican movement. The PIRA follows the old IRA in not accepting that the majority will should prevail if it is incorrect. In the 1920s a republican activist stated "The people of a nation may not voluntarily surrender their independence … if a majority is found that would vote for such a surrender, the vote is invalid legally and morally and a minority is justified in upholding the independence of their country."[10] Gerry Adams, President of PSF and allegedly a former PIRA chief of staff, has voiced similar sentiments.[11]

The PIRA claims to be a socialist organisation. In the early 1970s it is doubtful whether any coherent ideology apart from republican nationalism played a role. The late Seamus Twomey, a former Officer Commanding (OC) Belfast Brigade and PIRA chief of staff, is quoted as having said "At heart I am a socialist … I have been involved in setting up trade unions and so forth. But at the same time I am a right winger."[12] In a 1977 newspaper article journalist David Blundy judged that Twomey and Joe Cahill, OC Belfast April–August 1971, would feel ideologically at home on the right wing of the British Conservative Party.[13] Blundy also quoted Martin McGuiness, allegedly OC Derry and later PIRA Chief of Staff, as defining PIRA policy as "… blattering on until the Brits leave".[14]

PIRA military strategy is still largely concerned with "blattering away". In the early 1970s the PIRA tended to engage the British Army in gunbattles, whilst deploying car bombs in the city centres of Derry and Belfast. The deployment of car bombs forced the army to disperse its forces, thus precluding any army assaults upon the "no-go" areas of the Bogside and Lower Falls. The car bombs in commercial centres also formed part of an "economic campaign" by which PIRA hoped to turn Northern Ireland into an economic drain upon the British Treasury. The aim of the PIRA was to make Northern Ireland ungovernable.[15] Incidents such as the Falls Road Curfew of 1970, with its attendant house searches and use of tear gas, the introduction of internment in 1971, and the shooting dead of 13 nationalist demonstrators in Derry by the army on "Bloody Sunday" in January 1972, produced several recruits for PIRA.[16] In 1972 there were an estimated 700 volunteers in Belfast alone.[17] The successful smuggling into Northern Ireland of several hundred Armalite rifles in 1970–1971 and of a number of RPG7 shoulder-held rocket launchers in late 1972 meant that in some respects the PIRA were more heavily armed than the British Army (although the inexperience of the volunteers largely negated this).[18] The intensity of the fighting can be judged from the fact that in the period 1971–1974 over 20,000 shooting incidents were recorded, whereas in the period 1975–1988 there were less than 10,000.[19]

While this produced heavy army casualties, 232 regular soldiers being killed in the period 1971–1974, the PIRA also sustained heavy casualties, losing 106 volunteers dead in the period 1969–1973.[20] The PIRA also suffered badly from three factors. First, there was very little coordination between areas such as Belfast, Derry, and South Armagh, or indeed within Belfast itself. While this gave maximum scope to local initiative it precluded the simultaneous execution of operations in order to overstretch the army.[21] Second, the relatively large units in which PIRA operated were open to penetration by the Royal Ulster Constabulary (RUC) and informers.

The nominal organisation of the PIRA into companies, battalions, and brigades, with some Belfast companies containing up to 50 men, meant that one informer could name several men. As a result several experienced PIRA volunteers were arrested.[22]

Last, the PIRA's emphasis on physical force, largely to the exclusion of any other political philosophy, meant that it was unable to react to any change in the political climate, and in the absence of action was likely to atrophy. Thus, although the destruction of the Northern Irish government at Stormont had been the initial aim of the PIRA, when this occurred in July 1972 the first reaction of the PIRA leaders was to carry on fighting to force British withdrawal.[23] When the PIRA leaders negotiated with Government ministers in July 1972, apart from demanding the complete withdrawal of troops by 1975 they had no other long-term objectives and do not appear to have considered the consequences of withdrawal.[24]

The consequences of reliance on force were also seen in the period of the ceasefire of 1975–1976. Without the stimulus of action against the security forces, the PIRA degenerated into sectarian warfare with the Ulster Defence Association (UDA) and the Ulster Volunteer Force (UVF), and an internecine feud with the Official IRA (OIRA).[25] Martin McGuiness, allegedly OC Derry at the time, believes that the lack of action led to a drop in morale and recruiting.[26] According to Gerry Adams: "When the struggle was limited to armed struggle, the prolongation of the truce meant that there was no struggle at all. There was nothing but confusion, frustration, and demoralisation, arising directly from what I call 'spectator politics'." [27] As a result of the near debacle of the ceasefire period the then largely southern leadership was replaced over the next few years by younger men from the north. One major result was that the political tone of PIRA and PSF moved sharply leftwards. The "Green Book" specifically states that "All potential volunteers must be socialist in outlook".[28] On the other hand Adams himself has stated, "I don't think that socialism is on the agenda at all at this stage except for the political activists of the left. What's on the agenda now is an end to Partition. You won't get near socialism until you have national independence."[29] Interviews with ranking members of PIRA suggest that priority is given to winning the war against the British.[30]

Since the successful election of the H-Block hunger striker Bobby Sands to Westminster in 1981, PSF has evolved a political strategy which is complementary to, but not wholly dependent upon, the armed struggle. In 1982 PSF set up advice bureaux across Northern Ireland to help applicants in dealing with the authorities on social matters such as housing and social security benefits. According to Bishop and Mallie: "By 1984 Sinn Fein was established in the ghettoes of Belfast and Derry as the most efficient means of redress against the agencies of the State, with more advice bureaux than the rest of the Northern Ireland political parties put together."[31]

It has also contested elections in Northern Ireland at the local, national, and European level and has also contested elections in the Republic. At the 1981 PSF *ard fheis* (annual conference) the then Publicity Director Danny Morrison accurately described republican strategy as a combination of the ballot box and the Armalite. In the British general elections of 1983 and 1987 PSF managed to obtain between 35 and 42 per cent of the nationalist vote (11–13 per cent of the total Northern Irish vote) thus demonstrating a fairly solid bedrock of support for the militant republican line.[32]

In the Republic on the other hand, the PSF vote ranged from a modest 4.9 per cent in the 1984 European elections to a derisory 1.85 per cent in the 1987 elections to the Dail thus demonstrating the irrelevance of the North to southern voters, and their rejection of the PIRA's methods.[33] In 1985 at the PSF *ard fheis* the policy whereby elected PSF candidates abstained from taking up their seats in the Dail was overturned. Interestingly as well as many of the early leaders of PIRA, the last surviving anti-treaty deputy of the 1921 Dail, Tom Maguire, who had backed PIRA in the 1969 split, opposed the ending of abstentionism. He was ignored.[34]

On the military side, in 1976–1977 PIRA was reorganised in the cities from the above-mentioned semi-military structure to a system of 5-12-man cells, or Active Service Units (ASUs), linked only at brigade level by the cell leaders, with specialist cells dealing with sniping, bomb making and other specialised activities. In the rural areas the existing system was preferred by the local volunteers and was therefore retained. In theory a system of closed cells, operating on a "need to know" basis, should have greatly improved security. However, in closely knit societies such as West Belfast, where everybody knows everybody, it is very difficult to ensure that such hermetic isolation exists.[35] The highly decentralised nature of the PIRA, particularly since the formation of a separate Northern Command in 1976, has meant that to a very large extent local commanders, especially in the border areas, have a great deal of discretion in carrying out operations.[36] One commentator goes so far as to say that in order to avoid discouraging initiative and causing possible schisms, the PIRA leadership often retrospectively approves operations which given the choice it would not have authorised.[37] Complex or high profile operations on the other hand are usually planned by General Headquarters (GHQ) and executed by specially selected units.[38]

The military and political reorganisation was also a recognition that the British were not going to be forced to leave Northern Ireland soon, and that therefore the PIRA had to prepare for a long war. Up until March 1976 according to Bishop and Mallie, or March 1977 according to Kelley, the PIRA had publicly declared each year that the next year would be the "Year of Victory", and that "one more heave" would force the British to quit.[39] Thus long-term security and the need to build up a durable political base were not thought to be important. However, in a long war, it would be necessary to guard against deep penetration by informers and the security forces, and to build up a solid base of support among the northern Catholics. The reorganisation of the military structure was intended to achieve the former objective, the setting up of PSF advice bureaux and the "policing" role assumed by the PIRA in the ghettoes was to achieve the latter.[40]

PIRA military strategy is outlined in the "Green Book" as follows:

1   A war of attrition against enemy personnel which is aimed at causing as many casualties and deaths as possible so as to create a demand from their people at home for their withdrawal.
2   A bombing campaign aimed at making the enemy's financial interest in our country unprofitable while at the same time curbing long term financial investment in our country.
3   To make the Six Counties as at present and for the past several years ungovernable except by colonial military rule.
4   To sustain the war and gain support for its ends by National and International propaganda and publicity campaigns.
5   By defending the war of liberation by punishing criminals, collaborators and informers.[41]

Military strategy since the reorganisation has been affected by three factors; the available weaponry, the British government's policy of "Ulsterisation" – withdrawing the army into a supporting role, giving primacy to the RUC and the locally-raised Ulster Defence Regiment (UDR), and the perceived need to shape military strategy to meet political objectives. In terms of its weaponry the PIRA has proved capable of designing and manufacturing complicated devices such as mortars (since 1979) and radio-controlled bombs (since August 1974).[42] The introduction of new weapons such as the Armalite rifle, the RPG7 rocket launcher, the mortar, and the remote controlled bomb in the 1970s increased the capability of the PIRA to carry out operations in Northern Ireland. The development of the mercury tilt switch by the Irish National Liberation Army (INLA) in 1979, which they used to kill Airey Neave MP, has made it easier for assassins to plant a device, and be well clear when the movement of the car detonates it. Similarly, the PIRA now has devices, adapted from the technology used in video recorders, which allows bombs to be set to detonate months in advance. Such a device was used by the PIRA as early as 1977, and was the device used in the Brighton bombing of 1984.[43]

The extent to which the PIRA remains wedded to the use of a particular weapon whilst refining it in order to keep abreast of current developments can be seen in the deployment of the vehicle bomb. (Strictly speaking the term car bomb is too specific as other forms of vehicle such as buses and trucks have also been used.) The vehicle bomb can take the form of an explosive device, usually small, attached to a vehicle in the hope of killing the occupants. Alternatively, a vehicle can be loaded with a large amount of explosive in the hope of killing people or damaging structures in the vicinity.

In the former case the PIRA has made successful attacks against Ian Gow MP, and several members of the Crown forces in England and Northern Ireland.[44] People surviving such attacks include the former Cabinet Secretary, Lord Armstrong, and the Commandant-General of the Royal Marines, Sir Steuart Pringle, who lost a leg in the explosion.[45] In the early and mid-1970s such devices were bulky, and were detonated by relatively crude trembler devices which were oversensitive and prone to detonate prematurely, as occurred in 1975 when a bomb intended for an MP killed an eminent cancer surgeon.[46] With the development of the mercury tilt switch in 1979, and the acquisition of large quantities of Semtex plastic explosive in the mid-1980s, it became possible to develop small, reliable bombs, that would detonate only when the car was started.

Vehicles are also used as a means of transporting large bombs to locations where they can be detonated causing the maximum possible damage to the chosen target, preferably when the volunteer responsible is no longer in the vicinity. In the early 1970s most bombs were made from unstable ingredients and had fairly crude detonators, a problem which caused the premature death of 44 of the 106 PIRA volunteers killed between 1969 and 1973.[47] Furthermore, such bombs were bulky and were thus hard to carry without the use of several volunteers and the consequent risk of detection.[48] By placing the bomb in a vehicle and driving it to the target before priming the detonator, it was possible to safely transport a large bomb over a distance using only one volunteer.

The development of a reliable timing device in 1971, based upon the timer in a parking meter, meant that the volunteers parking car bombs had up to two hours to get clear of the scene of the explosion.[49] In 1971 and 1972 such devices were used effectively in the "economic campaign" in Belfast and Derry. Although the authorities were usually warned when a bomb was left in a public place, on some occasions civilians were killed, particularly when several bombs were placed in a short period and the authorities were unable to evacuate civilians in the time given. The prime example of such a case was "Bloody Friday" in July 1972 when 22 vehicle bombs exploded in central Belfast killing five members of the Crown forces and four civilians, and injuring nearly 300 civilians.[50] A car bomb killed six shoppers outside Harrods in London in December 1983, but, although planted by a PIRA cell, the organisation has always claimed that this was not an authorised operation.[51]

When combined with the use of remote-controlled detonators, vehicle bombs have been used to effect against targets thought likely to pass by a given spot. Thus in 1987 Justice Gibson and his wife were killed by a car bomb which exploded as they passed, just inside Northern Ireland as they returned from a holiday abroad. The PIRA had known that they would pass that way and had placed the car bomb accordingly, with an observer equipped with the remote trigger overlooking the location.[52] Such vehicle bombs have also been used against military targets. In July 1981 a van loaded with a large nail bomb exploded outside Chelsea Barracks in London as a coach containing soldiers passed by. This was the first use of a remote-controlled bomb in England.[53] The most effective use of such a device against the army occurred in August 1979 when a truck bomb, combined with another bomb, killed 18 soldiers at the Narrow Water near Warrenpoint, County Down in Northern Ireland.[54]

From 1972 onwards, and to a greater extent from 1974, the PIRA has used so-called "proxy bombs". In order to avoid the possibility of volunteers being arrested while stealing a suitable vehicle or driving the bomb to the target in a stolen car, the PIRA has forced civilians, by threatening themselves or their families, to drive a vehicle bomb to the intended target. Often the civilian's own car is used, thus avoiding the risk of it appearing on a police check list. On one occasion a bus driver was forced to drive his bus, laden with an 800lb bomb to an RUC station.[55] In these cases the bombs were detonated by a timing device and the "proxies" were given enough time to get clear before the bomb exploded.[56]

In a further refinement on 24 October 1990, the PIRA used what the press dubbed "human bombs". These were similar to the suicide bombings in the Lebanon with the difference that the drivers were not willing participants. In the three cases so far [January 1991], all on the same day but in different parts of Northern Ireland, the PIRA deliberately selected Catholics deemed to be "collaborators" (i.e. someone who worked in an army kitchen or sold goods or services to the Crown forces). The men were strapped into bomb-laden vehicles and, under the threat of harm to their families, drove the vehicles into army bases or checkpoints. Once there the bombs exploded, as a result of which six soldiers and one of the drivers were killed. It is not yet clear whether the bombs were detonated by timing devices, by remote control, or by a detonator triggered by the driver trying to escape. It is clear that the drivers were intended to be killed in the explosions. Thus the "human bombs" served the double purpose of getting bombs close to army posts and killing soldiers with the minimal risk to PIRA volunteers, and of discouraging "collaboration" by the Catholic population (thus minimising the risk of the Crown forces using such people, probably without their knowledge, as a source of inside information).[57] In an incident in November 1990 a so-called "collaborator" was forced to drive a vehicle containing a bomb of over 3500lb. The bomb failed to explode. The driver was not strapped into the vehicle and a timing device was used as the detonator.[58]

As an example of the integration of a weapon into overall strategy one can look at the use of mortars in the north. By attacking RUC stations with mortars, and then intimidating and killing contractors who repair the damage or help to build new stations, the PIRA has put the security forces in the position where either the RUC abandons the stations, or the work has to be carried out by the Royal Engineers. As the RUC expanded fourfold between 1969 and 1986, the repairs have to be made and new stations have to be built.[59] This exposes the soldiers to attack, thus fulfilling the PIRA's aim of killing them in preference to members of the RUC or UDR.[60] Off-duty RUC and UDR men present a softer target than soldiers, therefore several have been killed. However, in both 1988 and 1989 the number of soldiers killed exceeded the combined total of RUC and UDR killed.[61]

More recent developments have made it likely that the PIRA will be able to operate with increased effectiveness. Early in 1990 the security forces discovered that the PIRA were fitting their mortar bombs with a gyroscopic device which should mean that a greater percentage of impact-detonated mortar shells will land at an angle of 90 degrees and detonate.[62] A recent trial in the USA has shown that the PIRA has the potential to develop sophisticated anti-aircraft missiles using American technicians and laboratories.[63]

Although such developments are of importance, the PIRA's capability was most greatly enhanced by the armaments shipments supplied by the Libyan government between 1985 and 1987. The trial in France of the PIRA members involved in shipping the Libyan weapons has confirmed the vast size of the shipments.[64] Although no exact statistics are available, estimates suggest that the PIRA received from the Libyans up to 1,000 AK47 automatic assault rifles, several RPG7 rocket launchers, 12 SAM-7 shoulder-launched ground to air missiles, a number of DSKH 12.7mm heavy anti-aircraft machine guns, and over a tonne of the highly powerful plastic explosive Semtex.[65] Of all of the armaments Semtex is perhaps the most significant due to its power, malleability, and stability which have greatly increased the flexibility of the PIRA. Semtex has been used in car bombs, time bombs, armour-piercing "Drogue" grenades, and mortar bombs. According to journalist David McKittrick the PIRA has enough material to carry on its campaign for at least a decade.[66] Another journalist has stated that at least one PIRA member was trained in Libya in the use of the SAM-7 ground to air missile launcher and others may now be proficient.[67] In an interview in 1988, a senior republican indicated that the PIRA would use its new armaments to bring matters to a head when he said "This is the final phase. The next eighteen months to two years will be critical because the IRA has the resources and will know then if it has the capacity to end it."[68]

The PIRA has not confined its attacks in Northern Ireland to the security forces. In addition to the attacks on contractors, they have maintained their attacks on "economic targets". Following a car bomb explosion in central Belfast, a PIRA spokesman issued the following statement, which encapsulates part of the PIRA's thinking: "Economic investment in Belfast has recently presented the Brits with a propaganda platform from which they have been consciously proclaiming the return to normality. There is no normality."[69]

A further tactic used by the PIRA since 1973 has been attacks in England, and on the continent. These attacks are often carried out when the PIRA is finding it difficult to operate in the cities of Northern Ireland as was the case in 1973–1974, and has been the case for the past two years.[70] The more indiscriminate bomb attacks appear to be designed to bring the issue of Northern Ireland to the attention of the British people. A PIRA spokesman said in 1974, "Last year taught us that in publicity terms one bomb in Oxford Street is worth ten in Belfast."[71] The recent attacks upon military targets in England and the continent can be seen as PIRA fulfilling its desire to attack the British armed forces whilst taking fewer risks. Outside Northern Ireland the armed forces' security precautions are less stringent and targets are therefore "softer". Between December 1988 and June 1990, 18 soldiers were killed by PIRA in England and on the continent compared with 13 in Northern Ireland.[72]

In the past the PIRA has also targetted people and institutions which it has seen as representing the "Establishment". In 1974 Daithi O'Connell warned that PIRA intended to strike at mainland targets of an "… economic, judicial, military and political nature".[73] Between 1975 and the start of the current campaign a number of VIPs had either been assassinated or had had attempts made against them. These included such people as Hugh Fraser MP (car-bomb), Ross McWhirter (shot dead), the British ambassadors to both the Republic of Ireland and the Netherlands (the former killed by a culvert-bomb, the latter shot dead), and Lord Mountbatten (killed, with others, by a remote-controlled bomb). The PIRA also selected "Establishment" targets such as London clubs and high class restaurants.[74]

In 1984, in their most audacious operation so far, PIRA nearly succeeded in killed the then Prime Minister, Margaret Thatcher, and most of the cabinet by bombing the Grand Hotel during the Conservative Party Conference at Brighton. Gerry Adams has said that the Brighton bombing was intended to bring matters in Northern Ireland to a head by provoking massive repression, but, given the PIRA's hatred of Mrs Thatcher following the 1981 hunger strikes, it seems likely that a strong element of revenge was also present.[75]

In the current campaign, in addition to military targets, PIRA has targeted "Establishment" VIPs and institutions. Apart from the successful assassination of Ian Gow MP, attempts have been made upon notables such as the former Governor of Gibralter, Sir Peter Terry, the former Cabinet Secretary, Lord Armstrong, and a former paratrooper and Army commander in Northern Ireland

Sir Anthony Farrar-Hockley. Institutions which have been bombed include the London Stock Exchange, the Carlton Club, and the barracks of the Honourable Artillery Company. After the killing of Ian Gow and shooting of Sir Peter Terry, a PIRA spokesman said, "The IRA have quite forcibly told the British, the British Establishment, those who legislate for the war in Ireland, that they too will have to pay a price."[76]

In order to carry out attacks, both in Northern Ireland and outside, the PIRA needs information. In the case of the current mainland campaign much of the intelligence appears to have been collated from open sources such as *Who's Who, The Army List* and *The Civil Service Year Book*.[77] The so called "hit list" found at a PIRA safe house in Clapham, London, in 1988 appears to have been compiled from open and indeed obsolete sources as was shown by the attacks on the former home of Lord Armstrong, and on the former home of the Conservative Party Treasurer, Lord McAlpine.[78] The compilation of such VIP hit lists appears to be a prerequisite to sustained assassination campaigns, similar lists having been found in 1975 and earlier in 1990.[79]

In Northern Ireland PIRA is able to gather information both through local knowledge and through the infiltration of government institutions. As previously mentioned, the Catholic ghettoes are extremely close-knit, and therefore the PIRA would not find it difficult to collect local gossip and so forth. In addition, either PIRA recruits are told to work for bodies such as the Northern Ireland Housing Executive, tax offices, and social security offices where useful information can be obtained, or existing staff are identified and either bribed or intimidated into giving the PIRA information such as the home addresses of members of the RUC or of suspected loyalist paramilitaries.[80] In the late 1970s, the security forces feared that an elite RUC unit, as well as the UDR and the prison service had been penetrated by the PIRA's use of intimidation and bribery.[81] In a recent case a senior prison warder was ensnared in a so-called "honey-trap" by a suspected female member of the PIRA, and then intimidated into giving targetting information on colleagues to PIRA.[82] The PIRA is also reported to have successfully tapped the telephones at the Army HQ in Lisburn.[83]

The PIRA does have links with foreign terrorist groups but it is unclear how useful these links are in operational terms. PIRA spokesmen have denounced the German Red Army Faction and seem to regard them with some suspicion.[84] However, press reports suggest that left-wing groups in the Netherlands and Germany may have provided PIRA cells with safe houses and transport, and might have reconnoitred potential targets on their behalf.[85] In the case of the Basque group ETA, the PIRA has a far closer affinity due to the similarity of their respective nationalist struggles and their common Celtic bond. In 1979 one newspaper speculated thus on links between the PIRA and ETA, "Those Provisionals who have gone off to the Basque organisation ETA … have gone in order to learn how to attack policemen and other high value targets even more effectively."[86]

One possible foreign terrorist connection is with the Palestine Liberation Organisation (PLO). According to a NATO report, up to 44 PIRA operatives may have undergone training in the Lebanon during the late 1970s. However, this report appears to be inconclusive.[87]

At present the PIRA does not appear to be having any difficulty in recruiting. There are far fewer "professional" volunteers than in the early and mid-1970s (Bishop and Mallie estimate 250 compared with 1,000 in the mid-1970s), but PIRA does not require as many as it is no longer attempting to wage a fully-fledged guerrilla war. The PIRA's aim now is merely to maintain a level of violence which is too great to be ignored, and, in the words of a PIRA commander, to "… always retain the ability to bring the situation to a crisis".[88] According to a journalist, Cal McCrystal, one can place PIRA volunteers in one of four categories: the badly educated "lumpen bus-burners"; fairly well educated recruits who can infiltrate government bodies such as the civil service or the Housing Executive from which they can glean intelligence: graduates and tradesmen such as electricians, who provide the manpower for the ASUs; and the senior PIRA commanders, who may well have over ten years' experience of the Troubles.[89] As Bowyer-Bell points out, the PIRA leadership for the last twenty years has consisted of a small, tightly-knit group, and has thus built up a formidable wealth of experience, and continuity of purpose.[90]

McCrystal and other writers emphasise the extent to which antipathy to the security forces, due either to personal experiences or to nationalist sentiment, often provides a motive for joining the PIRA.[91] In the mid-1970s, a PIRA survey in the Maze prison found that 90 per cent of the Republican inmates had joined the PIRA in order to get revenge for "harassment" by the security forces.[92] One point which is fairly clear is that members of the PIRA are not psychopaths. They appear to be ordinary people, if anything more intelligent than the average, who believe that their cause is worth killing for, and have therefore to an extent repressed the usual moral restraint against killing.[93] A secret British Army report of 1978 confirmed that the average volunteers were not "mindless hooligans drawn from the unemployed or unemployable", but were chosen with some care and were growing in experience.[94] One problem which could arise is a result of the greater prominence given to PSF in the strategy of the Republican movement. If it is the case that most of the graduates and more experienced volunteers are being "creamed off" by PSF it is possible that the competence of the PIRA will be affected.[95]

The PIRA needs money in order to pay for weapons, pay for travel tickets and hotel rooms for ASUs in England and abroad, maintain safe houses and carry out general administration. In the case of the Republican movement there is also the need to fund PSF in order to fight elections. PIRA is involved in many ways of making money, legal such as running drinking clubs and taxi firms, others illegal such as bank robbery, tax fraud, and extortion.[96] A recent government announcement estimated PIRA income at £5.3 million, broken down as follows:

Legitimate business	£1,000,000
Tax fraud	1,000,000
Taxis	600,000
Drinking clubs	750,000
Gaming machines	250,000
Pirate videos and smuggling	600,000
EC fraud	300,000
Protection and extortion	500,000
Collections	200,000
NORAID and foreign	100,000
TOTAL	5,300,000[97]

In its long-term aim of achieving an independent, united Ireland, the PIRA has not yet achieved its objective. However, it has achieved many of the objectives listed in the section on military strategy in the "Green Book". In terms of affecting British public opinion by killing soldiers the PIRA appears to have had some, though limited success. A recent poll in *The Guardian* indicated that 59 per cent of those polled favoured the withdrawal of British troops from Northern Ireland.[98] The PIRA has certainly made Northern Ireland uneconomic, to the extent where a survey on behalf of the Bank of Ireland estimated that the current "Troubles" are costing Britain IR£358 million per year.[99] British government initiatives such as "Ulsterisation" and the various proposed forms of devolution certainly give the impression that the government wishes to keep the Irish problem at arm's length, and, if given the chance, would be glad to be rid of the problem permanently. In this respect Patterson may be right in his supposition that, provided the PIRA can survive militarily and maintain a bedrock of support in the Catholic community, they will wear down the will of the British government to remain in Northern Ireland.[100]

The PIRA have succeeded in forcing Britain to govern by "colonial military rule" in that they toppled Stormont, thereby forcing the British government to impose direct rule from Westminster, but have prevented the authorities from governing Northern Ireland in the same manner as they do in the rest of Britain. Furthermore, PIRA activities have forced the Government to adopt such expedients as the juryless "Diplock" courts and the censoring of Sinn Fein spokesmen on the broadcasting media, to maintain a semi-militarised police force in Northern Ireland, and to keep a large army presence in the Province.

The war in Northern Ireland has also had an adverse effect upon the British body politic. The demands of security mean that whilst increasing amounts of money are spent on the protection of politicians and public servants, they have become more remote from the people they govern.[101] Cases such as those of the Guildford Four, the Birmingham Six, and the Stalker affair have done much to diminish faith in the police, the judiciary, and the security services. Furthermore, the restrictions upon the broadcasting of comments by Sinn Fein spokesmen raise serious questions concerning the position of the media in a liberal democracy.

In terms of gaining national and international attention incidents such as the 1981 Hunger Strikes, "Bloody Sunday", the European Court ruling that Britain had treated internees in a degrading and inhuman manner and other embarrasments, have ensured that the "Troubles" have maintained a prominent place on the stages of world and domestic publicity. If it were not for atrocities, deliberate or not, such as the Enniskillen bombing, the PIRA might have quite a sympathetic audience.

Despite these achievements however, it is highly unlikely that the PIRA will succeed in achieving its ultimate aim. Although the PIRA claims, to some degree with justification, to be non-sectarian in the sense that sectarianism is not its main purpose, its aims and strategies almost totally ignore many of the realities of Northern Ireland. Representatives from PSF have spoken to Protestant organisations and at the 1990 *ardfheis* it was clear that the PSF leadership recognises that difficulties do exist.[102] However, the fact remains that not only do the vast majority of Protestants not want to join a united Ireland.[103], but, in addition, the PIRA campaign by killing members from the predominantly Protestant RUC and UDR, and by killing civilians makes such a result seem even more abhorrent.

In an interview with David McKittrick, a senior member of the PIRA makes it clear that, whatever the wishes of the loyalist majority, they are expected to go along with their incorporation into a united Ireland without a murmur.[104] Even though he accepts that the PIRA may have embittered many Protestants he does not seem to perceive that the British might be unwilling, or indeed unable, to disarm the largely loyalist-inclined RUC and UDR, as well as the various loyalist paramilitary groups. Despite attempts to devise a coherent political platform aimed at attracting fairly widespread support, the PIRA by its campaign, and PSF by its support for that campaign, have repelled Ulster Protestants from the idea of a united Ireland.[105]

The tradition of militant republican nationalism will almost certainly persist as long as Ireland remains partitioned. The social grievances of the northern Catholics, their fear of loyalist violence, and their perception of the Crown forces as repressive and partial will ensure that the PIRA or a similar organisation will continue to exist in Northern Ireland.[106] However, the activities of the PIRA have done much to discredit the concept of a united Ireland in the eyes of northern Protestants. The tragedy of the PIRA is that if a united Ireland ever does come about, it is extremely likely that it will be despite the efforts of the PIRA and not because of them.

Notes

1   See T.P. Coogan, *The IRA* (Glasgow: Fontana, 1987), p.685; J. Bowyer-Bell, *The Secret Army: The IRA from 1916* (Dublin: Academy Press. 1979), p.154.
2   See P. Bishop and E. Mallie, *The Provisional IRA* (London: Corgi, 1988), p.134; K.J. Kelley, *The Longest War: Northern Ireland and the IRA* (London: Zed Books. 1988), pp.88–89.
3   Bishop and Mallie, op. cit., p.133; Bowyer-Bell, op. cit., pp.363–364.
4   Kelley, op. cit., p.121: H. Patterson, *The Politics of Illusion* (London: Hutchinson, 1989). p.66.
5   Bishop and Mallie, op. cit., pp.112, 116, 121–122; Kelley, op. cit., p.121.
6   Bowyer-Bell, op. cit., p.135: Patterson, op. cit., p.98.
7   Bishop and Mallie, op. cit., pp.135–137: Patterson, op. cit., pp.126–127.
8   Coogan, op. cit., p.685.
9   M. Dillon, *The Dirty War* (London: Hutchinson, 1990), p.482.
10 Patterson, op. cit., p.23.
11 See G. Adams, *The Politics of Irish Freedom* (Dingle: Brandon. 1986), p.47; "Gerry Adams Takes Over as IRA Chief", *The Sunday Times,* 4 Aug. 1985.
12 Kelley, op. cit., p.283.
13 See "Inside the IRA", *The Sunday Times*, 3 July 1977.
14 Ibid. See also "Gerry Adams Takes Over as IRA Chief", op. cit.; Bishop and Mallie, op. cit., p.387.
15 Bishop and Mallie, op. cit., pp.192, 196–199, 220; Kelley, op. cit., pp.137, 157; S. MacStiofain, *Revolutionary in Ireland* (Edinburgh: Gordon Cremonesi, 1975), p.295.
16 Bishop and Mallie, op. cit., pp.152, 154, 188, 192, 202; Bowyer-Bell, op. cit., p.383.
17 "Inside the IRA", op. cit.
18 See J. Holland, *The American Connection: US Guns, Money and Influence in Northern Ireland* (Dublin: Poolbeg. 1987), p.89; Bishop and Mallie, op. cit., pp.169, 197.
19 Statistics on Security: Part 1 Statistics of Terrorist Activity. Yearly 1971–1988 (Northern Ireland Office, 1989).
20 Ibid. See also Bishop and Mallie, op. cit., p.193.
21 Bowyer-Bell, op. cit., pp.406, 437; Bishop and Mallie, op. cit., pp.171, 196.
22 L. Clarke, *Broadening the Battlefield: The H-Blocks and the Rise of Sinn Fein* (Dublin: Gill & Macmillan, 1987), pp.40–42; Bishop and Mallie, op. cit., pp.241, 247, 320.
23 Kelley, op. cit., pp.172, 175.
24 MacStiofain, op. cit., pp.281–285: Kelley, op. cit., pp.180–181.
25 Clarke, op. cit., p.35; Bishop and Mallie, op. cit., p.275.
26 Bishop and Mallie, op. cit., p.277.
27 Clarke, op. cit., p.29.
28 Coogan, op. cit., p.682.
29 See "What's on the Agenda Now is an End to Partition", *The Irish Times*, 12 Oct. 1986.
30 Coogan, op. cit., p.605.
31 Bishop and Mallie, op. cit., p.412.
32 Kelley, op. cit., pp.356–357; Bishop and Mallie, op. cit., pp.385, 458.
33 Kelley, op. cit., p.359; Bishop and Mallie, op. cit., p.451.
34 Kelley, op. cit., p. 127. See also "Veteran Opposes SF Going into Dail", *The Irish Times*, 29 Oct. 1985.
35 Clarke, op. cit., pp.41–42, 251–253; Bowyer-Bell, op. cit., p.437; Kelley, op. cit., p.285.
36 J. Bowyer-Bell, *IRA Tactics and Targets: An Analysis of Tactical Aspects of the Armed Struggle 1969–1989* (Dublin: Poolbeg, 1990), p.89; Bishop and Mallie, op. cit., p.312; Kelley, op. cit., pp.246–247.
37 Bowyer-Bell (1990), op. cit., pp.27, 48, 116.
38 Ibid., pp.63, 67, 115. Also the roll of honour on the 1990 Republican Resistance calendar lists the volunteers involved in the 1987 Gibraltar operation as GHQ members rather than as members of any geographic formation.
39 Bishop and Mallie, op. cit., p.331; Kelley, op. cit., pp.210, 265; Clarke, op. cit., p.42; Bowyer-Bell (1979), op. cit., p.404.
40 Bishop and Mallie, op. cit., pp.379, 412: Kelley, op. cit., pp.289–293. See also "This Town Ain't Big Enough", *New Statesman & Society*, 27 July 1990.
41 Coogan, op. cit., p.693.
42 Bishop and Mallie, op. cit., pp.204, 420.
43 Bishop and Mallie, op. cit., p.425.

44 See "MP Left Himself Open to Attack from Terrorists", *The Independent*, 31 July 1990; "Seven People Sought After Bomb Kills 11", *The Times*, 5 Feb. 1974. (This refers to a bomb explosion on board a bus, carrying soldiers and their families along the M62 motorway in England. The death toll subsequently rose to 12.) "London IRA Bomb Kills Soldier", *The Independent*, 17 May 1990; "IRA Bomb Kills Former Reservist", *The Independent*, 7 June 1990.

45 See "Car Bomb Attack on Thatcher Advisor Fails", *The Independent*, 7 Aug. 1990; "Booby-trap Bomb Maims General", *The Sunday Times*, 18 Oct. 1981.

46 See G. McKee and R. Faney, *Time Bomb: Irish Bombers, English Justice and the Guildford Four* (London: Bloomsbury, 1988), pp.307–308.

47 Bishop and Mallie, op. cit., p.193; see also J. Adams, *Trading in Death: Weapons, Warfare and the Modern Arms Race* (London: Hutchinson, 1990), pp.9, 35–36.

48 Bishop and Mallie, op. cit., p.220; Clarke, op. cit., p.18; Bowyer-Bell (1990). op. cit., pp.83–84.

49 Adams, op. cit., pp.35–36.

50 Bowyer-Bell (1990), op. cit., pp.85–88; Bishop and Mallie, op. cit., p.232; Coogan, op. cit., p.480.

51 See "Bomb Blitz at Harrods", *The Sunday Times*, 12 Dec. 1983; "Blast Highlights Provo Rift", *The Times*, 19 Dec. 1983.

52 See "Security Storm Over Blame for Judge's Murder", *The Sunday Times*, 26 April 1987; "Judge Booked Fatal Trip in his Own Name", *The Times*, 27 April 1987; "Judge was Irked by Security", *The Times*, 28 April 1987.

53 See "IRA Nail Bomb Kills One and Injures 40", *The Sunday Times*, 11 Oct. 1981.

54 See "15 Soldiers Die in Army's Worst Day", *The Daily Telegraph*, 28 Aug. 1979. The death toll subsequently rose to 18.

55 See "Four Held in Eire After Shots Hit British Helicopter", *The Times*, 15 Dec. 1972; "IRA 'Proxy Bombs' Blast Belfast", *The Times*, 26 July 1974; *Associated Press*, 16 Dec. 1986.

56 See "IRA's New Tactic Breaches Security Forces' Defences", *The Independent*, 25 Oct. 1990.

57 See "IRA Uses Human Bombs", *The Independent*, 25 Oct. 1990; "Deadly Precision of Terrorists' New Tactic", *The Sunday Correspondent*, 28 Oct. 1990.

58 See "IRA 'Human Bomb', Raid on Army Fails", *The Independent*, 24 Nov. 1990.

59 Bishop and Mallie, op. cit., p.421. See also "The Provos' Easiest Coup", *The Times*, 8 Aug. 1986; "The Gunman's Shadow Falls Across Ulster Business"? *The Financial Times*, 11 Aug. 1986: "IRA Kills Builder in War on Contracts", *The Independent*, 19 Aug. 1990.

60 See "The Men of War Promise Third Violent Decade", *The Independent*, 29 Sept. 1990: Adams, op. cit., p.121.

61 Richard Clutterbuck, *Terrorism, Drugs and Crime in Europe After 1992* (London: Routledge, 1990), p.73.

62 See "IRA's Deadly New Weapon", *The Independent*, 20 May 1990.

63 See "US Jury Convicts IRA Plotters", *The Independent*, 19 June 1990; "Four IRA Weapons Experts Jailed for Plot to Supply Weapons" *The Independent*, 21 Aug. 1990.

64 "French Court Told of Huge Libyan Arms Run by IRA", *The Independent*, 8 Jan. 1991.

65 See "Arming the IRA: The Libyan Connection", *The Economist*, 31 March 1990; "Libyan Arms Fuel Surge in Terrorism", *The Independent*, 8 May 1990.

66 "Libyan Arms Fuel Surge in Terrorism", op. cit.

67 Adams, op. cit., pp.21, 23.

68 See "The Provos' Resurgence: There's More to Come", *Fortnight*, Sept. 1988.

69 *Irish Times*, 2 Feb. 1987.

70 See "Shift in Politics Forces Move Out of Province", *The Sunday Correspondent*, 17 June 1990; "One Small Cell Attacking the Body Politic", *The Independent on Sunday*, 1 July 1990.

71 A.P. Schmid and J. de Graaf, *Violence as Communication: Insurgent Terrorism and the Western News Media* (London: Sage Publications, 1982), p. 43.

72 See "New Perils Facing UK Soldiers", *The Sunday Correspondent*, 3 June 1990.

73 Coogan, op. cit., p.583.

74 See "Echoes of the Clubland Bombings in 1970s", *The Independent*, 26 June 1990.

75 *Irish Times*, 15 Oct. 1984; Bishop and Mallie, op. cit., p.427.

76 See "The Men of War Promise Third Violent Decade", op. cit.

77 See "Bookworms Who Burrow for IRA", *The Sunday Correspondent*, 12 Aug. 1990.

78 See "McAlpine Bomb Indicates Switch in IRA Campaign", *The Independent*, 14 June 1990: "Car Bomb Attack on Thatcher Advisor Fails", op. cit.

79   Bishop and Mallie, op. cit., pp.256–257; see also "IRA Suspects had Cabinet Hit List", *The Independent*, 27 Nov. 1990.

80   See "Teenagers Who Enlist for Terror", *The Independent on Sunday*, 5 Aug. 1990; Bishop and Mallie, op. cit., pp.287–288.

81   *Associated Press*, 30 Oct. 1979.

82   See "Prison Warder Given Life for Role in IRA Murder", *The Independent*, 22 June 1990.

83   *Miami Herald*, 29 Jan. 1979.

84   Adams, op. cit., p.130; Bishop and Mallie, op. cit., p.308.

85   *Frankfurter Allemeine Zeitung*, 13 March 1980; see also "Meinhof Gang Helped IRA", *The Guardian*, 15 March 1980.

86   See "The Deceptive Calm in Ireland", *The Financial Times*, 2 Feb, 1979.

87   M. McKinley, "The Irish Republican Army and Terror International: An Inquiry into the Material Aspects of the First Fifteen Years", P. Wilkinson and A.M. Stewart (eds.), *Contemporary Research on Terrorism* (Aberdeen: Aberdeen University Press, 1989), p.201.

88   Coogan, op. cit., p.604.

89   "Teenagers Who Enlist for Terror", op. cit.

90   Bowyer-Bell (1990), op. cit., pp.13–14, 15–16.

91   Bishop and Mallie, op. cit., pp.152, 154, 349, 456; Coogan, op. cit., p.673; D. Beresford, *Ten Men Dead: The Story of the 1981 Irish Hunger Strike* (London: Grafton, 1987). pp.151–152; see also K. Heskin, "The Psychology of Terrorism in Northern Ireland", Y. Alexander and A. O'Day, *Terrorism in Ireland* (London, Croom Helm), p.97.

92   See "House Raids Earn the Security Forces New Enemies", *The Independent*, 6 Feb. 1989.

93   Heskin, op. cit., pp.91–94; "The Stable, Normal Minds of Terrorists Who Kill for a Cause", *The Independent*, 29 Nov. 1986.

94   S. Cronin, *Irish Nationalism: A History of Its Roots and Ideology* (Dublin: Academy Press, 1980), p.342.

95   Coogan. op. cit., p.604; Patterson, op. cit., p.195.

96   See "IRA Linked to £2m Extortion Threat", *The Independent*, 16 March 1990; "IRA Fund Raising Blamed for Surge in Irish Robberies", *The Independent*, 22 May 1990.

97   See "MP Calls for Tough Laws Against IRA Racketeering", *The Independent*, 6 Nov. 1990.

98   See "Ulster Catholics Split on Pull Out", *The Guardian*, 14 Nov. 1990.

99   See "'Troubles' cost UK and Ireland £410 m a year report says", *The Independent*, 22 May 1990.

100   Patterson, op. cit., p.207.

101   See "Bournemouth 'Under Siege' in £2m Security Operation", *The Independent*, 9 Oct. 1990; "Huge Cost Forces Yard to Review VIP Security", *The Independent on Sunday*, 4 Feb. 1990; "Anti-IRA Security Costs Must Rise, Police Say", *The Independent on Sunday*, 23 Sept. 1990.

102   See "Protestants 'Have a Role to Play in United Ireland'," *The Independent*, 2 Feb. 1990; Bishop and Mallie, op. cit., p.389.

103   See "Ulster Catholics Split on Pull Out", op. cit.

104   See "The Men of War Promise Third Violent Decade", op. cit.

105   "Ulster Catholics Split on Pull Out", op. cit.

106   See C. Hewitt, "Terrorism and Public Opinion: A Five Country Comparison", *Terrorism and Political Violence*, Vol.2, No.2 (Summer 1990), pp.165–166, 170.

12 Right-wing terrorism in a comparative perspective

The case of split delegitimization

Ehud Sprinzak

The case of particularistic terrorism

Insurgent terrorism usually evokes the association of an anti-regime terror and claims for a universal message. The atrocities involved are committed against an established regime that is charged with a flagrant violation of the fundamental human rights of either its citizens or subject nations. There is, however, one common form of insurgent terrorism which is not directed primarily against governments and is not committed in the name of universal values. The terror organizations involved, usually right-wing collectivities, vigilante groups or racist organizations, do not speak in the name of humanity. They are particularistic by their very nature and respond often to perceptions of insecurity and threats. They fight private wars against hostile ethnic communities, "illegitimate" religious denominations, classes of undesired people or "inferior races". The enemies they feel threaten them are, variably, Jews, Arabs, Catholics, Blacks, Communists, homosexuals, foreign workers or other classes of "inferior" human beings "who want to get more than they deserve".

The most significant political difference between "universalistic" terror organizations and "particularistic" ones lies in their relationship to the prevailing authority. While left-wing and nationalist radical movements are usually involved in a *direct* conflict with the ruling government and their terror campaign is directed against its emissaries, the conflict of many right-wing, religious or vigilante groups with the regime is secondary. The government is rarely considered an opponent and in many cases is expected to cooperate or remain uninvolved. Conflict with the authorities or occasional anti-regimist violence, while likely to develop in such cases, emerges, and often greatly intensifies, only after these radicals do not obtain official help, political understanding or favorable silence.

The purpose of this essay is to develop an analytical typology of right-wing terrorist groups and to demonstrate its usefulness for the organization of the large amount of historical and current information already gathered about these movements. The study is based on the conceptual framework of the process of delegitimization developed earlier by this author.[1]

Terrorism and the process of delegitimization

The analytical affinity between terrorism and the process of delegitimization is based on the understanding of insurgent terrorism as a product of a lengthy political process of group radicalization *vis-à-vis* the regime. The essence of this process is a slowly evolving legitimacy crisis between an insurgent movement and the government. Terrorism is the peak of the process of delegitimization. The movement involved is so vehemently opposed to the regime's legitimacy that it is ready to challenge it by the use of unconventional violence. What terrorists do – and other radicals do not – is to bring their rejection of the regime's legitimacy to the utmost and express it by extranormal violence.

The importance of the understanding of terrorism in terms of a process of delegitimization is that terrorism is identified as a behavioral stage in the life history of an extremist movement, a phase in which the organization is ready and willing to use unconventional violence against government's agents. The idea of the process of delegitimization implies, therefore, the presence of *pre-terrorist* and less radical stages in the evolution of the movement involved. It also recognizes the possibility of *post-terrorist* stages in which the group involved is no longer ready or able to use terrorism. This approach allows us to talk about terrorism as the peak of a historical cycle – the rise and decline of a militant political opposition. Terrorism, according to this approach, is not a detached state of mind of crazy misfits but a type of political behavior which evolves (and declines) gradually under certain identifiable psycho-political conditions.

While processes of delegitimization vary greatly, the typical process implies a struggle of a challenge group against the government, and is made up of three consecutive stages: *Crisis of Confidence, Conflict of Legitimacy*, and *Crisis of Legitimacy*.[2] Each of these stages pertains to a political protest group composed of activists and followers who interact with the regime as well as among themselves and who obtain in the process a collective psycho-political identity. The group identity, which often changes rapidly as radicalization proceeds, contains a combination of political behavioral components, ideological and symbolic tenets and psychological traits. A short examination of the three ideal-typical stages of the delegitimization trajectory reveals the following features.

Crisis of Confidence is the earliest and most moderate stage of group radicalization and involves no violence. It is experienced by a movement, or a challenge group, whose confidence in the existing political government is greatly eroded. Crisis of confidence implies a conflict with specific rulers or policies. It does not presume a structural delegitimation because the foundations of the established political system are not questioned or challenged.

Crisis of confidence is marked by the rise of a distinct ideological challenge group, movement, or counterculture which refuses to play according to the established rules of the game. The group articulates its critique of the establishment in loaded ideological terms, dissents from mainstream politics and opts for protests, demonstrations, symbolic resistance and other forms of direct action. While not illegal, its behavior, group mentality and language are likely to be provocative. Early confrontations with the authorities and the police, including small scale and unplanned events of violence, may occur.[3]

Conflict of Legitimacy is the radicalized continuation of the crisis of confidence. It is the behavioral stage that evolves when a challenge group, previously confined to criticizing the government, is ready to question the very legitimacy of the regime. Conflict of legitimacy implies the emergence of an *alternative ideological and cultural system*, one that delegitimizes the prevailing regime and its code of social norms in the name of a better normative political order.

Conflict of legitimacy usually begins when the challenge group is greatly disappointed with its previous stage of radicalization. The former "moderate" radicals become enraged and frustrated either by the government's hostile (sometimes excessively violent) response to their passionate critique, or by their own failure to reform the system. Mentally they now develop the need to channel their outrage into a more extreme form of protest. A proper course to follow seems to be the development of an *ideology of delegitimation* which communicates a complete chasm with the prevailing political order.

The evolution of the conflict of legitimacy is manifested by intense political action that ranges between angry protest (demonstrations, confrontations and vandalism) and the application of *intended low scale violence* against the regime. The challenge group now experiences considerable radicalization. The movement begins to solidify and closes rank. The individuals involved become revolutionary. Their jargon is slanderous and berates a totally discredited social order.[4]

Crisis of Legitimacy is the behavioral and symbolic culmination of the two preceding stages. Its essence lies in the extension of the previous delegitimation of the system to *every individual* person associated with it. Individuals who are identified with the "rotten" and "soon to be destroyed" social and political order are depersonalized and dehumanized. They are derogated into the ranks of the worst enemies or subhuman species. *Dehumanization* makes it possible for the radicals to disengage morally and to commit atrocities without remorse.[5]

The operational manifestation of the crisis of legitimacy is systematic terrorism. It usually amounts to the formation of a small terror underground, which is engaged in unconventional attacks on the regime and its affiliates, and which is capable of committing a wide range of atrocities. As a social unit, the terrorist underground is often isolated from the outside world. It constructs a reality of its own and a whole new set of behavioral and moral standards that are enforced in an authoritarian manner. The members of the group are so involved and entangled with each other that every individual act has a collective meaning of utmost importance. The psychodynamics of the whole unit, including its acts of terrorism against the outside society, assume a logic of its own and is, at many times, unrelated to any external factors.[6]

The three-stage process of delegitimization described above is the purest and most exhaustive form of insurgent terrorism. *It conveys the essence of the idea of terrorism, that is, the complete transformation of sane human beings into brutal and indiscriminate killers.* This is why I suggest calling it *transformational delegitimization*.[7] Terrorism reached through transformational delegitimization may represent the *ideal type* of terrorism, but is, of course, just one form of terrorism.

The case of split delegitimization

The fact that particularistic terror organizations usually avoid confrontation with the authorities and start their career by directing the majority of their operations at non-ruling groups suggests a different pattern of delegitimization than the typical transformational model presented above. It indicates the possible presence of a *dual process of delegitimization*: an intense delegitimization *vis-à-vis* the unaccepted non-governmental collectivity and a *diluted* delegitimization towards the regime. Thus, while the Crisis of Confidence, Conflict of Legitimacy and Crisis of Legitimacy are all present, their sequential order and direction are not the same. The issue at stake is one of *split delegitimization*, namely, *a case where an uneven radicalization of a group of extremists develops against two separate entities.*

The distinguishing feature of the radicalization of most particularistic terror organizations is that it *begins* with a Conflict of Legitimacy. The majority of right-wing movements are organized around the belief that the object of their intense opposition is *a priori* illegitimate. It does not belong to the same humanity that they see themselves part of, and should either be kept in an inferior legal status, expelled or even be eliminated. Such a belief, which is usually the product of a long held tradition or cultural heritage, does not require immediate violent action. As long as the particularistic movement involved does not monopolize political power, is systematically delegitimized by the established culture or feels an immediate existential threat, it will not resort to violence. Instead, it will do its best to strengthen and perpetuate the existing social and cultural mechanisms of discrimination. Violence, and gradually terrorism, only emerge when the group involved feels increasingly insecure or threatened. For instance, the Jews may suddenly appear too strong, the Blacks too influential, the Arabs too treacherous and the Communists too close to a Marxist revolution. Severe measures must be taken to restrict their movement. These measures are likely to begin with campaigns of intimidation and escalate (under specific conditions) to terrorism. A comparative examination of occasional terrorist eruptions by groups such as the Ku Klux Klan, other white supremacist groups in America, neo-Fascists in Italy, neo-Nazis in Germany, vigilantes of Gush Emunim, and the followers of the late Rabbi Kahane in Israel, the AWB paramilitary formations in South Africa and others, shows the same pattern of radicalization: a constant – but largely non-violent – sense of delegitimation regarding the "inferior" groups, a growing anxiety, efforts of low level intimidation and finally, outbursts of terrorism.

While much of the violence of particularistic terrorists is expected to involve non-ruling populations, at some point their violence may turn towards the political authorities. When vigilante movements, neo-fascists or neo-Nazis feel threatened by other groups, they often convince themselves that the government in charge is doing very little to protect their "legitimate" community. The rulers, or the most unfriendly elements among them, are then portrayed as "soft", "internationalist" or "leftist". Such projection implies a sense of betrayal and *a Crisis of Confidence* with the regime. While the government itself may not be declared illegitimate, and be an object of their rejection, the group's respect for its authority is dramatically eroded. With this comes flagrant disobedience of the law. This atmosphere often produces splinter groups which break from the mainstream because they feel that the leaders of their movement are not doing enough.

The presence of *split delegitimization* may not, necessarily, be permanent. There are increasing indications that very extreme right-wing organizations tend to close the legitimacy gap between their different hate targets. This happens when the radical group in question perceives the government to be identical with the illegitimate minority group, and when both are accorded the same level of illegitimacy. The theory behind the "disappearance of the split" is that the government has literally been taken over by the hated minority group and is no longer capable of reforming itself. It should therefore be destroyed with the same intensity as the original target group. The most significant example for the disappearance of split delegitimization is the recent rise of the imagery of ZOG (Zionist Occupation Government) in racist, neo-Nazi and millenarian circles, and the association of several Western governments with a Jewish-Zionist take over.[8] The ZOG imagery and its meaning will be discussed below in greater detail.

Unlike left-wing liberals, many particularistic terrorists, Fascists, Nazis, reactive vigilantes, racists and white supremacists do not feel remorse about their violence and the atrocities they cause. There is, in this case, no need to undergo a profound psycho-political transformation to become brutal killers. The desired world of most right-wing terrorists, with the notable exception of millenarian radicals, is not a reality of a non-violent universal humanity that is transformed temporarily – and for just reasons – into a bloody existence. Rather, it is a *Weltanschauung* which is predicated on conflict and dehumanization of specific classes of the population. From this perspective certain people just do not belong to the relevant community; they are outsiders and should be treated accordingly. Terrorism against these "inferiors" is a control mechanism, a means of assuring that they do not multiply and prevail. This attitude is perhaps the reason why most particularistic terrorists never attempt to apologize for their brutal actions and why so few explanatory ideologies of terrorism exist in this cultural milieu.[9] Acts that are reasonable and natural do not require justification.

Right-wing terrorism: a typology

The number of particularistic organizations which have resorted in the past century to terrorism is large, as are the variations among the respective organizations. Cultural and ethnic differences among nations increase this plurality significantly. This is why it appears useful to group them, for comparative purposes, into six general types: *revolutionary terrorism, reactive terrorism, vigilante terrorism, racist terrorism, millenarian terrorism* and *youth counterculture terrorism*. It is important to maintain that these six types of particularistic terrorism are not mutually exclusive. In reality we may find that reactive terrorism involves racism and that many racist and reactive terrorists see themselves as vigilantes, defenders of the normative order of society. Racist and reactive groups are often attracted to some type of fascist ideology as are youth countercultures. They are attracted not necessarily because of their fascination with fascist revolution. It may also be due to an emotional need to reject the normative order of liberal democracy and justify their violence. The following typology is based on the identification of the *dominant principle* around which the rightist group is organized and on its relation to the dynamics of split delegitimation.

A. Revolutionary terrorism

The most influential particularistic terrorism in modern time has been produced by right-wing revolutionary movements belonging to the Fascist and Nazi schools. Fascist insurgent movements were intensely active across Europe between the 1920s and 1940s, and produced an enormous amount of violence and terrorism. Two movements in particular, the Italian Fascists and the German Nazis, even succeeded in taking power in their respective countries. Their insurgent violence was converted into massive state terrorism with horrendous consequences.

The historical process of delegitimization undergone by the Fascist and Nazi movements was not short. Nor did it develop as a response to specific blunders of liberal democracy. It involved, instead, a lengthy trajectory of rejection of late nineteenth century bourgeois society and parliamentary democracy.[10] Part of the process was an early fascination with revolutionary socialism, which later developed into intense opposition. The Nazi variant of Fascism involved, in addition, rigid racist principles which added great impetus to the delegitimation of democratic culture. The radicalization of the European extreme right was enormously intensified by the violent experience of World War I and the post-1918 "culture of war".[11]

It is important to stress that the violence of both Italian Fascists and German Nazis was neither a behavioral product of their war experience nor of their increasing conflict of legitimation with their rivals. Violence was an essential part of their original philosophy of government. Fascist and Nazi ideologues glorified the use of violence. They saw it as an essential ingredient to virtuous politics.[12] Very few Fascists worried about justifying their use of force.[13] Violence and terrorism were perceived as essential parts of the Fascist *Weltanschauung* and, consequently, did not require explanation or justification.

While the Fascist road to power in both Italy and Germany involved *split delegitimization*, a primary conflict with the socialists and communists and a secondary conflict with their respective governments, the distinction between the two was tactical. The Fascists despised parliamentary democracy just as they rejected socialism and communism and all three were considered equally illegitimate. Fascist leaders believed, however, that it was too risky for them to confront the government directly. Instead, they assumed that they could rise to power through the flawed mechanisms of democratic politics. The overhaul of the system should come later. While postwar Italy was entangled in a virtual socio-political civil war, which allowed the *squadristi* to resort to terror and to the brutal killing of their direct enemies, the socialists and communists,[14] the Nazis were cautious not to alienate middle and higher class conservatives through the use of excessive terrorism. This required a "legalistic" strategy to get to power and implied violent but non-terroristic types of action.[15] Although post-World War I right-wing radicalism evolved in an intensely violent atmosphere, thereby producing much terror, terrorism was, with few exceptions, an unintended by-product of violent intimidation, brutal street hooliganism and aggressive propaganda.[16] For tactical reasons, then, the Fascist and Nazi delegitimation of their respective regimes rarely crossed the threshold of *conflict of legitimacy*.

The most significant difference between revolutionary right-wing terrorism of pre- and post-World War II is the socio-political marginality of the latter and their relative lack of confidence. Prewar European Fascists and Nazis were part of the main struggle for the future of Western civilization. Along with the socialists, the communists and the liberal democrats, they attracted millions of supporters, including highly educated and wealthy elites. Even their rivals considered the Fascists serious contenders for the hegemony of Western world. Its defeat in World War II, as well as the horrors of the Holocaust, gave Fascism an enormous blow. Most Fascist organizations were either totally eliminated or remained at the very illegitimate fringes of Western society. Many of their leaders who survived the war were executed as war criminals, put in jail for life or went into hidden exile.

Fascism survived, however, and small movements and parties of neo-fascists and neo-Nazis resurfaced in Europe, maintaining a low profile and a considerable sense of inferiority.[17] At the extreme margins they also created, since the late 1940s, small and unstable violent groups such as the Italian *Fasci Azione Rivolutionaria, Ordine Nouvo, Squadre Azuione Mussolini, Avanguardia Nazionale, Nuclei Armati Rivoluzionari* and *Ordine Nero*, the French *Occident, Omega, Odessa, Charles Martel Club, French National Liberation Front, Ordre Nouveau*, the German *Deutsche Aktionsgruppe, Wehrsportgruppe Hoffman, Deutsche Alternative*, and *Nationale Offensive*, the Swedish *Nordiska Rikspartiet, Vitt Ariskt Motstand* (VAM), *Riksfronten*, the Dutch *Jongeren Front Nederland* and many others. While committed to the old dreams of creating a fascist civilization, most of these minuscule groups have been unable to bring to full use the old strategies of street violence, bloody intimidation and armed propaganda. They certainly were in a no position to directly challenge their respective governments. Their repertoire of violence and terrorism, which seems to have come in unsystematic waves, has included desecration of Jewish cemeteries and synagogues, vandalism and arson, violent attacks on foreign workers in Europe, fire bombing of shelters housing foreign asylum seekers, rare assassinations and occasional spectacular bombings of public places such as the 1980 Munich Oktoberfest, the Italicus Express in Bologna and a Jewish synagogue in Rue Copernic, Paris. Italian, French and German neo-fascists appeared in the streets in the late 1960s and 1970s, violently confronting new left demonstrators. Since the mid-1980s, however, there has been a dramatic increase in European neo-Nazi and radical rightist violent attacks on foreign workers and asylum seekers, especially in Germany.[18] There has also been a significant development of an international neo-Nazi and racist communication network. It appears that the growing resentment in Western Europe of Third World immigrants and anxiety regarding the job market have played a considerable role in the increasing appeal and confidence of the European radical right.[19]

Careful not to confront the governments in their respective countries directly, many neo-fascists and neo-Nazis have also been involved in *tactical* Split Delegitimization. While hostile to and critical of liberal democracy, they have reserved their sporadic violence and terrorism almost exclusively for political movements or communities they believed to be weak and vulnerable. Rarely have they attacked agents of the governments or symbols of authority. In Italy, which never really rid itself of Fascism, many neo-fascists have come to believe since the 1950s that the communist threat – which was taken seriously by many respectable and established politicians – would slowly lead to the erosion of the nation's chaotic democracy, thereby facilitating a return of Italy to Fascism. Tactical terrorism was consequently recommended in order to further destabilize the political system and produce calls for strong national power.[20] Part of the neo-fascist effort involved attempts to attract military and police officers worried about a communist takeover.

A significant development in recent times has been the intensification of the "secondary" delegitimization processes of several European neo-Nazi organizations, that is, their radical confrontation with their respective governments. There are signs that the delegitimization of these organizations is not split any more. They are as negative about their respective governments as they are about the Jews, homosexuals, foreign workers and other "inferior" groups. Some of them may even be ready to conduct terror operations against government agents and agencies. A case in point is the Swedish VAM (White Aryan Resistance). In the spring of 1991 leading members of the VAM network went underground. After stealing arms from a police station and conducting a bank robbery, they vowed to prepare for the "Great Racial War", and made clear that their main target is none other than the government itself.[21] However, most were soon arrested and their declared war against ZOG has so far not got off the ground.

Why this development has taken place is not fully clear to me, but the rhetorical device that seems to have made it possible is identifiable. What is at stake is the rise to prominence of the ZOG (Zionist Occupation Government) language and imagery, and the increasing conviction among several European neo-Nazis that their governments have irreversibly been taken over by the Jews and their collaborators. If, in the past, there could be some hope of applying pressure on the respective governments to change their liberal policies towards the non-Aryan races, this is no longer the case. Governments that have been taken over by the Jews and their agents cannot be reformed. They must be brought down by force; and sabotage and terrorism are proper ways of starting the great struggle.[22]

One possible explanation for the radicalization of VAM and similar European neo-Nazis is the unprecedented growth of international neo-Nazi communication networks and the consequent feeling that the Nazi school is no longer small or isolated.[23] The very spread of the ZOG imagery is a good example. The discourse that the neo-Nazis have taken over was not invented in its present form in Europe. It was imported from the United States, where it had been developed and disseminated in the late 1970s and 1980s by several racist and Christian Identity organizations. For European right-wingers, just as for their American colleagues, it was an appealing post-communist answer to their quest for demons. The communist "evil empire", which had long haunted the extreme right and served as its great Satanic enemy, may be gone, but the real demonic people, the Jews, are still around. Better organized than ever around their Zionist center in Israel and heavily represented in government, business, the media, and the dominant liberal culture, the Jews are again considered the real threat for the Aryan race. And as in past European history, an unmasked Jewish threat may make it possible to get wide public support. Another potential explanation for the rising neo-Nazi confidence is the dramatic increase in the public concern over East European immigrants, third world workers and asylum seekers. There is now, so it appears to the neo-Nazis, a much greater appeal for their racist interpretation of reality and for the ZOG conspiracy theory.

B. Reactive terrorism

Particularistic terrorism is occasionally produced by status quo and conservative movements which react to real or perceived threats. This reactive terrorism is resorted to by organizations which have either lost their positions of power and social status or are fearful of such a development. The movements involved undergo an intense process of delegitimization *vis-à-vis* the forces that are out to take over. Terrorism is grasped as a means of last resort in order to restore the *status quo ante*, and is usually applied against organizations which themselves have reached power through the use of violence. The rightist orientation of most reactive groups is normally a response to two circumstances, the first being left-wing terrorism which earlier on was in some way responsible for their expropriation. It may also be a response to a universalistic (i.e., "leftist") frame of mind which threatens them by removing their privileged positions. While most reactive terrorists are not at first intensely preoccupied with right-wing ideology, they are often joined by old time fascists who hope to capitalize on their misery and recreate the glorious fascist past.

Reactive terrorists may be divided into two types: those who have already lost political power and are fighting an uphill battle to regain it, and those who have not yet been stripped of their power and privileges but are worried about such a development. Organizations which have lost political hegemony are usually weak and desperate. Their terrorism takes the form of sporadic revenge attacks and assassination attempts of government officials. This terrorism *does not involve split delegitimation* because the losers fight only the newly created government. In addition to the historical loss of power, which leaves them with few resources, they are vigorously pursued by the state's security apparatus. Members live either underground or in exile, and are usually ill-prepared for an effective campaign against the regime.

A historical example of an organization that seeks to regain lost power is provided by post-World War II Croat insurgents, who for years fought the communist regime of Yugoslavia. The Croats have a long history of right-wing violence and terrorism. In 1934 Croat assassins murdered Yugoslavia's King Alexander, together with French Minister of Foreign Affairs Louis Barthou. Throughout 1941–1945 the Croat *Ustasha* collaborated with the Nazis, controlling Croatia and other Yugoslav areas. Ardently Roman Catholic with a fascist inclination, they hated the Orthodox Christian Serbs, accusing them of unduly dominating the other peoples of Yugoslavia.[24] Hitler's defeat and Yugoslavia's takeover by the Communists ended Croatia's independence. Members of the old regime, who managed to escape Tito's retribution, resurfaced in several remote countries, most notably in Australia and Latin America. They vowed to return, retake Croatia from Tito and use all means necessary. The international rise of modern terrorism in the late 1960s and early 1970s and the reinstitution of the myth of terrorism as an effective revolutionary strategy had a great impact on the Croat diaspora. They believed terrorism could be used to publicize their cause among Croats to such an extent that it would make an invasion of Yugoslavia possible. Beginning in March 1971, when they blew up the Yugoslav consulate in Milan, the organization conducted several spectacular operations, including the successful hijacking of a Swedish airplane, of a TWA aircraft bound to Chicago and the planting of a bomb in Grand Central Station in New York.[25] In June 1972 the *Ustasha* attempted and failed at a raid into Yugoslavia.[26]

The desperate terrorism exercised by former *Ustasha* and several other groups of Croat émigrés did not help them politically. The Croat reactive struggle greatly declined in the 1980s. However, it did help reinvigorate Serb hatred which appeared in full force following the 1989 dissolution of Yugoslavia. The Civil War in that troubled country, launched in June 1991 among the Serbs, Croats, and Muslims of Bosnia and Kosovo, was not waged over the legacy of the émigrés, many of whom came back to retake Croatia. However, the historical memories of their reactive violence contributed to the easy passage to violence, terrorism and ethnic cleansing that continue to plague the region.

An example of reactive terrorism which started before the final loss of power is provided by the *Organization Armée Secret* (OAS), the terror organization established in 1961 by the French *Colons* in Algeria, in a last minute effort to stop the French retreat from the colony. In spite of their large concentration, the former French fascists in Algeria felt no desire to conduct a fascist revolution: the privileged French *pieds noirs* led a good colonial life in Algeria, and wanted to keep it that way. Full of contempt for the local population, they were consistently opposed to equal rights for the "natives".[27] An intense conflict of legitimation between these two populations was long in the making. The civil war which began in 1954 in Algeria triggered an intense radicalization between the *colons* and the local population. It also started a secondary process of delegitimization between the *colons* and the French government, which was seen as "too soft" on the Algerians.[28] In that context, the *ultras*, the most extreme among the settlers, even established small terror hit teams which "helped" the French Army launch counter strikes against the Algerians.[29] The situation deteriorated significantly between 1959 and 1960 when the *colons* found out that President Charles de Gaulle was ready to compromise with the FLN. Their process of delegitimization with the French government intensified dramatically.

The subtler sense of betrayal by France's historical hero was shared by several of the nation's most decorated generals, who vowed to keep Algeria French. By 1961, when de Gaulle's intentions to leave Algeria became a fact, the recently started process of delegitimization reached its peak. The disgruntled *pieds noirs* and the embittered generals established the OAS. Moving fast from conflict to crisis of legitimation with the French government, they launched a dual terror campaign. While applying vengeance terrorism against the Algerians in an effort to destroy the peace talks and accentuate the situation,[30] they also engaged in a massive terror campaign against the government. This they did in Algeria, in France and in Europe. OAS terrorism tragically backfired, however. In addition to its failure to stop the 1962 French retreat from Algeria, it destroyed the conditions for any kind of European-Algerian co-existence in the newly created Algerian republic. A massive exodus took place, which in a short time brought to France over one million former Algerian settlers.

Reactive terrorism, to conclude, usually starts with the terrorization of many non-governmental groups and communities. However, it is almost always transformed into an intense process of delegitimization with the government and anti-regimist terrorism.

C. Vigilante terrorism

A special variant of reactive terrorism is *vigilante terrorism*. Vigilante terror is used by individuals and groups who believe that the government does not adequately protect them from violent groups or individuals and that they must protect themselves. Vigilante movements rarely perceive themselves involved in conflict with the government and the prevailing concept of law. They are neither revolutionary nor interested in the destruction of authority. Rather, what characterizes the vigilante mind is the profound conviction that the government and its agencies have failed to enforce the law or establish order in a particular area.[31] Backed by the fundamental norm of self-defense and speaking in the name of the law of the land, vigilantes see themselves as enforcing the law and executing justice. Vigilantes are, therefore, particularistic supporters of the status quo and have no alternative political system in mind. They believe that they are acting legally against criminal elements because the authorities are either too weak to enforce the law or negligent in their duties.[32]

Vigilantism, it should be stressed, is by no means synonymous with terrorism. In reality, the majority of vigilantes rarely resort to atrocities in order to uphold the law. However, under circumstances of serious pressure, often involving violence against them, vigilantes undergo a process of delegitimization which pushes them toward the use of terror. Like most other particularistic terrorists, the primary process of delegitimization of the vigilante movement involves a non-governmental group or individuals who are believed to have broken the law. But vigilante terrorism, unless tacitly supported by the regime, is likely to trigger conflict with the government's agents. Most effective governments cannot tolerate systematic vigilantism and try to curtail its activity. If the stakes and the level of vigilante terror are high, this could lead to intense radicalization and serious conflict with the government. Two situations are particularly prone to the evolution of vigilante terrorism:

- lawlessness in border areas where the military and police are unable to fully protect the pioneering settlers;

- the presence of intense insurgent terrorism which cannot be effectively contained by the authorities.

Vigilante terrorism has developed, for example, in the occupied territories of Israel as a direct result of the rise of Palestinian violence and the inability of the Israeli Army to provide the settlers with complete protection. A group that was called the Jewish Underground by the Israeli press conducted several terror operations in the early 1980s in an attempt to restrain the Palestinians and maintain a system of control through terrorism. The most spectacular operation of the Jewish Underground was the blowing up of the cars of two Arab mayors believed by the group to be the major coordinators of PLO operations in the area. The vigilantes of Gush Emunim, a religious and messianic Israeli movement, believed they were upholding the law. They obtained rabbinical approval of the act based on the Jewish Halachic rule that, "he who comes to kill you, you kill him first", and argued in court that this was also the spirit of Israel's positive law.[33] Members of the Jewish Underground also convinced themselves that the military government of the area was tacitly behind them, and that several of the military officers involved, who knew the political constraints of the government, secretly encouraged them to carry out their plans. The decision of the Jewish underground to attack the mayors was exceptional and unprecedented in Jewish and Israeli contexts. It implied a serious secondary process of delegitimization with the government of Israel which was previously considered holy. However, the underground's conflict with the Israeli government never reached the point of a crisis of legitimacy and anti-Jewish terrorism.

Since the 1960s, vigilante killing of "subversive" elements has played an unprecedented role in Latin America, where the practice is long known and associated with the military and the police.[34] Following a wave of left-wing insurgent terror in the 1960s, a period which greatly destabilized countries such as Argentina, Brazil, El Salvador and Guatemala, a counterstrike was launched, with even worse human and political consequences. Unable to suppress terrorism through the ordinary legal system, police and military officers decided to take the law into their hands and to eliminate the leftist threat privately. They did this through the establishment of death squads which swept through the respective countries killing scores of suspected terrorists or alleged collaborators. What was unique about these vigilantes is that many of them were military officers acting in their free time. There is, in fact, a large body of information which shows that these operations were conducted with the full cooperation of the armies and governments involved, and that the whole idea was to free the officers from the legal constraints of due process.[35]

An early case in Argentina is that of President Isabella Peron's Minister of Social Welfare, José Lopez Rega, who established the Anti-Communist Alliance (Triple A). Rega recruited for the job federal and provincial policemen and armed them with weapons bought by state funds. Responding to the terror campaign of the *Ejército Revolucionario del Pueblo* and the *Montoneros* – organizations which had destabilized Argentina since the late 1960s – the Triple A assassinated over 200 people and intimidated many more in 1974–1975. In August 1976 Triple A killed 46 suspected terrorists.[36] Similar quasi-official vigilante groups operated in the 1960s and 1970s in Mexico, Brazil and El Salvador. In Guatemala, which between the mid-1950s and the mid-1980s witnessed a virtual civil war with three waves of intense terrorism, the right was represented by nearly 20 vigilante groups. These paramilitary organizations with such names as the New Anti-Communist Organization, the Purple Rose, and the White Hand, comprised supporters of the status quo such as landowners, police and military officers.[37] What marks the Guatemalan as well as many other Latin American vigilantes, is the nearly automatic support they receive from the government and the security forces. What is really occurring is state terrorism in disguise. Vigilantism in Guatemala, just as leftist insurgent terrorism, has become a way of life, a part of a "culture and counterculture of terror", which in the last 40 years took the lives of over 150,000 people.[38]

Vigilante terrorism often involves split delegitimization, but the secondary process of delegitimization rarely reaches terroristic maturation. People who believe they uphold the law of the land may get angry at the small support they receive from the authorities, but rarely, if ever, confront the government. Unless intensely abused and mistreated by government agents in jail, they are likely to restrict their occasional terrorism to the "law breakers".

D. Racist terrorism

Most particularistic terror organizations display some kind of racism, that is, a belief that race is an important organizing principle in society and that certain groups of "colored" people are inherently inferior. Several organizations, however, see race as the *main* organizational principle that counts, and devote all their energy to the struggle for racist supremacy. In contrast to revolutionary terrorists who dream about a total transformation of the social, cultural and political system and the creation of a fascist civilization, racist terrorists are usually political conservatives. Their sole desire is a social system which will either recognize their racial superiority officially or informally guarantee its perpetuation. Racist movements go into conflict with the prevailing government, namely, *engage in split delegitimization*, only after the regime involved has failed to support their platforms or has been actively engaged in their containment. Terrorism is often resorted to by these racists as a *control mechanism*, an effort to restore the previous caste structure of society in which the inferior race must remain, permanently, an underprivileged second class. In extreme cases racist terrorism is also utilized against government agencies or agents who are especially involved in law enforcement against the perpetrators of terror.

Racist terrorism has been almost synonymous with the American Ku Klux Klan, an umbrella secret society established in 1865, following the defeat of the Confederacy in the Civil War. The Klan underwent several historical transformations, and recently has been in a steady decline. Over the years, it has added to its original anti-Black platform new ideological concerns such as anti-Semitism, anti-Catholicism, anti-Communism and the idea of "100 per cent Americanism". Rarely as monolithic and centralized as its public image wants the average person to believe, the Klan has existed locally under a variety of names and titles. Since its foundation, however, the Ku Klux Klan *as an idea* has been the inspiration for many similar organizations.[39]

The "classic" KKK terror operation, a pattern developed in the late 1860s and maintained for generations, involved a small group of masked and hooded night raiders. A typical target was a black individual suspected of violating some "white man's values". Klansmen had all the advantages – darkness, disguise, superior numbers and armaments. Victims had an ingrained fear of the Klan and little or no military skills. In one given night, the Klan group might visit several black cabins to inflict "lessons" and punishment. Black suspects were often taken to a wooden area for a mock trial. Their homes were usually set on fire. Many trials were concluded by lynching the suspects, shooting them, or severely injuring them. An individual allowed to live was warned that there would be no second chance, and was sent to transmit the message to his peers and colleagues.[40]

The Ku Klux Klan and Klan-like organizations rarely attacked the Federal government or its agents directly, but have almost always been involved in a secondary process of *delegitimization* with Washington. In that respect, the Klan is a direct descendent of the influential American traditions of *populism* and *nativism*.[41] The role of the Federal government in the Civil War and the First Reconstruction, and its increasing involvement in public affairs in the post-1929 Franklin Roosevelt era, had constantly haunted the organization. KKK-like organizations argued persistently that the movement had been loyal to the Constitution of the United States, and that the original Constitution never intended to give the Federal government and Congress the degree of authority they came to possess. KKK's America grew up from individual settlers and independent local communities and was intended to remain that way.

The increased isolation of the Ku Klux Klan in America during the 1960s, the greater commitment of the Federal government to take anti-Klan action and the successful penetration of the organization by federal agents led to the organization's significant decline. The KKK lost its hold on the deep South and its followers became increasingly marginal. A resurgence attempt in the 1970s did not last long.[42]

Racist and white supremacist groups have not vanished from the American landscape, however, and several anti-communist paramilitary and survivalist groups gained some public notoriety between the 1960s and 1970s. The traumatic experience of the Vietnam War and the perception of an imminent communist threat were responsible for the rise of several paramilitary organizations and for the occasional resort of some of their members to violence.[43] Since the 1970s there has, furthermore, been a dramatic increase in the number and interaction of white supremacist groups with strong religious and millenarian inclinations. While marginalized and delegitimized by mainstream American culture, these groups and organizations seem to have been successful in the creation of a rather wide and self-supporting racist counter-culture.

E. Millenarian terrorism[44]

The fifth type of particularistic terrorism is millenarian terrorism, terrorism resorted to by religious groups which believe that the end of the world is imminent and that if spiritually prepared, they will be saved.[45] Terrorism and millenarianism, it must be stated at the outset, are by no means synonymous or even behaviorally interconnected. The majority of the millenarian sects are not terroristic. A typical feature of millenarianism is a peaceful withdrawal from the world.[46] The spiritual leaders of the group believe that only in a state of isolation and seclusion can they properly prepare themselves for the demise of the sinning world and for their own salvation. The millenarian separation from the rest of society implies either a simple conviction that God will punish the sinning people and that the group should mind its own spiritual business, or an admission of weakness and inability to struggle against the evil forces of society.

Millenarian sects that commit terrorist acts usually do so for reasons which are not directly related to their spiritual and chiliastic dreams. They resort to terrorism either because of the presence of individual leaders who are violence-prone, or because the external society or some of its agencies push them aggressively into a corner. So much hate, alienation and desperation are experienced by the group that on occasions, and after specific incentives have been created, it will resort to terrorism.[47] The occasional shift to terrorism implies the group's inability to fully seclude itself and sever all contacts with organized society.

Millenarian terrorists differ from most particularistic terrorists in their vision of the future. It was mentioned earlier that unlike left-wing terrorists, whose desired society is non-violent, many particularistic terrorists are convinced that violence and conflict are essential ingredients of the good society or are at least necessary for the preservation of their desired world. This is, however, not the case with millenarian terrorists. The ideal society of the millenarians is peaceful, harmonious and non-violent.[48] It is peaceful because the post-apocalyptic vision of the group leaves no room for conflict. The sinning world is expected to be destroyed and the future community will consist only of loyal believers. The terrorism committed by most millenarian groups is, thus, a necessary evil. It is often projected by the organization leaders as an act of self-defense against an aggressive and merciless external society. Bank robbery is not virtuous but may be justified by the legitimate financial needs of the group. An attack on a representative of the "Zionist controlled government" may, in the same spirit, be legitimate if that individual is perceived as an immediate threat to the organization. Terrorism may also help group members obtain the military experience that will be needed at the time of Armageddon.

Millenarian terrorism has occasionally been produced in the 1980s by several Christian Identity groups, an American umbrella subculture espousing a variety of racist, anti-Semitic, Christian-fundamentalist and anti-Federalist beliefs. The Christian Identity Movement seems to have grown up from the racist periphery of American fundamentalism and the extreme right, which in the last two decades has undergone a noteworthy revival. More radical and revolutionary than the Ku Klux Klan ever was, this plethora of millenarian sects, churches and small paramilitary organizations views the American political and cultural system as entirely illegitimate.[49] It is a decadent society hopelessly polluted by racially or ideologically inferior people such as Jews, Blacks, communists, homosexuals and liberals of all sorts. While many followers of the Identity schools are not full-time political revolutionaries, and may just be interested in a peaceful withdrawal from the world, their ideotheology indicates a profound Crisis of Legitimacy with the American system. It further implies considerable violent potential. The American government, according to the new movement, as well as the nation's most important institutions, have been totally taken over by the Zionist Occupation Government (ZOG) and are beyond repair. The Jews and their collaborators are all over the place. Not only are they in control of the nation's many established institutions such as government and mass media, but their organizations have intensely marginalized and delegitimized the entire patriotic American radical right.[50]

Much of the Christian Identity Movement's hopes for a better future relies on their messianic belief in the imminent Second Coming of a White Aryan Christ. This will occur after a seven year period of tribulation, a modern-day Armageddon, when the entire world will change dramatically. Jews and other "mud people" will be eliminated and genuine Anglo-Saxons will finally take over. For this reason, many Identity preachers recommend that their followers live in isolated encampments, mostly in the racially homogenous North-West, and arm themselves in preparation for the great moment.[51] While most of the arms are kept for the final struggle, it is legitimate also to use them, occasionally, against representatives and symbols of ZOG, which is presently in control of Washington. Bank robberies and other crimes aimed at strengthening the movements are also fully legitimate.[52]

Their ideo-theological rejection of the American system at nearly all levels, which is no longer different from their rejection of the original target communities such as Jews or Blacks, puts many Christian Identity groups at a very advanced position on both wings of the split delegitimization. While some of them express it by self-seclusion and withdrawal, others resort occasionally to terrorism, including direct attacks on government installations and symbols of authority. It appears, in fact, that if not for the persistent pressure and crack-downs of the Justice Department and the Federal Bureau of Investigation on white supremacist groups, several of them would have very likely resorted to intense anti-establishment terrorism in the 1980s.

F. Youth counterculture terrorism

A special type of particularistic terrorism which has grown since the mid-1970s, attracting increasing public attention, is right-wing terrorism conducted by alienated and isolated youth gangs. Many of these are shaven-headed and have come to be known as Skinheads or "Skins". Others are soccer rowdies involved in "spontaneous violence". The majority of them are very young and are more involved in a cultural than political crisis of legitimation with the democratic culture. Music is a key element in the Skinhead counterculture and serves as a recruiting tool, a propaganda weapon, a celebration of the gang ethic and a call for violence. The Skinhead "white power" music is aggressive, loud, and radiates a message of violent cultural revolt.[53] Just as their music expresses a rebellion against middle-class pop music, Skinhead behavior implies a rejection of the entire normative order of bourgeois society. The political essence of Skinheadism focuses on the glorification and perpetuation of brute violence against racial and ethnic minorities, homosexuals, leftists, and Jews. The adoption and glorification of racist and anti-Semitic violence seems to be less a logical conclusion of a certain political thinking and more of an emotional consequence of a youthful cultural rebellion and a denial of the normative status quo.[54]

The Skinheads, just as many other right-wing extremists, are by no means systematic terrorists and terrorism is only a small part of what a few of them do. Skinhead terrorism seems to be an unintended extension of non-political glorification of brutal physical force and symbolic excitement about violence. Many Skins come to their concerts armed with knives, axes, baseball bats and material for manufacturing firebombs. After several hours of listening to the throbbing beat of their wild bands and augmented by a flood of alcohol, they strike and occasionally kill. In the last decade Skinheads have been involved in fire bombings and murderous assaults which took the life of numerous innocent civilians in several Western countries. Moreover, these assaults left many more members of the targeted communities terrorized. The most notorious youth counterculture assault took place on 23 November 1992, in the German town of Mölln, where three Turkish women and girls were killed in a fire-bomb attack.

The Skinhead subculture, whose German annex has recently attracted much attention, originated in the 1970s in Great Britain and spread to several Western countries, including the United States. The shaven-headed Skinheads began to be seen in the streets in the early 1970s. Tattooed and wearing Doc Martens boots, they were reminiscent of the young thugs portrayed in the famous movie, *A Clockwork Orange*. Their style was aimed to stand in symbolic contrast to the liberal, pacifist, middle class values of the long hairs, and to stress patriotic, bellicose, anti-immigrant, working class attitudes. Skinheads can now be found in Germany, Hungary, Poland, Czechoslovakia, Italy, Sweden, Norway, Denmark, the Netherlands, Spain and the USA. The dislocation created by the unification of Germany and the demise of the GDR has led among other things to significant growth of a rather large Skinhead subculture in East Germany. In parts of East Berlin and in several border towns close to Poland, Skinhead gangs have virtually taken over, terrorizing both the opposition and local authorities into silence. Youth centers established by the government to provide housing and social care have been taken over by the Skins and turned into aggressive counterculture centers with strong neo-Nazi overtones. The nearby neighborhoods as well as bars have been terrorized into silence and acceptance of the Skinhead lifestyle. Much of the aggression of the gangs is directed against the huge number of immigrants, guest workers and asylum seekers in Germany, who are believed to have taken away jobs and opportunities.

As alarming as the rise of the violent right-wing youth counterculture may be, it appears that its real danger involves the interaction between these youngsters, other youth gangs and older and more experienced neo-Nazis. Even though Skins are not easy to organize, there are increasing indications that inexperienced Skins are occasionally mobilized for radical action and being used by several more experienced right-wing extremists.[55] The social marginality of the Skinheads and other youth gangs, their young age and their socio-economic detachment from organized society make some of them potential front-line "soldiers" for neo-fascist and neo-Nazi movements whose elderly members either cannot afford to get directly involved in extralegal activities or constantly suffer from manpower shortage. Most of the American Skinheads, for example, are affiliated with neo-Nazi organizations or the Aryan Nation and go by such names as Northern Hammerskins, SS of America and Aryan Resistance League. According to the American ADL, which has been carefully monitoring these groups, they have been put into destructive action by more experienced neo-Nazis. From 1987 to June 1990 there was a total of six cases of killing; but in the three years since, 22 murders were committed by Skinheads.[56] Most of the victims have been members of minority groups: Blacks, Hispanics, Asians, homosexuals and homeless persons. In addition, Skinheads had been involved in thousands of lesser crimes: stabbings, shootings, beatings, thefts and synagogue desecrations. The ADL has concluded that "Skinheads are today the most violent of all white supremacy groups. Not even the Ku Klux Klan, so notorious for their use of the rope and the gun, come close to the Skinheads in the number and severity of crimes committed in recent years."[57]

It appears that the conceptual framework of the process of delegitimization has almost no explanatory power for the terror produced by the youth counter-culture of the Skinheads, the soccer hooligans and other musical punks and youth gangs. What is involved is not a lengthy process of political delegitimization but a cultural rebellion of marginal youth groups who are in conflict with the demanding post-industrial society as well as with their parents, and who wish to provoke both. They are relevant to the present study because much of their cultural and experiential world is shaped by neo-fascist and neo-Nazi symbols and because their outrage is directed at enemies of the racist right. While much of this violence remains symbolic, criminal and non-political,[58] there is in the United States and certain European countries a feeling that a racist and neo-Nazi subculture has slowly been evolving at the margins of society since the 1980s, and that its effects are likely to be felt for a long time.

The modus operandi of right-wing terrorism: a part-time job

The huge political, historical and cultural variation among right-wing extremist groups makes it difficult to generalize about their behavioral dynamics. And yet it appears that there is a major difference in the *modus operandi* of universalistic and particularistic terror-producing organizations. While the former – usually extreme left, nationalist or anti-authoritarian terrorists – often operate in secret undergrounds, which presuppose full-time revolutionaries pursued by the law, the majority of right-wing terrorists do not devote their entire lives to the terrorist cause and rarely go underground. Many of them live almost a normal life, sustain families and perceive of themselves as distinguished members of the community. Their terrorism is, in most cases, a side function carried out after "working hours". As we shall see below, however, there are several exceptions to this rule.

The explanation for the part-time character of right-wing terrorism involves the nature of the delegitimization process undergone by particularistic terrorists and the target of their atrocities. Unlike universalistic terrorists who mostly fight repressive rulers and governments, the majority of particularistic terrorists do not directly challenge the structure of authority. The target of their outrage is a specific "inferior" community or individuals whom they wish to discriminate against and intimidate. In most cases they expect the government to fulfill this task and react only when government leaders are unwilling to cooperate or follow "their advice". This rule also applies, as was mentioned earlier, to revolutionary right-wing terrorists, whose ultimate goal is a structural change but who opt, for tactical reasons, for legalistic strategy. It goes without saying that legality does not preclude secrecy, and that most organizations involved in violence are extremely secretive about their terror plans. But in the majority of right-wing cases, the proponents of terrorism do not hide and are usually registered in the local telephone directory.

There are three exceptions to the part-time nature of right-wing terrorism: religious millenarian sects, youth counterculture groups and very extreme neo-Nazi organizations. Membership in these collectivities usually presupposes alienation from the community and rejection of its cultural and political norms. It further implies many fewer commitments to bourgeois society, including orderly family life and property ownership. The American millenarian organization of Robert

Mathews, the Order, or the Swedish VAM network, as well as several Skinhead groups can serve as examples for groups whose alienation and separation from organized society are almost total. But as we have seen, terrorism is not the main concern of these collectivities. Most millenarian groups withdraw from ordinary life and peacefully prepare themselves for the Second Coming of Christ. And the neo-Nazis and Skinhead counterculture is very much into noisy music, racist camaraderie, hostility to organized society and a culturally provocative lifestyle.

The legal status of most particularistic organizations involved in terrorism is also responsible for the low frequency of their terror operations. An organization which fulfills other social functions and is likely to be suspected of extremist operations is probably under constant surveillance by the security services of the regime. It must, therefore, keep a low profile. Its leaders, who are often much older than most active warriors in universalistic insurgency, wish to maintain their respectable community status, and simply cannot afford to be caught. One may also add that the kind of terrorism applied against "inferior" communities does not require great military skill or a highly sophisticated underground. Bruce Hoffman noticed back in 1984 that the favorite right-wing weapon is the bomb, the use of which does not require a sophisticated and well-organized conspiracy.[59]

Since the majority of present day right-wingers do not fundamentally challenge the structure of authority, their unsystematic terrorism is merely an additional method of coping with the socio-cultural anxieties they face. Four sets of circumstances seem to increase the likelihood that right-wing true believers will move from conflict to crisis of legitimation and resort to terrorism: (a) a sudden and intense sense of insecurity which produces emotional extremist action; (b) a conviction of right-wing leaders that they can rationally benefit from terrorism; (c) a sense of increasing public support for radical action against "undesirable people"; (d) the imposing presence of violent personalities whose resort to terrorism is made for purely personal-psychological reasons.

Small, isolated and poorly organized particularistic extremist groups are likely to respond to perceived threats without much calculation. A sudden anxiety, a decline in the group's sense of political control, a socio-economic recession, a fear of imminent leftist aggression or a profound outrage with certain acts of the authorities may drive members of such groups to occasional atrocities. Terrorism is resorted to emotionally in a desperate effort to restore the *status quo ante*. Many Ku Klux Klan and white supremacy organizations, small European neo-fascist cells in the 1970s and some Israeli right-wing extremists have acted in this fashion. Their terrorism has been an unplanned and unsystematic mechanism for the temporary release of group anxiety and tension.

More sophisticated and well-organized right-wing movements try not to act emotionally. Aware of their weakness and of the effectiveness of law enforcement agencies, their leaders order strikes only when convenient and when the government is seen to be in disarray. The presence of intense extralegal left-wing activity, which can be blamed for much of the violence, may be helpful, as was the case in Italy and France in the late 1960s and early 1970s. A special case in point is the "strategy of tension" of Italian neo-fascists since the 1950s. Responding to significant socio-economic strains, the rise in left-wing radicalism and a perception of potential support by the armed forces and police, group leaders like Pino Rauti recommended violent confrontation with the left and even terrorism.[60] Prudent leaders of reactive and vigilante groups may also use terrorism to attract public attention and place issues that trouble them on the public agenda.

Concluding remarks

Students of political violence have long been familiar with the positive correlation between the radical group's sense of public support and the likelihood that it will resort to violence.[61] This correlation appears to be holding for right-wing terror groups. A case in point is the enormous rise in the aggression and violence of Israel's Kach movement in the early 1980s. A strong anti-Arab sentiment which swept the country made Rabbi Meir Kahane, who for years was the isolated leader of the movement, a legitimate actor in Israeli politics.[62] The unexpected 1984 election of the rabbi to parliament surprisingly did not reduce the level of Kach's violence. On the contrary, their attacks on Arabs increased. In the same fashion it appears that the steady decline in violent operations of the Ku Klux Klan since the 1960s has had to do with, among other things, the dramatic decrease of public support. The rule seems to be holding currently in Germany where neo-Nazi violence has reached crisis proportions in the 1990s. The increasing confidence of the neo-Nazis in the rising anti-alien sentiment in Germany and several other European countries seems to have contributed to their daring activities.[63]

Psychologists and students of political violence have so far failed to fully explain the violent personality. We just know that the evolution and activity of certain violent groups, especially those that are small and poorly organized, cannot be reduced to socio-political factors. The heads of such groups just happen to be more violent than others, more excited with weapons, angrier at society or at its established leaders, or more moved by romantic dreams of virility and glorious violence. Such groups are almost always products of a single man. The leader's personality, more than the group's ideology or socio-political conditions, determines the level, repertoire and timing of violence. Unless developed into a larger and more broadly appealing movement, the death or arrest of the leader is often the end of the group. This seems to have been the case with neo-Nazi activists such as the German Karl Heinz Hoffman and his *Wehrsportgruppe Hoffman*, Robert Mathews of the American Order and to some extent even with Israel's Rabbi Kahane and several of his successors.[64]

Notes

1 Ehud Sprinzak, "The Process of Delegitimization: Towards a Linkage Theory of Political Terrorism", *Terrorism and Political Violence* [hereafter *TPV*] 3/1 (Spring 1991) pp.50–68. To clarify any possible confusion: I use the term "delegitimization" whenever I am talking about a behavioral process over time. The term "delegitimation" I use to denote an attitude. However, this distinction is of linguistic rather than theoretical significance, and I do not expect others to follow my usage.

2 Ehud Sprinzak, "The Psycho-political Formation of Extreme Left Terrorism in a Democracy: The Case of the Weathermen", in Walter Reich (ed.), *Origins of Terrorism* (NY: CUP, 1990), p.79.

3 Sprinzak (note 1), pp.54–55.

4 Ibid., pp.55–56.

5 Albert Bandura, "Mechanisms of Moral Disengagement", in Reich, *Origins of Terrorism* (note 2), pp.180–182.

6 Jeanne N. Knutson, "Social and Psychodynamic Pressures Towards a Negative Identity: The Case of an American Revolutionary Terrorist", in Yonah Alexander and John M. Glison (eds.), *Behavioral and Quantitative Perspectives on Terrorism* (NY: Pergamon Press, 1981), pp.211–215; Jerold M. Post, "Notes on a Psychodynamic Theory of Terrorist Behavior", *Terrorism: An International Journal* 7/3 (1984), pp.250–253.

7 Sprinzak (note 1), p.53. In addition to "transformational delegitimization", the article also identifies as a type "extensional delegitimization", which is more suitable for terrorism of national liberation movements. Extensional delegitimization implies a process which starts with long held cultural hostility towards a foreign ruler. The terrorism that develops does not represent a psycho-political transformation from early agreement to a bitter disagreement, but a rather radicalized and bloody extension of an already existing hostility and conflict.

8 This tendency within the ZOG discourse and related ideologies towards a complete identification of the hated minority with the government has been pointed out to me by Jeffrey Kaplan and Tore Bjørgo *Terrorism and Political Violence* 7:1.

9 Walter Laqueur, *The Age of Terrorism* (London: Weidenfeld, 1987) p.67.

10 Zeev Sternhell, "Fascist Ideology", in Walter Laqueur (ed.), *Fascism: A Reader's Guide* (Berkeley, CA: Univ. of California Press, 1976), pp.320–337.

11 Adrian Lyttelton, "Fascism and Violence in Post-War Italy: Political Strategy and Social Conflict", in W. J. Mommsen and Gerhard Hirshfeld (eds.), *Social Protest, Violence, and Terror in Nineteenth and Twentieth-Century Europe* (NY: St. Martin's Press, 1982); Peter Merkl, *The Making of a Stormtrooper* (Boulder, CO: Westview Press, 1987), pp.15–18; Jens Petersen, "Violence in Italian Fascism", in Mommsen and Hirshfeld cited above.

12 Merkl (note 11), pp.299–305; Ernst Nolte, *Three Faces of Fascism* (NY: Mentor Books, 1965), pp.260–263.

13 James A. Gregor, "Fascism: Philosophy of Violence and the Concept of Terror", in David C. Rapoport and Yona Alexander (eds.), *The Morality of Terrorism* (NY: Pergamon Press, 1982).

14 Petersen (note 11).

15 Jeremy Noakes, "The Origins, Structure and Functions of Nazi Terror", in Noel O'Sullivan (ed.), *Terrorism, Ideology and Revolution* (Boulder, CO: Westview, 1986).

16 Laqueur (note 9), pp.76–77.

17 Paul Wilkinson, *The New Fascists* (London: Grant McIntyre, 1981), Ch.3.

18 Anti-Defamation League, *The German Neo-Nazis: An ADL Investigative Report* (NY: ADL, 1993).

19 Tore Bjørgo and Robb Witte, *Racist Violence in Europe* (NY: St. Martin's Press, 1993).

20 Leonard Weinberg, "Italian Neo-Fascist Terrorism: A Comparative Perspective", in *Terrorism and Political Violence* 7/1 (1995), pp. 221–238.

21 Tore Bjørgo, "Militant Neo-Nazism in Sweden", *TVP* 5/3 (Autumn 1993).

22 Heléne Lööw, "The Cult of Violence: The Swedish Racist Counterculture", in Bjørgo and Witte (note 19), pp.67–70.

23 Erik Jensen, "International Nazi Cooperation: A Terrorist Oriented Network", in Bjørgo and Witte (note 19).

24 Albert Parry, *Terrorism: From Robespierre to Arafat* (NY: The Vanguard Press, 1976), p. 496.

25 Knutson (note 6), p. 116.

26 Parry (note 24), p.498.

27 Alistaire Home, *A Savage War Peace: Algeria 1954–1962* (London: Macmillan, 1977), pp.36–37.

28 Ibid., pp. 148–150.

29 Ibid., pp.349–350.

30 Martha Hutchinson (Crenshaw), *Revolutionary Terrorism: The FLN in Algeria 1954–1962* (Stanford, CA: Hoover Inst. Press, 1978), pp.58–59.

31 Jon H. Rosenbaum and Peter C. Sederberg, "Vigilantism: Analysis of Establishment Violence", *Comparative Politics*, Vol. 6 (July 1974).

32 Richard Maxwell Brown, "The American Vigilante Tradition", in Hugh Graham and Ted Robert Gurr, *Violence in America* (NY: Signet Books, 1969), pp.176–177.

33 Ehud Sprinzak, "From Messianic Pioneering to Vigilante Terrorism: The Case of Gush Emunim Underground", in David C. Rapoport (ed.), *Inside Terrorist Organizations* (London: Frank Cass, 1987), pp.210–214.

34 Martha K. Huggins, "Introduction: Vigilantism and the State – A Look at South and North", in Martha K. Huggins (ed.), *Vigilantism and the State in Modern Latin America: Essays on Extralegal Violence* (NY: Praeger, 1991), pp.1–4.

35 Ibid.

36 John Sloan, "Terrorism in Latin America", in Michael Stohl (ed.), *The Politics of Terrorism* (NY: Marcel Dekker, 1979), pp.389–390.

37 Ibid., pp.392–394.

38 Carlos F. Ibara, "Guatemala: The Recourse of Fear", in Huggins (note 34), pp.73–80.

39 David M. Chalmers, *Hooded Americanism* (Chicago: Quadrangle Paperbacks, 1968).

40 A. W. Trelease, *White Terror: The Ku Klux Klan Conspiracy and the Southern Reconstruction* (NY: Harper Torchbooks, 1971), pp.29–46.

41 Seymour Martin Lipset and Earl Raab, *The Politics of Unreason: Right-Wing Extremism in America 1790–1970* (New York: Harper and Row, 1970), pp.165–169.

42 Anti Defamation League, *Extremism on the Right: A Handbook* (NY: ADL, 1988), p.26.

43 Jerome H. Skolnick, *The Politics of Protest* (NY: Ballantine Books, 1969), pp.231–239.

44 I owe the inclusion of this category in the typology to Jeffrey Kaplan's constructive critique of an earlier version of my model (cf. his essay in *Terrorism and Political Violence* 7/1 (1995), pp. 44–95).

45 Michael Barkun, "Millenarian Aspects of 'White Supremacist' Movements", *TPV* 1/4 (Oct. 1989), pp.410–413.

46 Jeffrey Kaplan, "The Context of American Millenarian Revolutionary Theology: The Case of the 'Identity Christian' Church of Israel", *TPV* 5/1 (Spring 1993), pp.30–31.

47 Ibid., pp.54–56
48 Ibid., pp.31–32.
49 Ibid.
50 Leonard Weinberg, "The American Radical Right: Exit, Voice and Violence", in Peter H. Merkl and Leonard Weinberg (eds.), *Encounters with the Contemporary Radical Right* (Boulder, CO.; Westview, 1993), pp.186, 201.
51 Ibid, p.14.
52 Kevin Flynn and Gary Gerhardt, *The Silent Brotherhood: Inside America's Racist Underground* (NY: The Free Press, 1989), Ch.4.
53 Anti-Defamation League, *Sounds of Hate, Neo-Nazi Rock Music from Germany; An ADL Special Report* (NY: ADL, 1992).
54 Peter Merkl, "Conclusion: A New Lease on Life for the Radical Right?" in P. Merkl and L. Weinberg (note 50), pp.208–209.
55 Tore Bjørgo, "Terrorist Violence Against Immigrants and Refugees in Scandinavia: Patterns and Motives", in Bjørgo and Witte (note 19), p.30.
56 Anti Defamation League, *Young Nazi Killers, The Rising Skinhead Danger: An ADL Special Report* (NY: ADL, 1993), p.3.
57 Ibid.
58 Peter Merkl, "Conclusion: A New Lease on Life for the Radical Right", in Merkl and Weinberg (note 50), pp.212–214.
59 Bruce Hoffman, "Right-Wing Terrorism in Europe", *Conflict* 5/3 (1984).
60 Paul Furlong, "Political Terrorism in Italy: Responses, Reactions and Immobilism", in Juliet Lodge (ed.), *Terrorism: A Challenge to the State* (Oxford: Martin Robertson, 1981), p.70; Piero Ignazi, "The Changing Profile of the Italian Social Movement", in Merkl and Weinberg (note 50), pp. 80–82.
61 William Gamson, *The Strategy of Social Protest* (Homewood, IL: Dorsey Press, 1975), pp.81–82.
62 Ehud Sprinzak, "Violence and Catastrophe in the Theology of Rabbi Meir Kahane; The Ideologization of the Mimetic Desire", *TPV* 3/3 (Autumn 1991), pp.48–70.
63 Graeme Atkinson, "Germany: Nationalism, Nazism and Violence", in Bjørgo and Witte (note 19).
64 Peter Merkl, "Rollerball or neo-Nazi Violence", in Peter Merkl (ed.), *Political Violence and Terror: Motifs and Motivations* (Los Angeles: Univ. of California Press, 1986), pp.240–244; Flynn and Gerhardt, *Silent Brotherhood* (note 52); Robert I. Friedman, *The False Prophet: Rabbi Meir Kahane – From FBI Informant to Knesset Member* (NY: Lawrence Hill Books, 1990); Ehud Sprinzak, *The Ascendance of Israel's Radical Right* (NY: OUP, 1991), pp.211–214.

13 A subnational study of insurgency

FARC violence in the 1990s

Jennifer S. Holmes, Sheila Amin Gutiérrez de Piñeres and Kevin M. Curtin

Introduction

Many factors are theorized to be important to explain insurgency, including geography and history, the economy, government, and demography. Although Colombia is one of Latin America's oldest democracies, with a history of unusually consistent economic growth for the region, it is also home to one of the most entrenched leftist insurgencies in the world. Colombia is an ideal case to test these factors, due to the ability to analyze the issues at the subnational level and the variability of violence within the country. Although most of the research on Colombia is conducted at the national level, a subnational study of Colombia offers a unique opportunity to incorporate many of the theoretically important factors into a model of FARC violence. In this article, the analysis at the subnational level is based on unique dataset constructed from CINEP (Centro de Investigación y Educación Popular) and Colombian government sources. The subnational-level analysis can assist in the determination of whether the cross-national or national level results are supported at a disaggregated level. After extensive specification testing, the zero-inflated negative binomial regression was selected to model guerilla violence. In this analysis, a zero-inflated negative binomial regression model is utilized because the dependent variable (FARC human rights violations) is a count, with excess zeros and overdispersion. This model allows for different factors to account for the absence of violence (zeros) and the presence of violence (non-zeros). In this case, the forces that contribute to an absence of guerilla violence may be different from forces that explain the intensity of guerilla violence. Additionally, the model allows different processes to determine the absence of violence (zero counts). Based on the theories of guerilla violence, there could be multiple reasons why there is an absence of violence in a department—no exports to loot, high level of GDP or development, strong state presence, or other, unspecified factors.

When analyzing insurgencies, it is important to understand the origin and growth of the organization. Daniel Pecaut (1997) and Sánchez et al. (2003) remind scholars, especially in the case of the FARC, that factors contributing to later growth can be independent of factors that encouraged its emergence. Pecaut states that the pervasive Colombian violence has created its own influences on society, regardless of the original causes of the violence. Understanding old and new dynamics is essential to crafting an appropriate and effective policy response to the challenge of insurgency.

The FARC, the Revolutionary Armed Forces of Colombia (Fuerzas Armadas Revolucionarias de Colombia), is the dominant guerrilla group in Colombia, with approximately 17000 members.[1] The FARC, a dominant force in much of rural Colombia, also has a presence in the main cities (Petras 2000, 134). Formally, the FARC originated out of peasant self-defense groups in the 1960s. However, it has deeper historical roots, beginning in the 1920s and 1930s, in the early agrarian conflict of poor agricultural workers against the large landed estates (Pizarro 1992, 180, fn 26).

The FARC has continued to evolve since its founding, from a primarily localized movement, based on peasant support, to a revolutionary movement of national breadth, with fronts in both rural and urban areas. From the founding through the seventies, the FARC could still be considered a peasant movement of a limited geographic area. FARC support was based on their provision of basic order in parts of the country that did not have significant government presence (Rangel 1999; Vélez 2000; Medina Gallego 1990; Cubides 1998). The FARC builds on its original basis of demands for land reform, while adding charges of corruption, the perversion of capitalism, and U.S. imperialism to its motivations. Pecaut (1997, 915) argues that the motivations of the young guerrillas are very different than the older ones, in that the younger guerrillas tend to look at being a guerrilla as merely one potential job among many. Whether or not the group has become less ideological and more bureaucratized is not the subject of this study. Today the FARC consists of the following operational blocks. By the end of the twentieth century, the FARC had 67 rural and 4 urban fronts, composed of the Caribbean Block (Costa Atlántica), the Central Block (Tolima, Huila y Cundinamarca), the Southern Block (Nariño, Putumayo, and Caquetá), the Eastern Front (Meta, Vichada, and Guaviare), and the José María Córdoba Block (Urabá and Antioquia) (Vélez 2000, 6–9; Marks 2005[2]). By the 1990s, the FARC had been completely transformed.

The theoretical debate and testable hypotheses

Both economic and political factors are theorized to be essential in understanding the dynamics of insurgency. Economic factors can help understand both emergence and persistence of guerrilla conflict. Political factors can also inspire, suppress, or aggravate insurgency. This analysis examines traditional factors that have been purported to explain the prevalence of guerrilla violence at the subnational level.

Economic factors

There are two ways that economic factors can encourage insurgency. First, poor economic conditions may inspire sedition. In general, some scholars focus on hopelessness. Others, after controlling for the level of economic development, find no relationship between inequality and violence: Hardy (1979), Weede (1987), Weede and Tiefenbach (1981), and Collier (2000).[3] One direct connection between poverty and Colombian violence is that, in many cases, the guerrillas offer relatively higher wages than other available agricultural jobs (Sánchez 1998, 40).[4] In Colombia, there are long standing structural challenges in the countryside, resulting in persistent land conflict (Ortiz Sarmiento 1990–1991, Medina 1985–1986). As new crops become lucrative, old tensions reignite. For example, when new lands are brought into production (for coffee, coca, etc.) and peasants displaced, groups of bandits form to provide "protection" for the landowners from the recently displaced peasants. Beginning in the 1980s, with the advent of the drug agriculture, the aim has been to gain dominance, in the form of land ownership (Meertens 1997). Second, economic resources can serve as a financial basis for insurgent groups. Collier (2000) found:

> The factors which account for this difference between failure and success are to be found not in the "causes" which these two rebel organizations claim to espouse, but in their radically different opportunities to raise revenue ... the economic theory of conflict argues that the motivation of conflict is unimportant; what matters is whether the organization can sustain itself financially ...

> (Collier 2000, 2, 4)

In particular, primary commodity exports are "lootable because their production relies heavily on assets which are long-lasting and immobile" (Collier 2000, 9). Sánchez (1998, 39) documents that areas rich in primary export goods have become points of confrontation due to the importance of controlling these lucrative zones.

In addition to analyzing licit exports, it is important to examine illicit exports as a key source of financing of insurgent activities. Theoretically, illicit drugs can be conceptualized as a form of enclave production and thus more susceptible to predation. "It is evident that items produced in enclaves are more susceptible to predation. That makes them more attractive targets for both personal rulers and predatory rebels than are small agriculturalists because neither predation nor general state or market collapse will stop the revenue from flowing: even if their products are often looted, enclave producers will continue to generate goods because of extreme asset specificity, and because of general concentration, production will continue even in the face of general collapse" (Leonard and Straus 2003, 15). Given the combination of lucrative licit exports such as coffee, emeralds, coal, and oil in combination with illicit exports such as cocaine, Colombia is an ideal case in which to determine if predation is confined to licit exports, illicit exports, or exports in general.

Many scholars and U. S. officials cite the importance of coca production in fueling the Colombian conflict (Rochlin 2003; Byman et al. 2001; Pecaut 1997). For example, Francisco Thoumi (1995) pointed out "the drug trade has in fact weakened the country's economy by foster-ing violence and corruption, undermining legal activity, frightening off foreign investment, and all but destroying the social fabric." In Colombia, guerrillas fight for control of areas that can finance them (Bottía Noguera 2003, 44). Many scholars have discussed the financial basis of the group, but there is disagreement about the extent of the funding that comes from drugs. Some claim that the FARC is itself a cartel. For example, Villamarín Pulido (1996) cites military docu-ments claiming that the FARC is the third largest cartel in Colombia.[5] Despite suggestions that guerrilla groups such as the FARC are nothing more than another drug cartel, the reality is much more complicated. In areas where the guerrillas are too strong to eliminate, the drug traffickers pay the guerrillas a "tax' on their proceeds. Some scholars have probed the pragmatism of the relationship (Steiner 1999). In testimony to the U. S. House of Representatives, Marc Chernick dismissed claims of guerrilla groups operating as cartels as a distorted view of the true relationship between guerrillas and the drug trade. Instead, the groups tax the drug trade as any other source of income—illicit or licit (House of Representatives Committee on International Relations 104th Congress). The FARC's financial basis rests on extortion of both licit and illicit businesses in areas under its control and kidnapping (Shifter 1999, 15 and Sánchez et al. 2003, 12). Ortiz Sarmiento (1990–1991, 269) estimated that the group taxes production at rates of 10 percent and commerce at 8 percent. Some scholars cite particular times and circumstances in which there have been drug FARC ties. Edgar Torres (1995) tells of a 1977 decision of the narcos to locate processing facilities in guerrilla controlled areas, outside of the government purview. As the narcos purchased lands, their incentive to cooperate with guerrillas changed. Eventually, instead of having the guerrillas provide order (and impose their "tax"), the narcos funded their own paramilitary armies, often fighting the guerrillas for local control (Pecaut 1997, 908; Rochlin 2003, 100). How much of the recent growth of the FARC is due to funding from the drug trade? Rochlin (2003) discussed the complicated relationship between the FARC and coca. He cited an interview with the UNDCP, in which officials explain that some FARC members are involved, but it is not uniform among the leaders or the rank and file. However, he claims that much of the department by department spread of the FARC was due to drug cultivation in areas of its control (Rochlin 2003, 137, 99).

As applied in this analysis, the authors are able to operationalize economic factors in the following hypotheses.

Hypothesis 1. Guerrilla violence is positively associated with exports because easily lootable exports (illicit or licit) provide an accessible source of funding for non-state violent groups.

Hypothesis 2. Higher levels of insurgency will be associated with low levels of GDP per capita or negative growth rates.

Government factors

For 40 years, Colombia has faced an insurgency that the government has not been able to control. As recently as the last few years, some parts of the country did not have any government representatives in many municipalities. Power vacuums are then filled by leftist guerrilla groups or rightist paramilitary groups. Scholars such as Fearon and Laitin (2003, 76) hypothesize "that financially, organizationally, and politically weak central governments render insurgency more feasible and attractive due to weak local policing or inept and corrupt counterinsurgency practices." Other scholars recognize that cycles of violence can become established, with different types of violence (guerrilla, state, or paramilitary) intensifying conflicts as opposed to suppressing them. Hayes (2001) finds that widespread exposure to violence results in support for paramilitary movements and can create a cycle of perpetual violence. Mason and Krane (1989) highlight the importance of examining both state and paramilitary violence. In general, scholars such as Schock (1996) find that semi-repressive regimes have higher levels of violence.

These issues are well documented in the specific works on Colombia. Ortiz Sarmiento (1990–1991) generally found that violence during *La Violencia* was a product of an incremental chain of retaliation between the Liberals and Conservatives and that private justice has been common throughout Colombian history because of a relatively weak police and military presence. As Waldmann (1997) pointed out, Colombia has not had a unifying dictatorship, such as the Porfiriato in Mexico. For example, in 1949, there were only 15000 soldiers, compared to 4,500 guerrillas. Later, under Rojas Pinilla (1953–1957), the military increased to 42000, still a relatively small number in a country of 11.5 million (Ortiz Sarmiento 1990–1991, 253–254). Byman et al. (2001) criticizes contemporary Colombia for its low military spending, with only 3.1 percent of GDP spent on military expenditures in 1998. Power vacuums are then filled by leftist guerrilla groups or rightist paramilitary groups. Specifically within Colombia, Sánchez found large centers of guerrilla activity during *La Violencia* in parts of the country with recent settlement, land conflict, open frontier, rough topography, lack of state presence, and support of liberal landowners (Sánchez 1992, 92). Similarly, Ortiz Sarmiento (1990–1991) found a pattern of violence in areas of recent settlement. In particular, when settlement occurred without a robust state presence, insurgency tends to follow. In Colombia, certain areas tend to be conflict prone. Collier (2000) found that "if a country has recently had a civil war its risk of further war is much higher" (Collier 2000, 6). Previous wars, such as the war of the thousand days (1899–1901), and *La Violencia* (1946–1958) primarily occurred in the countryside, in remote regions, with little state presence (Waldmann 1997, 411). Some scholars, such as Pizarro, recognize a geographical overlap among successive Colombian conflicts (Pizarro 1992, 175). More recently, many blame the National Front for a legacy of political exclusion, insufficient legitimacy, and insurgency (Medina 1985–1986). Although the National Front, which lasted from 1958–1974, ended the war between the Liberals and Conservatives, the lack of mobility and flexibility of the National Front "gave rise to an opposition that, lacking a means of expression, turned toward a plan of radical rupture" (Pecaut 1992, 227).

The following hypotheses are tested to examine the relationship between political factors and FARC violence:

Hypothesis 3. Guerrilla violence is expected to emerge in the context of weak state presence.
Hypothesis 4. Higher levels of state repression will be associated with higher levels of insurgent
  violence.

In testing the stated hypotheses, the analysis needs to control for additional factors, such as
population, eradication of illicit crops, and general level of development. This literature review
highlights the importance of incorporating a broad range of explanatory factors into an analysis
of FARC violence. Although most of the research on Colombia is conducted at the national level,
a subnational study of Colombia offers a unique opportunity to incorporate many of the
theoretically important factors into a model of FARC violence.

Model specification, methodology, and analysis

Although at the national level, Colombia has seen a rise in drug cultivation and a concomitant
increase in violence, to claim that the increase in drug cultivation is the source of FARC violence
appears to be an oversimplification of the underlying causes of the violence. The national-level
data are not appropriate for time series analysis because of the limited data and the short time
span. Moreover, as Guillermo O'Donnell pointed out, "current theories of the state often make
an assumption which recurs in the current theories of democracy: that of a high degree of
homogeneity scope, both territorial and functional, of the state and of the social order it supports"
(O'Donnell 1999, 130). In the Colombian case, clarity may be gained by examining differences
among departments.[6] The country, in some respects, is a nominal nation, in which many parts
have never been under effective government control. In Colombia, there are 32 subnational
political territories called departments. From the original Spanish colonization through
contemporary times, significant differences persist into the current period. Examining the range
of FARC activity throughout the country, as opposed to examining only national level trends, will
provide a sharper focus to the Colombian internal dynamic. Sambanis highlighted that case
studies of civil war have "challenged the unit-homogeneity assumption that underlies current
quantitative work. This should prompt analysts to test for fixed effects by country, region, or
period" (Sambanis 2004, 273). An alternative approach to fixed effects is to use the zero-inflated
negative binomial regression to account for unobserved sources of heterogeneity (omitted
variables) that differentiate departmental violence. The zero-inflated negative binomial model is
particularly useful in situations with omitted variables, which can be captured in the respecified
error term. Year dummy variables capture unmodelled changes over time.

After extensive specification testing, the zero-inflated negative binomial regression was selected
to model FARC violence. In this analysis, a zero-inflated negative binomial regression model is
utilized because the dependent variable (FARC human rights violations) is a count, with excess
zeros and overdispersion. Almost 32 percent of the departments do not have FARC activity at one
time or another, making the data an appropriate candidate for the zero-inflated model. This
model allows for different factors to account for zeros and non-zeros. In this case, the forces that
contribute to an absence of FARC violence may be different from forces that explain the intensity
of FARC violence. Additionally, the model allows different processes to determine the zero counts.
In the Colombian case, there could be multiple reasons why there is no violence in a department—
no exports to loot, high level of GDP or development, strong state presence, or other, unknown
factors. (Table 13.1 presents the results.)

This is an original dataset, compiled from Colombian sources. The violence variables in the
data set used for this analysis were constructed from raw departmental data collected by the
Centro de Investigación y Educación Popular (CINEP) in Bogotá, Colombia and their Banco de
Datos sobre Derechos Humanos y Violencia Política.[7] The dependent variable, FARC human

Table 13.1 Zero-inflated negative binomial regression of human rights violations committed by the FARC 1993–1998

Independent variables	Logit		Negative binomial	
	Estimate	Z-score	Estimate	Z-score
Primary exports in millions US$1995	0.00949	0.52	.00102*	2.06
GDP in 1994 Pesos (Billions)	0.01496*	2.04	−.0003***	−3.34
Human rights violations by government forces	2.0500†	1.84	.0353**	2.74
Human rights violations by paramilitaries	1.4521†	1.92	.0052*	2.22
Population in millions	−9.1268	−1.55	.8156***	3.63
Coca cultivation	0.0068	0.00	.00001	1.46
Justice and security spending (Millions of 1998 pesos)	−0.6758*	−2.10	−.00396	−0.91
1994	3.569	0.90	0.7955***	3.25
1995	−6.696†	−1.82	0.6856**	2.57
1996	−0.2395	−0.06	0.5867*	2.33
1997	−0.5194	−0.15	0.5510*	2.13
1998	−0.4564	−0.17	0.8571***	3.39
Constant	−7.9118*	−1.94	0.3225	1.37
Ln α			−.6140***	−3.69
α			.5411	
Vuong test of zero inflated negative binomial standard negative binomial: z =	5.84***			
N	192			
(FARC H.R. Violations) > 0	138			
Mean FARC H.R. Violations	6.48			
LR χ^2 (12)	110.53***			

Logit model: Pr (Number of FARC human rights violations > 0).
*** = $p < .001$, ** = $p < .01$, * = $p < .05$, † = $p < .10$.
Note: The significant Chi-squared further reveals that taken as a group the estimated coefficients display a high degree of statistical significance.

rights violations, includes a spectrum of activity, ranging from threats to killings. The number of FARC human rights violations range from 0–93. This measure of violence facilitates an understanding of either an escalation or de-escalation of violence (Sambanis 2004). An important political factor, state strength, can be assessed by justice and security spending. Municipal justice and security spending (aggregated to the department level) are indicators of government police and military capability. These figures are provided by the Departamento Nacional de Planacion (DNP), in 1998 constant pesos and range from 0 to 313,000,000 pesos. Previous studies, such as that of Fearon and Laitin (2003), use per capita income as a proxy for these capabilities, instead of directly measuring actual security and justice expenditures as is done in this article. Gross domestic product per capita in constant 1994 pesos, obtained from Departamento Administrativo Nacional de Estadisticas (DANE), measures the general level of development. These estimates are provided at the department level and range from 624,787 to 6,872,523 pesos. Primary exports, on the other hand, are a measure of foreign exchange income streams, and are theoretically easily captured for the support of rebellious activities. Primary exports, in constant 1995 U. S. dollars, are from the Ministerio de Comercio, Industria y Turismo and range from 0 to $642,987,000. Coca estimates are incorporated into the model because it is a special category of "lootable exports." Coca cultivations numbers, in hectares, are provided by the Colombian National Police and range from 0–39,400 hectares. Other important factors included as control variables are population (from DANE), which range from 25,083 to 6,112,196, paramilitary violations (from CINEP), which range from 0–315, and state violence from 0–40 violations.

The results support the idea of a continuous cycle of violence. In general, it was found that for departments that have FARC violence in the initial year there is an increasing trend of FARC violence throughout the years from 1993–1998, reflecting an escalation of violence. However, in the departments that do not already have FARC violence, the probability of experiencing FARC violence does not significantly increase in any year. The intensity of guerilla violence increases over time; yet, the probability that a region will be newly infiltrated does not change over time.

Now the results in relation to the hypotheses studied are examined. Economic factors do explain some degree of the violence. Hypothesis one theorizes that guerrilla violence is positively associated with exports because easily lootable exports (illicit or licit) provide an accessible source of funding for non-state violent groups. As theorized by Collier (2000) and others, primary exports appear to attract guerrilla operations. In the logit model, departments that do not currently have FARC violence will not have a greater probability of experiencing FARC violence in the future, regardless of their resource base. On the contrary, in departments that already have FARC violence, there is a positive relationship between primary exports and FARC violence. Contrary to expectations, illicit exports, as represented by coca cultivation, are insignificant in all of the models. These results suggest that at least in the case of Colombia while licit exports may be a source of funding, illicit exports were not found to be a significant source of funding for the FARC.

Hypothesis two states that higher levels of insurgency will be associated with low levels of GDP per capita or negative growth rates. In the logit model, which measures the probability that a department will move from a zero to non-zero state of FARC violence, it was found that the higher the GDP, the more likely that FARC violence will follow. However, in departments that already have FARC violence, a positive relationship was found between lower GDP and FARC violence. These seemingly contrary results reflect the historical propensity of the FARC to operate in relatively underdeveloped areas, while reflecting the more recent FARC strategy of extending its areas of operation outside of its historic stronghold. These results suggest that although the FARC finds its historical stronghold in lesser developed regions of Colombia, it is now strategically moving into regions with the higher GDP.

Hypothesis three, the notion that guerrilla violence is more common in areas with a weak state presence, is partially supported in the models as indicated by aggregated municipal justice and security spending.[8] When examining departments without initial FARC violence, it was found that justice and security spending reduces the probability of future FARC violence. However, in areas where FARC violence is established, levels of justice and security spending are insignificant in explaining intensity. This suggests that increased justice and security spending in currently peaceful departments would deter the spread of FARC violence. Another indicator of state presence based on the number of municipal officials per thousand inhabitants, is available (see Figure 13.1). The authors are unable to include it in the regression model because the data only exists for 1995, but the trends can still be visualized. There is no apparent relationship between FARC violence and state presence, in the maps. The authors address the question of hegemonic dominance later in the article utilizing a more qualitative approach.

Hypothesis four theorizes that higher levels of state repression will be associated with higher levels of insurgent violence. Mason and Krane (1989) highlighted the importance of examining both state and paramilitary violence. Consistent across all models is the finding that high levels of repression are associated with higher levels of insurgent violence, although the causality is unclear.[9] Both government human rights violations and paramilitary violence are associated with higher levels of insurgent violence. Colombia may be experiencing a pattern in which the government loses popular support as a result of indiscriminate repression against suspected rebels (Holmes 2001; Schock 1996).

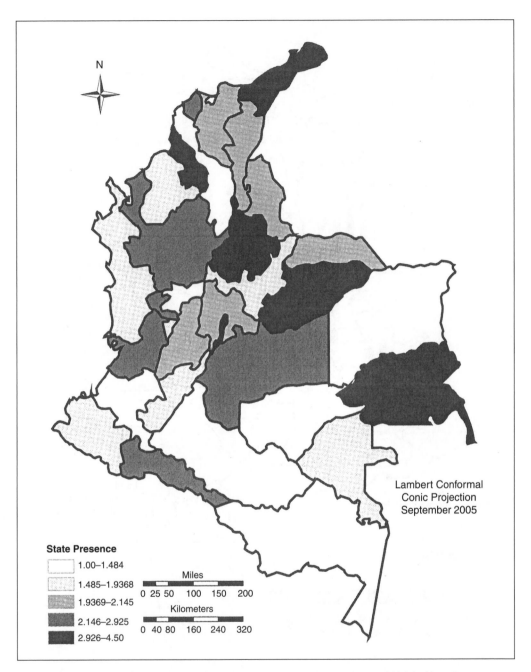

Figure 13.1 State presence in Colombia (in number of municipal officials per 1000 inhabitants).

Source: Banco de Datos sobre Derechos Humanos y Violencia Politica Centro de Investigacion y Educacion Popular (CINEP) Bogota, Colombia, 2002.

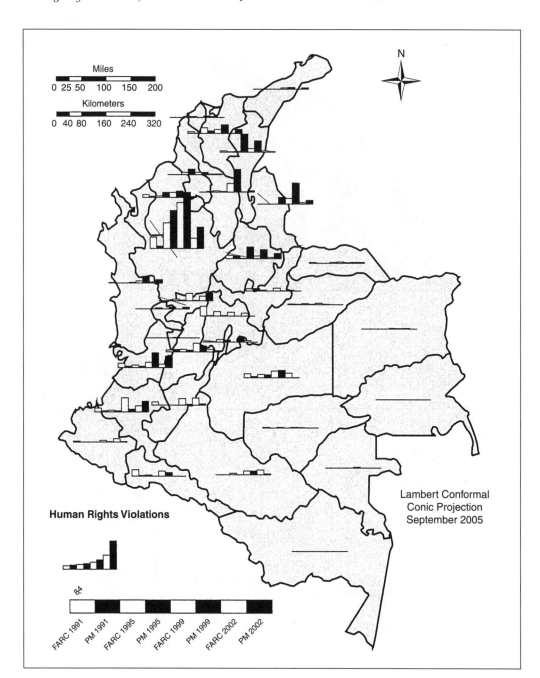

Figure 13.2 Incidents of FARC and Para military human rights violations in Colombia 1991, 1995, 1999, 2002.

Source: Banco de Datos sobre Derechos Humanos y Violencia Politica Centro de Investigacion y Educacion Popular (CINEP) Bogota, Colombia, 2002.

Some scholars may instead look for patterns of hegemony of different violent groups. In the formal model, no evidence of this is seen in either the logit model predicting the probability of experiencing FARC violence for the first time or the negative binomial regression to explain intensity of FARC violence. However, to explore these relationships further, the authors analyzed the patterns of conflict in departments that appeared to have a preponderance of one type of violence. Figure 13.2 maps FARC and paramilitary violence.

Four departments appear to have a relative predominance of violence. In Cesar and Santander, there appears to be more paramilitary violence. In Cundinamarca and Huila, the FARC appear to be more active. Presumably, if there is a hegemonic presence of one violent group, one would expect either generally low levels of conflict, reflecting an absence of conflict because effective monopoly of force had been established or a high level of one type of violence without violent challenges from other groups. To explore this, different types of violence were graphed from 1990 to 1998.

The category of social/political violence contains human rights violations that appear to be politically or socially motivated and where attributions of responsibility cannot be made. It is not included as an independent variable because these acts may contain incidents of unattributed FARC violence and also likely contain incidents of paramilitary or public forces violence. Including this category of violence in the regression analysis would affect the interpretation of the existing attributed violence variables of the paramilitary or public forces.[10] Although social/political violence cannot be included in the regression model, it does add to the qualitative analysis presented.

In Cesar and Santander, there appears to be a predominance of paramilitary violence in 1991, 1995, and 1999. When analyzed over time, however, the trends are more complex. In Figure 13.3,

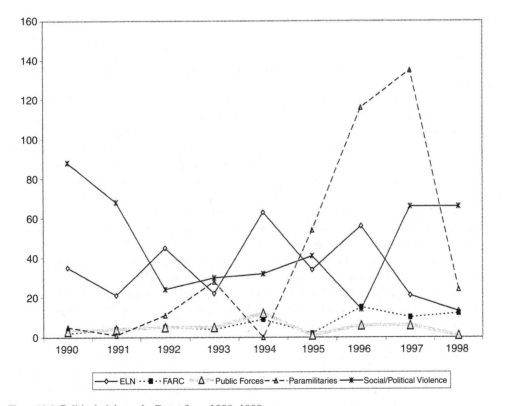

Figure 13.3 Political violence in Cesar from 1990–1998.

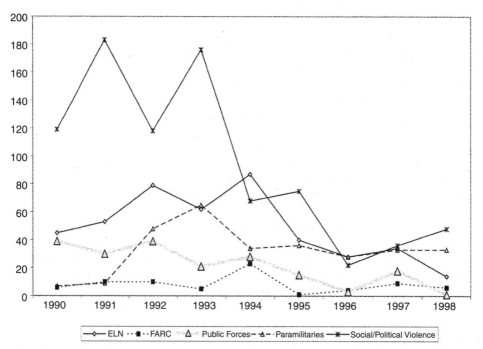

Figure 13.4 Political violence in Santander from 1990–1998.

although paramilitary violence is higher in those three years, there is still seen significant ELN violence, persistent modest levels of FARC violence, and high levels of unattributed violence. As paramilitary violence escalates in 1995 and 1996, ELN violence decreases in 1997 and 1998, and FARC violence increases in 1995. Moreover, unattributed violence spikes in 1997 and remains constant in 1998.

Trends of violence in Santander also appear to be significantly more complex than a simple story of hegemonic dominance (see Figure 13.4). In fact, unattributed social and political violence is the most dominant form of violence during this time period. FARC violence remains at a low level of activity, as does the ELN, despite a general decline after 1994. Even though violence appears to be generally tapering off in the later time period, all types of violence remain.

Figure 13.5 presents trends of violence in Huila. Here, as FARC violence greatly increases in 1991, unattributed and ELN violence fall. Furthermore, violence by public forces increases in 1992, as FARC violence begins to fall. However, by 1996, both FARC and paramilitary violence increase. In 1997 and 1998, unattributed violence drastically increases, whereas FARC violence remains stable and paramilitary violence declines.

In Cundinamarca, spikes in FARC violence accompany declines in both government human rights violations and paramilitary violence (Figure 13.6). However, the significant increase in unattributed violence is accompanied by stable FARC and paramilitary violence. A closer examination of these four departments demonstrates the difficulty of inferring hegemonic dominance of one group over another. Ideally, to examine the possibility of local control or hegemonic dominance by one group, municipal level data would be needed. Although some violence data is available at that level, the economic indicators necessary for a complete analysis are not. Moreover, Ortiz (2002, 140) noted that the FARC internal structure is unusual in that resources flow from the bottom of the organization up to general staff, who still maintains control of strategy and decisions. This further complicates a municipal level analysis.

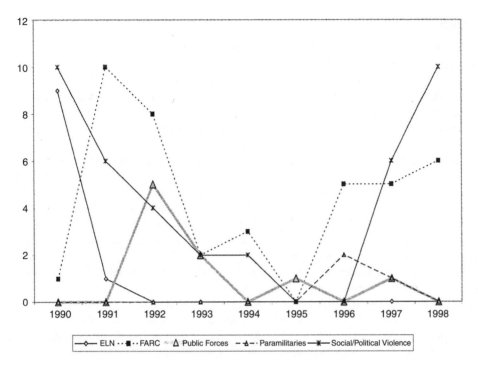

Figure 13.5 Political violence in Huila 1990–1998.

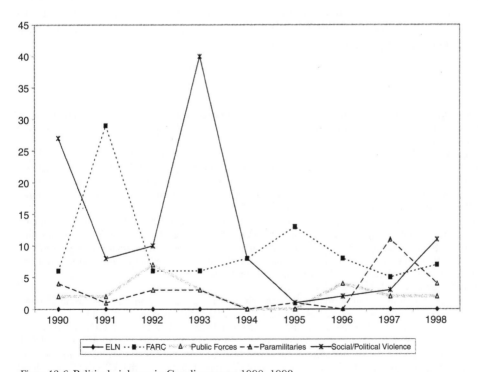

Figure 13.6 Political violence in Cundinamarca 1990–1998.

Conclusions

This analysis of Colombian FARC violence both sharpens the larger debate on insurgency and provides insight to the particular Colombian case. In Colombia, the utilization of a department level analysis is essential to uncover the factors fueling FARC insurgency. Theories of violence posit the importance of economic resources to explain the funding and activity of violent groups. Contrary to the expectations of many scholars and government officials, coca production does not explain either the onset of FARC violence or its intensity. Primary exports tend to increase the intensity of FARC violence, but do not make a department more likely to experience it if it was previously peaceful. As expected among areas with preexisting FARC, more FARC violence is present in areas of a low level of development or negative growth. However, consistent with FARC plans to move the conflict to new parts of the country, previously peaceful areas are more likely to experience FARC violence as their GDP rises. This analysis also suggests that FARC violence is positively correlated with both state and paramilitary violence in both initial and latter stages. Although the causality is not clear, this result suggests a possible counterproductive effect of repression or paramilitary violence on guerrilla activity.

In addition to increasing understanding of the Colombian conflict, this study refines general theory in the following ways. First, a more accurate measure of state strength or capacity should be used. The Colombian subnational analysis provided a precise measure—actual security and justice spending and a ratio of public officials to the population. Second, a subnational analysis provides an opportunity for increased rigor, through increasing the number of comparable cases, while encountering fewer problems associated with cross national studies. Finally, the importance of model specification in studying conflict is revealed. The zero-inflated negative binomial is a more appropriate model in that it allows both the analysis of zero and non-zero states in addition to the examination of the factors that lead to an increased probability of movement from a zero to non-zero state. Traditional OLS and Poisson models are inadequate in capturing the underlying dynamics of both intensity and onset of violence.

Notes

1   For the purpose of this article, only the FARC is included in the analysis. Another main group, the ELN, is smaller and concentrated in the oil-producing part of the country. The ELN has publicly criticized the FARC for its connection to the coca trade.
2   Special thanks to Thomas A. Marks for a current 2005 assessment of the FARC.
3   For the debate about violence and inequality, see Sigelman and Simpson (1977), Muller (1985), Muller and Seligson (1987), Boswell and Dixon (1990), and Schock (1996). For a relevant discussion of the debate as it pertains to Colombia, see Sanin, Francisco Gutiérrez, "Crimen e impunidad. Precisiones sobre la violencia" en *Revista de Estudios Sociales* (June 1999, no. 3), pp. 133–136.
4   For a discussion of these factors and homicide rates, see Sarmiento y Becerra (1998); Alfredo Sarmiento Gómez (1999) "Violencia y equidad," *Planeación y Desarrollo* 30(3), pp. 47–62; and, Echandía Castilla, Camilo (1999) "El conflicto armado y las manifestaciones de violencia en las regiones de Colombia," (Bogotá, Colombia: Oficina del Alto Comisionado para la Paz). A Colombian classic work attributing violence to poverty is Comisión de Estudios sobre la Violencia (1987).
5   See also *Semana* 354, 20 February 1989.
6   For a discussion of the role of subnational comparison in comparative research, see Arend Lijphart (1971, 689). *American Political Science.* More recently, see Snyder (2001) or Peters (1998, 44).
7   Some commentators and U.S. embassy officials have challenged the validity of CINEP's data. For example, Mary Anastasia O'Grady (2004) repeats State Department allegations that CINEP "methodology creates a heavy bias against the Colombian government while it grants a wide berth to guerrilla insurgents" (p. A17). O'Grady quotes an embassy report that claims that CINEP "follows legal conventions that define 'human-rights violations' as crimes that can only be committed by the state or

state-sponsored actors, which it presumes paramilitaries to be" (p. A17). In reality, CINEP tallies human rights violations among both state and non-state actors and differentiates between human rights violations committed by different actors, ranging from the FARC to the police. At times, CINEP includes incidents in multiple categories (see CINEP 2001), however, this issue is not relevant for this analysis because only one category is employed in this study. As with any dataset, the potential for bias exists. However, the authors believe any bias is consistent throughout time in this study because the included data were generated directly from CINEP's Base de Datos using consistent categories. Especially in politically sensitive areas such as violence statistics, it is prudent to compare nongovernment and government numbers because different groups may have incentives to over or under report, respectively. Because of this possibility and the controversy surrounding CINEP figures, this study compared official government data on terrorism with CINEP figures for this period. The correlations between CINEP numbers of total leftist guerrilla group violations and government numbers of terrorism is high (.7424) from 1991–1998. A comparison of terrorism incidents with human rights violations is not a direct comparison of exact same phenomenon, but the relatively high correlation provides confidence in CINEP numbers. Moreover, the CINEP database differentiates attribution of responsibility, which is essential when analyzing the violence of distinct groups with different goals.

8 Ideally, other factors, such as military presence, or a ratio of officials to citizens, would be incorporated into the model. However, these data are unavailable for each time period.

9 Different types of violence exist in Colombia, with distinct origins and effects. Because this study included different types of violence, it is prudent to check for multicollinearity—especially considering human rights violations by paramilitaries and government forces. To this end, all models were run using OLS to generate variance inflation factors (VIFs) for the independent variables specified in the models. In model one, the average VIF was 1.62. In model two, the average VIF was 1.61. Model three had an average of 1.59. Model four had an average VIF of 1.58. Only one variable had a score over 2—model 3 with human rights violations by public forces scoring 2.01. All others were under two. None of the scores indicate problems with multicollinearity.

10 During the years of 1990–1998, the correlations between unattributed social/political violence and attributed human rights violations is as follows: FARC .4790, ELN .5728, Paramilitary .2940, and Public Forces .6108.

References

Boswell, Terry, and William Dixon. 1990. "Dependency and rebellion: A cross-national analysis." *American Sociological Review* 55(4), pp. 540–559.

Bottía Noguera, Martha. 2003. "La presencia y expansión municipal de las FARC: Es avaricia y contagio, más que ausencia estatal?" Documento CEDE 2003–2003.

Byman, Daniel, Peter Chalk, Bruce Hoffman, William Rosenau, and David Brannan. 2001. *Trends in outside support for insurgent movements.* Santa Monica, CA: Rand.

CINEP. 2001. "Síntesis del marco conceptual." *Noche y Niebla* 22.

Collier, Paul. 2000. "Economic causes of civil conflict and their implications for policy." Washington, DC: World Bank.

Comisión de Estudios sobre la Violencia. 1987. *Colombia: Violencia y democracia.* Informe presentado al Ministerio de Gobierno. Bogotá: Universidad Nacional de Colombia.

Cubides, Fernando. 1998. "Los bemoles del despeje." *Coyuntura Política* No. 11

Fearon, James, and David Laitin. 2003. "Ethnicity, insurgency, and civil war." *American Political Science Review* 97(1), pp. 75–90.

Hardy, Melissa A. 1979. "Economic growth, distributional inequality, and political conflict in industrial societies." *Journal of Political and Military Sociology* 7(Fall), pp. 209–227.

Hayes, Bernadette. 2001. "Sowing dragon's teeth: Public support for political violence and paramilitarism in Northern Ireland." *Political Studies* 49, pp. 901–922.

Holmes, Jennifer S. 2001. *Terrorism and democratic stability. Perpectives on democratization.* Manchester: Manchester University Press.

Leonard, David K., and Scott Straus. 2003. *Africa's stalled development: International causes and cures.* Boulder, CO: Lynne Rienner.

Lijphart, Arendt. 1971. "Comparative politics and the comparative method." *American Political Science Review* 65(3), pp. 682–693.

Mason, T. David, and Dale A. Krane. 1989. "The political economy of death squads: Toward a theory of the impact of state-sanctioned terror." *International Studies Quarterly* 33(2), pp. 175–198.

Medina Gallego, Carlos. 1990. *Autodefensas, paramilitares y narcotráfico en Colombia: Origen, desarrollo y consolidación. El caso de Puerto Boyacá.* Bogotá: Editorial Documentos Periodísticos.

Medina, Mendofilo. 1985–1986. "Algunos factores de violencia en el sistema politico Colombiano 1930–1986." *Anuario Colombiano de Historia Social y de la Cultura* 13–14, pp. 281–297.

Meertens, Donny. 1997. *Tierra, violencia, y género: Hombres y mujeres en la historia rural de Colombia, 1930–1990.* Rotterdam: Katholieke Universiteit Nijmengen.

Muller, Edward, and Mitchell Seligson. 1987. "Inequality and insurgency." *American Political Science Review* 81(2), pp. 425–451.

Muller, Edward N. 1985. "Income inequality, regime repressiveness, and political violence." *American Sociological Review* 50(1), pp. 47–61.

O'Donnell, Guillermo. 1999. "A Latin American view." In *Counterpoints: Selected essays on authoritarianism and democratization,* ed. Guillermo O'Donnell. Notre Dame, IN: University of Notre Dame.

O'Grady, Mary Anastasia. *Wall Street Journal.* (Eastern edition). New York, 6 February, 2004, p. A17.

Ortiz, Román. 2002. "Insurgent strategies in the post-Cold War: The case of the Revolutionary Armed Forces of Colombia." *Studies in Conflict and Terrorism* 25, pp. 127–143.

Ortiz Sarmiento, Carlos Miguel. 1990–1999. "Violencia política de los ochenta: Elementos para una reflexión historica." *Anuario Colombiano de Historica Social y de la Cultura* 18, pp. 245–280.

Pecaut, Daniel. 1992. "Guerrillas and violence." In *Violence in Colombia: The contemporary crisis in historical perspective,* ed. Charles Bergquist, Ricardo Peñaranda, and Gonzalo Sánchez. Wilmington, DE: SR Books.

Peters, B. Guy. 1998. *Comparative politics: Theory and methods.* New York: New York University Press.

Petras, James. 2000. "The FARC faces the empire." *Latin American Perspectives* 27(5), pp. 134–143.

Pizarro, Eduardo. 1992. "Revolutionary guerrilla groups in Colombia." In *Violence in Colombia: The contemporary crisis in historical perspective,* ed. Charles Bergquist, Ricardo Peñaranda, and Gonzalo Sánchez. Wilmington, DE: SR Books.

Rangel, Alfredo. 1999. *Las FARC-EP: Una mirada actual.* Compilado por Malcom Deas y María Victoria Llorente en Reconocer la Guerra para construir la Paz. Bogotá: Editorial Norma.

Rochlin, James F. 2003. *Vanguard revolutionaries in Latin America.* Boulder, CO: Lynne Rienner.

Sambanis, Nicholas. 2004. "Using case studies to expand economic models of civil wars." *Perspectives on Politics* 2, pp. 259–279.

Sánchez, Fabio José, Ana María Díaz, and Michel Formisano. 2003. "Conflicto, violencia y actividad criminal en Colombia: Un análisis espacial." *Archivos de Economía* Documento 219.

Sánchez, Gonzalo. 1992. "The violence: An interpretative synthesis." In *Violence in Colombia: The contemporary crisis in historical perspective,* ed. Charles Bergquist, Ricardo Peñaranda, and Gonzalo Sánchez. Wilmington, DE: SR Books.

Sánchez, Gonzalo. 1998. "Colombia: Violencias sin futuros." *Foro Internacional* 38(1), pp. 37–58.

Schock, Kurt. 1996. "A conjunctural model of political conflict: The impact of political opportunities on the relationship between economic inequality and violent political conflict." *Journal of Conflict Resolution* 40(1), pp. 98–133.

Shifter, Michael. 1999. "Colombia on the brink." *Foreign Affairs* 78(4), pp. 14–20.

Sigelman, L., and M. Simpson. 1977. "Cross national test of linkage between economic inequality and political violence." *Journal of Conflict Resolution* 21(1), pp. 105–128.

Snyder, Richard. 2001. "Scaling down: The subnational comparative method." *Studies in Comparative International Development* 36(1), pp. 93–110.

Steiner, Roberto. 1999. "Hooked on drugs: Colombian-US relations." In *The United States and Latin America: The new agenda,* ed. Victor Bulmer-Thomas and James Dunkerly, 159–175. London: Institute of Latin American Studies, University of London.

Thoumi, Francisco. 1995. *Political economy and illegal drugs in Colombia.* Boulder, CO: Lynne Rienner.

Torres Arias, Edgar. 1995. *Mercaderes de la muerte.* Bogotá: Inermedio Editores, Circulo de Lectores.

Vélez, María Alejandra. 2000. "Farc—Eln evolución y expansión territorial." CEDE. Centro de Estudios sobre Desarrollo Económico. Universidad de los Andes. Documento CEDE 2000–2008.

Villamarín, Pulido, and Mayor Luis Alberto. 1996. *El cartel de las FARC.* 2nd edn. Editorial El Faraón.

Waldmann, Peter. 1997. "Cotiianización de la violencia: El ejemplo de Colombia." *Ibero-Amerikanisches Archiv* 23(3/4), pp. 409–437.

Weede, Erich, and H. Tiefenbach. 1981. "Some recent explanations of income inequality." *International Studies Quarterly* 25(2), pp. 255–282.

Weede, Erich. 1987. "Some new evidence on correlates of political violence: Income inequality, regime repressiveness, and economic development." *European Sociological Review* 3(2), pp. 97–108.

14 Al Qaeda

A different diagnosis

Xavier Raufer

What is really dangerous today?

The demise of the bipolar world order has caused more than walls to crumble, which, in Berlin and elsewhere, had rendered impassable the frontiers of the former Eastern Bloc. Other, psychological, obstacles have also disappeared. Thus the binary representations of yesterday's world—East versus West, political against criminal—now no longer make sense. "Political" players (guerrillas, militias, liberation movements, terrorist groups) and "common criminals" (organized crime, mafias, cartels) that yesterday were evolving differently and distinctly suddenly occupied the same stage. By choice? No, but without their former sponsors, their only option was either mutation or disappearance.

First, do these mutant entities represent a new threat? Yes, indeed. This can be easily demonstrated using an image from Karl Marx, who compared the revolution with heating water over a fire. Until it reaches boiling point, water only experiences a change of degree. Once it turns to steam at 100°, it changes character. In contrast to political unrest, insurrection, or riot, a revolution marks a change of character—and no longer of degree—in a country's sociopolitical reality. The same applies to these new threats. None of them is either original or recent in their own right. Just an example: there have always been Islamists, smugglers, and criminals in Algeria. But when a hybrid/symbiotic, fundamentalist–outlaw–thug entity like the GIA (Islamic Armed Group) wages an armed struggle, resists the most radical repression, summary executions, and so forth, and within three years of its appearance is able to put Algeria to the sword and the torch, hijack a French airliner, and carry out a wave of bomb attacks in France, through recruitment from within French territory, there is a situation without precedence. Failing to understand this means failing to understand the shape that real warfare will adopt in this new century.

Mutations: why and how

In scientific parlance, the end of the bipolar order has caused the mutation of a host of organisms that used to be purely terrorist groups or purely criminal groups. In other words, they have abruptly and unexpectedly shifted from machines (technomorph structures) to lifeforms (biomorph entities).

Machines. During the Cold War, most transnational terrorism was waged by groups organized or recruited by intelligence agencies working for states. Secretly obeying orders, they operated like machines, following start/stop signals.

Lifeforms. Since the collapse of the bipolar world, we are witnessing an almost biological, uncontrollable, and, thus far, unrestrained, proliferation of dangerous, complex entities that are very hard to identify, understand, and define within inadequately explored territories or movements.

The new dangerous entities: a typology

Diverse they may be, but these dangerous entities have nonetheless some common characteristics:

*   De-territorialization, or location in inaccessible areas.
*   Usually, an absence of state sponsorship, which makes them more unpredictable and uncontrollable.
*   A hybrid character, partly "political" or religious-fanatic, partly criminal.
*   An ability to rapidly mutate, according to the almighty dollar, now essential.
*   A pragmatic approach, following the old Maoist doctrine of "waging guerrilla to learn about warfare" (hence the GIA's primitive bombs in France, between July and November 1995).
*   Enormous killing power, compared with Cold-War terrorism, which was usually little more than symbolic; in April 1995, the Aum sect only failed to kill 40,000 in the Tokyo Metro because an aerosol blocked. And the 9/11 attacks killed fifteen times more people than the bloodiest terrorist attack of the twentieth century.

Keeping this in mind, this article's first prognosis is that Al Qaeda looks much like one of these chaotic, dangerous new entities. But before trying to prove it, thus transforming this prognosis into a diagnosis, this article examines why finding Al Qaeda's real character is so important. Why bother?

Why it is important to know

When SARS erupted in China, spread in Hong Kong, then elsewhere in the world, the first move of the concerned authorities (World Health Organization, etc.) was to define this new and atypical disease, that is, find the exact germ causing it. In less than a month, a virus had been identified. All the further programs aimed at combating the disease (tests, vaccine, etc.) would from now on stand on a firm ground.

Surprisingly, and even if Al Qaeda constitutes the most serious immediate threat to the security of the United States and has committed the worst terrorist attacks ever, no one in the United States seems, to this day, really sure of what Al Qaeda is. Even worse, the question "what is Al Qaeda?" seems futile, even meaningless, to an American administration persuaded it knows what Al Qaeda really is—a well-known entity, clearly defined and devoid of mystery.

Do they? Is it? No. Reading the available documentation shows it—these texts are like a pyramid sitting on its point. Because of a lack of initial definition, Al Qaeda is floating between contradictory descriptions, comparisons and metaphors. It remains an "unidentified terrorist object." This lack of definition is all the more curious given that in some of these texts, various technical points are clearly and specifically defined, showing the authors are conscious of the importance of definitions. One example: "systems: we use the word system in the sense of ..."

So, in the end, is Al Qaeda a "clearinghouse," an "extremist islamist group," a "global network," an "entity," an "organization," a "system," a "secret international brotherhood," a "powerful Islamic force," a "dispersed and amorphous terrorist foe"? Is it "more than an organization, also a process"? Is it "a dispersed and amorphous foe"? Does it have cells, operatives, members, a leadership? Does it "function like a cult" or like an "enterprise"? No one seems to know for sure.

Now the contradictions:

*   Can a "powerful force," an "organization" be "dispersed and amorphous" and have "no central command"?

- Does an "amorphous and dispersed" entity have an "operational philosophy" or a "center of gravity"?
- Does a "network" have a "leadership" and "members"?
- Either Al Qaeda is a conglomerate of "frustrated immigrants in Europe and America, drifters living on the margins of society, seekers of absolute truth or greater meaning in their lives, lonely souls with varying levels of education," or "bin Laden and many of his lieutenants and agents have not been the victims of poverty or deprivation." Can it be both simultaneously?

Finally, if the goal is the "pursuit," then the "destruction of Al Qaeda," how will it be achieved, if no one has a precise idea of what the target is and without at least a faint idea of the phenomenon's root causes? Was it possible to eradicate malaria without clearly understanding the links between swamps and some mosquito species? In the United States, why is it near impossible to read an accurate analysis on which mistakes gave birth to bin Laden and the Taliban? Where do the Taliban and bin Laden really come from? Are they a collective case of terrorist spontaneous generation?

Is Al Qaeda an organization?

If in its public declarations, the American administration has no definition for Al Qaeda, it has a preconceived idea about it, and a strong one. Since the August 1998 attacks on the U.S. embassies in Nairobi and Dar es-Salaam, and even more so since 9/11, the U.S. administration as a whole—with some dissenting voices, of course—considers Al Qaeda a Western-style organization, as some kind of an Islamist Euskadi Ta Askatasuna (Basque country & freedom) (ETA) or Irish Republican Army, with a central committee, a general headquarters, and so on, and a chief named Osama bin Laden.

Of course, there is an entity of some sort, or an Islamic nebula, working with bin Laden, and responsible for, among others, the 9/11 attacks. But is there really an Al Qaeda organization? Asking these questions is not academic finessing because what American officials call Al Qaeda may well differ greatly from the West's concept of an organization.

Why is this difference so important?

Using a word creates a representation in the human mind. When you present as a fact that there actually exists an Al Qaeda organization, you create a common perception of a mechanical structure, like a motor car or clock. You press a button, and you honk the horn. You touch another button, and the windscreen wiper works. This mechanical model is the West's terrorism model: pyramidal, hierarchical. The "strategic leadership" issues an order, then an attack occurs. Finally, the act is claimed on the organization's letterhead.

But what about Al Qaeda? Is Al Qaeda an Islamic Komintern? Has anyone seen an Al Qaeda letterhead or any authentic document using the word Al Qaeda as a brand, like IRA or Rote Armee Fraction (Red Army Fraction) (RAF)?

More to the point: has Osama bin Laden ever publicly used, on an authentic document, the word Al Qaeda (again, as a brand) himself? No, bin Laden never speaks for an organization, and always speaks as himself: he encourages Muslims to revolt, he is happy to see infidels punished, and so on because even if he's not a first class mufti himself, he knows very well what any decent Muslim knows: jihad is an individual act, nothing else. You may pose as a model; you may preach *jihad fi sabil'Allah*; you cannot force anyone to join it. You cannot order anyone to join a *jihad*.

Finally, the 9/11 attacks required a centralized coordination and planning, but does Al Qaeda have a unique command and control center able to plan and centralize each and every operation, one after the other, or has an ad hoc apparatus been created for each big operation (African embassies, U.S.S. *Cole*, 9/11, etc.)?

So, is this Al Qaeda-as-an-organization the only possible definition? No. Another way of thinking exists: since the beginning, Al Qaeda is nothing more than a nebula, a protoplasm with not one mold, no unique way to organize, but rather each group (e.g., the Egyptians or Pakistanis) creating its own cells within the nebula, out of its own jihadi culture, its own local habits. This is what the eminent Indian expert M. J. Gohel says: "It is important to understand that what is referred to as the 'Al Qaeda network' is in reality a conglomerate of a number of terror groups and their cells, of varying autonomy but who share a common ideology and who cooperate with each other." Recently the criminologist R. T. Naylor also depicted the Al-Qaeda entity in these terms: "In reality, al-Qaeda seems less an organization than a loose association of independent cell-like entities that change form and personnel ad hoc in response to threat and opportunities." ... al-Qaeda seems less an entity than a shared state of mind, less a political organization than a cult of personality. ..."[1]

Common in Europe, this way of thinking also exists in the United States. Bruce Hoffman's article "Al Qaeda, Trends in Terrorism and Future Potentialities: An Assessment," published in this issue of *Studies in Conflict & Terrorism*, also clearly shares this view, and shared doubts about an Al Qaeda monolithic organization.

How does such a chaotic-protoplasmic entity work? If any of these Salafist-activist cells or groups plans either to build a new mosque, or fund a new charity, or launch a terrorist attack, they will need a religious sanction and then funds for the operation they plan. Funding from whom? From some "jihadi philanthropy," or "terrorist philanthropy" active in Uzbekistan, Indonesia, Chechnya, Philippines, Bosnia, Kashmir, Algeria, and so on. A "philanthropy" in which Osama Bin Laden (OBL) plays, of course, a major role.

As said before, this is no mechanical model. This is a biological model. These Islamic cells appear like mushrooms after rain. They grow on the same ground. Their roots are mingled underground. All these mushrooms look more or less the same.[2]

But there is a huge difference between a mechanical and a biological model. If a car is damaged, it needs external help to be repaired. A watch or a car has a precise and definite set of parts; more important, they are dead. A mechanism is not alive. Of course, a biological entity is alive. When skin is scratched, it cicatrizes. Lizards even grow a second tail if the first one is broken.

Trying to destroy a biological entity while simultaneously thinking about it and describing it as a mechanical one, looks like a rather big intellectual mistake.

The fact that Al Qaeda is not a mechanism, with a precise set of parts, but a biological entity, able to grow new roots or branches, is easy to prove: since 1998, and the first U.S. reactions to the attacks against the embassies in Nairobi and Dar es-Salaam, around 5,000 (maybe more) OBL-related fanatics have been jailed worldwide; they have been captured in perhaps as many as 70 countries, the jihadi themselves coming from as many various nationalities (maybe more). Also, Al Qaeda-related funds (around US $130 million) have been frozen, or confiscated, in 129 countries. Now, imagine a company, or agency, with global markets, or an international mission, say IBM or the CIA. If their offices have been raided worldwide, or bombarded, tens of millions of dollars confiscated from them, all their known bank accounts blocked, their computers seized, their electronic communication systems destroyed, thousands of their employees and part of their leadership arrested—even killed sometimes—could these organizations still function? No, of course not. Still, after almost five years of this treatment, OBL-related fanatics were able to hit last spring in Riyadh and Casablanca—as always, where it hurts most. Obviously, Al Qaeda is not something as simple as an organization. It's the human-fanatic equivalent of AIDS. Thus, as long as the present U.S. administration fights this mutant and proteiform entity with the intellectual tools designed to confront organizations, it will risk being constantly one battle late.

Anatomy of the mind of the Islamic militant and Western perceptions

Anyone who has met Salafists (that is, in their familiar surroundings, when they feel safe to discuss; not in a prison cell or in a tribunal …), and has even a remote idea of their psychology, culture, and doctrine, should be surprised by the following judgments: "mission success is very important and leaders are in some way risk-adverse," or "their leaders are deeply concerned with control." This is a pure and simple projection of a Westerner's mental landscape. And bin Laden is not a "Fortune 500" CEO, but a Hadramaout Arab of Wahhabi persuasion. Given the immense importance of apostasy in Wahhabism, how could such an individual "see himself as a prophet" (for the non-Muslims, conversion to Islam means pronouncing the following sentence, known as *shahadat*, or testimony: "I attest that only God is God, and Mohammad, his last prophet and messenger"), or join a crusade?

Since 9/11 we have been subjected to massive amounts of such "information" on Islamic militants, especially Osama bin Laden and his Salafi followers and supporters. A lot of this information only shows how the West misunderstands the Islamic militant mindset.

In the last 15 years or so, from Lebanon to Algeria, from the Arabian peninsula to Sudan, the author has held discussions with many Islamic fanatics. But when comparing the picture of these fanatics as painted by Western officials, media, and some academicians, to what the author has seen and heard in discussions with these jihadists, he does not recognize the picture. There is a major disconnection between how the West perceives militant Islam and the reality of the situation. Some of the author's French and Algerian colleagues who have long conversed with these salafi militants share this concern.

This is a crucial point. Since ancient Greece, "know your enemy" has been a cardinal rule of warfare. If you want to determine what your enemy's targets and tactics will be, you must identify and understand its inner logic and comprehend the core elements of its motivations and objectives.

But to truly understand bin Laden, it is not enough to just collect and process facts about his finances, tactics, communications, and organizational skills. One has to try and understand his vision and worldview. In this way, we might be able to hazard a guess as to what his reactions would be to certain events, developments, or incidents. This vision and worldview comes from the subtle interaction of an individual psychology with a very specific culture. They cannot be easily programmed or captured and wrapped up in a computer's hard disk. Two examples follow.

Dates

One year after 9/11, precisely 11 September 2002, the Western world became hysterical. Commercial flights were empty. Each and every Western police force, army, navy, or air force was on high alert. Whereas, for a Salafi Muslim of the Arabian Peninsula, dates simply do not matter; they are meaningless. In the mindset, in the culture of a desert Bedouin, anniversaries, and birthdays do not exist. Children's and mothers' birthdays are not celebrated. Salafists even consider commemorating the Prophet's anniversary a major sin. Calendar obsession is a Westerner's disease. Not so for a fundamentalist desert Arab. After 9/11, in bin Laden's propaganda, that day became *yom al-moubarak* (the Holy Day) and that is it. Which precise calendar day it was is absolutely devoid of interest. Anyone having had an appointment with a Bedouin (moreover with a shiekh) will understand what the author means.

What is important is that all the Islamic militants the author has met are absolute literalists, obsessed by the Koran's literal meaning, by the Prophet's actual deeds. They will do something only if it's in the Koran—and indeed they only act and dress as the Prophet did. The Prophet used to squat before drinking water, so they do. The Prophet advised a true believer to enter a mosque right foot first, so they do. And so on.

Ninety percent of their exchanges (verbal, Internet, telephones) are about what is licit or illicit, what would the Prophet do if ..., etc. (As the major French antiterrorist judges teach in the author's research center, he knows this as a fact.) If it's not in the Koran, if the Prophet did not do it, it's worse than *haram* (unlawful), it's *bida* (innovation), the biggest sin for a Salafi, deserving a swift death penalty.

9/11 has been accepted by bin Laden's *shura* council because it's in the Koran:[3] what happened that day is a *ghazwah*, a raid. As an emir (military leader), the Prophet conducted many raids, for territorial conquest, loot, or revenge. He even said in the Koran "A raid on the path of God is better than this world and what's in it." So okay, the Salafist reasons, *ghazwah* is *halal* (lawful).

Biological or nuclear terrorism?

This is even more important. Among the serious, proven facts available on 9/11 (not so many, actually) there is a five-page document found by the FBI in Mohammad Atta's luggage, in a car left outside Dulles Airport; also found in several other *shahids* (martyrs') bags, and in the wreckage of the plane that crashed in Pennsylvania. Most probably this document, hand-written by the (unknown) organizer of the attacks, was given to all the hijackers. This text is a spiritual guide for the 19 terrorists' last day of life. It's not a technical or practical document, but a religious, even mystical one—it could have been written in the Prophet's times. Containing a list of rituals to be performed, starting with "The last night," it helps the future martyr achieve body and spirit unity in the last day of his mission.

The last paragraph of the letter is terrible: "When the moment of truth comes near, and zero hour is upon you, open your chest, welcoming death in the path of God. Always remember to conclude with the prayer, if possible starting it seconds before the target, or let your last words be: there is none worthy of worship but God, Muhammad is the messenger of God. After that, God willing, the meeting is in the highest paradise, in the company of God."

Among many tactical problems mentioned in this text (Why kill, and how to kill, the pilots or resisting passengers) a word is pointedly chosen: *dhabaha* (slit, rip something open) and not *qatala* (any way of killing). *Dhabaha* means slit the jugular vein of an animal or human being. It is a ritual slaughter, what Abraham was about to do to his son: sacrifice him on God's order. It is a physically close act, commited with a blade: the blood must actually flow. It's impossible to perform *dhabaha* from afar, with any other type of weapon.

Now, back to 2003: it's been seen that *ghazwah* is *halal*. With explosives, at a close distance and with a lot of blood flowing, *shahadat* (martyrdom) is acceptable to the Hamas *shura* council. Spreading poison in a public place should also be *halal*: poison is known in the Islamic tradition. Ten out of 12 Shi'a imams died from poisoning. Saladin ordered the Crusader's wells, in their fortresses, to be poisoned.

But biological or nuclear weapons? You spread a substance, and people die maybe months later from a disease. What about radiation? Experimenting with it, at the jihadi level, why not? But bin Laden's *shura* council, some very old and reactionary bigots, having spent their lives commenting on the only book they know by heart (the Koran); would they sanction an attack with such weapons? This is at least doubtful.

Is fighting terrorism a state-to-state problem?

Finally, there is a common perception in the present U.S. administration that the main strategic danger now comes from "rogue states." Following 9/11, the United States reacted to terrorism by a strong military operation against Afghanistan, as a rogue state. The plan—a state-to-state issue, a military reply to the "Taliban regime"—was to "find and punish culprit states behind 9/11." Now it has been Iraq's turn. But does this strategy address the real problems of today's chaotic world—and specifically, the terrorism problem? Indeed, since the end of the Cold War, the real threatening entities have been: terrorist nebulas, degenerated guerrillas, criminal cults, narcoterrorists, militarized mafias, warlords' savage armies, and so on. None of these entities are, have been, or will be any time soon, states. None of them has a vital need of any state to survive.

Thus, even if destroying dictatorships is morally important, does targeting "rogue states" really solve today's strategic security problems, terrorism and organized crime? The author seriously doubts it.

Notes

1   R. T. Naylor, *Wages of Crime: Blackmarkets, Illegal Finances and the Underworld Economy* (Ithaca, NY and London: Cornell University Press, 2002).
2   Most of the jihadi are between 25 to 50 years of age, Wahhabi in religious preference, middle-class, well educated, and trained in Afghanistan or Pakistan.
3   On this point, in English, read the excellent and erudite Kanan Makiya and Hassan Mneimneh, "Manual for a raid," in "Striking terror," *New York Review of Books*, 2002.

Section 5

Terrorist behaviour

Readings

della Porta, D. (1992). On individual motivations in underground political organizations. In Social movements and violence: Participation in underground organizations *(International Social Movement Research)*, *4*, 3–28.

Crenshaw, M. (1992). Decisions to use terrorism: Psychological constraints on instrumental reasoning. In Social movements and violence: Participation in underground organizations (*International Social Movement Research*), *4*, 29–42.

Pape, R. A. (2003). The strategic logic of suicide terrorism. *American Political Science Review, 97*, 21–42.

Bloom, M. M. (2004). Palestinian suicide bombing: Public support, market share, and outbidding. *Political Science Quarterly, 119*, 61–88.

Introduction

While the previous section presented you with a selection of case studies of terrorist movements, here we look a little closer at terrorists by exploring a series of contributions that examine individual, group, community and cultural dimensions to the development of terrorism. Donatella della Porta highlights the role of individual motivation, but presents an integrated framework that helps link individual trajectories and life histories with the broader social and political context that gives rise to and sustains involvement. She also focuses on the kinds of psychological factors that help us understand why people commit to a life in an "underground" movement. Martha Crenshaw examines the nature of decision-making by terrorists, and highlights the role of psychology and emotion in that process. We conclude this section by presenting the work of two scholars of terrorist suicide bombing. Robert Pape examines the role of strategic logic in the decision to use suicide bombing, while Mia Bloom considers not only strategic factors such as the need to gain public support, but efforts to "outbid" similar attempts by other movements bent on gaining market share.

Discussion questions

By the end of this section, you should be able to answer:

- What role can psychology play in understanding terrorism?
- Are terrorists rational?
- How is the individual psychology of the terrorist influenced by the terrorist organization?
- What factors drive the decision by an organization to engage in suicide bombing?

Further reading

Atran, S. (2003). Genesis of suicide terrorism. *Science, 299*, 1534–1539.

Bloom, M. (2005). *Dying to kill: The allure of suicide terror.* New York: Columbia University Press.

Borum, R. (2004). *Psychology of terrorism.* Tampa, FL: University of South Florida Press.

Gill, P. (2007). A multidimensional approach to suicide bombing. *International Journal of Conflict and Violence, 1*, 142–159.

Hafez, M. (2006). Suicide terrorism in Iraq: A preliminary assessment of the quantitative data and documentary evidence. *Studies in Conflict and Terrorism, 29*, 591–619.

Kydd, A., & Walter, B. (2002). Sabotaging the peace: The politics of extremist violence. *International Organization, 56*, 263–296.

McCauley, C., & Moskalenko, S. (2008). Mechanisms of political radicalization: Pathways toward terrorism. *Terrorism and Political Violence, 20*, 415–433.

McCormick, G. H. (2003). Terrorist decision making. *Annual Review of Political Science, 6*, 473–507.

National Commission on Terrorist Attacks. (2004). The 9/11 Commission report: Final report of the National Commission on Terrorist Attacks Upon the United States. New York: W. W. Norton & Company.

Pape, R. (2006). Dying to win: The strategic logic of suicide terror. *Australian Army Journal, 3*, 25–38.

Post, J. (2005). When hatred is bred in the bone: Psycho-cultural foundations of contemporary terrorism. *Political Psychology, 26*, 615–636.

Post, J. (2007). *The Mind of the terrorist: The psychology of terrorism from the IRA to Al-Qaeda.* Palgrave MacMillan.

Sageman, M. (2004). *Leaderless jihad.* Philadelphia, PA: University of Pennsylvania Press.

Sageman, M. (2004). *Understanding terror networks.* Philadelphia, PA: University of Pennsylvania Press.

Silke, A. (2003). *Terrorist, victims, and society: Psychological perspectives on terrorism and its consequences.* Hoboken, NJ: Wiley.

Sprinzak, E. (2000). Rational fanatics. *Foreign Policy, September–October,* 66–73.

Victoroff, J. (2005). The mind of the terrorist: A review and critique of psychological approaches. *Journal of Conflict Resolution, 49*, 3–42.

15 On individual motivations in underground political organizations

Donatella della Porta

The research on individual motivations in underground political organizations

The opening volume of this series on "International Social Movement Research"—*From Structure to Action* (Klandermans, Kriesi and Tarrow 1988)—emphasized the need for research on political mobilization which links processes occurring at different analytical levels, and identifies connections between social conflicts and individual involvement. The contributors to this volume* have attempted to fill this need, following several suggestions from the earlier volume to look at a very special kind of political organization: underground groups. I hope that this collection of papers can broaden the understanding of a phenomenon—normally referred to as "terrorism"—that sociological investigation has, so far, done little to illuminate, despite the enormous number of essays devoted to the topic. The need for deeper insight into individual motivations in the underground—or on "terrorism" tout court—is easy to substantiate. According to one recent commentator, this field of study is characterized by "a disturbing lack of good empirically-grounded research" (Gurr 1988, p. 115) and by "naive descriptions, speculative commentary and prescriptions for 'dealing with terrorism' which would not meet minimum research standards in the more established branches of conflict and policy analysis" (Gurr 1988, p. 143). Weakness and bias are even more visible in the studies on "terrorists," which have produced the impression that, to quote Zwerman's essay in this volume, several authors are "more concerned with generating antipathy toward the subject than with theory or scholarship." Especially in the seventies, when terrorist activities peaked in several countries, the majority of scientific as well as journalistic works presented "terrorists" as crazy people or cold-blooded murderers. In most of these works: "well-known personalities of the terrorist scene [were] utilized as show-pieces for propagating the authors' own ideas ... to denounce the offenders simply as paranoids, neurotics, or psychopaths" (Rasch 1979, p. 79). Analysts therefore showed little interest in explanations of individual motivations, which were considered irrelevant or simply untruthful. To interview militants was then deemed a sign of dangerous sympathy for, or even connivance with, political criminals.

In the 1980s, attitudes changed. The perception of what was sometimes called "the end of the terrorist emergency" provided a more congenial atmosphere for research projects focusing precisely on the nature of the individual motivations in the underground. The papers collected in this volume report the results of several of these research projects. All the contributions attempt to link individual motivations with structural conditions and group dynamics, focusing in particular

---

* Mention of 'this volume' refers to the original publication this article appeared in: della Porta, D. (1992). Social movements and violence: Participation in underground organizations, (*International Social Movements Research*) 4.

on the "social construction of reality" (Berger and Luckmann 1966) taking place in the underground. Underlying this research is the assumption that a phenomenon such as terrorism cannot be understood unless we take into account the interactions between structural conditions and symbolic meaning, "objective" and "subjective" reality, public activities, and private life.

Research in the sociology of knowledge has identified multiple realities. Our perceptions are influenced by the frames we use to understand events; events themselves are not "objective": they can be "fabricated" or simply misinterpreted. Thus, for a number of reasons experiences are vulnerable to manipulation (see, e.g., Goffman 1974). Further, the formation of perceptions and images is an interactive process. Because what is perceived as real produces real consequences, individual motivations evolve through, as it were, the concatenation of different subjective realities. From different perspectives, the studies in this book examine individual choices and rationale for such choices, as they emerge from the transformation of "historical" facts in the individual or subcultural mind, from the effects of some dramatic public event on the activist's private life, and from the activist's perceptions of the external world. A primary object of the book is therefore to explain the distinctive—socially constructed—"reality" shared by members of the underground.

This purpose is reflected in the methodological approach shared by all the researchers whose work is represented in this volume: that is, the use of biographical materials that enable us to see "inside" the underground organizations. Several of these studies—in particular those of White, Moyano, Passerini, Zwerman, and della Porta—are based on in-depth interviews with former or current members of underground organizations. The remaining studies rely on written sources, such as newspapers, autobiographies, police archives, and trial records. These different research techniques produced slightly different results. Printed sources provided more information on the external environment in which the underground organizations developed; life-histories offered a more "inward," subjective perspective; and semistructured interviews focused on opinions. But because they share the biographical method, all these essays produced highly comparable information about the macro-, meso-, and micro-processes that shape individual motivations in the underground.

The primary aim of this volume is therefore to approach the phenomenon of "terrorism" through the understanding of individual motivations and perceptions, and to present some results of a methodology rarely applied to the study of political radicalism (della Porta 1987, 1990b). In addition, the authors attempt to provide material for a comparative analysis in a field in which it is particularly needed. Labels such as "terrorism" or "underground political organizations" in fact describe a range of very disparate phenomena: right-wing and left-wing groups, political violence in democratic and authoritarian regimes, class-oriented and ethnically based conflicts. Not only do the underground organizations differ according to their goals, they also have varying organizational models and favor different forms of action. Any attempt to develop interpretative hypotheses about "terrorism" is therefore destined to fail without a typology that can identify their range of application.

Although this collection of papers does not attempt to describe all the main terrorist organizations, it provides a large sample of studies on the different forms of political violence which developed in the last two decades. The various contributions examine underground organizations in European countries—Northern Ireland, Spain, West Germany, Italy, and France—and in America—the United States, Canada, and Argentina. In assembling information on different national cases, we hope to "relativize" and specify hypotheses and explanations.

This intention is expressed in the structure of the volume. In Part I, this introduction and Crenshaw's paper offer observations toward a theory on individual motivations in underground organizations. In the remainder of this introduction, I discuss some results of the research presented in this volume, analyzing in particular the ways in which individual motivations are affected by the activists' social networks, the political environment's predispositions to violence, and the totalizing commitment required by terrorist organizations. Crenshaw presents some hypotheses on decision making in underground groups, and then deduces several conclusions about the counterproductive effects of over-repressive antiterrorist policies.

Part II consists of three case studies of different forms of underground organizations. Braungart and Braungart describe the environmental conditions and group dynamics that can explain individual motivations in the left-wing Weather Underground in the United States, an organization that emerged from the radicalization of the protest of the 1960s. White examines one of the oldest terrorist organizations in Europe, the Irish Republican Army, studying the development of "injustice" frames based on ethnic discrimination in a special group of militants: those living in the Irish Republic. And Moyano's interviews with Argentinian militants on the context and dynamics of political violence reveal the workings of yet another type of underground organization—the South American "guerrilla."

Part III contains two papers on women's studies in the field. Zwerman, a sociologist and psychotherapist, analyzes images of militant women in the academic field, in antiterrorist agencies, and in the feminist press, and compares them with the self-images of militants in the various American underground organizations she is studying in a project on American female prisoners. The oral historian Passerini reflects on the imagery and mentality of the Italian female militants whose life histories she collected during a seminar in the Turin prison.

Part IV makes an explicit attempt to develop typologies of underground organizations. Comparing left-wing and right-wing militants in West Germany, Neidhardt emphasizes the wide range of differences in the mobilization capacity of the various underground groups. Waldmann's study of left-wing and ethnic organizations reveals, in addition, significant differencies in the nature of membership in the two kinds of groups. In my own comparison of life histories of Italian and West German militants, I stress the relevance of historical circumstances and national contexts—such as the legitimation of political violence—in predisposing the individuals to engage in terrorism.

Individual motivations and social networks in underground organizations

On psychological characteristics: a critique of some prejudices and stereotypes

In the past, commentators have often explained participation in underground groups as the manifestation of some psychological pathology, such as personality dependence, low intelligence, egocentrism (Livingstone 1982; Wasmund 1986), and as a frustrated attempt to build a positive identity (Billig 1984; Ivianski 1983; Russel and Miller 1983; Knutson 1981; Schmidtchen 1981). These claims have never been substantiated by empirical research. Even in the few cases in which militants have been given personality tests, the subjects were individuals who had passed through two "total institutions"—the clandestine organization and the prison system—which had influenced their personalities (della Porta 1988, p. 156). In accord with a more recent trend in research all the papers in this volume share the assumption that no specific personality traits are "typical" of terrorists. As Braungart and Braungart state, militants are impelled to engage in destructive action not because of a "single orientation toward aggression" but for a "variety of reasons."

In addition, past research has found no sign of any typical pattern in the primary socialization of militants, no sign of particular family problems or of an authoritarian upbringing. On the contrary, Passerini's subjects, for example, remembered their childhood as serene and happy. My research among Italian militants confirms Passerini's findings: 85% of a total of 29 former militants described their family atmosphere as "good" or "very good." Moreover, the interviews indicate that, far from conflicting with the values of their parents the radical commitment of the young activists often reflected a continuity with the political traditions of their families (significantly, this relation appear to hold true among protest activists as well [see, e.g., Keniston 1968]). In fact, more than half of the militants of left-wing underground organizations grew up in left-wing families (della Porta 1990a).

Thus personality traits and family pathologies turn out to be very poor predictors of the propensity to engage in radical political activism. And comparative analysis shows that the extent to which a given society resorts to psychopathological explanations reflects the degree of political violence that society will tolerate. Waldmann observed, for instance, that in societies in which ethnic groups operate, the militants are generally perceived as demonstrating positive personality traits—determination, initiative, leadership ability—and are seen as integrated into their society. In societies in which underground organizations are more isolated from their environment, however, analysts favor interpretations of militance that stress pathological characteristics. Thus, in West Germany, for example, "the efforts at interpretation by psychological, psychiatric or psychoanalytical theories outnumber those afforded by sociology and political science" (Rasch 1979, p. 79).

Social networks and political motivations

Pathological personality types or deficient primary socialization, therefore, do not seem to account for motivations to join underground organizations. But, all the contributors to this volume agree, one further stage in the socialization process *is* highly relevant: the construction of peer groups during adolescence. That social networks play a vital role in political socialization as well as in personality building is not a new finding. Many empirical studies on social movements have shown that social movements recruit in dense social networks and, more particularly, among individuals who are already members of preexisting formal and informal groups. Further, friendship ties within social movement organizations have proven to be a prime inducement to participation (see, e.g., Zald and Ash 1966; Wilson 1973; Snow, Zurcher and Ekland-Olson 1980; Reynaud 1982; Snow and Machalek 1983; Klandermans 1984). Past research has already revealed the function of these ties in the evolution of political involvement: they provide a sense of cohesiveness in the face of opposition from the surrounding community, they encourage a desire for acceptance and cognitive coherence which produces conformity; and they filter political messages and information (Keniston 1968; see also Verba 1961).

Indeed, earlier research has demonstrated that participation in interpersonal networks is very important in all stages of involvement in the underground. In the case of the German and Italian militants, it was clear that the more time an individual spent on political activities, the more contact he or she had with political comrade-friends. And as his or her friendship ties became stronger, the value of the political activities increased (see my paper in this volume and also della Porta 1990a). Among the Irish militants, too, friendship and political ties were intertwined: as one militant interviewed by White declared, for instance, "most of my friends developed from ... my political involvement." Thus an individual's participation in militant activities increased at an "incredible speed," as the Italian and German militants said, and in a natural and almost unconscious way.

It was precisely these affective ties that prompted activists to make the transition from nonmilitant groups to the underground. For one thing, underground organizations were founded by cliques of friends (see, e.g., Franceschini, Buffa and Giustolisi [1988], on the Red Brigades) or, in some cases, by what Moyano has called "family dynasties," composed of couples and several siblings. Moreover, recruitment to the underground took place via the same channels that provided recruits for nonmilitant groups: "entering in the area of the armed struggle presupposed previous relational networks" (Novaro 1988, p. 287). Many German and Italian militants, for example, explained that joining an underground organization was an act either of solidarity with a friend "in danger" (in prison or in clandestinity) or of revenge for the death of a fellow comrade during a "militant" action (see my paper in this volume and also della Porta 1990a). In some cases, these affective ties developed during activities in the so-called organizations of solidarity with political prisoners, which in West Germany represented almost the only channel of recruitment for the second generation of left-wing terrorists.

Loyalty to the peer group was therefore an important motive as activists moved toward an ever-deepening political commitment (for a similar analysis on commitment in religious sects, see Lofland and Stark [1965]). They forged this commitment by dismissing all ties with outsiders, thus restricting themselves to relations within the group. Integration in the friendship networks within the social movement—in what Useem (1972) called "movement solidarity"—enabled activists to shift from their moderate initial stance to a radical political position. As McAdam (1986) observed about the passage from low-risk to high-risk activities in general, increased interactions within activist networks, ideological socialization and construction of an activist identity all served to enforce an individual's commitment. Commitment was thus "self-generating" (Becker 1960).

Although affective networks always play a role in politics, they operate in a special way in underground organizations, for in this context strong ties are more important than weak ties, which represent the primary channel of expansion for nonmilitant social movement organizations (Granovetter 1973). In underground organizations illegality produces a risk and so a need for secrecy; and, as in other secret societies, this need becomes the single most important determinant of the organization's structure and strategy (Erikson 1981). Recruitment in the underground therefore depends on strong confidence ties between recruitors and recruitees. Consequently, the possibilities for recruitment for the underground groups are always limited.

Furthemore, social networks have a peculiar function in maintaining loyalty to terrorist organizations. One characteristic of affective ties among comrade-friends in the underground is their intensity. Relations within the small community are given particular prominence, Passerini notes; and individual identities are so embedded in the group that the militants believe it is not possible to live outside the group or, indeed, it is not worth living outside it. In this volume, Moyano suggests that, in the isolation of clandestinity, the guerrillas' comrades served as a functional surrogate for their families, with whom they could not keep in contact. In the underground, as in high-risk secret societies (Erikson 1981), the excitement of shared risks strengthened friendships among the members. As a former Argentinian militant recalled, "you had people around you whom you knew would be ready to die in order to save you." Danger and isolation thus heightened emotional intensity.

Scholars have offered various explanations for the "strength" of these bonds. One of these explanations focuses on the degree of affective identification required by the total changes in an individual's life that adherence to an underground organization creates. As Berger and Luckmann observe, processes of re-socialization, or "alternations,"

> resemble primary socialization, because they have radically to reassign reality accents and, consequently, must replicate to a considerable degree the strongly affective identification with the socializing personnel that was characteristic of childhood. They are different from primary socialization because they do not start *ex nihilo*, and as a result they must cope with a problem of dismantling, disintegrating the preceding nomic structure of subjective reality.
>
> (Berger and Luckmann 1966, p. 157)

Thus, the new values must be mediated to the individual through "significant others" with whom he or she has established strong affective identifications: "No radical transformation of subjective reality (including of course identity) is possible without such identification, which inevitably replicates childhood experiences of emotional dependency on significant others" (Berger and Luckmann 1966, p. 157). Activists entering the underground, like individuals in other "novitiate" phases, "nihilated" those who inhabited their world before their conversion; in Berger and Luckmann's words, "People and ideas that are discrepant with the new definitions of reality are systematically avoided" (1966, p. 159).

A second explanation for the intensity of friendships in the underground is related to the militants' youth. Peer groups, we know, exert a different kind of influence in the different stages of an individual's life. Because the activists' participation in underground organizations often coincided with their search for emotional independence from the family, their loyalty to the peer group—an important element in the evolution of an adult personality—was especially strong. We can understand why underground organizations attract the young—youth is perhaps the only characteristic "terrorists" share—when we remember that young people are relatively unconstrained by obligations, responsibilities, and conventions, and that the underground mentality depends on certain psychological characteristics of adolescence. As the Braungarts' research on the Weathermen makes clear, such typically youthful characteristics as energy, utopianism, the need for autonomy, openness to experimentation, a search for identity and fidelity are conducive to total adherence to a "negative identity" and enhance the attraction of the "adventure" in the underground. Several other militant groups described in this volume also emphasized "adventure" and "action." The imagery of Italian militants, Passerini observed, revealed a great sensitivity to spectacular effects and a preoccupation with the illusion of an intense, free, and thoughtless life. Several former members of the underground quoted in this volume said they felt they were living "in a movie" or "in science fiction." Moreover, the biographies disclose the militants' fascination with action as opposed to "mere talking," and their positive emphasis on what Passerini has called "rebellion."

Having emphasized the importance of friendship ties throughout the process of political socialization—from the individual's first experiences of protest activism, to the radicalization of this experience, to his or her participation in the underground—and having observed the vital role that affective ties play in clandestine organizations, we must consider another question: how are the networks of "rebels" created? Focusing on affective ties provides only a partial explanation of individual motivations, since they cannot account for the specific form that social networks take. In the following section, then, I focus on the environmental conditions that make an individual receptive to the use of political violence.

Individual motivations and the escalation of political conflicts

Social origins of the underground organizations' activists

In looking for explanations of individual motivations at a macroanalytical level, we must consider the hypotheses that posit a correlation between political violence and social strata. One such hypothesis holds that political deviance—as well as other kinds of deviance—is accepted more readily in the marginal strata of the population, than in any others. And its general "subculture of violence" (Wolfgang and Ferracuti 1967) makes it hospitable to specifically political forms of violence as well. Lacking legal means to challenge the system, individuals in the marginal strata would also have a higher propensity for violence. But at least in the historical cases discussed in this book, this hypothesis did not hold true.

Proponents of a second, quite opposite, hypothesis focus on the middle class, maintaining that the radicalization of a working-class ideology in a middle-class environment is a psychological device to "compensate" for bourgeois origins. Apropos of the Weathermen, for instance, the Braungarts refer to one source that explains the behavior of these militants as a reaction to the cognitive dissonance created by the contrast between their own comfortable backgrounds and their awareness of poverty and racism. This hypothesis too proved misleading. First, several ethnic underground organizations—Waldmann cites the IRA and ETA—were composed mainly of militants from the lower or lower-middle classes. Further, Neidhardt's comparative study shows that right-wing terrorists came from poorer backgrounds than did their left-wing counterparts and were less educated than the left-wing terrorists. The hypothesis also misrepresents left-wing ideological terrorism. My research on more than 1,000 Italian militants, for instance, shows that only a few had an autonomous "bourgeois" profession (about 9%, including 2.2% who were lawyers); a larger group came from the new middle class (30%, about 5% of whom were teachers); but the highest number (41.8%) had working class positions (della Porta 1990a).

Generalizing from the Italian case, we can state that "terrorists belong to different social groups; no single social class is responsible for their production and reproduction, for their ideology or for their behavior" (Pasquino and della Porta 1986, p. 180). The social origins of terrorists varies with the organization and with the context. In our cases, political violence does not seem to depend on a subculture of violence among "poor people" or on a frustrated reaction of bourgeois revolutionaries. Rather, the social origins of the militants of terrorist organizations reflect those of the protest movements in which they were recruited. Accordingly, we should examine the dynamics of those social movements.

Social protest and political violence

In traditional studies, terrorism has been defined according to its more singular aspects: terrorism, it is said, uses an "intolerable" level of violence, aims at "scaring" people, and breaks the "rules of the game" (della Porta 1983). Without denying these singularities, the research collected in this volume demonstrates that underground organizations can be seen as part of a larger "social movement sector" (as defined in Garner and Zald [1983]). The definition of a social movement organization as "a self-conscious group which acts in concert to express what it sees as the claims of challengers by confronting elites, authorities, or other groups with these claims" (Tarrow 1989; see also Zald and McCarthy 1987) aptly characterizes the underground political organizations studied in this volume, for they clearly were "self-conscious groups" that expressed what they saw as "the claims of challengers." They were founded by social movement activists—often as a result of splits in social movement organizations—as a by-product of those interactions between challengers and opponents which constitute the essence of a social movement (Tilly 1984, p. 299). And not only did the militants perceive themselves as part of the social movement sector, the social movement activists (from whom the underground drew its new recruits) often recognized the militants as "comrades"—albeit as "comrades who were wrong."

The contributors to this volume agree that future terrorists can be described as small minorities within larger political subcultures or countercultures. The militants of the underground themselves defined their role as that of actors in a political conflict. Of course, as Waldmann rightly states, ethnic and left-wing terrorists operated within quite different political contexts. Ethnical militants reacted to what they perceived as an external threat coming from a power foreign to their own ethnic, regional, or religious group, with which they identified deeply. The left-wing militants, in contrast, rejected their own society and, in their search for an alternative, came to identify with external groups. Despite this difference, however, ethnic and left-wing militants did have something in common: the existence of—smaller or larger—networks of political activists for which political violence gradually became an everyday experience.

In all the cases analyzed in this book, protest repertoires gradually escalated toward violence. In the United States, protest actions became more and more radical after the Democratic convention in Chicago and the uprisings at Columbia University in 1968. In 1970, when the Weathermen went underground, as many as 5,000 bombing attempts for political reasons occurred. In Italy, the number of protest events characterized by organized and small-group violence increased dramatically during the first half of the 1970s (della Porta and Tarrow 1987). When the student movement declined in West Germany, the hope that the newly elected SPD government would adopt a reformist policy impelled several activists to return to conventional politics. But after a few years the activists became disillusioned and violence escalated during "squatting" incidents in houses and youth centers in the big cities (Klein 1980). In Ulster, the nonviolent civil rights movement faded away in the face of a violent opposition. And in Argentina, although reformers had some hope at the beginning of the sixties, political interactions soon degenerated into physical fights, and a bloody repression decimated the democratic opposition.

These environmental conditions fostered the rise not only of some underground organizations but also, to paraphrase Garner and Zald (1983), of national "terrorist sectors" composed of several clandestine groups, sometimes competing, sometimes collaborating with each other. In most of the historical cases dealt with in this volume, terrorist organizations claimed to represent the same social groups. Furthermore, adversaries—or countermovements—also organized in the underground. In Italy throughout the 1970s brutal conflicts escalated among young members of right-wing and left-wing nonunderground groups who fired at each other, sometimes killing each other, right in front of the high schools. Neo-Nazis and "anti-fascists" clashed in West Germany at the end of the 1970s. Civil rights advocates opposed the Ku Klux Klan in the United States. In Ulster and in the Basque country, armed groups of "loyalists" attacked IRA and ETA members respectively, setting off a spiral of violent reciprocal revenge. And in Argentina, Moyano shows, on the day of the Peron's definitive return street fights between rightists and Montoneros triggered an escalation of violence (during which 16 people died and 433 were wounded). A few months later, the terrorist anticommunist alliance (Triple A) was founded and began persecuting democratic Argentinians, driving the Montoneros further and further underground.

In these volatile climates, individual motivations for joining the underground proliferated. The atmosphere of violence had a particular influence on those who were just beginning to take an interests in political activities. Braungart and Braungart observe, for example, that the Weathermen and the older SDS leaders grew up under qualitatively different historical conditions: the nonviolent SDS in a period that valued peaceful protest; the militant Weathermen in a period accostumed to radical forms of action. Similarly, in West Germany and Italy, activists, socialized to politics in the violent first half of the 1970s and enrolled in the underground in the second half of that decade, formed a "second generation" of terrorism more populous and more violent than the first.

We can explain this self-sustaining proliferation of motivations for engaging in political violence in various ways. First, through experience, activists gradually acquired "skills," and structures for the use of violence were gradually created. The case of the New Left groups in Italy provides an illustration: as a result of their street fights with police and right-wing radicals, more or less autonomous "marshal bodies" sprang up within their main organizations. Through shisms and secessions, these small groups themselves sometimes became the foundation of underground groups (Novelli and Tranfaglia 1988; della Porta 1990a). These radicalized small groups also formed the reservoir for recruitment for the underground organizations. Similarly, the biographies of German militants testify to a (in Neidhardt's words) "militarizing" effect of involvement in radical legal groups, an effect that helped to "presocialize activists to militancy."

In addition to refining martial skills and creating structures for violence, the experience of daily fights with adversaries transformed the activists' attitudes toward politics. Physical conflicts with opponents produced a kind of battle spirit toward politics, much like that which emerged in the street violence between young communists and Nazi storm troopers in the early 1930s in Berlin. As Merkl reports: "According to accounts on both sides, the street fighters were motivated far more by the escalating physical confrontations than by ideological beliefs … the reality of the clashes had a great deal more to do with aroused emotions, brawny fists, and weapons than with these ideological concepts" (1986, p. 43). Street fights, then, produced ex post facto justifications and rationalizations for violence. As the biographies describe in detail, the militants engaged in long debates on the different "right" forms of violence; nevertheless, the empirical boundaries between "right" violence and "wrong" violence, "defensive" violence and "offensive" violence, "mass" violence and "elite" violence remained quite vague.

As attitudes and behaviors became radicalized, the "armed struggle" became easier for activists to accept—so much so that, as Passerini notes in her essay, several activists came to consider violence as "natural" and were able to move into the underground so smoothly that they did not perceive they had made an important choice. In most of the biographies I analyzed, the militants were unable to isolate a particular moment in which they decided to join the underground. Because the perceptions and attitudes of the young militants were similar to those that dominated their political environments, joining the underground was not a traumatic step for them. And because they saw only marginal difference between the normal and the deviant (on this point, see Matza [1969]), they could not clearly perceive any "deviation" from the norms. For the activists, the reality of everyday life—that is, the "reality par excellence," in which "the tension of consciousness is highest" (Berger and Luckmann 1966, p. 21)—created the conditions for a gradual acceptance of violence as a political means. Justifying violence was thus an integral part of constructing alternative systems of values and norms. As Passerini clearly illustrates, shared representations of the reality then "short-circuited" with the "primacy of action" mythicized by the young militants.

The effects of antiterrorist policies

Political conflicts are often further radicalized by the effects of antiterrorist policies. Several of the papers in this volume examine what in terms of the sociology of deviance could be defined as the role of deviance-control institutions in selecting those who will become deviant and in helping to create a "deviant" personality. In the late 1960s and early 1970s, state institutions often reacted to protest in over-repressive ways. To cite just one by no means extreme example: in the United States, Braungart and Braungart recall, the Nixon administration countered social protest by escalating surveillance, resorting to intimidation, establishing special congressional committees to investigate leftists, using informants and infiltrators, approving FBI controls over all SDS members, and creating the CIA's "operation chaos." In this way, it not only prosecuted illegal political behavior, but "criminalized" protest. Zwerman notes that the Reagan administration implemented a similar policy in the 1980s, when "terrorists" were defined as those who "support" or are "associated" with terrorist groups or "activities," engage in "previolent" forms of protest, and commit actions that have the "potential" to "evolve" into terrorism. This vague definition makes even noncriminal political behavior a possible target of repression. All the countries surveyed in this volume present similar examples of "criminalizing" the opposition. Moreover, in such countries as Argentina and Italy, many people believed that state apparatuses were involved in protecting the radical Right and thus in a "dirty war" against the political opposition on the Left.

Although they were intended to isolate the radical Left, the repressive measures of these governments often produced the opposite effect. First, they delegitimized the state not only by creating "injustice frames" (Gamson, Fireman and Rytina et al. 1982) but also by arousing the sense of an "absolute injustice" (Manconi 1988)—that is, the belief that the state had committed the most serious violation of the rules of the game. Following the delegitimation of the state, which was then perceived as an "unfair" enemy that used brutal repression, activists entered the underground. The interviews with the militants provided several examples of a sense of deep "injustice." For the Irish republicans, the British policy of "internment"—the imprisonment of suspected IRA members without trial—reinforced the image of the central authorities as illegitimate (White 1989). The Italian militants saw the neo-fascist massacre of Piazza Fontana as a turning point, proof that the state, which was alleged to have taken part in the terrorist plot, had violated its own democratic rules. Perceptions of an "absolute injustice" varied with the degree to which violent behavior was tolerated in the different countries and periods. In West Germany, a country with a very low tolerance for political violence, the death of the protestor Benno Ohnesorg and the attempt on the life of the student movement leader Rudi Dutschke were sufficient to produce the feeling that, as Baumann (1976) said, "they were firing at you." In an authoritarian regime such as that of Ongania's Argentina in the sixties, the shocking sense of a deep injustice grew out of the much more dramatic acts of military brutality, vividly described by Moyano: the "Cordobazo" (with 14 protestors killed), the "Viborazo" (with other 2 protestors killed), and the cold-blooded murder of 16 guerrillas in an Argentinian prison.

The fear of being the direct target of repression also impelled activists to join underground groups. In their biographies, several Italian militants recounted that they decided to join an underground organization only after the police began to pursue them (they joined in order to find support for escaping arrest) or after they had been arrested and had shared a prison cell with members of terrorist groups. A few members of the West German radical groups that supported the "political prisoners" said that they had felt harrassed or endangered by close police scrutiny and had reacted by joining the underground. Another impetus that often pushed rank-and-file militants deeper into the underground was the very severe penalties that the courts imposed for acts of political violence, such as the condemnation of some Weathermen, as early as in 1970, for a crime as serious as "conspiracy." Thus for many activists joining a terrorist formation was what Crenshaw calls an "unforeseen consequence" of nonterrorist actions.

Accordingly, the material effect of the "ban"—in Matza's (1969) words—was to "force" activists into contact with more experienced militants who were already engaged in clandestine activities. The ban had relevant psychological effects as well. Zwerman, for instance, observes that, among the American underground groups, getting arrested often "initiated" activists of radical groups "into their status as terrorists" and into an "array of exceptional, erratic, experimental procedures." The common reaction of these militants was to hide their feelings and fears behind what Zwerman calls a "grandiose self-definition" of their own heroic role and of the imminent revolution. In addition, many of the biographies of German and Italian militants indicate that harsh prison conditions and long sentences made them determined to stick to their "freedom-fighter" identity, which allowed them to see themselves as soldiers of a revolution that would soon free them. Imprisonment in high-security sections produced what Passerini calls a rigidity in memory and an "inability to go forwards or backwards." And, Crenshaw notes, coercive counterterrorist reactions often made terrorism self-sustaining insofar as these measures proved the militants' expectations of hostility to be correct, reinforced injustice frames, and set off a spiral of revenge. Over-reactions to political violence fostered what the neo-Chicago school has called "secondary deviance"—the identification of a "specifically deviant" individual with his or her "primary" deviation—and therefore the identification with the underground organization. The militants thus adopted alternative systems of norms and values, roles and rules, in order to transform stigma into prestige symbols (Goffman 1963).

Individual motivations and political socialization in the underground

We have already noted that the resources and meaning that foster underground organizations are produced by a variety of processes. The primary determinants of the militants' perceptions and behavior, however, can be traced to the very same characteristics of the terrorist groups. For underground groups as for religious sects, "the 'whys' or 'reasons' for joining arise out of the recruitment itself" (Snow, Zurcher and Eckland-Olson 1980, p. 799). The experience inside the terrorist organizations was then what shaped their dispositions. All the papers in this volume underline the relevance of the particular group situation the individual encounters on joining the underground. As the Braungarts emphasize, the real transformation in individual motivations begins within the terrorist organizations. "Terrorist" motivations are largely a product of what Crenshaw calls the "psychology of small, radical, illegal groups."

State control agencies usually operate on the assumption that underground organizations are criminal groups. Without denying the validity of this assumption, I feel it is necessary to point out another characteristic of these organizations which helps explain their behavior: they are ideological groups. In a study based on autobiographical materials concerning members of Russian underground groups in the second half of the nineteenth century, Nahirni tried to define the particular characteristics of ideological groups: they are, he said, groups "which require their members to orient themselves to one another primarily in terms of some central symbols and ideas" (Nahirni 1962, pp. 397–398). The distinctive feature of these groups is the members' total commitment to a cause, to which they must subordinate all personal ties. This description aptly characterizes underground political organizations as well.

Structures in the underground: "greedy institutions"

The obvious peculiarity of terrorist organizations is that they are underground. This characteristic has a profound effect on individual motivations: underground groups demand the total involvement of their members. Like the "greedy institutions" analyzed by Coser, they "seek exclusive and undivided loyalty and they attempt to reduce the claims of competing roles and status positions on those they wish to encompass within their boundaries" (Coser 1974, p. 4). To enforce loyalties, terrorist groups developed negative incentives, such as the threat of punishment for traitors. More effectively, they developed a value system in which, as in an army (so Crenshaw notes), betrayal was considered the most serious violation of group norms.

Terrorist organizations devoted much energy to developing systems of rules that their members had to respect at all times. The "handbooks for urban guerrillas" produced by most of the groups went well beyond the "logistic" needs of clandestinity. Their main effect was to ensure the organization's control of its members through domination on the more private aspects of their lives. The underground groups required their members to provide such extreme "testimony" of commitment as the total renunciation of privacy regarding both material and affective ties (and, in the case of the Weathermen, even in sexual relations). Lacking a private life, the militants experienced what Passerini calls the loss of individual identity, which in turn compelled them to rely more and more on the group. A reduced sense of the self obscured their perception of personal responsibility.

Once having joined an underground group, he or she would be required to participate at increasingly demanding levels of activity, whether in terms of the risk or the time involved.

Militants usually began their careers in the underground by distributing leaflets or renting an apartment. The longer they remained underground, the more likely they were to end up in participating in robberies and assassinations. In their biographies, several militants testify to the accelerating effect that a warrant of arrest had on their promotion in the internal hierarchy of the underground: from rank-and-file members they rapidly advanced to national leaders. Moreover, many recall the time they spent in the underground as a period of frenetic activism: they organized attacks, wrote documents, looked for refuge, and planned to free their comrades. The result of this "24-hours-a-day" commitment to the organization was, as one Italian militant put it, the lack of any time for "thinking," for critically reflecting on the sense of the crimes the terrorists had carried out. The biographies of the Italian and German militants demostrate that this process of material and emotional involvement culminated in the militants' almost complete identification with a "community of the armed struggle."

Another factor that strengthened total commitment in the underground was the militants' isolation from external channels of information. It is well known that the kind of clique to which people belong determines to a large extent the political message they receive and the ideological appeals they translate into concrete action. Earlier research has established that the media alone are not an effective conduit for political information; such information acquires meaning and relevance only when it is channeled through social networks (Smith, Lasswell and Casey 1946; McPhail 1971; McPhail and Miller 1973). The more "total" the activists' involvement in a political network, the more insulated they were from information that could threaten their political beliefs. As my comparative analysis of Italian and German militants illustrates, the militants' source of values and information rapidly shrank to the small circles of those who were underground. As a result, they lost a sense of reality, constructing images that were increasingly remote not only from the "dominant" culture but also from the counterculture. And because they were so isolated from external reality, the militants of the underground groups had great difficulty in perceiving the defeat of their project.

The degree to which these processes of commitment governed an underground organization seemed to vary according to the organization's degree of isolation. Waldmann notes, for example, that left-wing groups were far more isolated from their environment than were ethnic groups. In ethnic organizations, peer groups in the underground enforced the same norms and values that prevailed in their environment, whereas in left-wing groups, members had to enforce an alternative value system. As several studies indicate, however, under the pressure of internal conflicts and the specialization of state repression, all the underground groups tended to become more and more isolated and ended up concentrating their efforts simply on their survival.

Commitment to a cause: ideologies in the underground

Individual motivations were also shaped by the characteristics of the ideologies of the underground groups. Using a typology proposed by Sartori (1969), we can identify the major formal peculiarities of these ideological systems: they refuse factual arguments, they are abstract, they base their appeal on emotions, and they are accessibile to only a very small public. In order to ensure total commitment, underground ideologies exalt "powerful," strong, and abstract ideas. Because proponents of these ideologies never refer to the preconditions and the progression of a revolutionary process, the ideological beliefs seem "impermeable" to external defeats. In the underground, as in secret societies, symbolism and rituals which are needed to legitimize alternative authority, render the ideologies particularly rigid (Simmel 1950). Terrorist groups develop special languages, cryptic to anyone outside the group but possessing a highly symbolic value for their members.

Some of these characteristics can exist, to a different degree, in social movement organizations as well. Students of social movement ideologies have, for instance, defined social movement ideologies as "dogmatic" and have observed that motivating radical behavior requires a high degree of "certainty" about the external world (Gerlach and Hine 1970). Moreover, they noted that it is to a movement's advantage to maintain a certain level of ambiguity, which enables leaders to escalate their requests in order to keep protest alive after initial victories or to conceal moments of weakness (Gerlach and Hine [1970]; on a similar phenomenon in religious sects, see Lofland and Stark [1965]). Researchers have also stressed the positive role that rhetoric and rituals play in social movement organizations that must substitute symbolic for material incentives.

Nevertheless, social movement ideologies differ from underground ideologies in many ways. Social movement organizations, which hope to reach a large public, must try to balance the need for internal coherence with the often conflicting need for communication with external elements (Boucher 1977); underground groups, which are essentially insular organizations, focus mainly on internal functions. Their ideologies are what Moyano calls "an instrument for internal consumption." Consequently, the more isolated the groups are, the more abstract, ritualistic and inaccessible to factual argument their ideologies become. The experience of the German and the Italian militants indicate that the less time and energy they gave to recruitment, the more ingrown they became, abandoning the imagery and the language they shared with the counterculture and constructing an "alternative" reality. The Montoneros' "hedge theory"—according to which Peron supported the guerrilla but could not express his support because of his wife and the Right—exemplifies the extremes this "loss of the sense of reality" can reach.

The ideologies of underground organizations exhibit certain peculiarities in their political content as well as in their form. Members of the underground organizations, like members of other political groups, develop ideologies in order to define the organization's field of action and its role in it—that is, "the reasons for its existence, the embodiment of its values, its analysis of society and its prescriptions for change" (Boucher 1977, p. 25). Terrorist organizations, including right-wing groups, do not act randomly or because they are "blood-thirsty." On the contrary, they devote a great deal of energy to the elaboration of what Crenshaw called a "cognitive restructuring," through which reprehensible conduct is presented as honorable. Historical, linguistic, and religious "macronarratives" that justify violence are encompassed in eclectic ideological frames (Toloyan 1987). Processes of "frame amplification" (Snow et al. 1986) allow militants to accept the "armed struggle" on the basis of social movement discourses.

Frame amplification is evident in underground ideologies, first of all, in their elitist self-definition of the actors. It has been noted, in fact, that small radical organizations in general favor the image of a close community of the elect, emphasizing purity rather than proselytization, exclusivity rather than expansion (O'Toole 1975). The militants of the underground organizations described in this book "amplified" this claim of belonging to an "elite," although an "alternative" one. When they were linked to a larger social movement, they presented themselves as the "vanguard of the revolutionary masses." When they were isolated, they claimed to be the only "beacon" of resistance opposing the total dominion of capitalism. And we find that the German and Italian militants, for example, justified the use of violence through highly abstract and simplified images of the world in which small elites of "freedom fighters" were in charge of administering the real "justice." According to Crenshaw, the self-images of an "elite with high consciousness" and of the "hero" were widespread among the militants.

Elitism accomplished an important function: it made isolation appear to be a positive, self-imposed quality. An organization's lack of support became a sign of superiority, rather than an indication of its mistakes and defeat. Members cultivated their differences from others as proof of their being among the few "elect." Similarly aristocratic conceptions of self-identity are characteristic of other small totalistic groups, such as secret societies (Simmel 1950; Hazelrigg 1969) and sects (Niebuhr 1937; Wilson 1959).

Frame amplification is evident as well in the way terrorist groups define their adversary. Social movement ideologies, it has been said, tend to adopt a dicotomous image of the world, based on an inward-outward definition (Gerlach and Hine 1970). They represent the movement's counterculture as enacting "collective dramas" or rhetorical "phantasy themes" in which the actors in the conflict are "heroes" and "villains" and the setting consist of "profane" and "sacred" ground (Rogers 1985a, 1985b). The peculiarity of underground organizations is that they amplify the dichotomous confrontation. First, they define an "absolute" enemy. Among the Italian militants, Passerini observes, the widely accepted idea of "militant" antifascism provided the rationale for a process of frame amplification that would justify violence. The enemies were "fascist" and therefore responsible for all the enormities of the Mussolini dictatorship. In an even more abstract way, the terrorists described the victims of their attacks as "wheels of the capitalist machine" and therefore as responsible for all capitalist evil. The militants denied the possibility that there could be any mediate positions between the two adversaries. In the words of Ulrike Meinhof, the world is divided into "human beings and pigs." Their conflict is not reconcilable. The dichotomous image of conflict was "amplified" into an image of military war. Both the German and the Italian militants described how they perceived reality in military terms: they adopted a military jargon to define the external world; they divided the world into dangerous and free zones; and they judged successes and defeats in a military way.

Like the term "partisan" applied to forces in a war (Schmitt 1975) the terrorists' image of an "absolute enemy" imply an alternative "legal" system, while denying the legitimacy of a foreign ruler or a political regime because of its "crimes." Moreover, in order not to appear inhuman, anyone who assumes the self-appointed right to kill requires an absolutely evil enemy as justification. Contrasting one's own behavior with the more "inhuman" acts of the enemy is a technique for displacing responsibility. Dehumanizing the enemy is a way to deny any responsibility for one's victims (Crenshaw 1988). In other words, the war analogy allows for a suspension of normal values and behavior. As a result, the social and political dimensions of the activists' motivations gradually dissipate, and the "military" metaphor becomes real and self-sustained in the militants' continuous clashes with the state apparatuses. As Crenshaw has observed, terrorist and counterterrorist groups tend to become mirror images of each other, each consciously imitating the other. Thus, both underground groups and antiterrorist policies become more and more "militarized," each side fueling the violence of the other and so reducing the possibility of political solutions to the conflict.

To conclude, we should note that some organizational processes and dynamics typical of underground groups appear as well in the legal activism of social movements. In social movements as in the underground, activists construct "new" cultures, and commitment transforms the individual's private life. Social movements also produce collective identities to which the members willingly subordinate their own identities or roles. Further, social movements, Roots (1983) has observed, are particularly sensitive to the participants' structure of perceptions and the distribution of knowledge. Collective identities and the activists' motivations to participate are enforced by the integration of the individual into a movement counterculture built on alternative value systems and social structures. Activism in the social movement organizations strongly influences the "lenses" through which reality is perceived, information is selected, and motivations are produced.

Terrorist organizations, of course, differ from other social movements organizations in significant ways—most of which arise from the terrorists' isolation from the external world and from their almost daily use of criminal forms of action. Nevertheless, because it is important for empirical research on social movements to analyze the effects of organizational structure and violent interactions on activists' motivations, the study of underground organizations is entirely relevant, for like a kind of magnifying glass, it can clarify processes and dynamics that may also be present—though to a different degree—in nonunderground political organizations.

Conclusion

In this introduction, I have surveyed some of the major results of research on individual motivations in underground organizations. In the first part, I stressed that to understand differential recruitment and escalation of commitment in terrorist groups as well as in social movement organizations, we must look not at the psychological characteristics of the activists but at their relational positions. Accordingly, we examined the role personal networks played in the different stages of an activist's involvement in radical politics, including the decision to join the underground. The militants' youth and the high risks involved in militance in the underground appeared as factors that strengthened affective ties with comrade-friends.

Friendship ties, however, could not account for the environmental conditions that allowed for the radicalization of action strategies. As we saw, several processes contributed to the escalation, both symbolic and actual, of political conflict. To identify these processes, we examined some of the ways in which physically violent interactions and state repression affected the prominent images in political countercultures. The networks in which the underground organizations found their recruits were part of a larger political counterculture. As protest strategies confronted counterstrategies, the repertoires of collective actions expanded and became increasingly violent. In this process, activists developed new skills and new structures for carrying out violent action. The second generation of activists, which was socialized to politics after violence had become accepted in larger or smaller wings of the social movement sector, thus accepted radical action as routine. Moreover, the militants' attitudes toward politics changed, and they began to find justifications for the more radical forms of action which developed in their everyday experiences. As a result of its over-repressive counterstrategies, the state was perceived throughout the counterculture as nondemocratic and unfair. A "military attitude" toward political conflicts became pervasive.

These processes underwent a qualitative change in the underground organizations. Once an activist was recruited into an underground group—having been compelled to join by a combination of individual motives and environmental preconditions—the very specific conditions of participation in such a group determined the characteristics of further commitment. As "greedy institutions," these groups required a total commitment from their members, thus isolating them from the outside world and making them completely dependent on the organizations. Accordingly, the individual's value systems and perceptions of the external world became those of the group, and his or her motivational structure was transformed. By internalizing the group's rigid ideological systems, characterized by extreme elitism and "absolute" enmity, the militants accepted the definition of the situation as a war. This militaristic outlook in turn shaped their perceptions and motivations.

These findings, among others presented in the essays that compose this book, can greatly improve our understanding of individual militance in underground groups. By integrating macro-, meso- and micro-processes, we can in fact explain the complex mechanisms through which reality is constructed in the underground. The biographical method allows us to follow the gradual evolution of political commitment and of images of social conflict. Given this framework, we have been able to offer much more comprehensive explanations for individual motivations in underground than we could devise with models of "strategic" but "evil" behavior or of "craziness." Thus we have arrived at some important answers to the main question that students of underground organizations often ask: How do "normal" activists evolve into "terrorists"?

This collection presents some of the first research to adopt the biographical method. But the sociological literature on individual motivations in the underground contains several gaps, and much remains to be done. The first gap lies in the amount of material we have on militants in different forms of underground organizations. The comparative papers in this volume indicate that the degree to which a terrorist organization is isolated from its external environment differs significantly with the type of organization. But we have still to make a comparative assessment of the effects of the various forms of underground organizations on the motivational dynamics of their members. To make a systematic comparison, however, we will need to collect and analyze much more biographical material.

A second major gap in the literature is an "exogenous" one. We will be able to state what is "typical" of underground groups only when we have gathered enough biographical material on those activists in the broader countercultures—indeed, the majority—who did not join underground groups. With few exceptions (see della Porta [1990b] for a review), research on the life histories of social movement activists is almost nonexistent. Another serious deficiency in social movement research is the lack of studies on the effects of movement participation on the individual, or on "the ongoing dynamics of individual activism" (McAdam, McCarthy and Zald 1988, p. 729). Following this line of thought, Neidhardt and Rucht (1990) have stressed the need for studying the characteristics of the subcultural milieus of social movements—of their network structures and alternative life styles. Only by working within this broad research frame, can we hope to understand fully the evolution of individual motivation from nonviolent to radical forms of action.

We can identify a third major gap as the underdevelopment of methodologies appropriate for the study of the interactive dynamics that explain individual motivations. While researchers have elaborated sophisticated techniques to measure causal correlations, they have done much less for an empirical study of complex sets of interactions. Rational strategic action has received far more attention than self-sustaining escalation produced by miscalculations, which, according to several studies, were often the source of political violence. Commentators have singled out a similar deficiency in the sociology of social movements, namely the underdeveloped state of knowledge on the dynamics of collective action once the movement has emerged (McAdam, McCarthy and Zald 1988). In particular, social movement research has paid surprisingly little attention to the interactions between social movement organizations and their opponents and has neglected the black-and-white perceptions of reality these interactions tend to produce (Klandermans 1989, p. 302). Indeed, one of the main areas for future research is the analysis of the ways in which specific conflicts escalate into "metaconflicts" as movement and countermovement strategies interact (Neidhardt and Rucht 1990). The more information on these dynamics that becomes available, the more urgent the need for methodological techniques to analyze the empirical data and for appropriate concepts to transform the new findings into theoretical knowledge. The authors of this book hope to stimulate both empirical research and reflection on methodological and theoretical tools suitable for analyzing apparently "absurd" phenomena.

References

Baumann, M. 1976. *Tupamaros Berlin-Ouest* [Tupamaros West Berlin]. Paris: Les Presses d'aujourd'hui.

Becker, H. S. 1960. "Notes on the Concept of Commitment." *American Journal of Sociology* 66:32–40.

Berger, P. and T. Luckmann. 1966. *The Social Construction of Reality: A Treatise in the Sociology of Knowledge*. Garden City, NY: Anchor Books.

Billing, O. 1984. "The Case History of a German Terrorist." *Terrorism* 7:1–10.

Boucher, D. 1977. "Radical Ideologies and the Sociology of Knowledge: A Model for Comparative Analysis." *Sociology* 11: 25–46.

Coser, L. A. 1974. *Greedy Institutions: Patterns of Undivided Commitment*. New York: Free Press.

Crenshaw, M. 1988. "The Subjective Reality of Terrorists: Ideological and Psychological Factors in Terrorism," Pp. 12–46 in *Current Perspectives on International Terrorism*, edited by R. O. Slater and M. Stohl. London: Macmillan.

della Porta, D. 1983. "Le cause del terrorismo nelle società contemporanee" ["The Causes for Terrorism in Contemporary Societies]." Pp. 9–47 in *Terrorismo e violenza politica. Tre casi a confronto: Stati Uniti, Germania e Giappone* [Terrorism and Political Violence. A Comparison of Three Cases: United States, Germany and Japan], edited by D. della Porta and G. Pasquino. Bologna: Il Mulino.

———. 1987. "Storie di vita e movimenti collettivi. Una tecnica per lo studio delle motivazioni alla militanza politica" ["Life Histories and Collective Movements. A Technique for the Study of Motivation in Political Activism"]. *Rassegna italiana di sociologia* 28:105–131.

———. 1988. "Recruitment Processes in Clandestine Political Organizations: Italian Left-Wing Terrorism." Pp. 155–169 in *New Social Movements in Western Europe and the United States*. edited by B. Klandermans, H. Kriesi and S. Tarrow. Greenwich, CT: JAI Press.

———. 1990a. *Il terrorismo di sinistra* [Left-wing Terrorism]. Bologna: Il Mulino.

———. 1990b. *Biographies of Social Movement Activists: State of the Art and Methodological Problems*. Paper presented at the ECPR Joint Sessions, Bochum, April.

della Porta, D., and S. Tarrow. 1987. "Unwanted Children. Political Violence and the Cycle of Protest in Italy, 1966–1973." *European Journal of Political Research* 14:607–632.

Erikson, B. H. 1981. "Secret Societies and Social Structures." *Social Forces* 60: 188–210.

Franceschini, A., P. Buffa, and F. Giustolisi. 1988. *Mara, Renato ed io. Storia dei fondatori delle Brigate Rosse* [Mara, Renato and I. The Story of the Red Brigades' Founders]. Milan: Mondadori.

Gamson, W. A., B. Fireman and S. Rytina. 1982. *Encounters with Unjust Authorities*. Homewood, IL: Dorsey Press.

Garner, R. and M. N. Zald. 1983. *Social Movement Sector and Systemic Constraints: Toward a Structural Analysis of Social Movements*. CRSO Working Paper no. 238. University of Michigan.

Gerlach, L. P. and V. Hine. 1970. *People, Power, Change: Movements of Social Transformation*. New York: Bobbs-Merrill.

Goffman, E. 1963. *Stigma: Notes on the Management of Spoiled Identity*. Englewood Cliffs, NJ: Prentice-Hall.

———. 1974. *Frame Analysis. An Essay on the Organization of Experience*. Cambridge: Harvard University Press.

Granovetter, M. 1973. "The strength of weak ties." *American Journal of Sociology* 78:1360–1380.

Gurr, T. R. 1988. "Empirical Research on Political Terrorism: The State of the Art and How it Might Be Improved." Pp. 115–154 in *Current Perspectives on International Terrorism*, edited by R. O. Slater and M. Stohl. London: MacMillan.

Hazelrigg, L. E. 1969. "A Reexamination of Simmel's 'The Secret and the Secret Society': Nine Propositions." *Social Forces* 47: 323–330.

Ivianski, Z. 1983. "A Chapter in the Story of Individual Terror: Andrey Zhelyabol." Pp. 85–96 in *Perspectives on Terrorism*, edited by L.Z. Freedman and Y. Alexander. Wilmington, DE: Scholarly Resource Inc.

Keniston, K. 1968. *Young Radicals: Notes on Committed Youth*. New York: Harcourt, Brace and World.

Klandermans, B. G. 1984. "Mobilization and Participation in Social Movements: A Socio-Psychological Expansion of the Resource Mobilization Theory." *American Sociological Review* 49:583–600.

———. 1989. "Introductions." Pp. 1–17; 21–32; 117–128; 215–224; 301–314 in *Organizing for Change*, edited by B. Klandermans. Greenwich CT: JAI Press.

Klandermans, B.G., H. Kriesi, and S. Tarrow (eds.). 1988. *From Structure to Action: Comparing Social Movement Research Across Cultures*. Greenwich CT: JAI Press.

Klein, H.-J. 1980. *La mort mercenaire. Temoignage d'un ancient terroriste ouest-allemand* [The Mercenary Death: Testimony of a West-German Former Terrorist]. Paris: Seuil.

Knutson, J. N. 1981. "Social and Psychological Pressures Toward a Negative Identity: The Case of an American Revolutionary Terrorist," Pp. 105–150 in *Behavioral and Quantitative Perspectives on Terrorism*, edited by Y. Alexander and J. M. Gleamson. New York: Pergamon Press.

Livingstone, N. C. 1982. *The War Against Terrorism*. Lexington, KY: Lexington Books.

Lofland, J. and R. Stark. 1965. "Becoming a World-Saver: A Theory of Conversion to a Deviant Perspective." *American Sociological Review* 30:362–374.

Manconi, L. 1988. "Il nemico assoluto. Antifascismo e contropotere nella fase aurorale del terrorismo di sinistra" [The Absolute Enemy: Anti-fascism and Counter-Power at the Dawn of Left-Wing Terrorism]. *Polis* 2:259–286.

Matza, D. 1969. *Becoming Deviant*. Englewood Cliffs, NJ: Prentice-Hall.

McAdam, D. 1986. "Recruitment to High-Risk Activism: The Case of Freedom Summer." *American Journal of Sociology* 92:64–90.

McAdam, D., J.D. McCarthy and M. Zald. 1988. "Social Movements." Pp. 695–737 in *Handbook of Sociology*, edited by N. J. Smelser. Beverly Hills, CA: Sage.

McPhail, C. 1971. "Civil disorder participation: A critical examination of recent research." *American Sociological Review* 36:1058–1073.

McPhail, C., and D. Miller. 1973. "The Assembling Process: A Theoretical and Empirical Examination." *American Sociological Review* 38:721–735.

Merkl, P. H. 1986. "Approaches to the Study of Political Violence." Pp. 19–59 in *Political Violence and Terror. Motifs and Motivations*, edited by P. H. Merkl. Berkeley: University of California Press.

Nahirni, V. C. 1962. "Some Observations on Ideological Groups." *American Journal of Sociology* 67: 397–405.

Neidhardt, F. and D. Rucht. 1990. "The Analysis of Social Movements: The State of the Art and Some Perspective for Further Research." In *Research on Social Movements: The State of the Art in Western Europe and the USA*, edited by D. Rucht. Frankfurt/M. and Boulder: Campus and Westview Press.

Niebuhr, R. H. 1937. "Sects." Pp. 624–631 in *Encyclopaedia of the Social Sciences*, Vol. 13. New York: Macmillan.

Novaro, C. 1988. "Reti amicali e lotta armata" [Friendship Networks and Armed Struggle]. *Polis* 2:287–320.

Novelli, D. and N. Tranfaglia. 1988. *Vite sospese. Le generazioni del terrorismo*. [Suspended Lives: The Generations of Terrorism]. Milan: Garzanti.

O'Toole, R. 1975. "Sectarianism in Politics. Case Studies of Maoists and Leninists." Pp. 162–190 in *Sectarianism: Analysis of Religious and Non-religious Sects* edited by R. Wallis. New York: Wiley.

Pasquino, G. and D. della Porta. 1986. "Interpretations of Italian Left-Wing Terrorism." Pp. 169–189 in *Political Violence and Terror. Motifs and Motivations*, edited by P. H. Merkl. Berkeley: University of California Press.

Rasch, W. 1979. "Psychological Dimensions of Political Terrorism in the Federal Republic of Germany." *International Journal of Law and Psychiatry* 2:79–85.

Reynaud, E. 1982. "Identites collective et changement social: les cultures collectives comme dynamique d'action." *Sociologie du travail* 2: 159–177.

Rogers, K. L. 1985a. *Decoding a City of Words: Fantasy Theme Analysis and the Interpretation of Oral Interviews*. Paper.

———. 1985b. "Words Testify in Spite of Us": The Experience of CORE As a Subculture. Unpublished paper.

Roots, C. A. 1983. "On the Social Structural Sources of Political Conflict: An Approach from the Theory of Knowledge." *Research in Social Movements, Conflict, and Change*. 5:33–54.

Russel C. A. and B. H. Miller. 1983. "Profile of a terrorist." Pp. 45–59 in *Perspectives on Terrorism*, edited by L. Z. Freedman and Y. Alexander. Wilmington, DE: Scholarly Resource Inc.

Sartori, G. 1969. "Politics, Ideology, and Belief System." *American Political Science Review* 63:398–411.

Schmidtchen, G. 1981. "Terroristische Karrieren" [Terrorist Careers]. Pp. 14–77 in H. Jaeger, G. Schmidtchen, and L. Suellwold, *Lebenslaufanalysen* [Analysis of Life Careers]. Opladen: Westdeutscher.

Schmitt, C. 1975. *Teoria del partigiano. Note complementari al concetto di politica* [Theory of the Partisan. Complementary Notes to the Concept of Politics]. Milan: Il saggiatore.

Simmel, G. 1950. "The Secret and the Secret Societies." Pp. 345–376 in *The Sociology of George Simmel*, edited by K. H. Wolff. New York: Free Press.

Smith, B. L., H. D. Lasswell, and R. D. Casey. 1946. *Propaganda, Communication, and Public Opinion. A Comprehensive Reference Guide*. Chicago: University of Chicago Press.

Snow, D. A. and R. Machalek. 1983. "The Convert As A Social Type." Pp. 259–289 in *Sociological Theory*, edited by R. Collins. San Francisco: Jossey-Bass.

Snow, D. A., E. B. Rochford, S. K. Worden, and R. D. Benford. 1986. "Frame alignment processes, micromobilization, and movement participation." *American Sociological Review* 51: 464–481.

Snow, D. A., L. A. Zurcher, and S. Ekland-Olson. 1980. "Social networks and social movements: A microstructural approach to differential recruitment." *American Sociological Review* 45:787–801.

Tarrow, S. 1989. *Struggle, Politics, and Reform: Collective Action, Social Movements, and Cycle of Protest*. Western Societies Program Occasional Paper no. 21, Ithaca NY.

Tilly, C. 1984. "Social Movements and National Politics." Pp. 297–317 in *Statemaking and Social Movements: Essays in History and Theory*, edited by C. Bright and S. Harding. Ann Arbor: University of Michigan Press.

Toloyan, K. 1987. "Culture Narrative and the Motivation of the Terrorist." *Journal of Strategic Studies* 10:217–233.

Useem, M. 1972. "Ideological and Interpersonal Change in the Radical Protest Movement." *Social Problems* 19:451–469.

Verba, S. 1961. *Small Groups and Political Behavior. A Study of Leadership*. Princeton: Princeton University Press.

Wasmund, K. 1986. "The Political Socialization of West German Terrorists." Pp. 191–228 in *Political Violence and Terror: Motifs and Motivations*, edited by P. H. Merkl. Berkeley: University of California Press.

White, R. W. 1989. "From Peaceful Protest to Guerrilla War: Micromobilization of the Provisional Irish Republican Army." *American Journal of Sociology* 94:1277–1302.

Wilson, B. R. 1959. "An Analysis of Sect Development." *American Sociological Review* 24:3–15.

Wilson, J. 1973. *Introduction to Social Movements*. New York: Basic Books.

Wolfgang, M. and F. Ferracuti. 1967. *The Subculture of Violence*. London: Tavistock.

Zald, M. and R. Ash. 1966. "Social Movement Organizations: Growth, Decay, and Change." *Social Forces* 44:327–341.

Zald, M., J. D. McCarthy, et al. 1987. *Social Movements in an Organizational Society*. New Brunswick, NJ: Transaction.

16 Decisions to use terrorism

Psychological constraints on instrumental reasoning

Martha Crenshaw

Terrorism is often considered the result of a strategic choice based on instrumental reasoning (Crenshaw 1990; DeNardo 1985). In this perspective, terrorism is analyzed as a form of political violence designed to affect the attitudes of specific audiences whose reactions determine political outcomes. Terrorism is interpreted as a calculated course of action, chosen from a range of alternatives according to a ranked set of values. The efficacy of terrorism as a means of political influence is assumed to be the primary criterion of choice. Decision makers in the organizations that use terrorism are supposed to rely on explicit strategic conceptions to guide group behavior. These conceptions then become the focus of analysis. To explain a particular terrorist action, one asks what strategic purpose it was meant to accomplish.

Like all rational choice explanations of political action, this one is incomplete. My intention is not to contest the premise that terrorism is often strategic behavior, but to describe possible psychological barriers to purely strategic calculation in underground organizations. Psychological factors influence both the initiation and the conduct of terrorism and may be the source of actions that are incomprehensible if interpreted strictly as external goal-oriented behavior. We may be misled if we assume that such outcomes are the result of deliberate choice. Psychological interactions within underground organizations can provoke groups to action that is counterproductive in terms of long-term goals. Although psychological factors may occasionally reinforce the grounds for decisions that are instrumentally based, they may also interfere with strategic calculation of ends and means. I ask how group dynamics and collective belief systems influence the use of terrorism by making it possible, motivating it, determining its forms, and instigating its escalation or decline.

Any such analysis must be sensitive to variations in context. Terrorism is the resort of numerous groups acting in terms of different social and political situations, ideological backgrounds, and prospects of ultimate success. Yet there is a psychology of small, radical, illegal conspiracies that distinguishes them from other political and social actors. The hypotheses I suggest may be applicable primarily to underground organizations without substantial ethnic or other ascriptive constituencies and which are consequently isolated from society. Groups that are closed rather than open to contacts outside the group may be less likely to be strategic in their reasoning.

Group dynamics

The appropriate focus for a psychological explanation is the interaction of individuals within the group, not individual personality. The idea of terrorism as the product of mental disorder or psychopathology has been discredited. In a recent review of the literature, Maxwell Taylor concludes that it is inappropriate to think of the terrorist as mentally ill in conventional terms and that the individual psychology of the terrorist cannot be characterized in general (Taylor 1988).

Such groups recruit selectively and exclude aspirants who are undisciplined or untrustworthy. Furthermore, the group takes on an independent collective identity that transcends individual characteristics. Radical organizations typically unite people of different backgrounds and temperaments. Participation in the extremist group and commitment to a collective belief system, rather than any shared propensity for violence or inclination toward aggression, bind members together. As Albert Bandura (1979, p. 338) notes, "it requires conducive social conditions rather than monstrous people to produce heinous deeds." Jerrold Post (1987, pp. 25–26) also emphasizes that "once individuals join a terrorist group individual differences disappear in the face of the powerful unifying forces of group and organizational psychology" and that "group psychology provides a powerful explanation for this uniformity of behavior within the diverse population of terrorist groups." Thus the topics of most interest to the researcher are group recruitment and socialization processes, not individual personality characteristics prior to joining the group.

For political oppositions, the initial decision to use terrorism against the state usually requires a transition to clandestine life in the underground, a decision that in many contexts is irreversible. "The roads of retreat are all closed; one blows up all the bridges behind one in the truest sense of the word," explains Michael "Bommi" Baumann, a member of a West German terrorist group (Baumann 1977, p. 109). The move to the underground may even be precipitated by acts of nonterrorist violence. For example, the West German Red Army Fraction's attempt to rescue Andreas Baader from prison resulted in the accidental killing of a guard and thus criminality and illegality: "From this point on there was no going back but only the 'forward escape'" (Wasmund 1986, p. 199).

The transition to clandestinity requires total commitment from an inner core of militants. Some undergrounds form a kind of counterculture, resembling that of religious cults or youth gangs. Illegality isolates the members of the group from society and encourages the development of distinctive values, norms, and standards of behavior. The collectivity usually demands the complete obedience of members. For reasons of security as well as discipline, the organization usually prohibits personal relationships outside the group. Contacts with the outside world are mediated through the institutions of the group. Insiders are trusted; outsiders are distrusted.

Relationships of leaders to followers in the group may contribute to the isolation of the group from society and to the growth of interdependence among members. A leader of the Uruguayan Tupamaros, in a prison interview with a journalist, explained that rather than trying to select recruits who possessed specific traits, the "Movement" tried to "proletarize" the new member: "the most important thing is to create in him a feeling of dependence on the group. He has to be aware of the fact that he cannot be self-sufficient—that the others are essential to him" (Gilio 1972, p. 137). In addition to explicit indoctrination procedures, the structure of an underground organization creates dependence on a central leadership, because, for security reasons, it is essential to restrict knowledge of the overall organizational structure. Leaders usually control contacts with the outside world as well as the dissemination of information within the group. The authority of leaders within extremist undergrounds may be based on command of ideology (intellectual authority), operational expertise (military authority), or charisma (personal authority). Leaders also base their authority on the ability to manipulate incentives for followers. These incentives are both political—the ability to move the group toward accomplishment of collective goals—and psychological. For example, threatening expulsion from the group or from the inner circle is a powerful way of inhibiting dissent. In addition, leaders are under pressure to conform to group norms and to preserve ideological purity. Their freedom of action is thus limited.

In general, the members of such organizations are not suddenly converted to terrorism but acquire their commitment gradually, often through belonging to a group, set of friends, or family unit that collectively turns to terrorism. That is, people are recruited into terrorism through personal associations that precede or accompany political commitment. With regard to the West German left-wing groups, Klaus Wasmund (1986, p. 204) notes that "Most terrorists, in fact, have ultimately become members of terrorist organizations through personal connections with people or relatives associated with appropriate political initiatives, communes, self-supporting organizations, or committees—the number of couples, and brothers and sisters is astonishingly high." Leonard Weinberg and William Lee Eubank found in Italy that "it seems reasonable to suspect that the decision to become a terrorist was often not that of individual choice. Likely it involved a decision, and a gradual one at that, by a primary group whose members reached consensus over the desirability of violent political engagement" (1987, p. 83). Ties to other members of the group are independent of commitment to collective goals. As a consequence, the importance of the group to the individual is heightened. Loyalty is primarily to the group or entity, not to abstract objectives or ideology. At the least, the individual is unable to separate these two emotional and cognitive commitments—the one to friends, the other to ideals.

Therefore the pressures toward cohesion and uniformity that exist in all primary groups are likely to be intensified under the circumstances of underground life. Solidarity is all the more critical because the group usually lives under conditions of acute threat and high stress. Exposure to danger increases cohesion. The tension created by the underground situation may lead to high levels of anxiety, aggravated by fatigue. Such conditions decrease a group's ability to identify alternatives, estimate costs and benefits, assess outcomes, evaluate audience perspectives, and adjust to changes in the environment (Holsti 1972, pp. 7–25).

Furthermore, underground organizations usually suffer high rates of attrition. The death or imprisonment of group members may lead to the activation of the defense mechanism of identifying with the lost comrade. Through a process of introjection, the remaining members of the group take on the values of the dead or captured members (Janis 1968, pp. 84–85). As a result, adherence to group standards is strengthened because abandonment would be viewed as an act of disloyalty. In some ways, the behavior of members of such groups resembles that of soldiers under combat conditions. Disloyalty to one's comrades constitutes betrayal, the most serious violation of group norms.

Thus deviation from group standards is probably rare because of mutual interdependence, peer pressure, sensitivity to betrayal, and security risks. Ordinarily, members of these groups seek above all to avoid the disapproval of their peers. Dissent is emotionally painful. Both external danger and internal dissent may stimulate a need for reassurance, leading the faithful and loyal members to become more dependent on the group, its leaders, and collective beliefs. Thus where factionalism occurs—and it is common to many groups such as the Palestinian and Basque movements—solidarity within "survivor" groups may be intensified. Furthermore, the dissenters who form new factions are also likely to feel acutely dependent on the new group because they have sacrificed so much to join. The high entrance fee is likely to discourage exit (Hirschman 1970).

Whereas some groups such as the IRA permit their members to leave the group so long as they do not inform on it, others punish defection as "betrayal." There are then physical as well as psychological penalties associated with exit. One would expect dissent to be even more distressful under circumstances of high personal risk, which includes the prospect of punishment from the government as well as retribution from one's comrades.

Belief systems

A key role of the leadership is to develop or maintain a collective belief system that links overall ideological orientation to the environment in which the group operates. Ascertaining what terrorists believe is not a simple task (Crenshaw 1988). Appropriate sources are difficult to acquire.

It is difficult to distinguish motive from rationalization. The beliefs of violent extremists are often quite complex as well as hard to know. Nevertheless, understanding how underground groups view the world and themselves is essential to explaining terrorism. In particular, one must ask if their perceptions of the effects of their actions on audiences become distorted because of simplifying beliefs that guide action. For example, Alessandro Silj (1979) observed that the Italian Red Brigades "lost perspective on the situation" upon entering the underground; their misinterpretation of the likely reactions of relevant audiences resulted from isolation. "In part, the very logic of clandestinity, the dynamic of a process which, once set in motion, was irreversible, contributed to such a misperception" (Silj 1979, p. 115). Mistakes—particularly the false expectation that the Italian government was on the verge of collapse in 1971—were encouraged by the movement into the underground.

The sharpest and clearest aspect of the beliefs that may be conducive to terrorism is identification and characterization of the enemy. In a pattern that is typical of much social conflict, the enemy is portrayed as an undifferentiated and monolithic entity, usually an abstraction such as a system or a class. Wasmund (1986, pp. 215, 218) observes that "a friend-enemy mentality exists which is typical of all totalitarian groupings" and that the enemy is a figure that symbolizes everything "bad." The stereotypical enemy is both unrelentingly hostile and morally corrupt. Society as well as the state may be perceived as the enemy—the bourgeoisie, for example, or capitalism. The enemy may even be international; multinational imperialism is often a common enemy of the radical right and the radical left.

The self-image of the terrorist is ambivalent, even contradictory. Terrorists need to see themselves as doing good, to justify their actions, and to maintain morale. Consequently "auto-propaganda" may be more critical to group survival than are attempts to persuade external audiences, whether governments, constituencies, or likeminded groups (Cordes 1988). The users of terrorism often see themselves as victims, but also as an avant-garde acting on behalf of victims of injustice. They act for "the people" who are unable to act for themselves. They are simultaneously victims and righteous avengers, targets of oppression and soldiers. This conviction may be strengthened by the belief that they do not stand to gain personally from their efforts. Altruism and self-sacrifice are dominant themes, yet the key metaphor in terrorist literature is struggle and combat. A strong trace of millenarianism, with its faith in personal redemption through violence, is evident (Rapoport 1987).

Beliefs about enemy and self overshadow references to the actual victims of terrorism, whose deaths or injuries are usually blamed on others (governments who refuse to heed warnings, for example). They do pay attention, however, to the audiences for terrorism and interpret the world in causal terms (Hopple and Steiner 1984). The image of the "people" in Western democracies, for example, is based on imperfect assumptions of benevolence and ignorance. The physical victims of terrorism, whatever their personal identity, are never seen as members of the social classes whom the terrorists claim to represent.

The sources of these beliefs, which justify terrorism, lie in political culture and in psychological needs. Beliefs are selectively derived from the group's political, social, and cultural environment and thus reflect prevailing ideologies as well as socialization patterns. The intellectuals who lead or participate in groups that use terrorism are rarely philosophical or ideological innovators. Beliefs also serve important psychological needs, such as compensation for an inability to deal with aggressive feelings. They may aid in the external attribution of blame and the projection of hostility onto the enemy. Ideological rationalizations may mask a form of generational rebellion against authority displaced onto political figures. The low self-esteem exhibited by some individuals in these groups and their view of the enemy as omnipotent may be signs of developmental immaturity. The fact that most terrorists are young provides some support for this hypothesis. People who commit acts of violence may also need to neutralize guilt—guilt over their victims, survivor guilt when comrades are lost, or guilt over aggressive impulses toward parents or surrogate authority figures.

Psychological research in different theoretical traditions suggests that individual beliefs are likely to be stable rather than volatile. Even greater stability should characterize collective attitudes that are constantly reinforced by group interaction. Theories of cognitive consistency indicate that individuals absorb only information that supports their beliefs, ignore disconfirming evidence, fail to recognize value conflicts, and neglect to reconsider decisions once they are reached. Other approaches emphasize the emotional conflict that lies behind decision making. The more costly the consequences of a decision, the more painful the reassessment. Members of the groups who use terrorism may engage in what Irving Janis and Leon Mann call "defensive avoidance" (Janis and Mann 1977). Ego involvement in prior commitments is bound to be strong, and the cost of abandoning them unacceptably high. Furthermore, the nature of a belief system itself may preclude change. The least systematic beliefs are the most resilient, and the least empirically relevant are the most incontrovertible because they cannot be tested or falsified. Vague and distant long-term goals can be an advantage. "True believers" are not by nature skeptical (Snow and Machalek 1982).

It is also possible that the resort to terrorism precedes and consequently determines beliefs. That is, rather than acting as a result of preconceptions, people may act impulsively or unthinkingly and then rationalize their actions. "Self-perception theory" is based on the assumption that individuals use their own actions as a guide to the formation of attitudes and beliefs, through a process of self-inference (Larson 1985, pp. 42–50). Engaging in terrorism, perhaps because of coincidence or group pressures, leads the individual to adopt beliefs and images that explain the moral necessity and practical efficacy of terrorism. Once convinced that terrorism is intellectually justified, an individual is persuaded in retrospect that the initial use of terrorism was based on prior ideological beliefs. Because terrorism is extreme behavior, usually condemned by society, it is important for the individual to generate an explanation for it. When terrorists are students, the need to intellectualize terrorist activity may be particularly strong. Groups formed of people with diverse social backgrounds (such as the Provisional IRA) may feel less need for intellectual rationalizations or self-inference. The Provisional IRA appears to feel that the reasons for terrorism are self-evident.

Jeanne Knutson (1980) effectively described the relationship between group pressures and rigid but subjective belief systems: "Doubts are muted and are continuously attacked by the group, which employs great psychological pressure toward conformity. Basic concepts are challenged with great difficulty. ... There is no real debate over primary assumptions" (p. 213). The group seeks a "homogeneous level of ... thought which stifles self-doubt and a consideration of alternatives" (p. 213). She quoted one of her interviewees as admitting that "we were increasingly losing our grip on reality" and that cutting off contacts with the outside world led to a "group personality" with its own deadly internal momentum (pp. 213–214). She concluded, "In such an atmosphere, group actions take on a predetermined, fatalistic quality in which *responsibility* for the occurrence of specific actions is progressively shifted onto the opposition players in the government, general social forces, or an inactive populace, and terrorist players come to experience themselves as guided by an externally perceived necessity" (p. 214; also Wasmund 1986, pp. 218–220). The cohesiveness of the group strengthens adherence to beliefs, and in turn beliefs reinforce solidarity.

Implications for the practice of terrorism

These psychological factors have important implications for terrorist behavior. On a general level, members of groups may act simply to maintain a collective identity and thus seek to keep the group alive whatever its political accomplishments. Baumann (1977, p. 76) explains, "I saw that it was going to go a hundred percent wrong . ... I only participated out of solidarity." Dependence on the group is likely to lead members to value the approval of other members of the group more than the achievement of long-term political goals. Thus an objective definition of success, predicated on the achievement of political ends, may not be appropriate. When extremist organizations such as ETA and the Provisional IRA persist despite objective failure, one must ask whether or not simply keeping the group together has become more important than a Basque homeland or a united Ireland.

One consequence of the centrality of the group is that motives that unite its members, such as vengeance, take precedence over instrumental calculations, which can be deeply divisive. Newman and Lynch (1987) argue that terrorism may be a "cycle of violence" fueled by vengeance, leading to its self-perpetuation. They argue that the only possible common ideology associated with terrorism is one of vengeance, a code of conduct that shapes behavior. The code of vengeance embodies its own justification, giving the terrorist not only a moral claim but an obligation. Terrorism thus becomes a sophisticated modern form of feuding. Vengeance, which is motivated by a sense of injustice and of powerlessness, is based on the principle of reciprocity. Escalation occurs because the act of retribution is never an exact match for the original offense. Those who administer it cannot resist adding an element of coercion, trying to make the response to perceived injustice sufficiently strong to deter counterretribution. The avenger develops identity through violence, thus generating a process without limits. Only vengeance can defend one's honor, which is an essential component of identity.

The intense loyalty that members of the underground group feel for each other, a loyalty strengthened by bonds of kinship or personal affection, makes revenge imperative when government security forces kill or imprison comrades. Such an outcome is highly likely once a group resorts to terrorism, which is bound to provoke a repressive government reaction. Because revenge motivates both sides, terrorism and the response to terrorism create an independent and self-contained logic. Eventually repression from the authorities provokes actions intended only to avenge comrades, not to change the positions of government or society (Silj 1979, p. 219). Revenge is part of a process of using violence in order to strengthen group cohesiveness, confirm beliefs about self and world, and maintain group morale and individual self-esteem. These needs are frequently characterized in terms of upholding "honor."

Jerrold Post (1987, p. 33) notes, moreover, that government "retaliation may actually strengthen the group and promote increased terrorist activity" because the terrorists' worldviews are confirmed and their cohesiveness is enhanced by threat and shared danger. Coercive government responses thus make terrorism self-sustaining because the terrorists' expectations of hostility are proved right. Terrorism can then be justified as defensive. But, as noted earlier, governments may not be able to control their own response or prevent the development of a cycle of vengeance and retribution. Once terrorism begins, both sides are likely to lose control.

Terrorist and counter-terrorist forces are often mirror images of each other. Each consciously imitates the other—terrorists act as "armies," while national armies develop specialized elite intervention forces that operate covertly. Each side's reputation is caught up in the struggle. The purpose of terrorism and of repression becomes to outdo the other. Each small, self-contained, and specialized unit tends to become autonomous from central authority. Examples include the Combat Organization of the Socialist Revolutionary Party in Russia, combatting the czarist secret police or Okhrana, and the Algiers terrorist units of the FLN against the French paratroopers. In these situations, the phenomenon of the double agent or agent-provocateur takes on special importance as the communication link between the two sides. The role of the informant or double agent remains a "neglected category" for analysis, as Gary T. Marx claimed (1974).

Because internal conflict threatens group cohesion and identity, leaders may try to deflect aggression onto external targets. For example, one reason for the creation of the Black September organization was apparently to absorb the intense frustration of younger militants over the Palestinian expulsion from Jordan in 1970. Arafat apparently decided to permit, if not direct, terrorism outside the Middle East in order to prevent internal dissent within Fatah.

Furthermore, adherence to the group and to its standards helps to overcome guilt. Even if group values are internalized, some individuals will experience anxiety and self-doubt. Peer pressure encourages members of the group to commit actions they would normally find morally reprehensible, such as killing children. Distress engendered by guilt leads to greater dependence on the group, increased group influence over the individual, and consequently more terrorism. The unpleasant prospect of accepting responsibility and suffering remorse may then prevent the individual from leaving the group.

The collective belief system can aid in assuaging guilt. Albert Bandura explains that "people do not ordinarily engage in reprehensible conduct until they have justified to themselves the morality of their actions. What is culpable can be made honorable through cognitive restructuring. In this process, reprehensible conduct is made personally and socially acceptable by portraying it in the service of moral ends" (1979, p. 351). He refers to mechanisms such as contrasting one's behavior with the more inhumane practices of one's enemy (palliative comparison), using euphemistic language to disguise violence and make it respectable, obscuring the consequences of one's actions, dehumanizing the enemy, blaming the victim, or displacing responsibility onto others or in fact onto a collective instrumentality. All collective arrangements, he notes, obscure individual responsibility. He further explains that "people frequently engage in violent activities not because of reduced self-control but because their cognitive skills and self-control are enlisted all too well through moral justifications and self-exonerative devices in the service of destructive causes" (p. 356). In effect, the beliefs of terrorist actors serve as a mechanism of "moral disengagement" (Bandura 1987). Upon entering an underground organization, the individual does not undergo a psychological conversion but comes to see violence as morally sanctioned.

Legal and military terms of discourse reinforce the image of the terrorist as the impersonal agent of larger forces. In the euphemistic language of terrorism, victims are "executed" after "trials." Terrorism becomes "urban guerilla warfare." Seeing oneself as a victim makes it hard to conceive of others as victims or oneself as an aggressor. The idea of acting on behalf of an oppressed but faceless constituency (the proletariat, the Third World, or prisoners) justifies practices that would be abhorrent if performed out of pure self-interest. William Ascher (1986), in interviewing Armenian and Irish supporters of terrorism (admittedly not the terrorists themselves) identifies moral indignation as a critical attitude and links it to "disinterestedness" or "distance": the less one has to gain personally from the outcome of violence, the more sincere and righteous one feels.

Psychological considerations may also explain the particular form terrorism takes. Hostage taking, for example, can be interpreted rationally as a form of coercive bargaining, a means of compensating for the greater power of governments, since weakness is not a disadvantage in situations of blackmail (Crenshaw 1990). Yet, it is also possible that a desperate need to free imprisoned comrades genuinely motivates hostage taking. "Second generation" successor groups in West Germany and Italy devoted themselves to freeing imprisoned "historic" or "founding" leaders. The demand for the release of prisoners may thus be sincere rather than a disguise for publicity-seeking behavior. Dependence on the group and its leaders, fear of a hostile government, or survivor guilt, may combine to make hostage takers feel desperate. Hostage taking may also be a search for recognition by the government, a result of the terrorists' collective self-image as powerless victims (Knutson 1980).

The desire to avoid responsibility for violent outcomes may also affect the form of terrorism. Terrorists wish to blame casualties on the government. The attribution of blame begins with an assignment of responsibility and a judgement about causality (Shaver 1985; Bandura 1987, p. 23). Terrorists may not see themselves as morally accountable because they believe that they did not originally intend or foresee a negative outcome. Their initial expectations upon seizing hostages, for example, are optimistic because they believe that the government will comply. Terrorists may be likely to think that governments have a certain knowledge of the outcome if concessions are refused. Furthermore, one way of reducing cognitive dissonance, induced by having to choose between the two negative options of killing hostages or giving up, is to believe that the only escape from the dilemma rests with the opponent (Holsti 1972). The terrorists are also likely to see themselves as having been coerced, rather than seeing the government as having been blackmailed. They do not perceive the killing of hostages as a voluntary action but as something the government compelled them to do. Terrorists can thus not only exonerate themselves but feel self-righteous and see their image of the evil state confirmed.

Similarly, in leaving bombs a group may accept responsibility but not blame, which perhaps reveals an interesting ability to separate these two processes. Maria McGuire, an early member of the Provisional IRA, describes a car-bomb in Belfast in 1972 that killed six and injured 146 people. In this case, the Provisionals falsely accused the security forces of deliberately muddling the telephoned warning in order to discredit the IRA. McGuire continues, "despite blaming the security forces, the movement 'accepted responsibility' for the explosion, and it was a curious thing that the Provisionals felt that by doing so they somehow atoned for the casualties. … I admit that at times I did not connect with the people who were killed or injured in such explosions. I always judged such deaths in terms of the effect they would have on our support, and I felt that this in turn depended on how many people accepted our explanation" (1973, p. 113).

In barricade and hostage situations, where stress and tension are high, hostage takers may be prone to panic. Their behavior, Janis and Mann (1977) would suggest, is likely to be erratic. They are tempted to precipitous action. If all choices appear unpleasant and time pressures are severe, their judgement will be poor. The responsibility for averting disaster will be seen to rest with the government. For example, during incidents such as the takeover of the Achille Lauro or the attempted hijacking of a Pan Am jet in Karachi, the aggressive behavior of the hijackers may have been the result of loss of emotional control, not deliberate calculation. What an instrumental approach would interpret as sequential killing of hostages in order to reinforce the credibility of a threat, a psychological approach would interpret as a panic reaction. The so-called Stockholm Syndrome, a shorthand term for the hypothesis that with time hostages and their captors will become attached to each other because of the phenomenon of identification with the aggressor, is thus unlikely to operate. Hostage takers or kidnappers are acting as agents of a group on which they are emotionally dependent in the extreme; letting the group down is probably a worse alternative than killing hostages of whom one has grown reasonably fond or even confronting death. The relationship with the group also enables the hostage takers to think of themselves as impersonal agents of the collective entity and thus avoid assuming individual responsibility.

The escalation of terrorism to greater levels of destructiveness may also result from psychological processes. For example, it is possible that the "risky shift" that research in experimental social psychology finds characteristic of small groups applies to political undergrounds (Crenshaw 1986, p. 397). Participation in group discussions leads to a heightened propensity to take risks. The individual's reluctance to let the group "down" or lose face in the eyes of peers may encourage this process. Yet, we also know that most groups are risk-averse in the sense of selecting soft, unprotected targets. The expansion of targets toward increasingly innocent victims is a form of escalation. A group setting facilitates brutalization. Participation in terrorism conditions and desensitizes the individual. Discomfort with violence is overcome by performing it. Routine sets in. Thus the absence of conditioning may impede the adaptation of "second generation" recruits who enter the group after its values have been formed. They may be the most likely defectors. On the other hand, candidates for membership in established organizations may be attracted to violence, while the founding members were attracted to the group.

To note the phenomenon of brutalization, however, is not to claim that all members of such groups actually participate in or are capable of participating in physical violence. Only a few elite members of the underground organizations are sharpshooters or bombers; most are support personnel. Role differentiation enables many members of the group to dissociate themselves from violence. Responsibility is diffused through the division of labor (Bandura 1987). Few group members confront their victims face-to-face. Reluctance to deal personally with victims may partially explain the popularity of bombings as opposed to other forms of terrorism.

Moreover, a common method of dealing with stress is to focus narrowly on the task at hand, rather than to reflect on the implication of one's actions (Roth 1982, pp. 52–53, referring to Finz 1975). This psychological defense or coping mechanism becomes less necessary as the task becomes habitual. Both compartmentalization and routinization reduce the discomfort an individual might initially feel upon committing an act of terrorism. When terrorists claim that they are only "soldiers," they are trying to achieve detachment and impersonality as well as to legitimize their actions.

Conclusions

This analysis suggests that a radical group's decision to enter the underground and isolate itself from society may be a decisive event in the development of terrorism. In circumstances where this decision entails extreme isolation from social support networks, clandestinity strengthens solidarity and dependence on group beliefs that justify violence. The more terrorism is used, the more it needs to be justified by moralistic attitudes. It may develop into a cycle of vengeance and retribution that is self-defeating.

Furthermore, this analysis suggests that justifications for terrorism and emotional support, both provided by the group, are critical. From this point of view, terrorism is likely to end when the bonds that link members of the group to each other are dissolved or when beliefs that justify violence break down or are discredited. But, as Franco Ferracuti has observed, "what happens in the mind of the terrorist who decides to abandon terrorism is not known" (1987, p. 13). Future research should focus on the psychology of dissent and of exit, as well as on the personal interactions and collective beliefs of groups.

References

Ascher, W. 1986. "The Moralism of Attitudes Supporting Intergroup Violence." *Political Psychology* 7, 3:403–425.

Bandura, A. 1979. "Psychological mechanisms of aggression." In *Human Ethology: Claims and Limits of a New Discipline,* edited by M. von Cranach, K. Froppa, W. Lepenies, and D. Ploog. Cambridge: Cambridge University Press.

_____. 1990. "Mechanisms of Moral Disengagement." In *Origins of Terrorism: Psychologies, Ideologies, Theologies, States of Mind,* edited by W. Reich. Cambridge: Cambridge University Press and Woodrow Wilson International Center for Scholars.

Baumann, B. 1977. *Wie Alles Anfing-How it all Began: The Personal Account of a West German Urban Guerilla.* Vancouver: Pulp Press.

Cordes, B. 1988. "When Terrorists Do the Talking: Reflections on the Terrorist Literature." In *Inside Terrorist Organizations* edited by D. Rapoport. New York: Columbia University Press.

Crenshaw, M. 1986. "The Psychology of Political Terrorism." In *Political Psychology,* edited by M. G. Hermann. San Francisco: Jossey-Bass.

_____. 1988. "The Subjective Reality of the Terrorist: Ideological and Psychological Factors in Terrorism." In *Current Perspectives on International Terrorism*, edited by R. O. Slater and M. Stohl. New York: St. Martin's.

_____. 1990. "The Logic of Terrorism: Terrorism As a Product of Strategic Choice." In *Origins of Terrorism: Psychologies, Ideologies, Theologies, States of Mind*, edited by W. Reich. Cambridge: Woodrow Wilson International Center for Scholars and Cambridge University Press.

DeNardo, J. 1985. *Power in Numbers: The Political Strategy of Protest and Rebellion.* Princeton: Princeton University Press.

Ferracuti, F. 1990. "Ideology and Repentance: Terrorism in Italy." In *Origins of Terrorism: Psychologies, Ideologies, Theologies, States of Mind*, edited by W. Reich. Cambridge: Cambridge University Press and Woodrow Wilson International Center for Scholars.

Finz, W. D. 1975. "Strategies for Coping with Stress." In *Stress and Anxiety.* Vol.2, edited by I. G. Sarason and C. D. Spielberger. New York: Wiley.

Gilio, M. E. 1972. *The Tupamaros.* London: Seeker and Warburg.

Hirschman, A. O. 1970. *Exit, Voice, and Loyalty: Responses to Decline in Firms, Organizations, and States.* Cambridge: Harvard University Press.

Holsti, O. R. 1972. "Crisis, Stress and Decision Making." In *Crisis Escalation War.* Montreal: McGill-Queen's University Press.

Hopple, G. W. and M. Steiner. 1984. *The Causal Beliefs of Terrorists: Empirical Results.* McLean, VA: Defense Systems, Inc.

Janis, I. 1968. "Group Identification Under Conditions of External Danger." In *Group Dynamics: Research and Theory,* edited by D. Cartwright and A. Zander, 3rd ed. New York: Harper and Row.

Janis, I. L. and L. Mann. 1977. *Decision-Making: A Psychological Analysis of Conflict, Choice, and Commitment.* New York: Free Press.

Knutson, J. 1980. "The Terrorists' Dilemmas: Some Implicit Rules of the Game." *Terrorism: An International Journal* 4(1–4):195–222.

Larson, D. 1985. *Origins of Containment: A Psychological Explanation.* Princeton: Princeton University Press.

Marx, G. T. 1974. "Thoughts on a Neglected Category of Social Movement Participant: The Agent Provocateur and the Informant." *American Journal of Sociology* 80(2):402–440.

McGuire, M. 1973. *To Take Arms: My Year with the IRA Provisionals.* New York: Viking Press.

Newman, G. R. and M.J. Lynch. 1987. "From Feuding to Terrorism: The Ideology of Vengeance." *Contemporary Crises* 11:223–242.

Post, J. M. 1987. "Rewarding Fire with Fire: Effects of Retaliation on Terrorist Group Dynamics." *Terrorism: An International Journal* 10: 23–36.

Rapoport, D. C. 1990. "Messianic Sanctions for Terror." In *Origins of Terrorism: Psychologies, Ideologies, Theologies, States of Mind*, edited by W. Reich. Cambridge: Cambridge University Press and Woodrow Wilson International Center for Scholars.

Roth, W. T. 1982. "The Meaning of Stress." In *Victims of Terrorism*, edited by F. M. Ochberg and D. A. Soskis. Boulder, CO: Westview.

Shaver, K. G. 1985. *The Attribution of Blame: Causality, Responsibility, and Blameworthiness.* New York: Springer-Verlag.

Silj, A. 1979. *Never Again Without a Rifle: The Origins of Italian Terrorism.* New York: Karz.

Snow, D. A. and R. Machalek. 1982. "On the Presumed Fragility of Unconventional Beliefs." *Journal for the Scientific Study of Religion* 21:15–26.

Taylor, M. 1988. *The Terrorist.* London: Brassey's.

Wasmund, K. 1986. "The Political Socialization of West German Terrorists." In *Political Violence and Terror: Motifs and Motivations*, edited by P. H. Merkl. Berkeley: University of California Press.

Weinberg, L. and W.L. Eubank. 1987. *The Rise and Fall of Italian Terrorism.* Boulder, CO: Westview Press.

17 The strategic logic of suicide terrorism

Robert A. Pape

Terrorist organizations are increasingly relying on suicide attacks to achieve major political objectives. For example, spectacular suicide terrorist attacks have recently been employed by Palestinian groups in attempts to force Israel to abandon the West Bank and Gaza, by the Liberation Tigers of Tamil Eelam to compel the Sri Lankan government to accept an independent Tamil homeland, and by Al Qaeda to pressure the United States to withdraw from the Saudi Arabian Peninsula. Moreover, such attacks are increasing both in tempo and location. Before the early 1980s, suicide terrorism was rare but not unknown (Lewis 1968; O'Neill 1981; Rapoport 1984). However, since the attack on the U.S. embassy in Beirut in April 1983, there have been at least 188 separate suicide terrorist attacks worldwide, in Lebanon, Israel, Sri Lanka, India, Pakistan, Afghanistan, Yemen, Turkey, Russia and the United States. The rate has increased from 31 in the 1980s, to 104 in the 1990s, to 53 in 2000–2001 alone (Pape 2002). The rise of suicide terrorism is especially remarkable, given that the total number of terrorist incidents worldwide fell during the period, from a peak of 666 in 1987 to a low of 274 in 1998, with 348 in 2001 (Department of State 2001).

What accounts for the rise in suicide terrorism, especially, the sharp escalation from the 1990s onward? Although terrorism has long been part of international politics, we do not have good explanations for the growing phenomenon of suicide terrorism. Traditional studies of terrorism tend to treat suicide attack as one of many tactics that terrorists use and so do not shed much light on the recent rise of this type of attack (e.g., Hoffman 1998; Jenkins 1985; Laqueur 1987). The small number of studies addressed explicitly to suicide terrorism tend to focus on the irrationality of the act of suicide from the perspective of the individual attacker. As a result, they focus on individual motives—either religious indoctrination (especially Islamic Fundamentalism) or psychological predispositions that might drive individual suicide bombers (Kramer 1990; Merari 1990; Post 1990).

The first-wave explanations of suicide terrorism were developed during the 1980s and were consistent with the data from that period. However, as suicide attacks mounted from the 1990s onward, it has become increasingly evident that these initial explanations are insufficient to account for which individuals become suicide terrorists and, more importantly, why terrorist organizations are increasingly relying on this form of attack (Institute for Counter-Terrorism 2001). First, although religious motives may matter, modern suicide terrorism is not limited to Islamic Fundamentalism. Islamic groups receive the most attention in Western media, but the world's leader in suicide terrorism is actually the Liberation Tigers of Tamil Eelam (LTTE), a group who recruits from the predominantly Hindu Tamil population in northern and eastern Sri Lanka and whose ideology has Marxist/Leninist elements. The LTTE alone accounts for 75 of the 186 suicide terrorist attacks from 1980 to 2001. Even among Islamic suicide attacks, groups with secular orientations account for about a third of these attacks (Merari 1990; Sprinzak 2000).

Second, although study of the personal characteristics of suicide attackers may someday help identify individuals terrorist organizations are likely to recruit for this purpose, the vast spread of suicide terrorism over the last two decades suggests that there may not be a single profile. Until recently, the leading experts in psychological profiles of suicide terrorists characterized them as uneducated, unemployed, socially isolated, single men in their late teens and early 20s (Merari 1990; Post 1990). Now we know that suicide terrorists can be college educated or uneducated, married or single, men or women, socially isolated or integrated, from age 13 to age 47 (Sprinzak 2000). In other words, although only a tiny number of people become suicide terrorists, they come from a broad cross section of lifestyles, and it may be impossible to pick them out in advance.

In contrast to the first-wave explanations, this article shows that suicide terrorism follows a strategic logic. Even if many suicide attackers are irrational or fanatical, the leadership groups that recruit and direct them are not. Viewed from the perspective of the terrorist organization, suicide attacks are designed to achieve specific political purposes: to coerce a target government to change policy, to mobilize additional recruits and financial support, or both. Crenshaw (1981) has shown that terrorism is best understood in terms of its strategic function; the same is true for suicide terrorism. In essence, suicide terrorism is an extreme form of what Thomas Schelling (1966) calls "the rationality of irrationality," in which an act that is irrational for individual attackers is meant to demonstrate credibility to a democratic audience that still more and greater attacks are sure to come. As such, modern suicide terrorism is analogous to instances of international coercion. For states, air power and economic sanctions are often the preferred coercive tools (George et al. 1972; Pape 1996, 1997). For terrorist groups, suicide attacks are becoming the coercive instrument of choice.

To examine the strategic logic of suicide terrorism, this article collects the universe suicide terrorist attacks worldwide from 1980 to 2001, explains how terrorist organizations have assessed the effectiveness of these attacks, and evaluates the limits on their coercive utility.

Five principal findings follow. First, suicide terrorism is strategic. The vast majority of suicide terrorist attacks are not isolated or random acts by individual fanatics but, rather, occur in clusters as part of a larger campaign by an organized group to achieve a specific political goal. Groups using suicide terrorism consistently announce specific political goals and stop suicide attacks when those goals have been fully or partially achieved.

Second, the strategic logic of suicide terrorism is specifically designed to coerce modern democracies to make significant concessions to national self-determination. In general, suicide terrorist campaigns seek to achieve specific territorial goals, most often the withdrawal of the target state's military forces from what the terrorists see as national homeland. From Lebanon to Israel to Sri Lanka to Kashmir to Chechnya, every suicide terrorist campaign from 1980 to 2001 has been waged by terrorist groups whose main goal has been to establish or maintain self-determination for their community's homeland by compelling an enemy to withdraw. Further, every suicide terrorist campaign since 1980 has been targeted against a state that had a democratic form of government.

Third, during the past 20 years, suicide terrorism has been steadily rising because terrorists have learned that it pays. Suicide terrorists sought to compel American and French military forces to abandon Lebanon in 1983, Israeli forces to leave Lebanon in 1985, Israeli forces to quit the Gaza Strip and the West Bank in 1994 and 1995, the Sri Lankan government to create an independent Tamil state from 1990 on, and the Turkish government to grant autonomy to the Kurds in the late 1990s. Terrorist groups did not achieve their full objectives in all these cases. However, in all but the case of Turkey, the terrorist political cause made more gains after the resort to suicide operations than it had before. Leaders of terrorist groups have consistently credited suicide operations with contributing to these gains. These assessments are hardly unreasonable given the timing and circumstances of many of the concessions and given that other observers within the terrorists' national community, neutral analysts, and target government leaders themselves often agreed that suicide operations accelerated or caused the concession. This pattern of making concessions to suicide terrorist organizations over the past two decades has probably encouraged terrorist groups to pursue even more ambitious suicide campaigns.

Fourth, although moderate suicide terrorism led to moderate concessions, these more ambitious suicide terrorist campaigns are not likely to achieve still greater gains and may well fail completely. In general, suicide terrorism relies on the threat to inflict low to medium levels of punishment on civilians. In other circumstances, this level of punishment has rarely caused modern nation states to surrender significant political goals, partly because modern nation states are often willing to countenance high costs for high interests and partly because modern nation states are often able to mitigate civilian costs by making economic and other adjustments. Suicide terrorism does not change a nation's willingness to trade high interests for high costs, but suicide attacks can overcome a country's efforts to mitigate civilian costs. Accordingly, suicide terrorism may marginally increase the punishment that is inflicted and so make target nations somewhat more likely to surrender modest goals, but it is unlikely to compel states to abandon important interests related to the physical security or national wealth of the state. National governments have in fact responded aggressively to ambitious suicide terrorist campaigns in recent years, events which confirm these expectations.

Finally, the most promising way to contain suicide terrorism is to reduce terrorists' confidence in their ability to carry out such attacks on the target society. States that face persistent suicide terrorism should recognize that neither offensive military action nor concessions alone are likely to do much good and should invest significant resources in border defenses and other means of homeland security.

The logic of suicide terrorism

Most suicide terrorism is undertaken as a strategic effort directed toward achieving particular political goals; it is not simply the product of irrational individuals or an expression of fanatical hatreds. The main purpose of suicide terrorism is to use the threat of punishment to coerce a target government to change policy, especially to cause democratic states to withdraw forces from territory terrorists view as their homeland. The record of suicide terrorism from 1980 to 2001 exhibits tendencies in the timing, goals, and targets of attack that are consistent with this strategic logic but not with irrational or fanatical behavior.

Defining suicide terrorism

Terrorism involves the use of violence by an organization other than a national government to cause intimidation or fear among a target audience (Department of State 1983–2001; Reich 1990; Schmid and Jongman 1988). Although one could broaden the definition of terrorism so as to include the actions of a national government to cause terror among an opposing population, adopting such a broad definition would distract attention from what policy makers would most like to know: how to combat the threat posed by subnational groups to state security. Further, it could also create analytic confusion. Terrorist organizations and state governments have different levels of resources, face different kinds of incentives, and are susceptible to different types of pressures. Accordingly, the determinants of their behavior are not likely to be the same and, thus, require separate theoretical investigations.

In general, terrorism has two purposes—to gain supporters and to coerce opponents. Most terrorism seeks both goals to some extent, often aiming to affect enemy calculations while simultaneously mobilizing support for the terrorists' cause and, in some cases, even gaining an edge over rival groups in the same social movement (Bloom 2002). However, there are trade-offs between these objectives and terrorists can strike various balances between them. These choices represent different forms of terrorism, the most important of which are demonstrative, destructive, and suicide terrorism.

Demonstrative terrorism is directed mainly at gaining publicity, for any or all of three reasons: to recruit more activists, to gain attention to grievances from soft-liners on the other side, and to gain attention from third parties who might exert pressure on the other side. Groups that emphasize ordinary, demonstrative terrorism include the Orange Volunteers (Northern Ireland), National Liberation Army (Columbia), and Red Brigades (Italy) (Clutterbuck 1975; Edler Baumann 1973; St. John 1991). Hostage taking, airline hijacking, and explosions announced in advance are generally intended to use the possibility of harm to bring issues to the attention of the target audience. In these cases, terrorists often avoid doing serious harm so as not to undermine sympathy for the political cause. Brian Jenkins (1975, 4) captures the essence of demonstrative terrorism with his well-known remark, "Terrorists want a lot of people watching, not a lot of people dead."

Destructive terrorism is more aggressive, seeking to coerce opponents as well as mobilize support for the cause. Destructive terrorists seek to inflict real harm on members of the target audience at the risk of losing sympathy for their cause. Exactly how groups strike the balance between harm and sympathy depends on the nature of the political goal. For instance, the Baader-Meinhof group selectively assassinated rich German industrialists, which alienated certain segments of German society but not others. Palestinian terrorists in the 1970s often sought to kill as many Israelis as possible, fully alienating Jewish society but still evoking sympathy from Muslim communities. Other groups that emphasize destructive terrorism include the Irish Republican Army, the Revolutionary Armed Forces of Colombia (FARC), and the nineteenth-century Anarchists (Elliott 1998; Rapoport 1971; Tuchman 1966).

Suicide terrorism is the most aggressive form of terrorism, pursuing coercion even at the expense of losing support among the terrorists' own community. What distinguishes a suicide terrorist is that the attacker does not expect to survive a mission and often employs a method of attack that requires the attacker's death in order to succeed (such as planting a car bomb, wearing a suicide vest, or ramming an airplane into a building). In essence, a suicide terrorist kills others at the same time that he kills himself.[1] In principle, suicide terrorists could be used for demonstrative purposes or could be limited to targeted assassinations.[2] In practice, however, suicide terrorists often seek simply to kill the largest number of people. Although this maximizes the coercive leverage that can be gained from terrorism, it does so at the greatest cost to the basis of support for the terrorist cause. Maximizing the number of enemies killed alienates those in the target audience who might be sympathetic to the terrorists' cause, while the act of suicide creates a debate and often loss of support among moderate segments of the terrorists' community, even if also attracting support among radical elements. Thus, while coercion is an element in all terrorism, coercion is the paramount objective of suicide terrorism.

The coercive logic of suicide terrorism

At its core, suicide terrorism is a strategy of coercion, a means to compel a target government to change policy. The central logic of this strategy is simple: Suicide terrorism attempts to inflict enough pain on the opposing society to overwhelm their interest in resisting the terrorists' demands and, so, to cause either the government to concede or the population to revolt against the government. The common feature of all suicide terrorist campaigns is that they inflict punishment on the opposing society, either directly by killing civilians or indirectly by killing military personnel in circumstances that cannot lead to meaningful battlefield victory. As we shall see, suicide terrorism is rarely a one time event but often occurs in a series of suicide attacks. As such, suicide terrorism generates coercive leverage both from the immediate panic associated with each attack and from the risk of civilian punishment in the future.

Suicide terrorism does not occur in the same circumstances as military coercion used by states, and these structural differences help to explain the logic of the strategy. In virtually all instances of international military coercion, the coercer is the stronger state and the target is the weaker state; otherwise, the coercer would likely be deterred or simply unable to execute the threatened military operations (Pape 1996). In these circumstances, coercers have a choice between two main coercive strategies, punishment and denial. Punishment seeks to coerce by raising the costs or risks to the target society to a level that overwhelms the value of the interests in dispute. Denial seeks to coerce by demonstrating to the target state that it simply cannot win the dispute regardless of its level of effort, and therefore fighting to a finish is pointless—for example, because the coercer has the ability to conquer the disputed territory. Hence, although coercers may initially rely on punishment, they often have the resources to create a formidable threat to deny the opponent victory in battle and, if necessary, to achieve a brute force military victory if the target government refuses to change its behavior. The Allied bombing of Germany in World War II, American bombing of North Vietnam in 1972, and Coalition attacks against Iraq in 1991 all fit this pattern.

Suicide terrorism (and terrorism in general) occurs under the reverse structural conditions. In suicide terrorism, the coercer is the weaker actor and the target is the stronger. Although some elements of the situation remain the same, flipping the stronger and weaker sides in a coercive dispute has a dramatic change on the relative feasibility of punishment and denial. In these circumstances, denial is impossible, because military conquest is ruled out by relative weakness. Even though some groups using suicide terrorism have received important support from states and some have been strong enough to wage guerrilla military campaigns as well as terrorism, none have been strong enough to have serious prospects of achieving their political goals by conquest. The suicide terrorist group with the most significant military capacity has been the LTTE, but it has not had a real prospect of controlling the whole of the homeland that it claims, including Eastern and Northern Provinces of Sri Lanka.

As a result, the only coercive strategy available to suicide terrorists is punishment. Although the element of "suicide" is novel and the pain inflicted on civilians is often spectacular and gruesome, the heart of the strategy of suicide terrorism is the same as the coercive logic used by states when they employ air power or economic sanctions to punish an adversary: to cause mounting civilian costs to overwhelm the target state's interest in the issue in dispute and so to cause it to concede the terrorists' political demands. What creates the coercive leverage is not so much actual damage as the expectation of future damage. Targets may be economic or political, military or civilian, but in all cases the main task is less to destroy the specific targets than to convince the opposing society that they are vulnerable to more attacks in the future. These features also make suicide terrorism convenient for retaliation, a tit-for-tat interaction that generally occurs between terrorists and the defending government (Crenshaw 1981).

The rhetoric of major suicide terrorist groups reflects the logic of coercive punishment. Abdel Karim, a leader of Al Aqsa Martyrs Brigades, a militant group linked to Yasir Arafat's Fatah movement, said the goal of his group was "to increase losses in Israel to a point at which the Israeli public would demand a withdrawal from the West Bank and Gaza Strip" (Greenberg 2002). The infamous fatwa signed by Osama Bin Laden and others against the United States reads, "The ruling to kill the Americans and their allies—civilians and military—is an individual duty for every

Muslim who can do it in any country in which it is possible to do it, in order to liberate the al-Aqsa Mosque and the holy mosque [Mecca] from their grip, and in order for their armies to move out of all the lands of Islam, defeated and unable to threaten any Muslim" (World Islamic Front 1998).

Suicide terrorists' willingness to die magnifies the coercive effects of punishment in three ways. First, suicide attacks are generally more destructive than other terrorist attacks. An attacker who is willing to die is much more likely to accomplish the mission and to cause maximum damage to the target. Suicide attackers can conceal weapons on their own bodies and make last-minute adjustments more easily than ordinary terrorists. They are also better able to infiltrate heavily guarded targets because they do not need escape plans or rescue teams. Suicide attackers are also able to use certain especially destructive tactics such as wearing "suicide vests" and ramming vehicles into targets. The 188 suicide terrorist attacks from 1980 to 2001 killed an average of 13 people each, not counting the unusually large number of fatalities on September 11 and also not counting the attackers themselves. During the same period, there were about 4,155 total terrorist incidents worldwide, which killed 3,207 people (also excluding September 11), or less than one person per incident. Overall, from 1980 to 2001, suicide attacks amount to 3% of all terrorist attacks but account for 48% of total deaths due to terrorism, again excluding September 11 (Department of State 1983–2001).

Second, suicide attacks are an especially convincing way to signal the likelihood of more pain to come, because suicide itself is a costly signal, one that suggests that the attackers could not have been deterred by a threat of costly retaliation. Organizations that sponsor suicide attacks can also deliberately orchestrate the circumstances around the death of a suicide attacker to increase further expectations of future attacks. This can be called the "art of martyrdom" (Schalk 1997). The more suicide terrorists justify their actions on the basis of religious or ideological motives that match the beliefs of a broader national community, the more the status of terrorist martyrs is elevated, and the more plausible it becomes that others will follow in their footsteps. Suicide terrorist organizations commonly cultivate "sacrificial myths" that include elaborate sets of symbols and rituals to mark an individual attacker's death as a contribution to the nation. Suicide attackers' families also often receive material rewards both from the terrorist organizations and from other supporters. As a result, the art of martyrdom elicits popular support from the terrorists' community, reducing the moral backlash that suicide attacks might otherwise produce, and so establishes the foundation for credible signals of more attacks to come.

Third, suicide terrorist organizations are better positioned than other terrorists to increase expectations about escalating future costs by deliberately violating norms in the use of violence. They can do this by crossing thresholds of damage, by breaching taboos concerning legitimate targets, and by broadening recruitment to confound expectations about limits on the number of possible terrorists. The element of suicide itself helps increase the credibility of future attacks, because it suggests that attackers cannot be deterred. Although the capture and conviction of Timothy McVeigh gave reason for some confidence that others with similar political views might be deterred, the deaths of the September 11 hijackers did not, because Americans would have to expect that future Al Qaeda attackers would be equally willing to die.

The record of suicide terrorism, 1980 to 2001

To characterize the nature of suicide terrorism, this study identified every suicide terrorist attack from 1980 to 2001 that could be found in Lexis Nexis's on-line database of world news media (Pape 2002).[3] Examination of the universe shows that suicide terrorism has three properties that are consistent with the above strategic logic but not with irrational or fanatical behavior:

(1) *timing*—nearly all suicide attacks occur in organized, coherent campaigns, not as isolated or randomly timed incidents; (2) *nationalist goals*—suicide terrorist campaigns are directed at gaining control of what the terrorists see as their national homeland territory, specifically at ejecting foreign forces from that territory; and (3) *target selection*—all suicide terrorist campaigns in the last two decades have been aimed at democracies, which make more suitable targets from the terrorists' point of view. Nationalist movements that face nondemocratic opponents have not resorted to suicide attack as a means of coercion.

Timing

As Table 17.1 indicates, there have been 188 separate suicide terrorist attacks between 1980 and 2001. Of these, 179, or 95%, were parts of organized, coherent campaigns, while only nine were isolated or random events. Seven separate disputes have led to suicide terrorist campaigns: the presence of American and French forces in Lebanon, Israeli occupation of West Bank and Gaza, the independence of the Tamil regions of Sri Lanka, the independence of the Kurdish region of Turkey, Russian occupation of Chechnya, Indian occupation of Kashmir, and the presence of American forces on the Saudi Arabian Peninsula. Overall, however, there have been 16 distinct campaigns, because in certain disputes the terrorists elected to suspend operations one or more times either in response to concessions or for other reasons. Eleven of the campaigns have ended and five were ongoing as of the end of 2001. The attacks comprising each campaign were organized by the same terrorist group (or, sometimes, a set of cooperating groups as in the ongoing "second *intifada*" in Israel/Palestine), clustered in time, publically justified in terms of a specified political goal, and directed against targets related to that goal.

The most important indicator of the strategic orientation of suicide terrorists is the timing of the suspension of campaigns, which most often occurs based on a strategic decision by leaders of the terrorist organizations that further attacks would be counterproductive to their coercive purposes—for instance, in response to full or partial concessions by the target state to the terrorists' political goals. Such suspensions are often accompanied by public explanations that justify the decision to opt for a "cease-fire." Further, the terrorist organizations' discipline is usually fairly good; although there are exceptions, such announced ceasefires usually do stick for a period of months at least, normally until the terrorist leaders take a new strategic decision to resume in pursuit of goals not achieved in the earlier campaign. This pattern indicates that both terrorist leaders and their recruits are sensitive to the coercive value of the attacks.

As an example of a suicide campaign, consider Hamas's suicide attacks in 1995 to compel Israel to withdraw from towns in the West Bank. Hamas leaders deliberately withheld attacking during the spring and early summer in order to give PLO negotiations with Israel an opportunity to finalize a withdrawal. However, when in early July, Hamas leaders came to believe that Israel was backsliding and delaying withdrawal, Hamas launched a series of suicide attacks. Israel accelerated the pace of its withdrawal, after which Hamas ended the campaign. Mahmud al-Zahar, a Hamas leader in Gaza, announced, following the cessation of suicide attacks in October 1995:

> We must calculate the benefit and cost of continued armed operations. If we can fulfill our goals without violence, we will do so. Violence is a means, not a goal. Hamas's decision to adopt self-restraint does not contradict our aims, which include the establishment of an Islamic state instead of Israel. … We will never recognize Israel, but it is possible that a truce could prevail between us for days, months, or years.

(Mishal and Sela 2000, 71)

Table 17.1 Suicide Terrorist Campaigns, 1980–2001

Date	Terrorist Group	Terrorists' Goal	No. of Attacks	No. Killed	Target Behavior
		Completed Campaigns			
1. Apr–Dec 1983	Hezbollah	U.S./France out of Lebanon	6	384	Complete withdrawal
2. Nov 1983–Apr 1985	Hezbollah	Israel out of Lebanon	6	96	Partial withdrawal
3. June 1985–June 1986	Hezbollah	Israel out of Lebanon security zone	16	179	No change
4. July 1990–Nov 1994	LTTE	Sri Lanka accept Tamil state	14	164	Negotiations
5. Apr 1995–Oct 2000	LTTE	Sri Lanka accept Tamil state	54	629	No change
6. Apr 1994	Hamas	Israel out of Palestine	2	15	Partial withdrawal from Gaza
7. Oct 1994–Aug 1995	Hamas	Israel out of Palestine	7	65	Partial withdrawal from West Bank
8. Feb–Mar 1996	Hamas	Retaliation for Israeli assassination	4	58	No change
9. Mar–Sept 1997	Hamas	Israel out of Palestine	3	24	Hamas leader released
10. June–Oct 1996	PKK	Turkey accept Kurd autonomy	3	17	No change
11. Mar–Aug 1999	PKK	Turkey release jailed leader	6	0	No change
		Ongoing Campaigns, as of December 2001			
12. 1996–	Al Qaeda	U.S. out of Saudi Peninsula	6	3,329	TBD[a]
13. 2000–	Chechen Rebels	Russia out of Chechnya	4	53	TBD
14. 2000–	Kashmir Rebels	India out of Kashmir	3	45	TBD
15. 2001–	LTTE	Sri Lanka accept Tamil state	6	51	TBD
16. 2000–	Several	Israel out of Palestine	39	177	TBD
Total incidents	188				
No. in campaigns	179				
No. isolated	9				

Source: Pape (2002).
[a]To be determined.

If suicide terrorism were mainly irrational or even disorganized, we would expect a much different pattern in which either political goals were not articulated (e.g., references in news reports to "rogue" attacks) or the stated goals varied considerably even within the same conflict. We would also expect the timing to be either random or, perhaps, event-driven, in response to particularly provocative or infuriating actions by the other side, but little if at all related to the progress of negotiations over issues in dispute that the terrorists want to influence.

Nationalist goals

Suicide terrorism is a high-cost strategy, one that would only make strategic sense for a group when high interests are at stake and, even then, as a last resort. The reason is that suicide terrorism maximizes coercive leverage at the expense of support among the terrorists' own community and so can be sustained over time only when there already exists a high degree of commitment among the potential pool of recruits. The most important goal that a community can have is the independence of its homeland (population, property, and way of life) from foreign influence or control. As a result, a strategy of suicide terrorism is most likely to be used to achieve nationalist goals, such as gaining control of what the terrorists see as their national homeland territory and expelling foreign military forces from that territory.

In fact, every suicide campaign from 1980 to 2001 has had as a major objective—or as its central objective—coercing a foreign government that has military forces in what they see as their homeland to take those forces out. Table 17.2 summarizes the disputes that have engendered suicide terrorist campaigns. Since 1980, there has not been a suicide terrorist campaign directed mainly against domestic opponents or against foreign opponents who did not have military forces in the terrorists' homeland. Although attacks against civilians are often the most salient to Western observers, actually every suicide terrorist campaign in the past two decades has included attacks directly against the foreign military forces in the country, and most have been waged by guerrilla organizations that also use more conventional methods of attack against those forces.

Even Al Qaeda fits this pattern. Although Saudi Arabia is not under American military occupation per se and the terrorists have political objectives against the Saudi regime and others, one major objective of Al Qaeda is the expulsion of U.S. troops from the Saudi Peninsula and there have been attacks by terrorists loyal to Osama Bin Laden against American troops in Saudi Arabia. To be sure, there is a major debate among Islamists over the morality of suicide attacks, but within Saudi Arabia there is little debate over Al Qaeda's objection to American forces in the region and over 95% of Saudi society reportedly agrees with Bin Laden on this matter (Sciolino 2002).

Still, even if suicide terrorism follows a strategic logic, could some suicide terrorist campaigns be irrational in the sense that they are being waged for unrealistic goals? The answer is that some

Table 17.2 Motivation and targets of suicide terrorist campaigns, 1980–2001

Region Dispute	Homeland Status	Terrorist Goal	Target a Democracy?
Lebanon, 1983–86	US/F/IDF military presence	US/F/IDF withdrawal	Yes
West Bank/Gaza, 1994–	IDF military presence	IDF withdrawal	Yes
Tamils in Sri Lanka, 1990–	SL military presence	SL withdrawal	Yes (1950)[a]
Kurds in Turkey, 1990s	Turkey military presence	Turkey withdrawal	Yes (1983)[a]
Chechnya, 2000–	Russia military presence	Russian withdrawal	Yes (1993)[a]
Kashmir, 2000–	Indian military presence	Indian withdrawal	Yes
Saudi Peninsula, 1996–	US military presence	US withdrawal	Yes

Sources: Pape (2002). Przeworski et al. 2000 identifies four simple rules for determining regime type: (1) The chief executive must be elected, (2) the legislature must be elected, (3) there must be more than one party, and (4) there must be at least one peaceful transfer of power. By these criteria all the targets of suicide terrorism were and are democracies. Przeworski et al, codes only from 1950 to 1990 and is updated to 1999 by Boix and Rosato 2001. Freedom House also rates countries as "free," "partly free," and "not free," using criteria for degree of political rights and civil liberties. According to Freedom House's measures, Sri Lanka, Turkey, and Russia were all partly free when they were the targets of suicide terrorism, which puts them approximately in the middle of all countries, a score that is actually biased against this study since terrorism itself lowers a country's civil liberties rating (freedomhouse.org).

[a]Date established as a democracy (if not always a democracy).

suicide terrorist groups have not been realistic in expecting the full concessions demanded of the target, but this is normal for disputes involving overlapping nationalist claims and even for coercive attempts in general. Rather, the ambitions of terrorist leaders are realistic in two other senses. First, suicide terrorists' political aims, if not their methods, are often more mainstream than observers realize; they generally reflect quite common, straight-forward nationalist self-determination claims of their community. Second, these groups often have significant support for their policy goals versus the target state, goals that are typically much the same as those of other nationalists within their community. Differences between the terrorists and more "moderate" leaders usually concern the usefulness of a certain level of violence and—sometimes—the legitimacy of attacking additional targets besides foreign troops in the country, such as attacks in other countries or against third parties and civilians. Thus, it is not that the terrorists pursue radical goals and then seek others' support. Rather, the terrorists are simply the members of their societies who are the most optimistic about the usefulness of violence for achieving goals that many, and often most, support.

The behavior of Hamas illustrates the point. Hamas terrorism has provoked Israeli retaliation that has been costly for Palestinians, while pursuing the—apparently unrealistic—goal of abolishing the state of Israel. Although prospects of establishing an Arab state in all of "historic Palestine" may be poor, most Palestinians agree that it would be desirable if possible. Hamas's terrorist violence was in fact carefully calculated and controlled. In April 1994, as its first suicide campaign was beginning, Hamas leaders explained that "martyrdom operations" would be used to achieve intermediate objectives, such as Israeli withdrawal from the West Bank and Gaza, while the final objective of creating an Islamic state from the Jordan River to the Mediterranean may require other forms of armed resistance (Shiqaqi 2002; Hroub 2000; Nusse 1998).

Democracies as the targets

Suicide terrorism is more likely to be employed against states with democratic political systems than authoritarian governments for several reasons. First, democracies are often thought to be especially vulnerable to coercive punishment. Domestic critics and international rivals, as well as terrorists, often view democracies as "soft," usually on the grounds that their publics have low thresholds of cost tolerance and high ability to affect state policy. Even if there is little evidence that democracies are easier to coerce than other regime types (Horowitz and Reiter 2001), this image of democracy matters. Since terrorists can inflict only moderate damage in comparison to even small interstate wars, terrorism can be expected to coerce only if the target state is viewed as especially vulnerable to punishment. Second, suicide terrorism is a tool of the weak, which means that, regardless of how much punishment the terrorists inflict, the target state almost always has the capacity to retaliate with far more extreme punishment or even by exterminating the terrorists' community. Accordingly, suicide terrorists must not only have high interests at stake, they must also be confident that their opponent will be at least somewhat restrained. While there are infamous exceptions, democracies have generally been more restrained in their use of force against civilians, at least since World War II. Finally, suicide attacks may also be harder to organize or publicize in authoritarian police states, although these possibilities are weakened by the fact that weak authoritarian states are also not targets.

In fact, the target state of every modern suicide campaign has been a democracy. The United States, France, Israel, India, Sri Lanka, Turkey, and Russia were all democracies when they were attacked by suicide terrorist campaigns, even though the last three became democracies more recently than the others. To be sure, these states vary in the degree to which they share "liberal" norms that respect minority rights; Freedom House rates Sri Lanka, Turkey, and Russia as "partly free" (3.5–4.5 on a seven-point scale) rather than "free" during the relevant years, partly for this reason and partly because terrorism and civil violence themselves lower the freedom rating of these states. Still, all these states elect their chief executives and legislatures in multiparty elections and have seen at least one peaceful transfer of power, making them solidly democratic by standard criteria (Boix and Rosato 2001; Huntington 1991; Przeworski et al. 2000).

The Kurds, which straddle Turkey and Iraq, illustrate the point that suicide terrorist campaigns are more likely to be targeted against democracies than authoritarian regimes. Although Iraq has been far more brutal toward its Kurdish population than has Turkey, violent Kurdish groups have used suicide attacks exclusively against democratic Turkey and not against the authoritarian regime in Iraq. There are plenty of national groups living under authoritarian regimes with grievances that could possibly inspire suicide terrorism, but none have. Thus, the fact that rebels have resorted to this strategy only when they face the more suitable type of target counts against arguments that suicide terrorism is a nonstrategic response, motivated mainly by fanaticism or irrational hatreds.

Terrorists' assessments of suicide terrorism

The main reason that suicide terrorism is growing is that terrorists have learned that it works. Even more troubling, the encouraging lessons that terrorists have learned from the experience of 1980s and 1990s are not, for the most part, products of wild-eyed interpretations or wishful thinking. They are, rather, quite reasonable assessments of the outcomes of suicide terrorist campaigns during this period.

To understand how terrorist groups have assessed the effectiveness of suicide terrorism requires three tasks: (1) explanation of appropriate standards for evaluating the effectiveness of coercion from the standpoint of coercers; (2) analysis of the 11 suicide terrorist campaigns that have ended as of 2001 to determine how frequently target states made concessions that were, or at least could have been, interpreted as due to suicide attack; and (3) close analysis of terrorists' learning from particular campaigns. Because some analysts see suicide terrorism as fundamentally irrational (Kramer 1990; Merari 1990; Post 1990), it is important to assess whether the lessons that the terrorists drew were reasonable conclusions from the record. The crucial cases are the Hamas and Islamic Jihad campaigns against Israel during the 1990s, because they are most frequently cited as aimed at unrealistic goals and therefore as basically irrational.

Standards of assessment

Terrorists, like other people, learn from experience. Since the main purpose of suicide terrorism is coercion, the learning that is likely to have the greatest impact on terrorists' future behavior is the lessons that they have drawn from past campaigns about the coercive effectiveness of suicide attack.

Most analyses of coercion focus on the decision making of target states, largely to determine their vulnerability to various coercive pressures (George 1972; Pape 1996). The analysis here, however, seeks to determine why terrorist coercers are increasingly attracted to a specific coercive strategy. For this purpose, we must develop a new set of standards, because assessing the value of coercive pressure for the coercer is not the same problem as assessing its impact on the target.

From the perspective of a target state, the key question is whether the value of the concession that the coercer is demanding is greater than the costs imposed by the coercive pressure, regardless of whether that pressure is in the form of lives at risk, economic hardship, or other types of costs.

However, from the perspective of the coercer, the key question is whether a particular coercive strategy promises to be more effective than alternative methods of influence and, so, warrants continued (or increased) effort. This is especially true for terrorists who are highly committed to a particular goal and so willing to exhaust virtually any alternative rather than abandoning it. In this search for an effective strategy, coercers' assessments are likely to be largely a function of estimates of the success of past efforts; for suicide terrorists, this means assessments of whether past suicide campaigns produced significant concessions.

A glance at the behavior of suicide terrorists reveals that such trade-offs between alternative methods are important in their calculations. All of the organizations that have resorted to suicide terrorism began their coercive efforts with more conventional guerrilla operations, nonsuicide terrorism, or both. Hezbollah, Hamas, Islamic Jihad, the PKK, the LTTE, and Al Qaeda all used demonstrative and destructive means of violence long before resorting to suicide attack. Indeed, looking at the trajectory of terrorist groups over time, there is a distinct element of experimentation in the techniques and strategies used by these groups and distinct movement toward those techniques and strategies that produce the most effect. Al Qaeda actually prides itself for a commitment to even tactical learning over time—the infamous "terrorist manual" stresses at numerous points the importance of writing "lessons learned" memoranda that can be shared with other members to improve the effectiveness of future attacks.

The most important analytical difficulty in assessing outcomes of coercive efforts is that successes are more ambiguous than failures. Whenever a suicide terrorist campaign, or any coercive effort, ends without obtaining significant concessions, presumably the coercers must judge the effort as a failure. If, however, the target state does make policy changes in the direction of the terrorists' political goals, this may or may not represent a coercive success for suicide attack in the calculations of the terrorists. The target government's decision could have been mainly or partly a response to the punishment inflicted by the suicide attacks, but it also could be a response to another type of pressure (such as an ongoing guerrilla campaign), or to pressure from a different actor (such as one of the target state's allies) or a different country, or the target's policy decision may not even have been intended as a concession but could have been made for other reasons that only coincidently moved in a direction desired by the terrorists. Different judgments among these alternatives yield different lessons for future usefulness of suicide attack.

Standard principles from social psychology suggest how terrorists are likely to resolve these ambiguities. Under normal conditions, most people tend to interpret ambiguous information in ways that are consistent with their prior beliefs, as well as in ways that justify their past actions (Jervis 1976; Lebow 1981). Suicide terrorists, of course, are likely to have at least some initial confidence in the efficacy of suicide attack or else they would not resort to it, and of course, the fact of having carried out such attacks gives them an interest in justifying that choice. Thus, whenever targets of suicide terrorism make a real or apparent concession and it is a plausible interpretation that it was due to the coercive pressure of the suicide campaign, we would expect terrorists to favor that interpretation even if other interpretations are also plausible.

This does not mean that we should simply expect terrorists to interpret virtually all outcomes, regardless of evidence, as encouraging further terrorism; that would not constitute learning and would make sense only if the terrorists were deeply irrational. To control for this possibility, it is crucial to consider the assessments of the same events by other well-informed people. If we find that when suicide terrorist leaders claim credit for coercing potential concessions, their claims are unique (or nearly so), then it would be appropriate to dismiss them as irrational. If, on the other hand, we find that their interpretations are shared by a significant portion of other observers, across a range of circumstances and interests—from target state leaders, to others in the terrorists' community, to neutral analysts—then we should assume that their assessments are as rational as anyone else's and should take the lessons they draw seriously. In making these judgments, the testimony of target state leaders is often especially telling; although states like the United States and Israel virtually never officially admit making concessions to terrorism, leaders such as Ronald Reagan and Yitzhak Rabin have at times been quite open about the impact of suicide terrorism on their own policy decisions, as we see below.

Finally, understanding how terrorists assess the effectiveness of suicide terrorism should also be influenced by our prior understanding of the fanatical nature of the specific terrorists at issue. If the most fanatical groups also make what appear to be reasonable assessments, then this would increase our confidence in the finding that most terrorists would make similar calculations. Hamas and Islamic Jihad are the most crucial case, because these groups have been considered to be fanatical extremists even among terrorists (Kramer 1996). Thus, detailed examination of how Hamas and Islamic Jihad leaders assessed the coercive value of suicide attacks during the 1990s is especially important.

The apparent success of suicide terrorism

Perhaps the most striking aspect of recent suicide terrorist campaigns is that they are associated with gains for the terrorists' political cause about half the time. As Table 17.1 shows, of the 11 suicide terrorist campaigns that were completed during 1980–2001, six closely correlate with significant policy changes by the target state toward the terrorists' major political goals. In one case, the terrorists' territorial goals were fully achieved (Hezbollah v. US/F, 1983); in three cases, the terrorists' territorial aims were partly achieved (Hezbollah v. Israel, 1983–1985; Hamas v. Israel, 1994; and Hamas v. Israel, 1994–1995); in one case, the target government entered into sovereignty negotiations with the terrorists (LTTE v. Sri Lanka, 1993–1994); and in one case, the terrorist organization's top leader was released from prison (Hamas v. Israel, 1997). Five campaigns did not lead to noticeable concessions (Hezbollah's second effort against Israel in Lebanon, 1985–1986; a Hamas campaign in 1996 retaliating for an Israeli assassination; the LTTE v. Sri Lanka, 1995–2002; and both PKK campaigns). Coercive success is so rare that even a 50% success rate is significant, because international military and economic coercion, using the same standards as above, generally works less than a third of the time (Art and Cronin 2003).

There were limits to what suicide terrorism appeared to gain in the 1980s and 1990s. Most of the gains for the terrorists' cause were modest, not involving interests central to the target countries' security or wealth, and most were potential revocable. For the United States and France, Lebanon was a relatively minor foreign policy interest. Israel's apparent concessions to the Palestinians from 1994 to 1997 were more modest than they might appear. Although Israel withdrew its forces from parts of Gaza and the West Bank and released Sheikh Yassin, during the same period Israeli settlement in the occupied territories almost doubled, and recent events have shown that Israel is not deterred from sending force back in when necessary. In two disputes, the terrorists achieved initial success but failed to reach greater goals. Although Israel withdrew from much of Lebanon in June 1985, it retained a six-mile security buffer zone along the southern edge of the country for another 15 years from which a second Hezbollah suicide terrorist campaign failed to dislodge it. The Sri Lankan government did conduct apparently serious negotiations with the LTTE from November 1994 to April 1995, but did not concede the Tamil's main demand, for independence, and since 1995, the government has preferred to prosecute the war rather than consider permitting Tamil secession.

Still, these six concessions, or at least apparent concessions, help to explain why suicide terrorism is on the rise. In three of the cases, the target government policy changes are clearly due to coercive pressure from the terrorist group. The American and French withdrawal was perhaps the most clear-cut coercive success for suicide terrorism. In his memoirs, President Ronald Reagan (1990, 465) explained the U.S. decision to withdraw from Lebanon:

> The price we had to pay in Beirut was so great, the tragedy at the barracks was so enormous. … We had to pull out. … We couldn't stay there and run the risk of another suicide attack on the Marines.

The IDF withdrawal from most of southern Lebanon in 1985 and the Sri Lankan government decision to hold negotiations with the LTTE were also widely understood to be a direct result of the coercive punishment imposed by Hezbollah and LTTE respectively. In both cases, the concessions followed periods in which the terrorists had turned more and more to suicide attacks, but since Hezbollah and the LTTE employed a combination of suicide attack and conventional attack on their opponents, one can question the relative weight of suicide attack in coercing these target states. However, there is little question in either case that punishment pressures inflicted by these terrorist organizations were decisive in the outcomes. For instance, as a candidate in the November 9, 1994, presidential election of Sri Lanka, Mrs. Chandrika Kumaratunga explicitly asked for a mandate to redraw boundaries so as to appease the Tamils in their demand for a separate homeland in the island's northeast provinces, often saying, "We definitely hope to begin discussions with the Tamil people, with their representatives—including the Tigers—and offer them political solutions to end the war … [involving] extensive devolution." This would, Kumaratunga said, "create an environment in which people could live without fear" (Sauvagnargues 1994; "Sri Lanka" 1994).

The other three concessions, or arguable concessions, are less clear-cut. All three involve Hamas campaigns against Israel. Not counting the ongoing second intifada, Hamas waged four separate suicide attack campaigns against Israel, in 1994, 1995, 1996, and 1997. One, in 1996, did not correspond with Israeli concessions. This campaign was announced as retaliation for Israel's assassination of a Hamas leader; no particular coercive goal was announced, and it was suspended by Hamas after four attacks in two weeks. The other three all do correspond with Israeli concessions. In April 1994, Hamas began a series of suicide bombings in retaliation for the Hebron Massacre. After two attacks, Israel decided to accelerate its withdrawal from Gaza, which was required under the Oslo Agreement but which had been delayed. Hamas then suspended attacks for five months. From October 1994 to August 1995, Hamas (and Islamic Jihad) carried out a total of seven suicide attacks against Israel. In September 1995, Israel agreed to withdraw from certain West Bank towns that December, which it earlier had claimed could not be done before April 1996 at the soonest. Hamas then suspended attacks until its retaliation campaign during the last week of February and first week of March 1996. Finally, in March 1997, Hamas began a suicide attack campaign that included an attack about every two months until September 1997. In response Israeli Prime Minister Netanyahu authorized the assassination of a Hamas leader. The attempt, in Amman, Jordan, failed and the Israeli agents were captured. To get them back Israel agreed to release Sheikh Ahmed Yassin, spiritual leader of Hamas. While this was not a concession to the terrorists' territorial goals, there is no evidence that Hamas interpreted this in any way different from the standard view that this release was the product of American and Jordanian pressure. Accordingly the key Hamas campaigns that might have encouraged the view that suicide terrorism pays were the 1994 and 1995 campaigns that were associated with Israel's military withdrawals from Gaza and the West Bank. Terrorists' assessments of these events are evaluated in detail.

The crucial case of Hamas

The Hamas and Islamic Jihad suicide campaigns against Israel in 1994 and 1995 are crucial tests of the reasonableness of terrorists' assessments. In each case, Israel made significant concessions in the direction of the terrorists' cause and terrorist leaders report that these Israeli concessions increased their confidence in the coercive effectiveness of suicide attack. However, there is an important alternative explanation for Israel's concessions in these cases—the Israeli government's obligations under the Oslo Accords. Accordingly, evaluating the reasonableness of the terrorists' assessments of these cases is crucial because many observers characterize Hamas and Islamic Jihad as fanatical, irrational groups, extreme both within Palestinian society and among terrorists groups in general (Kramer 1996). Further, these campaigns are also of special interest because they helped to encourage the most intense ongoing campaign, the second *intifada* against Israel, and may also have helped to encourage Al Qaeda's campaign against the United States.

Examination of these crucial cases demonstrates that the terrorist groups came to the conclusion that suicide attack accelerated Israeli's withdrawal in both cases. Although the Oslo Accords formally committed to withdrawing the IDF from Gaza and the West Bank, Israel routinely missed key deadlines, often by many months, and the terrorists came to believe that Israel would not have withdrawn when it did, and perhaps not at all, had it not been for the coercive leverage of suicide attack. Moreover, this interpretation of events was hardly unique. Numerous other observers and key Israeli government leaders themselves came to the same conclusion. To be clear, Hamas may well have had motives other than coercion for launching particular attacks, such as retaliation (De Figueredo and Weingast 1998), gaining local support (Bloom 2002), or disrupting negotiated outcomes it considered insufficient (Kydd and Walter 2002). However, the experience of observing how the target reacted to the suicide campaigns appears to have convinced terrorist leaders of the coercive effectiveness of this strategy.

To evaluate these cases, we need to know (1) the facts of each case, (2) how others interpreted the events, and (3) how the terrorists interpreted these events. Each campaign is discussed in turn.

Israel's withdrawal from Gaza, May 1994

THE FACTS

Israel and the Palestinian Liberation Organization signed the Oslo Accords on September 13, 1993. These obligated Israel to withdraw its military forces from the Gaza Strip and West Bank town of Jericho beginning on December 13 and ending on April 13, 1994. In fact, Israel missed both deadlines. The major sticking points during the implementation negotiations in Fall and Winter of 1993–1994 were the size of the Palestinian police force (Israel proposed a limit of 1,800, while the Palestinians demanded 9,000) and jurisdiction for certain criminal prosecutions, especially whether Israel could retain a right of hot pursuit to prosecute Palestinian attackers who might flee into Palestinian ruled zones. As of April 5, 1994, these issues were unresolved. Hamas then launched two suicide attacks, one on April 6 and another on April 13, killing 15 Israeli civilians. On April 18, the Israeli Knesset voted to withdraw, effectively accepting the Palestinian positions on both disputed issues. The suicide attacks then stopped and the withdrawal was actually conducted in a few weeks starting on May 4, 1994.[4]

These two suicide attacks may not originally have been intended as coercive, since Hamas leaders had announced them in March 1994 as part of a planned series of five attacks in retaliation for the February 24th Hebron massacre in which an Israeli settler killed 29 Palestinians and had strong reservations about negotiating a compromise settlement with Israel (Kydd and Walter 2002). However, when Israel agreed to withdraw more promptly than expected, Hamas decided to forgo the remaining three planned attacks. There is thus a circumstantial case that these attacks had the effect of coercing the Israelis into being more forthcoming in the withdrawal negotiations and both Israeli government leaders and Hamas leaders publically drew this conclusion.

ISRAELI AND OTHER ASSESSMENTS

There are two main reasons to doubt that terrorist pressure accelerated Israel's decision to withdraw. First, one might think that Israel would have withdrawn in any case, as it had promised to do in the Oslo Accords of September 1993. Second, one might argue that Hamas was opposed to a negotiated settlement with Israel. Taking both points together, therefore, Hamas' attacks could not have contributed to Israel's withdrawal.

The first of these arguments, however, ignores the facts that Israel had already missed the originally agreed deadline and, as of early April 1994, did not appear ready to withdraw at all if that meant surrendering on the size of the Palestinian police force and legal jurisdiction over terrorists. The second argument is simply illogical. Although Hamas objected to surrendering claims to all of historic Palestine, it did value the West Bank and Gaza as an intermediate goal, and certainly had no objection to obtaining this goal sooner rather than later.

Most important, other observers took explanations based on terrorist pressure far more seriously, including the person whose testimony must count most, Israeli Prime Minister Yitzhak Rabin. On April 13, 1994, Rabin said,

> I can't recall in the past any suicidal terror acts by the PLO. We have seen by now at least six acts of this type by Hamas and Islamic Jihad. ... The only response to them and to the enemies of peace on the part of Israel is to accelerate the negotiations.
>
> (Makovsky and Pinkas 1994)

On April 18, 1994, Rabin went further, giving a major speech in the Knesset explaining why the withdrawal was necessary:

> Members of the Knessett: I want to tell the truth. For 27 years we have been dominating another people against its will. For 27 years Palestinians in the territories ... get up in the morning harboring a fierce hatred for us, as Israelis and Jews. Each morning they get up to a hard life, for which we are also, but not solely responsible. We cannot deny that our continuing control over a foreign people who do not want us exacts a painful price. ... For two or three years we have been facing a phenomenon of extremist Islamic terrorism, which recalls Hezbollah, which surfaced in Lebanon and perpetrated attacks, including suicide missions. ... There is no end to the targets Hamas and other terrorist organizations have among us. Each Israeli, in the territories and inside sovereign Israel, including united Jerusalem, each bus, each home, is a target for their murderous plans. Since there is no separation between the two populations, the current situation creates endless possibilities for Hamas and the other organizations.

Independent Israeli observers also credited suicide terrorism with considerable coercive effectiveness. The most detailed assessment is by Efraim Inbar (1999, 141–142):

> A significant change occurred in Rabin's assessment of the importance of terrorist activities. ... Reacting to the April 1994 suicide attack in Afula, Rabin recognized that terrorist activities by Hamas and other Islamic radicals were "a form of terrorism different from what we once

knew from the PLO terrorist organizations. ... Rabin admitted that there was no hermitic solution available to protect Israeli citizens against such terrorist attacks. ... He also understood that such incidents intensified the domestic pressure to freeze the Palestinian track of the peace process. Islamic terrorism thus initially contributed to the pressure for accelerating the negotiations on his part.

Arab writers also attributed Israeli accommodation to the suicide attacks. Mazin Hammad wrote in an editorial in a Jordanian newspaper:

> It is unprecedented for an Israeli official like Y. Rabin to clearly state that there is no future for the settlements in the occupied territories. ... He would not have said this [yesterday] if it was not for the collapse of the security Israel. ... The martyrdom operation in Hadera shook the faith of the settlers in the possibility of staying in the West Bank and Gaza and increased their motivation to pack their belongings and dismantle their settlements.
>
> ("Hamas Operations" 1994)

TERRORISTS' ASSESSMENTS

Even though the favorable result was apparently unexpected by Hamas leaders, given the circumstances and the assessments voiced by Rabin and others, it certainly would have been reasonable for them to conclude that suicide terrorism had helped accelerate Israeli withdrawal, and they did.

Hamas leader Ahmed Bakr (1995) said that "what forced the Israelis to withdraw from Gaza was the intifada and not the Oslo agreement," while Imad al-Faluji judged that

> all that has been achieved so far is the consequence of our military actions. Without the so-called peace process, we would have gotten even more. ... We would have got Gaza and the West Bank without this agreement. ... Israel can beat all Arab Armies. However, it can do nothing against a youth with a knife or an explosive charge on his body. Since it was unable to guarantee security within its borders, Israel entered into negotiations with the PLO. ... If the Israelis want security, they will have to abandon their settlements ... in Gaza, the West Bank, and Jerusalem.
>
> ("Hamas Leader" 1995)

Further, these events appear to have persuaded terrorists that future suicide attacks could eventually produce still greater concessions. Fathi al-Shaqaqi (1995), leader of Islamic Jihad, said,

> Our jihad action has exposed the enemy weakness, confusion, and hysteria. It has become clear that the enemy can be defeated, for if a small faithful group was able to instill all this horror and panic in the enemy through confronting it in Palestine and southern Lebanon, what will happen when the nation confronts it with all its potential. ... Martyrdom actions will escalate in the face of all pressures ... [they] are a realistic option in confronting the unequal balance of power. If we are unable to effect a balance of power now, we can achieve a balance of horror.

Israel's withdrawal from West Bank Towns, December 1995

The second Hamas case, in 1995, tells essentially the same story as the first. Again, a series of suicide attacks was associated with Israeli territorial concessions to the Palestinians, and again, a significant fraction of outside observers attributed the concessions to the coercive pressure of suicide terrorism, as did the terrorist leaders themselves.

THE FACTS

The original Oslo Accords scheduled Israel to withdraw from the Palestinian populated areas of the West Bank by July 13, 1994, but after the delays over Gaza and Jericho all sides recognized that this could not be met. From October 1994 to April 1995, Hamas, along with Islamic Jihad, carried out a series of seven suicide terrorist attacks that were intended to compel Israel to make further withdrawals and suspended attacks temporarily at the request of the Palestinian Authority after Israel agreed on March 29, 1995 to begin withdrawals by July 1. Later, however, the Israelis announced that withdrawals could not begin before April 1996 because bypass roads needed for the security of Israeli settlements were not ready. Hamas and Islamic Jihad then mounted new suicide attacks on July 24 and August 21, 1995, killing 11 Israeli civilians. In September, Israel agreed to withdraw from the West Bank towns in December (Oslo II) even though the roads were not finished. The suicide attacks then stopped and the withdrawal was actually carried out in a few weeks starting on December 12, 1995.[5]

ISRAELI AND OTHER ASSESSMENTS

Although Israeli government spokesmen frequently claimed that suicide terrorism was delaying withdrawal, this claim was contradicted by, among others, Prime Minister Rabin. Rabin (1995) explained that the decision for the second withdrawal was, like the first in 1994, motivated in part by the goal of reducing suicide terrorism:

> INTERVIEWER: Mr Rabin, what is the logic of withdrawing from towns and villages when you know that terror might continue to strike at us from there?
>
> RABIN: What is the alternative, to have double the amount of terror? As for the issue of terror, take the suicide bombings. Some 119 Israelis … have been killed or murdered since 1st January 1994, 77 of them in suicide bombings perpetrated by Islamic radical fanatics. … All the bombers were Palestinians who came from areas under our control.

Similarly, an editorial in the Israeli daily *Yediot Aharonot* ("Bus Attack" 1995) explained,

> If the planners of yesterday's attack intended to get Israel to back away from the Oslo accord, they apparently failed. In fact, Prime Minister Y. Rabin is leaning toward expediting the talks with the Palestinians. … The immediate conclusion from this line of thinking on Rabin's part—whose results we will witness in the coming days—will be to instruct the negotiators to expedite the talks with the Palestinians with the aim of completing them in the very near future.

TERRORISTS' ASSESSMENTS

As in 1994, Hamas and Islamic Jihad came to the conclusion that suicide terrorism was working. Hamas's spokesman in Jordan explained that new attacks were necessary to change Israel's behavior:

> Hamas, leader Muhammad Nazzal said, needed military muscle in order to negotiate with Israel from a position of strength. Arafat started from a position of weakness, he said, which

is how the Israelis managed to push on him the solution and get recognition of their state and settlements without getting anything in return.

(Theodoulou 1995)

After the agreement was signed, Hamas leaders also argued that suicide operations contributed to the Israeli withdrawal. Mahmud al-Zahhar (1996), a spokesman for Hamas, said,

> The Authority told us that military action embarrasses the PA because it obstructs the redeployment of Israeli forces and implementation of the agreement. ... We offered many martyrs to attain freedom. ... Any fair person knows that the military action was useful for the Authority during negotiations.

Moreover, the terrorists also stressed that stopping the attacks only discouraged Israel from withdrawing. An early August Hamas communique (No. 125, 1995) read,

> They said that the strugglers' operations have been the cause of the delay in widening the autonomous rule in the West Bank, and that they have been the reason for the deterioration of the living and economic conditions of our people. Now the days have come to debunk their false claims ... and to affirm that July 1 [a promised date for IDF withdrawal] was no more than yet another of the "unholy" Zionist dates. ... Hamas has shown an utmost degree of self-restraint throughout the past period. ... but matters have gone far enough and the criminals will reap what their hands have sown.

RECENT IMPACT OF LESSONS LEARNED

In addition to the 1994 and 1995 campaigns, Palestinian terrorist leaders have also cited Hezbollah experience in Lebanon as a source of the lesson that suicide terrorism is an effective way of coercing Israel. Islamic Jihad leader Ramadan Shallah (2001) argued that:

> The shameful defeat that Israel suffered in southern Lebanon and which caused its army to flee it in terror was not made on the negotiations table but on the battlefield and through jihad and martyrdom, which achieved a great victory for the Islamic resistance and Lebanese People. ... We would not exaggerate if we said that the chances of achieving victory in Palestine are greater than in Lebanon. ... If the enemy could not bear the losses of the war on the border strip with Lebanon, will it be able to withstand a long war of attrition in the heart of its security dimension and major cities?

Palestinian terrorists are now applying the lessons they have learned. In November 2000, Khalid Mish'al explained Hamas's strategy for the second *intifada*, which was then in its early stages:

> Like the intifada in 1987, the current intifada has taught us that we should move forward normally from popular confrontation to the rifle to suicide operations. This is the normal development. ... We always have the Lebanese experiment before our eyes. It was a great model of which we are proud.

Even before the second *intifada* began, other Hamas statements similarly expressed,

> The Zionist enemy … only understands the language of Jihad, resistance and martyrdom, that was the language that led to its blatant defeat in South Lebanon and it will be the language that will defeat it on the land of Palestine.
>
> (Hamas Statement 2000)

The bottom line is that the ferocious escalation of the pace of suicide terrorism that we have witnessed in the past several years cannot be considered irrational or even surprising. Rather, it is simply the result of the lesson that terrorists have quite reasonably learned from their experience of the previous two decades: Suicide terrorism pays.

The limits of suicide terrorism

Despite suicide terrorists' reasons for confidence in the coercive effectiveness of this strategy, there are sharp limits to what suicide terrorism is likely to accomplish in the future. During the 1980s and 1990s, terrorist leaders learned that moderate punishment often leads to moderate concessions and so concluded that more ambitious suicide campaigns would lead to greater political gains. However, today's more ambitious suicide terrorist campaigns are likely to fail. Although suicide terrorism is somewhat more effective than ordinary coercive punishment using air power or economic sanctions, it is not drastically so.

Suicide terrorism is unlikely to achieve ambitious goals

In international military coercion, threats to inflict military defeat often generate more coercive leverage than punishment. Punishment, using anything short of nuclear weapons, is a relatively weak coercive strategy because modern nation states generally will accept high costs rather than abandon important national goals, while modern administrative techniques and economic adjustments over time often allow states to minimize civilian costs. The most punishing air attacks with conventional munitions in history were the American B-29 raids against Japan's 62 largest cities from March to August 1945. Although these raids killed nearly 800,000 Japanese civilians—almost 10% died on the first day, the March 9, 1945, firebombing of Tokyo, which killed over 85,000—the conventional bombing did not compel the Japanese to surrender.

Suicide terrorism makes adjustment to reduce damage more difficult than for states faced with military coercion or economic sanctions. However, it does not affect the target state's interests in the issues at stake. As a result, suicide terrorism can coerce states to abandon limited or modest goals, such as withdrawal from territory of low strategic importance or, as in Israel's case in 1994 and 1995, a temporary and partial withdrawal from a more important area. However, suicide terrorism is unlikely to cause targets to abandon goals central to their wealth or security, such as a loss of territory that would weaken the economic prospects of the state or strengthen the rivals of the state.

Suicide terrorism makes punishment more effective than in international military coercion. Targets remain willing to countenance high costs for important goals, but administrative, economic, or military adjustments to prevent suicide attack are harder, while suicide attackers themselves are unlikely to be deterred by the threat of retaliation. Accordingly, suicide attack is likely to present a threat of continuing limited civilian punishment that the target government cannot completely eliminate, and the upper bound on what punishment can gain for coercers is recognizably higher in suicidal terrorism than in international military coercion.

The data on suicide terrorism from 1980 to 2001 support this conclusion. While suicide terrorism has achieved modest or very limited goals, it has so far failed to compel target democracies to abandon goals central to national wealth or security. When the United States withdrew from Lebanon in 1984, it had no important security, economic, or even ideological interests at stake. Lebanon was largely a humanitarian mission and not viewed as central to the national welfare of the United States. Israel withdrew from most of Lebanon in June 1985 but remained in a security buffer on the edge of southern Lebanon for more than a decade afterward, despite the fact that 17 of 22 suicide attacks occurred in 1985 and 1986. Israel's withdrawals from Gaza and the West Bank in 1994 and 1995 occurred at the same time that settlements increased and did little to hinder the IDF's return, and so these concessions were more modest than they may appear. Sri Lanka has suffered more casualties from suicide attack than Israel but has not acceded to demands that it surrender part of its national territory. Thus, the logic of punishment and the record of suicide terrorism suggests that, unless suicide terrorists acquire far more destructive technologies, suicide attacks for more ambitious goals are likely to fail and will continue to provoke more aggressive military responses.

Policy implications for containing suicide terrorism

While the rise in suicide terrorism and the reasons behind it seem daunting, there are important policy lessons to learn. The current policy debate is misguided. Offensive military action or concessions alone rarely work for long. For over 20 years, the governments of Israel and other states targeted by suicide terrorism have engaged in extensive military efforts to kill, isolate, and jail suicide terrorist leaders and operatives, sometimes with the help of quite good surveillance of the terrorists' communities. Thus far, they have met with meager success. Although decapitation of suicide terrorist organizations can disrupt their operations temporarily, it rarely yields long-term gains. Of the 11 major suicide terrorist campaigns that had ended as of 2001, only one—the PKK versus Turkey—did so as a result of leadership decapitation, when the leader, in Turkish custody, asked his followers to stop. So far, leadership decapitation has also not ended Al Qaeda's campaign. Although the United States successfully toppled the Taliban in Afghanistan in December 2001, Al Qaeda launched seven successful suicide terrorist attacks from April to December 2002, killing some 250 Western civilians, more than in the three years before September 11, 2001, combined.

Concessions are also not a simple answer. Concessions to nationalist grievances that are widely held in the terrorists' community can reduce popular support for further terrorism, making it more difficult to recruit new suicide attackers and improving the standing of more moderate nationalist elites who are in competition with the terrorists. Such benefits can be realized, however, only if the concessions really do substantially satisfy the nationalist or self-determination aspirations of a large fraction of the community.

Partial, incremental, or deliberately staggered concessions that are dragged out over a substantial period of time are likely to become the worst of both worlds. Incremental compromise may appear—or easily be portrayed—to the terrorists' community as simply delaying tactics and, thus, may fail to reduce, or actually increase, their distrust that their main concerns will ever be met. Further, incrementalism provides time and opportunity for the terrorists to intentionally provoke the target state in hopes of derailing the smooth progress of negotiated compromise in the short term, so that they can reradicalize their own community and actually escalate their efforts toward even greater gains in the long term.[6] Thus, states that are willing to make concessions should do so in a single step if at all possible.

Advocates of concessions should also recognize that, even if they are successful in undermining the terrorist leaders' base of support, almost any concession at all will tend to encourage the terrorist leaders further about their own coercive effectiveness. Thus, even in the aftermath of a real settlement with the opposing community, some terrorists will remain motivated to continue attacks and, for the medium term, may be able to do so, which in term would put a premium on combining concessions with other solutions.

Given the limits of offense and of concessions, homeland security and defensive efforts generally must be a core part of any solution. Undermining the feasibility of suicide terrorism is a difficult task. After all, a major advantage of suicide attack is that it is more difficult to prevent than other types of attack. However, the difficulty of achieving perfect security should not keep us from taking serious measures to prevent would-be terrorists from easily entering their target society. As Chaim Kaufmann (1996) has shown, even intense ethnic civil wars can often be stopped by demographic separation because it greatly reduces both means and incentives for the sides to attack each other. This logic may apply with even more force to the related problem of suicide terrorism, since, for suicide attackers, gaining physical access to the general area of the target is the only genuinely demanding part of an operation, and as we have seen, resentment of foreign occupation of their national homeland is a key part of the motive for suicide terrorism.

The requirements for demographic separation depend on geographic and other circumstances that may not be attainable in all cases. For example, much of Israel's difficulty in containing suicide terrorism derives from the deeply intermixed settlement patterns of the West Bank and Gaza, which make the effective length of the border between Palestinian and Jewish settled areas practically infinite and have rendered even very intensive Israeli border control efforts ineffective (Kaufmann 1998). As a result, territorial concessions could well encourage terrorist leaders to strive for still greater gains while greater repression may only exacerbate the conditions of occupation that cultivate more recruits for terrorist organizations. Instead, the best course to improve Israel's security may well be a combined strategy: abandoning territory on the West Bank along with an actual wall that physically separates the populations.

Similarly, if Al Qaeda proves able to continue suicide attacks against the American homeland, the United States should emphasize improving its domestic security. In the short term, the United States should adopt stronger border controls to make it more difficult for suicide attackers to enter the United States. In the long term, the United States should work toward energy independence and, thus, reduce the need for American troops in the Persian Gulf countries where their presence has helped recruit suicide terrorists to attack America. These measures will not provide a perfect solution, but they may make it far more difficult for Al Qaeda to continue attacks in the United States, especially spectacular attacks that require elaborate coordination.

Perhaps most important, the close association between foreign military occupations and the growth of suicide terrorist movements in the occupied regions should give pause to those who favor solutions that involve conquering countries in order to transform their political systems. Conquering countries may disrupt terrorist operations in the short term, but it is important to recognize that occupation of more countries may well increase the number of terrorists coming at us.

Appendix: suicide terrorist campaigns, 1980–2001

Date	Weapon	Target	Killed*
		Completed Campaigns	
Campaign #1: Hezbollah vs. US, France			
1. April 18, 1983	car bomb	US embassy, Beirut	63
2. Oct 23, 1983	car bomb	US Marine barracks, Beirut	241
3. Oct 23, 1983	car bomb	French barracks, Beirut	58
4. Dec 12, 1983	grenades	US embassy, Kuwait	7
5. Dec 21, 1983	car bomb	French HQ, Beirut	1
6. Sept 12, 1984	truck bomb	US embassy, Beirut	14
Campaign #2: Hezbollah vs. Israel			
1. Nov 4, 1983	car bomb	IDF post, Tyre, Lebanon	50
2. Jun 16, 1984	car bomb	IDF post, south Lebanon	5
3. Mar 8, 1985	truck bomb	IDF post	12
4. Apr 9, 1985	car bomb	IDF post	4
5. May 9, 1985	suitcase bomb	Southern Lebanese Army checkpoint	2
6. June 15, 1985	car bomb	IDF post, Beirut	23
Campaign #3: Hezbollah vs. Israel and South Lebanon Army			
1. July 9, 1985	car bombs	2 SLA outposts	22
2. July 15, 1985	car bomb	SLA outpost	10
3. July 31, 1985	car bomb	IDF patrol, south Lebanon	2
4. Aug 6, 1985	mule bomb	SLA outpost	0
5. Aug 29, 1985	car bomb	SLA outpost	15
6. Sept 3, 1985	car bomb	SLA outpost	37
7. Sept 12, 1985	car bomb	SLA outpost	21
8. Sept 17, 1985	car bomb	SLA outpost	30
9. Sept 18, 1985	car bomb	SLA outpost	0
10. Oct 17, 1985	grenades	SLA radio station	6
11. Nov 4, 1985	car bomb	SLA outpost	0
12. Nov 12, 1985	car bomb	Christ, militia leaders, Beirut	5**
13. Nov 26, 1985	car bomb	SLA outpost	20
14. April 7, 1986	car bomb	SLA outpost	1
15. July 17, 1986	car bomb	Jezzine, south Lebanon	7
16. Nov 20, 1986	car bomb	SLA outpost	3
Campaign #4: Liberation Tigers of Tamil Eelam vs. Sri Lanka			
1. Jul 12, 1990	boat bomb	naval vessel, Trincomalee	6
2. Nov 23, 1990	mines	army camp, Manakulam	0
3. Mar 2, 1991	car bomb	defense minister, Colombo	18**
4. Mar 19, 1991	truck bomb	army camp, Silavathurai	5
5. May 5, 1991	boat bomb	naval vessel	5
6. May 21, 1991	belt bomb	Rajiv Gandhi, Madras, India	1**
7. June 22, 1991	car bomb	defense ministry, Colombo	27
8. Nov 16, 1992	motorcycle bomb	navy commander, Colombo	1**
9. May 1, 1993	belt bomb	president of Sri Lanka, Colombo	23**
10. Nov 11, 1993	boat bomb	naval base, Jaffna Lagoon	0
11. Aug 2, 1994	grenades	air force helicopter, Palali	0
12. Sept 19, 1994	mines	naval vessel, Sagarawardene	25
13. Oct 24, 1994	belt bomb	presidential candidate, Colombo	53**
14. Nov 8, 1994	mines	naval vessel, Vettilaikerny	0
Campaign #5: LTTE vs. Sri Lanka			
1. Apr 18, 1995	scuba divers	naval vessel, Trincomalee	11
2. Jul 16, 1995	scuba divers	naval vessel, Jaffna peninsula	0
3. Aug 7, 1995	belt bomb	government bldg, Colombo	22

Date	Weapon	Target	Killed*
4. Sep 3, 1995	scuba divers	naval vessel, Trincomalee	0
5. Sep 10, 1995	scuba divers	naval vessel, Kankesanthurai	0
6. Sep 20, 1995	scuba divers	naval vessel, Kankesanthurai	0
7. Oct 2, 1995	scuba divers	Naval vessel, Kankesanthurai	0
8. Oct 17, 1995	scuba divers	naval vessel, Trincomalee	9
9. Oct 20, 1995	mines	2 oil depots, Colombo	23
10. Nov 11, 1995	belt bombs	army HQ, crowd, Colombo	23
11. Dec 5, 1995	truck bomb	police camp, Batticaloa	23
12. Jan 8, 1996	belt bomb	market, Batticaloa	0
13. Jan 31, 1996	truck bomb	bank, Colombo	91
14. Apr 1, 1996	boat bomb	navy vessel, Vettilaikerni	10
15. Apr 12, 1996	scuba divers	port building, Colombo	0
16. Jul 3, 1996	belt bomb	government motorcade, Jaffna	37
17. Jul 18, 1996	mines	naval gunboat, Mullaittivu	35
18. Aug 6, 1996	boat bomb	naval ship, north coast	0
19. Aug 14, 1996	bicycle bomb	public rally, Kalmunai	0
20. Oct 25, 1996	boat bomb	gunboat, Trincomalee	12
21. Nov 25, 1996	belt bomb	police chief vehicle, Trincomalee	0***
22. Dec 17, 1996	motorcycle bomb	police unit jeep, Ampara	1
23. Mar 6, 1997	grenades	air base, China Bay	0
24. Oct 15, 1997	truck bomb	World Trade Centre, Colombo	18
25. Oct 19, 1997	boat bomb	naval gunboat, northeastern coast	7
26. Dec 28, 1997	truck bomb	political leader, south Sri Lanka	0***
27. Jan 25, 1998	truck bomb	Buddhist shrine, Kandy	11
28. Feb 5, 1998	belt bomb	Air Force headquarters, Colombo	8
29. Feb 23, 1998	boat bombs	2 landing ships off Point Pedru	47
30. Mar 5, 1998	bus bomb	train station, Colombo	38
31. May 15, 1998	belt bomb	army brigadier, Jaffna peninsula	1
32. Sep 11, 1998	belt bomb	mayor of Jaffna	20**
33. Mar 15, 1999	belt bomb	police station, Colombo	5
34. May 29, 1999	belt bomb	Tamil rival leader, Batticaloa	2
35. Jul 25, 1999	belt bomb	passenger ferry, Trincomalee	1
36. Jul 29, 1999	belt bomb	Tamil politician, Colombo	1**
37. Aug 4, 1999	bicycle bomb	police vehicle, Vavuniya	12
38. Aug 9, 1999	belt bomb	military commander, Vakarai	1
39. Sep 2, 1999	belt bomb	Tamil rival, Vavuniya	3**
40. Dec 18, 1999	2 belt bombs	president of Sri Lanka, Colombo	38***
41. Jan 5, 2000	belt bomb	prime minister of Sri Lanka, Colombo	11***
42. Feb 4, 2000	sea diver	naval vessel, Trincomalee	0
43. Mar 2, 2000	belt bomb	military commander, Trincomalee	1***
44. Mar 10, 2000	belt bomb	government motorcade Colombo	23
45. Jun 5, 2000	scuba diver	ammunition ship, northeast coast	5
46. Jun 7, 2000	belt bomb	Industries Minister, Colombo	26**
47. Jun 14, 2000	bicycle bomb	air force bus, Wattala Town	2
48. Jun 26, 2000	boat bomb	merchant vessel, north coast	7
49. Aug 16, 2000	belt bomb	military vehicle, Vavuniya	1
50. Sep 15, 2000	belt bomb	hospital, Colombo	7
51. Oct 2, 2000	belt bomb	political leader, Trincomalee	22**
52. Oct 5, 2000	belt bomb	political rally, Medawachchiya	12
53. Oct 19, 2000	belt bomb	Cabinet ceremony, Colombo	0
54. Oct 23, 2000	boat bombs	gunboat/troop carrier, Trincomalee	2

(Continued)

Appendix: suicide terrorist campaigns, 1980–2001 *(Continued)*

Date	Group	Weapon	Target	Killed*
Campaign #6: Hamas vs. Israel				
1. Apr 6, 1994	Hamas	car bomb	Afula	9
2. Apr 13, 1994	Hamas	belt bomb	Hadera	6
Campaign #7: Hamas/Islamic Jihad vs. Israel				
1. Oct 19, 1994	Hamas	belt bomb	Tel Aviv	22
2. Nov 11, 1994	Islamic Jihad	bike bomb	Netzarim, Gaza	3
3. Dec 25, 1994	Hamas	belt bomb	Jerusalem	0
4. Jan 22, 1995	Islamic Jihad	belt bomb	Beit Lid Junction	21
5. Apr 9, 1995	IJ & H	2 car bombs	Netzarim, Gaza	8
6. July 24, 1995	Hamas	belt bomb	Tel Aviv	6
7. Aug 21, 1995	Hamas	belt bomb	Jerusalem	5
Campaign #8: Hamas vs. Israel				
1. Feb 25, 1996	Hamas	belt bomb	Jerusalem	25
2. Feb 25, 1996	Hamas	belt bomb	Ashkelon	1
3. Mar 3, 1996	Hamas	belt bomb	Jerusalem	19
4. Mar 4, 1996	Hamas	belt bomb	Tel Aviv	13
Campaign #9: Hamas vs. Israel				
1. Mar 21, 1997	Hamas	belt bomb	café, Tel Aviv	3
2. Jul 30, 1997	Hamas	belt bomb	Jerusalem	14
3. Sept 4, 1997	Hamas	belt bomb	Jerusalem	7
Campaign #10: Kurdistan Workers Party (PKK) vs. Turkey				
1. Jun 30, 1996		belt bomb	Tunceli	9
2. Oct 25, 1996		belt bomb	Adana	4
3. Oct 29, 1996		belt bombs	Sivas	4
Campaign #11: PKK vs. Turkey				
1. Mar 4, 1999		belt bomb	Batman	0
2. Mar 27, 1999		grenade	Istanbul	0
3. Apr 5, 1999		belt bomb	governor, Bingol	0
4. Jul 5, 1999		belt bomb	Adana	0
5. Jul 7, 1999		grenades	Iluh	0
6. Aug 28, 1999		bomb	Tunceli	0

Ongoing Compaigns

Date	Group	Weapon	Target	Killed*
Campaign #12: Al Qaeda vs. United States				
1. Nov 13, 1995		car bomb	US military base, Riyadh, SA	5
2. Jun 25, 1996		truck bomb	US military base, Dhahran SA	19
3. Aug 7, 1998		truck bombs	US embassies, Kenya/Tanzania	250
4. Oct 12, 2000		boat bomb	USS Cole, Yemen	17
5. Sep 9, 2001		camera bomb	Ahmed Shah Massoud, Afghanistan	1**
6. Sep 11, 2001		hijacked airplanes	WTC/Pentagon	3037
Campaign #13: Chechen Separatists vs. Russia				
1. Jun 7, 2000		truck bomb	Russian police station, Chechnya	2
2. Jul 3, 2000		truck bomb	Argun, Russia	30
3. Mar 24, 2001		car bomb	Chechnya	20
4. Nov 29, 2001		belt bomb	military commander, Chechnya	1
Campaign #14: Kashmir Separatists vs. India				
1. Dec 25, 2000		car bomb	Srinagar, Kashmir	8
2. Oct 1, 2001		car bomb	Legislative assembly, Kashmir	30
3. Dec 13, 2001		gunmen	Parliament, New Delhi	7

Date	Group	Weapon	Target	Killed*
Campaign #15: LTTE vs. Sri Lanka				
1. Jul 24, 2001		belt bomb	international airport, Colombo	12
2. Sep 16, 2001		boat bomb	naval vessel, north	29
3. Oct 29, 2001		belt bomb	PM of Sri Lanka, Colombo	3***
4. Oct 30, 2001		boat bomb	oil tanker, northern coast	4
5. Nov 9, 2001		belt bomb	police jeep, Batticaloa	0
6. Nov 15, 2001		belt bomb	crowd, Batticaloa	3
Compaign #16: Hamas/Islamic Jihad vs. Israel				
1. Oct 26, 2000	Islamic Jihad	bike bomb	Gaza	0
2. Oct 30, 2000	Hamas	belt bomb	Jerusalem	15
3. Nov 2, 2000	Al Aqsa	car bomb	Jerusalem	2
4. Nov 22, 2000	Islamic Jihad	car bomb	Hadera	2
5. Dec 22, 2000	Al Aqsa	belt bomb	Jordan valley	3
6. Jan 1, 2001	Hamas	belt bomb	Netanya	10
7. Feb 14, 2001	Hamas	bus driver	Tel Aviv	8
8. Mar 1, 2001	Hamas	car bomb	Mei Ami	1
9. Mar 4, 2001	Hamas	belt bomb	Netanya	3
10. Mar 27, 2001	Hamas	belt bomb	Jerusalem	1
11. Mar 27, 2001	Hamas	belt bomb	Jerusalem (2nd attack)	0
12. Mar 28, 2001	Hamas	belt bomb	Kfar Saba	3
13. Apr 22, 2001	Hamas	belt bomb	Kfar Saba	3
14. Apr 23, 2001	PFLP	car bomb	Yehuda	8
15. Apr 29, 2001	Hamas	belt bomb	West Bank	0
16. May 18, 2001	Hamas	belt bomb	Netanya	5
17. May 25, 2001	Islamic Jihad	truck bomb	Netzarim, Gaza	2
18. May 27, 2001	Hamas	car bomb	Netanya	1
19. May 30, 2001	Islamic Jihad	car bomb	Netanya	8
20. Jun 1, 2001	Hamas	belt bomb	nightclub, Tel Aviv	22
21. Jun 22, 2001	Hamas	belt bomb	Gaza	2
22. Jul 2, 2001	Hamas	car bomb	IDF checkpt, Gaza	0
23. Jul 9, 2001	Hamas	car bomb	Gaza	0
24. Jul 16, 2001	Islamic Jihad	belt bomb	Jerusalem	5
25. Aug 8, 2001	Al Aqsa	car bomb	Jerusalem	8
26. Aug 9, 2001	Islamic Jihad	belt bomb	Haifa	15
27. Aug 12, 2001	Islamic Jihad	belt bomb	Haifa	0
28. Aug 21, 2001	Al Aqsa	car bomb	Jerusalem	0
29. Sept 4, 2001	Hamas	belt bomb	Jerusalem	0
30. Sept 9, 2001	Hamas	belt bomb	Nahariya	3
31. Oct 1, 2001	Hamas	car bomb	Afula	1
32. Oct 7, 2001	Islamic Jihad	car bomb	North Israel	2
33. Nov 26, 2001	Hamas	car bomb	Gaza	0
34. Nov 29, 2001	Islamic Jihad	belt bomb	Gaza	3
35. Dec 1, 2001	Hamas	belt bomb	Haifa	11
36. Dec 2, 2001	Hamas	belt bomb	Jerusalem	15
37. Dec 5, 2001	Islamic Jihad	belt bomb	Jerusalem	0
38. Dec 9, 2001	???	belt bomb	Haifa	0
39. Dec 12, 2001	Hamas	belt bomb	Gaza	4
Isolated Attacks				
1. Dec 15, 1981	???	car bomb	Iraqi embassy, Beirut	30
2. May 25, 1985	Hezbollah	car bomb	Emir, Kuwait	0***
3. Jul 5, 1987	LTTE	truck bomb	army camp, Jaffna Peninsula	18
4. Aug 15, 1993	???	motorcycle bomb	Interior Minister, Egypt	3***
5. Jan 30, 1995	Armed Islamic Group	truck bomb	crowd, Algiers	42

(Continued)

Appendix: suicide terrorist campaigns, 1980–2001 *(Continued)*

Date	Group	Weapon	Target	Killed*
6. Nov 19, 1995	Islamic Group	truck bomb	Egyptian embassy, Pakistan	16
7. Oct 29, 1998	Hamas	belt bomb	Gaza	1
8. Nov 17, 1998	???	belt bomb	Yuksekova, Turkey	0
9. Dec 29, 1999	Hezbollah	car bomb	South Lebanon	1

Note: Several reports of PKK suicide in May and June 1997 during fighting between PKK and Kurdish militias in Iraq, but coverage insufficient to distinguish suicide attack from suicide to avoid capture.
* Not including attacker(s).
** Assassination target killed.
*** Assassination target survived.
??? = unclaimed.

Notes

1   A suicide attack can be defined in two ways, a narrow definition limited to situations in which an attacker kills himself and a broad definition that includes any instance when an attacker fully expects to be killed by others during an attack. An example that fits the broad definition is Baruch Goldstein, who continued killing Palestinians at the February 1994 Hebron Massacre until he himself was killed, who had no plan for escape, and who left a note for his family indicating that he did not expect to return. My research relies on the narrow definition, partly because this is the common practice in the literature and partly because there are so few instances in which it is clear that an attacker expected to be killed by others that adding this category of events would not change my findings.

2   Hunger strikes and self-immolation are not ordinarily considered acts of terrorism, because their main purpose is to evoke understanding and sympathy from the target audience, and not to cause terror (Niebuhr 1960).

3   This survey sought to include every instance of a suicide attack in which the attacker killed himself except those explicitly authorized by a state and carried out by the state government apparatus (e.g., Iranian human wave attacks in the Iran-Iraq war were not counted). The survey is probably quite reliable, because a majority of the incidents were openly claimed by the sponsoring terrorist organizations. Even those that were not were, in nearly all cases, reported multiple times in regional news media, even if not always in the U.S. media. To probe for additional cases, I interviewed experts and officials involved in what some might consider conflicts especially prone to suicide attacks, such as Afghanistan in the 1980s, but this did not yield more incidents. According to the CIA station chief for Pakistan from 1986 to 1988 (Bearden 2002), "I cannot recall a single incident where an Afghan launched himself against a Soviet target with the intention of dying in the process. I don't think these things ever happened, though some of their attacks were a little hare-brained and could have been considered suicidal. I think it's important that Afghans never even took their war outside their borders—for example they never tried to blow up the Soviet Embassy in Pakistan."

4   There were no suicide attacks from April to October 1994.

5   There were no suicide attacks from August 1995 to February 1996. There were four suicide attacks in response to an Israeli assassination from February 25 to March 4, 1996, and then none until March 1997.

6   The Bush administration's decision in May 2003 to withdraw most U.S. troops from Saudi Arabia is the kind of partial concession likely to backfire. Al Qaeda may well view this as evidence that the United States is vulnerable to coercive pressure, but the concession does not satisfy Al Qaeda's core demand to reduce American military control over the holy areas on the Arab peninsula. With the conquest and long term military occupation of Iraq, American military capabilities to control Saudi Arabia have substantially increased even if there are no American troops on Saudi soil itself.

References

al-Shaqaqi, Fathi. 1995. "Interview with Secretary General of Islamic Jihad." *Al-Quds*, 11 April. FBIS-NES-95–70, 12 April 1995.

al-Zahhar, Mahmud. 1996. "Interview." *Al-Dustur* (Amman), 19 February. FBIS-NES-96–034, 20 February 1996.

Art, Robert J., and Patrick M. Cronin. 2003. *The United States and Coercive Diplomacy*. Washington, DC: United States Institute of Peace.

Bakr, Ahmed. 1995. "Interview." *The Independent* (London), 14 March. FBIS-NES-95–086, 4 May 1995.

Bearden, Milton. 2002. Personal correspondence. University of Chicago, March 26.

Bloom, Mia. 2002. "Rational Interpretations of Palestinian Suicide Bombing." Paper presented at the Program on International Security Policy, University of Chicago.

Boix, Carlos, and Sebastian Rosato, 2001. "A Complete Dataset of Regimes, 1850–1999." University of Chicago. Typescript.

"Bus Attack Said to Spur Rabin to Speed Talks." 1995. *Yediot Aharonot*, July 25. FBIS-NES-94–142, 25 July 1995.

Clutterbuck, Richard. 1975. *Living with Terrorism*. London: Faber & Faber.

Crenshaw, Martha. 1981. "The Causes of Terrorism." *Comparative Politics* 13 (July): 397–399.

De Figueiredo, Rui, and Barry R. Weingast. 1998. "Vicious Cycles: Endogenous Political Extremism and Political Violence." Paper presented at the annual meeting of the American Political Science Association.

Department of State. 1983–2001. *Patterns of Global Terrorism*. Washington, DC: DOS.

Edler Baumann, Carol. 1973. *Diplomatic Kidnapings: A Revolutionary Tactic of Urban Terrorism*. The Hague: Nijhoff.

Elliott, Paul. 1998. *Brotherhoods of Fear*. London: Blandford.

George, Alexander, et al. 1972. *Limits of Coercive Diplomacy*. Boston: Little, Brown.

Greenberg, Joel. 2002. "Suicide Planner Expresses Joy Over His Missions," *New York Times*, 9 May.

Hamas Communique No. 125. 1995. *Filastin al-Muslimah* (London), August. FBIS-NES-95-152, 8 August 1995.

"Hamas Leader Discusses Goals." 1995. *Frankfurter Runschau*, 3 May. FBIS-NES-95-086, 4 May 1995.

"Hamas Operations Against Israel Said to Continue." 1994. *Al-Dustur* (Amman, Jordan), 14 April. FBIS-NES-94–072, 14 April 1994.

Hamas Statement. 2000. *BBC Summary of World Broadcasts*, 23 July.

Hoffman, Bruce. 1998. *Inside Terrorism*. New York: Columbia University Press.

Horowitz, Michael, and Dan Reiter. 2001. "When Does Aerial Bombing Work? Quantitative Empirical Tests, 1917–1999." *Journal of Conflict Resolution* 45 (April): 147–173.

Hroub, Khaled. 2000. *Hamas: Political Thought and Practice*. Washington, DC: Institute for Palestine Studies.

Huntington, Samuel P. 1991. *The Third Wave: Democratization in the Twentieth Century*. Norman: University of Oklahoma Press.

Inbar, Efraim. 1999. *Rabin and Israel's National Security*. Baltimore: John's Hopkins University Press.

Institute for Counter-Terrorism (ICT). 2001. *Countering Suicide Terrorism*. Herzliya, Israel: International Policy Institute for Counter-Terrorism.

Jenkins, Brian N. 1975. "Will Terrorists Go Nuclear?" Rand Report P-5541. Santa Monica, CA: Rand Corp.

Jenkins, Brian N. 1985. *International Terrorism*. Washington, DC: Rand Corp.

Jervis, Robert. 1976. *Perception and Misperception in International Politics*. Princeton, NJ: Princeton University Press.

Kaufmann, Chaim D. 1996. "Possible and Impossible Solutions to Ethnic Civil Wars." *International Security* 20 (Spring): 136–175.

Kaufmann, Chaim D. 1998. "When All Else Fails: Ethnic Population Transfers and Partitions in the Twentieth Century." *International Security* 23 (Fall): 120–56.

Kramer, Martin. 1990. "The Moral Logic of Hizballah." In *Origins of Terrorism*, ed. Walter Reich. New York: Cambridge University Press.

Kramer, Martin. 1996. "Fundamentalist Islam at Large: Drive for Power." *Middle East Quarterly* 3 (June): 37–49.

Kydd, Andrew, and Barbara F. Walter. 2002. "Sabotaging the Peace: The Politics of Extremist Violence." *International Organization* 56 (2): 263–296.

Laqueur, Walter. 1987. *The Age of Terrorism*. Boston: Little, Brown.

Lebow, Richard Ned. 1981. *Between Peace and War: The Nature of International Crisis*. Baltimore, MD: Johns Hopkins University Press.

Lewis, Bernard. 1968. *The Assassins*. New York: Basic Books.

Makovsky, David, and Alon Pinkas. 1994. "Rabin: Killing Civilians Won't Kill the Negotiations." *Jerusalem Post*, 13 April.

Merari, Ariel. 1990. "The Readiness to Kill and Die: Suicidal Terrorism in the Middle East." In *Origins of Terrorism*, ed. Walter Reich. New York: Cambridge University Press.

Mish'al, Khalid. 2000. "Interview." *BBC Summary of World Broadcasts*, 17 November.

Mishal, Shaul, and Avraham Sela. 2000. *The Palestinian Hamas*. New York: Columbia University Press.

Niebuhr, Reinhold. 1960. *Moral Man and Immoral Society*. New York: Scribner.

Nusse, Andrea. 1998. *Muslim Palestine: The Ideology of Hamas*. Amsterdam: Harwood Academic.

O'Neill, Richard. 1981. *Suicide Squads*. New York: Ballantine Books.

Pape, Robert A. 1996. *Bombing to Win: Air Power and Coercion in War*. Ithaca, NY: Cornell University Press.

Pape, Robert A. 1997. "Why Economic Sanctions Do Not Work." *International Security* 22 (Fall): 90–136.

Pape, Robert A. 2002. "The Universe of Suicide Terrorist Attacks Worldwide, 1980–2001." University of Chicago. Typescript.

Post, Jerrold M. 1990. "Terrorist Psycho-Logic: Terrorist Behavior as a Product of Psychological Forces." In *Origins of Terrorism*, ed. Walter Reich. New York: Cambridge University Press.

Przeworski, Adam, Michael E. Alvarez, Jose Antonio Cheibub, and Fernando Limongi. 2000. *Democracy and Development: Political Institutions and Well-Being in the World, 1950–1990*. Cambridge, UK: Cambridge University Press.

Rabin, Yitzhaq. 1994. "Speech to Knessett." *BBC Summary of World Broadcasts*, 20 April.

Rabin, Yitzhaq. 1995. "Interview." *BBC Summary of World Broadcasts*, 8 September.

Rapoport, David C. 1971. *Assassination and Terrorism*. Toronto: CBC Merchandising.

Rapoport, David C. 1984. "Fear and Trembling: Terrorism in Three Religious Traditions." *American Political Science Review* 78 (September): 655–677.

Reagan, Ronald. 1990. *An American Life*. New York: Simon and Schuster.

Reich, Walter, ed. 1990. *Origins of Terrorism*. New York: Cambridge University Press.

Sauvagnargues, Philippe. 1994. "Opposition Candidate." *Agence France Presse*, 14 August.

Schalk, Peter. 1997. "Resistance and Martyrdom in the Process of State Formation of Tamililam." In *Martyrdom and Political Resistance*, ed. Joyed Pettigerw. Amsterdam: VU University Press, 61–83.

Schelling, Thomas. 1966. *Arms and Influence*. New Haven, CT: Yale University Press.

Schmid, Alex P., and Albert J. Jongman. 1988. *Political Terrorism*. New Brunswick, NJ: Transaction Books.

Sciolino, Elaine. 2002. "Saudi Warns Bush." *New York Times*, 27 January.

Shallah, Ramadan. 2001. "Interview." *BBC Summary of World Broadcasts*, 3 November.

Shiqaqi, Khalil, et al. 2002. *The Israeli-Palestinian Peace Process*. Portland, OR: Sussex Academic Press.

Sprinzak, Ehud. 2000. "Rational Fanatics." *Foreign Policy*, No. 120 (September/October): 66–73.

"Sri Lanka Opposition Leader Promises Talk with Rebels." 1994. *Japan Economic Newswire*, 11 August.

St. John, Peter. 1991. *Air Piracy, Airport Security, and International Terrorism*. New York: Quorum Books.

Theodoulou, Michael. 1995. "New Attacks Feared." *The Times* (London), 21 August. FBIS-NES-95–165, 25 August 1995.

Tuchman, Barbara W. 1966. *The Proud Tower*. New York: Macmillan.

World Islamic Front. 1998. "Jihad Against Jews and Crusaders." Statement, 23 February.

18 Palestinian suicide bombing

Public support, market share, and outbidding

Mia M. Bloom

Why have suicide bombings in the Middle East become so popular? In this article, I investigate how and why Palestinian public opinion increasingly supports suicide bombings even though support for such operations and for Hamas has fluctuated in the past. Since November 2000, Palestinian public opinion has alarmingly shifted its support toward radical Islamic organizations because of a number of factors endogenous to Palestinian society.[1] Under conditions of mounting public support, the bombings have become a method of recruitment for militant Islamic organizations within the Palestinian community. They serve at one and the same time to attack the hated enemy (Israel) and to give legitimacy to outlier militant groups who compete with the Palestinian Authority for leadership of the community.

Multiple organizations are engaged in this competition and use violence to increase their prestige. With every major attack since November 2000, support for suicide bombings has increased and support for the Palestinian Authority has decreased. In addition to building support for martyrdom, groups that use the tactic become more popular. The support for militant Islamic movements appears to capture previously nonaligned groups among the Palestinians, demonstrating that martyrdom operations boost the organizational profile of the groups using them.

Palestinian suicide bombings are violent, politically motivated attacks carried out in a deliberate state of awareness by persons who blow themselves up together with a chosen target.[2] Support for suicide operations works against the stated goals of a better future for Palestinian civilians. Public opinion polls indicate that Palestinians are worse off now than they were before the al-Aqsa *intifada* according to every indicator (economic, social, health, etc.). Yet, the majority of Palestinians support the continuation of the al-Aqsa *intifada* and martyrdom operations regardless of Israeli retaliatory policies.[3] The targets and modus operandi of suicide bombings vary, ranging from government officials to military or economic targets, and from scores of attacks to solitary or sporadic ones.[4] However, there is no single theory about what motivates suicide bombers and no firm opinion among Palestinians as to their usefulness.

Conventional explanations of Palestinian suicide bombings regard them as a way for radical Islamic organizations to slow or stem the improvement of relations between Israel and the Palestinian Authority. In this capacity, the bombings play a strategic "spoiler role" in regard to the peace process. Hamas has urged more violence as relations between Israel and the Palestinian Authority have improved. According to Palestinian Authority documents released in January 2004, "suicide bombings are a key element in the arena of the struggle between the Israelis and Palestinians, and an analysis of the circumstances of the timing and execution of the vast majority of the bombings, particularly the major ones conducted by the Hamas and Islamic Jihad, makes clear the timing was much more a purely political matter than a practical military one."[5] According to the report, Hamas and Islamic Jihad had agents who provided information on political developments, including inside information about negotiations with Israel and the United States, thus enabling Hamas and Islamic Jihad to respond accordingly.

An alternative explanation follows from the logic of Barry Weingast and Rui de Figueiredo, who have argued that violence is often retaliatory.[6] This school of thought traces Palestinian suicide bombings to Israeli provocations, beginning with the Hebron Massacre by Baruch Goldstein. As Mazin Hammad has commented: "The al-Ibrahimi Mosque massacre opened the doors of revenge in Palestine like never before."[7] Other provocations include the opening of the tunnel under the al-Aqsa Mosque and the Israeli policy of "targeted assassinations" of Palestinian militant leaders, for example, Hamas's bomb maker, Yahiyeh Ayyash,[8] Izz Eddin al-Qassam Brigade leader Salah Shchada and his family and, most recently, Sheikh Ahmed Yassin on 22 March 2004.[9]

The news media implies causality and linkage between the two explanations: "Signs of progress recorded by Middle East peace-brokers were obliterated in an orgy of terror as six Israelis were killed in a Palestinian suicide attack in January after Israelis killed Raed Karmi, the local militia leader in Tulkarm of [Yasser] Arafat's Fatah organization."[10]

Andrew Kydd and Barbara F. Walter have argued that violence plays a spoiler role to the peace process and is to be expected when negotiated settlements become imminent. "The purpose is to exacerbate doubts on the target side that the moderate opposition groups can be trusted to implement the peace deal and will not renege on it later on."[11] For Walter and Kydd, suicide bombing is a complex game dependent upon uncertainty between moderates and the target state and upon whether moderates are weak or strong vis à vis their opposition. They posit that weak moderates are less capable of stopping terrorism from within their own ranks, causing uncertainty in the other side that results in the cancellation of peace negations and a shift in Israeli voting in favor of antipeace candidates. Their model appears to explicate the bombings that surrounded the 1996 Israeli elections, although it fails to explain the whole story.

The attacks carried out in February and March 1996 were among several factors that influenced the outcome of the Israeli prime ministerial election of May 1996 that brought right-wing Benjamin Netanyahu into power and delayed the implementation of the Oslo and Wye Agreements. Netanyahu's victory was actually unexpected and occurred in the wee hours of election night by a slim margin of less than one half of one percent. This outcome was the product of several factors, including the boycott by Israeli Arabs of the election. Israeli Arabs, who comprise 20 percent of the electorate, boycotted the election after 102 men, women, and children were accidentally killed in an Israeli artillery attack on the UN compound in Kana, Southern Lebanon on 18 April 1996—six weeks before the election. The Kydd and Walter model fails to explain why bombings in 1995 did not have the same effect on the peace process when Yitzhak Rabin was still alive,[12] nor can it rationalize how a left-wing government under Ehud Barak was elected in 1999 despite their indication of two episodes prior to the election. However, according to my data, there were no suicide attacks during this period and it is documented that "there was relatively little Palestinian terror on Netanyahu's three-year watch. Due to Arafat's combination of threats, policing and political cajolery, Arafat got Hamas to cut down its violence."[13]

Their explanation partially explains what motivates the organizations but does not account for why public opinion supports or rejects the tactic and, finally, they conflate the results of suicide bombing campaigns with their underlying motivation. There have been periods of time when Hamas has willingly honored cease fires (*hudna*) to allow Arafat to pursue peace negotiations with the Israelis. For example, Arafat convinced Hamas to suspend military actions after 11 September 2001 on the condition that Israeli targeted assassinations stop. The Israelis continued their policy, and Hamas proceeded with their attacks.[14] This was repeated in June 2003, when Hamas called a *hudna*, only to resume operations after a failed attack on Dr. Abdel Aziz Rantisi.

Hamas may use suicide terror to deter policymakers from reaching agreements but only as long as Israeli policymakers transparently equate violence with non-negotiation, providing Hamas with its own "road map" of how to spoil a peace process that would, by definition, exclude them. Kydd and Walter correctly identify extremist violence as being strategic; the target of the violence is not only the moderates negotiating the peace treaties. There are actually two audiences for the violence, one domestic (within the Palestinian community) and one external (the "Zionist Entity").[15]

These existing interpretations (spoiler or retaliatory) ignore the internal state-building process and discount the competition for leadership under way within the Palestinian community that accounts for both the occurrence of bombings as well as the absence of attacks in the period from November 1998 to November 2000. Furthermore, the significant increase in attacks in March 2002 took place against a political backdrop with few substantive peace negotiations between Israel and the Palestinian Authority—limiting the explanatory power of the spoiler rationale to explain this phenomenon as a whole. James Bennet commented, "Having seen peace initiatives melt before previous waves of violence, Israelis, like Palestinians, were already deeply skeptical of the new plan [Bush's Road Map]. Many on both sides do not seem to be paying much attention to the renewed diplomacy."[16] So it is unclear how effective the attacks are at spoiling a peace no one believes in. Finally, these existing interpretations cannot account for the variance in public support for such operations over time.

Two phases of support for suicide terror

In the first period (1994–1996), support for suicide operations never exceeded a third of Palestinians polled, whereas after November 2000, support for operations jumped to two-thirds or more. The bombings are not just the result of impending implementation of peace treaties or part of tit-for-tat violence. Suicide bombings are more than just a reaction to external stimuli; we have to acknowledge the motivations for violence within Palestinian society. One should nuance support for the bombings and explain each phase separately. To do this, we need to better comprehend the internal dynamics of the Palestinian polity and the ways in which radical organizations have effectively penetrated civil society.[17]

Palestinians' disillusionment with Arafat, his Palestinian Authority, and the deadlocked peace process provided radical groups with an opportunity to increase their share of the political market by engaging in violence.[18] Finally, Israeli heavy-handed responses to the violence (incursions into Area A, targeted assassinations, use of helicopter gunships, and civilian casualties) make Hamas's rhetoric appear valid and prescient.[19]

The frustrations associated with the Oslo Process and with Camp David II, and the provocative visit in September 2000 of Ariel Sharon to the Haram al-Sharif and the al-Aqsa Mosque exacerbated negative relations between Palestinians and Israelis. Israeli sharpshooters inflicted heavy casualties on Palestinian demonstrators, who were initially comprised of unarmed youths engaged in symbolic stone throwing. Israel relied on excessive force, generating a cycle of violence that has been escalated by Israel at each stage, inflicting disproportionate casualties on the Palestinian side.[20]

In the first period, suicide bombings were intermittent and, according to Sheikh Yassin and Abdel Aziz Rantisi, *were* intended to both undermine the legitimacy of the Palestinian Authority and negatively affect the peace process.[21] The timing of the attacks was correlated to respond to Israeli actions, which provided defensive justifications for Hamas violence—in accordance with Islamic law. However, responsibility for the attacks during the first period was often not claimed by any group at the time. Later on, groups vied with one another to claim each incident.

Popular support for the bombings during this period remained low, and Hamas was unable to mobilize Palestinians by using violence. In 1996, the attacks were intended to disrupt the Israeli elections, but the missile attack on Kana and the subsequent boycott of the elections by Israeli Arabs also had a significant impact on the election results.

In the second period (after November 2000) and increasingly since, support for suicide operations increased exponentially and the waves of bombings demonstrated a competition between groups vying for power against a backdrop in which violence resonates with the rank and file. Furthermore, we can observe increasing popular support for groups after they perpetrate martyrdom attacks.

The bombings have effectively undermined Arafat's monopoly of the legitimate use of force in an emerging Palestinian state entity.[22] According to one Palestinian cabinet member, "When there is an ongoing peace process, the Palestinian Authority is empowered enough to exercise its control over all of the citizens … but after ten years of negotiations, Jewish Settlements have doubled since the signing of the Oslo agreement… Hamas and the Islamic Jihad are political organizations that now have substantial standing in the [Arab] street."[23]

In the period immediately after Oslo, Arafat suppressed Hamas and Islamic Jihad, arrested over 2,000 operatives, and killed twenty of their leaders. The period between the signing of the 28 September 1995 Interim Agreement ("Oslo II") until the suicide bombings of February and March of 1996 represented a high point for the Palestinian Authority. The January 1996 elections for an eighty-eight-member Palestinian Council and the election of Yasser Arafat as President of the Palestinian Executive Authority endowed the Palestinian Authority with sorely needed political legitimacy. The smooth transition to Shimon Peres after Yitzhak Rabin's assassination, and the Israeli public reaction, increased Palestinian hopes for genuine peace. The Palestinian opposition's decision to boycott Palestinian Authority institutions and the elections led to its further marginalization and to increased dissent within its already fragmented ranks.

During the Oslo process, opinion polls consistently showed that the majority of Palestinians opposed "martyrdom operations." In November 1998, most Palestinians (75 percent) ceased to support suicide operations altogether. In 1999, when over 70 percent of Palestinians had faith in the peace process, support for suicide bombings fell to 20 percent and support for Hamas was at its lowest point ever (below 12 percent).[24] When it appeared that the peace process would yield positive results, the bombings did not resonate for the majority of Palestinians, who preferred statehood and peace to violence and continued occupation (see Figure 18.1).[25]

In the aftermath of Wye, Arafat had the mandate to crack down on militants and reign supreme on the Palestinian scene. President Bill Clinton's visit to Gaza in December 1998 helped give Arafat the legitimacy to implement the Wye Accord, and the Palestine National Council voted to amend the Palestinian Liberation Organization (PLO) charter to rescind the call for the destruction of the state of Israel. In January, Israeli Knesset members from all sides of the political spectrum rebuked Netanyahu and called for new elections. On 17 May 1999, Ehud Barak won a landslide victory. The majority of Palestinians were cautiously optimistic that they would get statehood.[26]

By the summer of 1999, Arafat had neutralized the Izz Eddin al-Qassam Brigade (the military wing of Hamas) in coordination with Israeli intelligence forces and had cut off millions of dollars that Hamas received from outside aid organizations. Hamas's popularity fell to 10 percent, and the organization began to fracture and disintegrate from within. Because of the funding shortage, Hamas's extensive network of social services, which bolstered its popularity among impoverished Palestinians, declined overall.[27] In 1999, major schisms in Hamas emerged when its spiritual leader, Sheikh Ahmed Yassin, recognized Arafat's leadership and openly participated in meetings of the Palestinian National Council, proffering legitimacy to the Palestinian Authority. Yassin even

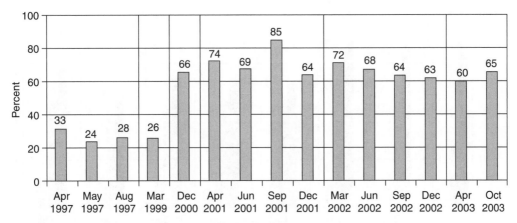

Figure 18.1 Support for Suicide Operations Among Palestinians

Sources: JMCC polls April 1997–October 2003.

Note: Months not present on the graph indicate that this question was not asked by the JMCC or that polls were not conducted because of the Israeli policy of closures, which hindered the JMCC's ability to conduct the research on a quarterly basis.

publicly endorsed Arafat's decision NOT to unilaterally declare independence in May/June of 1999, for which he was severely criticized by hardliners within his own organization.[28]

As Ehud Barak increasingly ignored the Palestinian issue in favor of a "Damascus-first strategy," Arafat's rule was increasingly questioned because of the peace deadlock and the Palestinian Authority's corruption.[29] Although Arafat was the unchallenged Palestinian leader in 1994–1996,[30] this was not the case during the second phase (1996–2000), when he appeared weak and incapable of delivering Palestinian support for his policies—partially explaining the much-touted refusal of Ehud Barak's peace deal in 2000.

In the second phase, Arafat's popularity occasionally plummeted to below 27 percent. The period of peace deadlock was closely correlated with an increase in Palestinian unemployment, decreasing per capita gross national product, and economic stagnation, which contributed to a poisoned atmosphere in which suicide bombings became more popular.[31]

Finally, the poor performance of the Palestinian Authority, the rife corruption of its leadership, and their inability to improve the daily lives of most Palestinians meant that by November 2000, Islamic Jihad and Hamas re-emerged to initiate a new cycle of violence. In the absence of funding to finance their benevolent activities, Hamas shifted the major focus of their efforts to martyrdom operations to raise their profile and win external donor support.

Public opinion polls showed a steady increase in support for martyrdom operations as Palestinian hopes for a peaceful future plummeted. After a series of suicide bombings in 2000, popular support for Hamas rose to over 70 percent, according to public opinion polls, and continued to rise over the next two and a half years. "Drawing sustenance from the demise of peace and Fatah's disarray and general despair, the group's popularity soared, reaching parity with Fatah's."[32] *The Economist*'s prediction of Hamas's parity with Fatah was realized by April 2003, when polls placed their popularity at approximately 22 percent each (see Figure 18.2).[33]

Violence now resonates with the larger population because of some of the Sharon government's counterterror tactics. Fewer than 17 percent of Palestinians are optimistic that the violence will end and peaceful negotiations will resume. Since the outbreak of the al-Aqsa *intifada* in September 2000, Israel has stepped up attacks on civilians, militants, the government, and civil infrastructure.

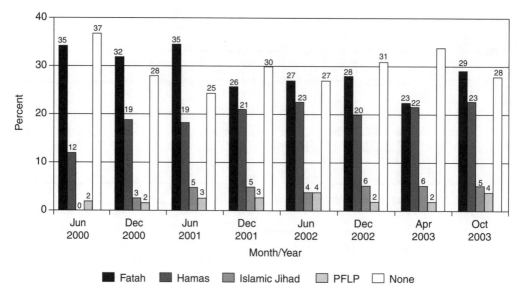

Figure 18.2 Trust in Palestinian Factions Over Time

Source: JMCC polls June 2000–October 2003.

Note: Support for Fatah did not change much at the outset of the al-Aqsa *intifada*. However, the level of support for Islamic factions (including Hamas, Islamic Jihad, Hezbollah, and other Islamic factions) increased from 12.0 percent in June 2000 to 23.9 percent in December 2000. Beginning in December 2000, the Islamic Jihad and Hamas organizations were ranked separately.

Under Sharon's government, Israeli soldiers have bombed Palestinian cities, sent tanks into Palestinian villages, assassinated Palestinian leaders, killed Palestinian youths, demolished Palestinian homes, blockaded Palestinian towns, mined Palestinian fields, and made Arafat a virtual hostage in the West Bank. But the suicide bombers keep coming.[34]

Most Palestinians view violence as their only option for achieving their goal of independence. Munir al Makdah, who trains suicide bombers, is quoted as saying, "Jihad and the resistance begin with the word, then with the sword, then with the stone, then with the gun, then with planting bombs, and then transforming bodies into human bombs."[35] Thus, suicide bombing develops as a strategy over time after other tactics fail to yield results.

After the outbreak of the *intifada*, support for the bombings and radical Islamic groups increased after every suicide bombing, and Arafat's support declined. According to Khalil Shikaki, the director of the Palestinian Center for Policy and Survey Research in Ramallah, young zealots hijacked the *intifada* and exploited Palestinian instability "to weaken the Palestinian old guard and eventually displace it."[36] Israeli intelligence officials predicted that Palestinian Authority rule in the Gaza Strip would "disintegrate and that Arafat will [eventually] be replaced by Hamas and the Islamic Jihad."[37]

By claiming responsibility for the attacks, Hamas made the PLO look moderate by comparison. The *New York Times* argued that Arafat benefited personally from extremist violence and that the suicide bombings gave him leverage in final status negotiations with Israeli Prime Minister Ariel Sharon.[38] Far from benefiting, Arafat was weakened by suicide bombing. Ziad Abu Amr, the chairman of the political committee of the Palestinian Legislative Council and Cabinet Minister, confirmed this: "Arafat should be empowered politically, not undermined. Only then can he move against the militants. Arafat was the only one who signed an agreement with Israel, and he is the only one who can. But Arafat is losing his popularity to suicide attacks. If there is nothing for him to brag about … nothing that he has accomplished … he has no standing. It all boils down to politics, power, and interests."[39]

Although directed at Israeli civilian and military targets, suicide bombings undermined Arafat's legitimacy. The attacks increased when Arafat was weakened by his inability to fulfill promises made to the Palestinian people and incapable of maintaining the monopoly of legitimate force.[40] In the absence of monopoly over force, groups competed and outbid each other with more spectacular bombing operations and competition over claiming responsibility. At the same time, the operations whipped up nationalist fervor and swelled the ranks of Islamic Jihad and Hamas, who used the bombings, in conjunction with the provision of social services, to win the hearts and minds of Palestinians.[41]

Hamas spokespersons acknowledge that the group sees its sizeable social programs as a means of building and maintaining popular support for its political goals and programs, including its militant and armed activities. "The political level is the face of Hamas, but without the other divisions Hamas would not be as strong as it is now," according to Ismail Abu Shanab. "… It needs the three parts to survive. If nobody supports these needy families, maybe nobody would think of martyrdom and the resistance of occupation."[42] Another Hamas leader, Ibrahim al-Yazuri, characterized Hamas's objective as "the liberation of all Palestine from the tyrannical Israeli occupation … which is the main part of its concern. Social work is carried out in support of this aim."[43]

During periods of deadlock, the Israeli policy of West Bank and Gaza closures causes severe economic stagnation. Terje Roed-Larsen, a United Nations representative, estimated that there is a 75 percent poverty rate in Gaza and a 53 percent unemployment rate in the Palestinian territories—exacerbated by restrictions on movement imposed by the Israeli security regime.[44] Thus, the bombings resonate against a dual backdrop of economic hardship and the disappearance of any possible peace dividend. Palestinians are convinced that military operations are the only way to wear down the Israeli resolve and weaken their desire to hold on to the Territories.[45] In sharp contrast to this, during periods of "peace progress," few Palestinians responded positively to the bombings in public opinion polls.[46] It is precisely during periods of deadlock that suicide bombings proliferate to augment the organizational profiles of Hamas or the Palestinian Islamic Jihad at the expense of the Palestinian Authority.[47]

Furthermore, the martyrdom operations allow Arafat's rivals to gain international prestige, foreign financial support, and increased domestic "market share" at his expense. The emerging groups of the Palestinian electorate—the young and the urban college-educated groups—typify this most clearly.[48] Among Palestinian youth, Arafat's popularity slips as suicide bombings proliferate. Arafat's approval rating was at 70 percent in September 2001, but within three months it slipped to 57 percent[49] and continued to decline until Israeli Prime Minister Sharon's incursions into the major West Bank towns in late March 2002 resuscitated Arafat's sagging popularity.

In most of the polls, more than 30 percent of the Palestinian public say that they "do not trust any of the current leaders"—leaving the field wide open for challengers. This group has potential for mobilization. Evidence suggests that with every suicide attack, the parties responsible for the bombings and other Islamic groups opposed to the Palestinian Authority are able to capture the support of people from this market share. Levels of support for Fatah might remain the same, but support for Hamas and Sheikh Yassin increases while the number of those polled who say they "don't trust any candidate" decreases at the same rate. Although there is some defection from Arafat's support base,[50] it is safe to assume that Hamas is winning the hearts and minds of the undecided. This is explained by the fact that groups engaged in suicide bombing appear to be proactive and capable of hurting the Israelis where they live. This positive image is something over which Palestinian organizations compete.

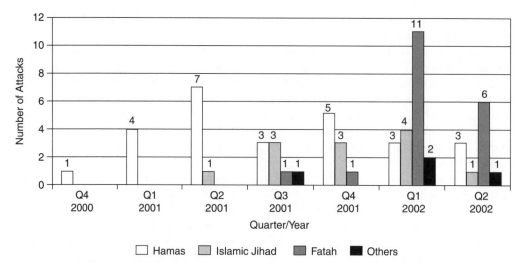

Figure 18.3 Proliferation of Groups Using Suicide Terror

Source: Assaf Moghadam, 2003 (from Israeli Ministry of Foreign Affairs, Ha'aretz, *Jerusalem Post*, and ICT).

Intragroup competition and outbidding

The suicide bombings have become bases of mobilization over which Hamas and Islamic Jihad compete for leadership by capturing the Palestinian imagination. Over time, more groups have jumped on the suicide-bombing bandwagon. There has been a proliferation of organizations using this tactic—some of which eschewed the tactic in the past. New groups have emerged, and previously secular groups have started using the language of religious holy war (*jihad*) to bandwagon onto Hamas's popularity, including: the DFLP (Democratic Front for the Liberation of Palestine), the PFLP (Popular Front for the Liberation of Palestine),[51] the al-Aqsa Martyrs' Brigade, and a new group calling itself an-Nathir (The Warning) (see Figure 18.3).

All of the groups vie for the right to claim each attack as their own. "Several Palestinian groups rushed forward to claim responsibility for the bus bombing—an indication of the competition among Palestinians for militant credibility."[52] Hamas and Islamic Jihad issued competing claims for responsibility for the 9 August 2001 attack on the Sbarro pizzeria (and rival claims that Izzedine al-Masri was *their* operative),[53] and Hamas and the PFLP issued competing claims for the 19 May 2002 attack on the Netanya market. No fewer than four different groups claimed credit for the bus bombing of 17 July 2002.

Al-Jazeera television reported that the attack was carried out by the al-Aqsa Martyrs' Brigade, in cooperation with Hamas. The DFLP also claimed responsibility for the attack in a statement faxed to Reuters, the authenticity of which was confirmed by a DFLP spokesman in Beirut. "The military wing of the Democratic Front for the Liberation of Palestine announces its responsibility for the courageous attack that targeted a bus full of settlers," it said. Hamas and Islamic Jihad also claimed (separately) that they were responsible.[54]

The PFLP and Hamas both claimed the bombing of Mike's Place on 30 April 2003, although two British citizens of South Asian descent were responsible. Violence has become *the* source of all honor among Palestinians. According to Nichole Argo, martyrdom is a public good and a major source of honor in Palestinian society. Individual esteem is bound to group status, physically and symbolically. Sacrifice and risk employed on behalf of the group become valuable virtues, rewarded by social status. A PFLP would-be bomber told her, "You cannot win by yourself, but your sacrifice will help show the world the true nature of your sacrificial self, and of your inhuman opponent."[55] At a profoundly important—albeit symbolic level—martyrdom is the final and irrefutable statement of group worth and dignity. The martyrs (*shahids*) gain increased social status as a result of suicide bombing operations. According to Sheikh Abdel Aziz Rantisi, "For Hamas, and Palestinian society in general, becoming a martyr is among the highest if not the highest, honor."[56]

The portraits of the bombers have become symbols of resistance as political groups vie to claim responsibility for the individual martyrs. The martyrs' posters covering the storefronts of West Bank towns pay homage to the *intifada* dead. With each incident, new posters cover over the tattered remains of the previous photos, proclaiming the Koranic slogan, "the martyr is not dead, but lives on," and displaying the martyrs' political affiliation prominently. The martyrs become the main topic of conversation. People discuss how they were killed, assess the posters for the kinds of weaponry displayed around them, and occasionally deride the political factions who vie for the right to claim the dead as members of their organizations. "Some of these guys were never political; the factions just want to bolster their popularity."[57]

George Habash answered allegations that he deliberately claimed the responsibility for operatives that were not actually PFLP members. His defense betrays the organization's competitive spirit: "The PFLP ... has never tried to take credit for operations or struggles that other heroes of the resistance from different patriotic or Islamic organizations have carried out. On the contrary, all of you know of the operations of our comrades who blew themselves up in occupied Jerusalem for which we did not announce our responsibility and which were claimed at that time by another organization. We in the Abu Ali Mustafa Brigades confirm again our responsibility for the heroic operation of blowing up the Zionist tank near the Netsarim Settlement. The first communiqué of the Brigades laid out the details of the operation just minutes after it took place. This can be considered clear proof that those who carried out the operation were the same ones who issued the communiqué with such precision and detail."[58]

In the polls conducted in 2000, support for the PFLP was lagging significantly. In 2001, the PFLP began to use suicide bombing as a strategy and even created, in the spring of 2001, a separate wing devoted exclusively to martyrdom operations called the Abu Ali Mustafa Brigades.[59] Between 2001 and 2002, the PFLP conducted 3 percent of all the attacks, and within months of its first attack (27 May 2001) and days after the PFLP exploded two car bombs, the Jerusalem Media and Communication Center (JMCC) poll of October 2001 placed PFLP support at 4.3 percent. The PFLP seemingly resuscitated its popularity by using suicide bombing as a tactic.

The al-Aqsa Martyrs' Brigades have also hinted at the competition between the various groups: "We announce with pride and dignity to you the martyrdom of Mohammed Hashaika from Tallouza village. This martyr who proved to all that there won't be peace, security or solution as long as ... Sharon insists on keeping occupation and commits all kinds of ugly and atrocious crimes against our people. Martyr Hashaika, member of al-Aqsa Martyrs' Brigades, *proved that our Brigades are leading the path of Jihad* [emphasis added] and resistance and martyrdom until the Zionist occupation leaves our homeland forever" (see Figure 18.4).[60]

Organizational backgrounds

Hamas is the Arabic acronym for the Harakat al Muqawamah al-Islamiyya (Islamic Resistance Movement), formed in 1987 as an outgrowth of the Muslim Brotherhood and the *Mujamma al-Islami*, and established in 1974 to provide much-needed social services to Palestinians under occupation. It operated out of the Gaza Strip and eventually spread to the West Bank.

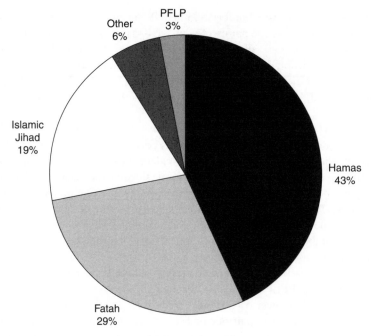

Figure 18.4 Percentages of Attacks by Organization, 2000–2002
Source: Assaf Moghadam, 2003.

Until the first *intifada* in 1987, the Israeli authorities avoided interfering with the organization as part of a strategy of divide and rule as a legitimate alternative to Yasser Arafat's Palestinian Liberation Organization. Shaul Mishal and Avram Sela note that the Israelis did not block the organization nor did they arrest any of its members and, in turn, the organization did not perpetrate any attacks against Israel for the first two years of its existence.[61] These two years of relative quiescence led to allegations from the mainstream PLO that Israel and Hamas were in collusion. Arafat subscribed to this conspiracy theory saying, "We must remember that these organizations were created by Israel, which also distributes arms to them."[62] When they did turn to violent protest, Hamas effectively augmented its reputation with rank and file Palestinians.

By its participation in street violence and murder during the first *intifada*, Hamas boosted its appeal in the eyes of the Palestinians, further enhancing its growth potential and enabling it to play a central role in the *intifada*. As a result of its subversive activity, Hamas was outlawed in September 1989.[63]

Hamas's popularity threatened PLO hegemony as it became the leading terrorist organization throughout the Territories as well as inside Israel. In 1991, Zaccaria Walid Akel, the head of the terrorist section of Hamas in Gaza, set up the first squads of the militant Izz Eddin al-Qassam Battalions, which operated throughout the West Bank and Gaza. In its early operations, they kidnapped and executed Palestinian collaborators and routinely threatened Arafat.[64]

However, in December 1991, the squads changed their modus operandi and began targeting Israelis. Hamas's leadership realized that militant activities and terror would not bring about their long-term goals, and so they devised long-term strategies and tactics. Earlier analysts stated that: "If suicide attacks, or the Israeli reaction to them, become harmful to the general Palestinian public and cause it to show qualms about them, Hamas might be forced to reconsider their value. For Hamas' leaders, the social and public meaning of their activity is no less important than its religious legitimacy."[65] In fact, the reverse happened; once Palestinians became convinced that military operations were their only option, support for suicide operations increased exponentially. According to Khalid Mish'al, Hamas recognized its limitations and its need to adjust its approach strategically: "We know that the current balance of power in the region does not allow us to achieve a decisive victory against the Zionists; however, we confidently believe that we are moving along the right path—the path of resistance. This choice will provide us with success in view of our accumulated achievements, our substantial ability to hold out, our will and strategic depth."[66]

Hamas's charitable associations had a dual function. On the one hand, they helped to channel funds into the region. While a portion of the funds was for charity, it was not always possible to distinguish between the charities and the funding of terrorist activities. The associations pay the fines and assist the families of operatives who have been arrested. Such donations are defined as charity but are directed only to the hard-core members. Hamas founds hospitals and pays for medical care, dentistry, and prenatal care within the Territories and provides multiple social services that the occupation does not provide. The benevolent associations have helped the organization gain credibility and support throughout all of Palestine. The fund pays $10,000–$25,000 per martyr, and so there is economic remuneration to underscore the institutionalization of suicide bombing.[67] Hamas appears to have several goals: to destroy Israel, to enhance its prestige among the Palestinians vis à vis the Palestinian Authority or other groups, to increase its appearance as a legitimate opposition, to promote ties with the Islamic world, to derail the peace process when it exists, and to defy the "Zionist entity."[68]

The Palestinian Islamic Jihad (*Harakat al Jihad al-Islami al Filastini*) was founded in 1979–1980 by Fathi Shikaki (assassinated by Israeli agents in 1995 in Malta), 'Abd al-'Aziz 'Odah, and Bashir Musa. It is a series of loosely affiliated factions rather than a cohesive group, and it is highly influenced by the Iranian revolutionary movement and focused exclusively on terrorism. Because of Israel's strong alliance with the United States, it also targets U.S. and moderate Arab governments that it believes are tainted by Western secularism.

In contrast to Hamas, Islamic Jihad does not have a network of social services (schools, mosques, clinics). Its charter promises to work for the destruction of the State of Israel through armed struggle, to replace Arafat's government with an Islamist state on the West Bank and Gaza, and to raise "the banner of Allah over every inch of Palestine."[69] Competition between Islamic Jihad and Hamas dates back to the first *intifada* when, according to Ahmad Rashad: "Jihad's spectacular acts of daring and courage in the 1980s lent credence to the Islamic movement in the occupied territories. Jihad's attacks against Israeli military targets set the stage for the Intifada … which spread rapidly due to the pride that Palestinians had begun to feel in the Jihad's actions. … Islamic Jihad's actions embarrassed Arafat and Hamas. But its brazen attacks increased the popularity of Islamic guerilla groups."[70]

The al-Aqsa Martyrs' Brigade, the military wing of Arafat's Fatah (Harakat al Tahrir al Falistiniya), was formally given the title after the September 2000 al-Aqsa *intifada*. The al-Aqsa Martyrs split off from the organization when the Palestinian Authority arrested the secretary-general of the PFLP, Ahmad Sa'adat, for killing Israeli right-wing Cabinet Minister Rechavam Ze'evi in October 2001. The PFLP claimed that Ze'evi was killed in retaliation for the killing of PFLP General Secretary Abu Ali Mustafa on 27 August 2001.[71] The al-Aqsa Martyrs' defection from Arafat demonstrated his growing weakness and isolation. However, in the raid of the Ramallah office of Fuad Shubeiki, head of the Palestinian Authority's financial apparatus, the Israel defence forces uncovered documents linking the Palestinian Authority and Fatah to the Brigades. The smoking gun document listed the financial demands of the al-Aqsa Martyrs' Brigade for bombings that had been carried out, and the fifth article on the document listed the costs for producing explosive devices and bombs.[72]

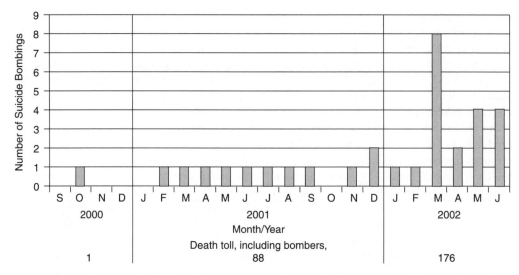

Figure 18.5 Suicide Bombings per Month since the Palestinian Uprising Began in September 2000
Source: *New York Times*, 19 June 2002.

The PFLP combines Arab nationalism with Marxist-Leninist ideology and views the destruction of Israel as integral to ridding the Middle East of Western influence.[73] In the fall of 2001, the PFLP shifted its emphasis and began using both the tactic of suicide bombing and the language of *jihad* to attract a greater constituency to swell its ranks.[74] Palestinian support for the PFLP was lagging until the organization turned to suicide bombing, putting them back on the political radar screen. They managed to capture 3 percent of Palestinian support after their operations in the fall of 2001 and the creation of a militant wing named after Abu Ali Mustafa. Not to be left out, the DFLP claimed responsibility for a bus attack in July 2002, and yet another organization, al-Nathir, was one of several groups that "claimed responsibility for the [18 July 2002] Tel Aviv bombing, identified the attackers, and said they had come from the Balata refugee camp in Nablus. The group said it was linked to Yasir Arafat's Fatah movement. ... The Islamic Jihad had previously claimed responsibility for the bombing."[75]

Since 1993, these groups have dispatched over 250 suicide bombers. The occurrences of suicide bombings do not correlate only with the peace process or negotiations. A broad examination of the number of attacks since Prime Minister Barak left office and Prime Minister Sharon took office indicates that suicide attacks are much more closely related to periods when Arafat is weaker and rival organizations compete to fill the power vacuum (see Figure 18.5).

Israeli counterterror policies

Faced with mounting attacks, Israeli policymakers responded with hard-line counterterror tactics of massive retaliation, targeted assassination of militant leaders, and demolitions to deter future bombings. Hamas and Islamic Jihad, as well as other groups, targeted Israeli civilians in public venues for maximum effect, killing and injuring as many civilians as they could. As *Jane's Defence Weekly* noted, "While some attacks are successful against military targets, most are carried out against civilians. As a Hamas training manual notes: 'it is foolish to hunt the tiger when there are plenty of sheep around.'"[76] The 27 March 2002 Passover bombing in Netanya prompted a rapid Israeli response launched on 29 March 2002.

Operation Protective Shield, launched to reoccupy seven of eight major Palestinian towns in Area A, had negative consequences for Israeli policy and its image abroad. Most countries rigorously condemned Israeli actions in Jenin and Qalqilya.[77] Surprisingly enough, Israelis rallied around the extreme right, thinking that hawkish policies would deter future attacks. In fact, the long-term ramifications on the Palestinian polity will encourage rather than deter future attacks. In essence, hard-line Israeli policy will probably backfire. The attacks after April 2002 and daily violence during the spring of 2003 demonstrated that despite Operation Protective Shield, reoccupation may temporarily slow the pace of the bombings but will not eliminate the scourge. These groups will engage in greater degrees of violence in competition for legitimacy and leadership of the Palestinian people. In fact, the present policy sows the seeds for future generations to swell the ranks of terrorist organizations by increasing incentives for groups to compete and outbid each other.

Motivations

In its constant quest for an explanation of why young men—and recently a few young women—decide to commit such acts, the Western press has primarily cited fanaticism and despair as reasons for suicide bombing.[78]

Some people allege that the bombers suffer from low social status, few economic opportunities, or personality disorders.[79] Bruce Bueno de Mesquita argues that the suicide bombers have a financial incentive. "They are young men with no economic prospects and little education."[80] He adds, "There is a rational expectation on the part of suicide bombers that they are providing for their families."[81] However, evidence shows that these explanations are not consistent with each other or with reality. Most suicide bombers are not undereducated religious zealots who blindly follow the commands of the religious leadership, but rather they come from a middle or upper class background and have comparatively high levels of education.[82]

Nasra Hasan argues that many of the bombers have suffered humiliation and persecution at the hands of Israeli forces. However, she insists that they are not suffering from mental illness or personality disorders.[83] The issue of pain and personal loss features prominently in any analysis of suicide bombing, yet pain and suffering alone do not create the phenomenon; they must be coupled with an environment in which there is no outlet for expressing the rage and frustration that would motivate someone to use suicide bombing as a weapon. The excessive use of force on Israel's part, as well as collective punishment, check points, closures, and economic sanctions, have all contributed to the delegitimization of the peace process and the Palestinian Authority, and a general feeling of hopelessness (see Figure 18.6).[84]

All of these factors appear to be necessary, although insufficient, to explain suicide bombing, given that the majority of Palestinians have experienced humiliation as part of the thirty-five-year occupation and yet the number of suicide bombers remains statistically irrelevant compared to the Palestinian population as a whole (until very recently). Customary media depictions of the average suicide bomber driven to self-destruction by despair fail to convince most Palestinians. All Palestinians living under occupation, they say, are desperate. Humiliation and persecution are a "constant" under the occupation and cannot account for why there has been an upsurge in this phenomenon or why public opinion shifts in favor of suicide attacks at different times. Many Palestinians view this portrayal as a way of denuding the attacks of their political aim: striking back at the Israeli occupation.[85]

Martyrdom reinforces the image of the Palestinians as an oppressed people, since this tactic is the quintessential "weapon of the weak." Terrorists make the moral claim that they are using such strategies only as a last resort and that only after peaceful means have failed or peace agreements

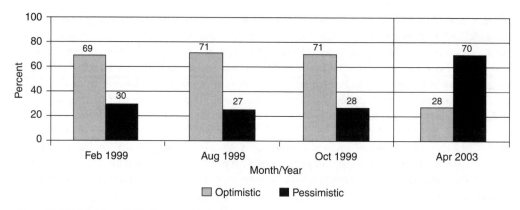

Figure 18.6 Palestinian Optimism for the Future
Source: JMCC polls February 1999–April 2003.

have been abrogated have they turned to violence. The Palestinians know that they could not win a shooting war against the Israelis; they would be grossly outnumbered, due to Israel's overwhelming military superiority. The bombings may be intended to invite reprisals, causing the Israelis to massively retaliate and overreact, causing the outside intervention for which Arafat has been calling since the al-Aqsa *intifada* broke out.[86]

Several things may motivate the individual suicide bomber,[87] whereas the leadership appears strategically minded vis à vis domestic rivals in the Palestinian Authority and vis à vis the international rival, Israel. Islamic extremist groups sending out suicide bombers are participating in a two-level game. Their attacks are intended to hurt Israel and at the same time undermine the legitimacy of the Palestinian Authority. Suicide bombing is an effort to punish and deter Israeli actions and to create a "balance of terror." The Palestinians seek to persuade Israelis that they will pay a high price for the occupation and to force them to pressure their government to withdraw from the Territories and thus end the occupation. The extension of the front to inside "green-line" Israel is to bring the war to the heart of Israel, where the majority of Israelis can no longer ignore the realities of the occupation. Through these attacks, they seek to wear down Israeli morale.[88]

This strategy has proven effective; inasmuch as Israelis fear going to public places, going shopping, or going out to eat, the suicide bombings have changed Israelis' lifestyles and assurance of security. During periods of deadlock, when most Israelis are comfortable with the status quo, Palestinian extremists know that something is required to tip the balance and change it. At the same time, with Arafat's leadership in crisis, several groups and individuals vie for control of a future Palestinian state and seek to place their imprimatur on what kind of state (for example, Islamic fundamentalist) will emerge.

Cycles of violence

The unprecedented Israeli siege of the occupied territories constituted a turning point for Palestinian public opinion. The hermetic closure of the West Bank and Gaza Strip and the policy of "separation" removed any remaining ambiguities about the nature of post-Oslo Israeli-Palestinian relations (see Figure 18.7).

The defection of Fatah loyalists has swelled the ranks of the al-Aqsa Martyrs and al-Nathir. The violence has increasingly assumed a pattern of attrition. Although seemingly irrational,

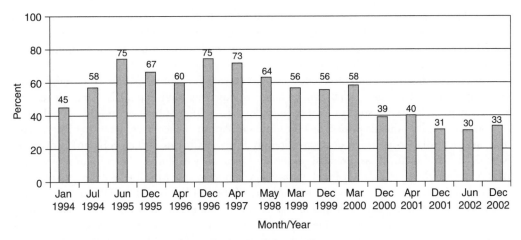

Figure 18.7 Support for Oslo Agreements Among Palestinians
Source: JMCC Poll December 2002.

because the attacks and counter measures have only generated more victims, Israel answers Palestinian suicide bombing by assassinating Hamas and Islamic Jihad leaders, the Palestinians respond with more bombings, and the Israelis retort with yet more assassinations.[89] The Israelis and Palestinians appear to be in a deadlocked battle of assassination-suicide bombing-assassination-suicide bombing in an unending causal loop. This call-and-response blood bath has radicalized the Palestinians, encouraging yet more "martyrs."

> Since Israel's first assassinations in 1995 and 1996, which reached a climax with the killing of Hamas's Yahiyeh Ayyash ("The Engineer") and the Islamic Jihad's leader, Fathi Shikaki, all of the assassinations have generated acts of revenge that have cost the lives of dozens of Israelis. The policy of assassination is a boomerang that hurts Israel badly.[90]

These tactics make a perverted kind of sense. Targeted assassination, renounced by almost every other democratic government and proscribed by international law, has been a standard operating procedure for Israel since the Black September Organization massacred eleven Israeli athletes at the 1972 Munich Olympics.[91] Israel has assassinated dozens of Hamas and Islamic Jihad members. The logic of targeted assassination is that murdering their operatives saps the effectiveness of Hamas and Islamic Jihad. The targeting not only neutralizes the dead men, but also forces the other terrorists to go underground. Because they know that Israel will kill them if they are found, the terrorists spend much of their time running or hiding and less time plotting terrorist attacks. Without skilled bomb makers and planners, Hamas and Islamic Jihad, it is reasoned, would have more difficulty in infiltrating Israel and carrying out their missions. Israel's logic, however, has proven fallible. Although several Palestinians have been caught before their bombs could detonate or have been killed or wounded while making the bombs,[92] the events of March 2002 demonstrated that the extremists' organizations are fully capable of replacing operatives as fast as Israeli targeted assassinations eliminate them. The suicide bombers have metamorphosed into a multiheaded hydra; for every one killed by Sharon's policies, another two appear to take his (and potentially her) place.

Targeted assassinations have a political utility for the Israelis and are more media friendly—without the negative reputational effect that shooting stone-throwing children had during the first *intifada*. The most important benefit to Israelis might have been a psychological one. Assassination showed that the government was being proactive, counteracting the chaos brought about by the bombings and bringing precision and order back to the conflict. According to public opinion polls in Israel, this policy was widely supported.

Thus, suicide bombings and targeted assassinations may be considered case studies in the law of comparative advantage. Israel, where labor is expensive and capital is cheap, invests in assassinations, a high-tech strategy that requires lots of equipment but does not risk Israeli lives. By comparison, Palestinians possess neither tanks nor Apache helicopters. Thus, the Palestinians have adopted a labor-intensive strategy—literally throwing bodies at the problem.[93] Advocates have described the attacks as the most important "strategic weapon" of Palestinian resistance.[94] And while religious justification for the attacks is important for Muslims, secular groups have resorted to similar tactics.[95] George Habash, leader of the PFLP, substantiated this as a deliberate strategy: "The losses in manpower that the Israelis are sustaining are very high. The Zionist entity has not witnessed the likes of this high rate of loses in any period of battle in any of the past decades. According to the latest figures, the rate is one Israeli killed for every three Palestinian martyrs. This is despite the great differential or the great imbalance of power and the minimal fighting means and equipment available to the Palestinian people."[96]

Suicide bombings exact no significant cost on Hamas, Islamic Jihad, or any of the secular groups. Although each bombing episode sacrifices one supporter, it recruits many more. More people are willing to become suicide bombers now than in the past. In response to the upsurge of bombings, Ariel Sharon initiated counterterror policies that further enraged Palestinians and swelled the ranks of militant organizations. Israel tried to degrade the ranks of Hamas and Islamic Jihad faster than new volunteers could restore them. This tactic has been proven unsuccessful because they underestimated Palestinian resolve against the occupation and outrage at Israeli reprisals, which have swelled the ranks rather than draw down the number of suicide bombers.

Conclusions

Suicide attacks serve multiple purposes in addition to that of inflicting damage. They generate a huge amount of publicity for the cause. The emergence of the "CNN factor" has enabled global awareness, much like airliner hijackings did for the Palestinian cause in the late 1960s and 1970s.

In settings in which the power disparities are as great as between the Israelis and Palestinians, the question is: which insurgent tactics are appropriate? Disparities in relation to power and force are accentuated by the degree to which the media portrays Israeli victimization as humanized, while Palestinian victimization is reduced to statistical abstraction and treated as an unintended by-product of legitimate Israeli reprisals or enforcement actions. Palestinian violence is viewed as an extreme form of terrorism, while Israeli responses, even when directed at civilian targets, are at most criticized as "excessive force."[97]

There is a sense that terrorism is the quintessential weapon of the weak, that if groups had the ability to, they would refrain from using terror instrumentally. To avoid charges of terrorism, Palestinians must find ways to resist that do not rely on violence directed at Israeli citizens. Such a burden may be difficult, given the harshness of the occupation, but it can only be lifted by Palestinian ingenuity. However, there is no moral concern with regard to the idea of civilian immunity. For most Palestinians, there is no civilian immunity, due to Israel's universal conscription of men and women. From this perspective, all Israelis are complicit in the immoral and illegal occupation of the West Bank and Gaza; moreover, these very same civilians willingly twice elected a hawkish government that pursues the maximalist goals of a "Greater Israel."

Finally, terrorists use these strategies to delegitimize the state of Israel. Part of the Palestinian goal has been to force Israel's hand, drive it to retaliate massively and betray democratic principles, force it to rip off the mask of legal justice, and show it to be the ravening beast that the Palestinians claim it is. There are no military solutions to terrorism; the challenge is to preserve the state's legitimacy and, even in the face of atrocious acts, to hold its high ground. The failure to do so is to hand the terrorists an absolute victory.

There is a failed state in Palestine. The systematic destruction of the political, administrative, and social apparatus of the Palestinian Authority—in Israel's campaign to weed out the terrorists—has crushed the Palestinian Authority as an authority. Without a legitimate authority in Palestine, there is no real security for the state of Israel. Destroying the Palestinian Authority leads to increased lawlessness and windows of opportunity for more violence and new groups who will use martyrdom operations to increase their popularity. According to local human rights organizations, more than 2,289 Palestinians and 440 Israelis have been killed (some statistics place the number at 572 Israeli civilians), including hundreds of children and ninety suicide bombers. Approximately 24,407 Palestinians were injured between September 2000 and January 2004.[98]

Ongoing closures and internal sieges have kept poverty and unemployment hovering just below 50 percent for months. A report from the Office of the United Nations Special Coordinator in the Occupied Territories put the initial cost of the al-Aqsa *intifada* between 2.4 and 3.2 billion dollars for the first year. Palestinian Authority revenues plummeted by 57 percent, and real income decreased by an average of 37 percent, resulting in 46 percent of Palestinians living below the poverty line—twice as many as previously.[99] In this environment, few Palestinians are prepared to disavow terror and more attacks will follow, regardless of Israeli countermeasures. It is only when Israeli policymakers conclude that force is not the solution and when the majority of the Palestinian polity feels a moral outrage against the martyrdom operations that suicide terrorism will cease to be a viable policy option.[100] In the short term, mass arrests, deportations, and targeted assassinations might have a nominal effect on the number of attacks inside Israel.

However, this research predicts that, in the long run, the number of attacks will increase because groups vying to lead the Palestinians will use violence as their main source of recruitment and mobilization. According to polls conducted by Khalil Shikaki, support for martyrdom operations against Israeli civilian and military targets remains high; however, there is also a willingness to return to the negotiation table if Israel is willing to fulfill the commitments made in Oslo. Consider Prime Minister Yitzhak Rabin's explanation to the Knesset on 18 April 1994 about why Israel should withdraw from Gaza:

> For 27 years we have been dominating another people against its will. For 27 years Palestinians in the territories … [have gotten] up in the morning harboring a fierce hatred for us, as Israelis and Jews … for which we are also, but not solely, responsible. We cannot deny that our continuing control over a foreign people who do not want us exacts a painful price: the price of continuing confrontation between us and them. … Hamas and Islamic Jihad … carried out most of the terrorist attacks, some on suicide missions. For two or three years, we have been facing a phenomenon of extremist Islamic terrorism, which recalls Hezbollah. … Israel and the Palestinian populations are so intertwined there are infinite opportunities for the rejectionist terrorists. There is no end to the targets. … Each Israeli, in the territories and inside sovereign Israel, including united Jerusalem, each bus, each home, is a target for their murderous plans. Since there is no separation between the two populations, the current situation creates endless possibilities for Hamas and the other organizations.[101]

The experience of the past and Rabin's clear-eyed assessment give us additional reasons to recognize that Israeli policy must change before the violence will end. It is difficult to expect a country under siege to reward violence, and yet the current policy is a prescription for an intensification of attacks in the long term. Inasmuch as Israel can alter Palestinian perceptions of the conflict, they can control the environment and backdrop against which the attacks occur. The only solution is to negotiate with the secular groups and provide the Palestinians with a hopeful future so that the bombings cease to resonate positively with the majority of Palestinians. Once the public ceases to support these attacks, they will fail to mobilize the new generation and the nonaligned voter.

Notes

1 See James Fallows, "Who Shot Mohammed al Durra?" *Atlantic Monthly* (June 2003): 49–56. The endogenous factors include the widely publicized and televised killing of Mohammed al-Durra on 30 September 2000 and seventy other Palestinians killed in the first two months alone, the failing economic situation, Palestinian disillusion with the deadlocked peace process, and Ariel Sharon's visit to the Temple Mount, which corroborated Hamas rhetoric that Israel would never fulfill its Oslo obligations. As much as Durra is a symbol, there are questions as to who is really responsible for his death.

2 Yoram Schweitzer, "Suicide Bombings: The Ultimate Weapon?" 7 August 2001, accessed on the JCT website at http://www.ict.org.il, 20 May 2002.

3 See JMCC Poll #47, December 2002, as well as interviews of Khalil Shikaki with the author, 17 October 2002.

4 Yoram Schweitzer, www.ict.org.il.

5 Arnon Regular, "PA Document: Hamas and Islamic Jihad Timed Bombings to Derail Peace Processes." 8 January 2004, accessed at http://www.Haaretz.com, 9 January 2004.

6 Rui de Figueiredo and Barry Weingast, "Vicious Cycles: Endogenous Political Extremism and Political Violence" (paper presented at the annual meeting of the American Political Science Association, Boston, September 1998).

7 "Hamas Operations Against Israel Said to Continue," *Al Dustur* (in Arabic), 14 April 1994.

8 The Council on Foreign Relations says that the five bus bombings in 1996 followed the killing of Hamas's chief bomb maker, Yahya Ayyash, "Terrorism: Questions and Answers, Hamas. Islamic Jihad," accessed at http://www.terrorismanswers.com, 10 May 2002.

9 Ehud Sprinzak, interview with the author, 1 April 2002. This is borne out by Palestinian public opinion surveys that cite the targeted assassinations as the factor most harmful to the Palestinians, see JMCC vol. 2 no. 6 October 2001 poll: 5, accessed at http://www.jmcc.org/publicpoll/pop/01/oct/pop6.htm, 10 May 2002.

10 Tony Karan, "Chronicle of a Massacre Foretold," *Time*, 18 January 2002; Robert Fisk, "Suicide Bombing on Passover Feast Wrecks US Peace Plan," *The Independent*, 28 March 2002.

11 Andrew Kydd and Barbara F. Walter, "Sabotaging the Peace: The Politics of Extremist Violence," *International Organizations* 56 (Spring 2002): 263–296.

12 "Peace, Terror and Dissent in Israel: Hamas Goal of Blocking Negotiations," *New York Times*, 23 August 1995.

13 Hillel Halkin, "Bye, Bye Bibi," *The New Republic*, 7 June 1999.

14 Interview with Ziad Abu Amr cited in Joyce M. Davis, *Martyrs: Innocence, Vengeance, and Despair in the Middle East* (New York: Palgrave, 2003), 171.

15 A senior Israeli security official said the attacks [in May 2003] were aimed both at Israel and at Mahmoud Abbas (Abu Mazen), the first Palestinian prime minister, who has promised to disarm militant groups. "Everyone in the terror chain is very worried about this development," he said of the appointment of Mr. Abbas. "They are determined to escalate and make every effort to carry out attacks in this period." James Bennet, "3 Israelis Killed and 50 Wounded in Blast at Mall," *New York Times*, 20 May 2003.

16 There was a series of failed or aborted peace missions. According to public opinion polls, fewer than 18 percent of those Palestinians polled had any confidence in the success of the Zinni or Powell Missions. After the election of Mahmoud Abbas as Prime Minister in the spring of 2003. Hamas justified its attacks to ensure that the "road map for peace" would fail. Bennet, ibid.

17 Mouin Rabbani, "Suicide Attacks in the Middle East are Fueled by Alienation and Futility," Palestinian Media Watch, 4 April 2001, *Middle East News Online*, accessed at http://www.merip.org/mero/mero10170.html, 20 May 2002.

18 Imad A. Faluji, *Darb al Ashwak: Hamas, al-Intifada, wa al Sultah* (The Path of Suffering: Hamas, the Intifada, and the Authority) (Arabic) (Amman, Jordan: Dar al Shuruq, 2002).

19 Interviews of Palestinians with the author, 12 April 2003, names withheld; see also Emile Sahliyeh and
    Zixian Deng, "The Determinants of Palestinians' Attitudes toward Peace with Israel," *International Studies
    Quarterly* 47 (December 2003): 706.
20 Richard Falk, interview with the author, 1 February 2002.
21 Ma'mun Basisu, Niqash Sarih li Muntaqidi al-amaliyyat al-istishadiyya (frank discussions with the critics
    of martyrdom operations), Arabic *al-Liwa'*, 6 July 2002; see also a Hamas statement that claimed that
    one purpose of the Netanya Park Hotel Passover Seder attack (27 March 2002) was to derail diplomatic
    initiatives at an Arab League summit in Beirut. "The summit resolutions are below the aspirations and
    the sacrifices of the Palestinian people," said 'Usama Hamdan, a Hamas spokesman in Beirut. The
    Palestinian Authority agreed that "this operation against Israeli civilians is in essence an attack against
    the Arab summit and against [U.S. Special Representative Anthony] Zinni's mission." WAFA (official
    Palestinian Authority news agency), 27 March 2002. Translated from Arabic by Human Rights Watch.
    HRW Report, *Erased in a Moment: Suicide Bombing Attacks Against Israeli Civilians* (New York: October 2002),
    33.
22 Andrew Bilski and Eric Silver, "Dashed Hopes: Rabin and Arafat have Become Prisoners of the Peace
    Process," *Maclean's* 108 (1995): 30–31.
23 Ziad Abu Amr, Palestinian Cabinet Member (Independent) and Minister of Culture, interview cited by
    Joyce Davis in *Martyrs*, 168–169.
24 When Palestinians were asked in 1999 about their level of optimism or pessimism about the future,
    70.7 percent of the respondents replied positively. There were no major differences in the level of
    optimism about the future between those surveyed in the West Bank and those in the Gaza Strip. By
    January 2001, when respondents were asked about their level of optimism or pessimism about the future,
    48.8 percent stated that they were optimistic and 50.2 percent were pessimistic about their futures, a
    significant change from 1999. JMCC Poll vol. 2 no. 2 (January 2001). By 2003, over 80 percent were
    now pessimistic (see Figures 18.1, 18.6, and 18.7).
25 Support for suicide operations varied by respondent characteristics. Those living in refugee camps were
    more supportive of military operations against Israeli targets than were respondents residing in cities
    and villages (79 percent, 75 percent, and 69 percent, respectively). Refugees and Gaza Strip residents
    were also more supportive of military operations than were nonrefugees or East Jerusalem residents, and
    there was 68 percent support among Palestinians with less than a high school education versus
    76 percent support among those with a high school education or higher; and 67 percent of Palestinians
    forty years or older versus 76 percent of respondents under forty supported suicide bombings. There has
    been a dramatic increase in the level of public support for military and suicide operations against Israeli
    targets. The level of support for suicide operations against Israeli targets is more than double the
    level of support during the past five years (26.1 percent in March 1999, 28.2 percent in August 1997,
    23.6 percent in May 1997, 32.7 percent in April 1997, and 32.8 percent in June 1995).
26 Yossi Beilin, chief Oslo negotiator, interview with the author, 16 April 2003.
27 "Hamas Divides Against Itself," *Middle East Intelligence Bulletin*, June 1999.
28 Yossi Beilin, interview with the author, ibid.
29 Fmr. Ambassador Itamar Rabinovitch, senior Israeli negotiator, interview with the author. 19 April
    2001.
30 Center for Palestinian Research Polls, CPRS Polls Survey Research Unit, accessed at http://www.pepsr.
    org/survey/cprspolls.html, 20 May 2002.
31 Assaf Moghadam, "Palestinian Suicide Bombing in the Second Intifada: Motivations and Organizational
    Aspects," *Studies in Conflict and Terrorism* 26 (2003): 75.
32 "Hamas Has the People's Heart," *The Economist*, 29 November 2001.
33 Shikaki, interview with the author, 17 October 2002; the April 2003 JMCC Poll #48, accessed at http://
    www.jmcc.org/publicpoll/results/2003/no48.htm, 30 April 2003.
34 Davis, *Martyrs*, 167.
35 Ibid., 150.
36 Khalil Shikaki, "Palestinians Divided," *Foreign Affairs* (January–February 2002): 89.
37 Arieh O'Sullivan, "IDF warns PA losing control of Gaza Strip," *The Jerusalem Post*, 19 November 2001,
    accessed at http://www.jpost.com/Editions/2001/11/19/News/News.38353.html, 20 May 2002.
38 Serge Schnemann, "Israelis and Palestinians Wait for Explosions, and Despair," *New York Times*, 8 March
    2002.
39 Abu Amr interview cited in Joyce Davis, *Martyrs*, 168.
40 John Kifner, "As Arafat Critics Close in, Deputies Vie in the Wings," *New York Times*, 21 May 2002.

41 Shaul Mishal and Avram Sela, *The Palestinian Hamas: Vision, Violence, and Coexistence* (New York: Columbia University Press, 2000). "One of 60 Operations That Hamas Has Planned To Carry Out against Israel," *al-Sharq al-Awsat* (London), 2 August 2002.

42 Megan Goldin, "Hamas Feeds Struggle against Israel with Charity," Reuters, 4 January 2001.

43 The interview in Hamas's *Filastin al-Muslimah* (no date cited) is translated and excerpted in "Summary of Information Provided by the FBI to the Department of Treasury in Support of the Designation of the Holy Land Foundation for Relief and Development," no date, provided to Human Rights Watch by the U.S. Department of the Treasury, August 2002.

44 Felicity Barringer, "Israel is Criticized for Restricting UN access in Gaza," *New York Times*, 20 May 2003.

45 George Habash, interview, 20 June 2002, accessed on the PFLP website at http://www.pflp-pal.org/opinion/habash29-6-02.html, 20 May 2003.

46 JMCC public opinion polls, "Palestinian Opinion Pulse," vol. 2 no. 4, June 2001, vol. 2 no. 6, October 2001, vol. 3 no. 7, January 2002, vol. 3 no. 8, April 2002, accessed at http://www.jmcc.org/publicpoll.opinion.html, 20 May 2002.

47 Ben Lynfield, "As Hope Dwindles, Hamas Thrives," *Christian Science Monitor*, 10 December 2001, accessed at http://www.csmonitor.com/2001/1210/p1s1-wome.html, 20 May 2002.

48 Roni Shaked, *Yedioth Ahronoth* (Hebrew), 25 April 2003, accessed through Lexis Nexis.

49 JMCC poll, vol. 3 no. 7, January 2002.

50 The August 2002 JMCC poll, *Ha'aretz*, "Poll: Majority of Palestinians Support PA Crackdown on Attacks," The Associated Press, 28 November 2002.

51 PFLP leader George Habash denounced suicide bombings in interviews up until 2001.

52 Joel Greenberg, "7 Killed, 17 Hurt in Ambush of Bus by Palestinians," *New York Times*, 17 July 2002.

53 Davis, *Martyrs*, 140.

54 "7 Die in Attack on Immanual Bus," *Ha'aretz*, 17 July 2002.

55 Nichole Argo, "The Banality of Evil: Understanding Today's Human Bombs," Policy Paper, Preventive Defense Project (Stanford, CA: Stanford University, unpublished ms., 2003), 13.

56 Interview with Abdul Aziz al Rantisi cited in Mark Juergensmeyer, *Terror in the Mind of God: The Global Rise of Religious Violence* (Berkeley: University of California Press, 2000), 187–188.

57 Lori Allen, "There Are Many Reasons Why: Suicide Bombers and Martyrs in Palestine," *Middle East Report: Barriers to Peace* 223 (Summer 2002), accessed at http://www.merip.org/mer/mer223/mer223.html, 20 May 2003.

58 Palestinian People's Resistance Forces, Martyr Abu Ali Mustafa Brigades, the military wing of the Popular Front for the Liberation of Palestine, press statement, 15 March 2002.

59 Mouin Rabbani, "A Tale of Two Assassinations: Mustafa Zibri and Rehavam Ze'evi," *Washington Report on Middle East Affairs*, August 2002, 13–14.

60 Press statement issued by Nasser Oweis, leader of al-Aqsa Martyrs' Brigades in Palestine, 22 March 2002 (Arabic).

61 Mishal and Sela, *Palestinian Hamas*, 36.

62 *Ash-Sharq al-Awsat*, 1 April 1996, in Foreign Broadcast Information Service, 2 April 1996.

63 www.ict.org.il; Haleh Hroub, *Hamas: Political Thought and Practice* (Washington, DC: Institute for Palestine Studies, August 2000).

64 CNN *World*, 16 January 2002.

65 Reuven Paz, "Sleeping with the Enemy, A Reconciliation Process as Part of Counter-Terrorism. Is Hamas Capable of 'Hudnah'?" *Institute for Counter-Terrorism, Israel*, 25 June 1998, accessed at http://www.ict.org.il/articles/articledet.cfm?articleid=37, 2 May 2002.

66 Khalid Mish'al, interview with Abdullah al-Qaq in Amman, *Amman al Dustur* (Arabic), 28 February 1998.

67 Human Rights Watch Report, *Erased in a Moment: Suicide Bombing Attacks Against Israeli Civilians* (New York: Human Rights Watch Report, October 2002).

68 Interviews/statements issued on al-Manar Television (Arabic): interview with Avi Jorisch, 13 February 2003.

69 Boaz Ganor, "The Islamic Jihad: The Imperative of Holy War," accessed at http://www.ict.org.il/articles/articledet.cfm?articleid=405 and http://www.ict.org.il/inter_ter/orgdet.cfm?orgid=28, 20 May 2002.

70 Ahmad Rashad, *Hamas: Palestinian Politics with an Islamic Hue* (Annandale, VA: United Association for Studies and Research, 1993), 4.

71 Graham Usher, "Arafat's Shrinking Dominion," *Al-Ahram Weekly Online*, 24–30 January 2002. Issue No. 570, accessed at http://weekly.ahram.org.eg/2002/570/rel.htm, May 2002.

72 Jonathon Lis and Amira Haas, "Israel Presents Document Linking the PA to Terror Attacks," *Ha'aretz*, 2 April 2002.

73 BBC News, 2 February 2002.

74 PFLP Abu Ali Mustafa Brigades letter to Sheikh Nasrallah of the Lebanese Hezbullah, 28 April 2002, accessed at http://www.tao.ca/~solidarity/texts/palestine/PFLPcommuniques.html, 30 April 2003. PFLP communiqués begin with "to the masses of the Arab nation." This letter begins with "in the name of Allah, the Mercy-giving etc. ..."

75 Joel Greenberg, "Shock at Charges Palestinians Were Sold Israeli Munitions," *New York Times*, 19 July 2002.

76 John Daly, "Suicide Bombing: No Warning and No Total Solution," *Jane's Defence Weekly*, 17 September 2001, accessed at http://www.janes.com/security/international_security/news/jtsm/jtsm010917_1_n.shtml, 20 May 2002.

77 See UN Security Council Resolution #1405, 19 April 2002; Human Rights Watch Report, "Israel/Occupied Territories: Jenin War Crimes Investigation Needed," accessed at http://www.hrw.org/press/2002/05/jenin0503.htm, posted 3 May 2002, 20 May 2003.

78 Allen, "Many Reasons Why."

79 Mouin Rabbanni, "Palestinian Authority, Israeli Rule: From Transitional Arrangement to Permanent Authority," *Middle East Report* (Fall 1996), accessed at http://www.merip.org/mer/mer201/rabbani.htm, 20 May 2002.

80 David Plotz, "The Logic of Assassination: Why Israeli Murders and Palestinian Suicide Bombings Make Sense," *Slate Magazine*, accessed at http://slate.msn.com/?id=113987, posted 17 August 2001, accessed 10 April 2002. Krueger and Malekova's research proves otherwise. Alan B. Krueger and Jitka Malekova, "Education, Poverty, Political Violence and Terrorism: Is There a Causal Connection?" Princeton University working paper, July 2002, 9.

81 Bruce Bueno de Mesquita, interview with the author, 18 March 2002.

82 Krueger and Malekova, "Education, Poverty, Political Violence and Terrorism," 4, 28.

83 Nasra Hassan, "Letter from Gaza: An Arsenal of Believers," *The New Yorker*, 19 November 2001, accessed at http://www.newyorker.com/fact/content/?011119fa_FACT1, 10 April 2002.

84 Dr. Khalil Shikaki, interview with the author, 17 October 2002.

85 Allen, "Many Reasons Why."

86 Alan J. Kuperman identifies a "moral hazard problem" in which minority groups deliberately incite the majority to act in a repressive fashion in order to force the hand of the international community to intervene. Palestinian calls for an international intervention after the Jenin massacre, the deliberate exaggeration of casualties, and fake bodies exhumed as evidence would appear to support Kuperman's hypothesis. "The Moral Hazard of Humanitarian Intervention" (paper prepared for the 2002 annual meeting of the International Studies Association, New Orleans, LA, 25–28 March 2002 and discussions with the author, 27 March 2002).

87 Amira Haas, "Confessions of a Dangerous Mind," *Ha'aretz*, 3 April 2003.

88 Patrick Seale interview, *Al Hayat* (London), 13 September 2001.

89 The killing of Raed Karmi, the head of Fatah's military wing, in Tulkarm resulted in the suicide bombings in early March 2002. In an aerial bombardment of Gaza, the Israeli Army killed Salah Shehada, head of Hamas's Izz Eddin al-Qassam Brigades, 22 July 2002. Hamas vowed retaliation. "There is nothing in our hands but to respond with whatever power we have," said Dr. Mahmoud al-Zahar, a political leader of Hamas. "Every Israeli is a target now. No one will stop us from defending ourselves." Abdel Aziz Rantisi vowed revenge against Israelis: "We will hit them hard, they will be targeted, their houses and their families." *New York Times*, 23 July 2002. On 28 April 2003, Israel killed Nidal Salameh of the PFLP.

90 Danny Rubinstein, "Assassination as a Boomerang," *Ha'aretz*, 6 March 2002.

91 Simon Reeve, *One Day in September* (New York: Arcade Books, 2000), 70–93, 160–175.

92 Joel Greenberg, "Coat, Backpack, Sweat: Close Call in Israeli Café," *New York Times*, 8 March 2002; see also Argo, "Banality of Evil," 13.

93 Plotz, "The Logic of Assassination," ibid.

94 Abd al-'Aziz Rantisi on *Al-Jazeera This Morning*, Al-Jazeera (Doha), 20 May 2002.

95 Haim Malka, "Must Innocents Die? The Islamic Debate over Suicide Attacks," *Middle East Quarterly* (Spring 2003), accessed at http://www.meforum.org/article/530, 20 May 2003.

96 George Habash Interview, 20 June 2002, accessed on the PFLP website at http://www.pflp-pal.org/opinion/habash29-6-02.html, 4 June 2003.

97   Richard Falk, interview with the author, 10 May 2002.
98   JMCC, 20 April 2003, accessed at http://www.jmcc.org/banner/banner1/listmartyr.htm, 20 May 2003; B'tselem and Palestinian Red Crescent websites, www.btselem.org, and http://www.idf.il/daily_statistics/english/1.gif, accessed 11 January 2004; http://www.palestinercs.org/crisistables/table_of_figures.htm, accessed 11 January 2004; and http://news.bbc.co.uk/1/hi/world/middle_east/3256858.stm, accessed 12 January 2004.
99   "Fifteen Months: Intifada, Closures, and Palestinian Economic Crisis—An Assessment," World Bank Report, 18 March 2002. The UNSCO data is included in the World Bank Report, accessed at http://lnweb18.worldbank.org/mna/mena.nsf/Attachments/complete/$File/complete.pdf, 20 April 2003.
100   Sunhi Asila, "Hal hana waqtu waqf al 'amaliyyat al-istishadiyya?" (Arabic) Has the time come to end martyrdom operations? *Al Ahram*, 10 September 2002, 7.
101   Robert A. Pape, unpublished manuscript citing an 18 April 1994 speech to the Israeli Knesset. "Rabin: Killing Civilians Won't Kill the Negotiations," *Jerusalem Post*, 13 April 1994; see also Robert A. Pape, "Strategic Logic of Suicide Terrorism," *The American Political Science Review* 97 (August 2003): 343–361.

Section 6

Counterterrorism

Readings

Pedahzur, A., & Ranstorp, M. (2001). A tertiary model for countering terrorism in liberal democracies: The case of Israel. *Terrorism and Political Violence, 13,* 1–26.

Dishman, C. (2005). The leaderless nexus: When crime and terror converge. *Studies in Conflict and Terrorism, 28,* 237–252.

Silke, A. (2005). Fire of Iolaus: The role of state countermeasures in causing terrorism and what needs to be done. In T. Bjorgo (Ed.), *Root causes of terrorism: Myths, reality, and ways forward* (pp. 241–255). Oxford, UK: Routledge.

Bin Hassan, M. H. (2006). Key considerations in counterideological work against terrorist ideology. *Studies in Conflict and Terrorism, 29,* 531–558.

Introduction

Up to this point, you have read a lot of material that has provided you with a solid conceptual, theoretical and methodological grounding in terrorism studies. This section will now turn to some very practical issues – namely, how is the threat of terrorism responded to, and why? Research on counterterrorism frequently lacks an understanding of "what works" – this section has been carefully constructed to allow for engaging these readings with that critical awareness that follows from the previous sections. Taking a critical stance on issues related to counterterrorism is imperative – knowing *how* or *why* a particular action may or may not be effective allows for sound strategic suggestions.

First, Ami Pedahzur and Magnus Ranstorp address a pressing question in the world today: can a democratic nation effectively fight terrorism while maintaining those values that make it free? Using Israeli responses to Jewish terrorists as data, the authors illustrate that the most effective anti-terrorist campaigns are often those that do not violate the civil liberties of citizens in the targeted nation. Next, Chris Dishman discusses the marriage of criminal and terrorist enterprises. Specifically, Dishman argues that the breaking down of hierarchical organizational structures among illegal organizations provides criminals and terrorists greater opportunity to collaborate with one another to achieve their respective goals. For counter-terrorist forces, this means criminal and terrorist organizations have more convenient resources at their disposal. Andrew Silke then takes an intriguing look at violent state counter-measures and their effectiveness in stamping out terrorist activity. Silke comes to the conclusion that while the use of violent action against terrorist organizations may be justified, legal and satisfying, aggressive measures may not diminish the incidence of terrorism in the long run. This prompts a debate about when and if to use violence to combat terrorism. Finally, Muhammad Haniff Bin Hassan provides a unique perspective that highlights the importance of fighting ideology as a means to fight terrorism. Through ideological "immunization" and "rehabilitation," Bin Hassan provides a framework with which an effective counter-ideological campaign could be employed to deter terrorism. As you will see from the readings in this section, careful consideration of counter-terrorism measures is extremely important if we are to avoid providing terrorist groups with propaganda that could be used to validate their actions.

Discussion questions

By the end of this section, you should be able to answer:

- What does it mean for a terrorist group to be "defeated?"
- In what ways can a terrorist group be defeated, if at all?
- What place do "soft" measures have in a state's counterterrorist strategy?
- How can counterterrorism and the civil liberties of a population be balanced?

Further reading

Arce, D. G., & Sandler, T. (2005). Counterterrorism: A game-theoretic analysis. *The Journal of Conflict Resolution, 49*, 183–200.

Chellaney, B. (2001). Fighting terrorism in southern Asia: The lessons of history. *International Security, 26*, 94–116.

Coll. S. (2004). *Ghost wars: The secret history of the CIA, Afghanistan, and bin Laden, from the Soviet invasion to September 10, 2001.* New York: Penguin.

English, R. (2009). *Terrorism: How to respond.* Oxford, UK: Oxford University Press.

Farley, J. D. (2003). Breaking al-Qaeda cells: A mathematical analysis of counterterrorism operations (A guide for risk assessment and decision making). *Studies in Conflict and Terrorism, 26*, 399–411.

Ganor, B. (2005). *The counterterrorism puzzle: A guide for decision makers.* Piscataway, NJ: Transaction.

Kilcullen, D. (2009). *The accidental guerrilla: Fighting small wars in the midst of a big one.* New York: Oxford University Press.

Lynch, T. (2002). Breaking the vicious cycle: Preserving our liberties while fighting terrorism. *Policy Analysis, 443*, http://www.cato.org/pubs/pas/pa443.pdf.

Metz, S. (2006). Insurgency and counterinsurgency in Iraq. *Washington Quarterly, 27*, 25–36.

Posen, B. (2001–2002). The struggle against terrorism: Grand strategy, strategy, and tactics. *International Security, 26*, 39–55.

Silke, A. (Ed.). (2010). *The psychology of counter-terrorism.* Oxon, UK: Routledge.

Wilkinson, P. (2011). *Terrorism versus democracy: The liberal state response* (3rd Ed.). London: Routledge.

19 A tertiary model for countering terrorism in liberal democracies

The case of Israel

Ami Pedahzur and Magnus Ranstorp

Introduction

For many years, scholars have been preoccupied with one of the central dilemmas facing liberal democracies that wish to maintain their legitimacy in view of the varying degrees of challenges posed by terror and political violence. At the core of this dilemma is to what degree a democracy can lead an effective struggle against subversive elements while at the same time uphold its liberal, or even democratic, character. In the effort to defend itself against terrorism, how can a liberal democratic state avoid the slippery slope that so easily may lead it to adopt the exact same methods as those who wish to undermine it? In his pioneering and exhaustive book, *Terrorism and the Liberal State*, Paul Wilkinson expounds upon this problem with great clarity:

> The primary objective of counter-terrorist strategy must be the protection and maintenance of liberal democracy and the rule of law. It cannot be sufficiently stressed that this aim overrides in importance even the objective of eliminating terrorism and political violence as such. Any bloody tyrant can "solve" the problem of political violence if he is prepared to sacrifice all considerations of humanity, and to trample down all constitutional and judicial rights.[1]

Two decades later, in response to this dilemma, Peter Chalk further advances the argument that the elusive ideal for any democracy is to adopt counter-terror measures which are both effective and, at the same time, conform with the underlying premises of a liberal democracy.[2]

In the years following the publication of Wilkinson's classic book, a great deal of research and academic debate have been devoted to the democratic dilemma of the fight against terror which in turn has spawned a number of different theoretical models.[3] In particular, two contrasting types of models of response have been identified and delineated, the "war" model and "criminal justice" model. In the "war" model, a stronger emphasis is placed on the actual restraint of terror than on the maintenance of liberal democratic rights, whereas in the "criminal justice" model, the preservation of democratic principles is a fundamental premise in the fight against terror, even at the expense of a reduced effectiveness of counter-terrorist measures. Despite the general usefulness of this broad conceptualization, these two models often do not concur with the reality on the ground. While most liberal democracies understandably try to refrain from using the "war" model, their attempts at complying with the "criminal justice" model and, at the same time, responding decisively to terrorism, have often resulted in the stretching of certain boundaries of the "criminal justice" model. Arguably, nowhere is this more evident than in the case of Israel's multifaceted policies and responses to its own internal Jewish terrorism and political subversion that has plagued Israeli society since the establishment of the state in May 1948. Unlike the often contentious and lively academic debate concerning whether Israel actually conforms to the principles of a liberal democracy, a debate that often focuses on the argument that Israel's relations with its Arab citizens are the sole factor for that compatibility, there is widespread consensus that Israel conforms to the liberal democratic model with regard to at least its Jewish population. Furthermore, the case of Israel does not deviate too far from Crelinsten's definition of a liberal democracy with regard to counter-terrorism applied to its own Jewish citizens, namely the "rule of law, the governing administration's openness and responsibility, and the preservation of trust between citizens and government based on citizen access to enough information as far as is allowed in the public interest".[4]

The primary aim of this article is to present an expanded taxonomy between the "war" and "criminal justice" models or, in other words, a tertiary, mediating model that reconciles the two aforementioned models and one that provides a more direct relation to the empirical reality of Israel's changing response to Jewish terrorism and subversion over the last fifty years. At the same time, this model is predicated upon two levels of analysis. The *exogenic* level stresses the cultural and social context of the process of determining policy and how policy-making is affected by these conditions. The *endogenic* perspective examines the degree in which the employment of the counter-terrorist model is based on consistent and professional grounds and whether it is possible to identify alternative motives for the use of one model of response over another.

Addressing the grey areas between the "war" and "criminal justice" models

The corpus of literature inquiring into counter-terrorism makes an analytical distinction between the "war" model and "criminal justice" model[5] on several levels. Terrorism, from the perspective of the "war model," is regarded as an act of revolutionary warfare, whereas the "criminal justice" model considers terrorism a criminal act. In line with these respective views are their correspondingly different responses to terror. The "war" model places the onus of response on a military that emphasizes the marshalling of all the means at its disposal in order to quash terrorist action. The "criminal justice" model accords the police with the primary responsibility for responding to terrorism, and its actions are naturally restrained by the state's criminal legal system.[6] As emphasized by Crelinsten in an attempt to further distinguish the two models:

> In a criminal justice model, the rule of law is paramount, while in the war model, it is the rules of war that prevail. In the criminal justice model, it is the police who exercise the state's monopoly on the use of violence. The rules of engagement, so to speak, involve the use of minimal force, which requires an exercise of judgment on the part of the officer(s) involved. Military rules of engagement, on the other hand, require the maximal use of force designed to overpower the enemy.[7]

Notwithstanding the above distinction, a review of the literature demonstrates that the attempt to apply theory to reality is often difficult and fraught with complexity. While the characteristics of the "war" model are quite clear and its boundaries well-defined, those of the "criminal justice" model suffer from ambiguity, especially as it often appears that the attempt to adhere to the "criminal justice" model leads policy-makers in liberal democratic states to an almost unrestrained elasticity of its boundaries. In particular, Crelinsten and Schmid argue that during times when democracies undergo a sense of an impending threat or crisis, they tend to extend the limits of the "criminal justice" model. This elasticity entails the application of special anti-terror legislation providing the police with greater authority, adjustment of judiciary processes to facilitate the prosecution of terrorists, and, occasionally, the establishment of special courts for trying accused terrorists.[8] However, Crelinsten later tried to tackle the elasticity from another angle. He argued that it is often difficult to draw clear boundaries with regard to political violence, especially because violent events of a criminal nature may tend to become enmeshed with those stemming from political motives. These developments make it difficult to formulate an unequivocal retaliatory policy and also lead to the mutual infraction of police and army forces – the encroachment of the military into the jurisdiction of police authority and vice versa.[9] Crelinsten and Schmid conclude by underscoring the significant disparity between the models and the reality of counter-terrorism. They argue that precisely because of these aberrations of the "criminal justice" model, liberal democracies attempting to exercise counter-terrorist strategies will tend to deviate from the "rule of law" and democratic standards.[10] As a consequence, the "criminal justice" model proves to be a hypothetical concept with very elastic boundaries, and in most cases cannot serve as a suitable vehicle for the assessment of various countries' capabilities to respond effectively to terror while also maintaining the conceptual and ethical boundaries of a liberal democracy. Consequently, the development of a third "mediating" model is necessary for assisting in the clarification of the boundaries between the "war" and "criminal justice" models, and may be referred to as the "expanded criminal justice" model. This model acknowledges the fact that the war against terror may often stray from liberal standards and employ means not necessarily accepted as principles of criminal law enforcement, but at the same time still significantly differs from the rules of war and customary military methods. The goal of this model is to include all those "gray" areas that are so commonly practiced in the war against terrorism yet are not accounted for in either the "war" or the "criminal justice" models as noted above. The advantages of the "expanded criminal justice" model are twofold. First, it allows the creation of a continuum between the first two models that will reduce the discontinuity between them. Secondly, the tertiary model will provide a framework for integrating theory and empirical reality, making it easier to classify and detect the changes in various countries' responses to terrorist threats. Based on a set of deductive inferences drawn from the literature in this field, the two traditional models as well as the proposed model can be classified according to the following criteria: general features, state interests, democratic acceptability, constitutional, legal and operational aspects (see Table 19.1).

An anatomic analysis of these three models reveals that in effect they consist of two principal parts, infrastructure and structure. The infrastructure is the numerous constitutional and judiciary arrangements whose absence, presence and character dictate the operational range of action. For example, the disregard of constitutional boundaries in the frame of the "war" model leaves much room for the manoeuvre of military forces whose goal is the elimination of terror. The "criminal justice" model endeavours to strike a balance between combat effectiveness and the maintenance of the liberal character of the state, subordinating the war against terror to rigid liberal constitutional principles and thus providing the police with only limited means for action. The "expanded criminal justice" model regards terror as an exceptional phenomenon and therefore, despite the aspiration to adhere as much as possible to the "rule of law", legal boundaries are extended to enable a more effective response to terror while partially foregoing certain liberal principles and in general abusing freedom of expression and action. Nevertheless, contrary to the "war" model, the means exercised in the frame of the intermediate model are not enough to violate completely the boundaries of the broad definition of the democratic political system.[11]

In order to overcome the methodological problems that may arise when attempting to confirm a theoretical argument using the "case analysis" method, the Israeli response to Jewish terror will be reviewed and analysed through a diachronic perspective. In fact, this type of analysis will give prominence to the advantages embodied in the three-model constellations as well as feature the delicate nuances of this taxonomy.

Table 19.1

Criteria	War model	Expanded criminal justice model	Criminal justice model
General feature	Terrorism is regarded as a tactic exercised in guerilla activities or even acts of rebellion.	Terrorism is regarded as an exceptional phenomenon that is not necessarily an act of war, yet also deviates from the standard definition of a felonious crime.	Terrorism is regarded as a crime.
State aims and means	Apprehending terrorists and the elimination of terrorism.	Arrest and penalization of terrorists.	Arrest and penalization of terrorists while adhering to the "rule of law" and liberal democratic standards with respect to the institution of law and enforcement.
Democratic acceptability	The exercise of military force and military strategies with the intention of eradicating terrorism in a certain society will lead the country significantly away from acceptable democratic standards.	The expansion of the concept of the rule of law by adopting special legislation in the battle against terrorism and administrative regulations will divert the regime away from liberal acceptability, yet will not completely violate democratic boundaries.	The use of this model corresponds with the elements to the liberal democratic orientation. Rigid constitutional boundaries.
Constitutional and legal aspects	Laws of war dictate counter-terrorism measures and consequently any constitutional or legal consideration is solely secondary.	The expansion of constitutional boundaries by adopting administrative regulations or special laws in the fight against terrorism, and the differential treatment by the court system of offences defined as terrorist.	The state responds to terrorist incidents in compliance with state criminal law and is subject to constant judiciary regulation.
Operational aspects	Forces responding to terrorism are the army and special units. The nature of their response resides in military doctrine.	Forces responding will be primarily police and secret service, occasionally complemented by special anti-terrorism units. The nature of the response will include preventive arrests, surveillance techniques and gathering intelligence date – typical methods used by secret services. All this with the intention of bringing suspects to trial.	The forces responding will be the police. The nature of the response is circumscribed by the standard rules of authority accorded to an anti-criminal police force.

The nature of Jewish terrorism in Israel

In the most comprehensive study of political violence in Israel written to date, *Brother Against Brother: Violence and Extremism in Israeli Politics from Altalena to the Rabin Assassination*, Ehud Sprinzak charts the map of violence and terror in Israeli society, originating as far back as the foundation of Israel. According to his methodology, it appears that nearly all forms of political violence documented in the professional literature have found expression in Israel, ranging from violent street demonstrations to the extremes of political assassinations and terrorism of a highly sophisticated nature.[12] Regarding the factors leading to the burgeoning of Jewish violence and subversion within Israel, Sprinzak proposes a trilateral classification:

1   violence of a political-ideological nature as exemplified by the struggle between the Israeli left- and right-wings over the country's borders;
2   violence evolving from feelings of ethnic deprivation, namely the struggle between those of Azhkenazim and Sephardim descent on the basis of socio-ethnic gaps and the resultant feelings of discrimination;
3   violence stemming from the conflict between ultraorthodox and secular Jews, or, more specifically, religious Jewish protest against the Israeli government and its policies.[13]

Complementing Sprinzak's comprehensive and analytically balanced approach of the phenomenon of political violence is a book written by Carmi Gillon, the former head of the Israeli Shabak or GSS (General Security Services), who deliberately adopts a much narrower approach.[14] Gillon's principle base of analysis is the political-ideological dimension, and not without reason. This dimension proved to be the dominant cause of numerous incidents of calculated and sophisticated violence, a fact also substantiated by Sprinzak, whereas the other sources (ethnic, economic and religious) provided for many years different forms of intriguing extra-parliamentary politics or, at the most, acts of hooliganism. This point is of great relevance because Gillon's perspective strikingly reflects the boundaries of political violence and terror as defined specifically by policy-makers and the security establishment in Israel.[15] Therefore, this is also the only aspect in which retaliatory measures were directly assigned to the GSS, whereas the response to violent incidents stemming from ethnic, religious and economic reasons was relegated to the criminal law enforcement system. In order to analyse the dynamics of Israeli counter-terror policy to Jewish terror and subversion, it therefore appears sensible to examine mainly the political-ideological axis.

The early years of the State of Israel – the predominance of the "war" model

The years prior to the founding of the State of Israel were marked by the Zionist movement's struggle to establish a sovereign state. Like other nationalist struggles, violent means were also used as an integral strategy or component in this venture. Two movements that were distinguished by ultra-nationalist right-wing notions – the Etzel (National Military Organization) and Lechi (Israeli Freedom Fighters) – were the most devoted to use of terror. Their tactics sparked fiery debate among the various political factions in the Jewish Yishuv,[16] which did not abate with the inauguration of the State of Israel and the cessation of the British Mandate in the spring of 1948. Approximately one month after the official declaration of the establishment of Israel, the nascent state's political leadership deliberately chose to adopt the "war" model and all it entailed in its attempt to put an end to the struggle over sovereignty and with the aim of dissolving the Etzel and Lechi. The incident most strikingly marking the assimilation of this model was the Altalena affair.

On 22 June 1948, the Army's Chief of Operations directly ordered his soldiers to fire a heavy gun barrage and sink the Altalena ship not far from the shores of Tel Aviv. On deck were Etzel members and in its cargo hold were significant stocks of weapons smuggled from France by the organization. This drastic step taken by Israel's first prime minister, Ben-Gurion, invites the question whether the weapons ship Altalena was indeed such a threatening element that it left the decision-makers with no alternative but to employ such extreme measures as prescribed by the "war" model. The answer to this question is multifaceted. Politically, behind the scenes of the Altalena affair, there was an attempt by the month-old state to raise quickly a state-run army that was to contend with the overall state of war with the neighbouring Arab states at that time. In order to organize such an army, it was necessary to combine all the clandestine elements that were in operation prior to the State of Israel's establishment into one unitary national framework.[17] However, the effort to unite hastily several hawkish factions, often separated by vast ideological chasms and a history of bitter confrontation, into one common framework was no mean feat. Furthermore, the various elements of the new army were not so willing to surrender their respective paramilitary distinctions and quickly subordinate to unite under a single national framework in which the Labour Movement had a highly dominant role. The Etzel, for example, strove to maintain a certain degree of autonomy in the new state-run army context, as revealed by the fact that its 5,000 members joined the Israeli Defense Forces as seven battalions operating under their own separate command.[18] In fact, Etzel requested that its members be accorded favoured status in the distribution of weapons seized from the Altalena.[19] In line with the conventional approach for countries adhering to the "war" model, the Israeli leadership saw this as a genuine direct threat, growing exponentially as the ship drew closer to the shores of Tel Aviv.[20] This sense of "crisis" stemmed from the belief of the Israeli leadership that members of the Etzel movement were attempting to form an alternative power centre and about to challenge the authority of the newly formed Israeli government.[21] As such, the odds favouring the military option increased. In the meantime, members of the Etzel movement, who had been conscripted into the burgeoning national army, abandoned their bases and made their way towards the location where the ship was expected to set ashore. The leader of the Etzel movement, Menachem Begin, in response to the escalation of the "crisis", endeavoured to reach a compromise with the Israeli political leadership, trying to prevent the sinking of the ship and the resultant loss of life. However, the new Prime Minister was apparently not too eager for such a resolution. According to the situation Ben-Gurion presented to his ministers, the Etzel movement represented an immediate and unacceptable challenge to the new sovereign government.[22]

The Altalena affair has itself provoked a fierce debate among Israeli scholars over whether Ben-Gurion perceived his own government to be truly in jeopardy or whether he simply used it to disable his political foes. Horowitz and Lissak advance the argument that applying "war" model tactics to the Altalena affair and the Etzel movement was deliberately undertaken in order to consolidate government stability. Accordingly, Israel's aggressive policy toward Altalena was only another variation on a universal theme where the group seizing power – within the context of the institutionalization of nationalist and social revolutions – needs to use force in order to rid itself of any radical elements carrying the potential of undermining the regime's stability.[23] In contrast, Barzilai emphasizes the political nature of Ben-Gurion's real concern over the build-up of hostile political forces, principally potential adversaries to his own party's government.[24] Whether Ben-Gurion's motives were driven by political considerations or were in the national interest, the Altalena affair signified the advent of a comprehensive campaign whose aim was to crush oppositionist militarist factors in the country. The operation included army raids on all Etzel military installations, arrest of the movement's leaders, and, in effect, the total dismantling of its military capacities.[25] With the dissolution of the Etzel movement, the use of the "war" model against Jewish political violence ended. Those in charge of the nascent State of Israel adopted instead the "expanded criminal justice" model, as an alternative course of countermeasures to internal subversion. The benefit of this option was that it sanctioned offensive action against terrorists and zealous politicians while it simultaneously protected the democratic basis of the state and prevented it from plunging into a crisis of legitimacy.

Adoption and institutionalization of the "expanded criminal justice" model

The operational foundations of the "mediating" model must include constitutional and judiciary versatility, making it possible for the state to respond to terrorist action using means that deviate from the criminal code. Except for Great Britain, Israel is the only democracy that does not have a written constitution ensuring basic individual rights, such as the freedom of speech and freedom of association. Notwithstanding the internal political reasons preventing the adoption of a formal constitution, the newly established State of Israel was under a genuine threat from its Arab neighbours, and this fact consolidated a sweeping public consensus on the issue of the precedence of security and military matters over civil rights. However, the sense of threat has persisted and this "security complex" has dominated policy and discourse for many years. Therefore, Israel has never really retracted the state of emergency under which it has operated all these years.

Hofnung argues that a "state of emergency" is a governmental declaration of the existence of an exceptional set of circumstances, which therefore demand the adoption of extraordinary measures.[26] As a result of the continuous state of emergency in Israel, the state has drafted a complex system of regulations intended to restrict basic individual rights. In an attempt to clarify this tangled web, it is possible to distinguish three strands of emergency legislation. First, there is the Defense (Emergency) Regulations (1945). Inherited from its predecessor, the British Mandatory authorities in Palestine, these regulations granted a great deal of power to the military command. High-ranking officers are authorized to order house demolitions, impose curfews, make arrests, carry out searches and detain suspects without judicial restraint. However, the enforcement of these regulations *within* Israeli borders is not common and is carried out only with the approval of the highest levels of the executive authority (the Cabinet or Minister of Defense). Secondly, section 9 of the Law and Administration Ordinance (1948) authorizes the executive authority to suspend, revoke or alter parliamentary legislative measures in cases of emergency. Finally, there is the Parliamentary emergency legislation.[27]

For the benefit of the present analysis, seven components from the 1945 security regulations have assisted in laying the foundations for counter-terror action in terms of the "expanded criminal justice" model:

1. *Military censorship* – the military censor is authorized to ban any publication (including daily newspapers) containing, according to the military censor, material that may endanger national security.
2. *Restrictions on freedom of movement* – an individual suspected of subversive activity may be subject to a restraining order that will restrict him to his area of residence and require that he report daily to the police station.
3. *Administrative detentions* – originally effected under the Emergency (Defense) Regulations (1945), this mandatory arrangement gained legislative endorsement in 1979. The 1979 statute gave license to the Minister of Defense and, under special circumstances, the Chief of Staff, to arrest a person without trial for a period of up to six months. Detention can be extended on condition that it is subject to judicial approval at each extension.
4. *Special courts* – defense regulations authorize the Chief of Staff to set up special courts for those suspected of activity that may jeopardize state security. Another legal proceeding is

putting such suspects on trial in a civil court of law on the condition that these courts sustain verdict in accordance with emergency legislation.[28]

5   One of the principal measures available to courts trying suspects of subversive offences is the *Prevention of Terrorism Ordinance No. 33 (1948)*. According to chapter 8, the executive authority is in charge of determining whether a political movement is a terrorist one or not. An illustration of the rigidity of the ordinance is found in chapter 2, which determines that an individual who takes part in the establishment or activity of a terrorist organization, or even dispenses propaganda in any form, will be guilty of an offense whose maximum sentence is twenty years imprisonment.

6   *Special legislation applying to the occupied territories* (territories occupied by Israel in 1976) and hence not in accordance with customary Israel legal standards (apart from East Jerusalem and the Golan Heights, which have been annexed by law). These areas are subject to international laws of occupation, which authorize the regional military commander to take any measures necessary to maintain control of, and order in, these territories.[29] In most cases, these measures were taken against the Palestinian population but, as Cohen-Almagor has pointed out, Jewish settlers were also occasionally subject to administrative detention orders. For example, following the Baruch Goldstein massacre at the Tomb of the Patriarchs in February 1994, eight Jewish extremists were put under administrative detention.[30]

7   The seventh course of action, which has received less than adequate academic attention, concerns the obscure *legal statutes of the internal Israeli security service*, otherwise known as Shabak (GSS).[31] Unlike other countries, such as Great Britain, where there is a robust system of public control over the secret services,[32] in Israel there is not only an absence of legislation which may have defined the limits and methods of the GSS, but public accountability of the security service is only partial.[33] A frail constitutional infrastructure enables the widespread existence of the phenomenon Crelinsten calls "provocative policing," that is, actions not necessarily designed to gather anti-terrorist evidence for the sake of prosecution, but rather in order to serve the intelligence aims of the security forces.[34] Furthermore, the absence of a genuine system of accountability also sanctions the adoption of patterns of actions verging on the illegal or what Gillon calls the "gray" areas.[35]

Following the above delineation of the legal foundations of the "expanded criminal justice" model, the process of its operational adoption will now be examined. The first indication of the abandonment of the "war" model was apparent already in the final stages of the dismantling of the Etzel movement when five members of the organization's command were placed under administrative arrest. They were allowed to appeal to the Supreme Court,[36] a fact that proved that the security forces were still liable to the civil court system even if this accountability was still partial. However, the most significant step towards the adoption of the "expanded criminal justice" model away from the "war" model became apparent in the actions taken in order to eliminate the smallest and most zealous underground right-wing movement – the Lechi. The incident that directly prompted this was the assassination of the Swedish diplomat, Count Folke Bernadotte, who had been assigned to be the United Nations mediator for Palestine, on 17 September 1948, in a well-planned ambush by Lechi members. While the initial Israeli response to the assassination was more in compliance with the "war" model, as soldiers from the Palmach (army elite squads) unit raided Lechi military camps, closed down Lechi organization's offices and arrested dozens of its members,[37] it quickly adopted several measures that relied completely on the judicial base of the "expanded criminal justice" model. Three days after the murder, the Israeli government declared Lechi to be a terrorist organization, thus expediting the process of the indictment of Lechi-affiliated members, including those whom had not been active participants in the terrorist operations. Israel's actions against Lechi indicated that Israel had become an established fact and a sovereign state bound to a system of rules. As such, every use of military force against civilians carried a genuine risk of harming the public legitimacy of the new government. As a result, the tertiary model was acknowledged as an option necessary for the stabilization of the government, both in order to gain legitimacy and also to justify the crackdown of violent antagonists. As for the motive behind the declaration of Lechi as a terrorist organization, Barzilai argues that the order was more directed toward subduing government opponents and de-legitimizing them than based on the rationale of taking counter-terror stabilizing action.[38] Despite the veracity of this argument, it seems that the disavowal of the "war" model in favour of the "expanded criminal justice" model demonstrates how Ben-Gurion, in his efforts to undermine his political opponents, chose a more restrained approach and abandoned any rigid methods employed in the struggle against Etzel.

Another indication of the institutionalization of the "expanded criminal justice" model, as the dominant doctrine in the struggle against Jewish terror, was the decision to favour the GSS over the army and police in the fight against terror. Isser Harel, founder of the GSS, began to isolate the secret services from the army and thus reinforce its status as an autonomous non-military body. According to Harel, this made it easier to reconcile the balance between security operational needs, on one hand, and the constraints of a democratic political system on the other. Harel also attempted to set the ground rules for GSS operations. As he saw it, the role of the organization in the war against terror should be limited to preventive measures. After the gathering of all available evidence, it was determined that the suspects would be transferred to the police for further investigation and prosecution, if necessary.[39] On the face of it, it seemed that Harel's aspiration was that Shabak's role in the war against Jewish terror would be limited to "reactive policing", a term Crelinsten defines as a method intended to restrict counter-terrorism to the "criminal justice" model. However, according to Carmi Gillon, who sat at the helm of Shabak for more that 40 years, the course chosen by his predecessor Harel and, in turn, his successors was undeniably "provocative policing". For instance, this involved security measures against regularly identified targets that appeared as potential threats (including political parties and movements), most notably employing surveillance of them in order to gather information and allow frequent pursuit of the leaders.[40]

The early 1950s were rife with events providing policy-makers with several opportunities to develop further actions that fall under the tertiary model. Three radical movements emerged at that time: Brit Hakanaim (Covenant of the Zealots), Hamachaneh (the Camp) and the Zrifin (the name of the prison where members were held) Underground.[41] The first two organizations eventually merged under a common leadership of militant Haredim (an ultra-orthodox sect), who vehemently objected to the Zionist character of the state. At the outset, their actions were primarily acts of hooliganism, yet the Israeli police was still quite powerless in restraining them. Therefore, the GSS assumed responsibility for dealing with this group, and Harel managed to plant two agents among its ranks, whose primary mission was to monitor and report member movements. After receiving intelligence reports regarding the intention of the organization to step up actions and engage in terrorist tactics, the GSS launched a comprehensive campaign against the group and its supporters, and 20 suspects were put under administrative arrest.[42] However, the handling of the Zrifin Underground is an even more striking example of the entrenchment of the "expanded criminal justice" model. The Underground, whose members were chiefly inspired by the *Lechi* tradition, began its foray into terror in the winter of 1953, and on 9 February 1953, it carried out its most violent and bold attack. A huge bomb was planted and detonated at the Soviet Embassy building in Tel Aviv and three diplomats were injured. Following a co-ordinated investigation between security service and police force, the Israeli government decided to enforce the Prevention of Terrorism Ordinance (PTO) on this group. In addition, for the first time, the Israeli government decided to establish a special military court in order to prosecute and sentence members of the Underground.[43] Some years later, as political violence subsided, counter-terrorist measures were relaxed and military courts were no longer convened for the trial of Jewish terror organizations.

From the "expanded criminal justice" model to the "criminal justice" model: paradoxes of Israel policy in response to Jewish terror

In the early 1970s, when Israeli political institutions approached the final stages of consolidation and the country achieved the status of a more stable democracy, it seemed that the adoption of the "criminal justice" model, as the dominant model in the fight against Jewish terror, was inevitable. But this, in fact, did not happened. A review of the factors forestalling the transition to the "criminal justice" model offers two principal types of explanation: factors rooted in the socio-political infrastructure of the country, so-called *exogenic* factors; and situation-specific motives affecting the nature of the response to various acts of terror, otherwise termed *endogenic* factors.

At the *exogenic* level, there are three principal factors that *prima facie* appear of consequence. The first is the frailty of the liberal tradition in Israeli political culture. This is due to the fact that Israel, the country of the "ingathering of the exiles", absorbed the majority of its immigrants from countries characterized by a dearth of liberal values. In addition, the pivotal role of religion in the Israeli political system has also hindered the liberalization of the political culture.[44] The absence of a liberal culture, among political elites as well as among the public, precluded the conditions that were suitable for the adoption of a liberal model in regard to various issues, *inter alia*, the fight against terror. The profound cleavages of this society are the second exogenic factor, or more specifically, the dispute among religious and secular leaderships in parliament, which has also undermined the drafting of a constitution.[45] Filling this constitutional void might have created the potential for the removal of the constructional-legal base of the tertiary model. Finally, the third factor relates to the ongoing Israeli–Arab conflict. The Israeli "society under siege", as it is often termed by sociologists, has constantly felt subject to a sense of threat and "exceptionalism",[46] and has consequently developed a great deal of reliance on its military establishment. This militarist orientation has occasionally bordered on a genuine glorification of the secret services and elite army units and has led to far-reaching implications. Israelis tend invariably to prefer security interests to other considerations, including proper government procedures. Even as recent as the early 1990s, following a period of erosion in the status of the military establishment in general and the GSS in particular, research confirmed the preference for security above all else. In particular, findings showed that more than 46 per cent of surveyed Israeli citizens totally rejected any judiciary intervention on behalf of the Supreme Court of Justice regarding decisions made by the Israeli Defense Forces. Fifty-eight per cent supported the Supreme Court's tendency during those years to interfere as little as possible in security affairs.[47] Therefore, the military apparatus in Israel enjoyed the almost unreserved trust of the public, a fact that awarded it with a great deal of freedom in its operations.

According to the above, at the *endogenic* level, the differential Israeli response to the four previously illustrated incidents raises a number of questions. The "expanded criminal justice" model should apparently have guided the state's response throughout the course of its war on Jewish terror. However, herein lies a paradox. Whereas in respect to political groups who constituted an almost negligible threat of terrorist action (such as Kach and the radical left), the tertiary model was practiced in full, but curiously the state chose to exercise the "criminal justice" model in regard to two of the most conspicuous incidents of Jewish terror and violence in the 1980s and

1990s – the Jewish Underground and Uzi Meshulam's group. This paradox can be explained by three principal causes. The first cause relates to the "marginality factor", which assumes that the smaller and more peripheral a group is, the more forceful the state's response will be, regardless of the degree of violence. This "policy" is a consequence of two stratagems: on the one hand, a society's need to mark its legitimate boundaries by denouncing radical elements, and on the other, the fact that marginal groups enjoy limited public and political support which in turn prevents them from mustering public sympathy against their exclusion. The second explanation in fact highlights a conceptual thread running throughout this article, and that is the intense politicization of counter-terrorism. This refers to the use of the means provided by the various models in order to advance aims that are not necessarily related to the war on terror, but rather associated with the political goals of the government in power. Finally, the third explanation refers to the military establishment's adherence to outdated conceptions regarding violent threats in general.

The Kach movement

Kach emerged in Israel in late 1971 and was in effect an offshoot of the Jewish Defense League (JDL), the violent and vigilant organization in the United States. When the leader of the movement, Rabbi Meir Kahane, immigrated to Israel, it seemed that his intention was to import the JDL's violent methods, especially as Kahane and his followers proved already in 1972 to constitute a significant challenge to the State of Israel. In August 1972, the Kach simulated a public trial against the Arab mayor of Hebron, Mohammed Ali Jabari, principally in response to his role in the 1929 massacre of Jews and the events of the 1948 War of Independence. In an effort to enact a public trial, Kahane and his adherents entered Hebron, a mostly Arab city, provocatively creating a significant potential for violent confrontation.[48] In the first years of Kahane's presence in Israel, the security forces were still trying to decide what he was actually capable of, preferring to look upon him as more of a provocateur than a terrorist. In 1973, he was the first individual to be sentenced to a two-month suspended prison sentence for conspiring to commit criminal offences in the US. In a large part, the conviction was based on evidence from letters that he wrote to his followers encouraging them to engage in acts of terrorism.[49] Seven years later, when his status as a terrorist was firmly established, Israel changed its policies and adopted the "expanded criminal justice" model in its treatment of Kahane and his adherents. The leader of Kach became a principal object of close surveillance by the security services, and the GSS adopted provocative policing methods on his organization.[50] This close surveillance of him led ultimately to the administrative arrest of Kahane for a period of nine months in relation to his organization's plot to fire a long-range missile at the Dome of the Rock mosque on the Temple Mount.[51] During the years 1984–1988, when Kahane served as a parliamentary member of the Knesset, the GSS suspended their surveillance due to a directive prohibiting the monitoring of elected public officials. Nonetheless, his supporters and party members remained under strict surveillance.[52]

In November 1990, the murder of Kahane in New York completely devastated his organization and led to the dispersal of his followers into two minor movements – Kach and Kahane Chai (Kahane Lives). Despite the peripheral status of these political movements in terms of their marginality within the Israeli political discourse, they still remained a principal target of the GSS. And in March 1994, in a wake of the massacre perpetrated by Baruch Goldstein (a former and active member of Kach) at the Tomb of the Patriarchs, the Israeli government decided to enforce the Prevention of Terrorism Ordinance on Kach and Kahane Chai. Notwithstanding the occasionally violent elements of these movements,[53] their place in the arena of radical violence at the time was minor, particularly in view of the radicalization of the Israeli Right, which included collective, or individual, blatant provocations against the rule of law and governmental legitimacy.

Not only does the enforcement of the ordinance specifically against these movements seem out of proportion, but also the pretext for this decision appears peculiar. Baruch Goldstein was identified as a "lone wolf" at the time – he committed the massacre at the Tomb of the Patriarchs on his own accord, unassisted by any organization. Yet, Cohen-Almagor explains, the inclusion of these organizations under the Prevention of Terrorism Ordinance was an inevitable development simply because the government of Israel had no other means of effectively dealing with these two movements.[54] He questioned the necessity to issue the Prevention of Terrorism Ordinance, suggesting that its enforcement was not particularly effective because the core of the movement would continue to remain active and unaffected, at the most under a different name and exercising more caution. Equally, while the rationale behind the governmental decree of the PTO seems to have been a strong declaration and denial of the legitimacy of these organizations in an attempt to expel them from the legitimate boundaries of society,[55] the enforcement of the PTO was supposed to have prevented the use of administrative procedures which are not legitimate means in the war against terrorism. However, the fact is that ex-movement activists are under the constant surveillance of the security services. In addition, the exercise of administrative procedures has not become any less prevalent. Warrants for the arrest and restriction of movement of activists in Judea and Samaria are issued on a regular basis[56] in addition to the use of the means imparted by virtue of the PTO.[57]

At a time when it seemed that even the use of the "criminal justice" model would have sufficed, it seems that the Israeli polity's decision to respond so severely was because of these movements' marginality. By exercising the PTO in relation to these groups, the Israeli government was able to send out a forceful message against those elements. The timing of this decision was also highly significant. It came immediately in the first few months after the signing of the Oslo Agreements, especially when a number of powerful political elements led huge demonstrations – some of them violent – against the government. The Kach and Kahane Chai movements were ideal targets for delivering a message in response, owing to their propensity for political dissent and to counter the mobilization of a parliamentary lobby for their cause. Another explanation for this iron-fist policy and isolated response against these two particular movements can also be found in the outdated and entrenched perspective of Israeli political elites and security services, which regard the Kach and Kahane Chai as the most extremist and violence-prone factions on the fringes of the Israeli radical right. In retrospect, particularly following the assassination of Rabin, this policy turned out to be misguided.[58] Furthermore, these movements proved to be easy targets for the enforcement of a harsh policy of response, a posture readily adopted by an entrenched intelligence outlook, preferring not to expand their view in the direction of the genuine threats evolving at that time.

Hanitzotz and the Revolutionary Communist League: the radical left in Israel

Another largely marginal group on the Israeli political scene, and hence also considerably vulnerable to the use of the "expanded criminal justice" model, was the radical left-wing element. Despite Sprinzak's argument that, in comparison with left-wing European organizations, the extreme left in Israel rarely needed to take violent action,[59] Israeli policy-makers tended to view organizations such as Hanitzotz (the Spark) and the Revolutionary Communist League as terrorist factions. The pretext for this was the fact that these organizations did not recognize the State of Israel's right of existence and they also received financial assistance from two Palestinian terrorist groups led by George Habash and Ahmad Jibril. Consequently, these movements were branded as targets for GSS intelligence surveillance. However, Carmi Gillon, one of the leaders of the struggle against these organizations, addressed them as "a completely marginal phenomenon, having no effect whatsoever on society and which never threatened the fragile consensus in this country".[60] Apart from reflecting the "marginality" factor, as these minimally subversive groups were given equal treatment as organizations that persistently used political violence, it also illustrates the "politicization" of the war on terrorism, reflecting the Israeli government's orientation toward the extreme left. According to Barzilai, a prominent example underscoring this politicization was the use of one of the amendments to the PTO in 1986, whose principal purpose (introduced and promoted by the Likud Movement) was the prevention of meetings between Israeli left-wing activists and Palestinian representatives. Ultimately, the Supreme Court was forced to decide on the controversial matter, choosing to avoid political confrontation by imposing prison sentences on those leftist activists that took part in such contacts. The inconsistencies in the amendment's selective application was evident following meetings between the Rabin Administration and PLO representatives in Oslo in the summer of 1993.[61] This incident lends further credence to the assumption that groups with weak political backing are more likely to be labeled "terrorist", regardless of whether they engage in violence or not. In the same vein, it is clearly apparent that counter-terrorist policy and the enforcement of counter-terrorism measures are substantially influenced by political interests – and in this particular instance, the political sway one party has over another in the attempt to preserve a coalition and balance of forces.

The Jewish Underground

A further confirmation of the "politicization" of counter-terrorism is the case of the Jewish Underground. But prior to an elaboration of this process, a brief historical account is necessary of the context and formation of the movement. The 1967 Six Day War culminated in the occupation of territories more than three times the size of Israel and completely rewrote the political discourse within Israel. The crucial change was the renewed prominence of the political division between left and right, and, in this case, the predominant issue was the future of territories seized in the war.[62] The right-wing maximalist camp coalesced around the idea of Erez Israel, a greater and indivisible Land of Israel, whereas the minimalist left-wing programme was the promotion of territorial compromises with the Arab world in exchange for peace.[63] This new prominence of the political-ideological cleavage put an end to a relatively lengthy period of time almost completely without Jewish terrorism. The most notable organization on the hawkish side of the Israeli political map, and which ultimately gave birth to the Jewish Underground, was Gush Emunim (Bloc of the Faithful),[64] a movement that was devoted to the ideology of Erez Israel and was inspired by the theology of Rabbi Kook.[65] Gush Emunim's principal mode of action was the construction of illegal settlements which occasionally led to confrontation with the official legal authorities, such as the case of the Sebastia settlements in July 1974.[66] Despite their illegal civil disobedience, the Israeli government and the Attorney-General, with the endorsement of Prime Minister Yitzhak Rabin, chose to avoid bringing the settlers to criminal trial. The decision to refrain from prosecuting these settlers, argued Gillon, was highly politicized, as the rule of law was subordinated to the Prime Minister's intention to avert needless political confrontation with settlers supported by a strong political lobby.[67] Gillon even asserted that the decision not to enforce the law against these offenders in practical effect opened a path towards the radicalization of several organizational members, which eventually led to the most sophisticated Jewish terror organization in Israeli history. Among other actions, the organization was responsible for severely injuring the mayors of Ramallah and Nablus in the summer of 1980 by sabotaging their cars,[68] and also for the attack on the Islamic College in Hebron three years later. In reaction to these incidents, Prime Minister Menachem Begin ordered the security service to take forceful action against the perpetrators. The GSS was activated, ordered to adhere to the "reactive policing" approach, and proceeded to gather evidence in a serious attempt to bring the culprits to trial. Following intensive investigations with the successful collection of enough incriminating evidence, the police and GSS carried out several arrests and proceeded to interrogate suspects.

According to both Gillon, who led the investigation, and Haggai Segal, one of the detainees, a notable fact surrounding the interrogation of suspects was the gentle manner in which they were conducted, without the use of traditional GSS interrogation methods.[69] As such, despite the involvement of the GSS in the investigation of the Jewish Underground, it would be difficult to classify this as a case of the "expanded criminal justice" model, especially as Shabak's (GSS) role in this case was in effect restricted to standard police procedures. Unlike the treatment of the underground movements of the 1950s, Israel elected this time not to use the "expanded criminal justice" methods, as it refrained from declaring the organization to be terrorist, establishing a special court or exercising other administrative measures against members and supporters of the Jewish Underground. In fact, all members of the movement stood criminal trial and were brought before a criminal court of law. However, after their convictions of serious criminal offenses (which included murder), extraordinary political pressure was applied to grant them pardon. This pressure was so effective that in a matter of years not one single prisoner member of the Underground remained behind bars. Among the reasons why Israel chose to adhere almost entirely to the "criminal justice" model in addressing the most sophisticated and brutal Jewish terror organization that Israel had known, is the fact that it was a result of exactly the same reasons that had led it to react to marginal and minimally threatening organizations with the security measures of the intermediate model – marginality factor. The Israeli ruling elite and shapers of defence policy opted not to respond to the Jewish Underground according to the reality of the threat it posed or the severity of its actions, but rather on the basis of the political clout to which it had access. The Underground movement benefited from broad public support, principally among religious Zionists and right-wing parties, such as the Mafdal and the Tehiyah. Even former Prime Minister Yitzak Shamir unequivocally supported the pardoning of members of the organization.[70]

An additional reason that explains this choice of action pertains to the cultural conceptions held by the security forces and the Israeli political elite. The alliance of the religious Zionists – and wellspring of the Underground – had struck a positive chord and earned a dependable reputation among participants in the Israeli political discourse. Many found them to be not terrorists but a rejuvenated image of the authentic Zionist pioneers. Unlike members of the Kach movement, who had mostly emigrated from the US and the USSR and were in effect strangers to Israeli culture, followers of the Jewish Underground represented the very heart and core of the Zionist-Israeli experience.[71] These devotees even "captured the hearts" of their interrogators. "The atmosphere in the interrogation of the Jewish Underground suspects", described Gillon, "was quite exceptional. Most of the people arrested were considered for all intent and purposes 'excellent boys', they were officers in the IDF and many of them had in fact served in units that had worked closely with Shabak. Then, all of a sudden, there was a situation of interrogator and suspect and they were sitting on the side of those being interrogated, in the role of the accused."[72] Despite the gravity of the acts they had committed, the personal background of the terrorists and their political backing as well were crucial factors that completely changed the counter-terror policy applied toward them.

Uzi Meshulam's group

The most evident use of the "criminal justice" model in Israel can be gauged from Israel's response to the Yehud affair. This incident began in the winter of 1994 when a religious sect, led by the charismatic Rabbi Uzi Meshulam, began to fortify and occupy his house. The declared goal of this small religious sect was to urge the government to investigate the disappearance of Jewish Yemenite children in the 1950s, a social wound that has yet to heal within Israeli society.[73] In order to cast off all doubt with regard to the group's unquestionable militancy and potential for terror, Assaf Hafetz (Chief of Police/Inspector-General at the time) described Meshulam and his followers as an "unprecedented and extreme nationalist terror group"[74] in a government session. In an effort to justify this description, Hafetz added that the actions committed by the group could not be anticipated and may lead to disastrous consequences. There were some grounds for these concerns, as Meshulam's group exhibited a dangerous potential in the first days of their fortification, especially when his followers threatened to use live weapons if security forces would take action against them. However, the Israeli response was to handle them with much restraint and to remain within the narrowest limits of the "criminal justice" model. The arrest of the members was conducted by Israeli Police, who opened fire only after the first shots were fired by the Meshulam house occupants. After their arrest, Meshulam and his followers stood trial under standard criminal procedure. Even during the course of the trial itself, there were reports that warned that Meshulam devotees (dispersed in different locations around the country) intended to attack law officials and take revenge with acts of violence in the wake of the outcome of the rabbi's verdict.[75] Nevertheless, these reports did not lead policy-makers to implement the Prevention of Terror Ordinance against the group or take administrative measures against its members.[76]

An effort to understand why Israel chose this course of action and strictly adhered to the "criminal justice" model, reveals similar underlying political factors to those that seem to have influenced official Israel's treatment of the Jewish Underground. As for the degree of the marginality factor, Uzi Meshulam and his believers were not favoured with a broad base of support similar to that enjoyed by members of the Jewish Underground. Nonetheless, they were successful in raising an issue onto the public agenda that touched a raw nerve in the history of Israeli society. Subsequent to the group's encampment in the Meshulam residence, a political front emerged consisting of public figures and members of the Knesset that demanded an official state-run commission of inquiry into the Yemenite children affair. As a result, the Israeli government was considerably interested in dropping the matter of the abducted Yemenite children from the political agenda, principally for fear that it would lead to ethnic-based riots. It became evident that any aggressive action taken by Israeli law enforcement against Meshulam and his followers would serve as a pretext for keeping the issue in the political spotlight.

While Uzi Meshulam's group operated out of socio-ethnic motivations, traditionally not included in areas considered to be Jewish terror, Israeli policy-makers' adherence to the notion that Jewish terror is solely a result of the ideological cleavage between right and left prevented them from perceiving the fortification of an armed sect with a charismatic leader as a terrorist threat. As a consequence, the security services and "expanded criminal justice" model measures were discarded, and instead the "criminal justice" model was applied. In July 1999, Uzi Meshulam was conditionally released from prison after serving nearly five and a half years of his sentence, as long as he would be responsible for severely restricting the number of people allowed in his house and limiting his connection with the media.[77] After Meshulam's release from prison, the leader chose to retire from political action and his followers have dispersed in all disparate directions.

Conclusion

The goals of this study were threefold. First, the elaboration of the operational aspects of the "war" model and "criminal justice" model in the war against terror and the presentation of the "expanded criminal justice model", whose primary function was to mediate between the two already existing models in the so-called "gray areas". The use of a range of three models offers the possibility of a dynamic continuum, whose main premise rests on the fact that the more aggressive the nature of the selected model of counter-terror, the more that democratic foundations will tend to be sacrificed in that process. For example, the transition from a "criminal justice" model to an "expanded criminal justice" model often requires the forfeit of some democratic fundamentals. The application of this continuum of models to a large extent served the second aim of this study, that is, the analyses of Israeli responses to Jewish terror. Although in the early stages of the state's existence those in charge elected to counter terror with the means of the "war" model, a democratization process of Israel has gradually pervaded over the course of years and this, to a certain degree, has restricted measures taken against Jewish terror, specifically limiting the approach to the "expanded criminal justice" model and, indeed, occasionally to the "criminal justice" model. This leads us to the third goal of trying to find causes for the transition from one model to another. Analysis of the Israeli context, from the perspective of the theoretical literature, yielded a two-dimensional analytical framework, exogenic and endogenic. At each level there are subordinate explanations. The exogenic explanation attempts mainly to underscore the weakness of the liberal element in Israel's political culture and, at the same time, give emphasis to the security element, a fact that enabled policy-makers to adopt militant counter-terror measures. At the same time, from another angle, it became clear that the endogenic approach provides three principal explanations. First, there is the marginality factor, that is, the smaller the organization and the less support it has, the greater its vulnerability and the chances that more rigid models will be applied against it even if the threat of terror is negligible. Secondly, there is the so-called politicization factor. According to this line of reasoning, the decision to adopt either model is a result of factors not necessarily related to the degree of threat posed by the organization, rather, they may reflect the political interests of leaders or certain demands made by other coalition parties. The third explanation focused on the prevalence and adherence of the defence establishment to past conceptions, a fact that led to inconsistencies in counter-terror policies when speaking of new and unfamiliar types of terror.

Notes

1   Paul Wilkinson, *Terrorism and the Liberal State* (Houndsmill: Macmillan 1986), p. 125.
2   Peter Chalk, "The Liberal Democratic Response to Terrorism", *Terrorism and Political Violence* 7/4 (1995), p. 17; and Peter Chalk, "The Response to Terrorism as a Threat to Liberal Democracy", *Australian Journal of Politics and History* 44/3 (1998), pp.373–388.
3   For example, see: Peter Chalk, "EU Counter-Terrorism, the Maastricht Third Pillar and Liberal Democratic Acceptability", *Terrorism and Political Violence* 6/2 (1994), pp.103–145; Peter Chalk, "The Liberal Democratic Response to Terrorism", *Terrorism and Political Violence* 7/4 (1995), pp.10–44; Peter Chalk, *West European Terrorism and Counter-Terrorism: The Evolving Dynamic* (Houndsmill: Macmillan Press 1996); Ronald D. Crelinsten, "The Relationship Between the Controller and the Controlled", in Paul Wilkinson and Alasdair M. Stewart (eds.), *Contemporary Research on Terrorism* (Aberdeen: Aberdeen University Press 1987), pp.3–23; Ronald D. Crelinsten, "Terrorism, Counter-Terrorism and Democracy: The Assessment of National Security Threats", *Terrorism and Political Violence* 1/2 (1989), pp.242–269; Ronald D. Crelinsten, "The Discourse and Practice of Counter-Terrorism in Liberal Democracies", *Australian Journal of Politics and History* 44/1 (1998), pp.389–413; Ronald D. Crelinsten and Alex Schmid, "Western Responses to Terrorism: A Twenty-Five Year Balance Sheet", *Terrorism and Political Violence* 4/4 (1992), pp.307–340; Charles Dunlop, "The Police-ization of the Military", *Journal of Political and Military Sociology* 27/2 (1999) pp.217–232; Fernando Reinares, "Democratic Regimes, Internal Security Policy and the Threat of Terrorism", *Australian Journal of Politics and History* 44/3 (1998), pp.351–371; G. Davidson Smith, *Combating Terrorism* (London: Routledge 1990); and Paul Wilkinson, "Pathways Out of Terrorism for Democratic Societies", in Paul Wilkinson and Alasdair M. Stewart (eds.), *Contemporary Research on Terrorism* (Aberdeen: Aberdeen University Press 1987), pp.453–465.

4   Ronald D. Crelinsten, "The Discourse and Practice of Counter-Terrorism in Liberal Democracies", *Australian Journal of Politics and History* 44/1 (1998), p.390.
5   Crelinsten, "The Relationship Between the Controller and the Controlled" (note 3), pp.3–23; and Crelinsten, "Terrorism, Counter-Terrorism and Democracy: The Assessment of National Security Threats" (note 3), pp.242–269.
6   Crelinsten and Schmid, "Western Responses to Terrorism: A Twenty-Five Year Balance Sheet" (note 3), pp.332–333.
7   Crelinsten, "The Discourse and Practice of Counter-Terrorism in Liberal Democracies" (note 3), p.399.
8   Crelinsten and Schmid, "Western Responses to Terrorism: A Twenty-Five Year Balance Sheet" (note 3), p.334.
9   Crelinsten, "The Discourse and Practice of Counter-Terrorism in Liberal Democracies" (note 3), pp.399–400.
10   Crelinsten and Schmid, "Western Responses to Terrorism: A Twenty-Five Year Balance Sheet" (note 3), pp.333–334.
11   See Robert A. Dahl, *On Democracy* (New Haven, CT: Yale University Press 1998), ch.4.
12   Ehud Sprinzak, *Brother Against Brother: Violence and Extremism in Israeli Politics From Altalena to the Rabin Assassination* (New York: The Free Press 1999).
13   Ibid., p.320.
14   Carmi Gillon, *Shin Beth Between the Schisms* (Tel Aviv: Yediot Aharanot Books and Chemed Books 2000) (in Hebrew).
15   Isser Harel, *The Truth about the Kasztner Murder* (Jerusalem: Edanim Yediot Aharanot 1985); and Yaakov Perry, *Strike First* (Tel Aviv: Keshet 1999).
16   Bruce Hoffman, *Inside Terrorism* (London: Victor Gollancz 1998), pp.48–56.
17   Dan Horowitz and Moshe Lissak, *Trouble in Utopia: The Overburdened Polity of Israel* (Tel-Aviv: Am Oved Publishers 1990), pp.59–60 (in Hebrew).
18   Martin Van Crefeld, *The Sword and the Olive: A Critical History of the Israeli Defense Force* (New York, NY: Public Affairs Books 1998), p.81.
19   Sprinzak (note 12), p.22.
20   Chalk, "The Liberal Democratic Response to Terrorism" (note 2), pp.17–18.
21   Horowitz and Lissak (note 17), p.60.
22   Sprinzak (note 12), p.24.
23   Horowitz and Lissak (note 17), p.60.
24   Gad Barzilai, "Centre Against Periphery: Law of 'Prevention of Terrorism' Acts", *Plilim*, 8 (1999), pp.238–239 (in Hebrew).
25   Uri Brener, *Altalena* (Tel Aviv: Hakibbutz Hameuchad 1978), pp.393–396 (in Hebrew), quoted in Sprinzak (note 12), pp.30–31.
26   Menachem Hofnung, *Democracy, Law and National Security* (Aldershot: Dartmouth Press 1996), p.26.
27   Ibid., pp.50–51.
28   Menachem Hofnung, "States of Emergency and Ethnic Conflict in Liberal Democracies: Great Britain and Israel", *Terrorism and Political Violence* 6/3 (1994), pp.347–351.
29   Ibid., p.351.
30   Raphael Cohen-Almagor, "Combating Right-Wing Political Extremism in Israel: Critical Appraisal", *Terrorism and Political Violence* 9/4 (1997), p.90.
31   Hofnung (note 26), pp.193–197.
32   Chalk, "The Response to Terrorism as a Threat to Liberal Democracy" (note 2), p.387.
33   Gillon (note 14), p.424.
34   Crelinsten, "The Discourse and Practice of Counter-Terrorism in Liberal Democracies" (note 2), p.402.
35   Gillon (note 14), p.425.
36   Sprinzak (note 12), p.31.
37   "The Searches and Arrests in Tel-Aviv are Continuing", *Yedioth Aharanot*, 19 Sept. 1948.
38   Barzilai (note 24), p.239.
39   Isser Harel, *Security and Democracy* (Tel Aviv: Edanim Publishers Yediot Aharanot 1989), pp.162–165 (in Hebrew).
40   Gillon (note 14), pp.407–412.
41   Sprinzak (note 12), p.61.
42   "Emergency Laws were Implemented against the Zealots", *Yediot Aharanot*, 17 May 1951.
43   "Bachar: 12 Years, Heruti: 10", *Yediot Aharanot*, 25 August 1953.

44   Benyamin Neuberger, *Democracy in Israel: Origins and Development* (Tel-Aviv: The Open University 1998), pp.30–55.

45   Shmuel Sandler, Robert O. Freedman, Shibley Telhami, "The Religious-Secular Divide in Israeli Politics", *Middle East Policy* 6/4 (June 1999).

46   Gil Merom and Robert Jervis, "Israel's National Security and the Myth of Exceptionalism", *Political Science Quarterly* 114 (autumn 1999).

47   Gad Barziliai, Ephraim Yuchtman-Yaar, Zeev Segal, *The Israeli Supreme Court and the Israeli Public* (Tel-Aviv: Papirus 1994), pp.100, 216 (in Hebrew).

48   Ehud Sprinzak, *Buds of De-legitimate Politics in Israel 1967–1972* (Jerusalem: The Levi Eshkol Center for the Study of Economics, Society and Policy in Israel 1973), p.190.

49   Yair Kotler, *Heil Kahane* (Tel Aviv: Modan Publishers 1985), pp.199–204 (in Hebrew).

50   Gillon (note 14), p.91.

51   Kotler (note 49), p.144.

52   Gillon (note 14), p.92.

53   Sprinzak (note 12), pp.124–130.

54   Cohen-Almagor (note 30), pp.85–86.

55   Ibid., pp.87–88.

56   Personal interview by Dr Pedahzur with Itamar Ben-Gvir, a leading activist of the ex-Kach movement on 1 March 1999.

57   Baruch Karah, "Is That a Way to Persuade a Judge?", *Haaretz*, 30 August 1999.

58   Gillon (note 14), ch. 16.

59   Sprinzak (note 12), p.121.

60   Gillon (note 14), p.70.

61   Barzilai (note 24), pp.242–243.

62   Sprinzak (note 12), p.115.

63   Rael Jean Issac, *Israel Divided* (Baltimore, MD: John Hopkins University Press 1976), chs.3–4.

64   Israel Shahak, "The ideology of Jewish Messianism", *Race and Class* 37/2 (October-December 1995).

65   See Ehud Sprinzak, "From Messianic Pioneering to Vigilante Terrorism: The Case of the Gush Emunim Underground", *Journal of Strategic Studies* 10/4 (1986), pp.194–216; and Ehud Sprinzak, *The Ascendance of Israel's Radical Right* (New York: OUP 1991).

66   Yossi Bar, "Since the Morning Hundreds of Soldiers Evacuated the Settlers without Resistance", *Yediot Aharanot*, 29 July 1974.

67   Carmi Gillon, *Ideologically Motivated Lawbreaking on the Extreme Right within the Context of the Arab–Israeli Conflict* (Thesis submitted in partial fulfillment of the requirements for the M.A. Degree: University of Haifa 1990), pp.121–122 (in Hebrew).

68   Eitan Haber, Taufik Huri, Gad Lior, Yisrael Tomer and Chaim Shibi, "It is Estimated that a Small Jewish Group is behind the Assassinations", *Yediot Aharanot*, 3 June 1980.

69   Gillon (note 14), ch.9; and Haggai Segal, *Dear Brothers* (Jerusalem: Keter Publishing House 1987), ch.17 (in Hebrew).

70   Gillon (note 14), p.156.

71   Noami Gal-Or, *The Jewish Underground: Our Terrorism* (Tel Aviv: Hakibbutz Hameuchad 1990), pp.38–40 (in Hebrew).

72   Gillon (note 14), p. 116.

73   The real motive behind the fortification was apparently the escalation of a quarrel between neighbours.

74   Reuven Shapira, "Meshulam's People Wrote Up a 'Death List' which included Peres, Shachal, Hafetz and Ben-Porat: This is a Nationalist Movement the Likes of Never Seen Before", *Haaretz*, 15 January 1996.

75   Reuven Shapira, "Fears in the Shabak that Meshulam's People Might Carry Out Exhibition Attacks", *Haaretz*, 17 February 1995.

76   Interview by Dr Pedahzur with Tzadok Chugi, Uzi Meshulam's lawyer, 2 March 1999.

77   Nina Pinto, "Uzi Meshulam Has Been Released from Prison", *Haaretz*, 8 July 1999.

20 The leaderless nexus

When crime and terror converge

Chris Dishman

International law enforcement pressure is forcing criminal and terrorist organizations to decentralize their organizational structures. Mexican law enforcement efforts are causing drug cartels in Mexico to break into smaller units. Many of the leaders who constituted Al Qaeda's command and control leadership are under arrest or dead, forcing bin Laden to play a more inspirational role, no longer micromanaging attacks as he did for the 11 September spectacular. Even groups that still maintain some hierarchical structure, like the terrorist group Hezbollah, have little control over their extensive networks.

The "flattening" of these groups is creating new and dangerous opportunities for collaboration between criminals and terrorists. The actions of criminal underlings or terrorist operatives are not as constrained because criminal or terrorist "headquarters" are no longer able to micromanage employees. Lower to mid-level criminals and terrorists are taking advantage of their independence to form synergistic ties between the two groups. Some political militant groups have also introduced financial incentive systems to recruit and retain militants. Because members join to make money, they will quickly set ideological goals to the side if it affects profits.

Criminals and terrorists have collaborated on some level for centuries. As many observers point out, the two groups work toward nefarious ends in the same underground community. This cooperation, however, was usually restricted to lower level criminals and terrorists and even then only for short durations. A Don, Colombian cartel boss, or Snakehead would not put his organization in bed with a terrorist group—not because of higher moral values—but because it was bad for business; cooperation with political radicals would turn unwanted attention onto his group. In the last two decades, however, these bosses have been forced to decentralize their organizations, and the managerial role of the leader has been replaced by a networked organization. In short, Don Corleone can no longer order his *mafiosi* to stay away from drug trafficking.

Nowhere is this dynamic more apparent than in the financing of terrorist and criminal cells that are forced to generate funds independently without assistance from leadership. International money laundering crackdowns are making it more difficult for terrorist financiers to quickly and continually send money to both their operatives and the more limited bank accounts of the terrorists themselves. Low- to mid-level terrorist and criminal actors are forced to find their funding sources, fraudulent documents, transportation, and safe houses. Mid to lower-level criminals—who have quickly risen to greater levels of prominence in decentralized structures—have few qualms working with terrorists, in spite of the fact their ultimate boss would certainly disapprove of such an arrangement. The result is that a *leadership nexus* has emerged between criminals and terrorists; a phenomenon with far-reaching implications that should be a major concern for law enforcement and intelligence.

The rise of networks in corporations, transnational criminal organizations (TCOs), and terrorist groups

Early in the twentieth century, industrialists like Henry Ford brought hierarchies to new heights. Hierarchies enabled businesses to mass produce and mass distribute goods and services. Companies were large, maintained tight control over their operations, provided clear roles for each worker, and asked workers to perform specialized tasks.[1]

The dawn of the Information Age, which brought a different set of factors for corporate success, quickly strained the rigid hierarchical organization. Speed, flexibility, integration, and innovation became ingredients for success in the modern era. In a hierarchy, boundaries exist between managers and the rank and file (ceilings and floors) and "walls" divide each function or specialization within the company.[2] Information is compartmented within the upper levels of the organization while the workers perform specialized tasks or functions.

Profits plummeted when hierarchical corporations could not adjust to the demands of the Information Age. Some companies realized that the hierarchy was impeding their success and radically changed their organizational structure to adapt to the new environment.[3] General Electric (GE), for example, implemented a "Workout" program that created permeable boundaries and shifted resources to support its processes versus functions. Workers learned new capabilities and assumed new responsibilities. Information was no longer compartmented and senior managers shared the company's goals and objectives with the rank and file.

The Information Age has not just had severe implications in the business sector, but also for terrorism and organized crime. In the last 20 years, criminal and terrorist organizations have undergone their own versions of GE's "Workout" program. Terrorist and criminal organizations began to transform their own hierarchical structures into networks. Some, like Al Qaeda, expanded the size and importance of networks already imbedded in their traditional hierarchical organizations, whereas others evolved from a networked group into a more complex horizontal design. Unlike the business community, low profits did not drive these organizations to seek change; law enforcement and intelligence, which began to successfully root out subversive organizations, forced illegal armed groups to find new ways to evade authority and become more resilient. Criminals and terrorists needed to ensure that their organization would not collapse if the main leader or leaders were arrested or killed.

John Arquilla and David Ronfeldt, pioneers in the discussion of network design, describe networks as the organizational cornerstone of a new mode of conflict.[4] Networks contain dispersed nodes—either cells or individuals—internetted together by similar beliefs, ideology, doctrine, and goals. There is no central command, headquarters, or single leader. Cells communicate horizontally and rely extensively on technology to facilitate the heavy communication necessary for networks to carry out operations or tasks. Participants in a network can range from the ultra-committed, to individuals who participate for only short periods.

Modern religious terrorist organizations, more so than criminal ones, have aggressively adopted networked structures in the face of intense counterterror actions. Domestic terrorist groups aiming to overthrow closed-political regimes learned quickly that a network provides resilience. Islamist groups in Egypt, for example, have been forced to radically change their organizational structure to be resilient in the face of suffocating counterterror operations.[5] Since 11 September, pressure against international terror organizations like Al Qaeda has also forced those groups to rely more on networks to organize, prepare for, and carry out attacks.

Terrorists have not always used networks extensively. Marxist terrorist groups, for example, were organized along hierarchical lines.[6] Many of these groups were state sponsored, which necessitated a tight line of control from the state liaison to the group's leader. The state needed a single person or group of persons to interface and give assurances about operations, goals, and so on. Any rogue actions by the terrorists could undermine the state's larger political objectives.

A networked organization can still contain hierarchical components. A command cadre, for example, can be imbedded within one node of the organization. There could also be an overarching hierarchy that only uses a network for tactical operations. Terrorist organizations that emerged in the 1980s and 1990s adopted this mix of network and hierarchy. Hezbollah, which emerged in earnest in 1982, is a purposeful blend of hierarchy and network.[7] While the hierarchy enables Hezbollah to control parts of Lebanon and participate in state politics, the network gives Hezbollah financial, religious, social, and military support inside and outside of the country. The network is comprised of Hezbollah followers guided by religious clerics on important political, social, or military subjects. As Hezbollah has no "membership," its leaders rely on the clerics and their own following to influence others to work toward the organization's interests. Hezbollah's hierarchy, in contrast, has formal and direct links between its organs. Its structure includes the highest authority, the decision-making *shoura* (council), which is made up of seven special committees: ideological, financial, military, political, judicial, informational, and social affairs. The committee's members are elected every two years and it is headed by the Secretary General. Hezbollah also contains other hierarchical elements including a Politburo and an Executive *shoura* that is responsible for implementing the high council's decisions. The Deputy Secretary General of Hezbollah outlined the decision to pursue a mixed structure: "We concluded at the end (of organizational discussions) that we needed a structural organization which was in some respects rigid enough to be able to prevent infiltration by the enemy and at the same time flexible enough to embrace the maximum sector of people without having to go through a long bureaucratic process of red tape."[8]

Another organization that maintained a mix of network and hierarchy was the Shining Path, a Maoist guerrilla group in Peru that aimed to overthrow the government with a People's Revolution. Before its dismantlement, the Shining Path's hierarchy consisted of a National Directorate, a Central Committee, and several regional commands.[9] Unlike Hezbollah, however, the hierarchy was not a collective body where everyone was given an equal vote. In fact, the hierarchy was designed to implement the decisions of one person, Abimael Guzman, who alone decided the group's strategy, objectives, and aims. The "rank and file" members comprised the network of the organization. They were organized into cells that had little contact with the hierarchy. The network allowed the Shining Path to operate over a vast geographic area because the widespread rank and file could make decisions without guidance from the command cadre.

Like modern terrorists, law enforcement crackdowns on transnational criminal organizations (TCOs) have forced criminals to expand their use of networks. Networks facilitate illegal commerce and help TCOs avoid and respond to law enforcement. Drug trafficking organizations in Mexico, in particular, have been forced to decentralize as law enforcement continues to decapitate the leadership of their organizations.[10] Mexican authorities have arrested key members of 3 different cartels within a 14-month period.[11] Mexico's senior counterdrug official noted that a result of the spate of drug arrests is that drug leaders are realizing that their organization will become disorganized and chaotic if its hierarchy is decapitated.[12] Cells begin to act independently without regard for the organization in order to make money. Leaders understand that this disarrayed organization is even more susceptible to continuing law enforcement pressure.[13] According to the official, one cartel has organized into a "horizontally-structured business council" to sustain its operations in face of intense law enforcement pressure.[14]

Members of drug trafficking organizations (DTOs), including Mexican drug trafficking organizations, are being pushed further from their traditional center of gravity, with the leadership forced to maintain distance from the members in order to evade law enforcement. Criminal expert Phil Williams notes that many criminal organizations still use some form of hierarchical design, only incorporating or expanding networks where needed. Williams outlines a framework for a networked criminal organization: a core, composed of tight-knit leadership and a periphery consisting of expendable, networked criminals.[15] This organizational mutation is probably only temporary—a transition point from a traditional hierarchical criminal group to a fully networked organization. The vulnerability of a core, even within a networked organization, will probably compel criminal leaders to further flatten their organizational structures.

The role of a terrorist leader in different organizational structures

Martha Crenshaw, an authority on terrorist organizations, believes that one of the most important jobs of a terrorist leader is preventing the defection of persons to the aboveground world or to another radical organization by creating an attractive incentive structure.

> Leaders ensure organizational maintenance by offering varied incentives to followers, not all of which involve the pursuit of the group's stated political purposes. Leaders seek to prevent both defection and dissent by developing intense loyalties among group members. ... Leaders maintain their position by supplying various tangible and intangible incentives to members, rewards that may enhance or diminish the pursuit of the organization's public ends.[16]

The creation of an incentive structure, as highlighted by Crenshaw, was an important characteristic of a leader managing an illicit hierarchy. Now, many terrorists groups have transformed into networked organizations, radically changing the role of the leader. At a minimum, a network has no single leader or command cadre that manages and oversees the organization. Sometimes there are no leaders at all, or leaders might be imbedded in various network nodes, or cells, but without authority over the broader organization (see Figure 20.1). One of the advantages of a network is that there is no leader who assumes so much responsibility that his or her arrest or death derails the organization's mission and capability. The use of networks is almost a natural evolution in response to a law enforcement strategy designed to decapitate the leadership of criminal or terrorist organizations—a hierarchy attacking a hierarchy. In addition to networks, there is another type of organization with no leader—leaderless resistance. This form of organization has no network, no leaders, and cannot be described as "flat" because it only consists of single individuals or very small groups who are not tied to any other organizations—vertically or horizontally.

The role of leaders in these types of organizations merits some discussion.

Hierarchical

In a hierarchical organization, the leader plays a direct role managing the activities of the organization. The leader acts as a Chief Executive Officer, delegating authority to subordinates and maintaining clear chains of command. The hierarchical organization is structured to facilitate top-to-bottom guidance. Ideas are rarely presented from the bottom-up, but even if they are, the group's leaders retain veto power over the idea. The leaders rely on subordinates with different areas of responsibility (i.e., security, financial, recruitment, etc.) to carry out their direction. Hierarchical leaders can be micro-managers; they will punish a low-level subordinate for a mistake, or direct a small activity or operation. Most importantly, however, the leader ensures the organization's operations ultimately support its goals and objectives. In sum, a hierarchy creates a cohesive monolithic unit that acts within well-defined parameters.

The Provisional Irish Republican Army (PIRA), a typical hierarchical organization, offers some insights. The PIRA is organized like a business, with positions, responsibilities, and authority dispersed in a pyramid-shaped organization. The Army Council controls and directs the military strategy and tactics of the PIRA, including ordering or vetoing the operations proposed by subordinate elements.[17] Military guidance is passed to either the PIRA's Northern or Southern Command—military elements with areas of responsibility, not dissimilar in organization to the U.S. Unified Command Plan. There is also a General Headquarters staff that oversees all PIRA activities through its ten departments. Overall, the organization proved very effective (although not resilient), because as one expert notes,[18] disputes were always ruled on by higher authorities ensuring a cohesive unit to carry out the leadership's guidance.

Decentralized cell structure

A decentralized cell structure is one characteristic of a networked organization, although not a defining trait. Understanding the leader's role in this form of organization—which is usually prominent in some form of a network—provides insights into the evolving role of leaders within a network.

Arquilla and Ronfeldt describe the structure and role of leaders in one form of network:

> The network as a whole (but not necessarily each node) has little to no hierarchy; there may be multiple leaders. Decision making and operations are decentralized, allowing for local initiative and autonomy. Thus the design may look acephalous (headless) at times, and polycephalous (Hydra-headed) at other times, though not all nodes may be "created equal." In other words, it is a heterarchy, or what may be better termed a "panarchy.[19]

As Arquilla and Ronfeldt note, the major difference in leadership in a decentralized cell structure versus a hierarchy is that a cell structure can have multiple leaders—a panarchy—whose functions and responsibilities change depending on circumstances. The leader is usually the person with the most experience in the cell, and its members naturally defer to this veteran. Within the cell, the leader ensures tasks are carried out appropriately without attracting law enforcement attention. The cell leader is also responsible for external relations, although contact is usually kept to a minimum and the cell retains extensive independence. Along these lines, Marc Sageman, whose examination of Al Qaeda focuses on social networks, believes that hub leaders are dynamic, outgoing personalities with extensive social reach. These persons are able to attract recruits and can help guide them to the training necessary to participate in jihad.[20]

The absence of the top-down guidance existing in a hierarchical organization makes it imperative for the nodes in the network communicate on a regular basis to ensure that each is operating within the context of a larger plan. He or she is also the ideological or doctrinal espouser and watchdog—ensuring that everyone maintains the ideological fervor necessary for the success of the cell and its broader networked organization. This is perhaps the most important responsibility, because the broader networked organization, of which the cell is a part, will only be successful if cell members retain similar goals, aims, and beliefs.[21]

Leaderless resistance

A third type of organization has been coined by experts as "leaderless resistance." Jeffrey Kaplan defines leaderless resistance as:

... A lone wolf operation in which an individual, or a very small, highly cohesive group, engage in acts of anti-state violence independent of any movement, leader, or network of support.[22]

In a leaderless organization, there are no leaders—only perpetrators—involved in an attack. Ideologues goal or motivate the radical masses into conducting attacks. As terrorism expert Jessica Stern notes, "inspirational leaders" encourage their followers to attack targets but the leaders do not provide funding, direct orders, or any other form of tangible support. Anti-abortionists, for example, will raise money for jailed militants, but never participate in any pre-attack measures.[23]

The White Aryan Resistance (WAR) urged followers to conduct violent attacks after Proposition 187, which would bar illegal immigrants from receiving government services in California, was stopped by a Federal court. The leader stated that "Today, California ceased to exist as an Aryan-dominated state. W.A.R. releases all associates from any constraints, real or imagined, in confronting the problem in any way you see fit."[24]

Leaderless resistance was popularized by the right-wing preacher and radical Louis Beam. Right-wing groups such as the Phineas Priesthood and the White Aryan Resistance embraced Beam's vision by ensuring that no formal organization existed in their movements. There is no hierarchy or chain of command between the group's activists and its leadership. Activists do not rely on support from other cells so there is very little—if any—communication between operatives or their cells. Each operative is self-sufficient; they will choose the site of an attack and plan the attack on their own. Interestingly, left-wing groups also adopted Beam's vision of a leaderless organization. The radical environmental group, the Earth Liberations Front (ELF) encourages its followers to create their own cell rather than joining an existing cell because efforts to locate an existing cell could compromise the organization.[25] ELF's cells are independent and autonomous, and members do not know the identities of members in a different cell; the cells are "linked" together by a shared ideology.[26]

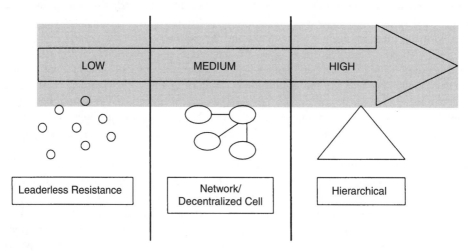

Figure 20.1 The degree of a leader's control in different forms of terrorist and criminal organizations. In a hierarchy, the leader controls almost all aspects of the organization, including recruitment, promotion, delegation of authority, and the planning of major events (i.e., terrorist attack or criminal undertaking). In a decentralized cell structure, there is no single leader or command element that controls all the various nodes in the network. Cell leaders guide the activities of individual cells. In a leaderless resistance movement, the leader's role is restricted to providing inspiration to its members (or potential members) to undertake tasks on behalf of the group.

Al Qaeda is forced to decentralize

Al Qaeda is the most salient example of a terrorist organization that has been forced to decentralize. Since 11 September Al Qaeda has lost roughly 70 percent of its leadership, which comprised the heart of Al Qaeda's command cadre. Experts have given different names to this centralized element, including the Al Qaeda hard core, Al Qaeda hierarchy, Al Qaeda's professional cadre, or Al Qaeda's central staff. This centralized element, created in 1998, coordinates and oversees the functions and tasks of Al Qaeda, including preparing for and executing terrorist attacks.[27]

Terrorist expert Peter Bergen believes Al Qaeda's centralized structure functions like a corporation, where bin Laden, acting as director, formulates policies in consultation with his top advisors.[28] These policies are implemented by a series of subordinate "committees," the most senior of which is the *shura majlis*, or "Advisory Council," which is attended by Al Qaeda's most veteran leaders and reports directly to bin Laden.[29] Under this council are at least four committees, including a military; finance and business; fatwa and Islamic study; and media and publicity committee.[30] Committee members can serve on more than one committee and sometimes individuals work directly for bin Laden on special assignments.[31] Committee membership is based on family, nationality, and friendship. In this regard, Al Qaeda's command element resembles the mafia: merit and performance play little role in success in the hierarchy.[32]

Bin Laden utilizes this structure to carry out spectacular mass attacks. The military committee, for example, plans and executes attacks for Al Qaeda, conducts surveillance, gathers intelligence, and trains members in military tactics.[33] The head of Al Qaeda's military committee prior to 11 September, Khalid Sheikh Muhammad, conceived and helped plan the plot to crash airliners into symbolic U.S. targets.[34] Bin Laden operates both within and outside this structure. For the most important terrorist attacks, bin Laden dealt directly with those executing the plot. The National Commission on Terrorist Attacks revealed, for example, that bin Laden played a very "hands-on" role in planning the 11 September attacks: he handpicked the operatives that participated in the operation; he cancelled a planned operation to crash airliners in Southeast Asia; he personally interceded to keep an operative in the plot who Muhammad wanted removed; and rejected several shura members' recommendations to abort the attacks.[35] Although the degree of bin Laden's involvement, as revealed by the Commission, could be overstated, it's clear that at a minimum he was heavily involved in operational decision making.

The loss of Al Qaeda's Afghanistan haven, and the death or arrest of many of its senior leaders, has forced Al Qaeda to decentralize. Because communication links between Al Qaeda's centralized command and its operatives have been disrupted, bin Laden and his central staff now play a less direct role in planning attacks.[36] Al Qaeda's operational commanders and cell leaders exert more authority and make decisions that used to be under bin Laden's purview.[37] Although it's unclear to what extent the committees are still functioning, bin Laden's essential need for secrecy since 11 September suggests that at a minimum, the committees are not operating as efficiently as before. According to J. Cofer Black, the State Department's Counterterrorism Coordinator, some terrorist cells have delayed attacks because of communication mix-ups between the group and Al Qaeda's leadership. Black cites the attack on the Muhaya housing compound in Riyadh as an example of the lack of clear direction Al Qaeda is providing to its network. The attack resulted in the deaths of many Muslims during Ramadan and as Cofer dryly noted, "was a public relations disaster"— the attack awoke the dormant Saudi counter-terrorism apparatus that began to flush out Al Qaeda cells.[38] Additionally, the international financial crackdown on Al Qaeda's finances has probably hurt the finance committee's ability to fund operations worldwide.

The negative results of decentralization: criminal, terrorist boundaries less clear

Al Qaeda provides a sharp illustration of a terrorist group forced to decentralize. Many other criminal and terrorist organizations also use networks to plan terrorist attacks or run illicit rackets. In the case of Al Qaeda, decentralization has probably hurt the organization's ability to carry out spectacular terrorist attacks. Nevertheless, the proliferation of international criminal and terrorist networks like Al Qaeda pose new threats to stability. Because networks marginalize or eliminate the command cadre, cells and nodes now have expanded roles and responsibilities. These lower to mid-level members define the organization, its actions, its direction and its goals. The activities of these operatives, who are the critical pillars of terrorist and criminal organizations, are no longer constrained by a leader or elder. This freedom allows individuals or small cells to pursue multiple nefarious ends, even at the expense of broader organizational goals. Although political[39] and financial aims are two distinct, usually incompatible ends, lower and mid-level operators do not wrestle with such academic distinctions. A criminal seeks to keep the status quo, stay out of the limelight, not commit collateral violence, and make money. A terrorist in contrast seeks attention, wants to commit collateral violence, and wants to alter the status quo. Lower to mid-level cell leaders are not concerned with incompatible goals, however, and without oversight will pursue personal and organizational agendas.

Historically, the distinction between a criminal and a terrorist has not always been clear. Many terrorists use crime to generate revenue to support their ultimate political goal, whereas some criminals use illicit funds to support radical political causes. Even prior to 11 September, Al Qaeda directed its cells to be financially self-sufficient.[40] Some criminals use terrorism (as a violent tactic) against authorities if a large-scale crackdown on their organization occurs. Nevertheless, within hierarchical organizations there is still some degree of leadership control that could bring the organization back on course should the organization's goals begin to stray from the original cause.[41] An organization that is completely decentralized, or contains a large decentralized component, is usually unwilling or unable to control the activities of its members. This dynamic

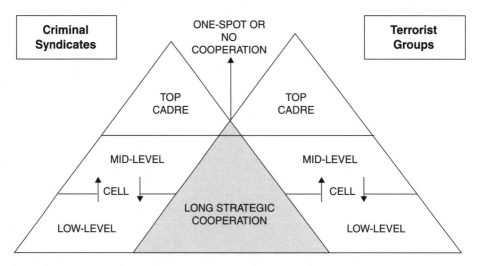

Figure 20.2 Graphic depiction of a new dynamic where low- to mid-level criminals and terrorists create strategic alliances with each other. These lower to mid-level members are the pillars of decentralized criminal and terrorist organizations, and cooperation between the two will lead to new challenges for law enforcement authorities.

is most applicable to criminal syndicates, where the transition from hierarchy to a decentralized network has sometimes created an "every cell for itself" atmosphere. Cash-strapped cells are now willing to conduct any crime in order to stay afloat.[42] These crimes could include operations previously "out of bounds" for most transnational organized criminal groups, including smuggling weapons of mass destruction, creating fraudulent documents for terrorists, or smuggling terrorist personnel. These cells are also no longer constrained by a leadership that prohibited interaction with terrorists because of the unwanted law enforcement attention such activities would bring.[43]

In addition to being unable to control its members, a decentralized network is unable to provide continuous financial assistance to its nodes. The need for secrecy and resiliency between nodes in the network means that money is not often passed between nodes or amassed in a single node in the network. There is no "terrorist bank" that a member can go to request funds in a decentralized network. Because of these financial difficulties, many terrorist nodes have taken an unprecedented foray into organized crime to raise money for their financially depleted cell or hub. Al Qaeda cells and hubs, for example, are deeply involved with drug trafficking in Afghanistan and have purchased illegitimate diamonds from rebels in Africa.[44] In December 2003 coalition forces seized three vessels smuggling heroin and hashish in the Persian Gulf that were probably tied to Al Qaeda operatives.[45] Far-flung Hezbollah networks have also generated a significant amount of money. According to one official, Hezbollah received anywhere from $50–$100 million from the tri-border region in South America. Two Hezbollah operatives in Cuidad del Este, Paraguay are estimated to have moved $50 million to Hezbollah from 1995 until their arrest in 2001. The cell raised money through counterfeiting, money laundering, and extortion.[46] A Hezbollah cell in North Carolina took advantage of the tax difference on cigarettes sold in North Carolina and Michigan to net over $7.9 million. Law enforcement authorities believe that terrorist groups in the United States continue to smuggle cigarettes, netting an average of $2 million on each truckload of the product.[47]

Dangerous dynamics emerge

Two phenomenon result from the increasing authority of low- to mid-level criminal and terrorist leaders and their need to survive in a decentralized environment. First, these leaders will increasingly seek to collaborate with criminal or terrorist counterparts outside of the organization for extended periods of time. These new cadre of leaders will be more likely to create strategic alliances with other terrorist or criminal subversives. Second, the decentralized organization will internally transform so that both criminals and terrorists are critical ingredients in the organization's structure.

External convergence

Past criminal/terrorist alliances were usually short-term relationships that existed on a case by case basis only. These were "one spot" arrangements, where terrorists or criminals would collaborate for only short periods of time.[48] Terrorists might provide bomb-making skills to a criminal group for a set fee, but the relationship would end after the training was over. In 1993, for example, some reports alleged that Pablo Escobar hired National Liberation Army (ELN) guerrillas to plant car bombs because Escobar's organization could not carry out such attacks.[49] One-spot arrangements can also include single transactions between criminal and terrorist groups. In one example, four members of the United Self-Defense Groups of Colombia were arrested in Houston, Texas when they tried to exchange $25 million of cocaine and cash for shoulder-fired anti-aircraft missiles and other weapons.[50]

From now on, criminal and terrorist cell or hub leaders will build long-term alliances with their criminal or terrorist counterpart, allowing each group to benefit from the other's knowledge and experience. In January 2002, members of a Hezbollah drug ring were arrested in "Operation Mountain Express" by U.S. and Canadian authorities. The Hezbollah ring was smuggling pseudoephedrine, a precursor chemical for methamphetamines, from Canada to Mexican criminal gangs in the Midwest. The Hezbollah operatives had established a long-standing criminal alliance with the Mexican drug dealers from which they netted at least millions of dollars that were laundered to terrorists in the Middle East.[51] Although this Hezbollah group laundered the proceeds to a Middle Eastern terrorist group, the cell could have also kept the money to sustain the cell and possibly prepare for an attack. In this respect, long-term alliances radically improve the effectiveness of each cell or small group. Terrorists will be able to raise more money from criminal actions. Ramzi Yousef, mastermind of the 1993 bombing of the World Trade Center, wanted to build a bigger bomb to topple one tower into the other, but he could not because he lacked the necessary funding.[52]

"External" alliances could become internal as the outside party becomes integrated into the network. A decentralized network facilitates these relationships by allowing cells or individuals to participate in the network in any capacity. As Williams states, "networks can be highly structured and enduring in nature or they can be loose, fluid, or amorphous in character, with members coming and going according to particular needs, opportunities and demands. Some individuals or even small organizations will drift in and out of networks when it is convenient for them to do so."[53] Businessmen and criminals who benefit from a guerrilla war economy would probably be folded into a network because their financial security is directly tied to the ongoing war and the guerrilla rebellion.

Hybrid organizations

A second and equally important dynamic is the "hybridization" of criminal or terrorist networks. A model example of a functioning network would consist of cells and members with similar ideologies, motives, and views of success or failure. When cells or nodes begin to pursue their own agendas, the like-minded identity that binds the network together dissolves and a hybrid organization emerges. The new hybrid organization is dominated by persons in cells, fronts, or other organizational components that retain multiple motives and desired end-states. Some Islamic militants, for example, are heavily involved in drug trafficking and reap major profits from the illegal activity. These militants justify drug trafficking because they believe their enemies suffer from drug consumption. In their view, they receive a dual benefit from the crime: they generate profits and hurt their enemies. These profits can be used to support the cell's activities, be invested in personal bank accounts, or given to friends and families. Hezbollah, for example, which has been involved in drug trafficking in Lebanon, views drug trafficking as another weapon to use against its enemies. One Hezbollah *fatwa* (religious edict) stated that "We are making these drugs for Satan America and the Jews. If we cannot kill them with guns, so we will kill them with drugs."[54] In more recent illustration, law enforcement officials investigating the Madrid bombings noted that one of the suspect bombers "justified drug trafficking if it was for Islam ... he saw it as part of jihad."[55]

Identifying a hybrid is difficult. Cells within hybrid organizations are chameleons—criminal by day, terrorist by night. A sleeper cell may not look like a sleeper cell at all; its activities focused on organized crime: extortion, counterfeiting, drug trafficking, and so on. Authorities investigating the Madrid train bombings stated that one of the suspect's drug trafficking activities masked his involvement in terrorism; authorities never considered him part of a terrorist plot.[56] Identifying a hybrid is also challenging because it has no hierarchy from which an analyst can determine aims, goals, and degree of control.

Hybrid organizations form synergistic ties internally to build criminal or terrorist expertise (see Figure 20.2). Cell leaders collaborate with other cells or nodes to maximize criminal gains or prepare for violent attacks. One result is that terrorist cells increase their financial intake by participating in sophisticated organized criminal rings. The examples shown earlier (Al Qaeda and Hezbollah) illustrate the millions of dollars that can be generated from organized crime. As noted earlier, emerging information about the Madrid bombings shows that many of the plotters were heavily involved in drug trafficking. Jamal Ahmidan, one of the cell's ringleaders, allegedly traded hashish for 220 pounds of dynamite used in the attack. He also brought in six drug traffickers who participated in the plot.[57] The result of this criminal, terrorist synergy was a devastating blast that killed 191 people.

Enforcement implications

The breakdown of hierarchical organizations poses a unique challenge for law enforcement and intelligence. Law enforcement's successful strategy of arresting high value targets has forced criminal and terrorist leaders to be less involved in the day to day direction of the organization. The result is a growing independence, sophistication, and number of small cells or criminal gangs that multiplies the number of targets law enforcement must pursue. Decentralized organizations leave few evidentiary trails between the leadership and its cells, and between the cells themselves. Many cell leaders cannot identify other cell members or their support personnel. In Colombia, for example, a senior law enforcement official noted that Colombian traffickers now operate in small, autonomous cells that make it more difficult for law enforcement to discover them.[58] Gathering information about a hierarchical organization was easier because law enforcement agents only needed to recruit one well-placed informant to break up the entire organization.[59]

The combustible mix of lower and mid-level profit-minded criminals and terrorists makes it difficult to delineate between the two. As a result, law enforcement agents working criminal cases could provide critical information on a terrorist cell or plot. Terrorists have traditionally used a criminal support structure in their operations, but now longer term relationships are being established between terrorist cells and criminal organizations. Terrorist cells could in fact become fully involved in profit-driven activities.

Since 11 September, many experts, think tanks, and commissions have debated the need to create a domestic counterterrorism intelligence service separate from the FBI. The 9–11 Commission, which is sure to make heavy recommendations for U.S. intelligence, has already hinted at the possibility of recommending the creation of a domestic intelligence service. Many proposals have emerged, some of which are tweaks of Britain's internal security service, MI5. Two proposals have received the most attention:

- *John Deutch's Proposal.* He proposed the creation of a domestic intelligence service under the Director of Central Intelligence, making the DCI responsible for both the foreign and domestic collection of terrorist threats. This is organizationally different than Britain's MI5 as Deutch's proposal places the service under the Director of Central Intelligence, versus Britain's Home Secretary—which is the closest equivalent of the Department of Homeland Security.
- *Gilmore Commission.* The Gilmore commission recommended the creation of a stand-alone agency to analyze domestic and foreign collected information on foreign terrorist groups. The agency would have the more muscular collection powers established under the post–11

September Foreign Intelligence Surveillance Act (FISA) regulations. It would be the primary coordinating point for sharing information with state and local officials, but would not collect or analyze information on national domestic terrorist groups.

Each proposal contains different components. Some place the new organization under the Director for Central Intelligence; others make it a stand-alone agency, and others not mentioned here recommend that the agency stay within the Department of Justice or the FBI. The common thread between all recommendations is that they separate the investigation of profit-driven crimes from terrorism investigations. At first glance, such a separation seems warranted. For years terrorism has been considered a law enforcement phenomenon, an issue that did not deserve the attention of other higher priority national security interests.

The problem, however, is that separating criminal from terrorist investigations could hinder, rather than help, identify and arrest terrorists. As this article has noted, it is increasingly difficult to label a terrorist a terrorist and a criminal a criminal. Many terrorists and guerrilla movements are engaged in organized crime, and many profit-minded criminals no longer have inhibitions about working with terrorists. Thus a criminal lead could very well trace back to a terrorist. The creation of a terrorism-only agency would create an institutional barrier between the criminal and terrorism analysts.

Conclusion

The transformation of terrorists and criminal organizations from hierarchy to network has dangerous and largely unnoticed implications. With the emergence of decentralized organizations, a centuries-old dynamic between hierarchical terrorist and criminal organizations has begun to change. Criminals and terrorists now have few reservations about cooperating with each other. Many will create long-term strategic alliances to harness each other's expertise—making their groups more dangerous and elusive than ever.

Notes

1   Ron Ashkenas, Dave Ulrich, Todd Jick, and Steve Kerr, *The Boundaryless Organization: Breaking the Chains of Organizational Structur* (Jossey-Bass, San Francisco, 2002).
2   Ibid.
3   Horizontal organization experts, however, still stress that some amount of hierarchy is necessary to guide and orchestrate the horizontal organizations. Ibid.
4   There are many works that provided the basis for this analysis. See John Arquilla and Theodore Karasik, "Chechnya: A Glimpse of Future Conflict," *Studies in Conflict & Terrorism*, 22, pp. 207–229 (1999). "Networks and Netwars," edited by John Arquilla and David Ronfeldt, RAND Report (2001). "In Athena's Camp: Preparing for Conflict in the Information Age," edited by John Arquilla and David Ronfeldt, RAND report (1997). "Networks, Netwar, and Information-Age Terrorism," John Arquilla, David Ronfeldt, and Michele Zanini, *Countering the New Terrorism* (Washington, DC: RAND, 1999).
5   Other paths were also chosen. Some organizations like Islamic Jihad chose to leave Egypt, while others, like the Muslim Brotherhood, gave up violence to pursue a political path.
6   Michele Zanini and Sean J. A. Edwards, "The Networking of Terror in the Information Age," in Networks and Netwars," edited by John Arquilla and David Ronfeldt, RAND Report (2001).
7   Magnus Ranstorp, "Hizbollah's Command Leadership: Its Structure, Decision-Making and Relationship with Iranian Clergy and Institutions," *Terrorism and Political Violence* (Autumn 1994) and from Hala Jaber, *Hezbollah: Born with a Vengeance* (New York: Columbia Press, 1997), pp. 63–66.
8   Hala Jaber, *Hezbollah: Born with a Vengeance* (New York: Columbia Press, 1997), p. 64.
9   Gordon McCormick, "The Shining Path and Peruvian Terrorism," *Inside Terrorist Organizations*, edited by David Rapaport. Also see Gordon McCormick, "The Shining Path and the Future of Peru," RAND report (March 1990).

10 The same dynamic exists in Colombia. See Joseph Contreras and Steven Ambrus, "The DEA's Nightmare: Colombian Targets Get Smart, Techno-Hip and Phenomenally Successful," *Newsweek*, 21 February 2000. Also see Jeremy McDermott and Oscar Becerra, "Mexican Drug Trade Faces Fragmentation," *Jane's Intelligence Review* (May 2003).

11 Ibid.

12 *Tijuana La Frontera*, UEDO Director Says Mexican Drug Cartels Operate Like Companies, 1 July 2003.

13 Ibid.

14 Ibid.

15 Phil Williams, "Transnational Criminal Networks," *Networks and Netwars*, edited by John Arquilla and David Ronfeldt, RAND Report (2001).

16 Martha Crenshaw, "Theories of Terrorism: Instrumental and Organizational Approaches," *Inside Terrorist Organizations*, edited by David Rapaport, p. 14.

17 John Horgan and Max Taylor, "The Provisional Irish Republican Army: Command and Functional Structure," *Terrorism and Political Violence*, 9(3) (Autumn 1997), pp. 1–32.

18 Ibid., p. 3.

19 The network form described in this section is an "all-channel network." See John Arquilla and David Ronfeldt "The Advent of Netwar: Analytic Background," *Studies in Conflict and Terrorism*, 2(1999), p. 193.

20 See Marc Sageman, *Understanding Terror Networks* (Philadelphia: University of Pennsylvania Press, 2004), pp. 70–71.

21 Jeremy Pressman, "Leaderless Resistance: The Next Threat?" *Current History* (December 2003).

22 Jeffrey Kaplan, "Leaderless Resistance," *Terrorism and Political Violenc* (Autumn 1997), p. 43.

23 Jessica Stern, *Terror in the Name of God: Why Religious Militants Kill* (New York: Harper Collins, 2003), pp. 148, 165.

24 Jo Thomas, "New Face of Terror Crimes: 'Lone Wolf' Weaned on Hate," *New York Times* (16 August 1999).

25 Stefan Leader and Peter Probst, "The Earth Liberation Front and Environmental Terrorism," *Terrorism and Political Violence* (Winter 2003).

26 Ibid.

27 "Overview of the Enemy," The National Commission on Terrorist Attacks Upon the United States, Staff Statement No. 15. Rohan Gunaratna, *Inside Al Qaeda* (New York: Berkeley Books, 2002), p. 76.

28 Peter Bergen, *Holy War, Inc.* (New York: Simon and Schuster, 2002), p. 31.

29 Rohan Gunaratna, *Inside Al Qaeda* (New York: Berkeley Books, 2002), p. 77.

30 A recent report by the National Commission on Terrorist Attacks cites two other committees: A foreign purchase committee and security committee. Rohan Gunaratna, *Inside Al Qaeda* (New York: Berkeley Books, 2002), p. 77. U.S.A. v. Usama bin Laden, 98 Cr. 1023 (SDNY) Indictment. Bergen, *Holy War, Inc.* (New York: Simon and Schuster, 2002), p. 31.

31 Rohan Gunaratna, *Inside Al Qaeda*, p. 77.

32 Rohan Gunaratna, *Inside Al Qaeda*, p. 76. U.S.A. v. Usama bin Laden, 98 Cr. 1023 (SDNY) Indictment.

33 Rohan Gunaratna, *Inside Al Qaeda* (New York, Berkeley Books, 2002), p. 77. U.S.A. v. Usama bin Laden, 98 Cr. 1023 (SDNY) Indictment.

34 "Outline of the 9/11 plot," The National Commission on Terrorist Attacks Upon the United States, Staff Statement No. 16.

35 "Overview of the Enemy," The National Commission on Terrorist Attacks Upon the United States, Staff Statement No. 16.

36 Testimony to the House Committee on International Relations, J. Cofer Black, "Al-Qaida: The Threat to the United States and Its Allies," 1 April 2004.

37 It is important to note that it's unclear to what extent Al Qaeda's centralized element still exists and functions. Rohan Gunaratana believes the four committees still existed after the U.S. invasion of Afghanistan. See Rohan Gunaratna, *Inside Al Qaeda*, p. 78. Also see "Overview of the Enemy."

38 Testimony to the House Committee on International Relations, J. Cofer Black.

39 The word "political" will be used loosely in this article. The purpose of "political" is to differentiate it from the financial goals of an organized crime group. As defined here, the word will encompass a wide range of motivations including irredentism, desire to overthrow a government, sectarian violence, and the host of religious motivations including establishment of an Islamic caliphate, pushing the United States out of the Middle East, overthrowing Western-minded Middle Eastern government, etc.

40 Mark Basile, "Going to the Source: Why Al Qaeda's Financial Network Is Likely to Withstand the Current War on Terrorist Financing," *Studies in Conflict & Terrorism*, 27, 169–185, 2004.

41 Some leaders might not be interested in steering the organization back to its original cause in which case the organization's ends and objectives have transformed. See Chris Dishman, "Terrorism, Crime, and Transformation," *Studies in Conflict & Terrorism*, 24, pp. 43–58 (January 2001).

42 *Tijuana La Frontera*, UEDO Director Says Mexican Drug Cartels Operate Like Companies.

43 Chris Dishman, "Terrorism, Crime and Transformation," *Studies in Conflict & Terrorism* (January 2001).

44 Rachel Ehrenfield, *Funding Evil—How Terrorism Is Financed and How to Stop It* (Chicago: Bonus Books, 2003), pp. 33–71. Al Qaeda reportedly taxes Afghanistan poppy growers and heroin refiners; launders money for the Taliban; purchases poppy crops directly; and distributes refined heroin throughout the Balkans to Europe. Al Qaeda cells also laundered over $20 million by purchasing illegitimate diamonds from Liberia and Revolutionary United Front rebels.

45 Series of CNN wire reports describe the boat seizures: 29 December 2003, "U.S. holds al Qaeda drug suspects: Navy intercepts hauls of hashish, heroin and methamphetamines," 20 December 2003, "U.S. seizes drugs on boats in Persian Gulf," 2 January 2004, "More drugs seized in Gulf–U.S."

46 Ehrenfield, *Funding Evil*, pp. 147–149.

47 Sari Horwit, "Cigarette smuggling linked to terrorism." *Washington Post*, 8 June 2004 (New York: St. Martins Press), p. 53.

48 Prepared testimony of Dr. Phil Williams before the House International Relations Committee, 31 January 1996.

49 Patrick Clawson and Rensselear Lee, *The Andean Cocaine Industry* 1998.

50 "Narco-Terrorism: International Drug Trafficking And Terrorism—A Dangerous Mix," United States Senate, Committee on the Judiciary, Opening Statement of Senator Orrin G. Hatch, Tuesday, 20 May 2003. Available at ⟨http://frwebgate.access.gpo.gov/cgibin/useftp.cgi?IPaddress=162.140.64.88& filename=90052.wais&directory=/diskb/wais/data/108_senate_hearings⟩.

51 See Ehrenfield, *Funding Evil*, pp. 11–12. "Drug Money For Hezbollah?," CBSNEWS.COM, Washington, D.C., 1 September 2002. Also see DEA transcript release, "More Than 100 Arrested In Nationwide Methamphetamine Investigation," available at ⟨http://www.usdoj.gov/dea/major/me3.html⟩.

52 Members of the cash-strapped cell were discovered when they attempted to get back their deposit on the rental van. Cited in Testimony of Matthew A. Levitt Senior Fellow in Terrorism Studies. The Washington Institute for Near East Policy Before the United States Subcommittee on International Trade and Finance, Committee on Banking, Housing, and Urban Affairs "Charitable And Humanitarian Organizations in the Network of International Terrorist Financing," 1 August 2002.

53 Williams, "Transnational Criminal Networks," p. 70.

54 Fatwa quoted in Ehrenfield, *Funding Evil*, pp. 143–145.

55 Sebastian Rotella, "The World; Jihad's Unlikely Alliance; Muslim extremists who attacked Madrid funded the plot by selling drugs, investigators say," *Los Angeles Times*, 23 May 2004.

56 Ibid.

57 One of the Madrid suspect bombers was also an informant for authorities investigating a drug gang. See Rotella, "The World; Jihad's Unlikely Alliance."

58 See Douglas Farah, "Colombian Drug Cartels Exploit Tech Advantage," *Washington Post*, 15 November 1999.

59 See Joseph Contreras and Steven Ambrus, "The DEA's Nightmare: Colombian Targets Get Smart, Techno-Hip and Phenomenally Successful," *Newsweek*, 21 February 21, 2000.

21 Fire of Iolaus

The role of state countermeasures in causing terrorism and what needs to be done

Andrew Silke

Introduction

In the nineteenth century, puerperal fever was one of the most feared diseases for women who were planning to deliver a child in a public hospital. Even in the most modern hospitals of the age, as many as one quarter of the patients would die as a result of this disease. Yet what were the root causes of the illness? On one level, child-birth itself was a cause. This, after all, was the reason the mothers were hospitalized and why they were receiving treatment. Yet, in 1847, an Austrian doctor, Ignaz Semmelweis, made a profound breakthrough. He discovered that while the hospital may be treating these women because of childbirth, vast numbers were dying not because labour itself was inherently so dangerous, but because the manner in which the hospitals treated these women was so misguided. Poor sanitary conditions and misguided medical practices rapidly spread infection and disease among patients. One could not solve the problem of patients dying from puerperal fever without first tackling the major cause of these deaths: the way in which hospitals managed people who came for treatment. When Semmelweis introduced the use of proper disinfectants, the death rate plummeted from nearly a quarter of all women to just one patient in a hundred.

The flawed manner in which the medical profession had responded to puerperal fever was a major cause of the disease's spread and lethality. Similarly, the issue of how states respond to terrorism raises questions about the nature of the drivers for terrorist violence. It has been argued by some that state countermeasures should not be seen as a root cause of terrorism. After all, they are primarily a reaction to something which is already occurring. Yet, as with the early medical countermeasures to puerperal fever, while a problem exists in some form before the countermeasures are introduced, these measures themselves can profoundly affect the nature and lethality of that problem. As a driver and facilitator of terrorist campaigns, state countermeasures can have a negative impact far greater than many of the issues which are traditionally seen as root causes of terror. Any comprehensive analysis of the causes of terrorism which does not consider state responses runs the risk of being as limited and flawed as an analysis of puerperal fever which did not consider the practices of doctors and hospitals in the treatment of that disease.

Fortunately, there already exists in the literature on terrorism some appreciation that countermeasures can inadvertently play a major role in causing and sustaining terrorism. Mythology often provides insight into modern life, and the fight against terrorism has on more than one occasion been likened to the mythological struggle against the monstrous Hydra (e.g. Wilkinson 1986). The Hydra was a beast with formidable resilience. In battle it could recover from even the fiercest strikes. When one of its heads was knocked off, two more would grow swiftly in place. Thus the creature could survive a barrage of savage blows, growing stronger in the aftermath of each one, until eventually its foe was exhausted and overwhelmed. Here is a form of violence which rather than being crushed by strong aggressive countermeasures can actually be stimulated and become an even greater threat. Yet, why exactly is this the case? And what lessons are there to be taken away at a time when a so-called "War on Terror" is being prosecuted across the globe?

Ultimately, there is no simple and single solution to terrorism, just as there is no simple and single cause. Responding effectively to terrorism is a very complex matter: a considerable array of responses are available to any regime facing a terrorist threat. As with many things in life, the easy and popular options are often also the most useless and unhelpful. Terrorism, itself the extreme use of violence and force, encourages a view that forceful and violent responses are not simply justified in combating it but are also obligatory. Such reactions are understandable but they can show a poor awareness of human psychology.

One conflict which has shown the painful consequences of forceful (yet popular) responses is that surrounding Northern Ireland. The "troubles" here offer many lessons for anyone interested in solving stubborn and costly terrorist campaigns, but a critical feature is that to get a useful answer one needs first to ask a useful question.

In 1968, the Irish Republican Army (IRA) was a moribund, shrivelled and irrelevant organization. Its membership was tiny and in long decline, its bantam resources diminished further with each year, and its political front, Sinn Fein, was an irrelevance boasting little electoral mandate. How, in the space of a handful of years, could this senile group turn into the largest, best equipped, best funded terrorist organisation in the Western world? From being a parochial joke, how did the IRA become a fiercely supported organization which enjoyed massive local endorsement and tolerance and become the benefactor of millions of pounds of donations from sympathizers spread around the world? A major factor in the growth of the IRA was not the skill and acumen of its leaders and members, but more the ineptitude of the manner in which the state chose to subdue it. As Sean MacStiofain, the Provisional IRA's first Chief of Staff put it:

> It has been said that most revolutions are not caused by revolutionaries in the first place, but by the stupidity and brutality of governments. Well, you had that to start with in the North all right.

> (MacStiofain 1975: 115)

In 1969, the Catholic minority in Northern Ireland were suffering considerable discrimination at the hands of the Protestant majority. Catholics were kept out of the civil service, the judiciary and managerial positions in Ulster's industries. Catholic families had more trouble acquiring state housing than their Protestant counterparts, and even in higher education Catholics were seriously underrepresented. Added to this, Protestant politicians manipulated voting boundaries to minimize Catholic influence in elections.

In August 1969, events came to a head as serious riots erupted first in Derry, then in Belfast. The riots followed in the wake of the annual Apprentice Boys March in Derry. Catholic crowds stoned the marchers and then were attacked themselves in a violent counter-reaction from the Royal Ulster Constabulary (RUC, the largely Protestant police force). The RUC actions were caught on television and led to a strong condemnation from the Irish government, which hinted they would invade the North to protect the Catholic population. Such hints provoked Protestant rioting in Belfast, and Protestant mobs invaded Catholic areas causing widespread violence. Three and a half thousand families (3,000 of them Catholic) were driven from their homes in Belfast during August and September. At least as many Catholics again would be driven from their homes over the next four years, in the largest case of ethnic cleansing in Europe since the Second World War. Protestants in their turn would be driven out of their enclaves in Catholic areas. The principle was the same. It just so happened that more Catholics were at risk (Lee 1989: 429).

As already stated, the IRA had been in serious decline since a failed campaign of violence in the North's border areas which lasted from 1956–1962. By the time of the 1969 riots, the organization was lethargic and lacked a clear structure and focus. The fervent republican ethos had become diluted with socialism, and even the traditional ban prohibiting active involvement in parliamentary politics was being reconsidered. When Protestant mobs swept into Catholic areas, the IRA lacked the manpower or the weapons to offer any kind of resistance. In the aftermath, the letters "IRA" became in Catholic minds, "I Ran Away".

Help for the beleaguered Catholics instead came from the British Army: in hindsight, a surprising source. In mid-August, to the frustration of the Protestants and the relief of the Catholics 10,000 British troops were sent to the North and the rioting was quelled. In the wake of the Army, the British Government imposed substantive reforms meeting virtually all of the demands of the civil rights movement (which shortly disbanded, its aims essentially achieved).

However, the Catholic experience at the hands of the Protestant mobs and the security forces in August meant the matter would not simply dissipate there. In Belfast, disgust at the IRA's failure during the riots led to a split in the organization, with a more focused and militant Provisional IRA (PIRA) abandoning the socialism and emerging politicization that characterized the 1969 IRA. The Provisionals provided a far more attractive and comprehensible façade to their Catholic neighbours, than the older IRA had. Initially they were almost a single-issue group, there largely just to protect the Catholic population. However, a united Ireland offered a long-term solution to this problem as well, and the Republican dimension was quickly to the fore again. Apart from being ideologically more accessible and acceptable, the PIRA benefited from a superior ability to acquire weapons and funds.

The emergence of such a vigorous militant force led to crackdown from the security forces, but this would have unforeseen repercussions. The PIRA benefited enormously from a massive influx of young recruits, who collectively became known as the "Sixty-niners" within Republican vocabulary (Bishop and Mallie 1987). However, it was only in 1970, when crude and oppressive security policies gave many previously uninvolved Catholics ample reason to hate the RUC and British Army, that the recruits began joining up en masse.

For example, in one two month period, over 1,183 Catholic homes were extensively vandalized by the security forces searching for weapons. The searches may not have been as extreme as Israeli demolitions of militants' homes in Gaza and the West Bank, but they were still highly ruinous. Carpets and floorboards were pulled up, doors kicked in, walls and ceilings knocked open with drills and sledgehammers. Yet in just 47 cases were weapons actually found. In 1971 alone, 17,262 Catholic houses were searched in this manner (Lee 1989: 433). The IRA themselves worked to provoke harsh measures from the unfortunate security forces, knowing full well the benefits it would reap in terms of support and recruits. For example, the IRA provoked a riot in Ballymurphy in April 1970. The security forces responded with the widespread use of CS gas alienating Catholics living in the area as well as the rioters.

As Bishop and Mallie astutely observe, it was not deeply felt republicanism which led to the IRA recruitment boom of the early 1970s,

> ... usually it was an experience or series of experiences at the hands of the Army, the police or the Protestants that left them with a desire to protect themselves in the future and also to get back at the state.
>
> (Bishop and Mallie 1987: 151–152)

The trend continued throughout the early 1970s, the IRA provoking the security services who generally lacked the restraint necessary to win the propaganda war. By the end of 1970, PIRA membership had grown from 100 to over 800 in the Belfast area alone. In an attempt to control the burgeoning growth of the PIRA, internment without trial was introduced by the Stormont government in August 1971. Theoretically internment was meant to allow the imprisonment of PIRA activists quickly and efficiently. The reality was that internment was the biggest miscalculation made in an attempt to end the violence. The intelligence on which people were detained was often appallingly poor. Of the first 2,357 people arrested, 1,600 were released without charge after humiliating interrogation (in some cases involving torture), leaving the innocent with a deeply unpleasant, offensive and bitter encounter with the security forces. In its wake and for as long as it continued, PIRA recruitment soared. The killing of 13 people on Bloody Sunday, 30 January 1972, by British Paratroopers in Derry added further to the vilification of the security forces, and did much to cement international support for the PIRA, particularly in the USA. Strong local support, ample manpower, and newly acquired funds and weapons allowed the PIRA to conduct an unprecedented campaign of violence against the RUC, judiciary and Army. The destruction and death toll escalated dramatically. Finally, the British Government stepped in and dissolved Stormont, implementing direct rule. Ultimately, the opportunity to bring about an end to the bloodshed had been lost for decades.

Feeding the Hydra

It has long been recognized that for most members a key motivation for joining a terrorist organization ultimately revolves around a desire for revenge (Schmid and Jongman 1988). Humans certainly have an incredibly strong sense of justice and a desire for vengeance represents a persistent darker side to this. It is not just humans either who can feel this way. Research on our nearest primate relatives reveals similar patterns. For example, Jennifer Scott at the Wesleyan University in Connecticut has found comparable behaviour in gorillas. Physically massive alpha males can still be given a hard time by their subordinates if they appear to behave unjustly (Tudge 2002).

Cota-McKinley *et al.* (2001: 343) define vengeance as "the infliction of harm in return for perceived injury or insult or as simply getting back at another person". These researchers carried out one of the few psychological studies on the subject in recent years and their thoughts on the subject are worth considering in more detail.

One important element of the desire for vengeance is the surprising willingness of individuals to sacrifice and suffer in order to carry out an act of revenge. As Cota-McKinley *et al.* (ibid.: 343) comment:

> Vengeance can have many irrational and destructive consequences for the person seeking vengeance as well as for the target. The person seeking vengeance will often compromise his or her own integrity, social standing, and personal safety for the sake of revenge.

This observation is supported by a number of research studies. For example, in one Swiss study, researchers gave students a cooperative task of the "prisoner's dilemma" kind: all students in the study benefit provided each behaves honourably, but those who cheat will benefit more provided they are not caught. The students were rewarded with real money if they did well and fined if they did not. They were also able to punish fellow players by imposing fines but could only do this by forfeiting money themselves. This meant that those who punished others frequently would end up with considerably less than those who punished others only a little. Despite this, the research found that the participants tended to punish cheats severely, even though they lost out by doing so. People seem to hate cheats so much that they are prepared to incur significant losses themselves in order to inflict some punishment on the transgressors (Tudge 2002).

The principle goes well beyond gorillas and university students. James Gilligan, a prison psychiatrist who encountered some incredibly violent and dangerous individuals during his career, judged that:

> I have yet to see a serious act of violence that was not provoked by the experience of feeling shamed and humiliated, disrespected and ridiculed, and that did not represent the attempt to prevent or undo this "loss of face": no matter how severe the punishment, even if it includes death. For we misunderstand these men, at our peril, if we do not realize they mean it literally when they say they would rather kill or mutilate others, be killed or mutilated themselves, than live without pride, dignity and self-respect.
>
> (Gilligan 2000: 110)

Yet why are people willing to pay such costs? What ends are served by a process which brings such cost to oneself? Cota-McKinley *et al.* (2001) highlight that revenge can fulfil a range of goals, including righting perceived injustice, restoring the self-worth of the vengeful individual, and deterring future injustice. Lying at the heart of the whole process are perceptions of personal harm, unfairness, and injustice and the "anger, indignation and hatred" associated with the perceived injustice (Kim and Smith 1993: 38).

Ultimately, the desire for revenge and the willingness to violently carry it out are tied both to the self-worth of the originally offended individual and also to a deterrent role against future unjust treatment. The vengeful individual "sends the message that harmful acts will not go unanswered" (Kim and Smith 1993: 40). Not only is the goal to stop this particular form of mal-treatment in the future, it is to deter the transgressor from wanting to commit similar crimes; additionally, vengeance may stop other potential offenders from committing similar crimes or from even considering similar crimes.

Not everyone though is equally content with the idea of vengeance or equally prepared to act in a vengeful manner. What little research that does exist indicates that some groups are more vengeance prone than others. Men hold more positive attitudes towards vengeance than women, and young people are much more prepared to act in a vengeful manner than older individuals (Cota-McKinley *et al.* 2001). It is not surprising to find that most recruits to terrorist groups then are both young and male. Some evidence exists too to suggest that religious belief also affects one's attitude to vengeance, with more secular individuals showing less approval to vengeful attitudes.

In-group and out-group stereotyping however can leave both sides depressingly blind to this reality. As Cota-McKinley *et al.* (2001) emphasized in their writing, revenge revolves around the idea of injustice and more particularly redressing injustice. However, appreciating this reality involves accepting that your in-group has behaved in an unjust manner. In a conflict situation, however, stereotyping does not easily allow for accepting ignoble behaviour of the in-group. We are good, they are bad. God is on our side. Everything we do is justified, everything they do is provocative, inhumane and cruel. We are innocent, they are guilty. Or at least, we are more innocent than they are.

Living in denial

In Northern Ireland, even after policies such as internment without trial were abandoned, there were many who continued to argue their benefits. It was argued that the aggressive tactics had after all resulted in weapons seizures and the incarceration of actual terrorists. These were significant achievements against a very serious problem. The counter-productive elements of such policies were ignored or dismissed. As a result throughout the conflict there remained voices who constantly advocated for these policies to be used. After the Shankill bombing in 1993, when a botched IRA bombing killed nine Protestant civilians (including two young girls), mainstream Unionist politicians argued strenuously in public that internment should be reintroduced. This was an understandable reaction given the human needs for justice and revenge. But it also displayed a blindness to the formidable costs hard-line policies bring in their wake. Northern Ireland is not the only arena to show such blindness, however.

On 5 April 1986, a bomb was detonated at La Belle discothèque club in West Berlin, a popular venue with off-duty American soldiers. The explosion killed three people and wounded more than 200 others. Two of the dead and some 80 of the injured were American servicemen. Intercepted embassy messages indicated that the Libyan government had been involved in the attack. In retaliation, the Reagan administration authorized a direct military strike on Libya, codenamed *Operation El Dorado Canyon*.

Ten days later, in the early morning of 15 April, over 40 US warplanes entered Libyan airspace. Flying just over 200 feet above the ground and at speeds of around 540 miles per hour, the planes closed in on targets in Tripoli and the important port city of Benghazi. The Americans devoted special attention to attacking Libyan leader Qaddafi's personal compound at the Sidi Balal naval base, dropping 2,000 pound, laser-guided bombs on buildings Qaddafi was believed to use. After the raid, the Libyans claimed that 37 people had been killed and nearly 100 wounded. Among the dead was Qaddafi's adopted daughter, and two of his sons were among those seriously injured. Qaddafi himself escaped the attack unharmed.

The military strike was extremely popular in the USA. Most Americans believed that the strike sent a powerful warning to states and groups who were contemplating terrorist attacks against American targets. The international community though reacted badly to the bombings and it was condemned outright by Arab nations. In Europe, only the UK provided support for the US action. The British Government allowed the Americans to use airfields in England to launch the attack. In contrast, other European countries, such as France and Spain, refused to even allow the US planes to fly through their airspace.

In the eyes of many experts and professionals, the raid came to be seen as having had a valuable deterrent effect on terrorist activity. For example, a research study conducted at Harvard University by Mark Kosnik (2000), a US Navy commander, concluded that the attack

> left Qaddafi weak, vulnerable, isolated and less able to engage in terrorism ... it put Qaddafi's terrorist apparatus on the defensive, rendering it less able to focus on new terrorist activities ... following the raid Qaddafi reduced his terrorist activity ... [and the attack] did not trigger a new cycle of violence against America.

Similar views are very common in the literature on terrorism and seen in such terms, the retaliation seems an unequivocal success. But is this an accurate assessment?

Many experts expressed serious doubts about the frequent claims of success surrounding *El Dorado Canyon*. Writing shortly after the attack, Michael Stohl (1987) warned against the back-slapping and congratulatory tone which dominated US political discourse on the bombing. The raid was being widely cited as being immediately effective in fighting terrorism, though Stohl pointed out that there was no reasonable evidence to support such claims. By 1998, Bruce Hoffman was able to comment that contrary to many claims, Libyan involvement in terrorism detectably increased in the immediate years after the raid (Hoffman 1998). He could not understand on what basis the original claims of a decrease were being made. Other studies agreed with Hoffman and judged that the accepted view of *El Dorado Canyon* being a success was badly misplaced (Enders *et al.* 1990; Enders and Sandler 1993). These studies were based on trends in international terrorism, and had uncovered that the retaliatory strike led to a significant short-term increase in terrorism directed against the USA and its close ally the UK. In the three months after the raid, terrorist bombings and assassinations against US and UK targets nearly doubled. Significant disruption was also caused when hoax attacks increased by 600 per cent. Libya, far from being cowed into submission, actually increased its commitment to terrorism and started to sponsor even more acts of terrorism than before. These new efforts included an attempt to launch a bomb attack in New York in 1988 (an attempt which was only foiled when the terrorist delivering the bombs was pulled over for a traffic offence in New Jersey). More tragically, the new terror campaign also included the bombing of Pan Am flight 103 in December 1988 over Lockerbie, Scotland, which left 270 people dead. In terms of saving lives, the *El Dorado Canyon* was a dismal failure. In the four years prior to the strikes, Libyan-supported terrorism killed 136 people. In the four years after the strikes, Libyan terrorism left 599 people dead (Collins 2004).

The UK also paid in other ways for its support of the US action. In the months after the raid, Libya secretly shipped an estimated 130 tonnes of weapons and munitions to the Provisional IRA. This haul included at least 5 tonnes of Semtex-H explosive (the bomb which brought down Pan Am 103 is believed to have contained just eight ounces of Semtex-H). Such a massive injection of weaponry virtually guaranteed that the IRA would have the means to continue their terrorist campaign for decades to come if they wished.

Stohl (1987) pointed out that the doctrine the USA adopted for responding to Libyan-sponsored terrorism in 1986 had been consciously modelled on the Israeli approach to tackling terrorism. The Israelis certainly had a deserved reputation for responding to terrorism in a highly aggressive and punitive manner. But how wise was the USA to follow in their wake?

On 11 March 1978, a team of Palestinian terrorists landed on the Israeli coast twenty miles south of Haifa. They promptly killed a US tourist, shot dead the occupants of a taxi, took hostage the passengers of a bus and then drove the bus to Tel Aviv, firing randomly at passing traffic as they went. The event ended in a violent shoot-out with the authorities. By the time it was all finished, 25 civilians were dead, as were nine of the 11 terrorists, and over 70 people had been injured. In response Israel launched a massive invasion of Southern Lebanon. Over 20,000 troops poured over the border backed up by tanks and jets. In the resulting fighting the Israelis killed 2,000 people and left a further 250,000 homeless.

Yet, Brophy-Baermann and Conybeare (1994) in an analysis of terrorist trends, found that the invasion, despite all the ferocity, failed to produce the expected decrease in terrorist attacks against Israeli targets. On the contrary, the level of attacks against the Israelis remained stubbornly stable. In the face of massive international condemnation the Israelis slowly pulled their troops back across the border. However, irked by continuing terrorist attacks, Israel invaded again a few years later in June 1982. This time they were determined to teach an even harsher lesson. In Operation *Peace in Galilee*, the Israelis forced their way deep into Lebanon and after four days of fighting they reached Beirut which was put under siege. The bombardment of the city lasted for over four weeks and casualties were horrendous. Over 18,000 people, most of them civilians, were killed and at least 30,000 were injured. Yasser Arafat and the PLO, the main targets of the Israelis, fled Beirut into exile. In the aftermath, over 1,000 Palestinian refugees were massacred in the city at the hands of paramilitaries allied to the Israeli army. Yet what did all this bloodshed achieve? Did terrorist attacks against Israel decline afterwards? Despite the violence, Brophy-Baermann and Conybeare (1994) again found that *Peace in Galilee* failed entirely to stop or reduce terrorism: attacks continued unabated and undiminished.

Though many continued to portray the various retaliations as successes, there was now mounting evidence that they were distinctly failing to deter terrorism. Worse, they could provoke a backlash of violence, a backlash which often included acts of terror more destructive and more costly than those which had originally goaded the Americans and Israelis to action. The retaliations, rather than cowing the Libyans and the Palestinians away from terrorism, had served only to increase support for extremists.

Why do military retaliations, pre-emptive strikes and other aggressive policies so often struggle to have more of an obvious detrimental impact on terrorism? Though many writers, analysts and security practitioners argue that they do work, the reality as testified by the actual records of terrorist attacks and activity is that retaliations do not have this effect. Why is this the case? The answer lies in understanding why people become terrorists and support terrorist groups to begin with. Labels like extremism, fundamentalism and fanaticism all work to help dismiss terrorism as the aberrant behaviour of an isolated few.

The true irony of retaliation and military force as a tool of counter-terrorism is that in the one moment it is a child of, and a father to, the cycle of vengeance and the common human desire for revenge and retribution. Social psychology has long appreciated that groups in conflicts become extremely polarized in their views of each other. There is a pervasive tendency to show increased appreciation of the traits and characteristics of the in-group (the group to which you as an individual identify with) and to denigrate the members of the out-group. Such denigration includes a tendency to dehumanize members of the out-group. Their members are described as "animals" or "monsters" rather than as people, and their psychology is regarded in suitably similar terms.

One unfortunate result of this common phenomenon is that as well as making it easier to tolerate and support the killing, suffering and harsh treatment of the out-group, it also lulls members of the in-group into thinking that the psychological response of out-group members to events will be qualitatively different to their own. For example, if the out-group kills our members we will not surrender but will continue to struggle on and will persevere to the end. However, if we kill members of the out-group, that will teach them that they cannot win against us and that they must surrender and give in to our will.

Colin Powell, as US Secretary of State, highlighted in his autobiography the dangers of such thinking. He made the point while discussing his reaction to the suicide attack against the Marine Barracks in Beirut in 1983 that killed 241 Marines. In the weeks prior to the attack, US ships off the coast of Lebanon had fired hundreds of shells into the hills around Beirut. This massive bombardment was supposed to support US allies in the area and deter attacks against US positions. Yet as Powell commented:

> What we tend to overlook in such situations is that other people will react much as we would. When the shells started falling on the Shi'ites, they assumed the American "referee" had taken sides against them. And since they could not reach the battleship, they found a more vulnerable target, the exposed Marines at the airport.
>
> (Powell 1996: 281)

Powell's point is an important one. Inevitably, both the out-group and the in-group are composed of people, and how they react to events will not escape this simple fact. The human desire for justice and for vengeance is an extremely common one. Indeed, it is arguably a universal trait of the human condition regardless of language, culture or racial background. Thus when Jews kill Arabs, and Arabs kill Jews, both sides can be expected to be equally vulnerable to issues pertaining to the psychology of vengeance and retribution.

A question of popularity

Because harsh countermeasures attend so closely with the human desire for revenge, they also possess an additional characteristic: they are very popular with domestic audiences. Though not commonly used by most Western democracies, military retaliations have generally been widely approved of in home opinion when they have been employed. In polls and surveys carried out in the aftermath of terrorist attacks, a clear majority consistently voice approval of their own government's use of military force against terrorism. In the USA, for example, although the government has only rarely resorted to such methods in recent decades, each occasion has been regarded with warm and overwhelming domestic approval. Though condemned internationally, the American strike against Libya in 1986 was approved by 77 per cent of US citizens polled. The two strikes authorized by the Clinton administration, first against Iraq in 1993 and then against alleged al-Qaeda interests in 1998, had approval ratings of 66 and 77 per cent, respectively, even though the latter occurred at a time when the president himself was embroiled in humiliating personal scandal (Kosnick 2000). After the terrorist attacks of September 11, the use of American military force in Afghanistan received massive domestic support with 87 per cent of the US population expressing approval. This high level of support remained solid over the following months of fighting as the Taliban collapsed and US troops scoured the countryside for al-Qaeda remnants. The levels of public support for these actions, from Libya to Afghanistan, have always been considerably higher than that seen for other harsh measures democracies utilize in the interests of security and law enforcement. For example, support for the use of capital punishment in the USA has normally fluctuated between 59 and 75 per cent. These are comfortable majorities, but the figures are less than those seen for the various retaliations. It is interesting that there is less public support for the killing of offenders whose culpability has been established by a rigorous, overt and lengthy judicial process, than for the swift elimination of alleged terrorist adversaries in a process which enjoys no such safeguards.

In Israel, too, support for retaliatory measures in response to terrorism has traditionally been high. Friedland and Merari (1985) found that 92 per cent of Israelis surveyed supported the assassination of terrorist leaders, 75 per cent supported the bombing of terrorist bases (even if it jeopardized civilian life), and 79 per cent supported the demolition of houses which harboured terrorists. Friedland and Merari found that males tended to support these measures more strongly than females. Also, religious respondents expressed more support for them compared to secular respondents.

The surveys and polls indicate, again, just how common vengeful attitudes are, and one does not have to be a terrorist (or support a terrorist group) to believe that the use of violence is appropriate and justified even when it incurs the loss of innocent life and bypasses non-violent means of responding to the problem. Ultimately, for any government which wishes to make a widely popular response to terrorist violence (at least among its own domestic population), aggressive military force is by far the most obvious choice.

Yet, despite this, the reality is that liberal democracies in general have tended to avoid overt military retaliations. Countries which have embraced the approach more fully have tended to be states whose status sits uncomfortably with the concept of a liberal democracy. Arguably, the two most ardent users in recent decades were the already much discussed Israelis followed then by apartheid South Africa. The USA, though siding with these two on many international counter-terrorism issues in the 1970s and 1980s, has been far more restrained. Between 1983 and 1998, there were some 2,400 terrorism incidents directed against US citizens and interests throughout the world. More than 600 US citizens were killed in these attacks and another 1,900 were injured (a casualty list which does not include the many non-US citizens killed and injured). Yet, in response to these 2,400 acts of terrorism the US government decided to take overt military reaction in just three cases.

The first of these three terrorist incidents was the already discussed bombing of a West Berlin discothéque in April 1986 which led to a retaliatory strike against Libya a few weeks later. The second was the attempt by Iraqi agents to assassinate former President George Bush using a car bomb when he visited Kuwait in April 1993. The third incident was the near-simultaneous destruction of the US embassies in Kenya and Tanzania by al-Qaeda terrorists in August 1998. These attacks killed 224 people, including 12 Americans, and more than 4,000 were injured.

It is revealing to ask why the USA responded violently to just these three incidents? After all, during that period the country and its citizens had endured thousands of terrorist attacks, but did not use overt military force in response. What was different about these three? Malvesti (2001) argued that while governments spoke about deterring and preventing terrorism in justifying the use of retaliatory military force, the reality was that there were other factors which actually predicted when the USA at least would resort to such measures. Malvesti identified six factors which were common to the three terrorist attacks but which were not seen in the others. She argued that it was this combination of factors which was important in leading to the use of military force. The factors she identified were:

- Relatively immediate positive perpetrator identification: the US authorities were quickly able to identify who they thought was responsible for the attack.
- Perpetrator repetition: this incident was not the first time the perpetrators had attacked US interests.
- Direct targeting of a US citizen working in an official US government-related capacity: Malvesti found that attacks against government officials, military servicemen, etc. seemed to ellicit a retaliatory response whereas attacks against civilians only did not.
- The fait accompli nature of the incident: it was completed by the time the response was being contemplated. So for example, retaliation was not used in response to sieges or kidnappings.
- Flagrant anti-US perpetrator behaviour: the perpetrator had a history of defying and denigrating US interests in a high-profile and open manner.
- The political and military vulnerability of the perpetrator.

The last factor is a particularly important one. When terrorist groups are not vulnerable in these terms, the USA did not move against them. Most of these factors probably also play a major role in explaining the decisions of other states to strike back. For example, these factors appear to be present for most Israeli strikes. The anti-Israeli terrorist groups, whether in the Palestinian territories, Lebanon or further afield are certainly militarily vulnerable to Israel's overwhelming conventional forces. This was proved in the invasions in the 1970s and 1980s and again more recently with the relative ease with which Israeli troops have been able to take control of towns and camps in the Palestinian Authority even when faced with determined opponents such as at Jenin in April 2002.

The political vulnerability of the groups is also well established. While most of the Islamic and Arab world is sympathetic to the Palestinian plight, and hostile towards Israeli military retaliations, the reality is that such states exert little political influence over Israel. The only foreign state with real political clout in Israel is the USA, and US governments have traditionally been tolerant or else largely ambivalent about hard-line Israeli measures in combating terrorism. While this is the case, the terrorist groups themselves will remain politically vulnerable and thus one can expect Israel to feel relatively unrestrained in considering military responses to terrorism.

While government spokespersons will make various defences of retaliatory responses to terrorism, Malvesti's research highlights that other undisclosed factors play an important role in the decision to use these measures. We have already seen though that retaliation does not seem to prevent or deter future acts of terrorism.

Conclusions

In considering the risks associated with the use of harsh measures to combat terrorism, it is worth returning to the story of the Hydra. As we have seen in this review, harsh blows administered in response to Irish, Palestinian and Libyan terrorism did not quell the conflict or subdue the protagonists. The violence continued, often more destructive and intense than before, consuming more lives and resources. How then does one overcome a Hydra?

According to myth, the Hydra was defeated by the most powerful of all the Greek heroes: Hercules. Yet crucially, it was not Hercules' great strength and power which proved the key to victory. In an insane rage, Hercules had killed his family. In order to atone for this act, the oracle of Delphi assigned him a series of labours and the second of these involved going to Lerna to kill the Hydra. The Hydra was the result of a mating between the monster Typhon and the Echidna, and was an enormous serpent with nine heads. Its den was a marsh near Lerna in Peloponnese. It would issue forth to ravage the herds and crops, and its breath was so poisonous that whoever smelt it fell dead. With the help of Athena (goddess of wisdom and prudent warfare), Hercules located the monster's lair. Accompanied by his nephew Iolaus, Hercules forced the monster to emerge from the marshes by means of flaming arrows. Hercules rushed forward to attack the beast, but every time he struck off one of the Hydra's heads two more grew in its place. Iolaus looked on in anxiety as his uncle became ever more entangled in the Hydra's growing heads. The tremendous power and force of Hercules' blows were proving useless in the struggle. Finally, with the great hero engulfed and on the verge of defeat, Iolaus grabbed a burning torch and dashed into the fray. Now, when Hercules cut off one of the Hydra's heads, Iolaus seared the wounded neck with flame, and prevented further heads from sprouting. Hercules cut off the heads one by one, with Iolaus cauterizing the wounds. Hercules succeeded in lopping off the last head, supposedly immortal, and buried it deep beneath a rock from where it could never do harm again.

Ultimately harsh, aggressive policies in response to terrorism fail so often in their stated aims, because they so badly misunderstand and ignore the basic psychology of the enemy and of observers. Strength and power alone are not enough to defeat terrorism. The Greeks had many gods of war, but the one who guided Hercules in his struggle with the Hydra was Athena, the goddess of prudent war. Athena, unlike the god Ares, did not glory in destruction and chaos. For her, violence had to have a clear and calm purpose and had to be guided in an effective and principled manner. Without the intervention of Iolaus, Hercules, for all his mighty strength, would have been undone. Aggression and force are too crude to resolve terrorist conflicts. They deceive by meeting the psychological needs of the state and its constituents and by offering up apparent indications of success. Their popularity gives the politicians and leaders who authorize them wider support, and the short-term results provide the security forces with evidence of apparent success: terrorists disabled, weapons and resources confiscated; operations and networks disrupted.

Yet, appearances and accolades can be deceiving. It is as if Hercules, when fighting with the Hydra, had paused to show each decapitated head to a cheering crowd. "Look another head … and another … and another … surely we are winning". But relying on such an approach brought Hercules to the edge of ruination. Without the fire of Iolaus, the great hero would have been vanquished.

Terrorist groups can endure military strikes, "targeted assassinations" and other harsh measures not because the people and resources lost are not important, but because the violence works to increase the motivation of more members than it decreases, and works to attract more support and sympathy to the group than it frightens away.

During the 1980s, the apartheid regime in South Africa sanctioned an organized campaign of assassination of Black activists and their prominent supporters, which resulted in scores of people being killed. The assassination campaign was intended to give the government better control over the process of change. However, as O'Brien (2001) argues the policy in all likelihood hastened the collapse of the system as wider support for the ANC and other opposition groups burgeoned in the face of the perceived injustice of the policy. When the British introduced harsh measures to tackle the IRA, recruits and support flooded to the organization. When the USA bombed Libya, the Libyans increased their involvement and buttressing of terrorism rather than pulling away from it. When Israel kills Hamas members and imposes other sanctions on Palestinian communities, they increase the sense of perceived injustice, particularly considering the high loss of innocent life, driving more recruits into extremist groups and facilitating increased sympathy and support for these groups not only within the West Bank and Gaza, but further afield among the international community. As a result, Israel may win skirmish after skirmish in these terms but still find itself unable to establish lasting peace and stability until other counter-terrorism policies are given greater priority and prominence. For similar reasons, the USA, aggressively chasing down al-Qaeda and its affiliates throughout the world, may find that a lasting resolution to the pursuit eludes it, regardless of how much energy and military force it invests in the campaign.

Ultimately, the use of aggressive measures to combat terrorism can be both justifiable and legal. Frequently, they also successfully fulfil a number of important (though usually short-term) objectives. However, if past experience is anything to go by, defeating or diminishing the threat of terrorism in the long term is not something that such measures are proficient at doing.

Though Hercules won the battle at Lerna, leaving the Hydra crushed and ruined in his wake, the monster nonetheless played a crucial part in the hero's eventual demise. After he had killed the beast, Hercules cut the snake's body open and dipped his arrows in the poisonous venom. Many years later, while living happily with his new wife, Hercules killed a centaur with one of the poisoned arrows. Before it died, the centaur tricked Hercules' wife into thinking that his now-poisoned blood was a love potion that would keep her husband faithful. She dipped one of Hercules' shirts in the centaur's poisoned blood and gave it to him later. When Hercules put it on, it burned his body to the bone and he died in agony. The ancients understood well that the apparent victory of today may simply be unlocking the door to future defeat.

Bibliography

Bishop, P. and Mallie, E. (1987) *The Provisional IRA*. London: Corgi.

Brophy-Baermann, B. and Conybeare, J.A.C. (1994) "Retaliating against terrorism: rational expectations and the optimality of rules versus discretion", *American Journal of Political Science*, 38, 196–210.

Collins, S. (2004) "Dissuading state support of terrorism: strikes or sanctions? (An analysis of dissuasion measures employed against Libya)", *Studies in Conflict and Terrorism*, 27, 1–18.

Cota-McKinley, A., Woody, W. and Bell, P. (2001) "Vengeance: effects of gender, age and religious background", *Aggressive Behavior*, 27, 343–350.

Enders, W., Sandler, T. and Cauley, J. (1990) "UN conventions, technology and retaliation in the fight against terrorism: an econometric evaluation", *Terrorism and Political Violence*, 2, 83–105.

Enders, W. and Sandler, T. (1993) "The effectiveness of antiterrorism policies: a vector-autoregression-intervention analysis", *American Political Science Review*, 87, 829–844.

Friedland, N. and Merari, A. (1985) "The psychological impact of terrorism: a double-edged sword", *Political Psychology*, 6, 591–604.

Gilligan, J. (2000) *Violence: Reflections on Our Deadliest Epidemic*. London: Jessica Kingsley.

Hoffman, B. (1998) *Inside Terrorism*. London: Victor Gollancz.

Kim, S. and Smith, R. (1993) "Revenge and conflict escalation", *Negotiation Journal*, 9, 37–43.

Kosnick, M. (2000) "The military response to terrorism", *Naval War College Review*, 53, 13–39.

Lee, J.J. (1989) *Ireland 1912–1985: Politics and Society*. Cambridge: Cambridge University Press.

MacStiofain, S. (1975) *Memoirs of a Revolutionary*. Edinburgh: Gordon Cremonesi.

Malvesti, M. (2001) "Explaining the United States' decision to strike back at terrorists", *Terrorism and Political Violence*, 13, 85–106.

O'Brien, K. (2001) "The use of assassination as a tool of state policy: South Africa's counter-revolutionary strategy 1979–1992 (Part 2)", *Terrorism and Political Violence*, 13, 107–142.

Powell, C. (with Persico, J.) (1996) *My American Journey*. New York: Ballantine.

Schmid, A. and Jongman, A. (1988) *Political Terrorism* (2nd edn.). Oxford: North-Holland Publishing Company.

Stohl, M. (1987) "Terrorism, states and state terrorism: The Reagan administration in the Middle East", *Arab Studies Quarterly*, 9, 162–172.

Taylor, P. (1993) *States of Terror*. London: BBC Books.

Tudge, C. (2002) "Natural born killers", *New Scientist*, 174, 36–39.

Wilkinson, P. (1986) "Fighting the Hydra: International Terrorism and The Rule of Law", in O'Sullivan, N. (ed.) *Terrorism, Ideology and Revolution: The Origins of Modern Political Violence*. Boulder, CO: Westview Press.

22 Key considerations in counterideological work against terrorist ideology

Muhammad Haniff Bin Hassan

Why ideological response?

Many scholars and analysts have said that terrorism cannot be defeated either by military or law and order means only. It requires a multipronged and multifaceted approach, which includes strategies to eliminate the roots and causes of terrorism.

One of the root causes of terrorism is the ideology that drives and motivates terrorists. This ideology can be ethno-nationalistic or politico-religious in nature or others.

Terrorism is committed when opportunity, motivation, and capability meet and ideology is one of many important elements that motivates a person to commit terrorism. Muslim terrorists, and Al Qaeda especially, are not excluded. In fact, the role of ideology is especially significant for Al Qaeda and its associates.

Prevention of terrorism requires the elimination of at least one of the three elements mentioned. One is motivation, which may be driven by an ideology.

Although it has been widely accepted that counterideology or ideological response to extremist groups' propaganda is an important part of counterterrorism strategy, up until now there is no one single concrete and coherent doctrine or framework for conducting it. This must be overcome to ensure the success of counterideological work against extremists' ideas. This article does not provide a comprehensive perspective on counterideological work but seeks to contribute in filling in the gap.

Ideological response: its importance, functions, and benefits

Ideology as the "centre of gravity" and tool for rallying support

Dr. Stephen Biddle concluded in his article "War Aims and War Termination" that the real enemy in the war against terrorism is not terrorism itself, but Al Qaeda's radical ideology. Unless the ideology is defeated, counterterrorist efforts will inevitably fail. This requires combining a war of military means and war of ideas to prevent their replacement from among the generally politically uncommitted Muslims. He asserted that military means should not be allowed to overpower the ideological means. He is of the view that the center of gravity in the war against terrorism lies in the hearts and minds of politically uncommitted Muslims. Terrorism is not the real enemy as declared in the "War on Terrorism." It is just a tactic.[1]

Often at its formative period, a terrorist organization will go through "a period of mobilisation of discontent" in which the ideology is formulated to help rally people toward common grievances.[2]

Three types of terrorists and the role of ideology

Generally, there are three types of terrorists: the Political Strategist, the Radical Theorist, and the Militant Activist.

- The *Political Strategist* strives for power so he can impose his will on society. He is politically driven.
- The *Radical Theorist* is more interested in the ideas that he believes in, than any political goal including power. He will not compromise his beliefs for the sake of power. The Radical Theorist may not be involved directly in terrorist acts, but acts as ideologue for the terrorist organisation. He develops and refines the belief system, and defends them from criticism. He is skilled in offering rational and religious justifications for the terrorists. To him, ideas are the ends, not the means.
- *Militant Activists* are those who are drawn to violence as an end in itself, either as a means of venting anger, or as a source of excitement and adventure. Even without any ideology, they will still be doing what they want to anyway.[3]

Based on these descriptions, the ideology is particularly important for the Political Strategist and Radical Theorist. The Political Strategist uses ideology to justify the imposition of his will and reduce resentment from the society, whereas the Radical Theorist considers ideology as the cause for his struggle.

Often the most dangerous terrorists are those who combine emotional, intellectual, and political drives. The Militant Activist who is purely emotionally inclined toward violence may not have enough discipline to plan and sustain effective terrorist activities, whereas the Political Strategist and the Radical Theorist without violent inclinations are likely to opt for other less dangerous means.[4]

Neutralizing threat from freelance terrorists

Counterideological work is also important in minimizing the threat of potential freelance terrorists, who may not be members of any group, but drawn into terrorism because they share the ideology or common grievances.[5] Terrorism committed by individuals not affiliated to any group is a known occurrence, which is increasingly becoming a threat due to the public availability and easy access to advanced and multipurpose technology.[6] Timothy McVeigh, the Oklahoma city bomber,[7] Baruch Goldstein, the attacker of the Cave of the Patriach in Hebron that killed 29 Muslims during Friday prayer,[8] and Theodore Kaczynski, known as the Unabomber,[9] are good examples.

Ideologically driven terrorists

The profile of Muslim extremists shows that not all of them commit terrorism because of poverty or economic marginalization.

Dr. Ayman al-Zawahiri, Al Qaeda's deputy leader, is a physician. Khalid Shaikh Mohammed, head of Al Qaeda's operations, reportedly attended Chowan College in North Carolina in the early 1980s before transferring to another American university, where he obtained an engineering degree. Dr. Azahari Husin, believed to be the Jemaah Islamiyah's bomb expert, was a lecturer at Malaysia Technological University. He holds a doctorate in engineering.[10] At least two of the Jemaah Islamiyah members detained in Singapore are holders of diplomas in engineering.[11] Jason

Burke described this type of jihadis as "intellectual activists"; "men who can justify their attraction to radical Islam in relatively sophisticated terms."[12]

The two explanations to this phenomenon could be psychological or ideological difficulties. These educated people could either have psychological problems or were driven by ideologies in which economic considerations were not a main factor.

Ideology and causes of terrorism

One may view the cause for terrorism at three levels. At the most superficial or immediate level, the cause may be seen to be implacable hatred, which drives terrorists to kill others, even by sacrificing their own lives. Proximate causes usually invoke historical and economic roots, such as the Muslim grievance that they are victims of a superpower's unfair policies, the Russian government's and its predecessors' long repression of the Chechen people, and the economic backwardness of the Pattani people in the Southern Thailand. Deeper causes mainly concern worldviews held by the terrorists, such as the bipolar view of good versus evil, the notion of "us" against "them," seeking the pleasure of God, and salvation from hell in the afterlife.[13]

Ideology and Al Qaeda's propaganda tool

It is evident that ideology plays a role in Al Qaeda's propaganda to attract followers and win sympathy from general Muslims. Al Qaeda makes it clear that it is striving for Islam and that its ideas represent the true Islam. In every statement it makes, Al Qaeda does not fail to cite verses from the Quran, quotes from the Prophet's tradition (*hadits*) and opinions of classical Muslim scholars, giving the impression that its ideas are founded on Islam. It continuously uses *fatwa* (religious rulings) of various Muslim scholars and does not hesitate to couch its opinion as *fatwa* for the Muslim *ummah*. Its struggle is based on ideas such as: armed jihad is the only means to change the current fate of the Muslims, Muslims should be in constant war against non-Muslims until they obtain glory for Islam, Muslims are obligated to re-establish the Caliphate, killing oneself is not suicidal but an act of martyrdom and the ultimate way is to sacrifice for the religion, and that Allah the Great will not neglect one who strives for the glory of His religion. Its ideas are founded on concepts such as submission and allegiance is to Allah alone and the supremacy of Islam above all.[14]

Al Qaeda views that the existing dominant culture founded by the West corrupts humanity and is destructive to the proper practice of faith and true Islam. To be a true and faithful servant of Allah one has to reject it totally and commit oneself to fight against it. Conflict between the West and Islam is thus inevitable and Al Qaeda is "unlikely ever to accept long-term co-existence even if its other aims were somehow realized." No compromise or concession will satisfy them ultimately except a "global imposition of their interpretation of the faith."[15] Therefore, refuting the ideas will help to neutralize the threat of Al Qaeda.

Whenever a leader of Al Qaeda is killed or captured, it will announce that its struggle will not die because it is founded not on individuals, but on ideas that its followers believe. Hence, there will always be many others who will continue with the struggle and be ready to replace the losses. Such a claim may be dismissed, but it shows that Al Qaeda strives to base its organization on its ideology, and not on individuals.[16]

What has been said so far clearly shows the importance and role of ideology in its recruitment, indoctrination and gathering of support and sympathy. Jason Burke described Al Qaeda as "less an organization than an ideology."[17] As such, delegitimizing and dismantling extremist ideology, indeed, is one of the important aspects of combating terrorism by Al Qaeda.[18]

In fact, the real target in the battle against Muslim extremist groups should not be the groups themselves, but their ideology, which should be stopped from spreading beyond their current members.[19]

Concept, objectives, and target groups for counterideological work

Adopting a counterinsurgency approach

Counterterrorism is not very different from counterinsurgency. It is a battle against an organized group motivated by a cause or ideology seeking to achieve its political aim through protracted campaign. By protracting the campaign, it seeks to win over the support of the people, thus weakening its enemy, which will eventually enable it to launch a final blow. A classic example of a successful insurgency campaign was the North Vietnamese Army and Viet Cong's struggle against America during the Vietnam War.

In counterinsurgency, the people are "the center of gravity" because the government and the army not only need their support, but also because the insurgents emerge from the people as well. By winning over the people, the flow of recruits and support would be cut off. This approach is popularly known as the "battle for the hearts and minds."[20]

However, this does not mean that winning the hearts and minds of the insurgents themselves are not important, because should the insurgents be persuaded to lay down arms, the insurgency would end immediately. Such a campaign may be launched to defeat the insurgents' "psychic forces" or "morale." General William Slim, commander of the Fourteenth Army in Burma during World War II, defined "morale" as a positive "state of mind" that has three components:

- "spiritual" confidence that the cause is just;
- "intellectual" confidence that the goal can be attained; and
- "material" confidence that the means of attaining the goal are available.[21]

One of the success stories of the battle for hearts and minds was that conducted during the Malayan Emergency by the British authority in Malaya, and subsequently the Malaysian government against local communist insurgents. During the Malayan Emergency, the threat against communist insurgents was countered not only through military means, but also through a comprehensive strategy encompassing ideological, economic, social, and law and order approaches.

On the ideological front, Muslim scholars were engaged effectively to counter communism as being against Islam, the religion of the predominant ethnic group, the Malays. This contained the influence of communism to largely the Chinese only.

As for the general population, especially the Chinese, their hearts and minds were won by attending to their needs.[22] For example, the Chinese were given rights of citizenship, which helped to provide them with social and political security.[23]

The successful counterinsurgency strategy of battling for the hearts and minds of the people holds many lessons for ideological response work against terrorist ideology. Admittedly, some modifications from counterinsurgency ideological propaganda may be required for counterterrorism ideological response, due to the specific characteristics of current threat of terrorism itself.

A comprehensive approach encompassing ideological response is necessary due to the fact that terrorism, like an insurgency, is rooted on various factors. In the case of Al Qaeda, its inclination toward terrorism is not only because of the ideology but also fueled by the context that provides them with the justification of their misinterpretation of Islam. The context also contributes in motivating Muslims to embrace the ideology. In many statements, Al Qaeda clearly strives to position itself as the champion for Muslims grievances, for example, in Kashmir under the rule of the predominantly Hindu India, the long oppression of Muslims in Chechnya by the atheist Russians, the suffering of the Palestinian at the hands of the Jews, the death of civilian Iraqis due to the economic blockade by the international community and the hypocrisy of the United States's foreign policies.

Ascertaining objectives and identifying target groups

The next step in counterideology work, after understanding its position within counterterrorism, is to have clear objectives. Important objectives for ideological response work should be to

- immunize general Muslims from extremist ideology,
- persuade less fanatic members of terrorist groups to abandon the ideology,
- create doubt and dissension within terrorist organisations,
- rehabilitate detained terrorist members, and
- to minimize non-Muslims' anxiety and suspicion by presenting alternatives to terrorist ideology.

It is important to note that the primary target group of the ideological response is not the terrorists but the majority of Muslims. The aim is to provide them with a correct understanding of the religion that is relevant to the contemporary context and current priorities, so that they will not be easily influenced by the terrorists' propaganda. The majority of Muslims should be "immunized" against the viral threat of extremist ideologies that are freely disseminated through the Internet.[24]

It might be impossible to persuade any fanatic hardcore members of Muslim terrorist groups to give up their ideology. Having been promised a place in paradise if they persevere in their cause, they will hardly be amenable to other inducements. However, in the battle for hearts and minds, the majority of Muslims can be convinced to desist Al Qaeda's ideology and to defuse any motivation to support it.[25]

Stephen Biddle wrote, "… so in this conflict we must look to a synergistic interaction between violence to root out terrorists and persuasion to prevent their replacement from among the great mass of politically uncommitted Muslims." He is of the view that the real challenge is to keep Al Qaeda's size fixed because sustained effort will eventually destroy any organization of fixed size, although it may be slow and laborious due to the covert nature of the process. In contrast, if Al Qaeda continues to succeed in recruiting new members through its ideological propaganda, or persuading non-members to conduct terrorist acts through sharing of ideas, then no military effort will be sufficient to prevail over it.[26]

Terrorist groups can only persist through popular support. Conversely, such support also "plays a fundamental role in the group's decline." Most terrorist groups disappear after an average of six and a half years of activity, due to the "disintegration of social support due to public backlash against terrorist acts, and in the fact that some of the issues raised by sympathizers were addressed."[27]

Another important target group, which is usually overlooked in counterideological work, are the non-Muslims at large. The aim is to provide them with alternative perspectives to terrorist ideas that hopefully will reduce their anxiety, concern, and misunderstanding of Islam and Muslims. In a multiracial and multireligious country, this is an important aspect of social harmony, which counterterrorism strategy needs to preserve and protect. Often, terrorism also aims to destabilize a society or a country. It may be a direct or indirect objective because instability will make counterterrorism operation more complicated and difficult.

The Singapore government's White Paper on The Jemaah Islamiyah (JI) Arrests and The Threat of Terrorism reported how the Singapore JI cell planned to attack key Singapore installations and to misrepresent them as acts of aggression by the Malaysian government. Their intention was to create distrust and animosity between "Muslim Malaysia" and "Chinese Singapore" and so cause ethnic conflict in both countries. By doing so, Muslims in Malaysia and Singapore would then respond to calls of jihad and turn both countries into Ambon-like crisis.[28]

That is why many country leaders have made appeals to non-Muslim citizens of their country not to blame Islam and Muslims for the tragic attack on the World Trade Center and the Pentagon.[29]

It can be concluded that there are three broad targets audience for counterideological effort. They are members of terrorist organizations and their sympathizers, general Muslims, and non-Muslims at large.

Mapping the ideas

The first step is to understand the ideology and main ideas of the extremist groups, especially Al Qaeda and its regional affiliate like Jemaah Islamiyah. Efforts should be made to draw up a key map of important ideas, which make up the belief system of the group.

The aim is to have a comprehensive view of the ideology. This will facilitate in devising appropriate response and establishing tools to monitor ideas on the ground.[30]

Sun Tzu wrote, "know yourself and know your enemy." Obviously, this is logical because, without proper understanding of the opposing view, no counterideology work will be effective and no correct alternative ideas can be offered. Clear understanding of the ideology also helps to distinguish the group's features better and so minimize the danger of mistakenly attacking wrong ideas and groups. Needlessly antagonizing others surely will only further complicate the problem.

To facilitate the mapping of the ideas, serious effort should be put into collating and compiling related materials. Specialists in the area should be recruited to analyze and to offer criticism and alternative views.[31]

Important approach

Equally important after understanding the idea is to adopt the appropriate approach. In this respect, it should be recognized that the "conventional lens" originating from the West might not necessarily work in understanding the cultural realities behind Muslim extremists; terrorism. They may not be able to prescribe the best approach.

There are various approaches in responding to the ideas of the terrorists but any meaningful approach should take into account the theological nature of terrorists' ideas, couched in juristic and jurisprudential pronouncements. Muslim terrorists do not believe in Western philosophy and ideals, considering them heretical.

It is also important to note that Muslims by and large are more comfortable with theological and juristic interpretations of religious questions. The opinion of the *ulama* still carries more weight than that of other scholars.[32] This is an important point to bear in mind, in any effort to get the ideological response to succeed and be widely accepted.[33] This underscores the importance of the theological and juristic approach in the ideological war against terrorism.

What is meant by the theological and juristic approach is the classical *ulama*'s methodology of *ijtihad* or deduction from the Quran and the *hadits*,[34] based primarily on three important sciences popularly known as *Usul Fiqh*,[35] *Usul Tafsir*,[36] and *Usul Hadits*.[37] This approach requires an exhaustive study of the classical *ulama*'s texts to investigate their stand on the pertinent issues. If the ideas propagated by the Muslim terrorists contradicts the opinions of those *ulama*, then it is a potent means to prove the terrorists wrong. This is especially so because Muslim terrorists argue for their ideas using the same approach, within what some call the classical or traditional approach.

Understanding this approach is important in developing "forensic theology" into a valuable intelligence tool. "Forensic theology" is also sometimes known as "ideological surveillance." France was probably the first nation to use this tool. In 1986, French security services worked with experts on Islam to learn the trademarks of extremist thought, and it have helped them to identify and disrupt militant cells and plots. The tool is used to authenticate terrorist documents, identify perpetrators, and targets for surveillance. Sometimes, it is more effective than conventional intelligence practices.[38]

Stephen Grey cited one example, which happened in France. A group of religious experts listening to sermons in various mosques pinpointed three clerics as probable extremists. Police investigators then found that all three had links to a terrorist group. They were expelled from France.[39]

It is also interesting to consider Dr. Stephen Biddle's proposal for "a third way," which is "neither separatist extremism nor imposed Westernism." The aim is not to approach the counterideological campaign as a war to convert Muslims to "our" [American/Western] way of life but to prevent mainstream Muslims "from being hijacked by a splinter group [Al Qaeda] whose view are now rejected."[40]

He is of the view that Al Qaeda and mainstream Muslims are now so far apart and there are many opportunities for "enabling the legitimate religious yearnings of everyday Muslims to see political expression without creating a dualistic struggle with Western ideals." Such alternatives should be identified and promoted, especially those alternatives that help to change the repressive and corrupted political regimes seen by many Muslims as inconsistent with their ideals.[41]

Both the "theological and juristic approach" and the "third way" can be combined together in that the "theological and juristic approach" is used as a key mechanism in offering alternatives that the Muslim community considers neither extremism nor Westernism.

Most important is to note that whatever approach is used, the war on terrorism will fail if it is perceived as a war on Islam. This will give credence to the call for Muslim solidarity in a jihad against America, thus falling into the trap of Al Qaeda.[42]

Important partners

The proposed "theological and juristic approach" as the primary approach for the "third way" will not be effective without the involvement of the *ulama*. Scholars who are not trained in this field still have a role to play in counterideological work, but they may not have the know-how and religious legitimacy to respond to the theological and juristic arguments of the extremists.[43]

Understanding Overlapping Grievances. Due to the overlapping grievances of general Muslims and the extremists, or the fact that the extremists are trying to manipulate Muslims grievances for their cause, one can often find a voice or view of a Muslim scholar that overlaps with those of the extremists, especially in criticizing the West, and in addressing the Israel–Palestine conflict and the establishment of an Islamic state.[44] One such example is Yusuf Al-Qaradhawi. He is criticized for supporting suicide attacks by Palestinian resistance groups against Israeli civilians.[45]

In this respect, it is important to ensure a holistic approach in assessing such scholars. It is not prudent to deny such scholars' roles in combating extremism and terrorism in society just because of a few views that one finds disagreeable.

In the case of Yusuf Al-Qaradhawi, despite his strong support for the Palestinian resistance and a hard-line position against Israel and American policies, he has devoted more than a decade in combating extremist ideas among Muslims through his seminal writings and speeches. Contrary to public expectations, he issued various *fatwas* condemning perpetrators of terrorism. He condemned the 9/11 attack and Bali bombing. He also ruled that hostage taking, kidnapping, targeting civilians by militants and killing of prisoners of war are prohibited in Islam.[46]

Amien Rais, former speaker of the People's Consultative Assembly on Indonesia and former Chairman of Muhammadiyah, is another good case in point. He was known for his role in the reform movement in Indonesia and a strong advocate of political reform and human rights. He embraced interfaith dialogue and denounced terrorism but at other times he showed support for Islamist policies and some of his views can be perceived as anti-Semitic and anti-Chinese.[47]

Although the broad moderate–radical categorization is a useful means of essentializing differences of tendencies among Muslim scholars, one should note that making a clear distinction between the "moderate" and the "radical" is difficult because in reality there is no such neat dichotomy. Community and political leaders all over the world behave in ways that defy such easy categorization. On certain issues, Muslim scholars can be "moderate" and "progressive" but on others they can be Islamist or sectarian. Thus, a more subtle or nuanced approach is needed when characterizing Muslim scholars and Islamic groups.[48] Amien Rais (mentioned earlier) and Gus Dur, former president of Indonesia and leader of Nahdhatul Ulama, the largest Islamic organization in Indonesia, are good examples.

In this respect, Jason Burke wrote that many of those who express their sympathy with bin Laden and take satisfaction at his ability to strike the United States do not genuinely subscribe to his ideology, neither does their anti-Western sentiment translate into rejection of Western values. This, he said, is indicated in surveys of public opinion in the Arab world by Zogby International and Pew Research center for the People and the Press that reveal strong support for Western practices such as elected government, personal liberty, and economic choice. Burke also highlighted that although Islamists often shared similar rhetoric such as "Islam is the solution" they disagree over what is the solution and how it might be achieved. Some Islamists, despite their criticism against contemporary political systems, still "want to appropriate the structures of the state, in varying degrees, Islamize them, usually with a view toward promoting greater social justice and outflanking undemocratic and powerful regimes." They are still useful as interlocutors for the West. "They should not be rejected out of hand as 'Islamists'; refusing to engage them only allows the extremists to dominate the political discourse."[49]

A more appropriate approach is to assess a scholar by looking at his views, opinions, and works in various issues, instead of judging him based on a specific issue only. Despite the hard-line position taken by such scholars in several issues, co-opting them into counterideological work provides opportunities for both parties to engage each other. This will facilitate better understanding of each other's perspective, which will help to build trust and confidence toward each other. Often, such engagement also helps to moderate the scholars' view.

Tolerating differences in political issues is a primary requirement in attaining the common goal of neutralizing extremist ideas, which are at the root of terrorism.[50] Secular government and Muslim scholars should join hands in the fight against terrorism despite their disagreement in issues like the role of religion in politics or the role of women in society or the limit of civil liberties.

Classical Scholars. Prudence is especially needed in dealing with the opinions of the classical Muslim scholars from centuries ago. One cannot definitively ascertain the link between the opinion of classical Muslim scholars with the ideology of Muslim terrorist groups. Ibn Taimiyah's works, for example, are alleged by some as the source of Muslim terrorist groups' ideology. But one can also find from his works many opinions that could be used to counter these groups.

Muslim extremists call for armed jihad against corrupt contemporary Muslim rulers. But Ibn Taimiyah said:

> He [the Prophet] has ordered them to obey and forbade them from removing the people from their positions and he has ordered them to stand for the truth.[51]
>
> The opinion of the *Ahl Sunnah* [Sunni] settled on the view that fighting must be avoided during civil wars due to the authentic *hadits* confirmed from the Prophet. They [the *Ahl Sunnah*] then began to mention their creeds. They ordered patience in the face of the injustice of the rulers and [they ordered] avoiding fighting against them. [This was their conclusion] although a number of people of knowledge and had fought in civil wars.[52]

The extremist rules that Muslims who hold positions in un-Islamic governments are apostates. Thus, shedding their blood is justified. However, when Ibn Taimiyah was asked whether Muslims should hold positions in an unIslamic government, he issued a *fatwa* saying:

> Praise be to Allah, yes [it is permissible] if he tries to implement justice and eliminate oppression according to his ability, and if his taking up the position is better for the Muslims than if the position were to be given to someone else, and if his authority over the area is better than the authority of another. Indeed, it is *mubah* (permissible) for him to remain in his position and there is no sin for him. In fact, it is preferred that he remains in that position rather than leave it.[53]

He cited the case of Negus, a Muslim ruler in a Christian country of Abyssinia,[54] and Prophet Yusuf's (Joseph) position as court treasurer of an Egyptian king who was not a Muslim.[55]

The extremists are taking a liberal approach in *takfir* (ruling others as apostates). Ibn Taimiyah warned against such practices in his work:

> Of the people of knowledge of the *Sunnah* (*hadits*), not to declare those who disagreed with them disbelievers, even if that opponent declared him a disbeliever. This is because *takfir* is a *syariah* ruling and it is not permissible to do it simply as a reciprocal act. ... Similarly, declaring another person a disbeliever is a right of Allah. Hence, one cannot declare a person an unbeliever save for that person whom Allah and His Messenger have declared a disbeliever [by virtue of a clear ad unassailable divine text in the Quran and *Sunnah* that such person is a disbeliever].[56]

Ibn Qayyim, Ibn Taimiyah's famous student, who is often quoted by Muslim extremists, also gave a wider definition of jihad, similar to his teacher's view, as opposed to the narrow application of *jihad* by the extremists. The general meaning of *jihad* was explained at length by Ibn Qayyim. He wrote that the Prophet was the best example in fulfilling the obligation of *jihad*. The Prophet, in fact, practiced *jihad* of all varieties and forms; with the heart, mind, and body and by the means of *dakwah* (propagation), explanation, and arms. All of his life was dedicated to *jihad* in all forms. Ibn Qayyim also wrote that *jihad* against oneself precedes *jihad* against the enemies outside, and the former is more important. Indeed as long as one does not perform *jihad* on oneself by fulfilling his obligations to Allah, one will not be able to perform *jihad* against the external enemies. Between the two (oneself and the enemy) is the third enemy, namely Satan.[57]

Role of Madrasah. Madrasahs should also be made an important partner in this effort, rather than be treated generally as a threat.[58] It is this institution that schooled many moderate Muslim scholars and thinkers.

Usually, *madrasahs* occupy a strategic position because they are the main provider for the right foundation to students keen on learning the mainstream Islam traditions and theology, which are important ballasts in combating extremist ideology. They also have the potential to function as the bastion for the preservation of mainstream Islam, which is the moderate and pragmatic strain, observed by Muslims in general.

The *madrasah* and the *ulama* are important conveyors of the message of Islam—peace and compassion. But this can only be achieved if their potential and role are recognized by the governments. A healthier relationship between the *madrasahs*, *ulama*, and the government is crucial in the ideological struggle against extreme militancy.[59]

Important considerations for effective counterideological work

Avoid generalization

It is very important in counterideological work to avoid generalizations, be it in making assessments, analysis, and conclusions.

Giovanni Caracci in his article "Cultural and Contextual Aspects of Terrorism" wrote that in the study of terrorism "it is easy to over-generalize and engage in reductionism."

He then quoted Walter Reich, "Researchers should take special care to identify the individual and the groups whose behaviour they are studying and limit their explanations to those individuals and groups, define the circumstances under which those explanations are valid, and not to suggest more that they do."[60]

Caracci suggested that terrorism must be studied in its cultural/contextual perspective to provide more focus to it. One cannot explain fully the motivation of terrorists without putting their act in its cultural and contextual milieu. For example, terrorist acts carried out by West European groups such as the Red Army from Germany differ significantly from others like the Shining Path in Peru in motivation, and cultural and contextual factors. Similar differences are also evident between nationalistic groups such as Basques to Muslim fundamentalists like the Egyptian Islamic Jihad. In reality the cultural matrix of terrorism differs from case to case.[61]

A study of extremist ideologies will show that it is often characterized by simplistic generalization and reductionism such as a Manichean view that sees the world divided into two camps only; the "good" versus the "evil," or "if you are not with us, you are against us."

Counterterrorism work should not fall into the same mistake. To be successful, counterideology should be specific in its response and not make sweeping statements or generalizations.

Generalization of Salafi-Wahabi

One example of generalization is the view that *Salafi / Wahabi* thought is a fertile ground that breeds ideology for extremism and terrorism. In the early period after 9/11, many expressed worries over the *Salafi / Wahabi*.

On the close connection of the *Salafi–Wahabi* relationship, Sheikh Hisham Kabbani views the contemporary *Salafi* movement as the modern outgrowth of the heretical teaching of Muhammad bin Abdul Wahhab, the founder of *Wahabi*. He wrote, "In essence, Salafism and Wahabism are the same but the latter is identified by the founder while the former takes the name of the salaf and makes it its own. Yet both Salafism and Wahabism depart from the same belief and practice of the Salaf."[62] He warns against contemporary *Salafi* and *Wahabi* as a source of radicalism.[63]

Similar views on the *Salafi–Wahabi* connection can be found also in the writing of Quinton Wiktorowicz, entitled *The New Global Threat: Transnational Salafis and Jihad*. He highlights the influence of *Salafi* thought on extremist groups such as the Gamaah Islamiyah in Egypt and the

Armed Islamic Group in Algeria. He infers the connection by saying "The Saudi state and its religious hierarchy are the major producers and exporters of Salafi publications, missionary operations and humanitarian assistance and the transnational organization of the movement, which incorporates a myriad of nationalities, render it an effective and influential force in the Muslim world."[64] In his conclusion he alluded that all *Salafis* carry the same view toward jihad as the means for spreading Islam. There is no "disagreement over whether jihad is needed, but rather the timing of any war."[65]

Jason Burke also categorized *Wahabis* as *Salafi*. He described bin Laden and his fellow extremists as "millinerian, fundamentalist, reformist, revivalist, Wahhabi/Salafi and, at least in their rootedness in modernity if not their programme, Islamist."[66]

Simon Reeve wrote for the Independent (London):

> Since the creation of the state, the House of Saud has partnered with clerics who espouse the strict form of Islam derived from the 250-year-old teachings of a preacher called Muhammad bin Abd al-Wahhab. Mercy and tolerance are hallmarks of Islam, but Wahhabi teaching declares that Muslims who do not adhere to his particular version of Islam are apostates, and thus deserving of death. For decades, strict Wahhabism has taught that Christians and Jews are infidels and heretics. Wahhabi clerics control education in Saudi, and they have raised many youngsters to hate.[67]

Mona Eltahawy, in her article *The Wahhabi Threat to Islam*, also wrote, "It is long past time for Muslims to question the Wahhabi ideology that is pulling the rug out from under Saudi life, for it is that same ideology that has been involved in militant movements throughout the Muslim world for years."[68]

Warren Fernandez, senior journalist at the *Straits Times*, wrote, "For some time, thoughtful commentators have been saying that the war on terror would not be won unless and until something was done to root out the source of the cancer in Saudi Arabia." He then refers the cancer to Wahhabism, "the obscurantist, severe and extreme form of Islam that Saudi Arabia has been supporting and exporting, including to this part of the world."[69]

However, the International Crisis Group (ICG) pointed out:

> One result of the "war on terror" in Indonesia has been increased attention to the country's links with religious institutions in the Middle East and the puritanical form of Islam known as salafism. Particularly, outside observers but some Indonesians as well, tend to assume that salafism is alien to Indonesian Islam, is growing by leaps and bounds, and is dangerous because it promotes violence. All three notions are misleading.[70]

Various colours of Salafi

Salafi is wider than Wahabism. *Salafi* thought has existed in the Muslim community for hundreds of years and has spread worldwide. Like many other school of thought, *Salafi* is not homogenous. It consists of various sub-cultures and orientations, from moderate to extreme.[71]

A good case in point is the Muhammadiyah, the second largest Islamic organization in Indonesia, with millions of followers. It has been recognized and has proved itself as a moderate organization. However, a study on Muhammadiyah's history will show that it has its origins in Saudi Arabia. Muslim scholars will acknowledge that up till now, the Muhammadiyah practice *Salafi-Wahabi* methodology in matters pertaining to rituals and its interpretation. Yet it remains moderate by adopting civil society approach in affecting changes or reform. Instead of condemning the authority, Muhammadiyah constructively offers alternative solution by establishing schools, hospitals, and social programs for the society.[72]

Although it is true that *Wahabi* is *Salafi*, it is but one of *Salafi*'s many orientations. *Salafi* and *Wahabi* are not two sides of the same coin.[73] There are *Salafis* who are not *Wahabis*. There are *Wahabis* who are not Saudis. There are also Saudis who are neither *Wahabis* nor *Salafis*.

A careful study of the early *Wahabis* will show that they were not politically inclined. That is why Sheikh Muhammad b. Abdul Wahab did not object to the political power of the Saud family,[74] as long as he was guaranteed freedom to do his reformation work of local Muslims who were mixing Islam with heretical practices.

The close relationship established between the Saud family as the political authority and the *Wahabi ulama* as the religious authority, has until recently contributed to the *Wahabi* stand of non-interference in politics. That is why they issued *fatwa* that reject the formation of political parties and disallowed revolt against the government.

The real problem actually lies with the Neo-*Wahabis*; that is, those who combine the tough character of the *Wahabi* with both a narrow interpretation of jihad and an obsession with political objectives. This is a recent development as a result of the prolonged problems of Palestine, economic backwardness, local political and global injustices, globalization and other factors, which color the ongoing Islamic revivalism. Today the extreme form of the Neo-*Wahabis* can be found in the ideology of Salafi–Jihadi movements and figures like Al Qaeda and Osama bin Laden.[75] It is not prudent to lump *Wahabi* and *Salafi* in one basket in the effort against extremism and terrorism.

One should also note that there are several sources of influence that have shaped Islamic revivalism in the Muslim world. The nature of these sources varies from spiritual introspection to comprehensive social action, from the Sanusi movement to the Ikhwan Muslimoon (the Muslim Brotherhood).

Due to its comprehensive approach to religious education, social activism, and political reform for justice and public good, Ikhwan's influence and ideas are pervasive throughout the Islamic world, Southeast Asia as well as the U.K., U.S., and Europe.

In Malaysia and Indonesia, manifestations of Ikhwan influence upon social and political reform thought may be seen in organizations such as PAS (Islamic Party of Malaysia), ABIM (Muslim Youth Movement), JIM (Jemaah Islah Malaysia), and Partai Keadilan Sejahtera, Indonesia (Justice Prosperous Party).

Ikhwan is *Salafi*. The organization openly declares this in many of the writings of its leaders, in particular those of Hasan Al-Banna.[76] However, the *Wahabis* do not accept Ikhwan as being *Salafi*.

Ikhwan's *Salafi* orientation in methodology of understanding Islam differs from the *Wahabi* understanding of *Salafi*. Hence, it is far from the truth to say that all *Salafis* are *Wahabis*.

Ikhwan is well known and acknowledged for its inclusivism. Ikhwan trains its followers to be tolerant to differences in opinion and approaches. Although Ikhwan strictly requires its followers to adopt the *Salafi* perspective in theology, it allows them to follow any of the four major schools of jurisprudence in matters of Islamic practices or juristic opinions (*fiqh*). Their slogan is "We cooperate in matters that we agree upon, and tolerate each other in matters that we disagree." Thus they are more inclined to "agree to disagree" and to be pragmatic.[77]

As such, one can find members of Ikhwan participating in political alliances and power-sharing with other parties, even secular or non-Muslim, to achieve the common good or interest. In 1976, members of the Ikhwan participated in Egypt's General Election under the ticket of Arab socialist party and as independent candidates and gained 15 seats. They collaborated with the New Wafd Party in 1984 in the General Election and won 8 seats. In 1987, they formed Labour Islamic Alliance with the Socialist Labour Party and the Liberal Socialist Party. The alliance won 60 seats, of which 37 were won by members of Ikhwan.[78] Ikhwan also "is willing to support a Christian candidate provided that he has good qualities, such as a nationalist position, honesty, straightforwardness and a clear position on Muslims and their legal rights."[79] Despite being critical toward the Egyptian government, Ikhwan does not close any opportunity for dialogue with the government's National Democratic Party.[80]

Because of their social activism and political reformism, many social analysts and political observers group them under the label of "Fundamentalist" and "Political Islamist" but the differences between both groups are marked enough to prove that not all *Salafis* are *Wahabis*, and that Ikhwan and the *Wahabis* are two different and distinct movements.

One may disagree with their religious–political aspirations, however, it is unwise to treat them in the same manner or classify them under one category.

Not all Saudis *are Wahabis*

Shirite Muslims make up 10–15 percent of Saudi Arabia's citizens[81] and they are clearly not *Wahabis*.

Just by looking at how some Saudis, either male or female, behave when they are abroad will help to understand the issue. The Saudi women who give up their veils and *abayas* the moment they leave their country and the Saudi men who seek entertainment in Bangkok will never be accepted nor accept themselves as *Wahabis*.

Many of the Bedouin Saudis are not *Wahabis*. The *Wahabis* are always harsh against them because they infuse Bedouin traditions in their practice of Islam.

Admittedly, a non-Muslim may find it difficult to differentiate the *Wahabis* among Saudis or even the Arabs due to the following:

a   Cultural homogeneity among Saudis.
b   The *Wahabi* school of thought is supported by the Saudi government. Thus they have free rein to voice and enforce their views in society and also to silence the others.
c   Lack of knowledge.

Although many non-*Wahabi* Saudis have a negative view of *Wahabis*, one must not underestimate the spirit of nationalism that binds the Saudis.

In Saudi society, as in many Arab countries, there remains entrenched the tribal ethos, which demands and honors loyalty and allegiance to one's social and national affiliations, especially in the face of foreigners, in spite of differences within the community.

Thus painting all Saudis with one brush is another imprudent move and may be counterproductive in the fight against terrorism in that region.

Similar generalizations can also be made about the Indonesians, or any of the other Muslim communities. The increase of Islamic revivalism among Muslims in this region had caused some commentators to classify all of them as *Wahabis*. Such generalizations only serve to galvanize what may otherwise be disparate elements within the community, in a mutual resistance against the unwarranted label and the accuser.

An ICG report concluded:

> The *Salafi* movement in Indonesia is not the security threat that it is sometimes portrayed as. It may come across to outsiders as intolerant and reactionary, but for the most part, it is not prone to terrorism, in part because it is inwardly focused on faith. … In some ways, the purist *salafis* are a more potent barrier against *jihadis* like JI than the pluralist Muslims who often become the recipients of Western donor aid.[82]

RAND has made a good study of Muslim thinking orientations and categorized them into the radical fundamentalist, scriptural fundamentalist, conservative traditionalist, reformist traditionalist, modernist, mainstream secularist, and radical secularist. One may disagree with this categorization and the proposals made by the study, but such an effort, which departs from a broad-brush approach, is commendable and should be encouraged.[83]

Generalization of madrasah

Another example is *madrasah/pesantren* as a terrorist "production factory." The discovery of the Jemaah Islamiyah (JI) connection with Pondok Al-Mukmin in Solo, Madrasah Lukmanul Hakim in Ulu Tiram Johor, and other Indonesian *pesantrens*, and several Pakistani religious schools' support of the Taliban has fuelled anxiety and suspicion[84] among the general public and political leaders that *madrasahs* are extremist and terrorist producing factories.

For example, Karvin Von Hippel wrote:

> The more hard-line Muslim theological schools are known as Deobandi *madrasa[h]s*, named after the original *madrasa[h]* established in 1867 in Deoband, an Indian town near Delhi. ... Thus, while the links between poverty and terrorism may not be so clear, what can be determined is that children who attend *madrasa[h]s* and other Qur'anic schools not only learn to despise "corrupting Western influences" from an early age, but also gain few practical skills.[85]

Similarly, Wayne A. Downing commented:

> Currently, a vast amount of hatred and distrust is being spawned in an insidious pan-Islamic education system. In the past 24 years, the radical Wahhabi sect from Saudi Arabia has sponsored religious schools and *madrassahs* [*madrasahs*] throughout the Islamic world. The Indonesians have seminaries called *pesandren* [*pesantren*]. Most of these schools spread a message of hatred and intolerance, radicalizing young Muslims and encouraging them to join the Holy War or Jihad.[86]

Various forms and types of madrasah

Such a generalization does not take into consideration the various forms of Islamic religious schools, for example, *pesantren, pondok, madrasah*.

Each of these forms carries different meanings depending on the context or country where they are operated. For example, *madrasahs* in Singapore are very different in many aspects than *madrasahs* in Pakistan. Even in Singapore, the word *madrasah* is used for two very different Islamic religious education platforms; full time and part time *madrasah*,[87] all privately run. In Indonesia, however, *madrasah* usually refers to government-run religious schools.[88]

The *pondok* system practiced in Indonesia is different from what is practiced in Malaysia. In Indonesia, there are *pondoks*, which are known as *Pondok Moderen* (Modern Pondok), which essentially operates just like mainstream schools. The only difference is that they offer religious subjects in addition to normal subjects.

In Indonesia, the bulk of the *pesantrens* (Islamic boarding schools) are run by Nahdhatul Ulama and Muhammadiyah. These are the two largest Islamic organizations in Indonesia, both well-known and internationally accepted as moderates. Jemaah Islamiyah and its like run only a small percentage of *pesantren*.[89]

In the case of Malaysia, only one religious school was linked to Jemaah Islamiyah, which was Sekolah Agama Tarbiyatul Islamiyah Lukmanul Hakim at Ulu Tiram, Johor.

Adil Mahdi pointed out that unlike the case of certain *madrasah* in Pakistan, no single *madrasah* in India has been involved in "terrorist" activities. He also spoke about the Deobandi's link with the Taliban, stressing that although the two shared a common vision, they differed in matters of strategy. The Taliban's rise to power owed more to support given by Pakistan, Saudi Arabia, and the United States than to Deobandi ideology.[90]

Dietrich Reetz of the ZMO mentioned that Deobandi *madrasah* has undergone a reform in 1982, in that English and computer applications were introduced. Yoginder Sikand highlighted that efforts were being made by the *ulama* and Muslim activists in India to introduce conventional subjects and teaching methods into *madrasahs*.[91]

As for *madrasahs* in China, some of these are part-time schools that cater for students who study full-time at regular schools and colleges. Except in the province of Sinkiang, *madrasah* in China are not a platform for antigovernment propaganda.[92]

The ISIM Workshop concluded that there seemed to be a near unanimity among the participants about the fallacy of labeling all or even most of *madrasahs* as "dens of terror," although they pointed out that some *madrasahs* in certain countries can be said militant or even terrorist. There has been a long history of intellectual and financial links between *madrasahs* and external parties but then, most with transnational connections have had nothing to do with terrorism. The report emphasized the importance of empirically grounded studies of *madrasahs* and the need to counter misleading stereotypes.[93]

In Singapore, there are only six full-time *madrasah*. They accommodate about 5,000 Muslim students from Primary 1 to Pre-University 2.[94] They make up 5 percent of the total number of overall Muslim students population. It is important to note that none of Jemaah Islamiyah detainees in Singapore were graduates of these *madrasahs*.

Contrary to common misperceptions, *madrasahs* in Singapore do not confine themselves to only religious subjects. Nor do they employ outdated modes of teaching and learning. The local *madrasahs* have been teaching non-religious subjects such as English, Science, and Mathematics for many years before the implementation of Compulsory Education, which requires such secular subjects to be taught in schools. Thus, local *madrasah* students have already been exposed to a mix of religious and secular education, albeit in varying degrees. Over the years, several graduates of local *madrasahs* have even been able to enroll in the National University of Singapore, with some emerging with honors.

Though the numbers are small, the significance of this is both symbolic and substantive—that local *madrasahs* can adapt and succeed.[95]

Even though local *madrasahs* are given some level of autonomy, the Islamic Religious Council of Singapore, which oversees Islamic education in Singapore, supervises and governs these schools.[96] This is unlike *madrasahs* in Pakistan and some *pesantrens* in Indonesia, which operate independently without supervision.[97]

Negative effect of generalisation

Stereotyped perceptions toward *madrasahs* will build psychological barriers between counterideology efforts and the community of the *madrasah*, which includes their staff, past and present pupils, and their families. This will cause difficulty in any collaborative effort.

Sweeping statements may also damage relations with the religious teachers and scholars, or even the majority of the Muslim community. It may be seen as an attack on a key Muslim institution, leading to a loss of potential partners and resources required for successful counter-ideology work.

Generalizations hamper counterideology work because it defines the threat too widely. Counterideology workers will have to face a wider "battlefront," larger target audience, or possibly creating too many unnecessary "battlefronts" for themselves. Most destructively, counterideology workers will end up creating more enemies for themselves by unnecessarily antagonizing others, for example, antagonizing the whole Saudi population by painting all of them as *Wahabis*.

It is in the interest of counterideology that governments take into account the heterogeneity of Muslims and Muslim organizations around the world, consider them as partners and assets, and not lump them as one malignant community to be distrusted.

Importance of understanding specifics

Counterterrorism measures, which involve counterideology, need to take into consideration different cultural and contextual realities. A policy that worked for one group or one area may not be successful for other groups or areas. Even within the same group, cultural and contextual differences will need to be addressed. Political, historic and socioeconomic considerations are all part of the contextual consideration in formulating policies at the national and international level.[98]

Optimism

Counterideological battle against Muslim extremism is a long-run effort, much like a marathon. To succeed, one requires strong stamina, which is facilitated by a sense of optimism that the effort is worth it and will produce positive results.

Although it is acknowledged that some of the hard-core extremists may not be persuaded by alternative arguments, it is wrong to conclude that such effort is futile or fruitless. Experience has shown that there were terrorists and extremists who left the group or abandoned their ideology.

Khaled Al-Harbi, known to be Osama's guest in a video shot in late 2001 in which he was shown speaking to Osama about the 9/11 attack, surrendered to the Saudi government during the one month period of amnesty that was offered to members of terrorist groups in Saudi Arabia. He was believed to be hiding on the Iran–Afghanistan border after the attack on Afghanistan by U.S. forces. After surrendering himself, he made a public statement, "I came because I abide by the word of God and that of the caretaker of the holy sites. This initiative from the caretaker of the holy sites and the king is an opportunity. And our country is the country of Islam. Undoubtedly, it is an opportunity any logical man would thank God—every logical man should take advantage of this opportunity."[99] Others who have also surrendered themselves are Mansoor Mohammad Ahmad Faqeeh, Abdullah bin Atiyyeh Al-Salami, Saa'aban bin Mohammed bin Abdullah Al-Shihari, Osman Hadji Al-Maqboul Al-Omary, and Ali Abdulrahman Sa'id Al-Faqsi Al-Ghamdi.[100]

Three ulama, Ali Fahd Al-Khudhair, Ahmed Hamoud Mufred Al-Khaledi, and Nasir Ahmed Al-Fuhaid, were arrested on May 2003 for issuing a statement of support for terrorist attacks in Riyadh. After going through a rehabilitation program, Al-Khudhair and Al-Fuhaid withdrew their opinion in November. Al-Fuhaid described his view as a "grave mistake." On December 2003, Al-Hamoud became the third ulama to denounce his previous statement.[101]

On 15 September 2004, Singapore's Ministry of Home Affairs announced that two detainees who were both members of the Jemaah Islamiyah *shura* (consultative council), were released on

Restrictive Order as "their preventive detention is assessed to be no longer necessary." Two others' Restrictive Orders were not extended.[102] They all had gone through religious counseling and responded positively. Mr. Wong Kan Seng reportedly said:

> Their release represents one of many steps forward in the long term resolution of the JI episode. Our approach in dealing with the JI and the MILF threat goes beyond preventive detention. It also involves the counselling of the detainees so that they understand where they have erred and their eventual release and re-integration back into society.[103]

Winning over the trust and addressing grievances

In the article "The Singapore Perspective—A War for Hearts and Minds in Southeast Asia," Mushahid Ali wrote:

> It is necessary for us, in general, and the West in particular, to understand that this is not just a security threat that can be crushed by military power but more of an ideological and political war for the hearts and minds of the Muslims...[104]

Winning "hearts and minds" will be an uphill task as long as some of the root causes of global Muslim grievances are not addressed. Three years after 9/11, one sore issue still is the uneven foreign policy of the United States in the Middle East, especially vis-à-vis Israel and Palestine, the occupation of Iraq, and the continued American "support" for undemocratic regimes in the region. Muslims all over the world share a deep sense of frustration with the injustices experienced across Muslim societies. As long as these issues are not resolved, the hearts and minds of Muslims may not be easily won.[105]

John E. Mack wrote that terrorism could not be checked, much less eradicated, if the affliction of millions of people in the Middle East who perceive themselves as victims of the policies of a superpower and its allies are not addressed: "This will require at the very least a reexamination of the U.S government policies that one-sidedly favor Israel in relation to the Palestinians."[106]

America must put an end to its practice of creating, nurturing, and supporting criminals, dictators, and terrorists, for example its previous support to Saddam Hussein, and currently its collaboration with the Northern Alliance in Afghanistan, which is infamous for its war-related crimes.[107]

Authoritarian governments, such as Egypt, Jordan, and Pakistan received support from Western countries in the form of credit and military assistance.[108]

Clark McCauley wrote: "It is important to recognize that it is not only Arab and Muslim countries in which U.S policies are seen as responsible for terrorist attacks against the United States." He then mentioned an IHT/Pew poll of 275 "opinion makers" in 24 countries on the issue of whether U.S. policies and actions in the world were a major cause of the 11 September attack. In 23 countries, an average of 58 percent of the respondent answered "yes." Seventy-six percent from Islamic countries and 36 percent from Western European countries said so.[109]

Importance of understanding the causes and contexts

Indeed, understanding the cause helps to understand terrorism's roots. In the case of the Chechen people for example, they are of the view that they are in a state of all-out-war against an enemy that is continuing its oppression, wanting nothing less than total domination, and possibly extinction of the Chechens. Such a view is not baseless if one looks at the long history of oppression by the Czarist Empire, Soviet Union communist regime, and the current Russian government against the Chechen.

So long as there is a precedent for the use of terror and attacking of non-combatants by the powers that be, the militants will reciprocate with the same, not to revenge, but to level the playing field. Thus also providing justification to invoke the "*Quranic* injunction" of an eye for an eye. If the international community continues to be ineffective in addressing these grievances, people will empower themselves.

Acts of terrorism cannot be stopped by defeating the terrorist forces only. Neither can the problem be overcome just by attacking the underlying values of the act, the obsession for revenge and its ideological motivations.[110] The ideas behind extremism and terrorism must be understood in its cultural and contextual milieu.

People who join terrorist organizations may adopt its ideology and belief system for a variety of reasons. Some do it only after careful study and analysis, whereas a few adopt it as a powerful tool for organizing and manipulating other people. "But some are filled with so much anger and frustration that they jump on the first bandwagon that comes along."[111]

In this regard, the problem lies in both the misinterpretation of the text and the opportunity and context that provide for the text to be misinterpreted in that manner. The answer therefore requires the political will of powers that be to address the root causes of the grievances that terrorist groups seize on and exploit in the name of avenging Islam.[112]

Terrorist leaders may be so committed to their ideas that nothing can change their minds. But they will not succeed unless there is a group of people who are susceptible to their recruitment and propaganda. Even hardcore terrorists are likely to become discouraged when support from the larger population withers away.[113]

The role of moderate non-Muslims against the radicals among them

Non-Muslims and Western governments must also make the effort not to allow the extremists among them to dictate the agenda of Muslim and non-Muslims relations by continuously casting doubts on general Muslims, or anticipating an inevitable clash between them.

In *The Clash of Civilisations*, Samuel Huntington wrote that, after the Cold War, the world will be divided into few major civilizations, namely the West, Latin American, African, Islamic, Sinic (Chinese), Hindu, Orthodox, Buddhist, and Japanese.[114] He claims that future world conflicts cannot be viewed through the old ideological struggle lens, that is, liberal democracy versus communism. Instead the source of conflict will be from various emerging antagonistic civilizations and so the "clash" will be between civilizations. But his main focus was on the imminent and inevitable clash between Asian, in particular Chinese/Confucianism, Islam, and Western civilization.[115]

Many Muslim and non-Muslim scholars have criticized and rejected the idea as failing to understand accurately the internal dynamics of the current Islamic world and its visible and heterogeneous communities, which defy simplistic generalizations and static characterizations. Unfortunately, the 9/11 incident has given the idea a new lease on life and probably thrust it as the most definitive thesis on Islam versus the West.[116]

Huntington rejects the argument that the West's problems are not with Islam but only with violent Islamist extremists. He writes that so long as Islam remains Islam, and the West remains the West, the fundamental conflict between the two will continue to define their relations in the future, as it has defined them for the past fourteen centuries.[117] He does not believe that multiculturalism will work in America[118] and Europe. In his new book *Who Are We?* he argues that multiculturalism is, in essence, "anti-European civilisation" because "it is basically an anti-Western ideology."[119]

The late Edward Said commented on Huntington's view: "'The Clash of Civilizations' thesis is a gimmick like 'The War of the Worlds,' better for reinforcing defensive self-pride than for critical understanding of the bewildering interdependence of our time."[120]

Another argument that does not help in promoting goodwill between the West and Muslims, and hence, in the war against extremism and terrorism, is Francis Fukuyama's opinion that only Western or probably American capitalism and democracy will and should prevail, after the collapse of communism, thus the end of history. In his book *The End of History and The Last Man*, he declared that capitalist democracy has succeeded in discrediting all forces such as fascism, socialism, monarchic rule, Islam, and other authoritarian varieties.[121]

Fukuyama may not agree with Huntington's idea of a clash of civilizations, but he applied the same broad-brush and generalizing approach in his view on Islam. He viewed Islam, or at least its fundamentalist branch, as not accepting modernity.[122] Islam, in his view, has defeated liberal democracy in many parts of the Islamic world and poses a grave threat to it in many other countries. He mentioned Iraq as challenger to the West after the Cold War, in which Islam arguably was a factor. On the limitless striving for conquest, he claims it sprang up among the Egyptians "after the conversion of Arabs to Islam, because of the emergence of an aristocratic order whose moral basis was oriented to war."[123] Therefore "it is not an accident that modern liberal democracy emerged first in the Christian West, since universalism of democratic rights can be seen in many ways as a secular form of Christian universalism."[124]

In a speech addressed to Europeans, he urged Europe to stop being intimidated in defending its own humanist culture. He was quoted as saying, "There is a European culture. It's subscribing to a broader culture of tolerance. It's not unreasonable for Europeans to say 'You have to accept this'. The Europeans have to end their political correctness and take seriously what's going on."[125]

He also wrote that Islam virtually has no appeal outside its traditional geographical areas. It has no resonance for young people in Berlin, Tokyo, or Moscow. It will not be able to challenge liberal democracy on its own territory on the level of ideas and would be vulnerable to liberal ideas.[126] If so, one wonders the reason behind his "alarmist" position and also, the fact that Islam is the fastest growing religion in Europe.[127]

Those who view Islam as a threat go to the extent of advising the United States government to unequivocally support regimes threatened by Islamists, even those such as Algeria and Egypt. They urge that the United States should not insist that those states implement political liberalization, because it will allow the participation of Islamists. These states are viewed as a lesser evil than Islam. If necessary, the United States may have to side with leftists against Islamists. For them, defending a global network of authoritarian political and social arrangements remains the most expedient way to maintain United States hegemony.[128]

American scholars and policymakers who view Islam as the "new Communism" and a grave threat to the West, draw on "neo-Orientalist" discourses that stress the inherently antimodern and antidemocratic nature of Islam. The proponents of this view even deride the notion of "Islamic moderates." They accuse those who view Islam as capable of reforms compatible with democracy and the West as "apologists" or "relativists."

Steve Niva offered that the "view is vigorously promoted by an alliance of frustrated Cold Warriors looking for a new threat to justify national security state and the pro-Israeli establishment led by AIPAC."[129]

In an interview with the *Straits Times*' journalist from Singapore, John Esposito warned about the presence of the militant Christian right who are like the right-wing nationalists in Europe in terms of their attitude toward foreigners, in particular Islamics. He also regretted that views by scholars like Bernard Lewis and Fukuyama have contributed to the post-9/11 hysteria about Muslims.[130]

He said:

> This argument is coming from people who are right-wing, who are not just anti-foreign, but in many ways anti-Muslim. It's Islamophobia. If—this is an important point—you were to write about the Jewish, for example, and substitute the word Judaism for Islam and Jews for Muslims, and you were to write the same kinds of pieces that these people write, use all the rest of the words, you would be accused of anti-Semitism. You couldn't do it. So why is it okay to write about Muslims that way?[131]

He said it is an irony that the American and European authorities want to hear the moderate Muslims, but they also fear the moderate Muslim voice, referring to the ban of Professor Tariq Ramadan and Yusuf Islam from entering the United States. He warned America and Europe of the danger that they play right into the hands of radicals because this will not only sideline the moderates among Muslims, but raise questions among them: Are there any Muslims who are acceptable? He described such people as anti-Islam because to them, it does not matter if Muslims are moderates or not, and the war is not against global terrorism, but it's a war against Islam and the Muslim world.[132]

The same message was raised by Sharif Abdullah in his article "The Soul of a Terrorist: Reflections on Our War With the 'Other.'" He wrote that Americans, in particular, should not forget that there are "homegrown versions of the Taliban" in their own country. "They are known as the Christian Identity movement."[133]

It takes two hands to clap. Thus, the war against terrorism is not only won by countering extreme ideology in the Muslim community, but also by countering prevailing prejudiced views among non-Muslims or Westerners that cast doubt on Muslims, antagozise them, and do not promote optimism for peaceful coexistence between the West and Muslims.

It is then important for the moderates among non-Muslims to reject such views and assure Muslims that the majority of them do not subscribe to them.

Conclusion

This study has argued the importance of counterideology in combating terrorism. It proposes a "theological and juristic approach" as one of the key approachs. This, then, requires co-opting the *ulama* and *madrasah* as strategic partners.

This study proposes that counterideology should not only be drawn up for the Muslims but also for non-Muslims, so as to reduce anxiety and create more understanding that will promote racial harmony in society. As a preventive measure, general Muslims should be the main audience for counterideology, to innoculate them from the influence of extremist ideas. But this is not to suggest that a counterideology work targeting terrorists is futile and not worthwhile.

As counterideology is a long battle, maintaining optimism is essential.

The study highlights one of the pitfalls in counterideology: generalization. The broad-brush approach must be avoided.

The important role played by counterideology work must include the need to address grievances held by Muslims.

It is true that the Muslim community has a major role to play in combating the ideology propounded by Muslim extremists and terrorists. Nevertheless, this does not discount the role of governments or policymakers because governments still remain the pivotal institution responsible for the social fabric.

Therefore, at least at the strategic level, governments must develop a comprehensive strategy against terrorism, that incorporates counterideology elements.

With the resource that governments have, their involvement will definitely enhance and multiply the effect of work done by the Muslim community. In fact, this study asserts that non-Muslims should also be incorporated in the work, although with a lesser role. Although Muslims are the best people to counter Muslim extremists and terrorists, non-Muslims are the best people to counter views that will antagonize Muslims at large as such feelings will only hamper counterideological work.

Notes

1   Stephen Biddle, "War Aims and War Termination," in *Defeating Terrorism: Strategic Issue Analyses*, Colonel John R. Martin, ed. (Strategic Studies Institute, U.S Army War College, January 2002), pp. 7–8.
2   Ibid., pp. 11–13; Ted G. Groetzel, "Terrorist Beliefs and Terrorist Lives," in *Psychology of Terrorism*, Chris E. Stout, ed. London, Praeger, 2002, vol. 1, p. 109.
3   Ted G. Groetzel, "Terrorist Beliefs and Terrorist Lives," pp. 99–100.
4   Ibid., p. 109.
5   M. E. Bowman, "Some-Time, Part-Time and One-Time Terrorism," *Intelligencer: Journal of U.S. Intelligence Studies* 13(2) (Winter/Spring, 2003), pp. 16–18. Available at ⟨http://www. fas.org/irp/eprint/bowman. pdf⟩ (24 October 2004).
6   See Walter Laqueur, *The New Terrorism: Fanaticism and the Arms of Mass Destruction* (London: Phoenix Press 1999), pp. 265–269.
7   "Timothy McVeigh profile: From decorated veterans to mass murder," in *CNN.com*, available at ⟨http:// www.cnn.com/CNN/Programs/people/shows/mcveigh/profile.html⟩ (21 February 2005).
8   "Excerpts from the report of the Commission of the Inquiry into the Massacre at the Tomb of the Patriarchs in Hebron," in *Report on measures taken to guarantee the safety and protection of the Palestinian civilians in the occupied Palestinian territory: Israel 03/05/95 CERD/C/282*, available at ⟨http://www.unhchr.ch/tbs/ doc.nsf/0/d6631f0eaea188fe8025675a005570fa?Opendocument⟩ (21 February 2005).
9   "The Unabomb case," in *CNN Interactive*, available at ⟨http://www.cnn.com/SPECIALS/1997/ unabomb/⟩ (21 February 2005).
10 "Tangkap Ketua Kumpulan Militan Malaysia Johor & Senarai Ahli KMM Yang Dikehendaki Polis," in *Royal Malaysian Police media release*, 17 September 2002, available at ⟨http://www.rmp.gov.my/ rmp03/020927kmm.htm⟩ (21 February 2005).
11 "Particular of detainees," in *Singapore government press statement on ISA arrests*, 11 January 2002, available at ⟨http://www2.mha.gov.sg/mha/ibrowse.jsp?type=1&root=1&parent= 1&cat=17⟩ (21 February 2005).
12 Jason Burke, *Al Qaeda: The True Story of Radical Islam* (London: Penguin Books, 2004), p. 281.
13 John E. Mack, "Looking Beyond Terrorism: Transcending the Mind of Enmity," in *Psychology of Terrorism*, p. 175–176.
14 "Bin Laden's fatwa," in *Online Newshour*, August 1996, available at ⟨http://www.pbs.org/newshour/ terrorism/international/fatwa_1996.html⟩ (21 February 2005); "Fatwa Urging Jihad Against Americans," in *Al-Quds Al-Arabi*, 23 February 1998, available at ⟨http://www.fas.org/irp/world/para/ docs/980223-fatwa.htm⟩ (21 February 2005); "A New Bin Laden Speech," in *The Middle East Media Research Institute*, Special Dispatch Series No. 539 (18 July 2003), available at ⟨http://www.memri.org/ bin/articles.cgi?Page=archives&Area=sd&ID=SP53903⟩ (21 February 2005); "Full transcript of Bin Laden's speech," in *Aljazeera*, 1 November 2004, available at ⟨http://english.aljazeera.net/NR/ exeres/79C6AF22–98FB-4A1C-B21F-2BC36E87F61F.htm⟩ (21 February 2005); "Imam Samudra: By Allah, It's Not Over Yet" in *Tempo, Special Commemorative Edition, Bali Bombing: One Year On*, 14–20 October 2003; Chistopher M. Blanchard, "Al Qaeda: Statements and Evolving Ideology," in *CRS Report for Congress*, 16 November 2004, available at ⟨http://www.fas.org/irp/crs/RS21973.pdf⟩ (21 February 2005); Christopher Henzel, *The Origins of Al Qaeda Ideology: Implications for U.S. Strategy* (20 April 2004), available at ⟨http://www.ndu.edu/nwc/writing/AY04/awardpapers/Nominated%20Paper–04– Henzel.pdf⟩ (21 February 2005); A. Maftuh Abegebriel, "Al-Qa'idah: Arabists or Islamists?" in *Negara Tuhan: The Thematic Encyclopaedia*, A. Maftuh Abegebriel and A. Yanti Abeveiro, eds. (SR-Ins Team, SR-Ins Publishing, Jogjakarta, 2004), pp. 574–576, 583–593, 607–629; Jason Burke, *Al Qaeda: The True Story of Radical Islam*, pp. 34–37.
15 Stephen Biddle, "War Aims and War Termination," in *Defeating Terrorism: Strategic Issue Analyses*, p. 9.

16 Jason Burke, "Think Again: Al Qaeda," *Foreign Policy* (May/June 2004), pp. 18–19, available at (http://www.foreignpolicy.com/story/cms.php?story_id=2536&print=1) (7 Mac 2005); Jason Burke, *Al Qaeda: The True Story of Radical Islam*, pp. xxv–xxvi.

17 Ibid.

18 See Llewellyn D. Howell, "Is The New Terrorism A Clash of Civilisations? Evaluating Terrorism's Multiple Sources," in *The New Global Terrorism: Characteristics, Causes, Controls*, Charles W. Kegley, Jr., ed. (New Jersey: Prentice Hall, 2003), pp. 179–184; see Paul K. Davis and Brian Michael Jenkins, *Deterrence and Influence in Counterterrorism: A Component in the War on al Qaeda* (Pittsburgh: RAND, 2002), pp. 46–47.

19 Biddle, "War Aims and War Termination," p. 10.

20 Kumar Ramakrishna, *Emergency Propaganda: The Winning of Malayan Hearts and Minds 1948–1958* (Surrey: Curzon, 2002), p. 11.

21 Ibid., p. 12.

22 Ibid., pp. 88–89; Richard Stubbs, *Hearts and Minds in Guerilla Warfare: The Malayan Emergency 1948–1960* (Singapore: Oxford, 1993), pp. 168–180.

23 Stubbs, *Hearts and Minds in Guerilla Warfare*, pp. 184–187.

24 Mushahid Ali and Muhammad Haniff Hassan, "Fighting Terrorism From Ideological Front," *Straits Times*, Singapore, 31 August 2004.

25 Thomas R. Mockaitis, "Winning Hearts and Minds in the War on Terrorism," in *Grand Strategy; In the War Against Terrorism*, Thomas R. Mockaitis and Paul B. Rich, eds. (London: Frank Cass, 2003) pp. 28–29.

26 Biddle, "War Aims and War Termination," p. 7; Jason Burke, "Think Again: Al Qaeda," p. 18.

27 Giovanni Caracci, "Cultural and Contextual Aspects of Terrorism," *Psychology of Terrorism*, 3, p. 66.

28 *The White Paper: The Jemaah Islamiyah Arrests and the Threat of Terrorism* (Ministry of Home Affairs, 2003), p. 11.

29 See full text of speech by Mr. George Bush, President of the United States, on 10 September 2002, at the Afghanistan Embassy Washington DC, available at (http://www.whitehouse.gov/news/releases/2002/09/20020910-7.html) (11 October 2004); Refer to question and answer text on the 9/11 attack, between the Prime Minister of England, Mr. Tony Blair, and journalists on 12 September 2001, available at (http://www.number-10.gov.uk/output/Page1597.asp) (11 October 2004).

30 See Caracci, "Cultural and Contextual Aspects of Terrorism," p. 58.

31 Ali and Hassan, "Fighting Terrorism From Ideological Front."

32 See Samuel Huntington, *The Clash of Civilizations and the Remaking of World Order* (New York: Simon & Schuster, 1997), p. 114.

33 Ibid.

34 Collection of Prophet Muhammad's deeds, statements, and concessions—as defined by Abdul Rahman b. Yusuf, *The Science of Hadith: An Introduction*, available at (http://www.sunnipath.com/resources/Questions/qa00002867.aspx) (11 October 2004).

35 The Science of Source Methodology of Islamic Jurisprudence. It has been defined "as the aggregate, considered per se, of legal proofs and evidence that, when studied properly, will lead either to certain knowledge of a Shari'ah ruling or to at least a reasonable assumption concerning the same; the manner by which such proofs are adduced, and the status of the adducer. As its subject matter, this science deals with the proofs in the Shari'ah source-texts, viewing them from the perspective of how, by means of Ijtihad, legal judgements are derived from their particulars; though after, in cases where texts may appear mutually contradictory, preference has been established." See Tahir Jabir Al-'Alwani, *Usul Al-Fiqh Al-Islami, Source Methodology for Islamic Jurisprudence: Methodology for Research and Knowledge*, Chapter One, available at (http://www.usc.edu/dept/MSA/law/alalwani_usulalfiqh/ch1.html) (11 October 2004); Hashim Kamali, *Introduction to Usul Fiqh*, available at (http://www.bysiness.co.uk/kitaabun01/introduction_to_usul_al.htm) (11 October 2004).

36 Also known as *Ulum Al-Quran*. It is the science of interpretation of Al-Quran. See Ahmad Von Denffer, *Ulum Al-Quran: An Introduction of Sciences of Al-Quran*, available at (http://www.islamworld.net/UUQ/) (11 October 2004).

37 Also known as *Mustalah Al-Hadits*. It is the science in the study of *hadits*. Its objective is to determine the authenticity of a *hadits* and how rulings can be deduced from it. See Suhayb Hasan, *An Introduction to the Sciences of Hadith*, available at (http://www.sunnahonline.com/ilm/sunnah/0008.htm#2) (11 October 2004); Abdul Rahman b. Yusuf, *The Science of Hadith: An Introduction*, available at (http://www.sunnipath.com/resources/Questions/qa00002867.aspx) (11 October 2004).

38 Stephen Grey, "Follow the Mullahs," in *The Atlantic Monthly* (November 2004, pp. 44–47, available at (http://www.theatlantic.com/doc/prem/200411/grey) (12 October 2004).
39 Biddle, "War Aims and War Termination, in *Defeating Terrorism: Strategic Issue Analysis*, p. 11.
40 Ibid.
41 Biddle, "War Aims and War Termination," p. 11; see also Sami G. Hajjar, "Avoiding Holy War: Ensuring That the War on Terorism is Not Perceived as a War on Islam," in *Defeating Terrorism: Strategic Issue Analyses*, pp. 17–19.
42 Mushahid Ali, "The Singapore Perspective—A war for Hearts and Minds in Southeast Asia," in *Terrorism: Perspective For the Asia Pacific*, Elina Noor and Mohamed Jawhar Hassan, eds. (Kuala Lumpur: ISIS, 2002), p. 104.
43 Yang Razali Kassim and Muhammad Haniff Hassan, "*Madrasah* can be key partners in war on terror," in *Straits Times*, Singapore, 22 September 2004.
44 Burke, "Think Again: Al Qaeda," pp. 20–22.
45 See ruling on martyrdom operation in Palestine, available at (http://www.qaradawi.net/site/topics/article.asp?cu_no=2&item_no=1461&version=1&template_id=130&parent_id=17) (13 October 2004); ruling by Yusuf Al-Qaradhawi on martyrdom operation by woman, available at (http://www.qaradawi.net/site/topics/article.asp?cu_no=2&item_no=2082&version=1&template_id=130&parent_id=17) and (http://www.islam-online.net/fatwa/english/FatwaDisplay.asp?hFatwaID = 68511) (13 October 2004); ruling on boycotting American and Israel's products, available at (http://www.qaradawi.net/site/topics/article.asp?cu_no=2&item_no=2090&version=1&template_id=130&parent_id=17) (13 October 2004).
46 See ruling on 9/11 attack, available at (http://www.qaradawi.net/site/topics/article.asp?cu_no=2&item_no=1665&version=1&template_id=130&parent_id=17) and (http://www.islamonline.net/*fatwa*/english/*Fatwa*Display.asp?h*Fatwa*ID=49756) (13 October 2004); ruling on hostage taking and kidnapping by militants, available at (http://www.qaradawi.net/site/topics/article.asp? cu_no=2&item_no=3423&version=1&template_id=130&parent_id=17) (13 October 2004); see ruling on terrorism against civilians, available at (http://www.islamonline.net/*fatwa*/english/*Fatwa*Display.asp?h*Fatwa*ID=49341) (13 October 2004); ruling on Bali bombing, available at (http://www.islamonline.net/*fatwa*/english/*Fatwa*Display.asp?h*Fatwa*ID=83718) (13 October 2004); Islam stance's on killing captives, available at (http://www.islamonline.net/fatwa/english/FatwaDisplay.asp?hFatwaID=114486) (21 February 2005).
47 Conference report, "Political Islam in Southeast Asia" by The Paul H. Nitze of Advanced International Studies John Hopkins University, 25 March 2003, p. 17.
48 Ibid.
49 Burke, "Think Again: Al Qaeda," p. 22.
50 Ali and Hassan, "Fighting Terrorism From Ideological Front."
51 Cited in Abdul Rahman b. Mu'alla Al-Luwaihiq, *Religious Extremism in the Life of Contemporary Muslims*, translated by Jamaal Al-Din M. Zarabozo (Al-Basheer, 2001), p. 452; see Ibn Taimiyah, *Al-Istiqamah*, Jami'ah Al-Imam Muhammad bin Sa'ud Al-Islamiah, Riyadh, 1403H, vol. 1, p. 41.
52 Ibid, p. 451. See Ibn Taimiyah, *Minhaj As-Sunnah An-Nabawiyah*, Jami'ah Muhammad bin Sa'ud Al-Islamiah, Riyadh, 1406, vol. 4, pp. 529–530.
53 Ibn Taimiyah, *Majmu' Al-Fatawa*, Matabi' Ar-Riyadh, Riyadh, 1372H, vol. 30, p. 357.
54 Ibid., vol. 19, pp. 218–219.
55 Ibid., vol. 20, p. 54.
56 Cited in Abdul Rahman b. Mu'alla Al-Luwaihiq, *Religious Extremism in the Life of Contemporary Muslims*, p. 338.
57 Ibn Qayyim Al-Jauzi, *Zad Al-Ma'ad*, Muassasah Ar-Risalah, Beirut, 1996, vol. 3, pp. 5–6, 8.
58 Christopher M. Blanchard, "Islamic Religious Schools, *Madrasas*: Background," in *CRS Report for Congress*, 10 February 2005, available at (http://www.fas.org/sgp/crs/misc/RS21654.pdf) (21 February 2005).
59 Kassim and Hassan, "Madrasah can be Key Partners in War on Terror."
60 Caracci, "Cultural and Contextual Aspects of Terrorism," p. 58.
61 Ibid.
62 Hisham Kabbani, *The Doctrine of Ahl Al-Sunna versus the "Wahabi-Salafi" Movement*, available at (http://www.islamicsupremecouncil.org/bin/site/ftp/SalafiDoctrine.pdf) (21 February 2005).
63 Hisham Kabbani, *"Salafis" Unveiled*, available at (http://sunnah.org/publication/salafi/salafi_unveiled/contents.htm) (21 February 2005), also *Islamic Radicalism: Its Wahhabi roots and current representation*, available at (http://www.islamicsupremecouncil.org/bin/site/wrappers/default.asp?pane_2=content-extremism_wahabroots) (21 February 2005).

64 Quinton Wiktorowicz, "The New Global Threat: Transnational Salafis and Jihad," in *Middle East Policy*, VIII (4) (December 2001), p. 20.

65 Ibid., p. 34.

66 Jason Burke, *Al Qaeda: The True Story of Radical Islam*, pp. 39–40, 55.

67 Simon Reeve, "Trouble in the Desert Kingdom: Saudi Arabia Racked by Fundamentalism and Political Unrest," *The Independent*, 14 July 2004, pp. 2–3.

68 Mona Eltahawy, "The Wahhabi Threat to Islam," *The Washington Post*, 6 June 2004, p. B07.

69 Warren Fernandez, "Root out cancer at the heart of Arab world; It is Saudi Arabia's Wahhbism that lies at the root of the violence fomented in the name of Islam," *Straits Times*, 31 May 2003.

70 International Crisis Group, *Indonesia Backgrounder: Why Salafism and Terrorism Mostly Don't Mix?*, ICG Asia Report No. 83, 13 September 2004, p. I.

71 See "Salafi," in *Wikipedia, the Free Encyclopedia*, available at (http://en.wikipedia.org/wiki/Salafi) (11 October 2004); see International Crisis Group, *Indonesia Backgrounder: Why Salafism and Terrorism Mostly Don't Mix?*, p. I.

72 See Abdul Mu'ti, "Boosting Moderate Islam," *The Jakarta Post*, 23 October 2003; see "Muhammadiyah," available at (http://philtar.ucsm.ac.uk/encyclopedia/indon/muham.html) (11 October 2004); Ahmad Syafii Maarif, Chairman of Islamic Movement Muhammadiyah, Indonesia wrote on the organization, available at (http://www.santegidio.org/uer/2003/int_508_EN.htm) (11 October 2004).

73 See brief introduction to "Wahhabis," in *The 1911 Encyclopedia Edition*, available at (http://3.1911encyclopedia.org/W/WA/WAHHABIS.htm) (11 October 2004).

74 See Abdul Aziz b. Al-Baz, *Imaam Muhammad b. Abdul Wahab—His Life and Mission*, available at (http://www.ahya.org/amm/modules.php?name=Sections&op=viewarticle&artid=180) (11 October 2004); see "Muhammad bin Saud," in *Wikipedia, the Free Encyclopedia*, available at (http://en.wikipedia.org/wiki/Muhammad_bin_Saud) (11 October 2004).

75 See Natana J. Delong-Bas, *Wahhabi Islam: From Revival and Reform to Global Jihad* (New York: Oxford University Press, 2004), pp. 257–279, 288–290.

76 Hasan Albanna, *Al-'Aqaa'id*, available at (http://www.youngmuslims.ca/online_library/books/the_creed/index.htm) (11 October 2004).

77 See Hasan Albanna, *Our Message*, available at (http://www.youngmuslims.ca/online_library/books/our_message/index.htm) (11 October 2004).

78 "Muslim Brotherhood—Egypt," in *the Encyclopedia of the Orient*, available at (http://icias.com/e.o/mus_br_egypt.htm) (23 Feb 2005); Federal Research Division of the Library of the Congress, "Egypt country studies," in *country—studies.com*, available at (http://www.countrystudies.com/egypt/the-opposition-parties.html) (23 February 2005) and (http://www.countrystudies.com/egypt/elections.html) (23 February 2005); Abdul Raheem Ali, "Seeking Reform, Egyption Opposition Closes Ranks," in *IslamOnline.net*, available at (http://islamonline.net/ English/News/2004–08/10/article06.shtml) (23 February 2005); Egypt's Culture Wars Lead to Crack-down on Labor Party, in *The Estimate*, 2 June 2000, available at (http://www.theestimate.com/public/060200.html) (23 February 2005); Amira Howeidy, "The Brother's Last Sigh?" in *Al-Ahram Weekly Online*, Issue No. 502, 5–11 October 2000, available at (http://weekly.ahram.org.eg/2000/502/ el1.htm) (23 February 2005); Khaled Dawoud, "Flat Tyres but no Regrets," in *Al-Ahram Weekly Online*, Issue No. 502, 5–11 October 2000, available at (http://weekly.ahram.org.eg/2000/502/el4.htm) (23 February 2005).

79 Amira Howeidy, "Running as religious duty," in *Al-Ahram Weekly Online*, Issue No. 502, 5–11 October 2000, available at (http://weekly.ahram.org.eg/2000/502/el2.htm) (23 February 2005).

80 Abdul Raheem Ali, "Muslim Brotherhood Seeks Mubarak Meeting," in *IslamOnline.net*, available at (http://islamonline.net/English/News/2004–09/05/article02.shtml) (23 February 2005).

81 Amer Taheri, "Saudi Shiites," in *National Review*, 23 May 2003, available at (http://www.nationalreview.com/comment/comment-taheri052303.asp) (11 October 2004); Hasan Abu Taleb, "The Shiite Question in Saudi Arabia," in *Centre for Political and Strategic Studies*, issue 9, (11 Mac 2004), available at (http://www.nationalreview.com/comment/comment-taheri052303.asp) (11 October 2004).

82 International Crisis Group, *Indonesia Backgrounder: Why Salafism and Terrorism Mostly Don't Mix?*, p. 29.

83 Cheryl Benard, *Civil Democratic Islam: Partners, Resources and Strategies* (Santa Monica: RAND Publication 2003), pp. 8–13.

84 See Leonard Sebastian, "Getting To the Root of Radicalism in Indonesia," in *Perspectives*, Institute of Defence and Strategic Studies, 2002, available at (http://www.ntu.edu.sg/idss/Perspective/research_050212.htm) (8 October 2004).

85 Karvin Von Hippel, "The Roots of Terrorism," in *Superterrorism: Policy Response*, Lawrence Freedman, ed. (United Kingdom: Blackwell Publishing, 2002), pp. 31–32.

86   Wayne A. Downing, "The Global on Terrorism: Focusing the National Strategy," in *Defeating Terrorism: Shaping the New Security Environment*, Russel D. Howard and Reid L. Sawyer, eds. (Connecticut: McGraw Hill, 2002), p. 152.

87   See ⟨http://www.madrasah.edu.sg/about.html⟩ (8 October 2004).

88   Martin Van Bruinessen, "'Traditionalist' and 'Islamist' Pesantren in Contemporary Indonesia," paper presented at the ISIM workshop on The *Madrasah* in Asia, 23–24 May 2004, available at ⟨http://www.let.uu.nl/~martin.vanbruinessen/personal/publications/pesantren_in_Indonesia.htm⟩ (13 October 2004).

89   Ibid. International Crisis Group, *Jemaah Islamiyah in Southeat Asia: Damaged but Still Dangerous*, ICG Asia Report No. 63, 26 August 2003, p. 26.

90   Yoginder Sikand, "Madrasah in Asia," in *ISIM Newsletter* 14 (June 2004), p. 56; Burke, *Al Qaeda: The True Story of Radical Islam*, pp. 92–94.

91   Ibid.

92   Ibid.

93   Ibid. See also Barbara D. Metcalf, "Traditionalist" Islamic Activism: Deoband, Tablighis and Talibs," available at ⟨http://www.ssrc.org/sept11/essays/metcalf_text_only.htm⟩ (14 October 2004).

94   See ⟨http://www.madrasah.edu.sg/about.html⟩ (8 October 2004).

95   Kassim and Hassan, "Madrasah can be Key Partners in War on Terror."

96   Ibid; also see ⟨http://www.madrasah.edu.sg/about.html⟩ (8 October 2004).

97   Christopher M. Blanchard, "Islamic Religious Schools, *Madrasas*: Background," in *CRS Report for Congress*, 10 February 2005 [online].

98   Caracci, "Cultural and Contextual Aspects of Terrorism," p. 78–79.

99   "Saudi: Bin Laden associate surrenders," in *CNN.com*, 14 July 2004, available at ⟨http://edition.cnn.com/2004/WORLD/meast/07/13/binladen.aide/⟩ (21 February 2005).

100 Saudi government report, "Initiative and actions taken by the Kingdom of Saudi Arabia to Combat Terrorism," March 2004, available at ⟨http://www.saudiembassy.net/ReportLink/WOT%20March%202004.pdf⟩ (21 February 2005); "Amnesty for Saudi Terrorist Nears End," in *FOXNews.com* (22 July 2004), available at ⟨http://www.foxnews.com/story/0,2933,126563,00.html⟩ (21 February 2005).

101 Ibid.

102 Singapore Government Press Statement, "Extension of 17 Detention Orders and One Restriction Order Release of Two Detainees and Lapse of Two Restriction Orders," (15 September 2004) available at ⟨http://www2.mha.gov.sg/mha/detailed.jsp?artid=1180&type=4&root=0&parent=0&cat=0⟩ (12 October 2004).

103 Teo Hwee Nak, "Detention extended for 17 of 19 men jailed for links to JI," in *Today* (16 September 2004) available at ⟨http://www.todayonline.com/articles/26027.asp⟩ (12 October 2004).

104 Ali, "The Singapore Perspective—A war for Hearts and Minds in Southeast Asia," p. 104.

105 Kassim and Hassan, "Madrasah can be Key Partners in War on Terror."

106 John E. Mack, "Looking Beyond Terrorism: Transcending the Mind of Enmity," *Psychology of Terrorism*, 1, p. 175

107 Sharif Abdullah, "The Soul of a Terrorist: Reflections on Our War With the 'Other,'" *Psychology of Terrorism*, 1, p. 139.

108 Clark McCauley, "Psychological Issues in Understanding Terrorism and the Response to Terrorism," *Psychology of Terrorism*, 3, p. 10.

109 Ibid.; see also B. Knowlton, "How the World sees the United States and Sept. 11," *International Herald Tribune*, 20 December 2001, pp. 1, 6.

110 Muhammad Haniff Hassan, "Beslan: Attack Grievances, Not Terrorist Only," in *Straits Times*, Singapore, 28 September 2004.

111 Goertzel, "Terrorist Beliefs and Terrorist Lives," p. 99.

112 Hassan, "Beslan."

113 Mack, "Looking Beyond Terrorism," p. 180.

114 Samuel Huntington, *The Clash of Civilizations and the Remaking of World Order*, pp. 26–27 (map 1.3), 45–48, 102, 109–111.

115 Ibid., p. 102, 109–111.

116 Ghada Hashem Talhami, "Muslim, Islamist and the Cold War," in *Grand Strategy in the War Against Terrorism*, p. 111.

117 Samuel Huntington, *The Clash of Civilizations and the Remaking of World Order*, p. 212.

118 Ibid., p. 318.
119 John Vicour, "Politcus: Trying to put Islam in Europe's agenda," in *International Herald Tribune* (21 September 2004), available at ⟨http://www.iht.com/articles/539686.html⟩ (11 October 2004).
120 Edward W. Said, "The Clash of Ignorance," in *The Nation*, 22 October 2001, pp. 11–13, available at ⟨http://www.thenation.com/doc.mhtml?i=20011022&c=2&s=said⟩ (7 October 2004).
121 Ghada Hashem Talhami, "Muslim, Islamist and the Cold War," p. 112; see Francis Fukuyama, *The End of History and the Last Man* (New York: Perennial, 2002), pp. 39, 42, 45–46.
122 Francis Fukuyama, "History is Going Our Way," in *Wall Street Journal* (5 October 2001), p. A14, available at ⟨http://www.opinionjournal.com/editorial/feature.html?id=95001277⟩ (3 October 2004).
123 Fukuyama, *The End of History and the Last Man*, p. 260.
124 Fukuyama, "History is Going Our Way."
125 John Vicour, "Politcus: Trying to put Islam in Europe's Agenda," *International Herald Tribune*, 21 September 2004, available at ⟨http://www.iht.com/articles/539686.html⟩ (11 October 2004).
126 Francis Fukuyama, *The End of History and The Last Man*, pp. 45–47.
127 "Interpreting the Prophet's Message," in *The Irish Times*, 27 November 2004, p. 1; Jeff Heinrich, "Two Thirds of our Muslims Regularly go to Mosque," in *The Gazzette (Montreal, Quebec)*, 24 July 2004, p. A4; Tamer Al-Ghobashy, "Fertile Crescent: Conversions to Islam on Rise in U.S.," in *The Daily News (New York)*, 26 December 2003, p. 35; Craig S. Smith, "Letter from Europe: Minarets and Steeples, can France Balance Them?" in *The New York Times*, 1 October 2003, p. 4; "Muslim in Western Europe," in *The Economist*, 8 August 2002, available at ⟨http://www.economist.com/displaystory.cfm?story_id=1270416#abroad_at_home,_by_satellite⟩ (21 February 2005), "Fast-growing Islam winning converts in Western world," in *CNN Interactive* (14 April 1997), available at ⟨http://www.cnn.com/WORLD/9704/14/egypt.islam/⟩ (21 February 2005); M. M. Ali, "Muslims in America: The Nation's Fastest Growing Religion," in *Washington Report on Middle East Affairs* (May/June, 1996), pp. 13, 107, available at ⟨http://www.washingtonreport.org/backissues/0596/9605013.htm⟩ (21 February 2005); "Islam to become 2nd largest faith practiced in US," in *The Times of India*, 12 July 2001.
128 Steve Niva, "Between Clash and Co-optation: US Foreign Policy and the Specter of Islam," in *Middle East Report* (Fall, 1998), pp. 27–28.
129 Ibid.
130 Mafoot Simon, "Islamophobia creates the very monster that it fears," in *Straits Times* (30 September 2004), available at ⟨http://straitstimes.asia1.com.sg/columnist/0,1886,1814–275252-,00.html?⟩ (7 October 2004).
131 Ibid.
132 Ibid.
133 Sharif Abdullah, "The Soul of a Terrorist," p. 136.

Section 7

Current and future trends in terrorism

Readings

Ackerman, G. (2005). WMD terrorism research: Whereto from here? *International Studies Review, 7,* 140–143.

Hoffman, B. (2004). The changing face of Al Qaeda and the global war on terrorism. *Studies in Conflict and Terrorism, 27,* 549–560.

Mueller, J. (2005). Six rather unusual propositions about terrorism. *Terrorism and Political Violence, 17,* 487–505.

Hafez, M. M. (2007). Martyrdom mythology in Iraq: How jihadists frame suicide terrorism in videos and biographies. *Terrorism and Political Violence, 19,* 95–115.

Cunningham, K. J. (2007). Countering female terrorism. *Studies in Conflict and Terrorism, 30,* 113–129.

Tonge, J. (2004). "They haven't gone away, you know': Irish republican "dissidents' and "armed struggle". *Terrorism and Political Violence, 16,* 671–693.

Vidino, L. (2009). Homegrown jihadist terrorism in the United States: A new and occasional phenomenon? *Studies in Conflict and Terrorism, 32,* 1–17.

Barkun, M. (2007). Appropriated martyrs: The Branch Davidians and the radical right. *Terrorism and Political Violence, 19,* 117–124.

Introduction

To this point, we hope that you have been provided with a very comprehensive introduction to almost all relevant issues in terrorism and political violence. While previous sections have provided a description of what terrorism is and how we understand it, this final section serves an important function by encouraging you to consider some of the ways in which terrorism is currently developing, and might continue to develop in the future. While Section 1 contained an important reading on how the "new" terrorism differs from the "old," this section explores these "new" characteristics in much more detail as well as considering what the implications of these will be for counterterrorism. Most of the contributions in this section will examine the global Salafi Jihad and developments within al-Qaeda. In addition, because the historical context to terrorism is so frequently overlooked, there is little appreciation of the need to look at future developments in the short, medium and long term. While this section focuses on many current trends in terrorism, it also looks forward to what issues may emerge as central in the realm of terrorism studies. First, Gary Ackerman takes a close look at one of the most distressing issues within terrorism studies – the potential use of weapons of mass destruction (WMD) by terrorist groups. Next, Bruce Hoffman provides a discussion of al-Qaeda and how it has changed since the September 11 attacks. Hoffman's examination highlights the affiliated groups and organizations that have emerged as "allies" to al-Qaeda and illustrates the extent to which it has transformed its structure and operations in the last decade. John Mueller then presents an argument for how to avoid the heavy costs typically associated with being subjected to a terrorist attack. Although he describes his propositions as "unusual," Mueller's arguments offer thought-provoking ways for states to deal with terrorism. Although we have considered suicide bombing in earlier sections, Mohammed Hafez investigates how killing oneself in the name of an ideology is currently framed by jihadists and how this framing can be used to persuade individuals to blow themselves up. Then, Karla Cunningham addresses an oft-ignored, but growing threat – the female terrorist. By examining terrorist activity in three geographical areas, Cunningham illustrates how the female terrorist emerged with such prevalence.

In a previous section, you were introduced to the Provisional IRA. In this section, Jonathan Tonge investigates those violent factions that split from the Provisionals when the Good Friday Agreement was signed. The Real IRA and the Continuity IRA, two extremely violent groups operating in Northern Ireland, are discussed. Next, we turn to what have been described as "homegrown terrorists," individuals who live among those they intend to target. Lorenzo Vidino takes a closer look at this phenomenon, comparing homegrown terrorists in the United States and Europe and counterterrorists' reactions to their activities. In light of arrests of homegrown jihadists in recent times, Vidino's work represents an emerging critical facet of U.S. counterterrorism policy. Finally, Michael Barkun investigates the extent to which the radical right values martyrs, even in spite of ideological inconsistency. Here, Barkun illustrates how the definition of "martyr" is largely flexible and can be changed based on the needs of a particular group.

Discussion questions

By the end of this section, you should be able to answer:

* How have terrorist groups and counterterrorist measures changed over the years (particularly after 9/11/01)?
* Can terrorism be an *individual* phenomenon?
* What do you think is the "next big terrorist threat?" Why?
* How do you think security forces should approach counterterrorism in the future, as groups become less hierarchical and more diffuse?

Further reading

Bloom, M. (2010). *Bombshell: The many faces of women terrorists*. Toronto: Penguin.

Conway, M. (2006). Terrorism and the Internet: New media – new threat. *Parliamentary Affairs, 59*, 283–298.

Gressang, D. (2001). Audience and message: Assessing terrorist WMD potential. *Terrorism and Political Violence, 13*, 83–106.

Horgan, J., & Braddock, K. (2010). Rehabilitating the terrorists? Challenges in assessing the effectiveness of de-radicalization programs. *Terrorism and Political Violence, 22*, 267–291.

Keohane, R. O. (2002). The globalization of informal violence, theories of world politics, and the "liberalism of fear'. *International Organisation, 1*, 29–43.

Krueger, A. B. (2008). What makes a homegrown terrorist? Human capital and participation in domestic Islamic terrorist groups in the U.S.A. *Economics Letters, 101*, 293–296.

Lia, B. (2005). *Globalisation and the future of terrorism: Patterns and predictions*. London: Routledge.

MacAllister, B. (2004). Al Qaeda and the innovative firm: Demythologizing the network. *Studies in Conflict and Terrorism, 27*, 217–239.

Nesser, P. (2006). Jihadism in Western Europe after the invasion of Iraq. *Studies in Conflict and Terrorism, 29*, 323–342.

Sageman, M. (2004). *Leaderless jihad*. Philadelphia, PA: University of Pennsylvania Press.

Schmid, A. (1999). Terrorism and weapons of mass destruction: From where the risk? *Terrorism and Political Violence, 17*, 106–132.

Webb, J. J., & Cutter, S. L. (2009). The geography of U.S. terrorist incidents, 1970–2004. *Terrorism and Political Violence, 21*, 428–449.

Weimann, G. (2006). *Terror on the Internet: The new arena, the new challenges*. Washington, D. C.: United States Institute of Peace Press.

23 WMD terrorism research

Whereto from here?

Gary Ackerman

Despite significant contributions in the past decade to our understanding of various aspects of WMD terrorism, the topic seems to have reached something of an "interpretive impasse." A recent survey of more than 120 books, journal articles, monographs, and government reports dealing with WMD terrorism indicated that the scholarly and policy-related literature has increasingly begun to recycle the same interpretations and staid shibboleths. This is not meant to denigrate several excellent works that have emerged, merely to point out that truly novel insights into WMD terrorism are becoming few and far between.

To some extent this is understandable, given the paucity of serious chemical, biological, radiological, or nuclear (CBRN) incidents and the absence of any true WMD attacks by terrorists upon which to base studies and against which to validate assertions. The answers to some of the questions surrounding WMD terrorism must, therefore, necessarily remain within the realm of the speculative as long as we do not experience any major attacks—and hopefully this will continue to be the case. There are, however, several aspects that seem to have been overlooked or given scant attention in the research program thus far. With the hope of broadening the research agenda for WMD terrorism, I offer the following three examples.

(1) Operationalizing WMD terrorism research by informing threat assessments

The current security situation, including recent indications of terrorist interest in using WMD, makes it untenable for scholars to act leisurely in applying their insights to practical purposes. Basic research needs to be operationalized as soon as possible in a form that analysts, investigators, and policymakers can deploy "in the field." A task that scholars should set for themselves in this regard is to actively work to incorporate the knowledge and insights we have gained over decades of study regarding motivational and other aspects of WMD terrorism into threat assessment methodologies that can be used by analysts with less experience and smaller knowledge bases than most scholars possess.

One means of informing threat assessments is to develop standardized methodologies for conducting in-depth, qualitative studies of particular extremist groups so that threat assessments encompass such factors as a group's history, ideology, life-cycle status, organizational structure, organizational dynamics, resources, operational capabilities, environmental factors, cognitive and affect-based distortions to perception and information processing, and operational objectives, to mention only some. In addition, scholars should not shy away from undertaking close qualitative studies themselves, given that intelligence and law enforcement analysts rarely possess the time or resources necessary to conduct comprehensive profiles of this sort. Such efforts, even those based solely on information found in unclassified sources, can yield considerable indicators of a group's or individual's future potential for various types of violence, including the use of WMD.

To provide but one example, a serious investigation of Aum Shinrikyo—which several Japanese newspapers did, in fact, carry out—should have been more than sufficient to alert domestic and international authorities to the dangers posed by the organization. If those warnings had been heeded and promptly acted upon, the 1995 sarin gas attack in the Tokyo subway could undoubtedly have been prevented. As Ehud Sprinzak (2000:5–6) has argued,

> the vast majority of terrorist organizations can be identified well in advance ... and the number of potential [WMD] suspects is significantly less than doomsayers seem to believe. Ample early warning signs should make effective interdiction of potential superterrorists much easier than today's prevailing rhetoric suggests.

Another way in which scholars can leverage their collective knowledge in the above mentioned pursuit is to combine empirical research (both of the large-N and case study varieties) on terrorist motivations and capabilities with the existing body of literature relating to terrorist decision making in order to produce usable and useful analytical tools. It needs to be emphasized that, despite the intent to provide analysts with analytical aids, there is no way to predict the timing, nature, or location of future WMD attacks with any degree of scientific certainty. In many ways the threat of WMD terrorism resembles a chaotic system, in the strict sense of the term, wherein tiny perturbations in any of a myriad of factors can result in significantly disparate outcomes. Moreover, the traditional analytical methods of the past have also served us rather poorly in predicting terrorist behavior—the failures in foreseeing such events as the 1995 Tokyo subway sarin release or the September 11 attacks were not solely the result of faulty intelligence. They were in many ways the consequence of a lack of imagination and innovation in thinking about such threats.

What is required is a synthesis—a marriage of the quantitative and the qualitative, the model and the empirical "actual." Combining real-world data with a new set of analytical tools—be they computational, statistical, or merely heuristic—could enable those involved in counterterrorism to reach a level of understanding that is both specific to the dangers of the terrorist group under consideration and sufficiently comparative to discern valuable trends and indicators that would otherwise go unnoticed.

(2) The need for second-order analysis and beyond

The consensus among scholars as well as in existing empirical evidence seems to suggest that, at present, WMD will not be the first choice of, nor is it within the capabilities of, most terrorists. Yet terrorism is an inherently dynamic phenomenon, and, if recent trends have taught us anything, it is that terrorists are nimble actors who can be innovative when necessary. This is especially true when considering such a diffuse, network-centric, and eminently adaptive set of groups and individuals as today's amorphous terrorist groups. At the same time, technological development is also inherently dynamic with one of the negative externalities of this dynamism being the opportunities it can provide for malefactors. Examples of such technologies include cheap, accessible sprayers for chemical weapons; nanotech, proteinacious microspheres; aerosol vaccine delivery; bioinformatics; single nucleotide polymorphisms (SNPs); and Bose-Einstein condensates.

A remarkable feature of the broader discussion regarding the likelihood of WMD terrorism is that hardly any commentators who believe terrorists currently lack the capacity mention anything about future developments. Even if one accepts that terrorists will eventually succeed in using WMD to cause mass casualties, how quickly this can happen is a very important question. Five years? Ten? Fifty? The speed with which a shift to possible WMD use might take place in the context of emerging technologies is a very important, yet underresearched, question. Also, many people assume that any transition to WMD use will be incremental and perceptible, with WMD incidents gradually increasing in frequency and severity. Will this necessarily be the case, or can technological or motivational developments cause a sudden shift toward WMD use? What we need to do is to consider "second-order questions" regarding when a potential transition to WMD use might occur and by what mechanisms it might take place.

Consideration of second-order questions may entail new analytical techniques and require a more diverse set of skills than scholars are accustomed to applying to the problem of WMD terrorism. One potentially fruitful source of insights in this regard is found in the business development literature that focuses on the impact of technological change on patterns of behavior. Various models of technological change, often based on a modified rational choice approach, may shed some light on the rate of WMD adoption by terrorists. As an example, consider a concept such as disruptive versus sustaining technologies (developed by Clayton Christensen at the Harvard Business School; see Bower and Christensen 1995). If WMD in the context of terrorism is likely to act as a disruptive technology (which *prima facie* indications suggest), then changes in terrorist behavior can be both swift and comprehensive instead of gradual and infrequent; in other words, the transition to the terrorist use of WMD as the strategic weapon of choice would be both sudden and permanent.

(3) **Where extremes touch**[1]

Another area that has thus far remained largely unexplored in the context of WMD terrorism involves the potential for and consequences of collaboration between terrorist groups. It is generally assumed that different types of violent extremists and terrorists operate within discrete ideological and cultural milieus that are relatively insular, if not entirely distinct from one another. This simplistic assumption ignores a far more complex and fluid reality, however, given that elements from different extremist milieus have frequently interacted and lent one another assistance in the past. And, indeed, there are indications that new patterns of ideological cross-fertilization and collaboration are presently emerging among terrorist groups.

It is important to recognize that one of the oldest alliance patterns adopted by states within the international system—that based on the notion that "the enemy of my enemy is my friend"—also influences the behavior of nonstate actors. Another potential motivation for adopting this collaborative approach would be to circumvent security measures taken against their own groups by engaging proxies to carry out attacks on their behalf. It is not necessary in this regard that the bulk of "mainstream" factions within each milieu find common ground. All that is necessary is for a small subset, perhaps even fringe elements, within each milieu to find ways to justify collaboration with one another, even though the majority of the respective ideologies' adherents continue to regard each other with antipathy.

Any type of operational cooperation between separate terrorist organizations is a potentially worrisome development, but it is even more ominous in an era in which terrorist attacks are becoming ever deadlier. Given the growing interest expressed by terrorists in using CBRN weapons, the establishment of symbiotic relationships with their counterparts from other ideological milieus and the possible combining of their efforts could result in groups that otherwise would lack the requisite capability to move beyond the WMD threshold.

Note

1   The following section is based on work prepared by Jeffrey Bale and the author (see Bale and Ackerman 2004). Thanks are due Bale for providing many of the observations noted below.

24 The changing face of Al Qaeda and the global war on terrorism

Bruce Hoffman

The Al Qaida of the 9/11 period is under catastrophic stress. They are being hunted down, their days are numbered.
—Amb. Cofer Black, U.S. State Department, Counter-Terrorism Coordinator, January 2004.[1]

The Americans only have predications and old intelligence left. It will take them a long time to understand the new form of al-Qaida.
—Thabet bin Qais, Al Qaeda spokesperson, May 2003.[2]

The plots were textbook Al Qaeda, even if the would-be perpetrators were not. Hijack a jet plane loaded with ordinary travelers and deliberately crash it into the tower of a prominent local landmark. Simultaneously dispatch multiple truck bombs to destroy embassies and other diplomatic facilities. Use a small boat laden with explosives to sink a large, powerful warship. Each reprised an infamous Al Qaeda operation: 9/11, the 1998 East Africa embassy bombings, and the attack on the *U.S.S. Cole*—but in this case all the attacks were to take place in Singapore. Moreover, the plotters were not battle-hardened *mujahideen* ("holy warriors") who had cut their teeth fighting Egypt's security forces or against the Northern Alliance in Afghanistan. Nor were they the usual Al Qaeda cadre favored for such spectacular operations: young, Arab males, mostly from Saudi Arabia, Yemen, or the Gulf, whose background, family ties, and bona fides inspired the trust and confidence of that movement's senior leadership. Rather, they were an utterly unremarkable group of middle-aged Singaporeans. Some were married and some were single. Some were businessmen with university-level degrees, whereas others were cab drivers or janitors. What they did have in common was a profoundly deep devotion to their Muslim faith alongside an all-consuming hatred of the United States and the West. They had acquired both convictions not as impressionable youths either as students in *madressehs* (Islamic schools) or worshippers in radical mosques, but comparatively late in life by attending small meetings and religious sessions held in the living rooms and kitchens of the ubiquitous high-rise apartments that dot Singapore. They were therefore likely regarded by the infamous KSM—Khalid Sheik Mohammed, the bin Laden lieutenant to whom their cell circuitously reported—as the "ultimate fifth column," whose age, background, and Asian—as opposed to Arab—appearance were calculated to allay rather than arouse the suspicions of domestic and foreign security and intelligence offices alike. The fact that many of the cell's members came from the traditionally moderate, English-speaking, expatriate community of Malabari Indian Muslims long resident in Singapore was an added bonus. Indeed, KSM and the group's other controllers would likely have known that although Singapore's highly efficient Internal Security Department would have kept close watch over newer immigrants and the more radicalized communities among that city-state's large Malay-speaking Muslim population, they might have paid less attention to such groups as the well-established Malabaris.[3]

The Singaporean cell embodies a new breed of post-9/11 terrorist: men animated and inspired by Al Qaeda and bin Laden, but who neither belong specifically to Al Qaeda nor directly follow orders issued by bin Laden. The Singaporeans were members of an entirely separate group, albeit one closely associated with Al Qaeda, known as Jemaah Islamiyah (JI, or the "Islamic Organization"). The aim of this predominantly Indonesian organization, whose origins can be traced to the early 1970s, is to establish a unified Islamic nation, guided by strict interpretation of *shari'a* (Islamic law) among the countries of Southeast Asia—including Indonesia, Malaysia, the Philippines, Brunei, and Singapore. Jemaah Islamiyah and the other radical Islamic Southeast Asian movements like it (e.g., the Moro Islamic Liberation Front in the Philippines, and the Kumpulan Mujahidin Malaysia) potentially represent an even more insidious and pernicious threat than Al Qaeda.

The Singaporean JI cell also reflects how, in the time since 9/11, Al Qaeda has deliberately sought to exploit local causes and re-align mostly parochial interests with its own transnational, pan-Islamist ideology. The transformation of the Islamic Movement of Uzbekistan (IMU) from an organization once focused mainly on Central Asia into one that now champions bin Laden's ambitious international vision of a re-established Caliphate is a case in point. In other instances, moreover, local cells have been surreptitiously co-opted by Al Qaeda so that, unbeknownst to their rank and file, the group pursues Al Qaeda's broader, long-range goals in addition to (or even instead of) its own, more provincial goals. This process has been particularly evident among some Algerian terrorist cells operating in European countries.

Finally, the Singapore cell encapsulates the terrorism-counterterrorism conundrum that exists today. As counterterrorism measures improve and become stronger, Al Qaeda and its affiliates and associates must constantly scramble to adapt themselves to the less congenial operational environments in which they now have to operate. For the terrorists, this inevitably entails tapping into new and different pools of recruits, adjusting targeting and modus operandi to obviate governmental countermeasures and an enforced evolutionary process on which their survival depends. Indeed, the main challenge for the radical jihadist movement today is to promote and ensure its durability as an ideology and concept. It can only do this by staying in the news. New attacks are therefore needed to maintain their relevance as a force in international politics and to enhance their powers of coercion and intimidation.

These processes largely explain the current patterns of terrorism being seen. Indeed, as military and government targets increase their protection levels, softer targets such as comparatively more vulnerable economic and commercial sites have thereby become more attractive. The attacks staged by Al Qaeda associates or affiliates such as JI in Bali in October 2002 and in Jakarta last August; by Assiriyat al-Moustaqim in Morocco in May 2003; by the Islamic Great Eastern Raiders Front in Turkey the following November;[4] by the jihadist cell comprised mostly of Moroccan nationals responsible for the bombings of commuter trains in Madrid last March (that killed more than 200 and injured over 1,600 others);[5] the semi-autonomous operations of Al Qaeda's Arabian Peninsula unit in Saudi Arabia; and that of Abu Musab Zarqawi and his Jamaat al Tawhid and Islam and Jihad organization in Iraq, evidence this pattern.

Al Qaeda today

Since 9/11, Al Qaeda has clearly shown itself to be a nimble, flexible, and adaptive entity. Because of its remarkable durability, the progress that the United States and allies achieved during the first phase of the GWOT—when Al Qaeda's training camps and operational bases, infrastructure and command-and-control nucleus in Afghanistan were destroyed and uprooted—has thus far proven elusive during this subsequent phase. In retrospect, the loss of Afghanistan does not appear to have affected Al Qaeda's ability to mount terrorist attacks to the extent hoped.[6] Afghanistan's main importance to Al Qaeda was as a massive base from which to prosecute a conventional civil war against the late Ahmad Shah Masoud's Northern Alliance. Arms dumps, training camps, staging areas, and networks of forward and rear headquarters were therefore required for the prosecution of this type of conflict. These accoutrements, however, are mostly irrelevant to the prosecution of an international terrorism campaign—as events since 9/11 have repeatedly demonstrated.[7] Indeed, Al Qaeda had rebounded from its Afghanistan set-backs within months of the last set-piece battles that were fought in the White Mountains along the Pakistani border at Shoh-e-Kot, Tora Bora, and elsewhere between December 2001 and March 2002. The attacks in Tunisia in April 2002 and in Pakistan the next month provided the first signs of this movement's resiliency. These were followed in turn by the attacks in Bali, Yemen, and Kuwait the following October, and then by the coordinated, near-simultaneous incidents in Kenya that November.[8]

Perhaps Al Qaeda's greatest achievement, though, has been the makeover it has given itself since 2001.[9] On the eve of 9/11, Al Qaeda was a unitary organization, assuming the dimensions of a lumbering bureaucracy. The troves of documents and voluminous data from computer hard disks captured in Afghanistan, for example, revealed as much mundane bumf as grandiose plots: complaints about expensive cell-phone bills and expenditures for superfluous office equipment[10] as well as crude designs for dreamt-about nuclear weapons.[11] Because of its logistical bases and infrastructure, that now-anachronistic version of Al Qaeda had a clear, distinct center of gravity. As seen in the systematic and rapid destruction inflicted during the military operations in Afghanistan during the GWOT's first phase, that structure was not only extremely vulnerable to the application of conventional military power, but played precisely to the American military's vast technological strengths. But in the time since 9/11, bin Laden and his lieutenants have engineered nothing short of a stunning transformation of Al Qaeda from the more or less unitary, near bureaucratic entity it once had been to something more akin to an ideology. Al Qaeda today, as other analysts have noted, has become more an idea or a concept than an organization;[12] an amorphous movement tenuously held together by a loosely networked transnational constituency rather than a monolithic, international terrorist organization with either a defined or identifiable command and control apparatus. Al Qaeda in essence has transformed itself from a bureaucratic entity that could be destroyed or an irregular army that could be defeated on the battlefield to a less-tangible transnational movement true to its name—the "base of operation" or "foundation" or, as other translations have it, the "precept" or "method."[13] The result is that today there are many Al Qaedas rather than the single Al Qaeda of the past. It has become a vast enterprise—an international movement or franchise operation with like-minded local representatives, loosely connected to a central ideological or motivational base, but advancing their common goal independently of one another.

Amazingly, Al Qaeda also claims that it is stronger and more capable today than it was on 9/11.[14] Al Qaeda propagandists on websites and other forums point repeatedly to a newfound vitality that has facilitated a capability to carry out at least two major attacks per year since 9/11 compared to the one attack every two years that it could implement before 9/11. "We are still chasing the Americans and their allies everywhere," Ayman al Zawahiri crowed in December 2003, "even in their homeland."[15] Irrespective of whether the U.S. definition of a major attack and Al Qaeda's are the same, propaganda does not have to be true to be believed: all that matters is that it is communicated effectively and persuasively—precisely the two essential components of information operations that Al Qaeda has arguably mastered.

That Al Qaeda can continue to prosecute this struggle is a reflection not only of its transformative qualities and communications skills, but also of the deep well of trained jihadists from which it can still draw. According to the authoritative annual *Strategic Survey*, published by the London-based International Institute for Strategic Studies, a cadre of at least 18,000 individuals who trained in Al Qaeda's Afghanistan camps between 1996 and 2001 are today theoretically positioned in some 60 countries throughout the world.[16] Moreover, Al Qaeda's management reserves seem to be similarly robust—at least to an extent perhaps not previously appreciated. A "corporate succession" plan of sorts has seemed to function even during a time when Al Qaeda has been relentlessly tracked, harassed, and weakened. Al Qaeda thus appears to retain at least some depth in managerial personnel as evidenced by its abilities to produce successor echelons for the mid-level operational commanders who have been killed or captured. It also still retains some form of a centralized command and control structure responsible for gathering intelligence, planning, and perhaps even overseeing more spectacular attacks against what are deemed the movement's most important, high-value targets in the United States. The computer records, e-mail traffic, and other documents seized by Pakistani authorities when a computer-savvy Al Qaeda operative named Mohammed Naeem Noor Khan was apprehended in August 2004 point to the existence of a more robust, centralized entity than had previously been assumed.[17]

Moreover, despite the vast inroads made in reducing terrorist finances and especially financial contributions, Al Qaeda doubtless still has sufficient funds with which to continue to prosecute its struggle. According to one open source estimate, some $120 million of *identifiable* Al Qaeda assets has been seized or frozen.[18] Given that bin Laden reputedly amassed a war chest in the billions of dollars, ample funds may still be at the disposal of his minions. At one point, for example, bin Laden was reputed to own or control some 80 companies around the world. In the Sudan alone, according to Peter Bergen, he owned all of that country's most profitable businesses, including construction, manufacturing, currency trading, import-export, and agricultural enterprises.[19] Not only were many of these well managed to the extent that they regularly turned a profit, but this largesse in turn was funneled to local Al Qaeda cells that in essence became entirely self-sufficient, self-reliant terrorist entities in the countries within which they operated.[20] The previously cited recent IISS report focuses on this issue as well. "While the organization and its affiliates and friends do not enjoy the financial fluidity that they did before the post-11 September counterterrorism mobilization," the report notes, "neither do they appear shorn of resources." The analysis disquietingly also explains that

> terrorist operations are asymmetrically inexpensive. The Bali bombing cost under $35,000, the *USS Cole* operations about $50,000 and the 11 September attacks less than $500,000. Moving large amounts of cash therefore is not an operational necessity. Furthermore, since the Afghanistan intervention forced al-Qaeda to decentralize and eliminated the financial burden of maintaining a large physical base, al-Qaeda has needed less money to operate.[21]

Finally, and above all, despite the damage and destruction, personnel and key leadership losses that it has sustained over the past three years, Al Qaeda stubbornly adheres to its fundamental strategy and objectives thereby continuing to inspire the broader radical jihadist movement. Bin Laden years ago defined this strategy as a two-pronged assault on both the "far enemy" (the U.S. and the West) and the "near enemy" (those reprobate, authoritarian, anti-Islamic regimes in the Middle East, Central Asia, South Asia, and South East Asia against whom the global jihadist movement is implacably opposed).[22] During the past year, for example, terrorist strikes have rocked Madrid and Istanbul (representing the "far enemy") as well as Riyadh, Baghdad, Islamabad and Jakarta (the "near enemies"). The periodic release of fresh targeting guidance and operational instructions has helped to give renewed focus and sustain this strategy. A particularly important guidance document, titled the "Camp al Battar [the sword] Magazine," was released around 31 March 2004. Reportedly written by the late Abdul Azziz al-Moqrin,[23] the reputed commander of Al Qaeda's operations on the Arabian Peninsula, it sheds considerable light on the current pattern of jihadist attacks in Saudi Arabia and Iraq. For example, it identifies as high attack priorities economic targets in the Middle East—and especially those connected with the region's oil industry. "The purpose of these targets," Moqrin wrote,

> is to destabilize the situation and not allow the economic recovery such as hitting oil wells and pipelines that will scare foreign companies from working there and stealing Muslim treasures. Another purpose is to have foreign investment withdrawn from local markets. Some of the benefits of those operations are the effect it has on the economic powers like the one that had happened recently in Madrid where the whole European economy was affected.[24]

To some extent, this strategy has already begun to bear fruit. The U.S. State Department, for example, has advised American workers and their families to leave Saudi Arabia. Following the murder in April of five expatriate employees of a petrochemical complex in the Saudi industrial city of Yanbu, foreign companies were reported to have evacuated personnel from the country.[25] Whatever optimism remained that the situation might quickly improve were dashed with the May attack on a housing complex in Khobar, where 22 foreigners were killed, and in the past weeks by the beheading of an American defense contractor, Paul M. Johnson, Jr.[26]

This same targeting guidance also explains the spate of kidnappings and execution of foreign workers in Iraq. Within a week of this targeting instruction's dissemination, for instance, the current wave of kidnapping of foreign nationals commenced in Iraq. The first victim was Mohammed Rifat, a Canadian, who was seized on 8 April and is still missing. Since then more than 60 others have been kidnapped. Although the majority has been released, to date five have been murdered and six are still missing. Among the dead is Nicholas Berg, who was kidnapped on 9 April and whose decapitated body was found a month later as well as a Korean national, Kim Sun II, who was kidnapped on 17 June and whose headless body was discovered five days later.[27] Moqrin deemed "[a]ssassinating Jewish businessmen" a special priority in order to "teach lessons to those who cooperate with them":[28] thus explaining why Berg, a Jewish-American, was doubtless symbolically so valuable a victim to Zarqawi and his followers.

Moqrin elaborated at some length on the "practical examples" of his targeting guidance. Following Jews—"American and Israeli Jews first, the British Jews and then French Jews and so on"—are "Christians: Their importance is as follows: Americans, British, Spanish, Australians, Canadians, Italians." Within these categories there are further distinctions: "Businessmen, bankers, and economists, because money is very important in this age"; followed by "Diplomats, politicians, scholars, analysts, and diplomatic missions"; "Scientists, associates and experts"; "Military commander and soldiers"; and, lastly, "Tourists and entertainment missions and anybody that was warned by mujahideen not to go to step in the lands of Moslems."[29] Jews and businessmen, as is seen, head the list.

The clearest explication of Al Qaeda's broad strategy in Iraq is perhaps the one provided by Zawahiri himself on the occasion of the second anniversary of the 9/11 attacks. "We thank God," he declared, "for appeasing us with the dilemmas in Iraq and Afghanistan. The Americans are facing a delicate situation in both countries. If they withdraw they will lose everything and if they stay, they will continue to bleed to death."[30] Indeed, what U.S. military commanders optimistically described last year as the jihadist "magnet" or terrorist "flytrap"[31] orchestrated by the U.S. invasion of Iraq, is viewed very differently by Al Qaeda. "Two years after Tora Bora," Zawahiri observed in December 2003, "the American bloodshed [has] started to increase in Iraq and the Americans are unable to defend themselves."[32] For Al Qaeda, therefore, Iraq's preeminent utility has been as a useful side-show: an effective means to preoccupy American military forces and distract U.S. attention while Al Qaeda and its confederates make new inroads and strike elsewhere. On a personal level, it may have also provided bin Laden with the breathing space that he desperately needed to further obfuscate his trail.

But most significant perhaps is that bin Laden and his fellow jihadists did not drive the Soviets out of Afghanistan by taking the fight to an organized enemy on a battlefield of its choosing. In fact, the idea that Al Qaeda wanted to make Iraq the central battle-field of jihad was first suggested by Al Qaeda itself. In February 2003, before the coalition invasion of Iraq even began, the group's information department produced a series of articles titled *In the Shadow of the Lances* that gave practical advice to Iraqis and foreign jihadists on how guerrilla warfare tactics could be used against the American and British troops. The call to arms by Al Qaeda only intensified after the fall of Baghdad, when its intermittent website, al Neda, similarly extolled the virtues of guerrilla warfare: invoking prominent lessons of history—including America's defeat in Vietnam and the Red Army's in Afghanistan. Under the caption "Guerrilla Warfare Is the Most Powerful Weapon Muslims Have, and It is The Best Method to Continue the Conflict with the Crusader Enemy," these lessons of history were cited to rally the jihadists for renewed battle. "With guerilla warfare," the statement explained,

> the Americans were defeated in Vietnam and the Soviets were defeated in Afghanistan. This is the method that expelled the direct Crusader colonialism from most of the Muslim lands, with Algeria the most well known. We still see how this method stopped Jewish immigration to Palestine, and caused reverse immigration of Jews from Palestine. The successful attempts of dealing defeat to invaders using guerilla warfare were many, and we will not expound on them. However, these attempts have proven that the most effective method for the materially weak against the strong is guerrilla warfare.[33]

But, as useful as Iraq undoubtedly has been as a rallying cry for jihad, it has been a conspicuously less prominent rallying point, at least in terms of men and money. The Coalition Provisional Authority (CPA) may be right that hundreds, perhaps even a few thousand, of foreign fighters have converged on Iraq. But few who have been captured have any demonstrable *direct* ties to Al Qaeda. Nor is there evidence of any direct command-and-control relationship between the Al Qaeda central leadership and the insurgents. If there are Al Qaeda warriors in Iraq, they are likely cannon fodder, possibly recruited through Al Qaeda networks and routed to Iraq via jihadist "rat lines," rather than battle-hardened, veteran mujahideen.

Al Qaeda's interest in Iraq, therefore, appears partly to exploit the occupation as a rousing propaganda and recruitment tool for the global jihadist cause.[34] Its primary intention may in fact have been to preoccupy the U.S with Iraq, thus enabling Al Qaeda and its affiliates to strike elsewhere. For them, Iraq is but one of many battlefields scattered throughout the world. Bin Laden and Al Qaeda's propagandists have long and repeatedly said as much. Indeed, while America has been tied down in Iraq, the international terrorism network has been active on other fronts. Various attacks undertaken by Al Qaeda and its affiliates since the occupation began have taken place in countries that are longstanding sources of bin Laden's enmity (e.g., Saudi Arabia)[35] or where an opportunity has presented itself (e.g., the suicide bombings by associated groups in Morocco last May,[36] Indonesia last August, and Turkey in November). In fact, although Saif al-Adel, the senior Al Qaeda operational commander who wrote the aforementioned *In the Shadow of the Lances* installments, is believed to have been behind the series of five suicide attacks that rocked Riyadh last May,[37] he has yet to be linked to any incidents in Iraq. Thus, it may not be a coincidence that, within weeks of President Bush's May 2003 declaration of the end of the war in Iraq, the jihadists struck in quick succession in Saudi Arabia and Morocco.

Finally, as America bears down on Iraq, Al Qaeda is doubtless bearing down on the United States. Chatter on Al Qaeda-linked web sites has revealed that the jihadists are constantly monitoring America, studying and gauging reactions to intelligence gathered on them and adapting their own plans accordingly. "If we know the importance of the information for the enemy, even if it is a small piece of information, then we can understand how important are [sic] the information that we know," was the admonition that appeared on a jihadist web site in June 2003.[38]

Conclusion: the future conduct of the GWOT

In summary, three main themes have framed this article:

* First, terrorism and the terrorist threat are changing. This is as much a reflection of success in the war against terrorism, as of the terrorists' own determination, adaptation, adjustment, and resiliency. There is no doubt, therefore, that the United States faces a formidable, capable, and implacable enemy.
* Second, the war on terrorism as it has unfolded over the past two plus years has come to bear little resemblance to any past conventional wars that the United States has fought. Because of the American military's overwhelming technological and doctrinal superiority, U.S. adversaries are deliberately using asymmetric warfare (e.g., terrorism and insurgency) and hopefully to lock the United States into a war of attrition. Indeed, whereas since the end of the Cold War the United States has become used to wars that last months if not weeks (e.g., the 1991 Gulf War and the 2002 invasion of Iraq), its adversaries have defined this conflict as a war of attrition: designed to wear down resolve, undermine confidence in U.S. leaders, and erode public support for the GWOT. In this respect, they have envisioned a struggle lasting years, if not decades. How this war is effectively fought will therefore require new approaches and perspectives and a different mindset from that which the United States brought to previous such conflicts.
* Third, terrorism itself is becoming a more diffuse and amorphous phenomenon: less centralized and with more opaque command and control relationships. The traditional way of understanding terrorism and looking at terrorists based on organizational definitions and attributes given Al Qaeda's evolution and development is no longer relevant. This inevitably will necessitate changes in how this evolving form of terrorism is studied and countered.

Given these observations, what can the United States do given these changed circumstances and this highly dynamic threat? Eight broad imperatives or policy options appear most relevant.

1   The preeminent lesson of 9/11 is not to be lulled into a false sense of complacency or to rest on past laurels: especially in a struggle that U.S. adversaries have defined as a war of attrition. In these circumstances, the main challenge faced is to retain focus and maintain vigilance and keep up pressure on terrorists by adapting and adjusting—rapidly and efficiently—to the changes unfolding with respect to terrorism. To do so, the United States needs to better understand Al Qaeda's operations and evolution and thus more effectively anticipate changes in radical international jihadism and better assess the implications of those changes.

2   It must be ensured that the new Iraq succeeds. The stakes are enormous. Regardless of whether or not it is Al Qaeda's central front, Iraq has become a critical arena and test of America's strength and resolve. That a democratic, stable government takes root in Iraq, that the Iraqi people are united in having a stake in that outcome, that security is achieved

throughout the country; and, that the January 2005 democratic elections are held have indisputably become among the most important metrics not only for assessing success in Iraq, but inevitably now in the war on terrorism. Ensuring that Iraq succeeds, however, is an international imperative, not only an American one. To that end, increased and active international involvement and assistance (including military commitments involving troop deployments along with civilian expertise) will be needed to strengthen the new Iraqi government and facilitate its ability to stabilize the country and promote the longevity of the democratic values to which it aspires.

3   America must systematically and thoroughly overhaul communications with, and create a more positive image of, the United States in the Muslim world. These communications were already fractured and efforts both stillborn and maladroit before the invasion of Iraq and the revelations about the treatment of Iraqi detainees at Abu Ghraib surfaced. Fixing these efforts and repairing the damage done has accordingly become critical. The United States today is increasingly viewed as a malignant force among Muslims throughout the world: thus furnishing Al Qaeda propagandists with fresh ammunition and alienating precisely that community that must be America's closest allies in the struggle against terrorism. Greater resources and more sustained focused efforts need to be committed to improving public diplomacy in the Muslim world as well as to develop more effective initiatives to counter the messages of radicalism and hate promulgated with greater fervor by the jihadists.

4   Part and parcel of this, the United States should recognize that it cannot compete with Al-Jazeera and Al-Arabiya and other Arab media simply by creating rival outlets such as the Arabic-language television station, Al-Hura, and radio station, Radio Sawa. In addition to those American-backed stations, which will inevitably take time to win their own significant audience share, America must meanwhile find ways to communicate more effectively using precisely those often hostile media like Al-Jazeera and Al-Arabiya to get its message across and directly challenge and counter the misperceptions that they foster.

5   America must address and conclusively resolve the open-ended legal status of the Guantánamo detainees and others held elsewhere. This is already a growing source of worldwide anger and opprobrium directed at the United States, especially in the aftermath of the Abu Ghraib revelations. Failure to arrive at an acceptable international legal determination regarding the detainees' status and ultimate disposition will remain an open sore in how the United States is perceived abroad and especially in the Muslim world.

6   America must embark on a renewed and concerted effort to resolve the Palestinian–Israeli conflict. Neither Americans nor anyone else should be under any illusion that resolving this conflict will magically end global terrorism. Bin Laden and Al Qaeda in fact took root and flowered in the late-1990s—precisely at a time when Palestinian-Israeli relations were at their zenith as a result of the Oslo Accords. But, it is nonetheless indisputable that being seen to play a more active and equitable role in resolving this conflict will have an enormously salutary effect on Middle Eastern stability, global Muslim attitudes toward the United States, and America's image abroad. The active involvement and assistance of its European allies and Russia as well as the United Nations will be a vital part of any reinvigorated peace process.

7   America must more instinctively regard its relations with friends and allies in the war on terrorism as a perishable commodity: not taken for granted and regularly repaired, replenished, and strengthened. Notwithstanding the sometimes profound policy differences that surfaced between the United States and even some of its closest allies over the war in Iraq, working-level intelligence and law enforcement cooperation in the war on terrorism has remained remarkably strong. However, these critically important relationships should neither

be taken for granted nor be allowed to weaken. This will entail repeated and ongoing sharing of intelligence, consultation and consensus, and continued unity of effort if America and its allies are to prevail against the international jihadist threat. Moreover, for the war on terrorism to succeed, enhanced multilateral efforts will need to be strengthened to accompany the already existent, strong bilateral relations.

8   Finally, the United States must enunciate a clear policy for countering terrorism and from that policy develop a comprehensive strategy. Nearly three years into this global war on terrorism there is no clear policy and there is, in turn, a too vague and ill-formed strategy. In the confrontation with communism following World War II, the United States did not declare a "war on communism." Rather, it articulated the policy of containment and within that intellectual framework developed a clever, comprehensive, multifaceted strategy—that did not rely exclusively on the military option—to serve that policy. Similar clarity of thought and focus is urgently needed today with respect to the global war on terrorism to guide and shape thinking and direct efforts through the subsequent phases of what will likely be a long struggle.

Notes

1   "U.S.: Al Qaida is 70 percent gone, their "days are numbered,'" *World Tribune. Com*, 23 January 2004.
2   Sarah el Deeb, "Al-Qaida Reportedly Plans Big New Attack," *Associated Press*, 8 May 2003.
3   Information provided by Singaporean authorities, June 2002 and September 2004. See also Ministry of Home Affairs, *White Paper: The Jemaah Islamiyah Arrests And The Threat of Terrorism: Presented to Parliament by Command of The President of the Republic of Singapore*, Cmd. 2 of 2003 (Singapore: Ministry of Home Affairs, 7 January 2003), pp. 10–17.
4   See, for example, Craig S. Smith, "Turkey Links Synagogue Bombers to Al Qaeda," New York Times, 18 November 2003; Louis Meixler, "Suicide bombers kill 27 in attacks on British consulate," *Associated Press*, 20 November 2003; Michael Isikoff and Mark Hosenball, "Al Qaeda's New Strategy: In Turkey, the terror group adopted a new strategy of directing home-grown militants," *Newsweek*, 10 December 2003.
5   See Associated Press, "Videotape Claims Responsibility for Madrid Attacks on Behalf of Al-Qaeda," New York Times, 13 March 2004; idem., "Transcript of Purported Al Qaeda Videotape," *New York Times*, 14 March 2004; CNN.com, "Video claims Al Qaeda to blame," 15 March 2004 available at ⟨http://www.cnn.worldnews/printthis.htm⟩; Glenn Frankel, Peter Finn and Keith B. Richburg, "Al Qaeda Implicated In Madrid Bombings," *Washington Post*, 15 March 2004; Craig S. Smith, "A Long Fuse Links Tangier to Bombings in Madrid," *New York Times*, 28 March 2004; Mark Huband, "Tangier's unlikely hothouse of radicalism" and Joshua Levitt, "Hunt for Madrid bomb suspects ends as four blow themselves up," *Financial Times* (London), 5 April 2004.
6   See, for example, Associated Press, "Expert Warns of al-Qaida-Linked Groups," 7 January 2004; Ellen Nakashima, "Thai Officials Probe Tie To Al Qaeda in Attacks," *Washington Post*, 9 January 2004; Associated Press, "Saudis Discover al-Qaida Training Camps," 15 January 2004.
7   Indeed, previous "high-end" Al Qaeda plots predating its comfortable relationship with the Taleban in Afghanistan demonstrate that the movement's strength is not in geographical possession or occupation of a defined geographical territory, but in its fluidity and impermanence. The activities of the peripatetic Ramzi Ahmad Yousef, reputed mastermind of the first World Trade Center bombing, during his sojourn in the Philippines during 1994 and 1995 is a case in point. Yousef's grand scheme to bomb simultaneously 12 American commercial aircraft in mid-flight over the Pacific Ocean (the infamous "Bojinka" plot), for example, did not require extensive operational bases and command and control headquarters in an existing country to facilitate the planning and execution of those attacks.
8   See William Wallis, "Kenya terror attacks 'planned from Somalia,'" *Financial Times*, 5 November 2003.
9   This point is also made in International Institute for Strategic Studies, *Strategic Survey 2003/4* (Oxford; Oxford University Press, 2004), p. 6, where the authors note: "The Afghanistan intervention offensively hobbled, but defensively benefited, al-Qaeda. While al-Qaeda lost a recruiting magnet and a training, command and operations base, it was compelled to disperse and become even more decentralized, 'virtual' and invisible."

10   See Alan Cullison, "Inside Al-Qaeda's Hard Drive: A fortuitous discovery reveals budget squabbles, baby pictures, office rivalries—and the path to 9/11," *The Atlantic Monthly* 294(2), no. 2 (September 2004), pp. 63–64.

11   Presentation by CNN correspondent Mike Boetcher, at the "Centre for the Study of Terrorism and Political Violence Symposium on Islamic Extremism and Terrorism in the Greater Middle East," University of St Andrews, St Andrews, Scotland, 7–8 June 2002.

12   See, especially, Jason Burke, "Think Again: Al Qaeda," *Foreign Policy* (May/June 2004), available at ⟨http://www.foreign policy.com⟩.

13   Ibid.

14   See Dana Priest and Walter Pincus, "New Target and Tone: Message Shows Al Qaeda's Adaptability," *Washington Post*, 16 April 2004; and Geoffrey Nunberg, "Bin Laden's Low-Tech Weapon," *New York Times*, 18 April 2004.

15   Associated Press, "Purported al-Qaida Tape Warns of Attacks," 19 December 2003.

16   International Institute for Strategic Studies, *Strategic Survey 2003/4* (Oxford; Oxford University Press, 2004), p. 6. As one commentary explained, the "IISS's figure of 18,000 potential operatives is calculated by deducting the 2,000 suspects killed or captured since the September 11, 2001 attacks from the estimated 20,000 recruits thought to have passed through al-Qaeda training camps in Afghanistan between 1996 and 2001." Mark Huband and David Buchan, "Al-Qaeda may have access to 18,000 'potential operatives', says think-tank," *Financial Times* (London), 26 May 2004. A figure of 20,000 is similarly cited in *Staff Report No. 15*, the National Commission on Terrorist Attacks Upon the United States ("9/11 Commission") on p. 10.

      Note that according to the report issued by the Joint Inquiry of the Senate and House Intelligence Committees, an estimated 70–120,000 persons trained in Afghanistan between 1979–2001, thus suggesting that the IISS estimate could be a conservative one. See Joint Inquiry of the Senate and House Intelligence Committees, p. 38; and "Al Qaeda Trained at Least 70,000 in Terrorist Camps, Senator Says," *Los Angeles Times*, 14 July 2003.

17   See, for example, David Johnston and David E. Sanger, "New Generation of Leaders is Emerging for Al Qaeda," *New York Times*, 10 August 2004; Josh Meyer and Greg Miller, "Fresh Details Back Threats," *Los Angeles Times*, 3 August 2004; Walter Pincus and John Mintz, "Pakistani-U.S. Raid Uncovered terrorist Cell's Surveillance Data," *Washington Post*, 2 August 2004; and, Glen Kessler, "Old Data, New Credibility Issues," *Washington Post*, 4 August 2004.

18   Electronic newsletter of the Orion Group, 24 April 2003.

19   Peter Bergen, *Holy Terror, Inc.: Inside the Secret World of Osama bin Laden* (New York: Free Press, 2001), pp. 47–49.

20   Anonymous, *Through Our Enemies' Eyes: Osama bin Laden, Radical Islam, and the Future of America* (Dulles, VA: Brassey's, 2002), p. 34. This book, written by a 20-year veteran of the CIA's operations directorate, is without doubt the preeminent work on bin Laden and Al Qaeda.

21   IISS, *Strategic Survey*, p. 8. In its *Staff Report No. 16*, the National Commission on Terrorist Attacks Upon the United States ("9/11 Commission") notes on p. 16 that the September 11th operation cost between $400–500,000 to mount.

22   Burke, "Think Again: Al Qaeda."

23   Moqrin was reportedly killed by Saudi security forces in Riyadh on 18 June 2004.

24   IntelCenter, al-Qaeda Targeting Guidance—v.1.0, Thursday, 1 April 2004 (Alexandria, VA: IntelCenter/ Tempest Publishing, 2004), pp. 6–9.

25   See Neal MacFarquhar, "As Terrorists Strike Arab Targets, Escalation Fears Arise," *New York Times*, 30 April 2004; idem., "Firm Pulls 100 From Saudi Arabia After 5 Deaths," 2 May 2004; idem., "After Attack, Company's Staff Plans to Leave Saudi Arabia" 3 May 2004; and Kim Ghattas and Roula Khalaf, "Shooting spree in Saudi city spreads jitters among western companies," *Financial Times* (London), 3 May 2004.

26   Craig Whitlock, "Islamic Radicals Behead American in Saudi Arabia," *Washington Post*, 19 June 2004.

27   Fabrizio Quattrocchi, an Italian and Henrik Frandsen, a Dane, and Hussein Ali Alyan, a Lebanese, are the other foreign kidnap victims who have been killed. See "Kidnapped in Iraq," *Washington Post*, 23 June 2004.

28   IntelCenter, al-Qaeda Targeting Guidance—v.1.0, Thursday, 1 April 2004 (Alexandria, VA: IntelCenter/ Tempest Publishing, 2004), pp. 6–9.

29   Ibid.

30 Quoted in Anonymous, *Imperial Hubris: Why America is Losing the War Against Terrorism* (Alexandria, VA: Brassey's, 2004), p. xxi.

31 Quoted in Bruce Hoffman, "Saddam Is Ours. Does Al Qaeda Care?" *New York Times*, 17 December 2003.

32 Quoted in Associated Press, "Purported al-Qaida Tape Warns of Attacks."

33 MEMRI Special Dispatch—Jihad and Terrorism Studies, 11 April 2003, no. 493 quoting (http://www.cubezero.nt/vhsvideo/imagis/?subject=2&rec=1043).

34 See, for example, Daniel Williams, "Italy Targeted By Recruiters For Terrorists," *Washington Post*, 17 December 2003 where it notes how a suicide bomber recruited in Italy is believed to have been responsible for the August 2003 bombing of the UN Headquarters in Baghdad and the rocket attack on the al-Rashid Hotel there in October.

35 See Simon Henderson and Matthew Levitt, "U.S.-Saudi Counterterrorism Cooperation In The Wake Of The Riyadh Bombing," Policywatch, No. 759, *Washington Institute of Near East Policy*, 23 May 2003; and, Craig Whitlock, "For Saudi Arabia, Al Qaeda Threat Is Now Hitting Home," *Washington Post*, 8 June 2004.

36 See, for example, Agence France Presse, "Qaeda 'paid' $50,000 to Morocco Bombers," 25 May 2003; Eliane Sciolino, "Moroccans Say Al Qaeda Was Behind Casablanca Bombings," *New York Times*, 23 May 2003; Jonathan Schanzer, "Intensify the hunt," *The Baltimore Sun*, 28 May 2003.

37 See Dana Priest and Susan Schmidt, "Al Qaeda Figure Tied to Riyadh Blasts," *Washington Post*, 18 May 2003.

38 "Do Not Be With the Enemy Against Us," article posted on *Islamic Studies and Research* (Al Qaeda-affiliated website), June 2003.

25 Six rather unusual propositions about terrorism

John Mueller

"The chances of any of us dying in a terrorist incident is very, very, very small," film-maker-provocateur Michael Moore happened to remark on 60 minutes on February 16, 2003. His interviewer, Bob Simon, promptly admonished, "But no one sees the world like that." Both statements, remarkably, are true—the first only a bit more so than the second.

This article investigates this incongruity. It is devoted especially to exploring the policy consequences that arise from what author Mark Bowden has characterized as "housewives in Iowa... watching TV afraid that al-Qaeda's going to charge in their front door,"[1] or more generally from the fact that many people have developed what Leif Wenar of the University of Sheffield has aptly labeled "a false sense of insecurity" about terrorism in the United States.

Terrorism generally has only limited direct effects

For all the attention it evokes, terrorism—in reasonable context—actually causes rather little damage and, as Moore suggests, the likelihood that any individual will become a victim in most places is microscopic. Although those adept at hyperbole like to proclaim that we live in "the age of terror," the number of people worldwide who die as a result of international terrorism is generally only a few hundred a year, tiny compared to the numbers who die in most civil wars or from automobile accidents. In fact, until 2001 far fewer Americans were killed in any grouping of years by all forms of international terrorism than were killed by lightning. And except for 2001, virtually none of these terrorist deaths occurred within the United States itself. Indeed, outside of 2001, fewer people have died in America from international terrorism than have drowned in toilets.

Even with the September 11 attacks included in the count, however, the number of Americans killed by international terrorism since the late 1960s (which is when the U.S. State Department began its accounting) is about the same as the number killed over the same period by lightning—or by accident-causing deer or by severe allergic reactions to peanuts. In almost all years the total number of people worldwide who die at the hands of international terrorists is not much more than the number who drown in bathtubs in the United States.[2]

Some of this is definitional. When terrorism becomes really extensive we generally no longer call it terrorism, but war. But people are mainly concerned about random terror, not sustained warfare. Moreover, even using an expansive definition of terrorism and including domestic terrorism in the mix, it is likely that far fewer people were killed by terrorists in the entire world over the last hundred years than died in any number of unnoticed civil wars during that century.

Obviously, this could change if international terrorists are able to assemble sufficient weaponry or devise new tactics to kill masses of people and if they come to do so routinely—and this, of course, is the central concern.[3] The weapons most feared in the hands of terrorists are so-called "weapons of mass destruction," a phrase systematically and extensively embellished after the cold war to embrace chemical and biological weapons as well as nuclear ones. This escalation of language is highly questionable.[4]

Chemical arms do have the potential, under appropriate circumstances, for panicking people; killing masses of them in open areas, however, is beyond their modest capabilities. Although they obviously can be hugely lethal when released in gas chambers, their effectiveness as weapons has been unimpressive, and their inclusion in the weapons-of-mass-destruction category is highly dubious unless the concept is so diluted that bullets or machetes can also be included. Biologist Matthew Meselson calculates that it would take a ton of nerve gas or five tons of mustard gas to produce heavy casualties among unprotected people in an open area of one square kilometer. Even for nerve gas this would take the concentrated delivery into a rather small area of about three hundred heavy artillery shells or seven 500-pound bombs. A 1993 analysis by the Office of Technology Assessment of the U.S. Congress finds that a ton of sarin nerve gas perfectly delivered under absolutely ideal conditions over a heavily populated area against unprotected people could cause between three thousand and eight thousand deaths. Under slightly less ideal circumstances— if there was a moderate wind or if the sun was out, for example—the death rate would be only one-tenth as great.[5] Although gas was used extensively in World War I, it accounted for less than 1 percent of the battle deaths.[6] In fact, on average it took over a ton of gas to produce a single fatality.[7]

Properly developed and deployed, biological weapons could indeed (if thus far only in theory) kill hundreds of thousands—perhaps even millions—of people. The discussion remains theoretical because biological weapons have scarcely ever been used. Belligerents have eschewed such weapons with good reason: biological weapons are extremely difficult to deploy and to control. Terrorist groups or rogue states may be able to solve such problems in the future with advances in technology and knowledge, but the record thus far is unlikely to be very encouraging to them. In the 1990s, Aum Shinrikyo, a Japanese cult that had some three hundred scientists in its employ and an estimated budget of $1 billion, reportedly tried at least nine times over five years to set off biological weapons by spraying pathogens from trucks and wafting them from rooftops, hoping fancifully to ignite an apocalyptic war. These efforts failed to create a single fatality—in fact, nobody even noticed that the attacks had taken place.[8] For the most destructive results, biological weapons need to be dispersed in very low-altitude aerosol clouds: aerosols do not appreciably settle, and anthrax (which is not easy to spread or catch and is not contagious) would probably have to be sprayed near nose level. Explosive methods of dispersion may destroy the organisms. Moreover, except for anthrax spores, long-term storage of lethal organisms in bombs or warheads is difficult and, even if refrigerated, most of the organisms have a limited lifetime. The effects of such weapons can take days or weeks to have full effect, during which time they can be countered with civil defense measures. And their impact is very difficult to predict and in combat situations may spread back on the attacker.[9]

The science with respect to chemical and biological weaponry has been known with considerable sophistication for more than a century, and that science has become massively more developed over the last hundred years. Moreover, governments (not just small terrorist groups) have spent considerably over decades in an effort to make the weapons more effective. Yet although there have been great increases in the lethality and effectiveness of conventional and nuclear weapons during that time, the difficulties of controlling and dispersing chemical and biological substances seem to have persisted.

Nuclear weapons, most decidedly, can indeed inflict massive destruction, and it is certainly reasonable to point out that an atomic bomb in the hands of a terrorist or rogue state could kill tens of thousands of people. But it may also be worthwhile to note that making such a bomb is an extraordinarily difficult task and that warnings about the possibility that small groups, terrorists, and errant states could fabricate nuclear weapons have been repeatedly uttered at least since 1947,[10] and especially since the 1950s when the "suitcase bomb" appeared to become a practical possibility. It has now been three decades since terrorism specialist Brian Jenkins published his warnings that "the mass production and widespread distribution of increasingly sophisticated and increasingly powerful man-portable weapons will greatly add to the terrorist's arsenal" and that "the world's increasing dependence on nuclear power may provide terrorists with weapons of mass destruction."[11] We continue to wait.

Actually, it is somewhat strange that so much emphasis has been put on the dangers of high-tech weapons at all. Some of the anxiety may derive from the post–September 11 anthrax scare, even though that terrorist event killed only a few people. The events of September 11, by contrast, were remarkably low tech and could have happened long ago: both skyscrapers and airplanes have been around for a century now.

Two careful reports from the late 1990s—one from the Gilmore Panel, the other from the General Accounting Office—stress the great difficulties a terrorist group would have in acquiring and developing devices with the capacity to cause mass casualties, and they pointedly warn against the worst case scenarios "that have dominated domestic preparedness planning."[12] The September 11 attackers did not use such weapons and the anthrax terrorism killed only a few people. Nonetheless, those events have caused these sensible warnings to become much neglected.

Thus, recent books by Graham Allison and Joshua Goldstein issue dire warnings about nuclear terrorism. Of particular concern in this are Russia's supposedly missing suitcase bombs—even though a careful assessment by the Center for Nonproliferation Studies has concluded that it is unlikely that any of these devices have indeed been lost and that, regardless, their effectiveness would be very low or even nonexistent because they require continual maintenance.[13] And in 2004 testimony, CIA adviser and arms inspector Charles Duelfer stressed that "nuclear weapons development requires thousands of knowledgeable scientists as well as a large physical plant."[14] It is also worth noting that, although nuclear weapons have been around now for well over half a century, no state has ever given another state (much less a terrorist group) a nuclear weapon that the recipient could use independently. There is always the danger that the weapon would be used in a manner the donor would not approve of—or even, potentially, on the donor itself. Allison thinks a dedicated terrorist group could get around these problems in time and eventually produce or procure a "crude" bomb—one that, by Allison's own admission, would be "large, cumbersome, unsafe, unreliable, unpredictable, and inefficient."[15]

Goldstein is alarmed because he considers nuclear terrorism to be "not impossible," and Allison more boldly declares his "own considered judgment" that, unless his policy recommendations (which include a dramatic push toward war with North Korea) are carried out, "a nuclear terrorist attack on America in the decade ahead is more likely than not."[16] Allison's declaration is far more likely to be remembered if it proves true than if, as is far more likely, it goes the way of C. P. Snow's once much-heralded alarmist broadside published in 1961:

> We are faced with an either-or, and we haven't much time. The *either* is acceptance of a restriction of nuclear armaments… The *or* is not a risk but a certainty. It is this. There is no agreement on tests. The nuclear arms race between the United States and the U.S.S.R. not only continues but accelerates. Other countries join in. Within, at the most, six years, China and several other states have a stock of nuclear bombs. Within, at the most, ten years, some of those bombs are going off. I am saying this as responsibly as I can. *That* is the certainty.[17]

It should also be kept in mind that September 11 was an extreme event: until then no more than a few hundred had ever been killed in a single terrorist attack, and during the entire twentieth century fewer than twenty terrorist attacks resulted in the deaths of more than one hundred people. The economic destruction on September 11 was also unprecedented, of course. However, extreme events often remain exactly that—aberrations, rather than harbingers.[18] A bomb planted in a piece of checked luggage was responsible for the explosion that caused a PanAm jet to crash into Lockerbie, Scotland, in 1988. Since that time, hundreds of billions of pieces of luggage have been transported on American carriers and none has exploded to down an aircraft.[19] This doesn't mean that one should cease worrying about luggage on airlines, but it does suggest that extreme events do not necessarily assure repetition— any more than Timothy McVeigh's Oklahoma City bombing of 1995 has. Since its alarming release of poison gas in the Tokyo subway in 1995, the apocalyptic group Aum Shinrikyo appears to have abandoned the terrorism business and its example has not been followed. Moreover, although there have been many terrorist incidents in the world since 2001, all (thus far, at least) have relied on conventional methods.[20]

This should not be taken, of course, to suggest that all extreme events prove to be the last in their line or that nothing bad ever happens. At the time, World War I—called the Great War for decades—was the worst war of its type. Yet an even more destructive one followed. Moreover, while Aum Shinrikyo and Qaddafi may be under control, Al Qaeda and like-minded terrorist groups are unlikely to die out any time soon: September 11, after all, marked their second attempt to destroy the World Trade Center. In addition, the suicidal nature of many attacks, while not new, can be very unsettling because deterring by threatening punishment to the would-be perpetrator becomes impossible. And, of course, terrorism itself will never go away: it has always existed and always will.

A central issue, however, is whether such spectacularly destructive terrorist acts will become commonplace and will escalate in their destructiveness. "Policy must consider the capacity for action," notes Russell Seitz, "not intent alone." The American communist party comprised a dedicated band of conspirators in league with foreign enemies who were devoted to using subversion and violence to topple democracy and capitalism and, if successful, they would presumably have established a murderous tyranny. The intent was there—but not, as it turned out, the capacity. In the present instance, one should not, as Seitz continues, "equate the modern ubiquity of high technology with terrorists becoming omniscient or infallible."[21] Although there is no reason to think Al Qaeda will never strike again, the record suggests that it will find it difficult to match or top what it accomplished on September 11 and that terrorism's destructiveness, despite the creative visions of worst case scenarists, may well fail to escalate dramatically. Moreover, the extreme destruction of September 11 has raised the bar, possibly reducing the impact of less damaging attacks.

The costs of terrorism very often come mostly from the fear and consequent reaction (or overreaction) it characteristically inspires

The costs of terrorism commonly come much more from hasty, ill-considered, and over wrought reactions (or overreactions) to it than from anything the terrorists have done. For example, responding to several vicious acts of terrorism apparently perpetrated by Chechens, the Russian government in 1999 reinstituted a war against the breakaway republic that has resulted in far more destruction of Russian (and, of course, Chechen) lives and property than the terrorists ever brought about. Ronald Reagan bombed Libya in 1986 after terrorists linked to that country had set off an explosive in a Berlin discotheque killing two people, a raid that then apparently led to the blowing up of an airliner, killing 270 and toppling the airline company into bankruptcy.[22]

When two American embassies in Africa were bombed in 1998, killing over 200 (including a few Americans), Bill Clinton retaliated by bombing a suspect pharmaceutical factory in Sudan, the loss of which may have led to the deaths of tens of thousands of Sudanese over time.[23] Also bombed were some of Osama bin Laden's terrorist training camps in Afghanistan, which caused the Afghan government—the Taliban—to renege on pledges to extradite the troublesome and egoistic bin Laden to Saudi Arabia, made him into an international celebrity, essentially created his Al Qaeda organization by turning it into a magnet for funds and recruits, and converted the Taliban from reluctant hosts to allies and partners.[24]

The costs of reaction outstripped those inflicted by the terrorists even in the case of the September 11 attacks, which were by far the most destructive in history. The direct economic costs of September 11 amounted to tens of billions of dollars, but the economic costs in the United States of the much-enhanced security runs several times that. The yearly budget for the Department of Homeland Security, for example, is approaching $50 billion per year while state and local governments spend additional billions.[25] The costs to the tourism and airline industries have also been monumental: indeed, three years after September 11 domestic airline flights in the United States were still 7 percent below their pre-September 11 levels, and one estimate suggests that the economy lost 1.6 million jobs in 2001 alone, mostly in the tourism industry.[26] Moreover, safety measures carry additional consequences: economist Roger Congleton calculates that strictures effectively requiring people to spend an additional half hour in airports cost the economy $15 billion per year; in comparison, total airline profits in the 1990s never exceeded $5.5 billion per year.[27] The reaction to the anthrax attacks will cost the U.S. Postal Service alone some 5 billion—that is, 1 billion for every fatality inflicted by the terrorist.[28] Various September 11-induced restrictions on visas have constricted visits and residencies of scientists, engineers, and businesspeople vital to the economy—restrictions that, some predict, will dampen American economic growth in a few years.[29]

The reaction to September 11 has even claimed more—far more—human lives than were lost in the terrorist attacks. Out of fear, many people canceled airline trips and consequently traveled more by automobile than by airline after the event, and one study has concluded that over one thousand people died in automobile accidents in 2001 alone between September 11 and December 31 because of this.[30] If a small percentage of the one-hundred-thousand-plus road deaths since 2001 occurred to people who were driving because they feared to fly, the number of Americans who have perished in overreaction to September 11 in road accidents alone could well surpass the number who were killed by the terrorists on that terrible day. Moreover, the reaction to September 11 included two wars that are yet ongoing—one in Afghanistan, the other in Iraq—neither of which would have been politically possible without September 11. The number of Americans— civilian and military—who have died thus far in those enterprises probably comes close to the number killed on September 11. Moreover, the best estimates are that the war in Iraq resulted in the deaths of one hundred thousand Iraqis during its first eighteen months alone.[31] This could represent more fatalities than were inflicted by all terrorism, domestic and international, over the last century.

In addition, the enormous sums of money being spent to deal with this threat have in part been diverted from other, possibly more worthy, endeavors. Some of that money doubtless would have been spent on similar ventures under earlier budgets, and much of it likely has wider benefits than simply securing the country against a rather limited threat. But much of it, as well, has very likely been pulled away from programs that do much good. As Clark Chapman and Alan Harris put it, "our nation's priorities remain radically torqued toward homeland defense and fighting terrorism at the expense of objectively greater societal needs."[32] Or, in the words of risk analyst David Banks, "If terrorists force us to redirect resources away from sensible programs and future growth, in order to pursue unachievable but politically popular levels of domestic security, then they have won an important victory that mortgages our future."[33]

The terrorism industry is a major part of the terrorism problem

The most common reaction to terrorism is the stoking of fear and the encouragement of overreaction by members of what might be called the "terrorism industry," an entity that includes not only various risk entrepreneurs and bureaucrats, but also most of the media and nearly all politicians.

There is no reason to suspect that George W. Bush's concern about terrorism is anything but genuine. However, his approval rating did receive the greatest boost for any president in history in September 2001, and it would be politically unnatural for him not to notice. His chief political adviser, Karl Rove, in fact had already declared in 2003 that the war on terrorism would be central to Bush's reelection campaign the next year.[34] It was, and it worked. The Democrats, scurrying to keep up, have stumbled all over each other with plans to expend even more of the federal budget on the terrorist threat, such as it is, than President Bush.

Meanwhile, Bush's hastily assembled and massively funded Department of Homeland Security seeks to stoke fear by officially intoning on the first page of its defining manifesto that "Today's terrorists can strike at any place, at any time, and with virtually any weapon."[35] This warning is true in some sense, of course, but it is also fatuous and misleading. As Benjamin Friedman notes, "Telling Kansan truck drivers to prepare for nuclear terrorism is like telling bullfighters to watch out for lightning. It should not be their primary concern. For questionable gains in preparedness, we spread paranoia." Such warnings, continues Friedman, also facilitate the bureaucratically and politically appealing notion that "if the threat is everywhere, you must spend everywhere," and they help develop and perpetrate "a myth of the all-knowing, all-seeing terrorists." Threat exaggeration is additionally encouraged, even impelled, because politicians and terrorism bureaucrats also have, as Jeffrey Rosen points out, an "incentive to pass along vague and unconfirmed threats of future violence, in order to protect themselves from criticism" in the event of another attack.[36]

Since September 11 the American public has been treated to endless yammering about terrorism in the media. Politicians and bureaucrats may feel that, given the public concern on the issue, they will lose support if they appear insensitively to be down-playing the dangers of terrorism. But the media like to tout that they are devoted to presenting fair and balanced coverage of important public issues. As has often been noted, however, the media appear to have a congenital incapacity for dealing with issues of risk and comparative probabilities—except, of course, in the sports and financial sections. If a baseball player hits three home runs in a single game, press reports will include not only notice of that achievement, but also information about the rarity of the event as well as statistics about the hitter's batting and slugging averages and about how many home runs he normally hits. I may have missed it, but I have never heard anyone in the media stress that in every year except 2001 only a few hundred people in the entire world have died as a result of international terrorism.

Even in their amazingly rare efforts to try to put terrorism in context— something that would seem to be absolutely central to any sensible discussion of terrorism and terrorism policy—the process never goes very far. For example, in 2001 the *Washington Post* published an article by a University of Wisconsin economist which attempted quantitatively to point out how much safer it was to travel by air than by automobile even under the heightened atmosphere of concern inspired by the September-attacks. He reports that the article generated a couple of media inquiries, but nothing more. Gregg Easterbrook's cover story in the October 7, 2002, *New Republic* forcefully argued that biological and especially chemical weapons are hardly capable of creating "mass destruction," a perspective relevant not only to concerns about terrorism, but also to the drive for war against Iraq that was going on at the time. *The New York Times* asked him to fashion the article into an op-ed piece, but that was the only interest the article generated in the media.

Moreover, the monied response to September 11 has created a vast and often well-funded coterie of risk entrepreneurs. Its members would be out of business if terrorism were to be back-burnered, and accordingly they have every competitive incentive (and they are nothing if not competitive) to conclude it to be their civic duty to keep the pot boiling. "Dependent on the public for status and recognition," notes Rosen, terrorism experts have an "incentive to exaggerate risks and pander to public fears."[37]

Doomsayers are difficult to refute in part because there is more reputational danger in underplaying risks than in exaggerating them. Disproved doomsayers can always claim that caution induced by their warnings prevented the predicted calamity from occurring (call it the Y2K effect). Disproved Pollyannas have no such convenient refuge.[38]

Not only are failed predicters of doomsday rarely held to account, but they have proved remarkably agile at creative nuance and extrapolation after failure. Thus, in 2004 the terrorism industry repeatedly insisted that some big terrorist event was likely in connection with (a) the Athens Olympics, (b) the Democratic Party convention in Boston, (c) the Republican parry convention in New York, (d) the election campaign, or (e) the presidential vote in November. When nothing happened (a terrorist wearing kilts did show up to disrupt the marathon in Athens briefly but this, I should think, did not count), the argument was floated that a taped encyclical issued by bin Laden in late October somehow demonstrated that he was too weak to attack before the election and also that he was marshalling his resources such that the several months *after* the election had now become especially dangerous.[39] A notable terrorist attack during that interval would have generated hundreds of thousands of news items not to mention a veritable paroxysm of breast-beating by the terrorism industry. The absence of an attack during the same time was scarcely noticed.

Members of the terrorism industry are truly virtuosic at pouring out, and poring over, worst case scenarios—or "worst case fantasies," as Bernard Brodie once labelled them in different context.[40] "Many academic terrorism analyses," notes Bruce Hoffman, "are self-limited to mostly lurid hypotheses of worst-case scenarios, almost exclusively involving CBRN (chemical, biological, radiological, or nuclear) weapons, as opposed to trying to understand why—with the exception of September 11—terrorists have only rarely realized their true killing potential."[41] That is, if terrorism is so easy and terrorists so omnicompetent, why isn't there more of it? For example, why don't they snipe at people in shopping centers, collapse tunnels, poison food, cut electrical lines, derail trains, set forest fires, blow up oil pipelines, and cause massive traffic jams?

Retaining his worst case perspective, however, Joshua Goldstein worries about terrorists exploding nuclear weapons in the United States in a crowded area and declares this to be "not impossible" or the likelihood "not negligible." Meanwhile, to generate alarm about such dangers and to reshape policy to deal with them, Graham Allison's recent book opens by grimly (and completely irrelevantly) recycling Einstein's failed half-century-old prediction about nuclear war: "Since the advent of the Nuclear Age, everything has changed except our modes of thinking and we thus drift toward unparalleled catastrophe." Both of these members of the terrorism industry want to massively increase expenditures to hedge against these "not impossible" scenarios, and Allison designates the North Korean problem a "supreme priority" and is fully prepared if necessary to launch a war, potentially costing a million lives, against that country (and presumably also against Iran) to reduce the likelihood that his worst case fantasy will materialize. (He would, however, humanely evacuate Seoul before attacking the North.)[42]

But there are, of course, all sorts of things that are "not impossible." Thus, a colliding meteor or comet could destroy the earth, Tony Blair or Vladimir Putin and their underlings could decide one morning to launch a few nuclear weapons at Massachusetts, George W. Bush could decide to bomb Hollywood, an underwater volcano could erupt and cause a civilization-ending Tsunami, bin Laden could convert to Judaism, declare himself the Messiah, and hire a group of Italian mafiosi to have himself publicly crucified.

That is, what we mostly get is fear-mongering, and much of it borders on hysteria. An insightful discussion seeking to put the terrorist threat into context was published in the journal *Skeptical Inquirer* by astronomers Clark Chapman and Alan Harris. They suggested that terrorism deserves exceptional attention only "if we truly think that future attacks might destroy our society." But, they overconfidently continued, "who believes that?"[43] The article triggered enormous response, and much of—to their amazement—came from readers who believed exactly that. Those readers have a lot of company in the terrorism industry.

Some prominent commentators, like David Gergen, have argued that the United States has become "vulnerable," even "fragile." Others, like Indiana Senator Richard Lugar, are given to proclaiming that terrorists armed with weapons of mass destruction present an "existential" threat to the United States—or even, in columnist Charles Krauthammer's view, to "civilization itself."[44] Allison, too, thinks that nuclear terrorists could "destroy civilization as we know it" while Goldstein is convinced they could "destroy our society" and that a single small nuclear detonation in Manhattan would "overwhelm the nation."[45] Two counterterrorism officials from the Clinton administration contend that a small nuclear detonation "would necessitate the suspension of civil liberties," halt or even reverse "the process of globalization," and "could be the defeat that precipitates America's decline," while a single explosion of any sort of weapon of mass destruction would "trigger an existential crisis for the United States and its allies."[46] A recent best-selling book by an anonymous CIA official repeatedly assures us that our "survival" is at stake and that we are engaged in a "war to the death."[47]

Apocalyptic alarmism by the terrorism industry reached a kind of pinnacle during the orange alert at the end of 2003. At the time Homeland Security czar Tom Ridge was given bravely to declaring that "America is a country that will not be bent by terror. America is a country that will not be broken by fear." Meanwhile, however, General Richard Myers, chairman of the Joint Chiefs of Staff, was assuring a television audience that if terrorists were able to engineer a catastrophic event which killed ten thousand people, they would successfully "do away with our way of life."[48]

The sudden deaths of that many Americans—although representing less than four thousandths of 1 percent of the population—would indeed be horrifying and tragic, the greatest one-day disaster the country has suffered since the Civil War. But the only way it could "do away with our way of life" would be if we did that to ourselves in reaction. The process would presumably involve repealing the Bill of Rights, boarding up all churches, closing down all newspapers and media outlets, burning all books, abandoning English for North Korean, and refusing evermore to consume hamburgers. It seems, then, that it is not only the most-feared terrorists who are suicidal. Ultimately the enemy, in fact, is us.

However, it does not seem unreasonable to point out that the United States regularly loses forty thousand lives each year in automobile accidents and still somehow manages to continue to exist. Or that countries have endured massive, sudden catastrophes without collapsing: in 1990 and then again in 2003, for example, Iran suffered earthquakes that nearly instantly killed some thirty-five thousand in each case, but the country clearly survived the disasters. They were major tragedies, of course, but they hardly proved to be "existential." In fact, there is extensive evidence that the most common reaction to disaster is not self-destructive panic, but "resourcefulness, civility, and mutual aid."[49] The main concern would be that in the aftermath people would adopt skittish, overly risk-averse behavior that would much magnify the impact of the terrorist attack, particularly economically. Most importantly in all this, public and private members of the terrorism industry must be able to restrain and contain any instinct to destroy their own societies in response should they ever be provoked. In the meantime, however, as Seitz puts it, "the rhetoric of extinction ... serves to inflate into satanic stature a merely evil man."[50]

All societies are "vulnerable" to tiny bands of suicidal fanatics in the sense that it is impossible to prevent every terrorist act. But the United States is hardly "vulnerable" in the sense that it can be toppled by dramatic acts of terrorist destruction, even extreme ones. In fact, the country can readily, if grimly, absorb that kind of damage—as it "absorbs" some forty thousand deaths each year from automobile accidents.

In 1999, the Gilmore Commission forcefully made a point they considered to be "self-evident," but one that nonetheless required "reiteration" because of "the rhetoric and hyperbole with which the threat of CBRN terrorism is frequently couched." The point was:

> As serious and potentially catastrophic as a domestic CBRN attack might prove, it is highly unlikely that it could ever completely undermine the national security, much less threaten the survival, of the United States as a nation... To take any other position risks surrendering to the fear and intimidation that is precisely the terrorist's stock in trade.[51]

The fact that terrorists subsequently managed to ram airplanes into three buildings does not render this "self-evident" point less sound, and "reiteration" continues to be required.

Policies designed to deal with terrorism should focus more on reducing fear and anxiety as inexpensively as possible than on objectively reducing the rather limited dangers terrorism is likely actually to pose

Where risks are real—as in the cases of smoking, obesity, alcoholism, and automobile driving—it makes sense to stoke fear: people should be *more* afraid, less complacent, and less in denial about these dangers than they are at present. However, where the real risks for any given individual are far smaller—as with terrorism, shark attacks, and airplane flying—fear becomes the problem, and accordingly it makes policy sense to use smoke, mirrors, and any other handy device in an attempt to reduce it.

Additionally the reduction of fear and anxiety is in fact actually quite central to dealing with terrorism. The revolutionary, Frantz Fanon, reportedly held that "the aim of terrorism is to terrify." And the inspiration of consequent overreaction seems central to bin Laden's strategy. As he put it mockingly in a videotaped message in 2004, it is "easy for us to provoke and bait... All that we have to do is to send two mujahidin ... to raise a piece of cloth on which is written al-Qaeda in order to make the generals race there to cause America to suffer human, economic, and political losses." His policy, he extravagantly believes, is one of "bleeding America to the point of bankruptcy," and it is one that depends on overreaction by the target: he triumphally points to the fact that the September 11 terrorist attacks cost Al Qaeda $500,000 while the attack and its aftermath inflicted, he claims, a cost of more than $500 billion on the United States.[52]

Since the creation of insecurity, fear, anxiety, and hysteria is central for terrorists, they can be defeated simply by not becoming terrified and by resisting the temptation to overreact: as Friedman aptly puts it, "One way to disarm terrorists is to convince regular Americans to stop worrying about them."[53] The 2001 anthrax attacks, Hoffman argues, suggest that "five persons dying in mysterious circumstances is quite effective at unnerving an entire nation."[54] To the degree that is true, policies for limiting terrorist damage should focus on such unwarranted reactions.

The shock and tragedy of September 11 does demand a dedicated program to confront international terrorism and to attempt to prevent a repetition, of course. But part of this reaction should include an effort by politicians, bureaucrats, officials, and the media to inform the public reasonably and realistically about the terrorist context instead of playing into the hands of terrorists by effectively seeking to terrify the public: in Friedman's words, "Policies that encourage fear are a self-inflicted wound."[55] What is needed then, as one statistician suggests, is some sort of convincing, coherent, informed, and nuanced answer to a central question: "How worried should I be?" Instead, the message, as one concerned Homeland Security official puts it, is "Be scared. Be very, very scared. But go on with your lives."[56]

Thus, a sensible policy approach for confronting terrorism might be to stress that any damage terrorists are able to accomplish likely can be absorbed and that, while judicious protective and policing measures are sensible, extensive fear and anxiety over what at base could well prove to be a rather limited problem is misplaced, unjustified, and counterproductive. In risk analyst Howard Kunreuther's words, "More attention needs to be devoted to giving people perspective on the remote likelihood of the terrible consequences they imagine."[57] That would seem to be at least as important as boosting the sale of duct tape, issuing repeated and costly color-coded alerts based on vague and unspecific intelligence, and warning people to beware of Greeks, or just about anybody, bearing almanacs.

What we need, then, is more pronouncements like the one in a recent book by Senator John McCain: "Get on the damn elevator! Fly on the damn plane! Calculate the odds of being harmed by a terrorist! It's still about as likely as being swept out to sea by a tidal wave... Suck it up, for crying out loud. You're almost certainly going to be okay. And in the unlikely event you're not, do you really want to spend your last days cowering behind plastic sheets and duct tape? That's not a life worth living, is it?"[58] But admonitions like that are exceedingly rare, almost nonexistent. Instead, we get plenty of alarmism from the terrorism industry and almost nothing—*nothing*— about realistic risks and probabilities.

For example, there is at present a great and understandable concern about what would happen if terrorists are able to shoot down an American airliner or two, perhaps with shoulder-fired missiles. Obviously, this would be a major tragedy in the first instance. But the ensuing public reaction to it, many fear, could come close to destroying the industry. It would seem to be reasonable for those with that fear to consider the following: how many airliners would have to crash before flying becomes as dangerous as driving the same distance in an automobile? It turns out that someone has made that calculation. The conclusion is that there would have to be one set of September 11 crashes a month for the risks to balance out. More generally, they calculate that an American's chance of being killed on one nonstop airline flight is about 1 in 13 million (even taking the September 11 crashes into account), while to reach that same level of risk when driving on America's safest roads (rural interstate highways) one would have to travel a mere 11.2 miles.[59]

Or there ought to be at least some discussion of the almost completely unaddressed but seemingly obvious observation that, in the words of risk analyst David Banks, "It seems impossible that the United States will ever again experience takeovers of commercial flights that are then turned into weapons—no pilot will relinquish control, and passengers will fight." The scheme worked in 2001 because the hijackers had the element of surprise working for them: previous airline hijackings had mostly been fairly harmless as hijackers generally landed the planes someplace and released the passengers. The passengers and crew on the fourth plane on September 11 had fragmentary knowledge about what the earlier hijackings that day had led to, and they prevented the plane from reaching its target. This is likely to hold even more for any later attempted hijackings. Nonetheless, notes Banks, "enormous resources are being invested to prevent this remote contingency." There is a distinction, he argues, "between realistic reactions to plausible threats and hyperbolic overreaction to improbable contingencies."[60]

It is easy, even comforting, to blame politicians, bureaucrats, experts, and the media for the distorted and context-free condition under which terrorism is so often discussed. In many respects, however, that circumstance arises not so much from their own proclivities, but rather from those of their customers. In Tocqueville's words, "the author and the public corrupt one another at the same time."[61] That is, hysteria and alarmism often sell.

In the end, it is not clear how one can deal with the public's often irrational, or at least erratic, fears about remote dangers. Some people say they prefer dangerous forms of transportation like the private passenger automobile (the necessary cause of over 3 million American deaths during the twentieth century) to safe ones like commercial airliners because they feel they have more "control." But they seem to feel no fear on buses and trains—which actually are a bit more dangerous than airplanes—even without having that sense of control and even though derailing a speeding train or crashing a speeding bus are likely to be much easier than downing an airliner. And people tend to be more alarmed by dramatic fatalities—which the September 11 crashes certainly provided—than by ones that cumulate statistically. Thus, in the United States the 3,000 deaths of September 11 inspire far more grief and fear than the 150,000 deaths from auto accidents that have taken place there since then.

In some respects, fear of terror may be something like playing the lottery except in reverse. The chances of winning the lottery or of dying from terrorism may be microscopic, but for monumental events which are (or seem) random, one can irrelevantly conclude that one's chances are just as good (or bad) as those of anyone else.

The communication of risk, then, is no easy task. Risk analyst Paul Slovic points out that people tend greatly to overestimate the chances of dramatic or sensational causes of death; that realistically informing people about risks sometimes only makes them more frightened; that strong beliefs in this area are very difficult to modify; that a new sort of calamity tends to be taken as a harbinger of future mishaps; that a disaster tends to increase fears not only about that kind of danger but of all kinds; and that people, even professionals, are susceptible to the way risks are expressed—they are far less likely, for example, to choose radiation therapy if told the chances of death are 32 percent rather than that the chances of survival are 68 percent.[62] Studies have also shown that when presented with two estimations of risk from reasonably authoritative sources, people choose to embrace the high risk opinion regardless of its source; that is, there is a "predilection toward alarmist responses and excessive weighting of the worst case scenario."[63]

Risk tends to be more nearly socially constructed than objectively calculated.[64] Nevertheless, risk assessment and communication should at least be part of the policy discussion over terrorism, something that may well prove to be a far smaller danger than is popularly portrayed.

An unorthodox, but potentially beneficial, policy approach might be systematically to determine which policy measures actually do reduce fear and then to put the least expensive of these into effect. If a measure actually does increase safety, that would be all to the good. But since the dangers terrorists present appear to be quite minor (barring some very massive technological breakthroughs on their part), the actual effect on safety would be only a secondary consideration. Indeed, any problems caused by radiological, chemical, and perhaps biological weapons are likely to stem far more from the fear and panic they may induce than from the direct harm the weapons may inflict themselves, so in these cases the potential for fear and panic should be a primary concern, not an ancillary one.

Thus, to the degree that people are less fearful when they have a sense of control, policies should seek to advance that rather vaporous quality whether it actually makes them safer or not.

For example, if some people somehow sense they gain control when they purchase duct tape and plastic sheeting, that act would be of value—not because it reduced danger but because it reduced anxiety.

Instead of maintaining that the terrorists might strike anywhere at any time, and thereby stoking the fear of random violence, it might make sense to suggest that only certain (relatively small) areas are primarily at risk. If the benefit from the reduction of fear in the excluded areas is greater than the costs of fear enhancement in the designated ones, the measure would presumably be, on balance, sound public policy.

Policy makers might also be on the lookout for cheap, even costless, measures that could reduce fear. For example, when concerns about shark attacks soared in the summer of 2001, a Florida commission heroically forbade the feeding of sharks.[65] Whether this measure actually reduced fears is a matter for empirical investigation, but if it did its value certainly outweighed its cost.

It might also be useful to plumb the "cry wolf" phenomenon for possibilities. The boy who repeatedly and alarmingly proclaims to his village that he has seen a wolf among the sheep ends up relaxing fear because people become less concerned about wolves when his alarms repeatedly prove false. Therefore if there are in fact no threatening wolves out there, or if the villagers generally are more concerned about wolf attacks than is objectively justified, he is providing a community service by reducing fear.

However, for this to work there are four special issues. First, because the people in charge are aware of the cry wolf problem, it is important that they not give in to the temptation to refrain from issuing too many warnings after they have been repeatedly mistaken: they must keep it up. Second, the warnings must be specific enough to be falsifiable: according to one version, Aesop's boy cries "Wolf! Wolf! The wolf is chasing the sheep!"—a claim the villagers are able quickly to falsify. He does not issue such unfalsifiable outcries as "I have intercepted some chatter recently suggesting that a wolf might chase the sheep at some time in the indefinite future, or, then again, maybe not." Third, it would be important to consider the cost of the alert itself: for example, orange alerts cost the Los Angeles airport alone $100,000 per day.[66] And fourth, it is crucial to the process that the community remembers the false alarms and tallies them up. In the real world, doomsday scenarists are rarely held to account because few remember their extravagant predictions when they fail to materialize.

Taking the last point more generally, a useful public service would be to cumulate a record of the many false warnings that have been issued by the Department of Homeland Security and by the terrorism industry, and to publicize them routinely and repeatedly. Although each warning has tended to elevate short-term concern, the cumulative impact of the series of false alarms could be—if people are jogged into remembering them—to reduce fears beneficially. There are, in this regard, a number of studies indicating that trust in the source of the information can be important.[67] The Department of Homeland Security and President Bush tend to enjoy considerable trust on this issue, and they have been, mostly inclined to stoke fears of terrorism. Efforts to undermine their credibility, therefore, could potentially have the effect of reducing fear.

Some studies suggest that people deeply angered at the September 11 attacks also tended to be less fearful.[68] It is not clear how one stokes anger rather than fear, nor is it clear that doing so would necessarily be a good idea. But further research on this issue might be of value.

Studies should also be made of safety measures currently in effect, with an eye toward reducing costs. For example, one might suspect that airline passengers are not made to feel any safer because they are often forced to remove their shoes as they pass through inspection, or because they are required to show their boarding passes twice to uniformed authority figures rather than once, or because cars picking them up are not allowed to loiter at curbside even when such traffic is light. Experimental studies could easily be set up in airports to test whether these suspicions are valid.

Also useful might be to reconsider the standards about what is harmful in some cases. For example, while a "dirty bomb" might raise radiation 25 percent over background levels in an area and therefore into a range the Environmental Protection Agency (EPA) officially considers undesirable, there ought to be some discussion about whether that really constitutes "contamination" or indeed much of a danger given the somewhat arbitrary and exceedingly cautious levels declared to be acceptable by the EPA.[69] If trusted governmental officials can truthfully say that the contamination does not reach levels considered unsafe, undesirable negative reactions might be beneficially reduced and might far outweigh any risks involved.

Doing nothing (or at least refraining from overreacting) after a terrorist attack is not necessarily unacceptable

Although it is often argued that it is imperative that public officials "do something"—which usually means overreact—when a terrorist event takes place, there are many instances where no reaction took place and the officials did not suffer politically or otherwise. Ronald Reagan's response to a terrorist bomb in Lebanon in 1983 that killed 241 American Marines was to make a few speeches and eventually to pull the troops out. Bill Clinton responded similarly after an unacceptable loss of American lives in Somalia ten years later. Although there were the (apparently counterproductive) military retaliations after the U.S. embassy bombings in Africa in 1998 as noted earlier, there was no notable response to terrorist attacks on American targets in Saudi Arabia (Khobar Towers) in 1996 or to the bombing of the USS *Cole* in 2000. The response to the anthrax attacks of 2001 was the same as to terrorist attacks against the World Trade Center in 1993 and in Oklahoma City in 1995— the dedicated application of police work to try to apprehend the perpetrator—and this proved to be politically acceptable.

The demands for retaliation tend to be more problematic in the case of suicide terrorists since the direct perpetrators of the terrorist act are already dead. Nonetheless, the attacks in Lebanon, Saudi Arabia, and against the *Cole* were all suicidal, yet no direct retaliatory action was taken.

Thus, despite short-term demands that some sort of action must be taken, experience suggests politicians can often successfully ride out this demand after the obligatory (and inexpensive) expressions of outrage are issued.

Despite U.S. overreaction, the campaign against terror is generally going rather well

Insofar as international terrorism—particularly Al Qaeda—is a problem, it seems likely that things are improving. This is not so much because the United States has spent so wisely and effectively, however.

In fact, the war in Iraq will probably prove encouraging to international terrorists because they will take even an orderly American retreat from the country as a great victory—even greater than the one against the Soviet Union in Afghanistan.[70] Osama bin Laden's theory that the Americans can be defeated, or at least productively inconvenienced, by inflicting comparatively small, but continuously draining, casualties on them will achieve apparent confirmation, and a venture designed and sold in part as a blow against international terrorists will end up emboldening and energizing them. A comparison might be made with Israel's orderly, even overdue, withdrawal from Lebanon in 2000 that insurgents there took to be a great triumph for their terrorist tactics— and, most importantly, so did like-minded Palestinians who later escalated their efforts to use terrorism to destroy Israel itself. People like bin Laden believe that America invaded Iraq as part of its plan to control the oil in the Persian Gulf area. But the United States does not intend to do that (at least not in the direct sense bin Laden and others doubtless consider to be its goal), nor does it seek to destroy Islam as many others also bitterly assert. Thus just about any kind of American withdrawal will be seen by such people as a victory for the harassing terrorist insurgents who, they will believe, are due primary credit for forcing the United States to leave without accomplishing what they take to be its key objectives.

Despite this, the campaign against terrorism is generally succeeding because, no matter how much they might disagree on other issues (most notably on America's war on Iraq), there is a compelling incentive for states—including Arab and Muslim ones, who are also being targeted— to cooperate to deal with this international threat. And since methodical, persistent policing of individuals and small groups is most needed, the process seems to be on the right track. It is not clear that this policing has prevented international terrorism in the United States, however. The number of such incidents in the three years after September 11 was zero, but that was the same number registered in the three years before the attacks at a time when antiterrorist policing exertions were much lower.

Actually, by some standards, it may all be nearly over. Stephen Flynn, like others in the terrorism industry, likes to begin articles with such dramatic lines as "the United States is living on borrowed time—and squandering it," and end them with "the entire nation… must be organized for the long, deadly struggle against terrorism." However, in midcourse he also supplies a standard for "how much security is enough" and determines that to be when "the American people can conclude that a future attack on U.S. soil will be an exceptional event that does not require wholesale changes in how they go about their lives."[71] It seems reasonable to suggest that they can so conclude right now, though that might require them to stop listening to the terrorism industry.

Hysteria and hysterical overreaction about terrorism are hardly required and can be costly and counterproductive. There are uncertainties and risks out there, and plenty of dangers and threats. But these are highly unlikely to prove to be existential. The sky, as it happens, is not falling—nor is apocalypse on the horizon. Perhaps we can relax a little.

Notes

1 Mark Bowden, remarks, *Tucker Carlson Unfiltered*, PBS, November 19, 2004.
2 In almost all years fewer than ten Americans die worldwide at the hands of international terrorists: U.S. State Department, *Patterns of Global Terrorism, 1997* (April 1998), 85. An average of ninety people are killed each year by lightning in the United States: National Safety Council, *Accident Facts* (Chicago: National Safety Council, 1997), 120. About hundred Americans die per year from accidents caused by deer: Andrew C. Revkin, "Coming to the Suburbs: A Hit Squad for Deer," *New York Times*, (November 30, 1998). And about 320 drown in bathtubs and 4 in toilets: John Stossel, *Give Me a Break* (New York: Harper Collins, 2004), 77.
3 See, for example, Walter Laqueur, *No End to War: Terrorism in the Twenty-First Century* (New York: Continuum, 2003), 226–228.
4 For an excellent overview of this issue, see Gregg Easterbrook, "Term Limits: The Meaninglessness of 'WMD,'" *New Republic*, October 7, 2002.
5 Matthew Meselson, "The Myth of Chemical Superweapons," *Bulletin of the Atomic Scientists*, April 1991, 13; Office of Technology Assessment, United States Congress, *Proliferation of Weapons of Mass Destruction: Assessing the Risks, OTA-559* (Washington DC: U.S. Government Printing Office, 1993), 54.
6 H. L. Gilchrist, *A Comparative Study of World War Casualties from Gas and Other Weapons* (Edgewood Arsenal, MD: Chemical Warfare School, 1928), 7.
7 Steve Fetter, "Ballistic Missiles and Weapons of Mass Destruction: What Is the Threat? What Should Be Done?" *International Security* 16, no.1 (1991): 15.
8 David C. Rapoport, "Terrorists and Weapons of the Apocalypse," *National Security Studies Quarterly* 5, no.1 (1999): 57.
9 Office of Technology Assessment, *Proliferation of Weapons*, 48–49, 62; Easterbrook "Term Limits."

10 Graham Allison, *Nuclear Terrorism: The Ultimate Preventable Catastrophe* (New York: Times Books, 2004), 104.

11 Brian Jenkins, "International Terrorism: A New Mode of Conflict," in *International Terrorism and World Security*, eds. David Carlton and Carlo Schaerf, 33 (New York: Wiley, 1975).

12 Norman J. Rabkin, "Combating Terrorism," GAO/T-NSIAD-00-145 (Washington DC: U.S. General Accounting Office, 2000), 4, 12.

13 "'Suitcase Nukes': A Reassessment" (Research Story of the Week, September 22, 2002), 4, 12.

14 Charles Duelfer, testimony before the Senate Select Committee on Intelligence (Washington DC, October 6, 2004); see also Russell Seitz, "Weaker Than We Think," *American Conservative*, December 2004.

15 Allison, *Nuclear Terrorism*, 97.

16 Joshua S. Goldstein, *The Real Price of War: How You Pay for the War on Terror* (New York: New York University Press, 2004), 128, 132. Allison, *Nuclear Terrorism*, 15; on Korea, 168–171.

17 C. P. Snow, "The Moral Un-Neutrality of Science," *Science*, January 1961.

18 See also John Mueller, "Harbinger or Aberration? A 9/11 Provocation," *National Interest*, Fall 2002; Seitz, "Weaker." By contrast, in 2004 Charles Krauthammer characterized the post–September 11 period as "three years in which, contrary to every expectation and prediction, the second shoe never dropped": "Blixful Amnesia," *Washington Post*, July 9, 2004. Allison also noted that "in the weeks and months following 9/11, the American national security community focused on what was called the question of the 'second shoe.' No one believed that the attacks on the World Trade Center and the Pentagon were an isolated occurrence": *Nuclear Terrorism*, 6.

19 And millions of passengers who checked bags at hotels and retrieved them before heading to the airport have routinely lied to an airline agent when answering the pointlessly obligatory question about whether their luggage had at all times been in their possession.

20 On the preference of terrorists for weapons that they know and understand, see Rapoport, "Terrorists and Weapons," 51.

21 Seitz, "Weaker."

22 Jeffrey D. Simon, *The Terrorist Trap: America's Experience with Terrorism*, 2nd ed. (Bloomington: Indiana University Press, 2001), 197–200.

23 Werner Daum, "Universalism and the West: An Agenda for Understanding," *Harvard International Review*, Summer 2001, 19.

24 Jason Burke, *Al-Qaeda: Casting a Shadow of Terror* (New York: Tauris 2003), 167–68; Steve Coll, *Ghost Wars* (New York: Penguin, 2004), 400–2, 414–15. On this process more generally, see David A. Lake, "Rational Extremism: Understanding Terrorism in the Twenty-first Century," *Dialog-IO*, Spring 2002. Reactions to terrorism have also often led to massive persecution. The Jewish pogroms in Russia at the end of the nineteenth century, for instance, were impelled in part because Jews were notable in terrorist movements at the time: David C. Rapoport, "The Four Waves of Modern Terrorism," in *Attacking Terrorism*, eds. Audrey Kurth Cronin and James M. Ludes, (68) (Washington DC: George-town University Press, 2004). On the often deadly and indiscriminant overreaction to anarchist terrorism in the United States and elsewhere, see Richard Bach Jensen, "The United States, International Policing and the War against Anarchist Terrorism, 1900–1914," *Terrorism and Political Violence* 13, no.1 (2002): 15–46.

25 Benjamin Friedman, "Leap before You Look: The Failure of Homeland Security," *Breakthroughs* 13, no.1 (2004): 35.

26 *Financial Times*, September 14, 2004, 8. Dean Calbreath, "Attacks to Cost 1.6 Million Jobs," *San Diego Union-Tribune*, January 12, 2002.

27 Roger D. Congleton, "Terrorism, Interest-Group Politics, and Public Policy," *Independent Review*, Summer 2002, 62.

28 Jeffrey Rosen, *The Naked Crowd* (New York: Random House, 2004), 68. On the $9 billion Los Angeles airport plan to (marginally) improve security from terrorist bombs, see Sara Kehaulani Goo, "Going the Extra Mile," *Washington Post*, April 9, 2004.

29 Kenneth Rogoff, "The Cost of Living Dangerously," *Foreign Policy*, November/December 2004.

30 Michael Sivak and Michael J. Flannagan, "Consequences for Road Traffic Fatalities of the Reduction in Flying Following September 11, 2001," *Transportation Research Part F* 7 (2004): 301–305.

31 See *Economist*, November 6–12, 2004, 81–82. The wars have also, of course, been quite costly economically.

32 Clark Chapman and Alan W. Harris, "A Skeptical Look at September 11th: How We Can Defeat Terrorism by Reacting to It More Rationally," *Skeptical Inquirer* 26, no.5 (2002): 30.

33 David L. Banks, "Statistics for Homeland Defense," *Chance* 15, no.1 (2002): 10.

34   Francis X. Clines, "Karl Rove's Campaign Strategy Seems Evident: It's the Terror, Stupid," *New York Times*, May 10, 2003. The war imagery suggests that people should be asked somehow to make sacrifices. This popular conclusion is at least partly fanciful. Few Americans except those directly involved in the wars in Korea or Vietnam really made much of a sacrifice and, although there were inconveniences on the homefront during World War II, consumer spending by the "Greatest Generation" generally surged. A goal of terrorism presumably is to hamper the economy, and therefore the best response to it—hardly much of a "sacrifice"—would be to go out and buy a refrigerator or to take an airplane to a vacation resort. The war imagery suggests we should be cutting back; but cutting back actually helps the terrorists.

35   Office of Homeland Security, "The National Strategy for Homeland Security," (July 2002).

36   Friedman, "Leap," 33–34, 36; Rosen, *Naked Crowd*, 79.

37   Rosen, *Naked Crowd*, 222.

38   See also Siobhan Gorman, "Fear Factor," *National Journal*, May 10, 2003, 1464.

39   Siobhan Gorman, "War on Terror, Phase Two," *National Journal*, November 20, 2004, 3534.

40   Bernard Brodie, "The Development of Nuclear Strategy," *International Security* 2, no.4 (1978): 68.

41   Bruce Hoffman, "Rethinking Terrorism and Counterterrorism Since 9/11," *Studies in Conflict and Terrorism* 25 (2002): 311–12. See also John Mueller, "Why Isn't There More Violence?" *Security Studies* 13 (2004): 191–203.

42   Goldstein, *Real Price*, 128, 132; Allison, *Nuclear Terrorism*, 1, 171. One Pentagon estimate is that a full-scale war on the peninsula could kill 1,000,000 people (including 80,000 to 100,000 Americans) cost over $100 billion, and do economic destruction on the order of $1 trillion. Don Oberdorfer, *The Two Koreas: A Contemporary History*, rev. ed. (New York: Basic, 2001), 324.

43   Chapman and Harris, "Skeptical Look," 32.

44   David Gergen, "A Fragile Time for Globalism," *U.S. News and World Report*, February 11, 2002 41; Richard Lugar, remarks on *Fox News Sunday*, June 15, 2003; Krauthammer, "Blixful Amnesia."

45   Allison, *Nuclear Terrorism*, 191. Goldstein, *Real Price*, 145, 179.

46   Daniel Benjamin and Steven Simon, *The Age of Sacred Terror* (New York: Random House, 2002), 398–399, 418.

47   Anonymous, *Imperial Hubris: Why the West Is Losing the War on Terror* (Dulles, VA: Brassey's 2004), 160, 177, 226, 241, 242, 250, 252, 263. For a contrast with such views, see Daniel L. Byman, "Al-Qaeda as an Adversary: Do We Understand Our Enemy?" *World Politics* 56, no.1 (2003), 160, 163; Seitz, "Weaker."

48   Jennifer C. Kerr, "Terror Threat Level Raised to Orange," Associated Press, December 21, 2003.

49   Thomas A. Glass and Monica Schoch-Spana, "Bioterrorism and the People: How to Vaccinate a City against Panic," *CID* 34 (2002), 214–215.

50   Seitz, "Weaker."

51   Gilmore Commission (Advisory Panel to Assess Domestic Response Capabilities for Terrorism Involving Weapons of Mass Destruction), *First Annual Report: Assessing the Threat* (1999), 37, http//www.rand.org/ nsrd/terrpanel/terror.pdf. Accessed 31 July 2005.

52   "Full transcript of bin Laden's speech," http://english.aljazeera.net/NR/exeres/79C6AF22-98FB-4A1C-B21F-2BC36E87F61F.htm. Accessed 31 July 2005.

53   Friedman, "Leap," 32.

54   Hoffman, "Rethinking Terrorism," 313.

55   Friedman, "Leap," 29.

56   Gorman, "Fear Factor," 1461–1462.

57   Howard Kunreuther, "Risk Analysis and Risk Management in an Uncertain World," *Risk Analysis* 22 (2002), 663. For a rare instance in which this is attempted, see Gwynne Dyer, "Politicking Skews Needed Perspective on Terror War," *Columbus Dispatch*, September 6, 2004 (also at www.gwynnedyer. com).

58   John McCain and Mark Salter, *Why Courage Matters: The Way to a Braver Life* (New York: Random House, 2004), 35–36. The imperatives of full disclosure require me to report that the ellipses in that statement conceal the following remarkable assertion: "Watch the terrorist alert and go outside again when it falls below yellow." Since the ever-watchful and ever-cautious Department of Homeland Security seems unlikely *ever* to lower the threat level below yellow, McCain's admonition seems effectively to contradict the spirit in the rest of the passage by encouraging everyone to cower inside for the rest of their lives. An e-mail inquiring about this curiosity was sent to Senator McCain's office in August 2004, but it has yet to generate a reply.

59   Michael Sivak and Michael J. Flannagan, "Flying and Driving after the September 11 Attacks," *American Scientist* 91, no.1 (2003): 6–9.

60 Banks, "Statistics" 10.

61 Quoted in Rosen, *Naked Crowd*, 77.

62 Paul Slovic, "Informing and Educating the Public about Risk," *Risk Analysis* 6 (1986): 403–15. On these issues, see also Cass R. Sustein, "Terrorism and probability neglect," *Journal of Risk and Uncertainty*, 26(2003): 121–136.

63 W. Kip Viscusi, "Alarmist Decisions with Divergent Risk Information," *Economic Journal*, November, 1997: 1669.

64 For a discussion, see Bernd Rohrmann and Ortwin Renn, "Risk Perception Research—An Introduction," in *Cross-Cultural Risk Perception: A Survey of Empirical Studies*, eds. Ortwin Renn and Bernd Rohrmann, (40–41) (Dordrecht, The Netherlands: Kluwer Academic Publishers, 2000).

65 Rosen, *Naked Crowd*, 79.

66 Goo, "Extra Mile."

67 Rohrmann and Renn, "Risk Perception," 31.

68 Jennifer Lerner, Roxana M. Gonzalez, Deborah A. Small, and Baruch Fischoff, "Effects of Fear and Anger on Perceived Risks of Terrorism," *Psychological Science* 14, no.2 (2003): 144–50.

69 Since "dirty" bombs simply raise radiation levels somewhat above normal background levels in a small area, a common recommendation from nuclear scientists and engineers is that those exposed should calmly walk away. But this bit of advice has not been advanced prominently (or even, perhaps, at all) by those in charge. Effectively, therefore, they encourage panic, and, as one nuclear engineer points out, "if you keep telling them you expect them to panic, they will oblige you. And that's what we're doing." Theodore Rockwell, "Radiation Chicken Little," *Washington Post*, September 16, 2003. See also Allison, *Nuclear Terrorism*, 8, 59, 220.

70 For discussion on this point, see John Mueller, "The Politics of Cutting and Running," *History News Network*, http//hnn.us/articles/5324.html. Accessed 31 July 2005. See also Neil MacFarquhar, "Rising Tide of Islamic Militants See Iraq as Ultimate Battlefield," *New York Times*, August 13, 2003.

71 Stephen E. Flynn, "The Neglected Home Front," *Foreign Affairs*, September/October 2004, 20, 27, 33.

26 Martyrdom mythology in Iraq

How jihadists frame suicide terrorism in videos and biographies

Mohammed M. Hafez

Introduction

Jihadists in Iraq confront a challenging communication problem. Their messages must achieve five goals: *appeal* to potential recruits inside and outside of Iraq; *justify* to the public the killing of civilians and fellow Muslims in insurgent attacks; *deactivate self-inhibiting norms* that may obstruct their cadres from killing civilians in suicide attacks; *legitimize* the organizations that engage in violence; and *counter the claims* of authorities in Iraq and around the Muslim world. Jihadists formulate a number of utilitarian, ideological, and theological arguments to achieve these tasks. However, to avoid overwhelming their audiences with information and complicated political and theological discourse, jihadists simplify their message by relying on emotional narratives that seek to construct the image of the "heroic martyr." Through online video clips and biographies of suicide bombers, they play on prevailing themes of humiliation, collusion, and redemption to demonize their enemies and motivate their cadres to make "heroic" sacrifices. They exaggerate mistreatment of women and appeal to the masculinity of men in order to shame them into protecting their "mothers and sisters." These emotive elements of their discourse are intended to galvanize support for their cause, not just from a narrow circle of activists, but also from the broader Muslim public.

The dominant narratives in insurgent videos, audio recordings, online magazines, and biographies revolve around three themes that are often presented in a sequence as if to show a play in three acts. Act one depicts the unmerciful humiliation and suffering inflicted on Muslims in Iraq and throughout the world, suggesting that there is a conspiracy by the Western "crusaders" to target Muslims and single them out for punishment. The second act shows the impotence of existing Muslim regimes and their collusion with the West, suggesting that they are not the true leaders of the Muslim world, but servants of their Western "masters." The final act insists on the inevitability of Muslim victory because pious and heroic cadres have stepped forward to redeem the suffering and humiliation of their fellow Muslims through faith in God, sacrifice on the battlefield, and righteousness in their cause. These three narratives are sometimes presented separately, but often they are woven together to suggest a problem, a cause of the problem, and a solution to the problem.

This article explores martyrdom mythologies in Iraq by drawing extensively on the literature of jihadists since the beginning of the Iraqi insurgency.[1] These include video clips,[2] audio recordings,[3] biographies of suicide bombers,[4] online magazines,[5] and still images posted online.[6] Special emphasis is given to how jihadists portray the fallen "martyrs." By elevating the suicide bombers to the status of extraordinary moral beings who make the ultimate sacrifice for God and the Muslim nation, jihadists deflect attention away from their atrocities and the victims they harm. It must be made clear from the outset that the portrayal of bombers in video clips and biographies is highly propagandistic and in all likelihood does not reflect the totality of their motivations. The point of focusing on martyrdom mythologies is to show how groups seek to achieve several communicative goals through manipulation of narratives, not to suggest that these mythologies reflect the true motivations of the suicide bombers. The latter is a complex research question that falls outside the scope of this article.

Discursive practices in and of themselves are not sufficient to mobilize people for action. Therefore, this study is not suggesting that mere "talk" by jihadists is sufficient to compel people to engage in suicide operations. A number of other factors such as societal conflicts, mobilizing networks, legitimating authorities, and permissive conditions are necessary for the phenomenon of suicide terrorism to develop on the scale witnessed in Iraq. However, discursive practices are a necessary component in the dynamic of violence, especially important in legitimating the indiscriminate killing of civilians. This research, therefore, is not intended to explain *why* suicide bombings take place in Iraq. Its intent is to explain *how* jihadists deploy emotional narratives to simplify their communication tasks as they attempt to mobilize their milieu and a sympathetic public for jihad in Iraq.

Background context

From March 22, 2003 to August 2006, more than 440 suicide attacks took place in Iraq. The overwhelming majority of these attacks have targeted Iraqi security forces and Shiite civilians, not coalition forces.[7] Many, if not most, of the perpetrators of these suicide bombings are non-Iraqis who volunteered to fight and die in Iraq. Most are connected to jihadi networks associated with "second generation" jihadists who trained in Afghanistan during the 1990s or militants fleeing arrest in their home or host countries.[8]

Suicide terrorism in Iraq began with the U.S.-led invasion of Iraq in March 2003. However, insurgent groups that deploy suicide terrorism in Iraq frequently do so not just to remove the occupation from the country, but also to collapse the emerging regime by intimidating and annihilating the newly formed Iraqi security forces and by fostering a sectarian war between Shiite and Sunni Muslims.[9] Insurgents regularly target new recruits to Iraq's security services. Approximately 44% of suicide attacks have targeted Iraqi security forces as of February 2006.[10] From June 2003 to April 30, 2006, approximately 4,550 Iraqi military and police personnel were killed.[11] As of April 30, 2006, 779 (35.5%) of the 2,400 U.S. troops killed in Iraq died in IED (improvised explosive devices) attacks; another 742 (30.9%) died in hostile fire that does not include car bombs, which killed only 121 (5.0%) American personnel. Given that the overwhelming majority of suicide attacks (70%) are conducted through car bombs, it is safe to conclude that most suicide attacks in Iraq do not target U.S. forces.[12] Kurdish, Shiite, and Sunni political figures operating in the new political process have also been attacked in suicide attacks as have militia members belonging to the Shiite Badr Corps, Mehdi Army, and Kurdish Peshmerga. The most gruesome suicide attacks have targeted Shiite civilians in markets, mosques, religious ceremonies, and funeral processions. As of February 2006, approximately 23% of suicide attacks targeted civilians in Iraq and 11% targeted government officials and parties.[13]

The Iraqi insurgents rely on a diverse tool kit of tactics and they deploy them across a range of targets. The deadliest tactics are the improvised explosive devices (IEDs), which are considered the most lethal in the insurgency, and car bombs driven by suicide bombers. However, insurgents also verbally and physically intimidate "collaborators" such as translators and manual laborers employed by the coalition forces; sabotage electric stations, oil and water pipelines and facilities, and coalition reconstruction projects; lob improvised rockets and mortar shells at coalition positions and fire surface-to-air rockets at airplanes and helicopters; kidnap local citizens and foreigners to exchange them for ransom or execute them, as well as kidnap members of the security services and "spies" to interrogate them and execute them; and carry out suicide attacks using explosive vests. Insurgents also attack international organizations such as the United Nations, non-governmental agencies such as the Red Cross, and representatives of foreign governments such as the Jordanian and Turkish embassies, and have killed Algerian, Egyptian, and Russian diplomats.

There is a strategic logic to why insurgents attack the targets they do. Expansive violence against foreigners, Shiite and Kurdish politicians and civilians, Iraqi security forces, international organizations, non-governmental agencies, journalists, and the physical and economic infrastructure is intended to create widespread insecurity among the public, engender sectarian polarization, and produce economic collapse. All of these outcomes delegitimize the new order; allow the insurgents to portray themselves as the sole protectors of Sunnis, thus being able to command their support; and create a failed state whereby the central authority does not have sole monopoly on the use of coercive force, which allows jihadists with an agenda beyond Iraq to establish a base for operations, recruitment, and training.

Ideological and instrumental justifications for suicide attacks

Al Qaeda in Iraq has declared responsibility for 30 percent of the claimed suicide attacks in Iraq as of February 2006.[14] Abu Musab al-Zarqawi offered an instrumental justification for these attacks in one of his audio recordings:

> [The holy warriors] faced the strongest and most advanced army in modern times. They faced its arrogance, tyranny and all its big numbers and advanced weapons... When the holy warriors noticed this huge disparity in numbers and armaments between them and the enemy, they looked for alternatives to amend this deficiency and fill this gap so that the light and the fire of jihad will not be extinguished. Brigades of martyrs, whose sole goals are to please God and rush to the heavens, have set out and attacked the sanctuaries of infidelity and broke its armies. They inflicted severe punishment and injuries on the enemy and hurt its reputation. They mobilized the sons of this nation against this enemy and revived hope in the souls once again, praises and gratitude is to God.[15]

Abu Dujana al-Ansari, the head of Al Qaeda's al-Bara Bin Malik Brigade (suicide bombing squad), similarly justifies suicide attacks in a montage dedicated to Zarqawi. Al-Ansari says that the suicide brigade was created following the earlier advice of Shiekh Osama Bin Laden to terrorize the enemy and penetrate its defenses in order to demoralize its soldiers.[16] Such attacks instill fear in their hearts and make them cower in the face of the Muslim fighters.

But how do they justify attacking Iraqi security forces? Insurgents in Iraq, not just those associated with Al Qaeda and Ansar al-Sunna Army, argue that the Iraqi security forces are a mere extension, an appendage, to the occupation forces in Iraq. Just as the U.S. recruited the northern alliance fighters in Afghanistan against the Taliban regime, it is doing the same in Iraq by relying on the Shiite militias of the Badr Corps (which insurgents derisively call the "Ghader"—betrayal—Corps) and the Kurdish militias known as the Peshmergas. The same goes for the newly-formed Iraqi security services (which they derisively call *al-haras al-wathani*—the idol-worshipping guard—as opposed to *al-haras al-watani*—the National Guard).[17] Striking at these "collaborators" is nothing less than striking at the U.S.-led occupation forces. In a 46-minute video montage dedicated to the theme of fighting the Iraqi police and security forces, Zarqawi rhetorically asks, "Why is it permissible to strike the enemy when he has blonde hair and blue eyes, but it is not permissible to strike him when he has dark hair and black eyes?" He concludes, "An American Muslim is our beloved brother, and an Arab infidel is our depraved enemy, even if we share with him the same spot of land."[18]

In justifying attacks against Shiite militias, Al Qaeda and Ansar Al-Sunna Army argue that these militias attack and kill Sunnis, torture them, abuse and humiliate them at checkpoints, and serve as spies for the occupation forces. Many video clips issued by Ansar Al-Sunna Army and by Al Qaeda in Iraq are dedicated to this theme. Therefore, the operations against the Shiites are intended as self-defense to protect the Sunni communities as well as to take revenge on those who would harm Sunnis and turn them over to the coalition occupation forces. Al Qaeda in Iraq formed the Umar Brigade specially to attack members of the Shiite Badr Corps.[19]

In justifying attacks against the ruling government, the nationalists and salafi jihadi insurgents argue that this is an illegitimate government—indeed a puppet regime—that came to power under unacceptable circumstances with the help of aggressive enemies of the Iraqi people. It rules only because the occupation forces allow it to rule, not because it is a genuine Islamic representative of the people of Iraq. The Iraqi government gives cover and legitimacy to the occupation when it should be fighting it and demanding the withdrawal of foreign forces from Iraqi land. Without this charade of parliamentary politics and constitutional conventions, the occupation would be exposed for what it is to the whole of the Iraqi people and the world.

Moreover, this government is part and parcel of a global conspiracy against Islam led by "Crusaders" and "Zionists." These forces fear the truth of Islam and the unification of Muslim lands under a single leader, *khalifa* (caliph), and consequently conspire to distort Islam and weaken the faith of Muslims in their religion. If Muslims are united in one entity, they would be able to counter the hegemony of the West and revive the glories of their golden ages. Secularism, nationalism, and Shiism are instruments of this nefarious plot to divide and conquer Muslims. Secularism divides the world into religious and non-religious spheres, which is antithetical to Islam. The latter is a comprehensive religion that regulates matters of faith *(Ibadat)* and social relations *(muamalat)*. Furthermore, secularism violates God's sovereignty *(hakimiyyat allah)* by allowing someone other than God to legislate right and wrong, permissible and forbidden. Nationalism, in turn, fosters narrow identifications with language, land, and borders, not a broader unity among the community of faithful and brotherhood of Muslims. As for Shiism, it gives ascendancy to a heretical creed, not Islamic law based on the proper *manhaj* (method or orientation). The Shiites are the most dangerous tool against the true believers because they appear Islamic, authentic, and of the people. In reality, they loathe the people of the Sunna and wait for the opportunity to betray them.[20]

These ideological justifications are intended for a narrow milieu of committed jihadists who may question certain tactics or targets of the insurgents, especially when it comes to indiscriminate attacks on fellow Muslims. To the extent that these highly controversial arguments are produced for the wider Muslim public, they are usually accompanied by vivid imagery and emotional narratives that shock the moral conscious of Muslims, demonize the Shiites and Iraqi security forces, and heighten the threat facing Muslims worldwide.

Emotional narratives to justify suicide attacks

Insurgents in Iraq do not depend solely on the force of ideology in mobilizing support for martyrdom. Insurgents seek to cut across ideological and political divides by appealing to emotional and personal themes embedded in the culture and ethos of Arabs and Muslims in Iraq and around the world. The narratives of insurgent groups rely on three themes: humiliation, impotence due to collusion, and redemption through faith and sacrifice. These themes are often presented separately, but sometimes they are delivered in a sequence as if to suggest a crisis, a causal explanation of the crisis, and the solution to alleviate the suffering of Muslims.

Humiliation

At the heart of the mobilizing narratives of insurgents is the theme of humiliation at the hands of callous and arrogant powers. Images from act one often begin with footage from the "shock and awe" phase of the invasion of Iraq in 2003. These images depict imperial arrogance and reflect the asymmetry in power between the aggressors and their victims. Photos of Iraqi women and children killed or bloodied by the bombardment, usually accompanied by chilling melancholic chants embedded in the clip; mosques and minarets purposely destroyed through bombardment while they are issuing the calls to prayer (*adhan*), suggesting a war on Islam, not just a war in Iraq; images of coalition forces storming into homes while women and children are crying out in terror, beseeching the foreigners to let their fathers and brothers go free; clips of a U.S. soldier shooting a wounded insurgent inside a mosque or occupation forces stepping with their boots on the backs of men that have just been bound and forced to the ground with black sacks covering their faces; and, above all, images of men and women enduring humiliating torture in Abu Ghraib prison— all these images personalize the suffering and heighten the sense of powerlessness and indignations that many Muslims feel.

The Mujahideen Army in Iraq issued a 60-minute, 45-second video entitled Courageous Men or Lions (*Usud al-Shara*).[21] It contains footage of destruction inside a mosque, a torn-up Quran and another one with the Christian cross hand-drawn on its cover. As these images appear, a child's voice is heard reciting poetry:

> *Where are our mosques?*
> *Where are our schools?*
> *Why do I see them in ruins after they were beacons?*
> *Where are my countrymen?*
> *Why are they not moving to free our captive brothers? Defend the honor of our sisters?*
> *Is this not in our religion?*

These images from Iraq are usually combined with stock images from other conflicts in Muslim countries, especially Palestine. We see images of the killing of the little boy Muhammad al-Durah while in the arms of his father during the opening days of the Al-Aqsa uprising in 2000. This image galvanized the world's attention and epitomized the suffering of the Palestinian people. This image along with others is intended to deliver two messages. First, the suffering and humiliation of Muslims around the world are not unconnected episodes, but a chain in a series of transgressions by the "Crusader-Zionist" alliance against Islam and Muslims. These images are intended to portray the war in Iraq as one of many wars on Islam. In doing so, the insurgents are heightening the sense of threat facing the Muslim world in order to justify extraordinary measures to fight back the manifest conspiracy against Islam. As Zarqawi declared in one of his video montages:

> Our Jihad in Iraq is the same as in Afghanistan, Kashmir, Chechnya, and Bosnia, an honorable jihad… We shed the dust of divisive nationalism and hopeless patriotism that tears asunder the ranks of Muslims and turns them into tasty bites for the infidels.[22]

In one of the biographies of "martyrs," the Kuwaiti suicide bomber Abdel Rahman Bin Shuja al-Utaybi (Abu Awf) is said to have been moved by suffering in Palestine: "One day we were watching a videotape of young stone throwers in Palestine and the tragedy there. There were heartbreaking scenes and one of the brothers shed so many tears. He was Abdel Rahman (Abu Awf), who could not stand the tragedies of Muslims."[23] In his last will and testament, the Saudi suicide bomber Abu Ans al-Tahami al-Qahtani writes:

> Whoever looks at the condition of the Islamic nation will find it is torn asunder and its cuts bleeding in every place. There is the wound of Palestine for nearly 50 years; and there are the wounds of Chechnya, Afghanistan, Kashmir, Indonesia, Philippines, and Iraq. We are immersed in our wants and desires while the sanctuaries are violated, the mosques demolished, and the holy books insulted. I do not know how we are living inside ourselves; do these wounds pain us or do we not care?[24]

The second message delivered by linking suffering in Iraq to other Muslim conflicts is that the struggle in Iraq is the central battlefield in which to fight the war against the enemies of Islam. Fighting in Iraq, in effect, is the same as fighting in Palestine, Chechnya, Kashmir, Saudi Arabia, and elsewhere in the Muslim world. These are all one struggle, not many separate wars. In framing the conflict in this light, insurgents can call on jihadists to come and fight in Iraq without feeling guilty that they abandoned their struggle at home. Victory in Iraq is victory in every Muslim land. One of the hymns chanted over and over in one of insurgent videos reflects this presumed unity in the struggles of Muslims:

> *With the Sharp Weapon of Truth*
> *We will liberate the lands of the free*
> *And bring back purity to the land of Jerusalem*
> *After the humiliation and shame.*[25]

Linking the war in Iraq to the liberation of Jerusalem "after the humiliation and shame" appeals to the emotional need for unity and solidarity among Muslims; it is reaching out to an identity rooted in shared suffering and collective yearning for a victory following decades of failure and defeat.

Jihadists in Iraq also rely on the theme of female dishonor and suffering at the hands of foreigners and Iraqi security forces to justify violence and mobilize people. Images of women terrified in their homes as soldiers storm in to search for insurgents; videos of women being frisked by foreign men; rumors of women abducted or taken into custody where they are humiliated or, worst, raped; stories of women being handed over by Iraqi forces as hostages to be exchanged for wanted insurgents are replete in jihadist video clips and montages, audio recordings, and online magazines. Insurgents undoubtedly are appealing to notions of masculinity that pervade tribal culture, in which *sharaf* (nobleness), *árd* (honor), and *Muruah* (chivalry or manliness) are of vital importance. These notions of masculinity are often judged by one's zealous protection of and control over women so they do not risk straying in their relations with men and, therefore, bring shame to the entire family or tribe. Shame brought about by violations of honor and norms of decency associated with the separation of the sexes can impel the traditionally-minded to engage in violence to redeem the honor of the violated female, including killing the "offending" women. Failure to take vengeance raises questions about one's nobility and sense of manhood. As we shall see below, this aspect of Arab culture is exploited to the hilt.

Impotence and collusion

Part and parcel of the mobilizing narrative in Iraq is to show the "arrogance" of the invading forces and the collusion of "so called" Muslim governments. Insurgent videos often show the clip of the gloating U.S. President, George W. Bush, on board a U.S. battleship declaring victory in Iraq. This image is often followed by images of U.S. troops marching in the streets of Iraq or walking through Saddam Hussein's palaces, smiling, confident in their triumphant conquest. Occasionally, one sees the famous image of a U.S. soldier placing the American flag atop the head of Saddam's statue in the center of Baghdad on the day the city fell. All these images are intended to portray the United States as an arrogant power proud of its unjustified aggression against a Muslim nation.

These images are closely followed by others showing Arab leaders—King Abdullah in Saudi Arabia, King Abdullah in Jordan, Hussni Mubarak in Egypt, and the post-invasion leadership of Iraq (Iyad Alawi, Ibrahim al-Jaafari, Jalal Tala-bani, and Abdel Aziz al-Hakim among others)—in the company of coalition forces officials, President Bush, and British Prime Minister Tony Blair. These leaders are laughing and sometimes embracing their Western "masters." The most commonly used image is that of King Abdullah of Saudi Arabia clenching hands with President Bush, suggesting a tight bond among the closest of friends. We also see the image of the late King Fahd of Saudi Arabia giving former U.S. President Bill Clinton a medallion. Other images include Arab and/or Western leaders in the company of Israeli leaders; the most commonly used image is that of President Bush shaking hands with former Israeli Prime Minister Ariel Sharon in the White House during the Aqsa uprising, suggesting approval of Israel's "iron fist" policies against the Palestinians.

In one of the videos of Ahl al-Sunnah wal-Jamaah Army, images of Muslim leaders in the company of Western dignitaries are contrasted in alternating frames with images of Iraqi fighters. Muslim leaders and their guests are enjoying themselves in lavish palaces and comfortable settings. The holy fighters are donning modest clothes and fighting in desolate towns and villages. The official leaders are laughing and smiling to their Western "masters," while the fighters are offering supplications to God, praying in the battlefield next to their weapons. Western leaders are shown with a superimposed Star of David on their foreheads, suggesting they are agents of Israel, while the fighters are chanting "God is great, glory to Islam."[26]

The sum of all these images is that the Arab and Muslim worlds are led by "puppets" that cannot be relied upon to liberate Iraq and end the suffering of the Muslim people. These are illegitimate governments that sold out to the arrogant occupiers who are conspiring against the Muslim world. This imagery is important for five reasons. First, it portrays anyone working for the official leaders and government in Iraq as part and parcel of the collusion with the Western aggressors. Given that these leaders are illegitimate sell-outs, it is not acceptable to work for them under the pretext of working for a Muslim or Iraqi government, not the occupation. Those who persist in working for the official Iraqi government are fair game and can be killed without moral compunction. Second, given that these leaders are collaborators working for foreign powers, their moral criticism of the jihadists and their tactics are without force; who are they to challenge the legitimacy of the insurgents? Third, given that these governments are impotent in the face of the suffering of Muslims, it is necessary for other Muslims to step forward to fight in their stead. Jihad is an individual obligation (*fard ayn*) because the existing governments have abdicated their duty toward protecting Muslim lands and liberating them from unbelievers. Fourth, given that jihadists do not have the support or resources of official governments, they have to rely solely on their faith and limited capabilities to repel the arrogant aggressors, justifying their demands for extraordinary measures and calls for martyrdom. Finally, these images frame the struggle in broader terms than simply liberating Iraq from a foreign occupation. Instead, they frame the struggle as one to replace the entire corrupt and "mercenary" regimes that currently rule in the Muslim world with ones that are truly Islamic and that protect Muslim interests, not their Western "masters."

Inevitable victory through faith and sacrifice

Acts one and two can be disempowering if not followed by act three. While act one frames the struggle in Iraq as unbearable suffering and humiliation that has afflicted the Muslim world, and act two frames existing rulers in the Muslim world as impotent individuals who are insufficient to reverse the suffering of Muslims in Iraq, act three presents the necessary solution for national salvation and redemption of Muslims around the globe. Salvation and redemption come through having faith in God and a desire to sacrifice in His path.

An important element in act three is the mythology surrounding martyrdom and martyrs. Al Qaeda in Iraq promotes the image of a heroic Muslim willing to make the ultimate sacrifice to redeem his nation and avenge the personal suffering inflicted on helpless Muslims, especially women. The propaganda surrounding the "martyrs" are issued on web postings, videos of operations, and in Al Qaeda's online journal entitled "Biographies of Eminent Martyrs." These productions reveal five themes that make up the mythology of martyrdom:

- Sincere devotion to religion
- Willingness to sacrifice one's wealth and personal ties for God
- Eagerness to carry out a "martyrdom operation"
- Success in sacrifice operations
- Confirmation of martyrdom through dream visions

It must be made clear from the outset that these biographies are often short, inconsistent in the information they present, and highly propagandistic. The point of the following analysis is to show how groups seek to promote the myth of heroic martyrdom through such stories, not to suggest that these biographies reflect the true motivations of the suicide bombers.

Sincere devotion to Islam

Insurgent videos are replete with images of pious Muslims praying, chanting "God is great" (*allahu akbar*), even as they are in the midst of an operation or while planting an IED. These "true" Muslims are intent on reversing the humiliation of their Muslim brethren around the world. One of the melodic hymns repeated over and over in several insurgent videos declares:

> *We shall not accept humiliation,*
> *We shall not accept humiliation,*
> *We shall not accept humiliation or subjugation,*
> *We will not bow our heads,*
> *We will not bow our heads,*
> *We will not bow our heads to the depraved.*[27]

As for suicide bombers in particular, almost invariably they are portrayed as genuinely religious people who love jihad more than they love life and fear God more than they fear death. The biographies often detail at length how the "martyr" used to pray incessantly and spent his time reading the Quran. The bombers are said to have prayed in the mosque, as opposed to praying at home, which is the best option in the eyes of God. They often pray more than the average Muslim, certainly more than is expected of them by God. They also wake up to make their pre-dawn prayers (*qiyam*), which is not a religious obligation, but a voluntary expression of devotion. Some are said to have memorized the Quran by heart at a very young age; others fast every Monday and Thursday, when they are not required to do so by religion (although it is part of the Sunna).

One Kuwaiti bomber, Abu Awf al-Kuwaiti (Abdel Rahman Bin Shuja al-Utaybi), is said to have cried as he was entreating God to grant the holy warriors victory everywhere.[28] The same is said of the Saudi suicide bomber Muhammad Bin Rahayman al-Tawmi al-Shamari (Abu Salih).[29] In the biography of Abu Umayr al-Suri (Syrian), the narrator mentions in passing that one of the martyrs did not want to stay in the same house of Abu Umayr because "he felt shame [out of guilt]; every time he woke up he would find Abu Umayr up already in the middle of his prayers."[30]

The emphasis on sincerity in devotion is important for Al Qaeda in Iraq and jihadi salafis in general. Suicide bombings can only be considered martyrdom in Islam if the individual bombers are adherent Muslims fighting out of faith in God and dying for His sake. One cannot expect to receive the rewards of martyrdom if he or she is motivated by something other than love of God and striving in His path. Perhaps more importantly, jihadi salafis are aware that Muslim governments attempt to portray jihadists as "deviants" and misguided individuals who know little about Islam and have been brainwashed into carrying out suicide attacks. Stressing the religiosity of the bombers, therefore, is Al Qaeda's attempt to counter the claims of existing governments and assure their supporting public that they are genuine Muslims doing their share to save the nation.

A video recording by Ansar al-Sunna Army shows an unidentified suicide bomber declare in his last will and testament:

> This is our religion and this is our path, to it we call, and for it we die, with God's blessings in order to meet him … What kind of a world is this where a nation's sanctity and honor are violated, its wealth robbed, and its scholars, pardon me, I mean the scholars of the sultans, discourage the youth from joining the jihad and raise doubts in their minds about jihad. Go forward my brothers and pay no heed. The land of jihad is calling you. How nice it will be if you answered the call. Oh God, accept me as a martyr…[31]

The suicide bomber is shown smiling as he waves goodbye to his brothers-in-arms.

The final will and testament sent by the Saudi suicide bomber Abu Hareth Abdul Rahman al-Dousry to his family reads: "To my mother, father, wife and brothers … I did not leave you to punish you, but instead to heed God's call to jihad. How can I live happily knowing that this country is being violated, usurped and raped, and that the infidels are storming our homes and sanctuaries and violating our religion? If we do not meet again on this earth, we shall meet in heaven."[32]

These and other insurgent productions are intended to affirm that the bombers are genuinely concerned Muslims who put their trust in God and sacrificed to redeem the suffering of their people.

Willingness to sacrifice personal wealth and family ties

The propaganda of Al Qaeda portrays the "martyrs" as people who have given up all things dear in order to fulfill a higher, more noble obligation: jihad and martyrdom in the path of God. Many of the bombers are said to be wealthy or from wealthy families (such as the previously mentioned

Abu Umayr al-Suri, who is an electrical engineer). Even those who are not wealthy have made personal sacrifices, such as selling their cars, using their meager savings, or relying on donations to make the trip to Iraq. Perhaps the most powerful imagery is that of a father leaving his newborn child or a husband leaving his newlywed to fight and die in the path of God.

The biography of Abu Osama al-Maghribi, a Moroccan from the city of Tangiers, is instructive. Abu Osama, we are told, was 26 years old when he carried out an operation. He worked with his father in a "fancy" restaurant that brings in about 3,000 dollars a month. At the age of 20, he bought a piece of land and got married. However, for six years he was unable to father a child. When the war broke out in Iraq, he decided to join the land of jihad. Abu Osama sold the piece of land and bought a ticket to "an Arab" country. As he was about to depart to Iraq, he found out that his wife was pregnant. He was overwhelmed with joy. However, this did not stop him from leaving for jihad.

After arriving in the Arab country, Abu Osama moved from mosque to mosque seeking someone to take him to Iraq. He ran into a group of Moroccans being led by Abu Khbab al-Falastini. They took him to Iraq to Abu Ismail al-Muhajir, who became Abu Osama's handler. Abu Osama made a vow with others to die in the path of God and eventually was the bomber in the operation against the United Nations' headquarters building. Like many of the other bombers, he was eager to do the operation. On the day he found out he was chosen for a suicide mission, he also received news that his wife bore him a son. She named him Osama after Bin Laden. This news did not deter him from carrying forward with his operation. On the contrary, he was happy for "two good pieces of news in the same day." On the day before the operation, he was left alone with his handler to reflect, pray, and cry. When the day came, he and his handler went to survey the target one more time. Abu Osama took hold of his new "wife," a reference to the explosive-laden vehicle, and drove off toward his target.[33]

This theme of leaving behind one's family is repeated over and over. In the biography of Abu Wadha al-Kuwaiti (Mansur al-Hajari), we are told that he was married but did not father any children for four years. Then he had a little girl he named Wadha. A week later he went to Iraq and eventually died in a suicide operation. The biographer draws the following lesson from the story of Abu Wadha: "The man was married and he did not have any children for four years. However, one week after he had a child he went to jihad. It is devotion and the love of faith."[34]

A similar narrative is presented for Abu Ahmed al-Kuwaiti (Abdel Aziz al-Shamari): "The hero got married to a relative but when he heard the call of God and saw the door of paradise open wide he could not sit around while his brothers were racing to reserve places in the highest paradise. The price of these places is sincere blood, truthful prayer, and tireless effort."[35] Abu Hamza al-Kuwaiti (Saíd al-Hajari) also gave up the good life for jihad: "His wedding was supposed to take place within a few months but he opted to marry the virgins of paradise."[36] The same is said of the Saudi suicide bomber Abu Ans al-Tahami al-Qahtani.[37]

These narratives are intended to set a new standard for heroism and devotion to the faith. It is not enough to be a good Muslim, pray regularly, and carry out one's ritual obligations. Even mere desire to join the jihad is not enough. One should exert as much effort as necessary to reach the land of jihad. These themes, undoubtedly, are intended to inspire others, particularly people in the Persian Gulf who live relatively decent lives, to abandon material wealth and join a more rewarding path in life.

Eagerness to conduct a "Martyrdom Operation"

Over and over we read in the biographies of the "martyrs" that they are eager to die in the path of God and are frustrated when they are denied or delayed. Almost every clip of the suicide bombers in Iraq shows the bombers as happy, eager to do the will of God. They usually wave goodbye with smiles on their faces, running toward their explosive-laden vehicles, reflecting the theme of joy in sacrifice in the path of God and assured in the rewards they will earn in paradise.

The Kuwaiti volunteer Abu Bara (Faysal Zayd al-Mutiri) is said to have declared to a friend: "My Brother, I cannot wait to meet God Almighty, can you?" When he died, "Abu Bara had an extraordinary smile on his bright face."[38] Another Kuwaiti, Abu Musab (Abdel Aziz Abdel Hadi Dayhani), is said to have told his friends: "I do not care if I get killed. I will not sit motionless while my brothers are under attack every day ... We should starve when the nation starves. We should share its joys and sorrows and we should die with it and for it ... God willing, we will meet in paradise if we do not meet in the land of dignity."[39] An Iraqi named Abu Faris al-Anbari is said to have been raring to go on a suicide mission and pestered Abu Musab al-Zarqawi to send him. He even cried profusely when he was wounded in a conventional operation—he did not cry out of pain, but because God did not bless him with martyrdom. Eventually he was killed by American forces while on his way to the hospital following a wound he suffered in an aerial bombardment.[40]

This theme of eagerness to carry out a suicide operation and joy expressed on the day of the operation is intended to counter the claims of authorities that the bombers are coerced or brainwashed into carrying out suicide attacks. Iraqi satellite channels often air "confessions" of foiled bombers who claim that they did not know that they were about to engage in a suicide operation because someone else was in control of the detonator while they were merely delivering the truck to the target. Some are said to have had their hands handcuffed to the steering wheel or to have been given drugs before their operations and shown pornographic materials to excite them into meeting heavenly maidens. The theme of eagerness to die, therefore, is intended to dispel these allegations and elevate the status of the suicide bombers to faithful and heroic martyrs fully in control of their choices and destinies. Many of these volunteers are said to have tried to go to Chechnya or Afghanistan following the 9/11 attacks, but they were prevented for one reason or another, suggesting a deep-rooted desire to engage in a jihad even prior to Iraq.

The biography of Azzad Akanji (Abu Abdullah al-Turki) is illustrative. Abu Abdullah is from Turkey. Prior to joining the jihad in Iraq, he went to Pakistan for two years and then to Afghanistan to train in combat. Following a stint in jihadi training camps, he returned to Turkey in order to make his way into Georgia. His ultimate goal was to join the jihad in Chechnya. However, he was unable to enter Chechnya and returned to Turkey.

While in Turkey, Abu Abdullah wanted to carry out a suicide operation against Jewish tourists. When this operation did not materialize, he wanted to participate in other suicide missions. However, he was not chosen for the operation against British and "Jewish" targets. Subsequently, he was wanted by the authorities in connection to the suicide bombings in Turkey. Undeterred, he made his way to Iraq and carried out an operation with two other bombers against the Khan Bin Saad police station in Diyali.[41]

The theme of eagerness to die is also intended to reinforce the idea that the bombers in Iraq are faithful Muslims who do not fear death because they know what awaits them in the afterlife. Like Hamas and Hezbollah, jihadi salafis in Iraq promote the idea that martyrdom is a gateway to another life, not an end to life. Dying in the path of God will achieve for the martyrs all the rewards of martyrdom, including:

- Remission of one's sins at the moment the martyr's blood is shed
- Immediate admission into heaven, so martyrs do not suffer the punishment of the tomb
- The privilege of accompanying prophets, saints, and righteous believers
- Marriage to heavenly maidens (*houri al-ayn*)
- The right to intercede with God on behalf of seventy relatives

- Protection against the pain of death
- Entry into the highest gardens of heaven (*jannat al-firdaous*)

The bombers are happy because they are abandoning this world of disgrace and shame to one in which they are venerated along with the honorable and righteous believers, enjoying for eternity all the fruits of their meager sacrifice. As proof of their happiness, jihadists often post on the web photos of dead jihadists who appear to be smiling or peacefully asleep. One caption points out that the martyr "is happy in the company of the heavenly maidens."

Success in martyrdom operations

Invariably, the biographies of the martyrs emphasize, or more often exaggerate, the success of the suicide mission as if to assure potential recruits that their worldly sacrifices will not be in vain. The number of "apostates," "crusaders," and "CIA agents" reported killed in these operations are often in the hundreds. One finds repeatedly in the biographies of the bombers that they killed more than is reported in the news, which "rely on American numbers." One often hears that the Americans dump their dead in rivers or in hastily-prepared graves in order to cover up their real losses. Given their "success," the biographers term each operation as "conquest" (*ghazwah*), such as *ghazwahit al-Nasiriyah* (the attack on Italian forces in Nasiriyah, which killed 31 people). The term *ghazwah* is an intentional allusion to battles in early Islamic history when Muslims fought against the unbelievers and ultimately triumphed over them.

Success, however, is not always just in numbers. The idea of vengeance against those who would violate the honor of Muslim women is important, playing on masculine expectations in the highly patriarchic Arab world. Insurgent groups often portray their attacks as revenge for personal violations of honor. In a communiqué declaring responsibility for an attack on a security building in Tikrit in April 2005, Al Qaeda congratulates one of its "lions" in the Martyrs Brigades for demolishing the site where "our women were imprisoned, and our elderly were humiliated, severely beaten, and tortured."[42] In another Al Qaeda video of a suicide attack on the Palestine Hotel in Baghdad, the suicide bomber is shown declaring before his operation that we will "regain the life of honor once more" and "we shall redraw for Islam a map, its borders are honor, might, and triumph."[43] The message delivered by this clip is that sacrifice is not merely for Iraq, but for the entirety of the Muslim world. Martyrdom in Iraq is the key to redeeming the Muslim nation the world over.

A clip by the Mujahideen Consultative Council in Iraq, titled "Fatimah's Fiancé," is illustrative. It shows Abu Muawiyah al-Shamali, a Saudi suicide bomber in his twenties. His operation was framed as a direct response to an alleged letter sent by a female detainee at Abu Ghraib prison named Fatimah. In December 2004, Fatimah called on the holy warriors to come to rescue all the female prisoners who were subjected to daily rape, torture, and humiliation at the hands of the "sons of the pigs and the monkeys" (referring to Jews). After describing the torture and humiliation, she asked the insurgents to save the prisoners. "Brothers," Fatimah writes, "I tell you again, fear God! Kill us with them so that we might be at peace. Help! Help! Help!" Abu Muawiyah al-Shamali then appeared with a big smile on his face reading a poem, with a gun and Quran nearby. After reciting the poem, he entreated God to grant him Fatimah's hand in marriage in paradise: "Oh, Lord, marry me to Fatimah who was martyred after they had violated her honor." The suicide bomber featured a big smile on his face throughout the taping of his farewell message. As he sat in the booby-trapped car, he smiled and patted the explosives that were going to end his life: "This is Fatimah's dowry." Waving back to his friends who were taping the operation, Abu Muawiyah drove his car toward an unidentified target.[44]

After portraying the jihadists as pious, sacrificing individuals who are eager to carry out the responsibilities that have been abdicated by their nominal Muslim leaders, we begin to see the results of their sacrifice. Image after image shows humiliation-in-reverse. Now it is the American soldiers who are bloodied, crying out of fear, embracing their fallen buddies. We see rows of coffins draped in American flags and families crying back in America. The "arrogant" have been humbled. One of the Islamic Army in Iraq videos begins with images of blown-up Humvees followed by images of President Bush, former Secretary of Defense Donald Rumsfield, Secretary of State Condoleezza Rice, and former Secretary of State Colin Powell appearing anxious and disturbed, suggesting that jihadi operations have shaken them and removed their exultant confidence.

In another insurgent video that ranked as number two in a montage of "Top Ten" attacks by the Islamic Army in Iraq, seven American soldiers are shown casually talking and walking as they converge on an object in the middle of a barren field with palm trees in the background. Suddenly, an IED explodes. All of the soldiers fall. The person taping the operation is overwhelmed with joy as he is heard sobbing uncontrollably, repeating, over and over, "God is great, God is great, God is great." Finally, he regains his composure and calmly says, "*al-hamdu lil-lah*," praise be to God. This clip ranked number two undoubtedly because of the powerful message it sends: God will reward the believers by punishing the unjust.[45]

Confirmation of martyrdom in dream visions

One of the surreal aspects of the martyrs' biographies is the theme of dream visions. There are two types of dreams that are narrated in these biographies. The first refers to suicide bombers having dreams about their operations or of previous suicide bombers, usually their friends, appearing in front of them. They sometimes hold conversations with the visions. The second type of dream involves the senders of the bombers confirming that they had a dream of a fallen martyr. The biographies of three Kuwaiti volunteers in Iraq are instructive.

Abu Bakr al-Kuwaiti (Faysal Ali Musa al-Rashidi) is said to have seen "a dream that he was in a waiting room in a hospital where a sign read: 'Martyr Faysal Ali Musa al-Rashidi.'" Abu Hamza al-Kuwaiti (Said al-Hajari) also had a dream: 'I saw myself swimming in a river with other people. The river led to a cave or a tunnel on which it was written: 'To the Highest Paradise.' The closer I came to the tunnel the fewer the swimmers. When I approached, something was dragging me to the bottom of the river. It was a beautiful young maiden of paradise. We hugged each other under water."[46]

Abu Awf al-Kuwaiti (Abdel Rahman Bin Shuja al-Utaybi), we are told, had a dream of his friend Mansoor al-Hajari, who died in an earlier operation. Al-Hajari was sitting next to him. He asked him "How are you Mansoor?" His friend replied, "Good, praise be to God." Abu Awf then said, "I would like to ask you what you witnessed immediately after you pressed the button that set off the explosion?" His dead friend smiled and said, "Come here, come here. God is generous. God is generous."[47]

A friend of Abu Awf begged him to pay him a visit in his dreams after Abu Awf had completed his mission. After the operation, in which "more than 60 apostates" were killed, Abu Awf fulfilled his friend's wish and came to visit him in his dream. "Where are you, Abdel Rahman [Abu Awf]? Are you alive?" Abu Awf replied, "I am alive. I am alive."[48]

The notion of visions (*ruyah*) in dreams has symbolic weight in the Islamic tradition, especially when the recipients of these visions are devout Muslims. Visions in dreams imply that God is communicating directly to His faithful. In the Quran, God communicated with the Prophets Abraham and Muhammad through dreams.[49] Dreams in Islam offer the faithful divine guidance, warn them of impending danger, and can foretell specific events. Many Muslims today, when facing tough decisions, rely on a Prophetic tradition that urges them to undertake a prayer for guidance (*istikhara*) in which they hope God would reveal to them the correct choice in a dream.[50]

The emphasis on bombers appearing in dreams is intended to assure future recruits that those who came before them were genuine and righteous Muslims who are still alive, in paradise, near God who is "generous." These visions appear to confirm the Quranic verses: "Whoever fights in the path of God, whether he be slain or victorious, on him We shall bestow a vast reward" (4:74); and "Think not of those, who are slain in the way of Allah, as dead. Nay, they are living. With their Lord they have provision" (3:169). Dream visions allow jihadists to circumvent the fact that the living cannot inquire of the dead what life is like after they have died. Not only is communication with the dead possible through dreams, it is also comforting because the dead appear happy, calling on others to "come here." Moreover, the mythology surrounding dreams is intended to counter the claims of authorities that the suicide bombers are misguided fanatics that unjustly kill themselves and other Muslims. If these claims were true, how could these "martyrs" appear in dreams over and over?

Weaving the narratives together

One of the most powerful series of clips that capture this narrative of humiliation, collusion, and redemption through sacrifice can be found in one of the montages issued by Al Qaeda in Iraq, which contained approximately 46 minutes of footage dedicated to the theme of fighting the Iraqi security forces.[51] The series of clips begin with an Iraqi woman donning the *hijab* (implying a pious "sister") and covered in a black shadow to hide her identity (implying she is not safe and needs continuous protection). In a tearful voice, she tells her story of suffering at the hands of an Iraqi policeman who was intent on turning her over to the occupation forces as a hostage to be exchanged for her wanted husband. According to her story, she begged her fellow compatriot: "I'm an Iraqi and you're an Iraqi; why are you doing this to me. Why?" She breaks down, uncontrollably sobbing, full of tears.

The Iraqi woman is unable to continue telling her story. As her voice fades, a melancholic hymn comes on accompanied by images of Iraqi policemen while they are smiling, singing, and dancing with American forces, apparently during a training session. The clip is juxtaposed to the clip of the Iraqi woman as she continues with her story of how she was bound and handed over to the Americans. In a tearful, but powerful voice, full of faith in God, she declares: "*hasbiyah allah wa niama al-wakil*" (Allah is sufficient for me, and He is an excellent Guardian). Yet, despite her faith in God, she is not strong enough to endure this suffering: "I would rather have died than suffer the humiliation and degradation that I saw." Then there is silence for a few seconds, giving viewers time to reflect on the woman in tears, letting her story sink in to their hearts and her image reach out to their consciences. As her image slowly fades, she is heard from once more: "*hasbiyah allah wa niama al-wakil, hasbiyah allah wa niama al-wakil.*"

The tenor of the video clip changes; now it contains an upbeat tone with more intensity, suggesting a turning point in the narrative. A new set of images show the jihadists marching in line, as if they came purposely to save none other that this suffering sister; it gives the impression that they are heroic and determined. The images are accompanied by a voiceover of marching feet and, almost subthreshold, a voice repeats: "They are coming, they are coming." Next, we see clips of suicide operations and jihadi attacks along with images of destroyed military vehicles belonging to the occupation forces and dead Iraqi security forces. These images are accompanied by a hymn that honors fighting in the path of God and venerates the sacrifice of one's blood for religion. Humiliation has turned into victory, powerless suffering into willing sacrifice, and shame into honor.

A poem recited by Zarqawi in one of his audio recordings also evokes the themes of humiliation, impotence, and redemption through faith and martyrdom:

> *Baghdad, we are shedding tears of sorrow and grief for you*
> *A Muslim town struck with humiliation at the hands of the worst of mankind, the Crusaders.*
> *I grieve for a girl as pure as snow, who is crying,*
> *Her chastity was violated by a dog and a pack of wolves.*
> *We go where thunder strikes but no Harun [al-Rashid] to stop them,*
> *And the heart is full of grief*
> *We go where thunder strikes while the [rest of the] Arabs bend their heads to them,*
> *But how can mice ever rise up.*
> *Woe unto my people, for they have strayed from the [right] path,*
> *By falsehoods and idols.*
> *Alas, there is no peace to unite us toward the great One,*
> *Nor do we have leaders among the people.*
> *Baghdad, do not be astonished, for the Arabs have no shame any longer;*
> *They live in sin and when the war heats up they abandon the battle.*
> *Dry your tears, for the people have strayed;*
> *The ammunition of war is faith before the sword.*
> *Where are the voices of the evil clerics whose rubbish we hear only when they are speaking against the holy*
> *   warriors? Where are they? Why are they not defending the honor of Muslim women?*
> *I wish they at least fight out of pride for the honor of [Muslim] women,*
> *Since they do not fight for religion.*
> *And [I wish] they at least join the battlefield even for material gains,*
> *Since they do not care to gain God's blessings.*
> *Here I am, oh mother,*
> *Here I am, oh sister,*
> *Here I am, oh honorable and pure one,*
> *By God, we shall not rest, nor sleep, nor put our swords back in their sheaths, until we avenge your honor and*
> *   dignity.*[52]

In summary, the ideological justifications for killing Muslims in Iraq are anchored with a poignant narrative that links the suffering and humiliation of Muslims to the collusion of nominal Muslim leaders and their agents with Western oppressors seeking to destroy Islam and subjugate Muslim lands. By framing the struggle in those terms, it becomes logical to strike at those who make Iraq safe for the invaders. The Iraqi security services and the Shiite and Kurdish political parties—and even those Sunnis willing to participate in the "farcical" democracy—are the flip side of the same "Crusader-Zionist" coin.

Conclusion

This study shows that jihadists rely, at least in part, on emotive narratives to construct the myth of heroic martyrdom. While groups like Al Qaeda in Iraq rely on a number of instrumental, ideological, and religious arguments that allow them, at least in theory, to circumvent Islamic prohibitions against Muslims killing themselves,[53] killing civilians,[54] and killing other Muslims,[55] their strategic use of emotion is intended to supplement these arguments and cut across ideological lines in order to appeal to a broader pool of supporters. Emotionally, jihadists in Iraq construct narratives rooted in themes of humiliation, collusion, and redemption to demonize their enemies and heighten the sense of threat facing Muslims to convince their coreligionists to accept the use of extraordinarily cruel measures to repel their foes. The mythology surrounding individual suicide bombers and other fallen jihadists is intended to appeal to potential recruits to make similar "heroic" sacrifices as well as counter the claims of authorities that the bombers are deviants, brainwashed youth who know little about Islam.

The theme of humiliation relies on framing the war in Iraq as one in a series of aggressions and defeats by Muslims at the hands of "crusaders," "Zionists," and "apostates." Just as important, humiliation is as much about personal stories of suffering and indignity as it is about collective deprivations and grievances. The theme of impotence due to collusion resonates with the wider Muslim public who live under oppressive regimes that do not challenge U.S. hegemony and have failed Muslims time and again in Palestine, Chechnya, and Iraq. Not only are Muslim governments not fighting back, they are perceived as active collaborators in the humiliation and subjugation of Muslims. The theme of redemption through sacrifice is presented as the way out of the malaise. Groups frame martyrdom as an act of redemption, empowerment, and defiance against unjust authorities. Volunteers for suicide attacks are not brainwashed victims of opportunistic recruiters, nor are they manipulated individuals who are fooled by calculating terrorists. Instead, groups portray suicide bombers as inspired individuals with heroic motivations seeking opportunities to fulfill their obligation to God, sacrifice for the nation, and avenge a grieving people. Jihadists weave together these three narratives to suggest a deleterious condition that requires an immediate action, offer an explanation of the causes of this persistent crisis, and present the necessary solution to overcome the problem.

As stated at the outset, discourse is necessary, but not sufficient, to mobilize people for violent action or suicide operations. Factors such as military and sectarian strife, preexisting jihadi networks, and permissive security and cultural environments are necessary for suicide terrorism to develop on the scale witnessed in Iraq. Martyrdom mythologies, therefore, are not sufficient to explain why suicide bombings have become almost a daily event in Iraq. However, ideology, religious framing, and emotional narratives that go into the construction of martyrdom mythologies help explain how jihadists deactivate self-inhibiting norms against murder and mayhem. These discursive ploys allow jihadists to appear as moral agents even when they are acting in immoral ways. Just as soldiers are trained to overcome their inhibitions against killing others in the service of their country, terrorists frame their violent deeds as moral acts in the service of their people, nation, or God. Understanding how violent militants are able to deactivate self-deterring norms against killing and injuring civilians is an important step to combating terrorism.

Notes

1 The source materials informing this article were collected through daily monitoring of pro-jihadist websites and forums. Some were collected through access to Open Source Center (OSC, formerly FBIS). Due to the regular displacement of these websites by authorities or other technical failures, the author has downloaded the materials on his personal computer. They can be acquired through a written request to hafezm@umkc.edu or mohammed_hafez@ hotmail.com.

2 The author reviewed 29 video clips that range from less than one minute to over one hour. Nine of the video clips belonged to Al Qaeda in Iraq or Mujahideen Consultative Council; three from the Islamic Army in Iraq; three from the Global Islamic Media Front, which is associated with Al Qaeda, but features clips from other insurgent groups; two from Ansar al-Sunna Army; two from Salah al-Din al-Ayubi Brigades; and one from each of the 1920 Revolution Brigades, Ahl al-Sunnah wal-Jamaah, Iraqi Jihadist League, and Mujahideen Army in Iraq. Six additional videos that incorporated clips from various groups were also reviewed.

3   The author reviewed five major audio recordings by Abu Musab al-Zarqawi, the founding leader of Al Qaeda in Iraq, killed in June 2006: Audio 1 is 74 minutes, entitled "The Descendents of Ibn al-Alqami Are Back," issued by the Ana Muslim Forum (www.muslm.net), in May 2005; Audio 2 is 59 minutes, and 29 seconds, entitled "Would the [Islamic] Religion be Degraded while I am Alive," issued by the Islamic Renewal Organization (www.tajdeed.org.uk) in July 2005; Audio 3 is 16 minutes, 47 seconds, entitled "Here is a Message for Mankind, Let Them Take Warning Therefrom," issued by the Global News Forum (www.bayanat.info) in September 2005; Audio 4 is 75 minutes, entitled "Obeying God and His Messenger is More Useful to Us," issued by the Islamic Renewal Organization (www.tajdeed.org.uk) in September 2005; and Audio 5 is 51 minutes, entitled "Do Ye Know Better than Allah," issued by the Returning Caravans bulletin board (www.goafalaladyn.com/vb) in October 2005.

4   The author reviewed issues 1 through 6 and 8, 10, and 11 of the Biographies of Eminent Martyrs online magazine series released by Al Qaeda in Iraq. This magazine is distributed through various forums, including Islamic Renewal Organization (www.tajdeed.org.uk), Al-Meer (www.almeer.net/vb), and Global News Network (www.w-n-n.net). As of July 2006, there are 19 issues of the Biographies of Eminent Martyrs.

5   The author reviewed three issues of Zarwat al-Sinam (The Highest Peak) online magazine issued by Al Qaeda in Iraq; 11 issues of Ansar Al-Sunna magazine issued by Ansar al-Sunna Army in Iraq; and one Fursan (Knights) magazine issued by the Islamic Army in Iraq. These magazines can be downloaded from the same forums cited above.

6   For an excellent collection of jihadists' imagery online, see the publication by the Combating Terrorism Center at West Point, entitled "The Islamic Imagery Project: Visual Motifs in Jihadi Internet Propaganda," (http://www.ctc.usma.edu/imagery.asp) March 2006.

7   Mohammed M Hafez, "Suicide Terrorism in Iraq: A Preliminary Assessment of the Quantitative Data and Documentary Evidence," *Studies in Conflict and Terrorism* 29 (2006): 1–27. See also Mohammed M. Hafez, *Suicide Bombers in Iraq: The Strategy and Ideology of Martyrdom.* (Washington, D.C.: United States Institute of Peace, July 2006).

8   Ibid.; Hamd al-Jaser, "Kuwaiti Jihadists in the Sunni Triangle," (Arabic) *Al-Hayat*, August 11, 2004; Hazem al-Amin, "Lebanese 'Jihadists' in Iraq: 'Salafis' from Peripheral Regions and Cities," (Arabic) *Al-Hayat*, 11 August 2004; Hazem al-Amin, "Jordanian 'Zarqawis' Visit Their Clerics in Jail and Await the Opportunity to Join Abu Musab [al-Zarqawi] in Iraq," (Arabic) *Al-Hayat*, December 14, 2004; Jean Chichizola, "Four Recruiters for Jihad in Iraq Arrested," (French) *le Figaro* (Paris), January 26, 2005; Muhammad al-Ashhab, "European Networks for Smuggling Jihadists," *Al-Hayat*, February 11, 2005; Saud al-Sarhan, "Al Qaeda in Saudi Arabia" (Arabic), *Asharq al-Awsat*, May 20, 2005; Eric Schmitt, "As Africans Join Iraqi Insurgency, U.S. Counters Military Training in their Lands," *New York Times*, June 10, 2005; Peter Beaumont, "Insurgents Trawl Europe for Recruits," *The Observer* (London), June 19, 2005; Ahmed al-Arqam, "The Moroccan Judiciary Sentences to Prison Deportees from Syria on their way to Fight in Iraq," *Asharq al-Awsat*, July 2, 2005; James Glanz, "In Jordanian Case, Hints of Iraq Jihad Networks," *New York Times*, July 29, 2005; and OSC, "Florence's Sorgane Mosque Identified as Site of Recruitment Cell for Iraq-Bound Suicide Bombers," August 29, 2005; Hazim al-Amin, "How Al Qaeda Searched for a Twin State to the Taliban Emirate," (Arabic) *Al-Hayat*, October 10, 2005; Ibrahim Hamaydi, "Islamic Trends Advance in Syria and the Authorities Wage 'Preemptive Operations' Against the Takfiris' (Arabic), *Al-Hayat*, January 4, 2006; Hazem al-Amin, "Strangers Come during "Al Qaeda Season" to Recruit Suicide Bombers to Iraq," (Arabic) *Al-Hayat*, January 26, 2006 (part 1) and January 27, 2006 (part 2); Nir Rosen, "Iraq's Jordanian Jihadis" *New York Times*, February 19, 2006.

9   Hafez, "Suicide Terrorism in Iraq," (see note 7 above), 6–8.

10   Ibid, 17.

11   The Brookings Institution Iraq Index (www.brookings.edu/iraqindex), May 1, 2006.

12   Hafez, "Suicide Terrorism in Iraq," 13.

13   Ibid, 17.

14   Ibid, 19.

15   Audio entitled "The Descendents of Ibn al-Alqami Are Back," issued by the Ana Muslim Forum (www. muslm.net), in May 2005.

16   The montage is 77 minutes, 47 seconds, entitled "Commander of the Slaughterers," issued by the Global Islamic Media Front in November 2005 and available at the OSC, "GIMF Issues 'Amir of the Slaughterers" Video,' December 14, 2005.

17   This analysis is made in the document "Jihad in Iraq: Hopes and Dangers." The document does not have an author or date, but it was dedicated to Yousef al-Ayiri, Al Qaeda leader in Saudi Arabia killed

in 2003. It was issued by The Media Commission for the Victory of the Iraqi People (The Mujahdin Services Center) sometime in 2003. Also, see article by Salah al-Muatasim, "The Truth about the Americans and the Collaborating Regime," (Arabic) *Ansar al-Sunna* (online magazine), issue 11, June 2004, 8–10.

18 Montage entitled "And Worship Shall be Only for Allah," issued by the Media Division of Al Qaeda in Iraq in June 2005. This argument was repeated in aforementioned "Commander of the Slaughterers" video by the Global Islamic Media Front. In it Zarqawi says, "after the Americans suffered major losses, they began to create the local police and security services to do their work. They have become infidels and apostates for serving the Americans ... Those that say you can kill those with blue eyes, but not those with black eyes love nationalism, not monotheism; they want this world, not the next. The Iraqi Army is the army of apostasy."

19 Zarqawi announced the formation of the Umar Brigades in an audio tape released on July 5, 2005. OSC, "New Al-Zarqawi Message," July 11, 2005.

20 See article by Abi Aisha al-Hashimi, "Bush ...The Angelical Crusader," (Arabic) *Zarwat al-Sinam* (Al Qaeda in Iraq's online magazine) issue 3, n.d., 18–22; OSC, "Al-Zarqawi Justifies Killing of Innocent Muslims, Condemns Shia 'Betrayal' of Sunnis," May 18, 2005; FBIS, "Text of Al-Zarqawi's Statement of Operations Against Iraqi Forces, President Bush's "Holy War,'" July 6, 2005; OSC, "Al-Zarqawi Calls for 'All-Out-War' Against Shia," September 14, 2005.

21 Issued in January 2006 at www.jaishalmugahideen.net/.

22 Montage entitled "And Worship Shall be Only for Allah," issued by the Media Division of Al Qaeda in Iraq in June 2005.

23 Abu-Maryam al-Kuwayti, "A Cry in the Face of Deception," n.d. This a 68-page pamphlet containing the biographies of ten Kuwaitis killed in Iraq. It was posted by al-Sham Islamic Forum (http://www.islam-syria.com/vb) in February 2006.

24 Information derived from a 157-page document entitled "Martyrs in Iraq," posted by Majidah Forum (www.majdah.com/vb). The document features information about 394 mainly Arab volunteers that perished in Iraq. Abu Ans al-Tahami al-Qahtani is 150 on the list.

25 Video is 55 minutes, 12 seconds, entitled "Persist" or "Continue," issued by the Islamic Army in Iraq and distributed through al-Meer Forum (www.almeer.net/vb) in January 2006.

26 Video is 37 minutes, 52 seconds, entitled "Takbir al-Id," issued by the Media Division of Ahl al-Sunna wal-Jamaah and distributed by al-Meer Forum (www.almeer.net/vb) in January 2006.

27 See, for example, the 1-minute, 50-second video by Al Qaeda in Iraq entitled "Hy al-Adl Martyrdom Operation," distributed by Al-Saqifa Forum in February 2005.

28 Abu-Maryam al-Kuwayti, "A Cry in the Face of Deception."

29 Information derived from a 157-page document entitled "Martyrs in Iraq," posted by Majidah Forum (www.majdah.com/vb). The document features information about 394 mainly Arab volunteers that perished in Iraq. Muhammad al-Shamari is 256 on the list.

30 See issue 3 of Al Qaeda in Iraq's "Biographies of Eminent Martyrs," distributed by al-Meer Forum (www.almeer.net/vb) in November 2005.

31 OSC, "Ansar al-Sunnah Posts Video of 'Martyrs' Will Before Attack in Balad," January 13, 2005.

32 Hala Jaber, "Suicide Bombers Stream into Iraq," *Sunday Times* (London), May 8, 2005.

33 See issue 1 of Al Qaeda in Iraq's "Biographies of Eminent Martyrs," distributed by Global News Network Forum (www.w-n-n.net/) in October 2005.

34 Abu-Maryam al-Kuwayti, "A Cry in the Face of Deception."

35 Ibid.

36 Ibid.

37 Information derived from a 157-page document entitled "Martyrs in Iraq," posted by Majidah Forum (www.majdah.com/vb). The document features information about 394 mainly Arab volunteers that perished in Iraq. Abu Ans al-Tahami al-Qahtani is 150 on the list.

38 Abu-Maryam al-Kuwayti, "A Cry in the Face of Deception."

39 Ibid.

40 Information derived from a 157-page document entitled "Martyrs in Iraq," posted by Majidah Forum (www.majdah.com/vb). The document features information about 394 mainly Arab volunteers that perished in Iraq. Abu Faris al-Anbari is 160 on the list.

41 See issue 10 of Al Qaeda in Iraq's "Biographies of Eminent Martyrs," distributed by Hanin Net Forum (www.hanein.net) in January 2006.

42 OSC, "Al-Zarqawi's Group Details Suicide Attack on 'US Intelligence Building' in Tikrit, Posts Video," April 25, 2005.

43 Video is 13 minutes, 47 seconds, entitled "Baghdad Badr Raid," issued by Al Qaeda in Iraq and distributed by Ana al-Muslim Forum (www.muslm.net/vb) in November 2005.

44 Video is 9 minutes, 2 seconds, distributed by al-Meer Forums (www.almeer.net/vb) in February 2006.

45 The video is 16 minutes, 22 seconds, issued by the Global Islamic Media Front and distributed by the al-Muntada forum in August 2005.

46 Abu-Maryam al-Kuwayti, "A Cry in the Face of Deception."

47 Ibid.

48 Ibid.

49 Abraham was commanded to sacrifice his son Ishmael in a dream vision. His willingness (and that of his son) to fulfill the divine command, which was a mere test of faith, was rewarded by God who withheld Abraham's hand as he was about to fulfill the deed: "We called unto him: O Abraham! Thou hast already fulfilled the vision. Lo! thus do We reward the good" (Quran 37:102–105). God also communicated to the Prophet Muhammad in dreams in order to strengthen his resolve before the battle of Badr, in which the Muslim forces were outnumbered 3 to 1 by the unbelievers: "Remember in thy dream Allah showed them to thee as few: if He had shown them to thee as many, ye would surely have been discouraged, and ye would surely have disputed in (your) decision; but Allah saved (you): for He knoweth well the (secrets) of (all) hearts" (Quran 8:43).

50 The tradition is narrated by Jabir bin Abdullah in *Sahih Bukhari*, Volume 2, Book 21, Number 263 in USC-MSA Compendium of Muslim Texts (http://www.usc.edu/dept/MSA/).

51 Montage entitled "And Worship Shall be Only for Allah," issued by the Media Division of Al Qaeda in Iraq in June 2005.

52 OSC, "Al-Zarqawi Uses Western Press, Poetry to Criticize US, Encourage 'Mujahidin,'" May 11, 2005.

53 Quranic verse 4:29–30: "Nor kill (or destroy) yourselves: for verily Allah hath been to you Most Merciful! If any do that in rancor and injustice, soon shall We cast them into the Fire: And easy it is for Allah." Prophetic tradition narrated by Abu Hurairah in *Sahih Bukhari* Volume 2, Book 23, Number 446 in the USC-MSA Compendium of Muslim Texts: "The Prophet said, "He who commits suicide by throttling shall keep on throttling himself in the Hell Fire (forever) and he who commits suicide by stabbing himself shall keep on stabbing himself in the Hell-Fire.'"

54 Quranic verse 2:190: "Fight in the path of God those who fight you, but do not transgress limits, for God does not love transgressors." Prophetic tradition quoted in *Sahih Muslim* Book 019, Number 4319 in the USC-MSA Compendium of Muslim Texts: "It is narrated on the authority of Abdullah that a woman was found killed in one of the battles fought by the Messenger of Allah (may peace be upon him). He disapproved of the killing of women and children."

55 Quranic verse 4:93: "If a man kills a believer intentionally, his recompense is Hell, to abide therein (For ever): And the wrath and the curse of Allah are upon him, and a dreadful penalty is prepared for him."

27 Countering female terrorism

Karla J. Cunningham

Women represent a growing, if not already established, presence in myriad terrorist organizations officially identified as national security threats to their respective states (e.g., Russia, India, Colombia, Israel, Britain). Importantly, the study of female terrorists is rarely acknowledged as a subject that can add to our understanding of terrorism. Similarly, the study of female terrorists is rarely, if ever, acknowledged as a subject that can add to our understanding of how to counter terrorism. At the simplest level, much in the way gender has been theoretically explored in the field of International Relations, "… a gender analysis of women's lives and experiences does not simply 'add something' about women but transforms what we know about men and the activities they undertake" (O'Gorman and Jabri 1999, 7–8).

By studying these women, scholars and analysts may move toward a better understanding of terrorism by considering the influence of gender on the theoretical and methodological approaches of the field and how these approaches may influence outcomes. Gender is a variable that is "in play" within the field, but it is extremely difficult to ascertain how officials are coming to terms with its impact. The success of female terrorists, combined with official reactions, indicates that analysts and leaders failed to anticipate the emergence and range of female militant actors. This failure must be acknowledged, examined, and rectified given the operational success of female militants.

This analysis will briefly explore three cases involving high levels of female involvement in organizations that are officially viewed as pressing terrorist threats: right-wing organizations in the United States, Palestinian militants confronting Israel, and Chechen separatists targeting Russia. The cases were chosen for the following reasons: first, all involve female participation levels that are either growing and/or diversifying; second, in all instances officials failed to anticipate increasing and/or altering female roles; third, in all cases officials have responded to female participation in a limited, and arguably predictable, manner; and finally, all three cases involve conservative/traditional socio-ideological settings or organizations that observers often view as especially hostile to female participation and activism.

From these cases six general counterterrorism deficiencies become apparent that influence how counterterrorism specialists anticipate, respond to, and interact with female militants: (1) exploiting female terrorists in custody; (2) organizational structures; (3) technology; (4) denial and deception; (5) tactical advantages; and (6) culture and ideology. To date, the cases of Palestine, Chechnya, and to a lesser extent right-wing organizations in the United States have challenged their respective states with often high levels of violence that was unforeseen and forced security elements into a reactive and defensive posture. Utilizing some of the counterterrorism lessons of these cases, this analysis will briefly explore how addressing these deficiencies may improve counterterrorism efforts by examining two cases that have considerable potential for female militancy and violence in the future—left-wing terrorism in the United States and global Islamist terrorism[1] by groups like Al Qaeda.

Selective cases involving female terrorism

Right-wing organizations in the United States: expanding female participation

Right-wing organizations have increasingly targeted women for recruitment in the past several years, especially with the advent of the Internet, and women's roles within the organizations are expanding (Blee 2001, 2002, 2005). Groups such as Stormfront and the World Church of the Creator (WCOTC) often include women's pages ("Women on the Web" 1999), and one of the more traditionally prolific writers within this movement has been Elisha Strom, otherwise known as the "Angry White Female" (Beirich and Potok 2003). Women such as Lisa Turner (WCOTC) and Rachel Pendergraft (Ku Klux Klan, KKK) have risen to positions of power and influence within their respective organizations, and women overall have become important agents for recruiting other members, especially women, through the Internet (Nesbitt 1999; Schabner 2002). Additionally, several women have become prominent over time for their activism within the movement, achieving "martyr" status, including Kathy Ainsworth who was killed when she tried to bomb a Jewish home in 1968, and Vicki Weaver who was killed at the standoff on Ruby Ridge in 1992.

Although women have tended to refrain from high levels of violence within the larger right-wing movement, and significant segments of the right-wing movement have exhibited a tactical shift toward less violent behavior overall, this should not be construed as a proclivity toward nonviolence by women associated with rightist organizations. Blee (2005) notes two areas of racial terrorism in which female violence is growing: strategic terrorism against the state and narrative terrorism against racial minorities (430). However, women's roles in strategic terrorism remains largely centered around lending legitimacy to this form of terrorism, whereas women engage in more overt acts of violence in narrative racial terrorism (Blee 2005, 428).

Anti-abortion groups share important similarities with the larger right-wing movement and one of the most politically violent organizations is the Army of God (AOG).[2] Although accurate dating of the AOG's origins is unclear, the organization has published three manuals that advocate escalating forms of violence to end abortion in the United States. The organization promotes loose structuring and lone-wolf actions to deter law enforcement intelligence gathering and interdiction. Women have been active members of the anti-choice movement, including within the Army of God. Of the eighteen listed "heroes" of the anti-abortion movement, five are women.[3] One of the most prominent female heroes is Shelley Shannon who is serving a thirty-one year prison sentence for the 1993 attempted murder of an abortion provider in Wichita, Kansas and a spate of arsons and bombings she committed in 1992. Shannon also committed two acid attacks against women's health centers in 1992.

Officials view right-wing organizations as a pressing threat to United States security (*Terrorism 2000/2001*; Gilmore Commission 2002), but the rising numbers of female participants within these organizations has not appeared to have attracted official interest. Reports by the Federal Bureau of Investigation (FBI) overwhelmingly focus on male leaders and perpetrators and official scenarios are devoid of female operatives (Cordesman 2001, "Countering Terrorism: Integration of Practice and Theory: An Invitational Conference" 2002). Furthermore, the FBI does not provide statistical data on the gender of hate crime offenders, leading one to conclude that of the reported 7649 incidents reported in 2004, all 7145 known offenders were male (*Hate Crime Statistics* 2004). Yet Blee's (2005) account of women involved in several hate crimes linked to racial terrorism suggests that this conclusion is likely false. Finally, officials do not generally publicize female actors within the right-wing movement and information regarding strategies and/or operational procedures for identifying, searching, interrogating, and/or exploiting female militant members of domestic organizations for counterintelligence purposes is not publicly available.

With respect to right-wing terrorism in the United States, all six counterterrorism deficiencies are apparent. Although female militants have been apprehended and successfully prosecuted by the federal government, it is not clear that officials have sought, much less successfully obtained, insight into the organizations with which the women were affiliated. It is also not clear how women are influencing, and being influenced by, organizational structures. As with Islamic terrorism and some left-wing groups, hierarchies are increasingly giving way to flatter structures and "leaderless resistance" frameworks and women's roles within these two differential organizational approaches, and women's influence on moving organizations structurally, is unknown. Interestingly, women's participation in racial terrorism in earlier historical periods increased as organizational structures became more rigid (Blee 2005,424), and there have been "… at least fledgling attempts to organize all-women racist skinhead groups under the banner of 'White power/women power', … efforts that would be unimaginable in other parts of the White supremacist movement" (Blee 2005, 429).

Technology is one of the most notable areas of activity with respect to female militancy in the right-wing movements, including anti-abortion groups. The Internet has become a critical arena for recruitment, propaganda dissemination, and intra-group participation for women. Further, the Internet creates transnational opportunities for women as exemplified by Melissa Guille who runs the Canadian Heritage Alliance website in Canada from her London home (Richmond 2005). Women's use of, and influence over, technology has the potential to affect female standing within groups and their overall operational roles.

Male leaders of various White supremacist groups have recognized that women attract publicity for their groups, and generate fear and discomfort in observers. Don Black, former leader of the Alabama KKK and creator of Stormfront in 1995, estimated that one-third of his members were female and one-third to one half of chat room participants were women by 1999 (Nesbitt 1999). This observation was reinforced by the Southern Poverty Law Center (SPLC) who estimated that women comprised at least 25 percent of many groups and up to half of new recruits ("All in the Family" n. d.). More interestingly is that women's participation is increasingly associated with strategic advantages, especially recruiting additional female and male members. What merits greater scrutiny is whether women's participation is being over or under reported for denial and deception purposes. Counterterrorism and counterintelligence elements need to investigate female activity through the use of female operatives and observe and compare public announcements by group leaders regarding female participation with data drawn from operatives within groups and arrest and incarceration statistics.

Right-wing White power movements in the United States have seen the success of female militancy in cases such as Palestine and Chechnya, as well as historical cases such as the Weather Underground and Black Panther party, which may result in growing female involvement in strategic and narrative violence (Blee 2005, 431). Stormfront chatrooms confirm that White supremacist groups are watching developments related to female militancy.[4] To date, for most observers, women are ignored in right-wing movements because they have had little to no role in violent organizations and/or actions, although this perception is increasingly being shown to be incorrect (Cunningham 2003; Blee 2005). Intensifying this factor is that most of the highly violent organizations that preoccupy U.S. counterterrorism specialists are also ideologically conservative, which is viewed as making these organizations uniquely hostile to female participation and operationalization. This is true of right-wing movements in the United States and it is true in settings such as Palestine, Chechnya, and global Islamism (Al Qaeda).

Palestinian organizations and the emergence of female suicide attackers

Women's involvement with politically violent organizations is not unheard of in the Middle East, including the use of female suicide bombers, contrary to popular perceptions that this is a new phenomenon. During the 1980s in Southern Lebanon, female suicide bombers were utilized, mainly by the Syrian Socialist Nationalist Party (SSNP) and two-thirds of the attacks undertaken by the Kurdistan Workers' Party (PKK) were by women in the mid- to late-1990s. There is some evidence that the last female suicide bomber in Lebanon acted on behalf of Hezbollah and in 2002 Sheik Muhammad Husayn Fadlallah publicly approved of female suicide bombers.[5] Since 2002, both secular and Islamist Palestinian groups have utilized women in eight successful suicide attacks against Israel including the Al-Aqsa Martyrs Brigades (an off-shoot of Fatah), the Palestinian Islamic Jihad, and Hamas. Reportedly there are at least a dozen incarcerated women whose suicide missions failed (Beyler 2005), and since 2000 ninety-six Palestinian women have been involved in violence against Israel (Daraghmeh 2005), with forty-one women (including the eight suicide attackers) having been recruited between 2002 and 2004 (Dudkevitch 2004). Further, Israel publicized the capture of the first Hamas female bombmaker in October 2005 (Daraghmeh 2005).

Israeli security sources claimed to have been aware of women's roles in terrorism from the beginning of the second *intifada*, however Wafa Idris's suicide bombing in January 2002 surprised the Israeli security apparatus (Gilmore 2002). Despite clear indicators, Israeli officials missed the signals that women's terrorist violence was possible, much less impending. Between 1998 and 2002, at least 18 Palestinian women were arrested for a variety of attacks that included stabbings of soldiers and police officers (8), attempted murder of a soldier (method unknown) (1), the murder of an Israeli boy (1), planting bombs (2), planned suicide bombings in 2002 (2), and a car bomb (1).[6] Palestinian males often escalated violence (e.g., stabbings and shootings) before turning to suicide bombings (Karmon 2000). Nevertheless, despite a pattern of escalating violence by Palestinian women during the second *intifada*, and earlier events in Lebanon (Beyler 2003), Israeli security forces failed to anticipate that they would face female suicide attacks.

The effects of female suicide bombers on Israeli officials should not be underestimated. In addition to the expanded field of possible threats that must now be addressed at border crossings, the psychological impact of female suicide bombers has been significant as these women challenge traditional Israeli assumptions regarding Palestinian women and society. Some of this effect is visible in Israeli efforts to downplay social fears associated with female militants. For example, the Israeli Ministry of Information has distributed information regarding female militants that portrays them as unwitting victims and/or desperate social failures. It is not unusual for male suicide attackers to be described as "sentient missiles" (Ucko and Langston 2002) as opposed to "real terrorists" who plan and organize attacks. Similarly, female suicide attackers are portrayed in both the Palestinian and Chechnyan cases as weapons-delivery-systems (WDS)[7] in the sense that they are little more than bombs with a brain. The danger is that women will be viewed as *limited* to the role of suicide attackers, raising the likelihood that observers will underestimate the actual recruitment and operational depth and range for female operatives, such as the emergence of Hamas's female bombmaker. The lessons of Hamas are particularly noteworthy because most observers were skeptical that Hamas would ever operationalize women. This was despite the fact that Islamic and Hamas leaders, including Hamas's spiritual leader Sheikh Ahmed Yassin, never ruled out the possibility and were intellectually setting the stage for several years (Cook 2005).

In the Palestinian setting, all of the counterterrorism deficiencies are identifiable, although there are important areas of convergence and divergence from U.S. right-wing movements. As of June 2005 Israel was holding at least twelve failed female suicide attackers (Beyler 2005) but Israeli attitudes toward these women will affect if and how they will be exploited as a meaningful source of intelligence. If women are simply WDS, then captured women have little usefulness aside from publicity for the Israeli state.

One of the reasons why Israeli officials were surprised by the emergence of female suicide bombers was the hierarchical nature of Palestinian groups. This factor also explains why Israelis tend to dismiss women as WDS rather than view them as meaningful members of their respective organizations. However, as the Palestinian setting demonstrates, operational success trumps hierarchy. Further, women's success in suicide attacks has precipitated a reaction by both women and men in the Palestinian setting that may have longer-term organizational implications for expanding women's roles and participation (Cunningham 2005). Here the role of technology may have future meaning. Although the Internet has not become a meaningful means to recruit and operationalize women in the Palestinian setting, the Internet and other media outlets such as satellite television and newspapers have been applied toward disseminating information about female militants to expatriates and regional audiences (Israeli 2004). Fund-raising activities by women in other Middle Eastern-based groups such as the PKK and the Mujahadeen-e-Khalq (MEK) in North America (Cunningham 2003) suggest that women's roles have the potential to be more expansive both within and outside of the Palestinian setting. Counterterrorism officials need to consider how technology may play a role in fostering women's participation both inside and outside the region with respect to the Palestinian uprising.

Three of the most clearly discernable and overlapping areas regarding counterterrorism deficiencies concern denial and deception, tactical advantages, and culture/ideology. Arafat initiated calls for female participation in the secular uprising in early 2002 (Victor 2003), while Islamist acceptance had been slower but emerging. Hamas's spiritual leader Sheikh Ahmed Yassin described the use of its first female suicide attacker as an "evolution" (Zaanoun 2004) and a "new beginning" (Barzak 2004). Idris's success, which related more to the public response than to the tactical nature of her attack, sent a clear and compelling message to all Palestinian organizations that women enjoy tactical advantages that their male counterparts do not. In the Israeli case, this success has had as much to do with being able to get close to intended targets as with undermining public confidence in Israeli security forces, jarring entrenched public attitudes regarding Palestinian society, and invigorating Arab publics. In the wake of successful female suicide attacks, Israel began to post female soldiers at security checkpoints but not until 2004 (Barzak 2004). However, even in secure settings female guards are limited, allowing women to detonate their explosives before they can be screened, as was the case with Reem Saleh Riyashi, Hamas's first female suicide attacker, in January 2004 (Moore 2004).

Significantly, Israeli officials and most Western observers not only had difficulty anticipating the emergence of female suicide attackers in Palestine, but they have continued to resist their presence by attempting to diminish them and explain them away. Entrenched attitudes regarding Islamic and Arab cultures have reinforced this process as culture is seen to trump operational success. Although this assumption has been shown to be incorrect, it is entrenched and highly resistant to change, thereby explaining counterterrorism failures in the Chechen case and the dangers facing an emergent case such as global Islamism.

Chechnya's "Black Widows": fear + sympathy + publicity = the perfect terrorist

To date, the literature on Chechnya is limited, and most accounts regarding female suicide bombers are journalistic and often sensationalist. Female suicide bombers have been used in a number of high profile attacks against Russian targets since 2002 including a Moscow rock concert in July 2003, the Moscow theater hostage-taking in October 2002, the Beslan elementary school attack in September 2004, and the downing of two planes in August 2004. Women were first used in suicide attacks beginning in June 2000 (Meier 2004) but since October 2002 the majority of suicide attacks have been undertaken by women (Abdullaev 2004). Nivat (2005) argues "... more Chechen women seem to be participating actively in the separatist-turned-jihadist struggle than in the larger and longer-running Palestinian conflict" (419). Given the limitations of the literature on Chechnya to date, it is difficult to form a complete picture of the true operational range of female Chechen rebels; however, there is reason to believe that it may be wider than the "Black Widow" phenomenon suggests.

Women have been participating in greater numbers, in more frequent attacks, and in more complex missions over the past three years. Forty-six percent (19/41) of the Moscow theater hostage takers were women and two to four of the roughly thirty hostage takers in Beslan were women. Their operational success is impressive with Chechen suicide bombers beating the world's average by more than double the number killed (Abdullaev 2004). Russian officials have been shocked and alarmed by the frequency and success of female suicide attacks, but as with the Palestinian case, officials should have at least anticipated this innovation by Chechen separatists given reports of female combatants in the first Chechen war from 1994 to 1996.

Nivat (2001) met two women, both of whom she refers to as "Larissa," who were female combatants years before women escalated into more substantial acts of violence. The first Larissa clearly served in combat roles but was sent home to attend to her daughter with the death of her husband. Once home she fulfilled a variety of roles, becoming a liaison officer in charge of counter-espionage, an intelligence agent, a sniper, a cook, and a nurse. The second Larissa, a female combatant in uniform, was able to join the rebellion after marrying a rebel. She told Nivat, "'[s]ince I was little... I wanted to make the *gazovat* [holy war]. And now, here I am'" (199). Unfortunately, there are few accounts such as Nivat's that provide any insight into women's roles within the Chechen uprising outside of the sensationalist "Black Widows" phenomenon.

Despite evidence that women were involved in a range of operational roles within the Chechen uprising including more generalized combat in Grozny, there has been little official acknowledgment of this operational range, or indications of Russian responses to women's roles. Until women became something the state could not ignore, officials dismissed early female suicide attacks as a "fiction" (Paukov and Svistunov 2003). Most official attention toward female suicide bombers has focused on their status as widows suggesting, much as in the Israeli case, that the women are naïve and irrelevant throwaways whose presence merits no additional explanation and/or understanding. Russian officials arguably have sought to arouse public sympathy for these women as victims of Chechen leaders to distract the public from focusing on how bad things must be to drive Chechen women to suicide attacks (Groskop 2004; Page 2004; Meier 2004). In general, Russian officials have sought to explain Chechen female militants using three techniques: the "Black Fatima" legend; the "zombification" of Chechen women; and foreign influence, especially the Islamicization of the conflict.

Harkening back to the Baba Yoga folklore (Meier 2004), the "Black Fatima" legend is furthered by Russian officials through the state-owned media, and was reinforced by the lone failed female suicide attacker, Zarema Muzhakhoyeva. "Black Fatima" is characterized as an older woman in black furs with a "hook nose" who recruits, trains, drugs, and then tasks young Chechen women for suicide attacks (Page 2004; Meier 2004). Others point to the "zombification" of Chechen women caused by grief and sorrow (Groskop 2004), whereas still others see them as evidence of the Islamicization of the conflict (Myers 2004) who are led by Arabs (Mainville 2003) or bankrolled by mercenaries (Page 2004). Russian officials prefer to utilize a "profile" of Chechen female terrorists as young, widowed, desperate for revenge, or hapless victims forced into attacks through blackmail or rape. However, this profile is not supported by observers who note that female suicide attackers are not necessarily young, religious, poor, widowed, grieving, or raped (Abdullaev 2004; Myers 2004). Instead of a profile what exists is an organization willing to apply this "high value franchise" (Abdullaev 2004).

The counterterrorism failure in the Chechen case conforms to the two earlier cases, especially that of Palestine. Several female Chechen combatants are in custody but it is not clear how Russian officials have exploited their presence for counterterrorism and counterintelligence purposes. Russian officials have been fairly aggressive in their physical responses to Chechen attacks, killing most perpetrators, and women's participation in suicide attacks negates the issue of capture and interrogation. Nevertheless, the potential for interrogating militant Chechen women exists, but Russian official statements peripheralizing and trivializing women's roles suggests that these intelligence avenues are likely underutilized.

The limits of information are telling in the Chechen case with respect to organization, technology, and denial and deception. Like the Palestinian and right-wing movements in the United States, Chechen groups remain hierarchical, which generally limits women's roles. Earlier accounts, while admittedly sparse, highlighted a range of operational roles for women including combatant, espionage, sniper, and support activities. Reportedly, women were being trained in explosives and Islam by Wahhabi Chechens several years before the first suicide attacks occurred (Meier 2004). Currently Chechen women are almost exclusively considered as suicide attackers. Importantly, women's success as suicide attackers has prompted their inclusion into larger and more complex missions such as Beslan in 2004 (Abdullaev 2004). It is clear that even within suicide attacks observers must move toward a more nuanced understanding of the roles women are filling.

The tactical advantage of females in suicide attacks has been readily apparent, yet women's potential role in other types of violence and technology-assisted recruitment, fund-raising, and propaganda activities is unknown. There is evidence that the Chechens are mobilizing women differently in the past year, pulling them straight from their homes into an attack rather than pulling them out of society and putting them in the mountains for training for attacks weeks later (Myers 2004). This shift will complicate Russian counterterrorism efforts and is muddying Chechen public attitudes toward attacks such as the plane bombings because the idea that women were in society one day and carrying out an attack the next is unsettling. It also weakens Russian perceptions, and to some extent that of the Chechen public, that Chechen female suicide attackers must be brainwashed to carry out their attacks. Finally, women's tactical advantage in the Russian context is reinforced by a unique feature with this case for the purposes of this study—corruption. The pervasiveness and depth of Russian corruption is well known, but the 2004 plane crashes highlights that this problem is exploitable by female militants who were able to bribe an airline official and by-pass police security to obtain access to the planes.

As in both the Palestinian and right-wing movement cases discussed earlier, much of what has limited counterterrorism success against female militants is centered in cultural and ideological assumptions. Chechen women were not on the counter-terrorism radar screen because of entrenched beliefs that cultural norms would prohibit their being included and operationalized in any militant setting. Despite evidence that women were participating in militant activities such as espionage and combat roles, and being trained in militarist activities by Wahhabis, the prospect of female suicide attacks seemed unthinkable because Islam and larger cultural mores were believed to be opposed to this possibility. Finally, in the face of women dying while undertaking suicide attacks, Russian leaders" willingness to peripheralize and diminish female activity has allowed cultural assumptions to remain unchanged and strategic perceptions of women's limited roles to go unchallenged.

Two possible future scenarios

The dangers of the counterterrorism failures highlighted by the preceding cases become more apparent when we look to the future and consider where terrorism has the potential to go and how women's participation in that future might look. Each of the counterterrorism failures examined earlier has resonance for two possible terrorism futures with the potential for significant female participation, whether in terms of overall numbers or with respect to operational success and effect. These cases are global Islamism and left-wing terrorism in the United States.

Global Islamism

Global Islamism fostered by groups such as Al Qaeda have frequently been considered the most uniquely hostile organizations to women because of their extreme religiously grounded ideological conservatism. Yet Cook (2005) observes that religious legal discussions do not severely impede the ideological use of women in *jihad*, but rather the absence of women in groups like Al Qaeda results from social conservatism in Muslim societies (383), or Arabism.

Information is scattered and difficult to obtain regarding global Islamist organizations but even a brief examination provides evidence of widening and deepening female participation and mobilization as of late 2005. Women have been supporters and family members of global Islamist groups like Al Qaeda for many years, but they have also reportedly been used to train women ("Mother of Usama"), run women's organizations and groups, participate as girls in Islamist summer camps, run Internet magazines, distribute Qur'ans in prisons and schools, create Islamist nongovernmental organizations and charities, participate in Muslim Student Associations (MSAs), and engage in illegal activities such as fund-raising (Ozment 2004; Scroggins 2004, 2005). Although these activities are nonviolent, they are also frequent pathways to militancy for male members of global Islamist groups and are critical sources for propaganda, recruitment, and fund-raising. Since 2003, women have also participated in suicide attacks, and several failed efforts, in Iraq and as of 2005 these attacks were claimed by Iraq's Al Qaeda. Overall, women have been associated with Islamist militancy, largely linked to Al-Qaeda, in Pakistan, Great Britain, the United States, Jordan, Iraq, the Philippines, and Uzbekistan since 2001.

Despite the operational success of women in Palestine and Chechnya, however, the presence of "Al Qaeda women" is hard for most Western observers to comprehend, much less prepare for, because culture is seen to trump operational considerations. Although Islamic scholarly discourse has clearly been coming to terms with the potential, if not probability, of female militancy for years (Cook 2005), Western observers remain resistant to this possibility, preferring to maintain cultural assumptions much in the way Israeli and Russian officials have done. The hierarchical features of the larger globalist Islamic movement will not preclude women's participation in the same way that these organizational features have not in Palestine and Chechnya. In an excellent move toward denial and deception, while Islamic scholars make way for the possibility of female terrorists, global Islamist leaders may continue to espouse rhetoric hostile to women in an effort to reinforce Western cultural assumptions while preparing to take advantage of the lack of Western preparedness for an attack involving women. Complicating this case is that, to date, few women have been visibly involved with global Islamist groups, preventing officials from exploiting captured females for counterterrorism and counterintelligence purposes.

Left-wing terrorism in the United States

The 1960s and 1970s were characterized by high levels of female participation in violent left-wing groups, including female leadership in developed states within North America, Europe, and Japan. Currently, ecoterrorism, especially from groups like the Earth Liberation Front (ELF) and Animal Liberation Front (ALF) is considered by the FBI to be one of the most significant domestic terrorist threats within the United States (*Terrorism 2000/2001*; Cunningham 2003). Yet most official observers are preoccupied with ideologically conservative, and particularly religiously grounded, terrorist organizations, especially those based in Islam.

Ecoterrorists in the United States have been seeking to link their movement with other "social justice" movements, providing an opportunity to broaden their ideological and geographic reach. Ideologically, antiwar, anarchist, antiglobalist, anticapitalist, and rights-focused (animals, women, racial, developing world) movements are logical targets for this effort. Ecoterrorists have engaged in transnational efforts to train like-minded activists that included animal rights advocates and anarchists in Kent in September 2004 (Taylor 2004; Nugent 2004). These linkages are not surprising considering leftist movements have a historical record of creating ties with one another (Zwerman 1995) and ecoterrorism originated in the 1970s.

Women have been active participants in the ELF and ALF although their overall levels are unknown (Cunningham 2003) and visible leadership is overwhelmingly male. Nevertheless women are clearly evident in training, violent actions such as arson, publicity especially on the Internet, and directing violent operations. The ALF's "Arson Guide" features a woman burning down a McDonalds entitled "Arson-Around with Auntie ALF" ("Ecoterrorism" n. d.). Significantly, women have undertaken many of these roles without attracting publicity. For both women and men in the ALF and ELF violence has become an acceptable and effective means to an end and this conviction is gaining cross-national currency. ALF activists who attended the Kent training event highlighted the fact that "direct action" has been the only thing that has raised the group's profile and attracted media attention (Taylor 2004). Although there is no established socioeconomic profile of female participants in the ecoterrorist movement, what is evident is that their age range is wide.

Ecoterrorist aspirations to link their movement to other "social justice" movements have the potential to extend the influence and organizational range of violent members. Leftist organizations have historically witnessed significant female participation and leadership and ecoterrorists seem to share this feature of leftist groups. One possible area for emergent female violence lies in the growing tension between conservatives and liberals in the United States. If the conservative agenda gains juridical success in limiting certain freedoms for women, especially with respect to abortion, then there is a possibility women could radicalize in the United States in similar ways to anti-abortion groups. Through over-lapping membership and ideological linkages, violent actions—and the training to do them—may potentially target conservative leaders (official, religious, and nongovernmental), judges, and media figures. The "women's liberation" association of many leftist groups in the 1970s and ongoing women's participation on leftist organizations such as the ELF/ALF contain both organizational and ideological features that facilitate high female participation levels and leadership roles in this type of scenario.

Summary

One of the most significant advantages held by female terrorists is that their potential is denied, ignored, and diminished and as a result they are almost always unanticipated, underestimated, and highly effective. Their effectiveness results from an important nexus: the ingenuity and capabilities of female attackers, the rational calculations and organizational capabilities of terrorist organization leaders, and the shortsightedness and denial of officials in the targets. The cases examined in this study demonstrate the importance of all three features but the only area that officials truly have the power to correct is their own. Counterterrorism efforts need to be directed toward learning from the past to anticipate possible futures and if these efforts fail to prevent female terrorism then a rapid effort needs to be made to effectively and neutrally respond to the innovation of female actors in violent settings. Initial steps can be taken in the six counterterrorism deficiency areas that emerged from existing cases of female militancy: exploitation, organization, technology, denial and deception, tactical advantages, and culture and ideology.

Because women are often not viewed as significant and meaningful actors in most organizations, women currently held in detention are unlikely to be seen as exploitable resources for intelligence on organizations, their leaders, and for developing scenarios. Observers must be willing to exploit the range of female participants in violent organizations, from female combatants to supporters because of their ability to provide fuller pictures of organizations and participants. Finally, observer preoccupation with violent actors runs the risk of overlooking participation trajectories that move from nonviolent to violent behavior. Men follow these trajectories and so do women; it is imperative that observers remain open-minded when observing female participation and capable of discerning when that participation is moving along a trajectory that may favor violent action.

Hierarchical organizations are often viewed as hostile to women's participation in terrorist organizations but not only has this assumption not held up, it has limited observers from anticipating other options including the formation of women's organizations and women's roles in less hierarchical settings. Similarly, observers are preoccupied by conservative/religious terrorist organizations and suicide attacks, two features that have heretofore been viewed as inhospitable to female participation despite historical precedents with the PKK and Sri Lanka. There is precedence for female participation in both secular and religious terrorism and both forms of terrorism remain ongoing threats to various states, including the United States.

Two areas where women have some of their greatest impact are actually nonviolent and include technology and denial and deception. Women's use of, and responsiveness to, technology has been significant in settings such as the right-wing movement in the United States, and there is precedence for women's effective use of technology for fund-raising, recruitment, and propaganda in other organizations including those from the Middle East. Additionally, technology gives women, and their organizations, transnational influence and access, creating an avenue to link expatriates with localized conflicts. Finally, the role and participation of women in terrorist settings has profound denial and deception potential, as terrorist organizations can use the cultural assumptions of their opponents to obscure meaningful assessments of female participation. To date, terrorist leaders in a variety of settings have sought to downplay and/or amplify female participation levels and roles in an effort to disrupt, disorient, and/or distract their opponents.

Five proposals to overcome these deficiencies

The challenge of overcoming the deficiencies discussed in this analysis may appear daunting; however, there are five immediate proposals that can be taken to address them and, more importantly, the issue that underlies them all. Perhaps the most significant lesson for counterterrorism scholars and officials of the three cases discussed in this analysis (United States, Israel, and Russia) is that women's emergence and participation in terrorist settings is not the "surprise" it often appears to be. Rather, all three cases demonstrate that if counterterrorism experts had looked, they would have seen women's entry into the respective terrorist settings years before violence occurred and, with respect to the right-wing groups in the United States, this pathway is arguably still emerging. Further, counterterrorism "surprise" has not been limited to women's entry into terrorist settings, but also the types of tactics they have been tasked with (e.g., violent versus nonviolent action), and ultimately the "promotional" opportunities for women within their respective organizations (e.g., becoming a suicide attacker versus not being limited to suicide attacks). These three areas of surprise are directly caused, and exacerbated, by the six counterterrorism deficiencies highlighted throughout this analysis.

Given limited resources and a seemingly endless list of emergent and ongoing threats, counterterrorism experts have downplayed both the possibility and probability of female terrorism. As a result, responses have been overwhelmingly inadequate and defensive despite the high operational success of female terrorist attacks. Yet there are five counterterrorism steps that officials and other experts can take to place their security apparatuses in a more responsive and anticipatory posture. Although this may not prevent the emergence and/or expansion of female participation in terrorist settings, it may very well deprive terrorist organizations and their leaders of two of the most important advantages associated with female terrorism: surprise and tactical access. Each of these suggestions, presented in no particular order of importance, should be relatively easy for states to implement as part of their overarching counterterrorism program and the implementation of all five would provide some of the best remediation for the six counterterrorism deficiencies discussed earlier.

Intelligence Communication between local, state, federal, and international elements is absolutely critical to identify, analyze, and respond to female participation in diverse violent settings. Particularly useful would be intelligence efforts directed toward identifying potentially emergent cases of female participation in violent, or potentially violent, settings and how this participation transforms over time. Further, official efforts must be reinforced with scholarly efforts by academics and researchers. Intelligence professional organizations and seminars would be useful settings for this type of information sharing. However, individual streams of information have little broad utility if they are not analyzed within larger frameworks.

As a result, an *International Database of Female Terrorism*, containing classified and unclassified information, should be considered. Ideally it would include a wide range of information on female participation in violent organizations, or with the potential for violence. Official information generated from incarceration interviews, statistics, and surveillance can be combined with broader trends identified from the media, scholarly research and interviews, and terrorist propaganda to provide cross-national data on the range, levels, and trends of female participation in violent settings. Additionally, earlier data sources should be reviewed to identify any overlooked information, such as the FBI's *Hate Crime Statistics*, and assess its implications. Established databases such as RAND's MIPT Terrorism Knowledge Database and the University of St. Andrew's Centre for the Study of Terrorism and Political Violence Database Project are two good models, and it is possible that a database of women's terrorist activity could be included in one or both of these established databases.

As communication and data expand, it is imperative that official and scholarly counterterrorism experts engage in *Scenario Development* that involves both "never" and "what if" components. First, experts must address the ongoing challenge of the impossible scenarios, or "nevers," such as the early reluctance noted by Shultz and Vogt (2002) to believe that Shi'a and Sunni groups would overcome their sectarian differences to cooperate with each other (376–377). This same tendency has been readily apparent in counterterrorism efforts, or the lack thereof, with respect to female terrorism, especially with ideologically conservative groups. Secondly, experts must engage in "what if" scenarios they develop with male actors to include women. For example, "what if" an attack by Al Qaeda included women? What would the impact be, how would this affect the operation's success, and would the psychological impact of the attack be amplified? How would the inclusion of a woman influence the response to the attack, the ability to prevent the attack, and/or the effect of the attack for the public, officials, and responders? Importantly, individuals developing scenarios must not only create scenarios that involve female perpetrators, they must also compare the same scenarios but where the only divergent variable is the gender of the perpetrator to assess how gender affects their larger security assessments, planning, and responses.

Counterterrorism efforts must also be made in two applied fields. First, *Security Protocols* must be evaluated and, where necessary, revised before an attack by a female perpetrator ever occurs. The case from Hamas is illustrative, in that Israeli officials were aware of female suicide attackers and had female security personnel available but not on hand. This allowed enough time for a female to detonate an explosive at a security checkpoint in a manner that a male would have been unable to achieve. In areas where female security personnel are necessary to inspect women for social proprietary and other reasons, those personnel must be trained and deployed in advance of attacks. Conversely, if this deployment is impossible, security precautions need to be taken to prevent females from obtaining sustained access to areas prior to security screenings.

Second, *HUMINT* efforts need to be implemented, deepened, and/or widened to include not only established threats to respective states but emergent threats as well. Further, female assets must be utilized to gain entry into various organizations to obtain information regarding female access, range, and internal mobilization potential. Intelligence gathered through these channels will provide a fuller picture of female participation in violent settings, especially when considered in tandem with information gathered through intelligence sharing, scholarly analysis, and other information sources such as terrorist propaganda and media reports.

Counterterrorism experts, and the state leaders who rely on them, should work together to implement the five counterterrorism proposals briefly discussed earlier because they will address the two most important issues related to female terrorism and counterterrorism: surprise and tactical advantage. By generating, sharing, and refining intelligence information, analytical efforts will be improved and threats (or potential threats) will become more visible and thereby less surprising. Through applied counterterrorism steps including more robust security protocols and the use of HUMINT, officials and analysts will have an infrastructure in place to respond to emergent and impending threats. Although none of these suggestions will deter violent organizations, or the women who participate in them, they will impact the ability of terrorist leaders to surprise officials and analysts with an unanticipated terrorist actor and will ensure that states are better able to handle this possible innovation in terrorist strategy.

Notes

1   Because the nature of Al Qaeda and its offshoots is unclear, this author prefers to utilize this term to capture groups such as Al Qaeda led by Osama bin Laden and/or his successor(s) and Iraq's Al Qaeda. These types of organizations are interested in the projection of global Islamist influence and control, as well as the replacement of their respective governments with an Islamic regime.

2   Overall, there have been more than 80,000 incidents of violence and/or disruption at United States and Canadian clinics since 1977 including: 7 murders, 17 attempted murders, 41 bombings, 166 arsons, 82 failed bombings and/or arson attempts, 100 butyric acid attacks, 654 anthrax threats, and 3 kidnappings (see "NAF Violence and Disruption Statistics: Incidents of Violence & Disruption Against Abortion Providers in the US & Canada," 2003, National Abortion Foundation (30 September), available at (http://www.prochoice.org/Violence/Statistics/default.htm), accessed 10 December 2003, p.1).

3   They include: Shelley Shannon, Betsy McDonald, Loretta Marra (Malvasi), Linda Wolfe, and Mary Stachowicz. Criteria for inclusion on the list are somewhat questionable. For example, although McDonald is best known as an avid supporter of James Kopp, who was convicted of murdering Dr. Barnett Slepian of Amherst, New York in 1998, Stachowicz was the victim of a "homosexual hate

crime" because she was allegedly murdered by a homosexual man. Finally, Wolfe's entry appears to be mistaken and should refer to a woman named Brenda Phillips.

4   A post by "Dr. A. Jurievich" in February 2004 under the discussion "Chechen soldiers for Kids" about female Chechen snipers included references to earlier female militancy of the legendary "White Stockings" snipers (http://www.stormfront.org/forum/showthread.php?t=158429&page=2&pp=10), accessed 22 November 2005.

5   See Cronin (2003), 12–14; Sprinzak (2000), 9; and Beyler (2003), 3, 7. For additional information see "Female Separatist Rebel Captured in Southeastern Turkey," 1998, *BBC* (15 August) Lexis/Nexis accessed 31 January 2002, pp. 1–2; "Turkey: Female 'Terrorist' Reportedly Carries Out Suicide Bombing," 1998, *BBC* (24 December) Lexis/Nexis accessed 31 January 2002, pp. 1–2; "Suicide Bombings Increase in South," 1985, *Facts on File* (16 August) Lexis/Nexis accessed 2 August 2002, pp. 1–2; and "Brazilian-Born Girl Carries Out Suicide Bombing, Report Says," 1985, *The Associated Press* (26 November) Lexis/Nexis accessed 2 August 2002, pp. 1–2.

6   See "Palestinian and Arab Women Political Prisoners," n. d., Addameer Prisoners' Support and Human Rights Association, Khalid Daromar, trans., available at (http://www. addameer.org/women), accessed 3 June 2002, pp. 1–5; "Deteriorating Conditions of Palestinian Female Prisoners Reach Dangerous Levels," 2001, Mandela Institute for Human Rights (30 September), available at (http://www.blythe. org), accessed 3 June 2002, pp. 1–3; "Palestinian Female Political Prisoners and Detainees in Israeli Jails," 2001, Democratic Palestine No. 98–99 (October), available at (http://www.democraticpalestine. net/article.php?article=7&issue=98), accessed 3 June 2002, pp. 1–3; and "LAW Report: 11 Female Palestinian Detainees in Israel, Three Under 15, Suffer Appalling ...," 2001, *Washington Report on Middle East Affairs* 20, 9 (December), available at (http://www.britannica.com), accessed 3 June 2002, pp. 1–6.

7   This terminology was used in a discussion with a confidential counterterrorism source in January 2004 describing official interpretation of female suicide bombing in Chechnya and Palestine.

References

Abdullaev, Nabi. 2004. "Women to the Forefront in Chechen Terrorism." International Relations and Security Network (ISN), available at (http://www.isn.ethz.ch), accessed 2 November 2005, pp. 1–4.

Anti-Defamation League. n.d. "Ecoterrorism: Extremism in the Animal Rights and Environmentalist Movements." Available at (http://www.adl.org/learn/ext_us/Ecoterrorism_print.asp), accessed 23 November 2005, pp. 1–14.

The Advisory Panel to Assess Domestic Response Capabilities for Terrorism Involving Weapons of Mass Destruction. (Gilmore Commission). 2002. *Fourth Annual Report to the President and the Congress of the Advisory Panel to Assess Domestic Response Capabilities for Terrorism Involving Weapons of Mass Destruction. IV: Implementing the National Strategy.* 15 December. Arlington, VA: RAND. Available at (http://www.rand.org/nsrd/terrpanel/terror4txt.pdf), accessed 3 December 2003, pp. 15–18.

Barzak, Ibrahim. 2004. "Hamas Leaders Says Era of Female Suicide Bombers Has Begun." *Associated Press Worldstream* (19 January) Lexis/Nexis accessed 19 November 2005, pp. 1–3.

Beirich, Heidi and Mark Potok. 2003. "40 to Watch." *Southern Poverty Law Center Intelligence Report*, available at (http://www.splcenter.org/intel/intelreport/article.jsp?aid=115), accessed 9 December 2003.

Beyler, Clara. 2005. "Women Weapons." *The New York Sun* (29 June) Lexis/Nexis accessed 18 November 2005, pp. 1–3.

Beyler, Clara. 2003. "Messengers of Death: Female Suicide Bombers." International Policy Institute for Counter-Terrorism (12 February), available at (http://www.ict.org.il/) accessed 3 December 2004, pp. 1–19.

Blee, M. Kathleen. 2005. "Women and Organized Racial Terrorism in the United States." *Studies in Conflict & Terrorism* 28(5) (September-October), pp. 421–433.

Blee, M. Kathleen. 2002. *Inside Organized Racism: Women in the Hate Movement.* Berkeley: University of California Press.

Blee, M. Kathleen. 1991. *Women of the Klan: Racism and Gender in the 1920s.* Berkeley, CA: University of California Press.

Cook, David. 2005. "Women Fighting in *Jihad?*." *Studies in Conflict & Terrorism* 28(5) (September-October), pp. 375–384.

Cordesman, Anthony H. 2001. *Defending America: Redefining the Conceptual Borders of Homeland Defense: The Risks and Effects of Indirect, Covert, Terrorist, and Extremist Attacks with Weapons of Mass Destruction, Challenges for Defense and Response.* Center for Strategic and International Studies. (14 February) Columbia International Affairs Online (CIAO), accessed 12 December 2003.

Cronin, Audrey Kurth. 2003. "Terrorists and Suicide Attacks." *CRS Report for Congress* RL32058 (28 August), pp. 1–22.

Cunningham, J. Karla. 2005. "Women, Political Violence, and Democratization," in *Democratic Development and Political Terrorism: The Global Perspective*, edited by William Crotty, (Boston, MA: Northeastern University Press), pp. 73–90.

Cunningham, J. Karla. 2003. "Cross-Regional Trends in Female Terrorism." *Studies in Conflict & Terrorism* 26(3) (May-June), pp. 171–195.

Daraghmeh, Ali. 2005. "22-Year-Old Said to Be Hamas Bomb Maker." *Associated Press Online* (11 October) Lexis/Nexis, accessed 28 November 2005, pp. 1–3.

Dudkevitch, Margot. 2004. "Suicide Attack was 8th by Female." *The Jerusalem Post* (23 September) Lexis/Nexis, accessed 18 November 2005, pp. 1–2.

FBI Academy. 2002. "Countering Terrorism: Integration of Practice and Theory: An Invitational Conference," Quantico, VA (28 February), available at ⟨http://www.fbi.gov/publications/counterr/counterterrorism.pdf⟩, accessed 10 December 2003.

Gilmore, Inigo. 2002. "Woman Suicide Bomber Shakes Israelis." *The Daily Telegraph* (28 January) Lexis/Nexis, accessed 15 April 2002, pp. 1–2.

Groskop, Viv. 2004. "Chechnya's Deadly 'Black Widows'; Young Chechen Women are Striking Fear in the Hearts of Russians by Staging Suicide Missions. But are they Willing Martyrs—or pawns in a male war? Only one has ever survived to tell her story." *New Statesmen* (6 September) Lexis/Nexis, accessed 18 November 2005, pp. 1–4.

Israeli, Raphael. 2004. "Palestinian Women: The Quest for a Voice in the Public Square Through 'Islamikaze Martyrdom'." *Terrorism and Political Violence* 16(1) (Spring), pp. 66–96.

Karmon, Ely. 2000. "'Hamas' Terrorism Strategy: Operational Limitations and Political Constraints." *Middle East Review of International Affairs (MERIA)* 4(1) (March) Columbia International Affairs Online (CIAO), accessed 20 December 2000, pp. 1–15.

Mainville, Michael. 2003. "Trained By Arabs, 'Black Widows' A Terrifying New Weapon." *The New York Sun* (10 December) Lexis/Nexis, accessed 18 November 2005, pp. 1–3.

Meier, Andrew. 2004. "Andrew Meier Discusses Chechen Women Who Become Terrorists." Interview with Noah Adams. *National Public Radio* (7 September) Lexis/Nexis, accessed 18 November 2005. pp. 1–3.

Moore, Molly. 2004. "Young Mother Kills 4 at Gaza Crossing." *The Washington Post* (15 January) Lexis/Nexis, accessed 18 November 2005, pp. 1–3.

Myers, Steven Lee. 2004. "From Dismal Chechnya, Women Turn to Bombs." *The New York Times* (10 September) Lexis/Nexis, accessed 18 November 2005, pp. 1–5.

Nesbitt, Jim. 1999. "The American Scene: White Supremacist Women Push for Greater Role in the Movement," available at ⟨http://www.newhousenews.com/archive/story1a1022.html⟩, accessed 24 July 2002.

Nivat, Anne. 2005. "The Black Widows: Chechen Women Join the Fight for Independence—and Allah." *Studies in Conflict & Terrorism* 28(5) (September-October), pp. 413–419.

Nivat, Anne. 2001. *Chienne de Guerre: A Woman Reporter Behind the Lines of the War in Chechnya.* Susan Darton, trans. (New York: Public Affairs), pp. 187–199, with the quotation located on p.199.

Nugent, Helen. 2004. "Classes in Death and Violence for Animal Activists." *The Times (London)* (6 September) Lexis/Nexis, accessed 18 November 2005, pp. 1–2.

O'Gorman, Eleanor and Vivienne Jabri. 1999. "Locating Differences in Feminist International Relations," in *Women, Culture, and International Relations*, Vivienne Jabri and Eleanor O'Gorman, eds. Boulder, CO: Lynne Rienner Publishers, Inc. CIAO accessed 9 December 2003, quoting V. Spike Peterson and Anne Sisson Runyan, 1993, *Global Gender Issues*. Boulder, CO: Westview Press, pp. 7–8.

Ozment, Katherine. 2004. "Who's Afraid of Aafia Siddiqui?" *Boston Magazine* (October) Lexis/Nexis, accessed 18 November 2005, pp. 1–8.

Page, Jeremy. 2004. "Spectre of the Chechen "Black Widows". *The Times (London)* (7 February) Lexis/Nexis, accessed 18 November 2005, pp. 1–2.

Paukov, Viktor, and Viktor Svistunov. 2003. "Black Widows Two Steps From the Kremlin." *Defense and Security (Russia)* (15 December) Lexis/Nexis, accessed 18 November 2005, pp. 1–2.

Richmond, Randy. 2005. "Who Are They?; Free Press Reporter Randy Richmond Profiles the Most Prominent White Supremacists in London. Their Backgrounds Range From University History Graduate to Digital Designer to Former Brinks Driver." *London Free Press (Ontario)* (28 March) Lexis/Nexis, accessed 18 November 2005, pp. 1–2.

Schabner, Dean. 2002. "Out of the Kitchen: Has the Women's Movement Come to the Extreme Right?" *ABCNews.com* (12 December), available at (http://www.abcnews.com), accessed 19 May 2003, pp. 1–2.

Scroggins, Deborah. 2005. "The Most Wanted Woman in the World; How Did A Boston-Educated Scientist and Mother of Three End Up On The FBI's List of Possible Top Al-Qaeda Terrorists? And After She Disappeared In Pakistan In 2003, Where Did She Go?" *Vogue* 195(3) (March) Lexis/Nexis, accessed 23 November 2005, pp. 1–10.

Scroggins, Deborah. 2004. "Inside Al Qaeda: The Role of Women." Interview with Wolf Blitzer. *CNN* (12 January) Lexis/Nexis, accessed 18 November 2005, pp. 1–4.

Shultz, Richard H. and Andreas Vogt. 2002. "The Real Intelligence Failure on 9/11 and the Case for a Doctrine of Striking First," in *Terrorism and Counterterrorism: Understanding the New Security Environment*, Russell D. Howard and Reid L. Sawyer. eds. (Guilord, CT: McGraw Hill, 2002), pp. 367–390.

Southern Poverty Law Center. 1999. Intelligence Report (Summer). "Women on the Web." Available at (http://www.splcenter.org/inel/intelreport/article.jsp?sid=2148&printable=1), accessed 28 November 2005.

Southern Poverty Law Center. n. d. "All in the Family: Women, Formerly the Helpmates of the Radical Right, are Becoming Increasingly Outspoken as a Debate on Female Roles in the Movement Takes Shape." Available at (http://www.splcenter.org), accessed 28 March 2002, pp. 1–8.

Sprinzak, Ehud. 2000. "Rational Fanatics." *Foreign Policy* 120 (September/October) ProQuest, accessed 25 March 2002, pp. 66–73.

Taylor, Matthew. 2004. "Animal Rights Activists Sharpen Up Their Battle Plans At Weekend Training Camp." *Manchester Guardian Weekly* (10 September–16 September) Lexis/Nexis, accessed 18 November 2005, pp. 1–3.

Ucko, David and Christopher Langton. 2002. "Suicide Attacks—A Tactical Weapons System." The International Institute for Strategic Studies (IIIS) (24 April) available at (http://www.mafhoum.com/press3/96P8.htm), accessed 10 January 2004.

United States Department of Justice. Federal Bureau of Investigation. 2004. *Terrorism 2000/2001*. FBI Publication #0308. Available at (http://www.fbi.gov/publications/terror/terror2000_2001.htm#page_35), accessed 28 November 2005.

United States Department of Justice. Federal Bureau of Investigation. 2005. *Hate Crime Statistics 2004*. November. Available at (http://www.fbi.gov/ucr/hc2004/tables/HateCrime2004.pdf), accessed 28 November 2005, pp. 1–173.

Victor, Barbara. 2003. *Army of Roses: Inside the World of Palestinian Suicide Bombers*. Emmaus, PA: Rodale.

Zaanoun, Adel. 2004. "Mother of Two Stuns Family With First Ever Hamas Female Suicide Attack." *Agence France Presse* (14 January) Lexis/Nexis, accessed 18 November 2005, pp. 1–2.

Zwerman, Gilda. 1995. "The Identity Vulnerable Activist and the Emergence of Post-New Left Armed, Underground Organizations in the United States." *Center for Studies of Social Change* (September) CIAO, accessed 14 December 2003, pp. 1–16.

28 "They haven't gone away, you know". Irish Republican "dissidents" and "armed struggle"

Jonathan Tonge

Introduction

The Irish Republican Army (IRA) has long been an organization prone to internal splits in its pursuit of British withdrawal from Northern Ireland and the establishment of a 32-county, united, independent Ireland. The Northern Ireland peace process and provisional IRA (PIRA) cease fires have revived the old adage of the first item on the Republican agenda being the split. Two small Republican groups, the Continuity IRA (CIRA) and the Real IRA (RIRA) emerged from the "mainstream" IRA in rejection to the constitutional and peace strategies adopted by PIRA and Sinn Féin. That such splits occurred is unsurprising, for two key reasons. First, an historically determinist view of Irish republicanism notes its tendency towards compromise and the subsequent marginalization of former "comrades". Second, the Republican movement has always been an eclectic, noncohesive body. Within its ranks have been found, in a far from exhaustive list, militant Nationalists, unreconstructed militarists, romantic Fenians, Gaelic Republicans, Catholic sectarians, northern defenders, international marxists, socialists, libertarians and liberal Protestants.

Given these factors, what may be remarkable about the current peace and political processes is the lack of defection to Republican ultra groups, following the acceptance by Sinn Féin of the 1998 Good Friday Agreement. The deal fell substantially short of the Republican goal of a united, independent Ireland, a point acknowledged by Sinn Féin. The relative unity of provisional Republicans is even more startling in view of the PIRA's willingness to decommission part of its weaponry, a move unprecedented in the history of the IRA. Critics of the PIRA/Sinn Féin strategy nonetheless emerged, such dissenters being a varied grouping. They range from anti-violence intellectuals and former prisoners, for whom a renewed armed campaign is viewed as pointless, to more traditional Republican diehards, unwilling to abandon violence as a route towards the achievement of a 32-county republic.[1]

These critics argue that a united Ireland cannot be achieved through the outworking of the Good Friday Agreement or similarly framed deal, even if Sinn Féin enjoys the benefits of, first, a presence in government north and south; second, cross-border bodies and, third, changing demographics with a growing Catholic-Nationalist vote in Northern Ireland. According to such critics, Sinn Féin has diluted its agenda; all-island bodies are merely symbolic and there is no demographic route to victory. The Catholic population, far from entirely Nationalist, rose by only 2 per cent between 1991 and 2001.[2] These Republican critics have commonly been labeled "dissidents", for rejecting Sinn Féin's strategy. The "dissidents" argue that they have remained true to Republican principles and the label "dissident" is perhaps misleading, offering a Herbert Morrison-type view of republicanism—that it is what (provisional) Sinn Féin does.

This article concentrates on these Republican groups unwilling to abandon the physical force tradition in Irish politics, exploring their historical development, rationale, strategy and impact.

The CIRA was the first "dissident" group to develop and, since 1996, has been responsible for scores of bombings, as has the RIRA emergent in 1997. Although most of the bombings have been minor, the groups combined have been responsible for 30 deaths, 29 in the bombing of Omagh in 1998.

The unfavorable political context to the maintenance of "armed struggle"

Republican ultras operate in perhaps the most unfavorable climate ever for the physical force tradition. Prior to 1998, Republicans could at least console themselves in that although their tactic of "armed struggle" to achieve Irish unity was eschewed, their ambitions were legitimized by the claim of the Irish Republic to Northern Ireland, embodied in the 1937 constitution. Partition was still seen as illegitimate and it remained a constitutional imperative of all Irish governments to seek its end, even if such governments did little to pursue unity. The PIRA was born in 1970, at a time when sections of the Irish government still strongly disliked the "Orange regime" in the north and British rule more generally. As such, the government lent some sympathy (if little else) to those who were prepared to complete the "unfinished business" of ending partition. The Irish government was critical of the excesses of the British security forces and Unionist government, which formed the basis for much PIRA recruitment. By the mid-1990s, however, it was evident that a political agreement would involve abandonment of Ireland's constitutional claim to Northern Ireland. In 1995, Bertie Ahern, the leader of the avowedly Republican party, Fianna Fail (then in opposition) conceded:

> Irish nationalism has changed. Irredentism is dead. I know of almost no one who believes it is feasible or desirable to attempt to incorporate Northern Ireland into the Irish Republic or into a united Ireland against the will of a majority there, either by force or coercion. Ireland is, in the view of the vast majority of us, one nation which is divided, because its two traditions have by and large chose up till now to live under two different jurisdictions. In my view we have to leave behind us the territorial claims.[3]

The constitutional claim to Northern Ireland was removed by the voters of the Irish Republic in the May 1998 referendum, only 6 per cent (85,748) opposing its downgrading to an aspiration and a further 1 per cent (17,064) spoiling their ballot paper. Although the modest turnout, of 56 per cent, meant that a majority of the electorate had still not endorsed partition, it was evident that an enforced reclaiming of Northern Ireland did not find many takers in the Irish Republic. Any legitimacy afforded to armed struggle as the "cutting edge" of Ireland's constitutional claim was now removed. While diehard Republicans were contemptuous of the government of the 26 counties, the constitutional claim of Articles 2 and 3 offered succor. The belief in a united Ireland was never more than a vague aspiration for many of the citizens of the Irish Republic (the same could be said of many Northern Catholics) and the lack of pressing desire for unity has always been a weakness for the Republican movement. There is evidence that the aspiration for unity remains as *extensive* as ever, but the lack of *intensity* remains problematic.[4]

There is some evidence that the British government can be moved by physical force republicanism, but such movement is not substantially in the direction of Irish unity. The large-scale bombings of London and Manchester undertaken by the Provisional IRA during the 1990s did force Sinn Féin into the political process. Indeed there is an argument that PIRA might have achieved more in terms of an Irish dimension to any settlement if, first, it had been able to maintain such bombings[5] and second, if Sinn Féin had negotiated strongly in the run-up to the Good Friday Agreement. Instead, Sinn Féin concentrated upon the release of prisoners, an issue necessary to sell the deal to the Republican base.[6] The British prime minister, in his first speech on the subject after the election in May 1997, made clear that British constitutional policy, based upon consent within Northern Ireland, would remain. Blair insisted that his agenda was "not a united Ireland", declaring that "a political settlement is not a slippery slope to a united Ireland. The government will not be persuaders for unity".[7]

Even worse for supporters of "armed struggle", the moves towards peace by the provisional IRA meant that any dissident IRA(s) could not enjoy a significant urban support base. A dissident campaign would have to be launched from border areas, reminiscent of the 1956–62 Operation Harvest Border Campaign, hardly an encouraging precedent for the IRA. That campaign petered out amid recrimination and acrimony, with Republicans claiming that the population had been "deliberately distracted from the supreme issue facing the Irish people—the unity and freedom of Ireland".[8] Dissident groups attempting to claim the IRA mantle and maintain armed struggle were confronted by a popular Republican party in Sinn Féin and a long-established, if largely redundant, provisional IRA. Sinn Féin enjoys substantial support among Catholics, particularly among the working class but with rising middle-class Catholic backing. Following the PIRA cease fire in 1994 (fractured in 1996 but restored in 1997), Sinn Féin's electoral support has increased markedly. The party overtook the Social Democratic and Labour Party (SDLP) as the majority representative of nationalism in the 2001 Westminster and council elections and confirmed its ascendancy with a substantial victory over the SDLP in the 2003 assembly elections.[9] The PIRA is the dominant paramilitary group in Nationalist working class areas, notably parts of West and North Belfast and is resistant to the formation of Republican rivals. This was evident in the PIRA's killing of the RIRA's Joe O'Connor in Belfast in 2000. The PIRA has "neutralized" rivals in earlier years, although its decisive movement against the self-styled Irish People's Liberation Organization (IPLO) in 1992 was partly due to that organization's involvement in the drug trade. Even "moderate" Republican dissenters from Sinn Féin's approach, who decline to support the CIRA or RIRA, have been marginalized.[10]

An unprecedented level of international hostility to terrorism, post 9/11 has also hindered dissident groups. The U.S. government declared the RIRA and CIRA terrorist organizations in May 2002 and prohibited fundraising for the dependants of prisoners. A paid FBI agent, operating largely outside the control of the Garda Siochana, was the main (almost sole) prosecution witness in the trial leading to the imprisonment of the RIRA leader, Michael McKevitt in 2003. The FBI also closed websites used to raise funds for RIRA and its political associates, the 32-County Sovereignty Committee.[11] Legislation designed to toughen measures against terrorism was introduced in the UK (in a single day) after the Omagh bombing and similar measures existing in the Irish Republic. Imprisoned dissident Republicans in the Irish Republic have also been subject to financial investigation by the Criminal Assets Bureau and, in one case, served with a 750,000 € bill, in relation to alleged smuggling. Republicans outside the mainstream could no longer look towards America for substantial funding. Instead, Republican ultras could only lament that "the Irish National Caucus, Ancient Order of Hibernians, Political Education Committee, Irish American Unity conference, Friends of Sinn Féin etc. have all been bought by the British peace process, which is not about Irish unity".[12]

The "dissident" critique of the provisionals

The Republican leadership has been able to prevent widespread defections to the dissidents, despite settling for a political deal it would have rejected dismissively during the 1970s and 1980s. The Good Friday Agreement keeps Northern Ireland in the UK for as long as the people there so desire. The Agreement created only six executive cross-border bodies, with their expansion conditional upon the approval of the Northern Ireland Assembly. As such, the Agreement, on a literal reading, is not transitory to a united Ireland. It provided, for the first time ever, Sinn Féin's acceptance of the "principle of consent" on Northern Ireland's constitutional future.[13] Previously, Sinn Féin had dismissed the idea of consent within Northern Ireland, a territory regarded as artificially created at partition and illegally held by Britain. The Agreement offers substantial internal change, but a reformed Northern Ireland under British jurisdiction was not the vision for which most Republicans had fought in a conflict in which almost 3,700 people died between 1969 and 1998. As Bernadette Sands-McKevitt, sister of Bobby Sands, the first imprisoned hunger striker to die in the Republican fasts of 1981 put it: "Bobby did not die for cross-border bodies with executive powers. He did not die for Nationalists to be equal citizens within the Northern Ireland state".[14] Republican ultras have highlighted the view of the Taoiseach's special adviser, Martin Mansergh, that "there is no evidence, let alone inevitability from international experience, that limited cross-border cooperation necessarily leads to political unification".[15]

Accordingly, dissidents argue that the Good Friday Agreement is "less than Sunningdale", the ill-fated power-sharing compromise of 1973–1974, which lasted a mere 5 months.[16] Outlining such criticism, Marian Price, a former PIRA prisoner, argues that "to suggest that a war was fought for what they have today…diminishes anybody who partook in that war, anybody who died in it and went out there and sacrificed their lives and liberty".[17] The dissidents offer a republicanism consistent with traditional doctrine, insisting that "the people who have changed their beliefs are the leaders of Sinn Féin, the likes of Gerry Adams".[18]

The critique offered by dissidents has not arrested the rapid pace of change within Sinn Féin. The party's President, Gerry Adams, informed the 2003 ard fheis (annual conference) that he envisaged a future without the IRA and that "full implementation of a new policing service" would lead to Sinn Féin taking seats on the board of the Police Service of Northern Ireland.[19] Such a move would result in Sinn Féin's leaders supporting imprisonment of erstwhile comrades, in a manner akin to Collins and De Yalera in previous eras. Republican critics adopt a historian's approach in their critique. Sinn Féin's support for the Good Friday Agreement and entry into the Northern Ireland Assembly at Stormont in 1999 are seen by Republican critics as analogous to the 1926 move of De Valera into Dail Eireann, the Irish parliament seen by Republican purists as illegal and partitionist. At that time, Fianna Fail possessed an armed wing, carried most Republicans and protested the evils of partition, yet the quest for power overtook the pursuit of Irish unity as the primary goal of the party.[20]

During the peace process of the 1990s and beyond, the extent of U-turns by mainstream Republicans was remarkable. The PIRA had always insisted that it would continue fighting until the British government offered a declaration of intent to leave Northern Ireland. The organization used the slogan "not an ounce, not a bullet" in rejecting calls for it to decommission its weaponry, yet by 2001, began decommissioning, seen as a "final betrayal" by ultras in order to "save the peace process".[21] In earlier difficult times for Republicans, such as the end of the failed 1956–1962 campaign, weapons were dumped, but never formally decommissioned at the behest of the "enemy". As late as 1997, Sinn Féin mobilized its supporters on a "no return to Stormont" platform. By late 1999, the party's ministers were running the health and education services of a state that Republicans had attempted to destroy. The commitment of the provisionals to the 32-county republic, even prior to the compromises of the peace process, has been questioned, McIntyre suggests that Catholic defenderism and responses to Unionist and British security force blunders provided stronger impetuses to the development of PIRA.[22] The lack of commitment to Republican theology may explain the apparent ease of policy reversal in recent years. However, the original PIRA leadership, if not many grassroots members, did pay homage to the 1916–1919 politics of rebellion.

A combination of factors, outlined here, explain the hegemony of PIRA/Sinn Féin within Republican circles and the relative lack of defections. First, there has been the marginalization of Republican ultras, both from governmental pressure as outlined above and through community ostracism. Second, the "military" performance of the ultras, described below, has often been abject, the obvious nadir being the 1998 bombing of Omagh, in which all 29 killed were civilians. The dissidents were dismissed as "militarily useless".[23] Third, there has been sufficient ambiguity in the messages from the PIRA to reassure hardliners, with a return to war being kept open as an option for a time. This reversion occurred once, in 1996–1997 and PIRA declines to say its war is over. Leaders of Sinn Féin have nonetheless stated that they have "ended the war in our streets'[24] and declared their opposition "to the use of threat of force".[25] The provisionals have tilted decisively towards the Adams' project of ending physical force Republicanism, but this was less obvious during the first PIRA cessation, the Sinn Féin president reassuring doubters that "They (the IRA) haven't gone away you know".[26] The Republican base was still being told, as late as 1999, that if negotiations fell apart, "we simply go back to what we know best", but post-Good Friday Agreement, a return to violence was not on the provisionals' agenda.[27]

Fourth, many of the credible "military" figures within PIRA have remained in the movement, often in prominent positions within Sinn Féin, a source of reassurance to doubters. Fifth, there is the belief, grounded in realism, that if PIRA, the best-equipped and most dangerous paramilitary group in Europe, could not shift the hold of the British government on Northern Ireland, tiny, ill-equipped "micro-groups" will barely register and the struggle becomes futile posturing. The newly moderate Republican movement insisted that "any struggle which adopts the tactic of armed force is in danger of succumbing to militarism…The continuation of the armed campaign itself becomes the objective," whereas Republicans were morally and politically bound to seek alternatives.[28] Indeed, supposed diehards such as Ruairi O'Bradaigh, president of the dissident Republican Sinn Féin (RSF), had themselves supported IRA cease fires during the mid-1970s, which had led to PIRA being run down.

Sixth, Sinn Féin electoral gains have helped mask the political reverses of the Good Friday Agreement, conveying an impression of a vibrant republicanism making gains at the expense of Unionist and Nationalist rivals. Seventh, Sinn Féin's ideological somersaults have been somewhat masked by the divisions within the Ulster Unionist Party, creating the impression that unionism, not Republicanism, is in retreat. Finally, support for "armed struggle" was always a minority taste among northern Catholics, few of whom thought a united Ireland was worth the sacrifices of an armed campaign, particularly one which provoked a determined Loyalist backlash. The overwhelming support of Catholics for the Good Friday Agreement, almost all voting in favor of a deal which kept Ireland partitioned for the foreseeable future, was indicative of the willingness of Catholics to prioritize internal political change over longer-term constitutional ambitions.[29] Furthermore, only a much smaller majority, 58 per cent, indicate they would support a united Ireland in a referendum (although only 20 per cent would vote against).[30] A majority of Nationalists nonetheless seem content with the assertion of a Sinn Féin ard chomhairle (executive) member, Francie Molloy, that "we are prepared to work an Executive. We are really prepared to administer British rule in Ireland for the foreseeable future. The very principle of partition is accepted and if the Unionists had that in 1920 they would be laughing".[31] From Sinn Féin and PIRA, the criticism of ultras was based upon (self)-awarded monopoly rights to Republican armed struggle, to which it was claimed there was "no alternative" prior to 1994.

Whatever the strength of the critique offered by "dissidents", the odds are stacked against the maintenance of a Republican armed struggle. Politically marginalized, short of weaponry, lacking popular support, heavily infiltrated and internally divided, Republican ultras plough infertile terrain. Nonetheless, the CIRA and RIRA continue to exist, fortified in the knowledge that mandates for armed struggle have never preceded the existence of armed groups in Ireland. In assessing their activity and rationale, it is necessary to examine how they evolved from their critique of Sinn Féin and the PIRA.

Purist and ultra: the continuity IRA and Republican Sinn Féin

Both the CIRA and RIRA and their political affiliates emerged from the PIRA and Sinn Féin. The CIRA and its political outlet, RSF are "purist" Republicans, opposing the "partitionist" institutions of the 26-county Irish state and those in Northern Ireland. They have their origins in the 1986 split in Sinn Féin over whether to lift the ban on elected party candidates taking seats in the Irish parliament. For Republican fundamentalists, the only true Dail Eireann was that established after Sinn Féin won the 1918 all-Ireland elections and created the First Dail. The election result and this parliament were vetoed by Unionists and the British government and replaced by "partitionist" political institutions; a 26-county parliament in the south and a six-county parliament in the north. Upon formation in 1969–70, PIRA and Provisional Sinn Féin (PSF) pledged allegiance to the First Dail, having split from what became "Official" IRA/Sinn Féin because it had voted to enter a "partitionist" parliament. Yet wheels began to turn circle by the mid-1980s, as abstention from Dail Eireann was seen by a majority within PIRA/PSF as inhibiting its development within the 26 counties. In 1986, the (provisional) Sinn Féin ard fheis voted to end abstention from the Irish Parliament, by a majority of 429 to 161. As the (then) IRA's Martin McGuinness told the conference:

> We are not at war with the government of the 26 counties…we have failed to convince a majority in the 26 counties that the Republican movement has any relevance to them. By ignoring reality we remain alone and isolated on the high altar of abstentionism, divorced from the people of the 26 counties and easily dealt with by those who wish to defeat us.[32]

McGuinness prefaced his remarks by offering "a commitment on behalf of the leadership that we have no intention of going into Westminster or Stormont" and a promise to continue the "war".[33] Thirteen years later, he was a minister at Stormont, dismissed as a "crown minister" by Republican ultras.[34] Sinn Féin's move has been seen as the beginning of the end for traditional republicanism in Ireland.[35] Opponents of change, led by founders of the provisional movement, Ruairi O'Bradaigh and Daithi O'Conaill, left the conference hall to announce the establishment of Republican Sinn Féin. The fundamentalist wing argued, with prescience, that the end of abstention in respect of Leinster House would lead eventually to Provisional Sinn Féin taking seats in Stormont. With the PIRA/Sinn Féin leadership insistent that the "war" could continue until the British left Northern Ireland and the IRA able to increase its campaign following the arrival of Libyan arms, there were few defectors to RSF.

O'Bradaigh's supporters propagandized through three editions of *Republican Bulletin* between November 1986 and April 1987. This was replaced in May 1987 by its existing publication, *Saoirse* (freedom). A feature of *Saoirse* is the amount of space devoted to criticisms of the Irish "Free State", with the 26 counties subject to almost as much criticism as British rule in Northern Ireland. The 26 counties are viewed as neo-colonial and the north is seen as a directly controlled British colony. There are "no stepping stones" to Irish unity according to RSF.[36] British withdrawal from Northern Ireland within the lifetime of a Westminster parliament is demanded, with a federal Ireland (Eire Nua) to be established, comprising parliaments for each of the historic four Irish provinces.[37] The Ulster parliament would offer some autonomy for Unionists. All this is identical to Provisional Sinn Féin policy until federalism was overturned in 1983. Republican Sinn Féin views involvement in pan-Nationalist alliances as a dilution of Republicanism, leading to acceptance of a form of Unionist veto upon constitutional change.[38] The belief in a distinctive Irish nation-state and unfettered national sovereignty is evident in RSF's political approach, which opposes European Union expansion. Unionists are viewed as Irish "fellow countrymen" (sic) who would come to accept Irish unity in the event of British withdrawal.[39]

Although a Continuity Army Council was formally created at the time of the split with the provisionals, a military wing to RSF did not emerge until 1996. Indeed, RSF occasionally denies it is the political wing of the Continuity IRA, but *Saoirse* publicizes the activities of CIRA and the link is symbiotic. The CIRA emerged with a 1,200 lb bombing of a Fermanagh hotel in 1996. The CIRA retained a "Dad's Army" image nonetheless, due to its association with RSF, seen as an elderly group of diehard Republicans still grounded in the "pike and Thompson gun" anti-treatyism of the early 20th century. This image persists, even though it was reported that the CIRA had used a small quantity of semtex in an attack on government offices in Londonderry in 1997.[40] Among other operations, the CIRA attacked the residence of the British Secretary of State for Northern Ireland in 2001; bombed a police training college in East Belfast in April 2002; attempted to leave a large bomb in city center Belfast in October 2002; injured six police officers in an Enniskillen bombing in February 2003 and planted a bomb near Dail Eireann to coincide with the visit of the British Prime Minister in May 2003. Republican Sinn Féin struggles to penetrate urban areas, but now has a permanent office in west Belfast. Backed by former arms suppliers or supporters of the PIRA, it has established fundraising bodies in the U.S., Cummann na Saoirse, with (small) branches in seven cities in Northeast America.[41] However, in common with the RIRA, the CIRA has been penetrated by informers. This has led to dozens of arrests, the seizure of large arms caches and the discovery of a "training camp" in Waterford in the Irish Republic in August 2003.

Republican Sinn Féin and the CIRA adopt a traditional, historical determinist approach to republicanism. According to the President of RSF, the "overwhelming" Irish historical lesson is "that there has always been resistance" and the CIRA's actions are "indications that militant republicanism is not dead", even if, "instead of a flame they are only a spark".[42] Resistance to colonial rule is justified on historical (tradition) and comparative (utility) grounds. The latter argument is based, first, upon a belief that the British have never left colonies on an entirely voluntary, peaceful basis and, second, that colonial powers leave countries when pressured through force, even where there is an indigenous minority population in favor of the colonial power (British Unionists are likened to French Algerians in this respect). British declarations of a lack of selfish strategic or economic interest in Northern Ireland have not impacted upon such Republicans. Republican Sinn Féin places itself within the Wolfe Tone tradition of unity of Catholic, Protestant and dissenter within an independent Ireland, a mantle claimed by Republicans of various other hues, even those who accept partition.[43] The CIRA and its associates are predictably dismissive of the diversion of Republican politics into social and cultural campaigns around the equality agenda of the Good Friday Agreement. Such militants criticize the manner in which "the provisional leadership are not fighting for 'Brits out'—instead they seek parity of esteem … We are not a defence committee; what we want is a campaign against the English".[44]

The Real IRA and the 32-county sovereignty movement: militarist and split

The RIRA and its political outlet, the 32-County Sovereignty Movement (32 CSM) have their origins in the transformation of Sinn Féin and PIRA during the peace process of the 1990s. Disinterested in RSF's anachronistic "purist" concerns over Dail Eireann, these dissidents stayed with the provisional Republican movement after 1986, reassured that the military campaign to remove British sovereignty from Northern Ireland remained as strong as ever. The catalyst for the formation of RIRA was the restoration of the PIRA's cease fire in July 1997, an event that occurred despite the British prime minister's insistence that there could not be a united Ireland. Although unhappy with the first cease fire, the PIRA Quartermaster, Michael McKevitt, had stayed with the organization, which had in any case temporarily returned to violence in 1996–1997. Renewal of the cease fire led to his resignation, along with that of one other senior figure in the PIRA. McKevitt was instrumental in forming the new IRA, being joined soon afterwards by nearly 40 serving or former PIRA members.[45] Although few others followed, the RIRA's expertise in the supply and construction of weapons made it a bigger threat than the CIRA. Despite drawing supporters from border areas less prone to leaks than elsewhere when PIRA was fully operational, the RIRA was heavily infiltrated by informers from the outset, with large bombs intercepted in March and April 1998.

Within Sinn Féin, the 32 CSM claimed to act as a pressure group, determined that the leadership did not "sell-out" in any political Agreement. The group had been unhappy with Sinn Féin's adherence to the six Mitchell Principles of nonviolence in 1996. The 32 CSM ruled out entry to Stormont and rejected any political deal maintaining the "Unionist veto". These dissidents were removed from Sinn Féin, speeding the Adams-McGuinness leadership's path to the political compromise of the Good Friday Agreement. According to Bernadette Sands-McKevitt, one of the founders of the 32 CSM, there was "nothing in the Agreement to suggest that there was a stepping-stone approach to a united Ireland".[46] Members of the 32 CSM, including a Sinn Féin councilor, were physically barred from entering Sinn Féin's ard fheis in April 1998 and the split was complete.[47] Without indicating its means, the 32 CSM declared its objective to "successfully pressure the British into relinquishing its (sic) claim to sovereignty over part of our country and withdrawing from Ireland".[48]

Concurrently, the RIRA launched its campaign in early 1998. It first appeared mounting roadblocks in South Armagh, when it awarded itself the title "Real IRA".[49] Prior to the Omagh bombing, RIRA bombs destroyed the town centers of Moira and Banbridge. Better armed than the CIRA, the RIRA further attracted a small influx of recruits after the first act of decommissioning by the PIRA in Autumn 2001.[50] The leadership of Sinn Féin acknowledged the sensitivity of the decommissioning issue, indicating that it had "caused little earthquakes" within the Republican constituency.[51]

Post-Omagh, RIRA has been beset by problems. Hampered by arrests and intercepted operations, a section of the organization decided that continued armed struggle against such overwhelming odds was pointless. Although unspoken, it was thought a prolonged cease fire or disbandment might open the possibility of early prison releases. Tactical divisions came to a head in October 2002 when the organization split. A number of RIRA prisoners and some non-incarcerated supporters outlined their views in a newly launched journal, *Forum*, a surprisingly professional-looking outlet. In the first edition in February 2003, they urged the RIRA leadership, which existed "in name only" to "stand down with ignominy", claiming it had neglected prisoners; fraternized with "criminals" and lacked strategy.[52] Most frankly, the journal argued that "it is obvious that there is no support for armed struggle in Ireland at this time."[53] Given that the RIRA had been formed to maintain an unpopular "armed struggle", this point appeared curious. Skeptics believed that the journal emerged as an indirect means of boosting the case of Michael McKevitt, although the publication did not figure during his trial.[54] Morale within RIRA was reportedly so low in 2002 that it sought a cease-fire deal with the Irish government, by which its 39 prisoners in the Irish Republic would be released.[55] Nonetheless, one faction of the RIRA continued its military campaign.

The publication *Sovereign Nation* propagandized the 32 CSM's "defense of the nation", especially its lodging of a challenge at the United Nations of the perpetuation of partition through the Good Friday Agreement. A 32 CSM delegation attended a session of the United Nations Human Rights Commission in 2001, on the basis that partition was a violation of "human rights" of sovereignty. To the derision of the Irish government, the delegation demanded "an end to Britain's illegal occupation in Northern Ireland and the restoration of Ireland's national sovereignty".[56]

A very thin, irregular pamphlet, *Beir Bua!* emerged in February 2001, with a brief "war news" column, although it was a pale shadow of the coverage under the same title found in the Provisionals' *An Phoblacht/Republican News* prior to 1994. It urged Republican unity, a most unlikely prospect given the decisive nature of the splits, insisting that it was "essential for the provisional movement to call time on the Good Friday Agreement, to sit down with the rest of us and plan how to defend Irish sovereignty".[57]

Political differences between the political outlets of the dissident organizations have created tensions, even if there has been "cooperation on the ground" between the paramilitary wings.[58] Amalgamation was an aim of the RIRA leadership, which had little regard for the military capacity of the CIRA and wanted to modernize the IRA, if necessary engaging in new practices, such as cyber-terrorism. However, the 32 CSC and RIRA were derided by the CIRA and its associates for wanting "total control" and for having "split from the Provos 10 years too late".[59] For its part, the CIRA declared that "we have no animosity towards the 'Real' IRA, but we are two entirely separate organizations and that is the way we will stay. There is no question of even cooperating with the 'Real' IRA".[60] Despite this assertion and the (irrelevant to Ireland's population) political wrangling over recognition of Dail Eireann between political wings, there has been cooperation between the RIRA and CIRA.[61] The CIRA denied responsibility for the Omagh bombing, although it emerged at the McKevitt trial that its members had planted the bomb and one of its members was convicted separately of a planning role in the atrocity.[62] The two groups have also struggled to form a representative group for their prisoners. For RIRA, this was difficult given its own split in 2002, but even more problematic have been differences between CIRA and RIRA. The Irish Republican Prisoners' Welfare Association aimed to act as an overall representative body, although it was seen as a RIRA creation, and RSF often prefers to campaign alone on behalf of CIRA prisoners.

Representatives of mainstream republicanism condemned dissident groups for engaging in precisely the type of operation they supported until the PIRA cease fires.[63] Sinn Féin argued that dissidents "have no strategy to secure a united Ireland and no support within the community".[64] Both claims were difficult to refute, even if both criticisms could be thrown back; Sinn Féin's own unification strategy was far from apparent and support for PIRA had been very much a minority Nationalist taste. When the RIRA killed a civilian worker at an army base, Sinn Féin's Martin McGuinness declared: "This was not a blow for Irish freedom. It was nothing of the sort".[65] Ten years earlier, the PIRA had killed eight civilians for working at an army base at Teebane. The CIRA dismissed provisional calls for its disbandment as emanating from "nauseating hypocrites".[66]

The continuing "armed struggle"

The bulk of "dissident" operations have been carried out by the RIRA. Between January 1999 and July 2002, the RIRA mounted 80 operations.[67] In August 2002, it claimed its first victim since 1998, a bomb at a territorial army base in Londonderry killing a civilian contractor. Like the CIRA, the RIRA has had more operations intercepted than it has executed, indicative of penetration by informers. In June 2003, a 1,200lb-primed bomb, one of the largest made in Northern Ireland, was discovered in Londonderry and explosives were discovered in County

Table 28.1 Real IRA bombings resulting in death or injury, 1998–2003

Location	Date	Deaths / Injuries
Moira	February 1998	7 injured
Banbridge	August 1998	35 injured
Omagh	August 1998	29 killed, 310 injured
BBC HQ, London	March 2001	1 injured
Ealing, London	August 2001	11 injured
Magilligan Army Camp	February 2002	1 injured
Ballymena (on police)	June 2002	2 injured
Portadown (on police)	July 2002	2 injured
Londonderry TA Camp	August 2002	1 killed
Belfast ("punishment")	September 2003	1 killed

Monaghan during the same month. A minority of RIRA actions have caused death or injury as detailed in Table 28.1.

Only 31 of the 101 killings by Republican and Loyalist paramilitaries between 1998, the year of the Good Friday Agreement, and July 2002 were committed by Republican dissidents and the two dissident groups were responsible for only 20 per cent of the 1,833 shootings (excluding "punishment" shootings) and bombings during this period.[68] The vast bulk of bombings, in particular, were committed by Loyalists. The scale of dissident IRA attacks is limited, compared even to previous periods when the IRA was isolated. In 1939, for example, the IRA detonated 127 bombs in its campaign in England, killing five civilians, compared to seven such bombings by the RIRA in 2000–2001, while the 1956–1962 campaign in Northern Ireland had an annual average of 100 operations.

The most significant dissident bombing, at Omagh, was also the most disastrous. The public outcry led to demonstrations even in the supposed RIRA heartland of Dundalk. Allied to warnings from PIRA to desist (Sinn Féin, for the first time, condemned a Republican bombing) a Real IRA cease fire followed. Although this was never formally revoked, the RIRA returned to violence in 2000. The Irish government was sufficiently concerned by the existence of the RIRA for the Taoiseach, Bertie Ahern, to send his own special adviser, Martin Mansergh, to meet the group's leader, Michael McKevitt twice, in July and December 1998, to "underline the Irish government's belief that there was no future in armed struggle" and to insist that the RIRA should disband.[69] Politically sensitive, the contact was initially denied by Ahern, who informed Dail Eireann in 2002 that "no member of the government" had met the RIRA, technically true, given Mansergh's status as an *ad hoc* special adviser. Mansergh had played an important role in steering the PIRA towards peace, but found RIRA unreceptive. The Fianna Fail senator claimed that "the gardai (Irish police) regarded them as a serious threat from the very beginning"[70] a position endorsed by the chief constable of the Police Service of Northern Ireland, Hugh Orde.[71] The previous chief constable had argued that, in respect to diehard Republican determination to disrupt the peace and political processes, "desire far exceeds their ability".[72] In 2003, with political institutions suspended, 68 per cent of Ulster Unionist Party supporters and 53 per cent of Sinn Féin supporters believed it "probable" or "very probable" that dissident Republican paramilitary groups would become more active.[73]

Such "recognition" by the Irish government might be viewed as a rare success by the dissidents. The other "gain" was the decision in 2003 of the Northern Ireland Security Minister to segregate Republican and Loyalist prisoners in Maghaberry Prison. The swelling number (approaching 100 by September 2003) of Republican prisoners was indicative of the extent to which the organizations had been penetrated.

Despite the protestations of the British government that there would be no return to a "Maze-type situation", it was apparent that such prisoners were not entirely being treated as common criminals, given that their organizations were now recognized. The segregation followed a short "dirty protest" by Republicans, in a manner briefly reminiscent of that undertaken in the late 1970s. There was little to indicate a wave of sympathy similar to that arising from the Republican hunger strikes of 1980–1981. Nonetheless, the ultras hoped to attract sympathy to their cause via the still potentially emotive issue of the holding of Irish prisoners in British jails. In the Irish Republic, Republican prisoners occupied their own wings in Portlaoise jail, but as in the North, were not awarded special category status. By August 2001, E-wing in Portlaoise contained 44 RIRA, three CIRA and 10 Irish National Liberation Army (INLA) prisoners, the latter group committed to a cease fire.[74] The assertion by a representative of Sinn Féin, many of whose own members had been incarcerated, that there were no political prisoners, merely increased determination on the issue.[75]

Despite the insistence of both groups of ultras that the problem was one of British occupation of Ireland, neither has engaged "crown forces" to a great extent, although attacks upon the police increased after mid-2002. After a period of quiet following the Omagh bombing, the RIRA revival in 2000 saw a bombing campaign in London, including a highly publicized attack outside the BBC and a similar car bomb in Ealing, which injured 11 people. This campaign spread to Birmingham in the autumn of 2001, but the RIRA cell was arrested and imprisoned shortly afterwards. Twenty-seven attacks were mounted by dissident Republicans in 2001, but made little impact. A RIRA attempt to establish an arms supply line from Iraq was thwarted after its team was arrested in Slovakia and convicted in May 2002. In 2003, it was claimed that RIRA was compiling lists of targets using hospital records and the Police Service of Northern Ireland warned 300 individuals that their names appeared on RIRA target lists. Devoid of "operators" in England, the CIRA has confined its attacks to Northern Ireland, generally attempting to bomb police stations and government offices, although "soft" targets such as hotels and shops have also sufficed. The CIRA launched an incendiary attack in 2001 in Newry to coincide with the visit of the Secretary of State, John Reid. In 2003, the RIRA began a campaign of intimidation at members of District Policing Partnerships, attacking vehicles and forcing resignations.

Is there *any* support for dissident republicanism?

Support for Republican armed struggle has always been a small minority taste in the Irish Republic and a larger minority stance in Northern Ireland. Sinn Féin won seats in the 1950s and two imprisoned anti-H Block candidates were elected to Dail Eireann in 1982, but the overall electoral message was one of rejection of political violence. During PIRA's campaign, Sinn Féin only averaged 2 per cent of the vote south of the border. A vote for Sinn Féin in Northern Ireland could readily be construed as a vote for armed struggle, not least because Sinn Féin candidates were mandated by party ardfheisanna (annual conferences) during the 1980s to offer unqualified support for the PIRA's campaign. The PIRA's cease fire has been accompanied by increased support for Sinn Féin, to 7 per cent, and the party won five seats in Dail Eireann in the 2002 Irish election. In Northern Ireland, one-third of Catholics supported Sinn Féin during the PIRA campaign, a figure that has risen to over 50 per cent as PIRA has maintained its cease fire and approaches disbandment, whether formal or evolutionary. A modern vote for Sinn Féin is cast for the stouter defender of the Nationalist ethnic bloc in a polity which has oscillated between consociational power sharing and direct British rule from Westminster in the post-Good Friday Agreement years.

Republican Sinn Féin and the 32 CSM disdain the electoral arena, although RSF does have a tiny number of elected councilors in the Irish Republic. As such, it is difficult to measure precisely their support, if any. Republican Sinn Féin wished to field an imprisoned CIRA member in the 2001 Westminster election, but was barred from doing so under electoral rules created after the British government was embarrassed by the election of Bobby Sands in 1981. Republican Sinn Féin urged voters in West Belfast to spoil their ballot papers. Over 1,500 did, way above the average of less than 300, but the protest was dwarfed by the amassing of three-quarters of all votes cast by Gerry Adams. In the 2003 assembly elections, RSF urged a boycott of the poll. Although the fall in turnout in majority Nationalist constituencies, at 9.4 per cent, was above the 5.3 per cent fall in majority Unionist areas, overall turnout in majority Nationalist areas, at 68.3 per cent, remained comfortably higher than the 60.1 per cent turnout in majority Unionist areas and RSF's call had little impact.[76] Sinn Féin hegemony has been a source of frustration to dissidents. Rory Dougan, of the 32-County Sovereignty Movement, urged the Republican grassroots to "seriously consider whether their allegiance is to one particular political party or to the goal of a 32-county, sovereign island".[77]

In October 2002, RSF and 32 CSM were listed as an option for the first time, in a BBC Northern Ireland *Hearts and Minds* poll examining which organization best represented the electorate's views.[78] The support for these Republican ultras amounted to 7.1 per cent of Nationalist preferences, obviously way below the figure for Sinn Féin of 49.8 per cent, but, nonetheless, perhaps surprisingly high given that the Omagh atrocity had occurred only 4 years earlier. Thirty-eight per cent of Nationalists supported Republican Sinn Féin, with a further 3.3 per cent backing the 32-County Sovereignty Committee. Given the propensity to provide pollsters with "socially acceptable" answers (Sinn Féin's support is still underestimated in such surveys), it is possible that the actual level of support for dissidents might be even higher. Against this, the poll was undertaken shortly after the nadir of devolved government at Stormont, the police raid upon Sinn Féin's office and subsequent collapse of the institution, a period when hard-line positions might more readily have been adopted.

The Republican theology of dissident groups dispenses with the need for mandates, no more required than was sanction for the subsequently legitimized 1916 rebellion against British rule. For the CIRA and RIRA and their political outlets, the mandate was provided historically in the last all-Ireland elections in 1918 and it remains a right to resist British rule. Until the 1990s, the PIRA regarded itself as government in waiting, a view hardly shared by the majority of Irish people and one abandoned by Sinn Féin in the 1990s. For CIRA, RIRA and their followers, the right of unfettered national self-determination must be obtained, by force if necessary. Support for armed struggle is viewed as consequential upon a campaign, rather than a prerequisite, with historical lessons of support "following on" provided by the rebellions of 1916 and 1970.

The dissidents offer an undiluted form of national self-determination, based upon the sovereignty of the Irish people as a single unit, although neither have indicated whether they would accept the result of an all-island referendum on unity (not that it will ever be awarded). Gerry Adams spent much of the 1980s engaging in private dialogue through an intermediary with the Irish and British governments in attempting to create a formula for Irish self-determination.[79] What emerged, following public dialogue with the SDLP leader, John Hume, was a heavily qualified form of codetermination, in which the future of Ireland, North and South was determined separately in either jurisdiction. For dissidents (and some others), this amounted to merely a modernization of a Unionist veto thinly concealed in "greener" language, given that even 100 per cent support for unity of the island in the Irish Republic would be nullified by rejection of the idea in the north. Irish unity is acknowledged as "the legitimate wish of a majority of the people of the island of Ireland" in the Good Friday Agreement, but the mechanics of self-determination precluded this as an option of choice for the island's citizens.[80]

Conclusion

Dissident Irish Republicans carry with them the "end-of-history" approach that has characterized a previous era of republicanism, in which the British withdraw from their "last colony" and an independent, 32-county Irish nation-state is established. Yet it is doubtful if even dissident groups believe that an armed struggle will remove the British government from Ireland, whatever their utterances, given the failure of PIRA to achieve such an outcome. Their *raison d'être* therefore is first, to emphasize the "colonial" nature of British rule, by (re)creating the need for repressive and visible security measures in Northern Ireland, giving the impression that the British Army and the police service are "forces of occupation". Second, continued violence stresses the abnormality of Northern Ireland. Entry into political institutions, as Sinn Féin has undertaken, allows the state to embed, whereas the logic of continued resistance is that Northern Ireland is not allowed to advance from a position of being, hitherto, a failed and insecure political entity. For Republican ultras, public support is viewed as a useful, but not necessary, prerequisite for a campaign. Instead they hope to keep alive what has been described by an anti-Republican commentator as a "sneaking regard for the violent Republican tradition", which, if it exists, is difficult to quantify.[81]

The Real and Continuity IRAs and their supporters carry the same weaknesses as previous generations of Republicans; a lack of cognizance of the Unionist position as the British presence in Ireland (whatever the federalism of Eire Nua offered by RSF); disinterest or hostility, especially post-Omagh, from the majority of the Irish people and an inability to sustain a campaign of violence. To these traditional problems can be added newer difficulties; Sinn Féin's dominance among Nationalists in Northern Ireland; the abandonment of even a rhetorical drive to Irish unity by the Dublin government and the broader contexts to national sovereignty in the modern age, diminishing the nation-state, even allowing that northern Nationalists have never truly had theirs. Militant Republicanism has, of course, survived bleak times in previous eras and uncertainty over the Good Friday Agreement has maintained its presence, solace for the lingering bearers of the Republican physical force tradition.

Notes

1 See the magazine, *Fourthwrite*, first published in Spring 2000. Although a broadly dissident forum of the Irish Republican Writers Group, *Fourthwrite* also published contributions from mainstream Sinn Féin members scorning Republican ultras. See, for example, the contribution by Sean Hayes, a Sinn Féin councilor in issue 2, Summer 2000. *The Blanket* later emerged as another dissident forum.

2 Northern Ireland Census, *Religion Report 2001* (Belfast: HMSO 2002).

3 Quoted in P. Bew, P. Teague and H. Patterson, *Between War and Peace. The Political Future of Northern Ireland* (London: Lawrence and Wishart 1997) p.228.

4 B. Hayes and I. McAllister, "British and Irish Public Opinion Towards the Northern Ireland Problem", *Irish Political Studies* 11 (1996) pp.61–82.

5 E. Moloney, *A Secret History of the IRA* (London: Penguin 2002).

6 T. Hennessey, *The Northern Ireland Peace Process* (Dublin: Gill and Macmillan 2000).

7 Quoted in J. Tonge, *Northern Ireland: Conflict and Change* (London: Pearson 2002) p.179.

8 IRA statement at the closure of its 1956–1962 campaign, cited in T.P. Coogan, *The IRA* (London: Fontana 1989) p.418.

9 Sinn Féin won 23.5 per cent of first preference votes in 2003, compared to the SDLP's 17.0 per cent. The trend of Sinn Féin dominance over the SDLP appears irreversible.

10 The most prominent intellectual critic is Anthony McIntyre, a contributor to the journals *Fourthwrite* and *The Blanket*. McIntyre was forced from his Belfast home in 2000.

11 For example, in 2002, the internet service provider Hypervine was threatened with closure if it did not close the website IRAradio.com.

12 "A Final Wake-Up Call to the Irish American Community", *Saoirse* 132 (April 1998) p.13.

13 For discussions on the modern nature of Republicanism (albeit excluding a dissident/ultra perspective), see J. Coakley (ed), *Changing Shades of Orange and Green* (Dublin: UCD 2002).
14 Quoted in Hennessey (note 6) p.112.
15 Quoted in *Saoirse* 162 (October 2000) p.1.
16 *Saoirse* 134 (June 1998).
17 Quoted in R. English, *Armed Struggle* (London: Macmillan 2003) p.317.
18 Quoted in "IRA Dissidents Claim Mantle of Adams's Father", *Times*, 7 September 2002, p.2.
19 Speech to Sinn Féin ard-fheis, Dublin, May 2003.
20 *Sovereign Nation* 4/2 (June/July 2001).
21 *Sovereign Nation* 4/5 (December 2001) p.1.
22 A. McIntyre, "Modern Irish Republicanism. The Product of British State Strategies", *Irish Political Studies* 10 (1995) pp.97–122; and "Modern Irish Republicanism and the Belfast Agreement: Chickens Coming Home to Roost, or Turkeys Celebrating Christmas?" in R. Wilford (ed), *Aspects of the Belfast Agreement* (Oxford: Oxford University Press 2001) pp.202–22.
23 Martin McGuinness, BBC Northern Ireland *Newsline*, 25 September 2003.
24 Mitchel McLaughlin, Chair of Sinn Féin, quoted in *Sunday Independent*, 19 October 2003, p.10.
25 Gerry Adams, Statement on Sinn Féin's position on the peace process, 21 October 2003.
26 Quoted in Moloney (note 5) p.437.
27 Quoted in "Talks Under Threat as IRA is Primed", *Daily Telegraph*, 17 November 1997, p.2.
28 *An Phoblacht/Republican News*, 20 August 1998.
29 B. Hayes and I. McAllister, "Who Voted for Peace? Public Support for the 1998 Northern Ireland Agreement", *Irish Political Studies* 16 (2001) pp.73–94.
30 R. MacGinty, "What our Politicians Should Know", *Research Update. Ark. Northern Ireland Social and Political Archive* 18 (April 2003).
31 Quoted in *Sunday Times*, 28 March 2003.
32 Quoted in B. Feeney, *Sinn Féin. A Hundred Turbulent Years* (Dublin: O'Brien 2002) p.332.
33 Quoted in B. Lynn, "Tactic or Principle? The Evolution of Republican Thinking on Abstentionism in Ireland, 1970–1998", *Irish Political Studies* 17/2 (2002) pp.74–94.
34 *Saoirse* 152 (December 1999).
35 M. Ryan, *War and Peace in Ireland. Britain and the IRA in the New World Order* (London: Pluto 1994).
36 *Saoirse* 1 (May 1987).
37 Republican Sinn Féin, *Towards a Peaceful Ireland* (Dublin: RSF 2001).
38 "Provisional Leadership has 'Abandoned Basis for War'", *Saoirse* 101 (September 1995).
39 See, for example, "Pledge to Pull Together Republican Constituency'", *Saoirse* 99 (June–July 1995) p.9.
40 *Times*, 5 November 1997.
41 "Aiming for a Federal Ireland", *Irish Post*, 9 November 1996.
42 Quoted in "Republican Diehard Awaits New Militancy", *Times*, 13 February 2003, p.4.
43 See, for example, "New Democracy, New Ireland", *Saoirse* 191 (March 2003) p.1.
44 "Continuity IRA to Target British Crown Forces", *Saoirse* 121 (May 1997) p.5.
45 B. O'Brien, *The Long War. The IRA and Sinn Féin* (Dublin: O'Brien 1999).
46 Quoted in E. Mallie and D. McKittrick, *Endgame in Ireland* (London: Hodder and Stoughton 2001) p.258.
47 *Sunday Tribune*, 19 April 1998.
48 *Sovereign Nation* 2/6 (2000) p.5
49 T. Harnden, *Bandit Country. The IRA and South Armagh* (London: Hodder and Stoughton 1999).
50 See a particularly well-sourced report "Disgruntled Provisionals Swell Real IRA Ranks", *Irish News*, 1 December 2001.
51 "IRA Arms Move 'Caused Little Earthquakes' in Republicanism", *Irish News*, 28 November 2001.
52 *Forum* 1 (February 2003).
53 Ibid., p.1.
54 Private information from two sources.
55 "Real IRA holds secret cease-fire talks with Dublin", *Times*, 2 July 2002.
56 *Sovereign Nation* 4/2 (June/July 2001).
57 *Beir Bua!* 12 (2003) p.3.
58 BBC Northern Ireland, *Spotlight*, 4 March 2003.
59 *Times*, 16 August 2003.
60 *Irish Times*, 21 February 2003; and *Saoirse* 191 (March 2003).
61 BBC Northern Ireland, *Spotlight*, 4 March 2003.

62   For the statement of denial, see *Saoirse* 197 (September 2003).
63   For a withering critique, see S. Breen, "A Word with No Meaning", *Fortnight* 407 (October 2002) p.6.
64   "Chaos Blamed on Dissident Group", *Irish News*, 1 December 2001.
65   "Three Held as Real IRA is Blamed for Killing of Taman", *Times*, 2 October 2002.
66   *Saoirse* 154 (February 2000).
67   Ibid.
68   Police Service of Northern Ireland, *Chief Constable's Report 2002–03* (Belfast: PSNI 2003); and *Times*, 25 July 2002.
69   *Sunday Times* (Irish) 19 October 2003.
70   "Mansergh Did Not Lie", *Sunday Times* (Irish ed) 19 October 2003.
71   http://news.bbc.co.uk/1/hi/northern_ireland/3185806.
72   Sir Ronnie Flanagan, *BBC Breakfast with Frost*, 4 November 2001.
73   C. Irwin, "Devolution and the State of the Northern Ireland Peace Process" *The Global Review of Ethnopolitics* 2 (March–June 2003) pp.71–82.
74   "Overcrowding Fear at Portlaoise", *Sunday Business Post*, 5 August 2001.
75   Martin Ferris, Sinn Féin, quoted in *Saoirse* 167 (March 2001) p.1.
76   Majority Nationalist defined as those electing more Nationalist candidates than any other type in each six-member constituency (nine in total); majority Unionist those electing more Unionist candidates than any other type (seven in total). Two constituencies did not have Unionist or Nationalist majorities re-elected candidates.
77   Quoted in "Republicans: Dissident Factions Hope to Recruit Those Who Still Believe in Violence", *Independent*, 25 October 2001, p.2.
78   www.news.bbc.co.uk/1/hi/northern_ireland, 12 November 2002.
79   Moloney (note 5).
80   *The Agreement* (Belfast: Northern Ireland Office 1998) p.2.
81   See E. O' Hanlon, "Michael McKevitt is Not the Only Monster", *Sunday Independent*, 10 August 2003.

29 Homegrown jihadist terrorism in the United States

A new and occasional phenomenon?

Lorenzo Vidino

On 9 March 1977, a group of 12 armed men, all African-American converts to Islam who called themselves Hanafi Muslims, brought havoc to the central area of Washington, D.C. Divided in three groups, the men stormed into the city's Islamic Center, City Council chambers, and the headquarters of B'nai B'rith, America's oldest Jewish organization. Wielding rifles, shotguns, and machetes, the men took about 150 people hostage.[1] They were led by Hamaas Abdul Khaalis, an African-American convert who had served as secretary to Malcolm X at Harlem's Temple #7 under the name of Ernest 2X McGhee before leaving the Nation of Islam to form his own sect, which referred to a more traditional form of Sunni Islam.[2] After seizing the buildings, Khaalis issued a series of demands. First he wanted authorities to hand over to him the five Nation of Islam members who had been arrested for brutally murdering several members of his family, including some infants, four years earlier. Then he demanded that authorities ban the showing of the movie *Mohammad, Messenger of God*, which he deemed offensive to Islam. This second request was granted and theaters nationwide stopped showing the controversial movie. The siege ended two days later, after extensive negotiations led by the Egyptian, Pakistani, and Iranian ambassadors to the United States, who read the men passages from the Quran about compassion and mercy. A security guard and a journalist were killed during the siege, and several others, including Washington mayor-to-be Marion Barry, were injured.

Three years later, another violent incident motivated by political Islam bloodied the streets of America's capital. On the morning of 22 July 1980, Ali Akbar Tabatabai, a former press attaché at the Iranian Embassy in Washington, was shot dead on the doorstep of his Bethesda home.[3] Since the 1979 Revolution, Tabatabai had been a staunch opponent of the Iranian regime and authorities immediately suspected a political motive for his murder. What they quickly came to learn was that Tabatabai's killer was a Long Island native and former Baptist named David Theodore Belfield. Belfield, an African-American convert to Sunni Islam who also went by the name Dawud Salahuddin, had been hired by Iranian officials to conduct the assassination. Belfield left America a few hours after the murder, reportedly finding shelter in the Geneva home of Said Ramadan, the right-hand man of Muslim Brotherhood founder Hassan al Banna and one of the movement's most important leaders of the last fifty years. Belfield eventually reached Iran, where he has been living ever since. "I was primed for violence, and I thought about cratering the White House a quarter century before Al Qaeda did," said Belfield in a 2002 interview with *The New Yorker*. "It would be accurate to say that my biggest aspiration was to bring America to its knees, but I didn't know how."[4]

The Washington siege and the Tabatabai assassination represent two early examples of a phenomenon that has been largely overlooked by experts and policymakers alike: homegrown terrorism of *jihadist* inspiration inside the United States. Over the last few years, and particularly after the July 2005 London bombings, much attention has been devoted to homegrown *jihadist* networks in the West. Academics and security services have been analyzing the growing threat coming from small clusters of Western-born, self-radicalized militants who look at Al Qaeda as an ideological inspiration but who act with varying degrees of independence from it. Yet most analyses have been based on the dual assumptions that this phenomenon has manifested itself only extremely recently and that it is largely limited to Europe. Although these two assertions are not completely unfounded, they do not take into consideration significant anecdotal evidence pointing to an extensive history of homegrown networks inspired by radical Islam operating within the United States.

Obviously the Washington siege and the Tabatabai assassination possess characteristics that set them apart from what could be described as today's prototypical homegrown terrorism of *jihadist* inspiration. For example, despite their demand to ban the movie *Mohammad, Messenger of God*, the actions of the 12 Hanafi Muslims that seized the heart of Washington for a day seem to have been motivated mostly by internal disputes among the most radical fringes of African-American Muslim groups.[5] In contrast, Belfield's actions appear to have been directed from abroad and should be interpreted as an attempt of the newly established Iranian regime to eliminate one of its opponents by using an American executioner. Today's homegrown networks, conversely, are predominantly motivated by a strict Salafi interpretation of Islam and have no links to foreign governments.

Nevertheless, despite these evident differences, the Washington siege and the Tabatabai assassination represent two of the first instances in which American-born and/or American-based individuals inspired by a radical and politicized interpretation of Islam decided to use violence inside the United States. They represent only some of the earliest examples that can be used to dispel the dual assumptions that homegrown *jihadist*-inspired terrorism is a recent phenomenon in the West and that it is largely limited to Europe. Although it is true that homegrown networks have become significantly more numerous and dangerous over the last few years, extensive anecdotal evidence shows that they have been present in the West for at least three decades. Moreover, although it is undeniable that Europe is home to a larger number of them, homegrown *jihadist* networks (both "atypical," such as the Washington siege's Hanafi Muslims, and others more commonly inspired by Salafism) have long been operating inside the United States as well.

Before going forth with this article's aim of analyzing the presence of homegrown terrorism of *jihadist* inspiration in America, it is necessary to clarify some definitions. The quintessential "homegrown network" is composed of individuals born in the West (second or third generation Muslim immigrants and/or converts) who embraced a radical interpretation of Islam autonomously and formed a more or less cohesive cluster that operates independently from any other organization. Nevertheless, a looser definition of "homegrown" focuses less on the individual's place of birth, but rather on where his or her radicalization has taken place. Using this standard, the mastermind of the wave of bombings that bloodied France in the summer of 1995, Khaled Kelkal, would be considered homegrown. Although born in Algeria, Kelkal moved to France when he was two, and his radicalization took place in the grimy suburbs of Lyon.[6] A network's independence from any organization also poses some challenges to the definition: Would clusters that formed autonomously in the West but later forged some kind of link with outside organizations, such as the 7/7 London bombers, qualify as homegrown?[7]

Given all these variables, definitions of homegrown vary significantly. For the purposes of this study, nevertheless, a cluster will be considered as homegrown if (a) irrespective of their place of birth, most of its members have spent most of their lives in the West and, most importantly, their radicalization took place in the West; and (b) the cluster itself was formed in the West. Based on this definition, the article will describe homegrown *jihadist* networks that have operated in the United States over the last 30 years. Particular attention will also be devoted to a sub-category of homegrown: the so-called lone wolves. Lone wolves, isolated individuals that, while operating outside any structure or chain of command, carry out violent acts in support of a terrorist group and/or a radical cause, have been a staple of political violence in America, encompassing notorious examples such as Atlanta Olympics bomber Eric Robert Rudolph and "Unabomber" Theodore Kaczynski. Over the last three decades, the United States has been home also to several cases of homegrown lone wolves that have taken their inspiration from radical Islam. Interestingly, this phenomenon seems to be uniquely American, as very few cases of *jihadist* lone wolves have been seen in Europe.

First tremors

As the Washington siege and the Tabatabai assassination show, the first violent acts motivated by radical Islam in the United States were committed by African Americans, a direct consequence of the history of Islam in the country. Aside from the isolated cases of scattered communities of Lebanese immigrants, the vast majority of Muslims living in the United States until the 1960s were African Americans. While present among West African slaves since the seventeenth century, Islam began to attract a following among Black Americans in the first decades of the twentieth century, as charismatic African-American Muslim preachers found a following among the masses of disenfranchised Blacks who had immigrated from the South to the large cities of the North.

One of the first of such Muslim organizations was the Moorish Science Temple of America, which was founded by Noble Drew Ali in Newark in 1913.[8] Ali's Islam was a personal interpretation and amalgamation of several religions, among which Islam was only nominally superior. Ali crafted for himself an almost mystical role, claiming to embody the spirits of Jesus, Mohammed, Buddha, Zoroaster, and Confucius. Similarly characterized by an unorthodox interpretation of Islam and a personality cult of the leader was the Nation of Islam, which was founded by Wallace Fard in Detroit in 1930.[9] The Nation's leadership was soon taken over by Elijah Mohammed, the son of a Baptist preacher who described himself as "Allah's special messenger to the so-called Negroes."[10] Mohammed's sect declared Fard as God personified, believed that Islam was the Black man's original faith and espoused the idea of Black superiority over the White race.

Movements such as the Moorish Science Temple and the Nation of Islam clearly started as religious alternatives to Christianity that would at the same time serve the political purpose of fostering Black pride. Their charismatic preachers portrayed Christianity as the White man's religion and Islam as the vehicle through which Blacks could recover their ethnic and cultural heritage. Some focused on a positive message of internal rebirth and political redemption, whereas others preached antagonistic messages that bordered on sheer hatred of Whites. Even though these movements had a positive influence on the life of many African Americans who found in them an alternative to crime, alcohol, and drugs, their history is deeply marred by episodes of violence. Throughout the years, several of their members engaged in violent actions, which, to be sure, were mostly motivated by acute internal rivalries, racial tensions, and purely criminal purposes, rather than by militant interpretations of Islam.

Most orthodox Sunni Muslims have often regarded the Moorish Science Temple and the Nation of Islam as heretical cults whose racial rhetoric, bizarre myths and rules, and personality cult of their leaders, make them completely at odds with traditional Islam. In the 1960s, a growing number of African-American converts, influenced by Arab and South Asian Muslim immigrants in the United States, also began to look with suspicion at traditional African-American Muslim organizations.[11] Mosques established in the country during those years by the Muslim Brotherhood also began to attract converts, thereby contributing to the spread of traditional Sunni Islam in

America.[12] But no factor contributed more to the switch from Black Particularism to traditional Sunni Islam than the influence of Saudi propaganda operating both in the United States and during the *hajj*, when thousands of American Muslims traveled to Mecca.[13] "He went to Mecca as a Black Muslim and there he became only a Muslim," said the wife of Malcolm X, describing her husband's 1964 journey to Saudi Arabia and, likewise, the spiritual journey of many other African-American Muslims.[14]

Throughout the 1970s many African-American Muslims followed the examples of Malcolm X and Hamaas Abdul Khaalis, breaking with organizations such as the Nation of Islam and embracing traditional Sunni Islam. As Saudi mosques and publications began to make their way into Black neighborhoods, some African-American Muslims went to study in universities and Islamic schools in Saudi Arabia.[15] Inevitably, some of these men embraced the most radical interpretation of Sunni Islam preached in Saudi Arabia. A small number of African-American Muslims, in fact, allegedly joined the group led by Saudi militant Juhayman al Uteybi, which, in November 1979, occupied Mecca's Grand Mosque, a violent protest against the Saudi monarchy that foretold the wave of violence and militancy that would sweep Saudi Arabia and the rest of the world in the following years.[16]

The movement of small numbers of African Americans to the Middle East continued in the 1980s, as some reached Afghanistan to join the anti-Soviet resistance. Whereas some of these volunteers were devout Muslims with no connection to any group, others belonged to an American-based movement called Jamaat al Fuqra (or Community of the Impoverished).[17] Al Fuqra was founded in 1980 by Sheikh Gilani, an influential Pakistani Sufi cleric who had begun preaching in New York City, attracting a following in some of the city's African-American mosques.[18] Speaking with an ammunition belt around his waist, Gilani urged American Muslims to join the Afghan *jihad* and to establish small communities "where they could raise their children in a wholesome environment and live a life of pure Islam, free from decadence of a godless society."[19] Heeding Gilani's advice, al Fuqra members have since developed small villages in rural parts of California, Virginia, Georgia, Colorado, and New York.[20] Al Fuqra members, who are predominantly African Americans, live in almost complete self-isolation, home-schooling their children and limiting their contacts with the outside world.[21]

Over the years several members of al Fuqra have been involved in violent and religiously motivated activities. Throughout the 1980s, several al Fuqra members have been convicted for a string of bombings targeting Hindu, Jewish, and Hare Krishna temples throughout the country and in Canada.[22] In September 1989, Colorado Springs police searched a storage locker rented by local al Fuqra members and found thirty to forty pounds of explosives, three large pipe bombs, a number of smaller improvised explosive devices, ten handguns, silencers, military training manuals, and detailed plans for attacks against various military facilities and places of worship located in the region.[23] Al Fuqra still operates today and authorities estimate that it has between 1,000 and 3,000 members nationwide. Although it is not formally designated as a terrorist organization, a 2005 Department of Homeland Security internal report cited al Fuqra as a domestic organization that needed continued monitoring, as it "continues to conceal its activities and prepare itself for a possible confrontation with U.S. authorities."[24]

Al Fuqra, a group formed in the United States by American converts who over the last 25 years have engaged in violent activities motivated by radical Islam, represents another proof of the long-established presence of homegrown networks of *jihadist* inspiration in America. Although the group operates autonomously, various incidents have revealed some links to Al Qaeda. Two al Fuqra members from Colorado have been convicted for the 1990 assassination of Rashad Khalifa, a Tucson moderate imam.[25] Investigations revealed that Tucson resident Wadih el Hage, bin Laden's personal assistant in the United States throughout the 1990s who is currently serving a life sentence for his role in the 1998 Embassy bombings, was involved in Khalifa's assassination.[26] Another African-American al Fuqra member and veteran of the Afghan *jihad*, Clement Rodney Hampton El, was sentenced to 35 years for his role in the 1993 Landmarks Plot, a plan hatched by various militants linked to the "Blind Sheik" Omar Abdel Rahman to bomb high-profile targets in the New York metropolitan area.[27]

The Landmarks Plot and the first bombing of the World Trade Center highlight the importance of the New York area in this phase of militant Islam in the United States. Both plots had been hatched by a New York-based cluster that cannot be considered homegrown, as it was composed and directed predominantly by radicals coming from outside the country. Yet the presence in the cluster of Hampton El, Indiana-native of Iraqi descent Abdul Rahman Yasin, and immigrants whose radicalization had taken place in the United States, testifies to the growing amalgamation of American homegrowns with foreign terrorists. By the early 1990s, in fact, foreign *jihadists* had begun to establish a presence in the country, interacting with local sympathizers and spreading their propaganda to attract new ones.

Traveling for *Jihad* in the 1990s

A key role in the formation of the New York cluster was played by the Masjid al Farooq, a Brooklyn mosque where the Blind Sheik used to preach. Al Farooq was the American headquarters of al Khifa, an organization founded by Al Qaeda founder Abdullah Azzam to recruit and fund-raise for the Afghan *jihad* among Muslims worldwide. Other branches of al Khifa were active in Atlanta, Boston, Chicago, Pittsburgh, and Tucson and around them the first networks of Al Qaeda supporters, both immigrants and American-born, started to grow.[28]

Al Khifa and other recruiting networks spread throughout the country continued their activities after the end of the Afghan war against the Soviets, as American Muslims continued to travel to Afghanistan and Pakistan for *jihad*. Pakistani authorities claim to have knowledge of at least 400 Americans who had received training in Pakistani and Afghan camps between the end of the Afghan war against the Soviets and 2001.[29] Al Fuqra officials openly admit to having sent more than 100 members to Pakistan during the time, but claim that the men received only religious training. Robert Blitzer, a former counterterrorism official who once headed the FBI's first task force on Islamic fundamentalism, estimates that in the 1990s, between 1,000 and 2,000 volunteers left the United States to fight or train with various *jihadist* outfits throughout the world, a number comparable to that of European Muslims who left the continent during the same years. In an interview with *U.S. News and World Report*, Blitzer also revealed that at the time authorities were monitoring two mosques in New York from which 40 to 50 aspiring *jihadists* were leaving every year.[30]

One of the most notorious examples of American converts who had fought in Afghanistan is John Walker Lindh, the so-called American Taliban, currently serving a 20-year prison sentence.[31] Lindh discovered Islam online and embarked on a long journey that led him through training camps in both Pakistan and Afghanistan before being detained by CIA officials after the bloody Qala-i-Janghi prison uprising.[32] Ohio native Christopher Paul is another convert who fought in Afghanistan. Paul reportedly joined Al Qaeda in 1991 and spent more than a decade shuttling between Columbus and Al Qaeda training camps. In 2007 he was indicted for his involvement in a plot to attack American diplomatic facilities and American tourists in Europe.[33] Less detailed information is available on Hiram Torres, a New Jersey native of Puerto Rican descent who used the name of Mohammed Salman after his conversion.[34] Torres, a freshman at Yale University when he left the country, reportedly ended up fighting with Harkat ul-Mujahedeen, a Pakistani *jihadist* group.

Torres was one of the first in a growing number of Americans of Hispanic origin who converted to Islam and then embraced the most radical interpretation of their new religion. The best known case of Hispanic convert is that of Jose Padilla, a New York-born convert who was accused of planning to carry out a "dirty bomb" attack inside the country (a charge later partially retracted). And whereas Torres seemed to have been a loner seeking adventure, Padilla was part of a well-established American-based network of militants. Padilla, a former gang member who converted in jail, had been recruited by militants operating in the Miami area.[35] He then left the country in 1998 and spent years in Egypt and other Middle Eastern countries, continuing his involvement with radical outfits.[36] After his 2002 arrest and extensive legal vicissitudes, Padilla was tried in 2007 and convicted of supporting terrorists along with his co-defendants Adham Amin Hassoun and Kifah Wael Jayyousi.[37]

Hassoun and Jayyousi were part of a South Florida-based network that, throughout the 1990s, recruited and fund-raised for various *jihadist* outfits throughout the world in close cooperation with a similar cluster of radicals based in San Diego. Operating out of the plush beach community of La Jolla, the San Diego cluster created an intricate web of front charities and organizations with innocent sounding names such as the American Islamic Group, Islamic Center of the Americas and Save Bosnia Now.[38] The group did not limit its activities to propaganda. Aukai Collins, a native of Hawaii who converted to Islam in San Diego, was sent by the group to Kashmir and Chechnya, where he lost a leg while fighting alongside Arab foreign fighters.[39] The leader of the group, the American-born son of Egyptian parents Mohammed Zaky, died in 1995 while fighting in Chechnya, the only American to be known to have done so.[40]

Post 9/11 boom

The San Diego and South Florida networks are just some of the examples of clusters operating inside the United States throughout the 1990s, many of which had homegrown characteristics. The number of such clusters increased significantly after 2001. An explanation for this increased mobilization can be found in the effect of the 9/11 attacks, which represented a powerful call to arms for many individuals who had only harbored sympathies for radical Islam, but had never acted on them. Following a global trend, more American Muslims embraced Al Qaeda's message after the 9/11 attacks and the subsequent wars in Afghanistan and Iraq. But the authorities' increased attention to *jihadist* networks, which were virtually ignored before 9/11, can also explain the higher number of clusters uncovered after 2001. Many of them, in fact, had operated well before 2001, but were subjected to the authorities' scrutiny only after the 9/11 attacks.

While some of the first arrests carried out in the United States after 9/11 involved foreign *jihadists*, as the months went by authorities uncovered a growing number of clusters that presented strong homegrown characteristics. In September 2002, federal authorities arrested six young residents of Lackawanna, a suburb of Buffalo, accusing them of having trained at an Al Qaeda-run camp in Afghanistan in the summer of 2001.[41] The men, all American-born citizens of Yemeni descent, later received sentences ranging from 7 to 10 years. A month later a Portland federal grand jury indicted five men and a woman for conspiracy to provide assistance to Taliban and Al Qaeda by planning to travel to Afghanistan. Members of the Portland cell, an odd group of well-integrated Middle Eastern immigrants and African-American converts, later received prison sentences ranging from 3 to 18 years.[42]

Lackawanna and Portland were just the first cases of a long list of American homegrown clusters seeking to travel overseas to join *jihadist* outfits. One of the most significant cases is represented by the so-called paintball *jihad* network, which was dismantled by authorities in 2003.[43] The network was formed by a dozen militants, mostly middle-class young men based in northern Virginia, who had trained in paintball to prepare themselves for real military training. Some of the men had also traveled to Pakistan immediately after 9/11, where they trained with Lashkar-e-Taiba. The cluster had typical homegrown characteristics, as it included nine U.S. citizens, five of whom were converts. Three of the men also had served in the U.S. military.[44]

The investigation into the "paintball *jihad*" network soon led authorities to other homegrown *jihadists*. A phone number connected to the cluster connected the men to Tarik Shah, a New York-based jazz player and martial arts expert. Shah, an African-American convert who had been affiliated with the Nation of Islam, was approached by an *agent provocateur* who recorded him expressing his desire to train other Muslims in martial arts so that they could wage *jihad* against the United States.[45] Investigating Shah, authorities also reached Rafiq Sabir, a New York native and an accomplished physician who graduated from Columbia University before opening his practice in Florida. Using the same technique, authorities taped Sabir pledging to use his medical skills to treat wounded *mujaheddin*. Sabir and Shah, who had developed contacts in Saudi Arabia and had attempted to travel to Afghanistan as far back as 1998, were convicted of conspiring to provide material support to Al Qaeda and sentenced to 25 and 15 years, respectively.[46] Other ramifications of the "paintball *jihad*" investigation led overseas. An associate of the cluster, Houston-born and Virginia-raised Ahmed Abu Ali, was convicted and sentenced to 30 years for conspiring to carry out attacks in the United States, including an assassination attempt on President Bush, with an Al Qaeda-linked cell he had teamed up with while studying in Saudi Arabia.[47]

Like Abu Ali, several Americans have been arrested since 9/11 for joining various *jihadi* outfits overseas. A small group of Americans fought in Somalia in December 2006, joining the Islamic Court Union, the Islamist militia that briefly took control of the country before being defeated by the Ethiopian army. The fate of only two of them is known. New Jersey resident Amir Mohamed Meshal, the American-born son of Egyptian immigrants, was reportedly detained in Ethiopia after admitting he had been at a training camp in Somalia.[48] One of his companions, Daniel Maldonado, was captured by the Kenyan military as he was trying to leave Somalia, and was later indicted in the United States. Maldonado, a Latino convert from Massachusetts, described his experience in the African country to FBI agents: "I would be fighting the Somali militia, and that turned into fighting the Ethiopians, and if Americans came, I would fight them too."[49]

A telling example of how American homegrowns follow patterns similar to those of their European counterparts is represented by the stories of Mohammad Junaid Babar and Syed Hashmi, two Pakistani-born youths who had immigrated to New York as young children.[50] While attending college in Queens and Brooklyn, respectively, Babar and Hashmi joined the American branch of al Muhajiroun, the London-based extremist group founded by Omar Bakri. Like many second generation Pakistani immigrants in the United Kingdom, after 9/11 Babar and Hashmi traveled to Pakistan to join various *jihadist* outfits. They both teamed up with different clusters of British-based militants and were later arrested for their involvement in the planning of thwarted terrorist attacks inside Britain.

Examples of American militants who have been recruited by foreign *jihadist* networks abound. Denver native James Ujaama, an African-American convert to Islam, was recruited in 1999 by a network headed by London-based cleric Abu Hamza and other Al Qaeda-affiliated individuals to establish a training camp in rural Oregon.[51] Majid Khan, a Pakistani native who immigrated as a teenager to the suburbs of Baltimore, became one of Al Qaeda mastermind Khalid Sheik Mohammed's top American operatives, tasked to conduct attacks against various targets in the New York area.[52] To be sure, these cases should not overshadow the fact that most of the attacks that have been plotted against the United States since 2001 have been conceived by purely homegrown, operationally independent, and, for the most part, quite amateurish clusters. An analysis of these plots shows, once again, the staggering ethnic diversity of American homegrown *jihadis.*

A Pakistani who had grown up in New York and the son of an Egyptian father and an Irish-American mother were behind the plot to bomb one of New York's busiest subway stations in concomitance with the 2004 Republican National Convention.[53] The two men had radicalized and met at the Pakistani's uncle's Islamic bookstore in Brooklyn. A year later, authorities in California arrested two African-American converts during a robbery of a Los Angeles gas station. The subsequent investigation revealed that the men belonged to Jam'iyyat Ul-Islam Is-Saheeh ("Authentic Assembly of Islam"), a group founded in 1997 in prison by Kevin James, another African-American convert. According to authorities, the group was using armed robberies to finance terrorist operations.[54] In December 2007, James and his right-hand man, Levar Washington, plead guilty to federal terrorism charges, admitting that they "conspired to attack United States military operations, 'infidels,' and Israeli and Jewish facilities in the Los Angeles area."[55]

African Americans were also behind a bizarre plot to target Chicago's Sears Tower and federal facilities in Florida. In June 2006, in fact, authorities arrested seven men against whom they had collected allegedly damning evidence with the help of an *agent provocateur* that had infiltrated the group.[56] The men belonged to the Seas of David, a spin-off of the Moorish Science Temple that had been created by the Chicago-born son of a Baptist preacher, Narseal Batiste.[57] The men lived in a sort of fraternity in a windowless warehouse in Liberty City, a predominantly Black and low-income area of Miami and, in keeping with the Moorish Science's traditions, wore uniforms with a Star of David and held Bible studies.[58] Batiste also organized martial arts classes and, when the *agent provocateur* purporting to be an Al Qaeda representative seeking to plan operations in the United States approached him, Batiste replied that he was building an Islamic Army to wage war in the United States himself. Batiste and his men then pledged allegiance to Al Qaeda and offered their support to carry out attacks throughout the country.[59]

A comparably independent and amateurish homegrown cluster was uncovered in May 2007, when authorities in New Jersey arrested six men allegedly planning to attack a local military base. The men had conducted firearms training in remote areas of Pennsylvania and were in possession of handguns and semi-automatic assault rifles.[60] According to authorities, they planned to enter the Fort Dix military base, on which the men had conducted surveillance thanks to the fact that the father of one of the suspects owned a pizza place that delivered inside the base, and kill as many soldiers as possible.[61] Three of the suspects were brothers of ethnic Albanian descent who had grown up in the suburbs of Philadelphia. None of them was known to be particularly religious and some had priors for drug possession, mirroring the fast radicalization process that has characterized many European *jihadis.*[62]

Lone wolves

John Walker Lindh and Jose Padilla, men who could represent the poster boys of the homegrown American *jihadist*, are commonly believed to be lone wolves, individuals who embarked on a solitary journey to fight *jihad* far from the United States. In reality, the two men had had extensive contacts with recruiting networks inside the United States before leaving the country and cannot fully account as lone wolves. The same goes for Adam Gadahn, the California native that has become the American face and voice of *al Sahab*, the multimedia wing of Al Qaeda. Before joining the upper echelons of Al Qaeda in Afghanistan, in fact, the former heavy metal fanatic had been groomed by an Orange County-based cluster of militants that was deeply involved in the Millennium plot to blow up tourist facilities in Jordan.[63]

If Lindh, Padilla, and Gadahn do not represent real lone wolves, American authorities have witnessed various cases since 9/11 that fit such a profile. In May 2005 authorities arrested Ronald Allen Grecula, a Pennsylvania engineer, for attempting to build and sell a bomb to a terrorist organization for use against the United States. Grecula had offered the device, whose effectiveness has been doubted, to an undercover officer.[64] A few months later, Idaho resident Michael Curtis Reynolds was arrested after offering his support to an FBI agent that had portrayed himself as an Al Qaeda operative. Reynolds had offered to carry out bombings against pipeline systems and energy facilities in exchange for money.[65]

If Grecula's and Reynolds's efforts seem to be motivated mostly by money, other American lone wolves appear to have acted out of true conviction. In October 2004, Ryan Anderson, an active duty National Guardsman from Washington State who had converted and went by the name Amir Abdul Rashid, attempted to make contact with Al Qaeda members online, volunteering to pass military secrets that could "take things to the next level in the fight against our enemy (the U.S. government)."[66] Anderson, who was about to deploy to Iraq with his battalion, passed information on the vulnerabilities of American tanks and the location of U.S. troops in Iraq to whom he believed to be an Algerian militant. In reality his interlocutor was Shannen Rossmiller, a former Montana municipal judge who surfs the net to uncover *jihadist* sympathizers. Anderson was arrested after Rossmiller passed the information to authorities and was later sentenced to life for seeking to aid the enemy during a time of war and attempted espionage.[67]

Another member of the U.S. military had better luck and found a way to send military secrets to actual Al Qaeda sympathizers. Paul Hall, a former U.S. Navy signalman, has been accused of sending military secrets from a computer on the destroyer U.S.S. *Benfold* to the webmasters of Azzam.com, a notorious Al Qaeda-affiliated website that operated out of London. Hall, who legally changed his name to Hassan Abujihaad after converting, sent detailed classified information on the movements of a U.S. Navy battle group and its formation when passing the Straits of Hormuz and indicated when and how the ships would have been more vulnerable to an attack.[68] At the trial, authorities also accused Abujihaad of planning an attack on the San Diego naval base in October 2006, a facility he knew well since he had been stationed there.[69] Abujihaad vaguely discussed the plan with his roommate Derrick Shareef, himself another American convert to Islam. Shareef was arrested two months later in his native Chicago while attempting to purchase grenades to attack a local shopping mall at the peak of Christmas shopping season. Shareef, who had already prepared his last will and claimed to be ready to die in the attack, did not realize that the man he had asked for the grenades was a federal informant.[70]

Anderson, Hall, and Shareef represent typical cases of lone wolves, individuals that have embraced the most militant interpretation of Islam and decided to act on it without any outside assistance. More puzzling are instances in which violent acts are carried out by lone wolves who had never displayed any sign of radicalization, leading normal lives until the day they carried out a seemingly unpredictable act. Over the last 15 years, in fact, authorities have witnessed various cases of Muslim immigrants who had lived a long and mostly successful life in the United States, had never showed any visible sign of extremism, and yet, who one day committed violent acts that seem to be dictated by radical Islamist motives. Some of these cases include Rashid Baz, a Lebanese cab driver who opened fire on a van full of Hasidic Jewish boys on the Brooklyn Bridge in 1994, killing one; Ali Hassan Abu Kamal, a Palestinian immigrant who killed a tourist and injured six other people on the observation deck of the Empire State Building in 1997 out of his self-declared hatred for Israel and America; and Hesham Mohamed Ali Hedayat, who began shooting at the El Al ticket counter at the Los Angeles International Airport in 2002, killing two.[71]

Whereas these attacks were perpetrated by immigrants, other similar actions have been committed by American natives or long-time residents, giving them the proper qualification of homegrown. Attributing these incidents solely to *jihadist* ideology is incorrect, as many of the perpetrators seem to have suffered from some form of mental disturbance. However, it is noteworthy that when these individuals decided to carry out acts of violence, the choice of their targets and the motivations expressed by them during or after the attack do not seem to be accidental, but influenced by political motives. An incident that seems to be motivated by such an odd mix of radical Islam and mental disturbances took place in Seattle in July 2006, when Naveed Haq, an American-born Muslim of Afghan descent, began shooting inside the city's Jewish Federation, killing one and injuring several others. Haq, who has been described as a problematic young man suffering from bipolar disorder, had reportedly converted to Christianity a few months before the shooting and told a ministry that he saw "too much anger in Islam and wanted to find a new beginning in Christianity."[72] Yet before opening fire, Haq reportedly made several statements "indicating anger at Jews" and, after the shooting, told a police dispatcher: "These are Jews and I'm tired of getting pushed around and our people getting pushed around by the situation in the Middle East."[73]

Mental disturbances have not been ruled out also in the case of Mohammed Reza Taheri-azar, an Iranian native who moved to the United States when he was two. In March 2006 Taheri-azar intentionally began hitting people with a sport utility vehicle on the campus of the University of North Carolina at Chapel Hill, the university from which he had graduated the year before, injuring nine.[74] His actions seemed at first those of a deranged loner taking revenge on his former classmates, given Taheri-azar's poor social life and marijuana abuse. Yet Taheri-azar's statements to police officers and a letter he wrote to a local TV station reveal the political nature of his motives. "The U.S. government," wrote the 23 year old, "is responsible for the deaths of and the torture of countless followers of Allah, my brothers and sisters. My attack on Americans at UNC-CH on March 3rd was in retaliation for similar attacks orchestrated by the U.S. government on my fellow followers of Allah in Iraq, Afghanistan, Palestine, Saudi Arabia, and other Islamic territories. I did not act out of hatred for Americans, but out of love for Allah instead."[75]

A delayed awareness

All the aforementioned examples, hardly an exhaustive list, clearly demonstrate this article's point that homegrown networks of *jihadist* inspiration have long existed in the United States and that their presence is hardly limited to a few cases. Nevertheless, despite such ample anecdotal evidence, for a long time the U.S. law enforcement and intelligence communities remained largely unable to detect and properly assess the growth of the phenomenon. Such failure is partially to be attributed to legal limitations that severely hampered American intelligence agencies' ability of monitoring U.S.-based individuals and organizations. But equally determining was, during the 1990s, the general lack of understanding of the magnitude of the threat posed by *jihadist* groups worldwide and domestically, which caused the lax attitude of most intelligence and law enforcement agencies.[76]

9/11 removed many of these legal and cultural impediments, and U.S. authorities began to frantically look for terrorist cells and sympathizers on American soil. As seen, such renewed attention led to the uncovering of several networks, many of them possessing the characteristics of a homegrown. Yet, in the lingo of most American officials and experts, the term "homegrown terrorism" was still reserved to domestic organizations such as antigovernment militia, White supremacists, or ecoterrorist groups such as the Earth Liberation Front. Such groups were termed as homegrown to distinguish them from *jihadist* terrorist networks, even though the latter possessed some of the very same characteristics (membership born and raised in the United States, focus on U.S. targets). Because the cause of the *jihadists* was perceived to be foreign, the U.S. government did not label them as homegrown, despite the typically homegrown characteristics of many of them.

The July 2005 attacks in London, which had been carried out by a quintessentially homegrown cluster, led U.S. authorities to look at the homegrown issue with renewed attention. As an increasing number of cells that clearly possessed homegrown characteristics were uncovered throughout the country, authorities began to re-assess the definition of homegrown. By 2006 top FBI and DHS officials began to openly speak of homegrown terrorism of *jihadist* inspiration inside the United States, even describing it as a threat "as dangerous as groups like Al Qaida, if not more so."[77] As a consequence of this reassessment, U.S. authorities began to ask themselves if the emergence of relatively large numbers of radicalized second generation Muslims that had been observed in Europe could also take place in the United States. This fear led to an increased attention on the dynamics and causes of radicalization among Muslims in both Europe and North America.

Four concurring reasons are often identified to explain the divergence between the levels of radicalization in Europe and the United States. The first one is related to significantly better economic conditions of American Muslims. Although European Muslims generally languish at the bottom of most rankings that measure economic integration, American Muslims fare significantly better, and the average American-Muslim household's income is equal to, if not higher, than the average American's.[78] As the many cases of militants who came from privileged background have proven, economic integration is not always an antidote to radicalization, but it is undeniable that radical ideas find a fertile environment among unemployed and disenfranchised youth. A direct consequence of economic integration is the lack of Muslim ghettoes in the United States. Areas of large European cities with a high concentration of poor Muslim immigrants have been ideological sanctuaries where radicals could freely spread their message and where radical Islam has become a sort of counterculture. The American Muslim community's economic conditions have prevented the formation of such enclaves in the United States.

Geographic dispersion, immigration patterns, and tougher immigration policies have also prevented the formation of extensive recruiting and propaganda networks as those that have sprung up in Europe. Although this article has demonstrated that networks have been operating inside the United States for the last 30 years, their activities cannot be compared in intensity to those operating in Europe. Although places such as Brooklyn's al Farooq mosque or Tucson's Islamic Center saw extensive *jihadist* activities in the 1990s, they pale in comparison to recruiting headquarters such as London's Finsbury Park, Hamburg's al Quds mosque, or Milan's Islamic Cultural Institute. Finally, the fact that large segments of the American-Muslim population belong to ethnicities that have traditionally espoused moderate interpretations of Islam can also be cited as a reason for America's lower levels of radicalism. In fact, Muslims from the Iranian- and Indian-American communities, which account for vast segments of America's Muslim population, have traditionally embraced moderate forms of Islam and have been, to varying degrees, almost impervious to radicalization.

Although all these characteristics still hold true, they no longer represent a guarantee. Cases such as Lackawanna or the "paintball *jihad*" have shown that economic integration does not always prevent the radicalization of young American Muslims. Factors such as perception of discrimination and frustration at U.S. foreign policies could lead to radicalization, irrespective of favorable economic conditions. Experts and community leaders have repeatedly warned about the growing alienation of American Muslims, particularly among those of the second generation. These frustrations could produce what Steven Simon refers to as "a rejectionist generation," which could embrace radical interpretations of Islam.[79] The same conclusion has been reached by a widely publicized report recently released by the New York Police Department Intelligence Division. "Despite the economic opportunities in the United States," reads the report, "the powerful gravitational pull of individuals' religious roots and identity sometimes supersedes the assimilating nature of American society which includes pursuit of a professional career, financial stability and material comforts."[80]

Cases such as Fort Dix or the Taheri-azar incident have shown that radicalization can touch also communities where extremism is rare, such as the Albanian and the Iranian American. Moreover, the fact that no organized group has an extensive network in the country is no longer a guarantee that radicalization cannot reach America's shores, as the Internet has, in many cases, replaced the need to have operatives physically spreading the propaganda on the ground.[81] Young American *jihadists*, given the easy access to the Internet that they enjoy, have been extremely active online. A search of *jihadist* chat rooms and even of subgroups in "benign" social network sites such as Myspace.com reveals the presence of many American-born youngsters that glorify Al Qaeda's ideology.[82]

By the same token, the Internet has become a way to connect American aspiring *jihadists* to like-minded individuals worldwide. The case of Syed Ahmed and Ehsanul Sadeque, two U.S. citizens living in Atlanta, perfectly epitomizes this new trend.[83] Ahmed and Sadeque had met in 2004 at a local mosque and had begun browsing radical websites together. They ended up communicating with Younis Tsouli, a London-based radical that served as a webmaster for a number of *jihadi* websites. Ahmed and Sadeque, who never met Tsouli, taped potential targets in Washington, D.C. and Virginia and sent the clips to Tsouli to disseminate to operatives for an attack.[84] Moreover, the two traveled to Toronto to meet members of a local cluster they had met on Tsouli's websites and discussed possible attacks inside the United States.[85]

The U.S. Government's response

Even though a full-fledged acknowledgment of the presence of homegrown networks of *jihadist* inspiration came only in 2006, U.S. authorities began to aggressively investigate *jihadist* networks operating in the country, both homegrown and not, immediately after 9/11. The authorities' approach toward the new domestic threat has been two-pronged. On one hand, agencies understood that the conviction-driven, *ex post facto* approach they had traditionally used toward *jihadist* terrorism inside the country was no longer sufficient. Arresting militants before or after they had carried out an attack or after they had committed criminal acts in support of a terrorist organization while closing the investigation after the case went to court (as it happened, for example, after the first World Trade Center bombing) came to be deemed an incomplete counterterrorism approach. In what represents a monumental cultural change reversing decades of practice, FBI officials are now instructed by the Bureau's leadership to prioritize intelligence gathering rather than dismantling cells and obtaining convictions.[86]

Although obtaining the full picture on the composition, *modus operandi* and aims of *jihadist* networks, both homegrown and not, operating inside the country is one the authorities' new priority, the occasionally diverging goal of dismantling them is equally important. Attacks in other countries have showed that, in many cases, homegrown clusters go from the radicalization phase to action within a very short time. Due to their lack of communication with outside groups such passage can be very difficult to detect. Consequently, U.S. authorities have often resorted to markedly aggressive tactics in order to dismantle them before they spring into action. In some cases authorities have employed the "Al Capone" law enforcement technique, arresting suspected terrorists for immigration, financial, or other non-terrorism-related offenses in order to neutralize them when they did not possess enough evidence to convict them for terrorism.

An even more aggressive technique occasionally employed in terrorism cases has been that of the introduction of *agents provocateurs*. Operating under the assumption that certain individuals or clusters that espouse *jihadist* ideology are likely, eventually, to go into action, U.S. counterterrorism officials have sometimes resorted to the idea of triggering themselves the passage from the radicalization phase to action. Therefore, since 9/11, various federal and local authorities (such as the New York Police Department, which has resorted to the tactic in numerous occasions) have infiltrated small clusters of known radicals, many of which are isolated and amateurish *jihadist* wannabes, with *agents provocateurs*. Under the strict direction of authorities such individuals approached their targets, led them to believe they belonged to Al Qaeda or other *jihadist* organizations, and encouraged them to either plan attacks or provide material support to terrorist organizations.

The tactic presents obvious advantages. Authorities can gain virtually complete insights on the activities of a radical cluster, even indirectly controlling its activities. Additionally, the evidence collected by *agents provocateurs* is likely to be much more extensive than what authorities would collect otherwise and has guaranteed, despite some occasional mishaps, several convictions. Nevertheless, the flipsides of using such technique are equally evident. Critics of the tactic argue that authorities use it to frame individuals that have radical ideas but would not necessarily act on them. Moreover, the reliability of some of the individuals used as *agents provocateurs* has been sometimes questioned, as many of them are convicted felons trying to gain a reprieve of their sentences or make money in exchange for their role in counterterrorism cases.

The efforts toward intelligence dominance and the use of aggressive counterterrorism techniques show the authorities' increased awareness of the existence of homegrown *jihadist* networks in the United States. Such networks have become the priority of U.S. counterterrorism authorities and, given their domestic nature, efforts have been made in order to increase intelligence sharing between federal, state, and local authorities.[87] Yet, while all these improvements address short-term security needs, the United States seems to be lacking a long-term strategy to confront the homegrown *jihadist* threat. Authorities, in fact, have so far been unable to conceive any coherent policy that would preemptively tackle the issue of radicalization, preventing young American Muslims from embracing extremist ideas in the first place.

Authorities are now well aware that America is not immune from the threat of homegrown *jihadist* terrorism and have taken various initiatives to discuss ways to prevent the spread of radicalism to the country's Muslim community, including a proposal to form a Congress-mandated National Commission on the Prevention of Violent Radicalization and Homegrown Terrorism.[88] Various intelligence and law enforcement agencies have reached out to the academic community to better understand the social, political, and psychological causes of radicalization. Nevertheless, the still limited understanding of the issue, coupled with the overlap of jurisdiction between often competing federal, state, and local authorities, have so far prevented the implementation of a systematic, nationwide antiradicalization program.

Solutions are, to be sure, hard to find. Europeans, who detected the problem of radicalization of segments of their own Muslim communities well before the United States, are still struggling with the same issue and are only now attempting to put in place coherent antiradicalization programs, the success of which must still to be verified. Equally challenging have been efforts, on both sides of the Atlantic, to find reliable and representative organizations within various Muslim communities to be employed as partners in antiradicalization activities. Clearly, more attention and analysis should be devoted to the issue. But the awareness that homegrown terrorism of *jihadist* inspiration, albeit less widespread than in Europe, has been a constant in the United States for the last 30 years can represent a useful starting point, providing authorities with abundant factual evidence that can make them uncover consistent radicalization patterns.

Notes

1 "The 38 Hours: Trial by Terror," *Time*, 21 March 1977.
2 Mattias Gardell, *In the Name of Elijah Muhammad: Louis Farrakhan and the Nation of Islam* (Durham, NC: Duke University Press, 1996), p. 189.
3 Ira Silverman, "An American Terrorist," *The New Yorker*, 5 August 2002.
4 Ibid.
5 Manning Marable, *Race, Reform and Rebellion: The Second Reconstruction in Black America, 1945–1982* (Jackson: University Press of Mississippi, 1984), p. 178.
6 Dietmar Loch, "Boyhood of a Terror Suspect," *Guardian*, 11 October 1995.
7 For an official account on the links between the 7/7 bombers and Al Qaeda, see: House of Commons, Report of the Official Account of the Bombings in London on 7th July 2005.
8 Robert Dannin, *Black Pilgrimage to Islam* (New York: Oxford University Press, 2002), pp. 26–31.
9 Edward E. Curtis, *Islam in Black America* (Albany: State University of New York University Press, 2002), pp. 63–84.
10 Richard Brent Turner, *Islam in the African American Experience* (Bloomington: Indiana University Press, 1997); Aminah Beverly McCloud, *African American Islam* (New York: Routledge, 1995), p. 28.
11 Curtis, *Islam in Black America*, pp. 2–20.
12 Ikhwan in America, Government Exhibit 003-0089 in United States v. Holy Land Foundation et al., 3:04-cr-240 (ND, Tex.).
13 Curtis, *Islam in Black America*.
14 Betty Shabazz, in Clifton E. Marsh, *From Black Muslims to Muslims: The Transition from Separatism to Islam, 1930–1980* (Metuchen, NJ: Scarecrow Press, 1984), p. 82.
15 Yaroslav Trofimov, *The Siege of Mecca: The Forgotten Uprising in Islam's Holiest Shrine and the Birth of al-Qaeda* (New York: Doubleday, 2007), pp. 36–37.
16 Ibid., p. 64.
17 David E. Kaplan, "Hundreds of Americans have Followed the Path to Jihad. Here's How and Why," *U.S. News and World Report*, 2 June 2002.
18 U.S. Department of State, *Patterns of Global Terrorism* (1999), p. 120; Yehudit Barsky, *Al Fuqra: Holy Warriors of Terrorism*, special report by the Anti-Defamation League, 1993.
19 Steven Emerson, *Jihad Incorporated: A Guide to Militant Islam in the US* (Amherst, NY: Prometheus, 2006), pp. 274–275.
20 *Patterns of Global Terrorism*; see also Sean Webby and Brandon Bailey, "The Mysterious Saga of Sister Khadijah," *San Jose Mercury News*, 11 February 2007.
21 *Patterns of Global Terrorism*.
22 *Patterns of Global Terrorism*; Barsky, *Al Fuqra*.
23 Information Regarding Colorado's Investigation and Prosecution of Members of Jamaat Ul Fuqra, Attorney General's Office, Colorado Department of Law, available at http://www.ago.state.co.us/pr/121001_link.cfm
24 Department of Homeland Security, Intergrated Planning Guidance, January 2005, p. 11.
25 Attorney General Salazar Announces 69 Year Sentence for "Fuqra" Defendant Convicted of Racketeering and Conspiracy to Commit Murder, Attorney General's Office, Colorado Department of Law, available at http://www.ago.state.co.us/press_detail.cfm?pressID=503
26 U.S. v. Usama bin Laden et al., U.S.D.C. Southern District of New York, S(7) 98 Cr. 1023, 15 February 2001, pp. 790–798; Oriana Zill, "A Portrait of Wadih el Hage, Accused Terrorist," *PBS Frontline*, 12 September 2001.
27 U.S. v. Omar Ahmed Ali Abdel Rahman, U.S.D.C. Southern District of New York, S5 93 CR 181, Indictment, 19 October 1994.
28 *The 9/11 Commission Report: Final Report of the National Commission on Terrorist Attacks upon the United States* (New York: Norton, 2004), p. 58.
29 Kaplan, "Hundreds of Americans have Followed the Path to Jihad."
30 Ibid.
31 U.S. v. John Lindh, U.S.D.C. for the Eastern District of Virginia, Plea Agreement, 15 July 2002.
32 U.S. v. John Lindh, U.S.D.C. for the Eastern District of Virginia, Criminal No. 02-37-A, 17 June 2002.
33 U.S. v. Christopher Paul, U.S. District Court, Columbus, Ohio, 11 April 2007.
34 David Rohde, James Risen, "Missing New Jersey Man's Name Turns up in Kabul," *New York Times*, 6 February 2002.

35 U.S. v. Adham Amin Hassoun et al., U.S.D.C. Southern District of Florida, 04-60001-CR-Cooke, Indictment, 17 November 2005.

36 Summary of Jose Padilla's Activities with al Qaeda, Department of Defense Memorandum, 28 May 2004; Declaration of Jeffrey N. Rapp, Director of the Joint Intelligence Task Force for Combating Terrorism, filed in the Padilla case, 30 August 2004.

37 "Jose Padilla and Co-Defendants Sentenced on Terrorism Charges," Department of Justice press release, 22 January 2008.

38 U.S. v. Adham Amin Hassoun et al.

39 Aukai Collins, *My Jihad* (New York: Pocket Star Books, 2002).

40 U.S. v. Adham Amin Hassoun et al.

41 *Terrorism in the United States, 2002–2005*, unclassified report by the Federal Bureau of Investigation, available at http://www.fbi.gov/publications/terror/terrorism2002_2005.htm

42 Ibid.

43 Ibid.

44 U.S. v. Royer et al., 03-CR-296, indictment, Eastern District of Virginia, 25 June 2003; "Defendants Convicted in Northern Virginia Jihad Trial," Department of Justice press release, 4 March 2004.

45 U.S. v. Tarik Ibn Osman Shah and Rafiq Sabir, Criminal Complaint, U.S.D.C. for the Southern District of New York, 27 May 2005.

46 "Bronx Martial Arts Instructor Pleads Guilty to Conspiring to Support al Qaeda," U.S. Attorney, Southern District of New York press release, 4 April 2007; "Florida Doctor Sentenced to 25 Years for Conspiring and Attempting to Support al Qaeda," U.S. Attorney, Southern District of New York press release, 28 November 2007.

47 *Terrorism in the United States, 2002–2005*; U.S. v. Ahmed Abu Ali, U.S.D.C. for the Eastern District of Virginia, Indictment, 3 February 2005.

48 Daily Press Briefing of State Department Spokesman Sean McCormack, 4 April 2007; Raymond Bonner, "New Jersey Man Who Fled Somalia Ends Up in an Ethiopian Jail," *New York Times*, 23 March 2007; Jonathan S. Landay, "U.S. Citizen is Said to Have Admitted al-Qaida Link," *McClatchy Newspapers*, 25 March 2007.

49 Affidavit of FBI Special Agent Jeremiah A. George in U.S. v. Daniel Joseph Maldonado, U.S.D.C. Southern District of Texas, H-07-125M, 13 February 2007.

50 Report by Mitchell D. Silber and Arvin Bhatt, New York Police Department Intelligence Division, *Radicalization in the West: The Homegrown Threat*, August 2007; *Terrorism in the United States, 2002–2005*; U.S. v. Syed Hashmi, U.S.D.C. Southern District of New York, 06-CRIM-442, 24 May 2006; Jon Gilbert, "The Supergrass I Helped to Create," *Times of London*, 3 May 2007; Alison Gendar, Angie Wallace, and Celeste Katz, "Disturbing Signs Early for a Zealot," *New York Daily News*, 10 June 2006.

51 U.S. v. Earnest James Ujaama, U.S.D.C. Western District of Washington, CR02-0283R, Plea Agreement, 14 April 2003; *Terrorism in the United States, 2002–2005*.

52 Summary of Evidence for Combatant Status Review Tribunal: Majid Khan, Department of Defense, Office for the Administrative Review of the Detention of Enemy Combatants, 28 March 2007; Summary of Evidence for Combatant Status Review Tribunal: Khalid Shaykh Muhammad, Department of Defense, Office for the Administrative Review of the Detention of Enemy Combatants, date unknown; Eric Rich and Dan Eggen, "From Baltimore Suburbs to a Secret CIA Prison," *Washington Post*, 10 September 2006; Katherine Shrader, "An Immigrant's Journey from Maryland to Gitmo," *Associated Press*, 22 March 2007.

53 Report by Mitchell D. Silber and Arvin Bhatt, New York Police Department Intelligence Division, *Radicalization in the West: The Homegrown Threat*, August 2007, pp. 66–73.

54 *Terrorism in the United States, 2002–2005*.

55 "Two Plead Guilty to Domestic Terrorism Charges of Conspiring to Attack Military Facilities, Jewish Targets," U.S. Department of Justice press release, 14 December 2007, available at http://www.usdoj.gov/opa/pr/2007/December/07_nsd_1006.html

56 U.S. v. Narseal Batiste, U.S.D.C. Southern District of Florida, 06-20373, 22 June 2006.

57 Doug Simpson, "Father of Man Accused as Ringleader in Terrorism Plot Can't Explain Arrest," *Associated Press*, 24 June 2006.

58 Toby Harnden, "Sect Inspired 'Leader of Sears Tower Plot,'" *Sunday Telegraph*, 25 June 2006.

59 U.S. v. Narseal Batiste.

60 "Attack Foiled: Undercover Probe Busts Terror Plot," FBI press release, 8 May 2007, available at http://www.fbi.gov/page2/may07/ftdix050807.htm

61 "Six Individuals Charged with Plotting to Murder U.S. Soldiers at New Jersey Military Base," U.S. Department of Justice press release, 8 May 2007, available at http://newark.fbi.gov/dojpressrel/2007/nk050807.htm

62 Anthony Faiola and Dale Russakoff, "The Terrorists Next Door?" *Washington Post*, 10 May 2007.

63 Raffi Khatchadourian, "Azzam the American: The Making of an Al Qaeda Homegrown," *New Yorker*, 22 January 2007.

64 US v. Grecula, U.S.D.C. Southern District of Texas, H-05-257-S, 8 August 2006.

65 *Terrorism in the United States*, 2002–2005.

66 Shannen Rossmiller, "My Cyber Counter-Jihad," *Middle East Quarterly* XIV(3) (Summer 2007).

67 United States of America, Department of the Army vs. Specialist Ryan G. Anderson, Fort Lewis, Army Base, Washington State; Rossmiller, "My Cyber Counter-Jihad."

68 U.S. v. Hassan Abujihaad, U.S. District Court of Connecticut, 3:07CR57(MRK), 7 March 2007.

69 Motion in Limine in U.S. v. Hassan Abujihaad, U.S. District Court of Connecticut, 3:07CR57(MRK), 19 October 2007.

70 Affidavit of FBI Special Agent Jarred Ruddy in U.S. v. Derrick Shareef, U.S.D.C. Northern District of Illinois.

71 Supreme Court of the State of New York, County of New York, People of the State of New York vs. Rashid Baz, Part 31/56, 1872–1894, Sentence, 18 January 1995, 24, pp. 17–21; Mahmoud Habboush, "Killer's Daughter Admits it was Political," *New York Daily News*, 16 February 2007; *Terrorism in the United States, 2002–2005*.

72 Scott Gutierrez, "Suspect in Jewish Federation Shootings Recently Baptized," *Seattle Post-Intelligencer*, 31 July 2006.

73 Seattle Police Department, Certification for Determination of Probable Cause in the case of Naveed Haq, 28 July 2006.

74 State of North Carolina v. Mohammed Reza Taheri-azar, 06-CRS-51275, 1 May 2006.

75 Text of Taheri-azar's letter, as published in "Taheri-azar Writes to Eyewitness News," *ABC 11 Durham*, 14 March 2006.

76 For the attitudes of the U.S. government toward Al Qaeda and the *jihadist* threat pre-9/11, see, for example, the *9/11 Commission Report*, particularly pp. 339–360.

77 Remarks of FBI Director Robert Muller, City Club of Cleveland, 23 June 2006.

78 *Muslim Americans: Middle Class and Mostly Mainstream*, Pew Research Center, 22 May 2007, pp. 24–25.

79 Steven Simon, Statement before the Senate Committee on Homeland Security and Governmental Affairs, 12 September 2006.

80 *Radicalization in the West*, p. 8.

81 Bruce Hoffman, "The Use of the Internet by Islamic Extremists," Testimony before the House Permanent Select Committee on Intelligence, 4 May 2006.

82 Extensive monitoring of the site conducted by the author between 2005 and 2006.

83 U.S. v. Ahmed (N.D. GA.), No 1:06-CR-147-CC, 19 July 2006.

84 Ibid.

85 U.S. v. Ehsanul Islam Sadeque, U.S.D.C. Eastern District of New York, M-06-335, Affidavit of FBI Special Agent Michael Scherck in Support of Arrest Warrant, 28 March 2006.

86 Interview with top FBI official, Boston, March 2007.

87 Ibid.

88 See, for example, the significant attention devoted to the issue by the National Strategy for Homeland Security, Homeland Security Council, October 2007; the bill for the formation of such Commission was introduced by Rep. Jane Harman (D-CA) in April 2007.

30 Appropriated martyrs

The Branch Davidians and the radical right

Michael Barkun

On April 19 of most years, a few obligatory articles still appear to mark the anniversary of the Oklahoma City Federal Building bombing in 1995. However, they rarely mention the other event that took place on April 19, the one that apparently motivated Timothy McVeigh and Terry Nichols to plan and carry out the Oklahoma City attack. That, of course, was the calamitous end of the Branch Davidian standoff outside Waco, Texas, in 1993.

When the Branch Davidian compound went up in flames, nearly all the sect's members perished, save for nine who got out of the burning compound, 35 who had left during the standoff with the FBI, and a handful who for one reason or another were not at Mt. Carmel, as the compound was known, when the standoff began. Eighty died in the fire, 59 adults (including the sect leader, David Koresh), and 21 children. So much is certain. Whether they were martyrs, however, depends upon whom one asks. It also is shaped by two other factors.

There is, first of all, the question of how and by whom the fire was started. This is bitterly contested. I will return to it, not in order to resolve it, but to suggest the paradoxical way in which it has affected judgments of martyrdom. Second, there is the question of what a martyr is. This would seem relatively simple, since the available definitions are remarkably consistent. Scholars and lexicographers understand martyrdom to be an act of fatal religious witness for the purpose of demonstrating one's faith and commitment.[1] The very word comes from the Greek for "witness." To be sure, issues remain in the conceptualization of martyrdom, as, for example, the question of whether it occurs only when one is passively killed for the faith or whether it also takes place when one dies fighting for the faith.[2] In any case, the connection among commitment, death, and intentional risk-taking remains. However, martyrs are made not only by themselves but also by martyrologists, those who come after and take it upon themselves to describe and characterize the deaths of others. The martyrologists who have interested themselves in the Waco victims have not felt themselves bound by the classical definition.

Of all those who consider the Branch Davidians martyrs, none have been more vocal than members of the far right. These have included not only Timothy McVeigh but libertarians, gun rights advocates, many members of militia groups, and other militantly anti-government organizations.[3] That the Davidians should have such champions is particularly strange in light of the fact that, as Jeffrey Kaplan observes, "the beliefs and lifestyle of David Koresh and his followers were utterly inimical to all that the right-wing holds dear."[4] The community was multi-ethnic and multi-racial, with members from Great Britain, Canada, Australia, Israel, Mexico, Jamaica, the Philippines, and New Zealand. Half of the roughly 130 members were people of color, 45 of them black.[5] The Davidians felt a strong connection to Israel. Koresh had traveled there in 1985, and he prophesied that his followers would fight on the Israeli side at the Battle of Armageddon.[6] David Koresh may well have been familiar with right-wing conspiracism through his frequent attendance at gun shows,[7] but his was decidedly not a group likely to commend itself to racists or anti-Semites. Nor is there any suggestion that Koresh and his followers stood in an adversarial relationship with the government, prior to the events of 1993.

Nonetheless, after April 19, 1993, the Branch Davidians took their place in right-wing martyrology alongside Gordon Kahl, the North Dakota tax protestor shot to death in 1983 after having killed two federal marshals; Robert Mathews, the leader of the white separatist guerrilla group known as The Order, who died in a shootout with the FBI on Whidbey Island, Washington, in 1984; and the wife and son of Randy Weaver, the Idaho Christian Identity survivalist, killed during an armed standoff with the FBI in 1992. Kahl, Mathews, and the Weavers were natural candidates for elevation, but the apolitical, racially integrated Branch Davidians seem decidedly out of place. April 19, 1995, the day McVeigh set off the bomb in Oklahoma City, was the second anniversary of the Waco fire. A commemorative observance was scheduled for the Mt. Carmel site, where the compound once stood. The Texas ceremony was to feature Ramsay Clark, along with journalists, lawyers, and academics interested in the Davidians' cause. However, also on the program were Ralph Turner, spokesperson for the North Texas Constitutional Militia; and James "Bo" Gritz, the former Green Beret who had become a notorious right-wing organizer.[8]

Those in the far-right subculture have glorified the casualties of the Waco fire in terms usually reserved for the hallowed dead of a religion's most devoted believers. To Roy Taylor, a Christian Identity pastor, the Waco dead are "Christian martyrs," killed by the "lackeys" of "Mystery Babylon."[9] To Shonda Ponder, a frequent webposter for right-wing causes, "the martyrs of Waco" have awakened the nation to the dangers of gun control and restrictions on religious freedom. "Waco became a door, and a finger of God for the nation."[10]

The radical right found it easy to hijack the Mt. Carmel community and engraft its history onto their own. This was made easier by the fact that few people knew much about Branch Davidian doctrine. The community was small and insular before the standoff, an obscure offshoot of Seventh Day Adventism, unknown even to most scholars of religion. Afterwards, the handful of survivors had meager resources and took support where they could find it. When support was offered from the extreme right, they took it. How the linkage was done is less interesting, however, than why. Here two issues intersect: the meaning of "martyr" and the contested accounts of the final fire.

In order for the Branch Davidians to have been martyrs, they would have had to have knowingly placed themselves at risk of death. Indeed, many outsiders thought they had actually done so. According to this scenario, the inhabitants of the compound started the fire to immolate themselves rather than submit to the government. Aside from the impossibility of definitively proving what happened during the compound's last hours, the mass suicide scenario introduces substantial complexity into the martyrdom question.

In the first place, the question of suicide has been a bitterly divisive issue, since belief in the suicide of the Mt. Carmel members appears to diminish the government's moral responsibility for their deaths. If they themselves set the fire in order to avoid the consequences of the standoff, then they, rather than the government, bear responsibility. Not surprisingly, the suicide theory has been rejected by surviving Davidians and by many scholars sympathetic to them. Opponents of the suicide theory point to the fact that in a 1992 conversation with a representative of the Texas Children's Protective Services and in discussions with the FBI during the standoff, David Koresh rejected the possibility of suicide.[11] In any case, suicide and martyrdom are not identical. The classical martyr places him/herself in a situation where the enemies of God will make death inevitable, but he/she does not take his or her own life. Making a distinction between suicide and martyrdom has been precisely the problem facing radical Islamic supporters of so-called "suicide bombers," for they must somehow deal with the Muslim prohibition on suicide while converting the bombers" deaths into acts of martyrdom.[12] The problem for the suicide theory in the Branch

Davidian case is even more formidable, for it assumes that if they had not taken their own lives, they would have been killed by the FBI.

Second, those who deem the Davidians to be martyrs—particularly those on the radical right— also reject the suicide scenario, insisting that the government deliberately set the fire. For them, the Davidians are martyrs *because* the government killed them. They reject the theory that the Davidians started the fire in order to martyr themselves and that, instead, they were the victims of the government's deliberate attack. They are, in other words, martyrs precisely because they died in a manner that fails to meet the requirements of martyrdom.

This paradoxical conclusion has important implications for an understanding of martyrdom, particularly where political causes are involved. It suggests, first, that the capacity to create martyrs rests not only, or even primarily, with the martyrs themselves but also with the subsequent martyrologists. An individual may deliberately choose to place his or her life at risk to demonstrate fidelity to some cause; and such knowing surrender of life has been at the root of the concept of the martyr. However, the manner in which a death is subsequently seen depends on how it is presented later, and after the moment of martyrdom, the martyr loses control of that process. The process is then driven by writers, organizers, and other symbol manipulators whose agendas may differ from the martyr's own.

A martyr is not, therefore, simply a creation of an individual who decides to die in a particular way. It is, rather, a persona that needs to be constructed, and at the least requires the cooperation of martyrologists who present the death in the desired way. However, the construction of martyrs places significantly more power in the hands of martyrologists than merely the power to record and transmit stories. For the very meaning of "martyr" turns out to be malleable.

As noted at the outset, there is little controversy among scholars about what a martyr is. That consensus, however, is not shared in American society generally, and many individuals who have not in fact died martyrs' deaths are nonetheless remembered as though they had. Among those often so designated are Abraham Lincoln, John F. Kennedy, and the World Trade Center dead. While these represent exceptionally loose applications of the word "martyr," the term has also been applied less than scrupulously in religious history as well. Ivan Strenski notes that during the Crusades, "popular and non-canonical piety" applied the term much more loosely than Church authorities.[13] Even so, these were differences at the margins, among individuals and institutions that shared the same moral universe. The same cannot be said of the Branch Davidians and their martyrologists on the right.

Loose designations of "martyr" typically occur in situations of widespread public mourning, either for a celebrated figure or for those who died through the actions of an enemy. Identifying them as "martyrs" elevates their death to an exalted level. However, neither condition was met in the Waco case. The Branch Davidians were virtually unknown outside the Waco area, and the government's decision to end the standoff on April 19 was widely applauded by the general public. In a subsequent CNN/Gallup poll, fully 93% of respondents blamed David Koresh for the deaths.[14] The surviving Davidians remained largely invisible and had few means by which to affect public perceptions of their deceased coreligionists. Finally, the right-wing groups and individuals who took up the cause of Davidian martyrdom were themselves marginalized. As far apart as the Branch Davidians were from their latter-day champions, the two were joined by common outsider status: the religiously marginal taken up by the politically marginal. The Branch Davidians, stigmatized in the eyes of the general public and unable to control the manner in which they were presented, were thus available to anyone who wished to craft an image.

The image constructed by the radical right is of religionists deliberately attacked and murdered by the federal government. The April 19 events fit into a larger right-wing conviction that a conspiratorial "global elite" is in the process of taking control of the world by imposing a "New

World Order." This world dictatorship would especially target gunowners, and the raid on Mt. Carmel by the Bureau of Alcohol, Tobacco, and Firearms arose out of allegations about gun-law violations. The standoff at Randy Weaver's Ruby Ridge, Idaho, cabin, which had taken place only a year earlier, had also arisen out of a gun violation. The Weaver family were Christian Identity survivalists who had retreated into the mountains. Not only had Weaver's wife and son been killed during the standoff, but Weaver's trial took place at the same time as the Waco siege. In response to Ruby Ridge, the Christian Identity pastor, Peter J. Peters, convened a "meeting of Christian men" in Estes Park, Colorado, in October 1992.

The Estes Park conference occurred only four months before the Waco standoff began. It did not explicitly address martyrdom, but its discussion of Ruby Ridge made imputations of martyrdom natural and established a foundation for the subsequent matryological treatment of the Branch Davidians. Pastor Peters began his Introduction to the conference report by quoting Numbers 35:33: "So ye shall not pollute the land wherein ye are; for blood it defileth the land: and the land cannot be cleansed of the blood that is shed therein, but by the blood of him that shed it."[15] The conference participants sent an "Open Letter to [the] Weaver Family" in which they spoke of "Vicki and Samuel [Weaver's] mortal sacrifices. …"[16] They also clearly believed that more violent episodes were imminent: "A concern of many was the antichrist's forces [sic] attempts to generate an opened [sic] armed confrontation of some sort."[17] The gathering at Estes Park is consequently often regarded as the catalyst for the growth of militia groups in the early 1990s. Finally, the conferees made no secret of their belief that FBI agents had murdered the Weavers. They spoke of "police state tactics" and "genocide."[18]

Hence by the time Waco occurred, the leadership stratum of the anti-government right was already preoccupied with killings by government personnel and anticipated more to come. They were already seeking to understand these deaths as part of a religious struggle between the forces of Christ and Antichrist. There were also hints that what mattered were government actions, not the conduct or motivations of the victims. Some at Estes Park advised caution in rising to Weaver's defense on the grounds that he "had a poor reputation as a Christian man." The dominant view, however, was that "reputation was not the issue at hand and that the issue was concerning the government killing of Mr. Weaver's wife and son."[19] This anticipates the right's later lack of interest in the actual beliefs of the Branch Davidians, even though many of those beliefs were contrary to their own. What mattered was the role of the government.

The right's disinterest in Davidian beliefs was matched by their desire to treat the Davidians as passive victims. Many with no extremist associations have questioned the government's view that the compound's inhabitants were responsible for the fatal fire. However, extremists have dramatically extended this position, particularly in two widely circulated films by Linda Thompson, *Waco: The Big Lie* and *II: The Big Lie Continues*. Thompson is an Indianapolis lawyer who has given herself the title of "Acting Adjunct General of the Unorganized Militia of the United States."[20] She claims that the ATF agents supposedly shot by the Davidians at the beginning of the standoff were actually executed by the government; that the tanks used by the FBI to insert CS gas into the compound were actually equipped with flamethrowers; and that the government shot survivors as they fled the burning buildings.[21] For the right, therefore, it was not sufficient to absolve the Davidians of blame for the fire. It was necessary that they be presented as completely uninvolved in their own deaths, in order to transfer complete responsibility to the government. As a result, the constructed martyrs were required to behave in a manner inconsistent with classic concepts of martyrdom.

By implication, then, the right has conflated martyrdom with victimization. By virtue of being victimized, an individual becomes a martyr regardless of his or her behavior or intent. Martyr status is assigned on the basis of the putative evil of the victimizer rather than the chosen self-sacrifice of the victim. In like manner, once the victim has been redefined as a martyr, his or her beliefs cease to be relevant. It does not matter that some, such as Vicki and Samuel Weaver, were ideologically compatible with the extreme right, while those at Waco were not.

Even as this process was unfolding, the anti-government right chose not to take advantage of an opportunity to articulate a more conventional concept of martyrdom. During the Estes Park conference, great attention was given to a paper written by Louis Beam. Beam, who has had long associations with both the Ku Klux Klan and Christian Identity,[22] has acquired a substantial reputation among extremists for his essays on movement strategy. The Estes Park gathering was particularly taken with his essay, "Leaderless Resistance," which was reprinted in full in the conference report.[23] "Leaderless resistance" stood for an entirely atomistic and non-hierarchical approach to anti-government violence, which was to be undertaken by separate individuals or small coteries acting independently of each other. Beam argued that the pervasiveness of government surveillance and infiltration was so great that organized insurgent activity was too dangerous. Instead, opponents of the "New World Order" needed to take action individually, at times and places of their own choosing, so that violence would be traceable only after the fact.

Beam's essay dealt with the strategic advantages of the concept, particularly as a defense against government penetration. However, the conference's so-called "SWAT Committee" (an acronym for "Sacred Warfare Action Tactics") interpreted leaderless resistance in religious rather than strategic terms: "... in light of the Christ being the head (i.e., leader) of His body of believers (Ephesians 1:22, 23) who function individually as members of His body (Eph. 5:30). Such people receiving their orders and instruction from their commander in chief through his word and Holy Spirit. [sic] (Romans 8:14)."[24] Thus, they were in effect saying that the individual who appears to commit acts of violence on his own initiative, actually does so at Christ's command.

Although this was written nearly a decade before 9/11, the resemblance to contemporary examples of Islamic terrorism is striking. There is, however, one important difference: Neither Beam in his essay nor the Estes Park group in their interpretation of it discussed situations in which the user of violence might himself be killed in the attack. Indeed, in none of the Biblical examples cited—such as Moses' killing of the Egyptian overseer (Exodus 2:12)—had the attacker died.[25] The unspoken assumption, both by Beam and by the Estes Park conferees, was that the attackers would survive to use violence another day.

Nonetheless, a different view of martyrdom had appeared almost simultaneously on the radical right, in a text that was to become virtually canonical for white racial separatists: *The Turner Diaries* by Andrew MacDonald (the pseudonym of William Pierce, leader of the National Alliance), a work published in 1980. It was widely publicized in 1995, after it became known that Timothy McVeigh had thought highly of it and might well have been influenced by it. The novel is in the form of the diaries of its eponymous hero, Earl Turner, a member of a quasi-monastic racist organization that seeks to overthrow the government. Turner's last mission is to detonate a nuclear warhead on his plane as he flies over the Pentagon. Before leaving on the suicide mission, he tells his colleagues, much in the manner of later Islamic suicide bombers, "I offer you my life." After the racist forces achieve victory, the date of Turner's mission is celebrated as the "Day of the Martyrs."[26]

The Turner Diaries is generally considered the most widely read book on the radical right. Pierce claimed that by 1995, 200,000 copies were in circulation.[27] Yet notwithstanding its wide circulation, the concept of martyrdom central to the story seems to have made little headway among its readership. It did nothing to dim the right's fixation on Waco and its embrace of the Branch Davidians. Appropriation of the Branch Davidians suggests that rightists have paid little attention to the putative martyrs themselves, either in terms of their intentions before death or their beliefs. It mattered only that their deaths could somehow be attributed to the federal government. Thus right-wing martyrology is a parade of diverse and sometimes incompatible victims, ranging from Robert Mathews, the Odinist racist insurgent, to the Waco dead. Martyrs are identified and honored, but there is almost no advocacy of martyrdom itself. Rather, martyrs are seen as accidental byproducts of conflicts with the state. Individuals may be killed or die defending themselves, but they do not function in the classic manner, as "witnesses."

Martyrs, in this case, are made by martyrologists, not by themselves. In a world replete with victims—many from groups that have no control over representations of themselves—a reservoir of potential martyrs is always available. Their deaths may be hijacked for whatever cause they seem to serve. Such appropriation was facilitated in this case by an accident of timing. The conflagration at Waco occurred just as the Internet was beginning its extraordinary growth, and the proliferation of far-right websites provided vehicles for views that might otherwise have been accessible only to tiny subcultures. Instead, Waco became the object of a kind of cultic fascination in which the received view of the government and the mass media was met with a counter-narrative glorifying the victims.[28] The construction of such martyrs is possible not only because, in the case of the Branch Davidians, they and their survivors are powerless to prevent it, but because "martyr" has become such a flexible concept. Those who operate within religious traditions that have theologies of martyrdom may be constrained by the conventions of those traditions,[29] but it is a far freer process for those who operate in relatively unsystematized traditions or, indeed, outside of any historic religious framework. For them, martyrology offers the continual temptation to glorify one's cause by enveloping it in the halo of the dead who are in no position to protest.

Notes

1   Mark Juergensmeyer, *Terror in the Mind of God: The Global Rise of Religious Violence* (Berkeley: University of California Press, 3d ed., 2003), 170–171.
2   Ivan Strenski, "Sacrifice, Gift and the Social Logic of Muslim 'Human Bombers,'" *Terrorism and Political Violence* 15 (Autumn 2003): 1–34.
3   Mark MacWilliams, "Symbolic Resistance to the Waco Tragedy on the Internet," *Nova Religio: The Journal of Alternative and Emergent Religions* 8 (March 2005): 59–82.
4   Jeffrey Kaplan, ed., *Encyclopedia of White Power: A Sourcebook on the Radical Racist Right* (Walnut Creek, CA: Altamira, 2000), 323.
5   James D. Tabor and Eugene V. Gallagher, *Why Waco?: Cults and the Battle for Religious Freedom in America* (Berkeley: University of California Press, 1995), 24.
6   Tabor and Gallagher, *Why Waco?*, 76, 207.
7   Mattias Gardell, *Gods of the Blood: The Pagan Revival and White Separatism* (Durham, NC: Duke University Press, 2003), 62–63.
8   Michael Barkun, *Religion and the Racist Right: The Origins of the Christian Identity Movement* (Chapel Hill: University of North Carolina Press, rev. ed., 1997), 263.
9   Royal Taylor, "Virtuous Israelite Women: The Song of the Lamb," http://www.roytaylorministries.com/am01152.htm (March 23, 2004).
10 Shunda M. Ponder, "Cornerstone," http://www.angelfire.com/wy/1000/cornerstone.html (March 23, 2004).
11 Tabor and Gallagher, *Why Waco?* (see note 5 above), 218.
12 David Cook, "Suicide Attacks or 'Martyrdom Operations' in Contemporary Jihad Literarture," *Nova Religio: The Journal of Alternative and Emergent Religions* 6 (October 2002): 7–44.
13 Strenski (see note 2 above), "Sacrifice, Gift…," 11.
14 Stuart A. Wright, "Another View of the Mt. Carmel Standoff," In Wright, ed., *Armageddon in Waco: Critical Perspectives on the Branch Davidian Conflict* (Chicago: University of Chicago Press, 1995), xv.
15 Peter J. Peters, "Introduction," "Special Report on The Meeting of Christian Men Held in Estes Park, Colorado October 23, 24, 25, 1992 Concerning the Killing of Vickie and Samuel Weaver by the United States Government," (LaPorte, CO: Scriptures for America Ministries, 1992), 1.
16 "Special Report on the Meeting of Christian Men," 25.
17 "Special Report on the Meeting of Christian Men," 24.

18 "Special Report on the Meeting of Christian Men," 7, 24.
19 "Special Report on the Meeting of Christian Men," 24.
20 "Paranoia as Patriotism: Far-Right Influences on the Militia Movement," The Nizkor Project, http://www.nizkor.org/hweb/orgs/American/adl/paranoia-as-patriotism/Linda-thompson.html (April 21, 2004).
21 Barkun, *Religion and the Racist Right* (see note 8 above), 319, fn. 11.
22 "The Firebrand," *The Southern Poverty Law Center Intelligence Report* (Summer 2002), 11–21.
23 "Special Report on the Meeting of Christian Men," 19–23.
24 "Special Report on the Meeting of Christian Men," 19.
25 "Special Report on the Meeting of Christian Men," 18.
26 Andrew MacDonald (pseudo. William Pierce), *The Turner Diaries* (Washington, D.C.: National Alliance, 2d ed., 1980), 204–205.
27 Marc Fisher and Phil McCombe, "Going By the Book of Hate," *Washington Post National Weekly* (May 1–7, 1995), 9.
28 MacWilliams (see note 3 above), "Symbolic Resistance in the Waco Tragedy on the Internet."
29 See, for example, David Cook, "Suicide Attacks or 'Martyrdom Operations'..." (see note 12 above).

Index